T0396092

THE ROUTLEDGE COMPANION TO THE PRACTICE OF CHRISTIAN THEOLOGY

This Companion introduces readers to the practice of Christian theology, covering what theologians do, why they do it, and what steps readers can take in order to become theological practitioners themselves. The volume aims to capture the variety of practices involved in doing theology, highlighting the virtues that guide them and the responsibilities that shape them. It also shows that the description of these practices, virtues and responsibilities is itself theological: what Christian theologians do is shaped by the wider practices and beliefs of Christianity. Written by a team of leading theologians, the Companion provides a unique resource for students and scholars of theology alike.

Mike Higton is Professor of Theology and Ministry at Durham University.

Jim Fodor is Professor of Theology and Ethics at St. Bonaventure University and editor of the journal *Modern Theology*.

ROUTLEDGE RELIGION COMPANIONS

Available:

The Routledge Companion to the Christian Church
Edited by Gerard Mannion and Lewis S. Mudge

The Routledge Companion to Religion and Film
Edited by John Lyden

The Routledge Companion to the Study of Religion
Edited by John Hinnells

The Routledge Companion to Early Christian Thought
Edited by D. Jeffrey Bingham

The Routledge Companion to Religion and Science
Edited by James W. Haag, Gregory R. Peterson, and Michael L. Spezio

The Routledge Companion to Theism
Edited by Charles Taliaferro, Victoria S. Harrison, and Stewart Goetz

The Routledge Companion to Modern Christian Thought
Edited by Chad Meister and James Beilby

The Routledge Companion to the Practice of Christian Theology
Edited by Mike Higton and Jim Fodor

The Routledge Companion to Religion and Popular Culture
Edited by John C. Lyden and Eric M. Mazur

Forthcoming:

The Routledge Companion to Christianity in Africa
Edited by Elias Bongmba

The Routledge Companion to the Qur'an
Edited by Daniel A. Madigan and Maria M. Dakake

The Routledge Companion to Death and Dying
Edited by Christopher Moreman

THE ROUTLEDGE COMPANION TO THE PRACTICE OF CHRISTIAN THEOLOGY

Edited by
Mike Higton and Jim Fodor

Routledge
Taylor & Francis Group

LONDON AND NEW YORK

First published 2015
by Routledge
2 Park Square, Milton Park, Abingdon, Oxon, OX14 4RN

and by Routledge
711 Third Avenue, New York, NY 10017

Routledge is an imprint of the Taylor & Francis Group, an informa business

British Library Cataloguing in Publication Data
A catalogue record for this book is available from the
British Library

Library of Congress Cataloging in Publication Data
The Routledge companion to the practice of Christian theology / edited by Mike
Higton and Jim Fodor. – 1st ed.
pages cm. – (Routledge religion companions)
Includes bibliographical references and index.
1. Theology, Practical. 2. Theology. 3. Christian life. I. Higton, Mike. II. Fodor, Jim.
BV3.R68 2015
230 – dc23
2014035437

ISBN: 978-0-415-61736-9 (hbk)
ISBN: 978-1-315-72479-9 (ebk)

Typeset in Goudy Old Style
by Taylor & Francis Books

CONTENTS

CONTENTS

CONTENTS

CONTRIBUTORS

Susan Abraham is Assistant Professor of Theological Studies at Loyola Marymount University. She is the author of *Identity, Ethics, and Nonviolence in Postcolonial Theory: A Rahnerian Theological Assessment* (Palgrave Macmillan, 2007) and co-editor of *Shoulder to Shoulder: Frontiers in Catholic Feminist Theology* (Fortress, 2009). Ongoing research projects include issues in feminist theology, theology and political theory, global Catholicism, and Christianity between colonialism and postcolonialism.

Nicholas Adams teaches philosophy and theology at the University of Edinburgh. His interests focus on the ways in which philosophical approaches fundamentally shape theological inquiry. He is the author of *Eclipse of Grace: Divine and Human Action in Hegel* (Blackwell, 2013) and *Habermas and Theology* (CUP, 2006) and editor of *The Impact of Idealism: Religion* (CUP, 2013).

John Bradbury is Vice-Principal and Director of Studies in Systematic Theology and Church History at Westminster College, Cambridge. He is the author of *Perpetually Reforming: A Theology of Church Reform and Renewal* (T&T Clark, 2013) and various articles in the area of ecclesiology. He is deeply engaged in ecumenical work, both on behalf of the United Reformed Church, and also the Community of Protestant Churches in Europe.

Jason Byassee is Senior Pastor of Boone United Methodist Church in North Carolina and a Research Fellow in Theology and Leadership at Duke Divinity School. He is author, most recently, of *Discerning the Body: Searching for Jesus in the World* (Cascade, 2013).

William T. Cavanaugh is Professor of Catholic Studies and Director of the Center for World Catholicism and Intercultural Theology at DePaul University. He holds degrees from the universities of Notre Dame, Cambridge, and Duke. He is the author of five books and editor of two more. His books have been translated into French, Spanish, Polish, and Norwegian.

Thia Cooper is Associate Professor of Religion and Director of Latin American Latina/o and Caribbean Studies at Gustavus Adolphus College in St. Peter, Minnesota. Author of *Controversies in Political Theology: Development or Liberation?* (SCM Press, 2007), she also recently edited *The Reemergence of Liberation Theologies: Models for the 21st Century* (Palgrave Macmillan, 2013).

Jenny Daggers is Associate Professor in Christian Theology at Liverpool Hope University. Daggers is author of a number of books, articles and chapters in theology, gender, and women's history, including *Postcolonial Theology of Religions* (Routledge, 2013) and collections co-edited with Grace Ji-Sun Kim, *Reimagining with Christian Doctrines* (Palgrave, 2014) and *Christian Doctrines for Global Gender Justice* (forthcoming, Palgrave, 2015).

Michael W. DeLashmutt is currently the Academic Dean and Vice President of Academic Affairs at Trinity Lutheran College in Everett, WA. His teaching and research interests focus on the interface between Christian beliefs and practices and everyday life, with a particular interest in popular culture, technology, and education. Before moving back home to the Pacific Northwest of the United States, Dr DeLashmutt taught and served at a number of higher education institutions in the UK and the US.

Jim Fodor is Professor of Theology and Ethics at St. Bonaventure University in Western New York. He is author and editor of several volumes, including (with Oleg Bychkov) *Theological Aesthetics After von Balthasar* (Ashgate, 2008), (with Frederick Christian Bauerschmidt) *Aquinas in Dialogue: Thomas for the Twenty-First Century* (Blackwell, 2004), and *Christian Hermeneutics: Paul Ricoeur and the Refiguring of Theology* (Clarendon, 1995). He is also editor of the journal *Modern Theology*.

Garrett Green is Professor Emeritus of Religious Studies at Connecticut College (New London, CT, USA). He is the author of *Imagining God: Theology and the Religious Imagination* (Eerdmans, 1998) and *Theology, Hermeneutics, and Imagination: The Crisis of Interpretation at the End of Modernity* (Cambridge University Press, 2000). He has also translated and introduced Karl Barth, *On Religion: The Revelation of God as the Sublimation of Religion* (T&T Clark, 2006; Bloomsbury, 2013).

Mike Higton is Professor of Theology and Ministry at Durham University, having previously worked in Cambridge and Exeter. He is the author of several books, including *A Theology of Higher Education* (Oxford, 2012), *Christian Doctrine* (SCM, 2008), *Difficult Gospel: The Theology of Rowan Williams* (SCM, 2004), and, with Rachel Muers, *Modern Theology* (Routledge, 2012) and *The Text in Play: Experiments in Reading Scripture* (Wipf and Stock, 2012).

Willie James Jennings is Associate Professor of Theology and Black Church Studies at Duke University Divinity School, in Durham, North Carolina. Dr Jennings teaches in the areas of systematic theology, black church and cultural studies. He is the author of *The Christian Imagination: Theology and the Origins of Race* (Yale, 2010).

Brad J. Kallenberg is Professor of Theology and Ethics at the University of Dayton in Dayton, Ohio. He is author of several books, including *Ethics as Grammar* (Notre Dame, 2001) and most recently, *By Design: Ethics, Theology and the Practice of Engineering* (Cascade, 2013), and numerous scholarly articles at the intersection of theology, virtue ethics, and Wittgenstein studies.

Karen Kilby is a systematic theologian who has written on Karl Rahner, Hans Urs von Balthasar, Thomas Aquinas, and the doctrine of the Trinity. She works in the

Centre for Catholic Studies in the Department of Theology and Religion at Durham University.

Gerard Loughlin is a Professor of Christian Theology in the Department of Theology and Religion at the University of Durham. His research interests include religion and film, gender and Christianity, and narrative theology. He is the author of *Telling God's Story: Bible, Church and Narrative Theology* (Cambridge, 1996), and a co-editor of the journal *Literature & Theology*.

Morwenna Ludlow of the University of Exeter has published widely on the church fathers and their modern reception, including *Gregory of Nyssa, Ancient and (Post) modern* (Oxford, 2007). Her survey, *The Early Church* (Tauris, 2009) has been well received. She is currently working on a project, *Art, Craft and Theology*, aimed at reconceiving the way in which scholars view early Christian writers' use of rhetoric.

Rachel Muers is Senior Lecturer in Christian Studies at the University of Leeds. She was previously a lecturer at the University of Exeter, and before that Margaret Smith Research Fellow at Girton College, University of Cambridge. Her publications include *Keeping God's Silence: Towards a Theological Ethics of Communication* (Blackwell, 2004); *Living for the Future: Theological Ethics for Coming Generations* (Continuum, 2008); (with David Grumett) *Theology on the Menu: Asceticism, Meat and Christian Diet* (Routledge, 2010); (with Mike Higton) *Modern Theology: A Critical Introduction* (Routledge, 2012).

Paul D. Murray is Professor of Systematic Theology in the Department of Theology and Religion at Durham University, England, where he is also Dean of the Centre for Catholic Studies. His first monograph was *Reason, Truth and Theology in Pragmatist Perspective* (Peeters, 2004). He is editor of *Receptive Ecumenism and the Call to Catholic Learning: Exploring a Way for Contemporary Ecumenism* (Oxford, 2008), and co-editor of *Ressourcement: A Movement for Renewal in Twentieth Century Catholic Theology* (Oxford, 2012).

Simon Oliver is Associate Professor of Philosophical Theology and Head of the Department of Theology and Religious Studies at the University of Nottingham, UK. He is author of *Philosophy, God and Motion* (Routledge, 2013) and editor, with John Milbank, of *The Radical Orthodoxy Reader* (Routledge, 2009). His research interests focus on the doctrine of creation and the relationship between theology and philosophy.

C. C. Pecknold is Associate Professor of Historical and Systematic Theology at The Catholic University of America in Washington, DC. He is the author of *Transforming Postliberal Theology* (Continuum, 2005) and *Christianity and Politics: A Brief Guide to the History* (Cascade, 2010). In addition, he has edited a number of volumes, most recently *The T&T Clark Companion to Augustine and Modern Theology* (Bloomsbury, 2014).

Stephen Plant is Dean and Runcie Fellow at Trinity Hall, Cambridge and an Affiliated Lecturer in the University of Cambridge, where he teaches Christian theology and theological ethics. He is editor and author of several books on modern theology, most recently of *Taking Stock of Bonhoeffer* (Ashgate, 2014). From 2007–13 he edited the journal *Theology*.

Kevin J. Vanhoozer is Research Professor of Systematic Theology at Trinity Evangelical Divinity School. Previously he was Senior Lecturer in Theology and Religious Studies at the University of Edinburgh, Scotland. He is the author of *Is There a Meaning in this Text?* (Zondervan, 2009), *The Drama of Doctrine* (WJKP, 2004), *Remythologizing Theology: Divine Action, Passion, and Authorship* (Cambridge, 2012), and *Faith Speaking Understanding: Performing the Drama of Doctrine* (WJKP, 2012).

Richard Viladesau is Professor of Systematic Theology at Fordham University in New York. A graduate of the Gregorian University in Rome, he was ordained a Roman Catholic priest in 1969. He has written extensively on philosophical questions in theology, comparative theology, and theological aesthetics.

1
GENERAL INTRODUCTION

Mike Higton and Jim Fodor

This is not yet another book that introduces the standard topics or themes of Christian theology ('trinity', 'incarnation', 'salvation' and the rest) – though many of those topics and themes will certainly come up. It is instead a book designed to introduce the *practice* of Christian theology.

We're not using the word 'practice' in the sense it has in the phrase 'practice makes perfect'. In other words, we're not primarily talking about the things that budding Christian theologians do when they are first starting off, in order to become proficient – before taking the trainer wheels off and doing it for real. We will certainly talk a bit, from time to time, about ways to get started on the practice of Christian theology, but that's not the main theme of the book.

Instead we're using the word 'practice' in the sense it has in a phrase like 'her normal practice'. That is, we're going to be talking about the ongoing habits, the persisting patterns of activity, involved in the pursuit of Christian theology. We're going to be talking about the craft of Christian theology; this is a book about what Christian theologians habitually do.

In particular, we're going to be asking what it means for Christian theologians to practise their craft *well*, so as to be – to the extent that this is possible at all – good Christian theologians.

Good practice

The Catholic philosopher Alasdair MacIntyre defined a practice as

> any coherent and complex form of socially established cooperative human activity through which goods internal to that form of activity are realized in the course of trying to achieve those standards of excellence which are appropriate to, and partially definitive of, that form of activity, with the result that human powers to achieve excellence, and human conceptions of the ends and goods involved, are systematically extended.[1]

So, we're talking about a human activity that is cooperative: it is not simply the activity of an isolated individual, but of multiple people interacting with one another.

It is complex: we are not simply talking about a simple activity like clapping, but about an activity that has many parts and processes to it. It is coherent: there may be fuzzy edges and grey areas, but when we talk about 'Christian theology' we are talking about an activity or family of activities that can be identified and discussed. We're talking about an activity that has 'standards of excellence which are appropriate to it': that is, we can meaningfully ask what it means to be a good theologian, and our answers are, on the whole, going to have to be specific to theology, rather than answers that could do just as well for other kinds of activity.

That much of MacIntyre's definition is clear. That leaves the phrases about 'goods internal to that form of activity' and about the systematic extension of 'human conceptions of the ends and goods involved'.

A 'good' is, roughly speaking, a desirable fruit. The goods of a practice are the desirable fruits that it yields. We are dealing with 'external' goods if we can separate these outcomes from the practice that yielded them – if we can separate ends and means. If you can say that you happen to have produced this particular good by means of this practice, but could have produced it in some quite different way, then you are talking about an external good.

An external good is therefore one where what you *get* (this external good) is detachable from what you have to *be* (good at this particular practice) in order to get it. Think, for instance, of money. You can acquire it by flipping burgers, winning games of poker, selling your paintings, or robbing banks, and quite possibly in other ways too. Getting rich (getting hold of lots of the desirable fruit produced by these activities) is a state of affairs with no inherent connection to being a skilled painter or deft burger-flipper.

MacIntyre therefore argues that an external good tends to be the kind that can be thought of as property or as a possession, something that could in principle be passed around or exchanged, but which I happen for now to own. They therefore tend to be the kind of goods for which there can be competition, because in general the more I have of one of these external goods, the less there will be for others.

Internal goods, on the other hand, although they can be the outcome of some competition to excel, tend not to result in situations where there must always be winners and losers. The characteristic form of a good internal to a practice is that it is the desirable fruit of becoming better at that practice – becoming a good practitioner. If we both become translators, for instance, we may end up competing for the same business – and if I end up cornering the market, my earning of the external good of payment for my work will mean you earning less of that external good. But we can both become, by means of diligent effort, better at speaking French – we can achieve the internal good of excellent linguistic ability – without being caught in the same kind of zero sum game. We will be extending 'the human powers to achieve excellence'.

Moreover, if I become better at speaking French, and you do too, there will simply be more good French speaking going on – we will become part of a community with greater linguistic resources than before: our achievement of the good will mean that there is more of the good around than before. In this sense, any practitioner who truly excels at a practice, and thereby promotes the goods internal to that practice, will also tend to enrich the whole relevant community (the community of people who value this kind of good).

MacIntyre also argues that the proficiency and confidence with which a practitioner carries out a practice are directly related to that person's recognition that the practice requires a certain kind of submission. The practitioner needs to recognize the authority of the community whose practice this is – a willingness to learn from that community how this practice goes, and what counts as being good at it. To enter into a practice is to enter into a relationship of apprenticeship not only to other contemporary practitioners, but also and especially to those notable exemplars who have preceded us in the practice. In other words, becoming a good practitioner requires not only the acquisition of certain requisite skills, but acquiring those skills in a tradition or community of practitioners. A good practitioner will therefore tend to have a sense of identity and/or 'belongingness' with respect to the tradition in which she sees herself embedded and against which her abilities, and the abilities of those she is either mentoring or being mentored by, or both, are judged.

MacIntyre also argued, however, that a person's own acquired excellence in the performance of this practice gives something back to that community. It is not just that the community – let's say the community of chess players – benefits from there being more of this good, more good chess playing around. Rather, to the extent that she becomes really good at chess, she shows that community *more* of what being good can mean. So although the standards of excellence by which an activity is judged arise from the very form of that activity itself, the goal or goals of that practice are not fixed for all time. Rather, the goals themselves are transmuted by the history of the activity, and 'human conceptions of the ends and goods involved' are extended, deepened, enriched.

When we speak about 'the practice of Christian theology', this is the kind of picture we have in mind. We are talking about the ongoing collaborative activity of theologians, learnt largely by apprenticeship but constantly evolving and developing, its boundaries stretched by each generation of practitioners. And we are talking about the standards of good practice, and the exemplars who embody those standards, that shape our notion of what it means to pursue this practice well. That's what this book is about: the evolving tradition of collaborative theological practice, and the standards to which its participants aspire.

Of course, by talking about the 'evolving tradition' of theology, we don't want to give the impression that there is some sort of inherent, guaranteed progress to the tradition of Christian theological practice. That would be both naïve and delusional. There are all too many challenges and threats to good theological practice, and all too many ways in which that practice can be distorted and corrupted. That is also a central theme of this book: the ways in which we might identify and respond to distortions and corruptions in the practice of theology.

A spiritual discipline?

There is something important missing from this discussion, however. We've talked about the 'desirable fruit' of the practice of Christian theology. We've mentioned the possibility of 'distortions and corruptions'. And we've referred, using MacIntyre's language, to 'human conceptions of the ends and goods involved' and to 'human powers to achieve excellence'. Yet in the Christian community, the 'ends and goals' of the practice of theology have normally been understood to include knowing God more truly, following God more faithfully, living more transparently to the ways of God's kingdom, and participating more deeply in the gracious love of God.

There is, therefore, something odd, something not quite right, about describing this practice as if it were simply the way of life of a particular human community – without going on to say something about this community's, and this practice's, relationship to God.

If the practice of Christian theology is indeed involved in some way – sometimes perhaps for good and sometimes perhaps for ill – in the processes by which Christians pursue truthfulness, faithfulness, holiness, or righteousness before God, then that will make a difference to how we talk about it. If we follow the deep patterns of Christian thinking about growth in holiness, justice or righteousness, we will not be able to think about these ends and goals simply as something that we might, with the right effort and the right training on our part, be able to *achieve*. Rather, we will think about them as something into which we might, by the grace of God, be drawn. Just as we can think of prayer both as something that we do, *and* as something that God does in us, so we can think of good theology as something that we do, *and* as something that we receive, something that God does in us – working in us by the Spirit to conform us to Christ.

We can therefore take the ideas about 'submission' and 'apprenticeship' discussed a few paragraphs ago, and recast them in the language of discipleship – and we can, perhaps, also take the whole description of Christian theology as a practice, and recast it in the language of spiritual discipline. Different theologians will do this in different ways: they will understand the relationship of this practice to discipleship differently; they will understand the relationship of divine grace and human effort differently; they will understand the relationship between theology and other Christian practices differently. You will find some of these differences if you compare the various chapters of this book. Nevertheless, in and through these differences, this too is a central theme of this book: the practice of Christian theology as a practice of discipleship, a form of spiritual discipline, closely entwined with practices of prayer, worship, and the pursuit of just and holy living.

Reason, Scripture, tradition, experience

You will see that we have arranged the chapters of this book under four headings – headings that may well be familiar. You may have come across reference to 'Scripture, tradition and reason' or 'Scripture, tradition, reason, and experience' when people are talking about the ways in which theology should be developed. The threefold list gets attributed to the sixteenth-century Anglican divine Richard Hooker; the four-fold form is Methodist, and gets attributed to John Wesley – though in both cases the neat formulation is a twentieth-century summary.[2]

In some discussions of these lists, the idea seems to be that these are three or four distinct sources from which theological claims can be generated, and that the theologian's job is to know how to balance, integrate or prioritize them. So we might have the Bible telling us that God is the God of Abraham, Isaac, and Jacob; tradition telling us that God is Triune; reason telling us that God is omnipotent, omniscient, and omnipresent; and experience telling us that God is intimately present to us – and the theologian's job would be to work out how those four claims go together, and which should have priority.

That is not the way we are using the headings in this book. We are, after all, interested in the practice or activity of Christian theology, and we are using these four headings to point to four aspects of that one activity.

To put it simply, a Christian theologian is someone who in some specific contexts thinks about the Scriptures in company with others.

When we use the heading 'reason', we are simply focusing on the fact that the theologian is someone who thinks. What kind of thinking, drawing on what resources, governed by what standards, to what end – all these are questions that we're going to be exploring. We are not particularly interested in using 'reason' to name an independent human faculty that, if left to its own devices, could produce answers to theological questions independent of the Scriptures, tradition or experience.

When we use the heading 'Scriptures', we are focusing on the fact that the thinking that Christian theologians do is carried out, more and less directly, in engagement with the Christian Scriptures. What kind of engagement, treating the Scriptures in what way, acknowledging what kind of authority, and with what fruit – all these, too, are questions that we're going to be exploring.

When we use the heading 'tradition', we are focusing on the fact that Christian theologians don't and can't operate alone. Their thinking is a practice that exists in a tradition of practice (even if some theologians end up being reformers of that tradition), and their thinking therefore always, more or less explicitly, takes the form of conversation with theology's past and present practitioners – a conversation that will more or less directly be a conversation about how best to engage with Scripture. We will be asking what shape that conversation should have, and what kinds of humility and boldness Christian theologians should have as they participate in it.

Finally, when using the heading 'experience', we are interested in the fact that this thinking – this conversational thinking that engages with the Scriptures – always takes place somewhere specific. Christian theologians each have a location – and not just a literal geographical location, but a cultural location, a gender location, a class location, a historical location. They write from contexts of specific kinds of privilege and specific kinds of deprivation. They write in the wake of specific histories of peace and violence, inclusion and exclusion, liberation and oppression. And Christian theologians write at specific points in the lives of their churches, and specific points in their own journeys of discipleship, in the midst of all this. And their location makes a difference to what they see and how they see it – to how they engage in conversation with the tradition, to how they read the Scriptures, to how they think – just as how they think, read, and converse makes a difference to how they navigate their lives in their specific locations.

The four sections therefore belong together. The reasoning discussed in section one is always scriptural, conversational, and contextual; the engagement with Scripture always involves thinking and conversation in some specific location – and so on. These are not four sources that can be separated out, but four vantage points from which to look at, and ask questions about, the same activity.

The chapters in this book

Each of the four sections of the book has its own introduction, which will set the scene, and explain more about what we mean by 'reason', 'Scripture', 'tradition' and 'experience'. It will also explain how the individual chapters in that section fit in to that scene. A few initial words about the nature of the various chapters might be useful here, however.

First, the authors who have contributed to this book don't all agree. You will be able to find disagreement on specific points of substance, if you read carefully enough, but you will also find different visions for how theologians should work. Sometimes those visions differ only in emphasis, but at other times there is a wider gap between them. We've not tried to smooth those differences out – and you should stay alert for them as you read.

Second, we have not tried to be comprehensive, and the chapters don't cover every base. Between them, they do not discuss every kind of activity that can plausibly fall under the heading 'theology'. Even a book this size is unavoidably selective – and the selection we have gathered inevitably reflects our contexts, the way we happen to read the Christian tradition, our relationships to Scripture, and in general our specific patterns of thinking. Nevertheless, we hope that you will find a rich and varied diet here – and that it will fire your imagination, and help you see what might be involved in becoming a Christian theologian.

Notes

1 Alasdair MacIntyre, *After Virtue: A Study in Moral Theory*, 2nd edn, London: Duckworth, 1985, p. 187.
2 For Hooker, see Peter Toon, 'Scripture, Tradition and Reason: Hooker's Supposed Three-legged Stool' (no date), The Prayer Book Society of the USA; available online at http://pbsusa.org/Articles/Hooker%27s%20stool.htm. For Wesley, see Albert C. Outler, 'The Wesleyan Quadrilateral – in John Wesley', *Wesleyan Theological Journal* 20.1 (1985), 7–18; available online at Wesley Centre Online: http://wesley.nnu.edu/wesleyan_theology/theojrnl/16–20/20–01.htm.

Part I
REASON

2
REASON

Mike Higton

Every word that you speak or write as a theologian will be a product of human reason. What else could it be? As soon as you have put a moment's thought into what you say, or as soon as you accept that what you say might be open to any kind of correction, you have already become involved in reasoning. It makes no more sense to ask whether your words are too much or too little the product of reason than it does to ask whether the words I am writing now are too much or too little the product of my typing. What matters is not the quantity, but the quality and kind of reasoning involved.

The fact that 'reason' is the first of this book's four main sections does not imply that we think reason is somehow more authoritative than Scripture, or tradition, or experience. As we have explained in the introduction, we don't find it particularly helpful to think of theology as an attempt to balance the claims derived from four different sources, and to get the priority among those four sources right. To say that theology is reasoning all the way through is not yet to say anything – whether positive or negative – about theology's relation to the Bible, or to tradition, or to experience. Different qualities and kinds of reasoning will relate to Bible, tradition, and experience in very different ways.

But what is reasoning? In order to provide an initial answer to that question, I am going to begin with an analogy. Reasoning is, I claim, like the building of a child's wooden railway. I'm thinking of the kind of railway that comes as a set of wooden track sections – straights, curves, junctions, bridges – ready to be fitted together into networks. My family is, I think, typical in having a rather random collection of pieces, some inherited, some bought. The attempt to make a coherent layout from them all (such that the train will be able to navigate the whole network without having to be lifted from the tracks), still more to make a *complete* layout (one that uses all the pieces and leaves no loose ends), is no easy business. You get a certain way through, and then realize that you do not have enough curves left to join the two remaining ends – so you take a curve out here and a straight there in order to free up an extra piece, only to find that now you have a spare junction, and nowhere to put it. Working towards a coherent and complete layout – if that is indeed what you want – is a complex process. You can't simply start at the beginning, add the pieces one by one, and carry on all the way to the end. You have to experiment with a possibility, then unpick it a little and rebuild slightly differently, so as to respond to what that experiment has shown you.

It is a matter of ongoing, iterative, unpredictable negotiation. 'Ongoing', because you try experiment after experiment, and it all takes time; 'iterative', because each experiment responds to the problems exposed by the last experiment, and you try again and again to make the layout work; 'unpredictable', because nothing can tell you in advance how thoroughgoing the reworking of your existing layout will need to be as you face any particular inconsistency; 'negotiation', because every change you make involves seeking some agreement between the connection you want to make and the tolerances of the connections already made.

Of course, when one has, with triumph, produced a workable network, all pieces in place (and without too much strain on any of the joints), it inevitably happens that some small child (probably in revenge for the adult takeover of his or her playthings) will discover an extra piece of track from behind the sofa. And the finding of that extra piece will start the whole iterative process going again.

We can use the noun 'settlement' to refer to a coherent track layout: a workable arrangement in which all the presently available pieces have been placed together, to the present satisfaction of the builders. However, we can also use the verb 'to settle' to denote the activity of *seeking* a settlement: the active process of iterative renegotiation and repair by which broken networks are remade in pursuit of settlement. And though the application to theology may not yet be clear, my claim is that 'reasoning' is, at its most basic, simply *the faculty of settling*: the faculty by which one thinkingly pursues ongoing, iterative, unpredictable negotiation with the materials given to one, in search of a settlement. It involves serious playfulness (the willingness to experiment, to unpick and remake again and again); it involves a quick imagination (the ability to see possible reworkings of the materials one has to hand); and it involves various kinds of practical know-how (familiarity with how tight a curve one can persuade the pieces to yield, or with the ways in which an articulated bridge can be put together). It is a skill, or set of skills: one can practise it, learn, and get better at it – though however skilled one becomes, the game never loses its iterative, negotiable character.

When you hear the word 'reason', therefore, try not to think too quickly of an argument written down in clear steps on a page. That is not reasoning but the record of some reasoning, like the diagram of a completed train track. Think instead of an activity, of people seeking a settlement: an ongoing, iterative, unpredictable negotiation.

Reasoning in theology

Theology involves reasoning – or, better, theology *is* a practice of reasoning – in precisely this sense. It is an ongoing, iterative, unpredictable negotiation. Think, for instance, of an individual theology student. She brings with her some set of inherited ideas (a settlement of some kind), and finds herself faced with all sorts of new ideas from her teachers, her fellow students, and from the books and articles she reads. (She's presented with the extra track piece, from behind the sofa – or has someone take away the piece that currently joins her bridge to her turntable.) Her existing settlement involves certain ways of using the Bible, which imply certain claims about what it is and how it should be read. It involves some claims about earlier generations of Christian settlers, and what notice deserves to be taken of *their* attempts at settlement. It involves claims about the nature of the world she inhabits, and about the proper ways of living in it. But the new claims that she encounters unsettle her settlement: they call it into question, or present her with ideas that she does not know how to assimilate. She becomes engaged in active settling, in *reasoning*, to the extent that she tries to make sense of these new ideas – trying to see how they might fit in to her settlement, trying to see what alteration to that settlement might be necessary, trying to do justice to what she believes ought to remain central to that settlement, trying to decide what might need to be rejected.

The process of settling might be set off by something relatively trivial. Perhaps she hears one of her lecturers confidently arguing that the book of Isaiah is not a unified whole, but includes material by Proto-, Deutero-, and Trito-Isaiah. As well as assessing the cogency of the lecturer's arguments, she finds herself wondering whether and how such a conclusion affects other things she has been taught as she grew up. Does it call into question things she's been taught about the reliability and integrity of biblical authors, or the nature of prophecy? Can she adjust this track piece without having to rearrange the whole layout? It is unlikely that she'll find answers to these questions immediately, or that she'll know quickly what ripples of change might spread out around her settlement from this point. Making sense of this claim will involve an ongoing, iterative, unpredictable negotiation.

This example risks missing something important, however – something that has been visible when I have, on occasion, made the train track analogy very practically in class. I have sometimes brought in a bag of track pieces, tipped them onto a table, and asked a group of students to make a coherent and complete layout. It is fascinating to watch. Various members of the group propose possible settlements. They argue. Often, a loud and plausible voice manages to dominate early on, until the settlement that he was working towards fails, and other participants take over. The activity becomes a mixture of cooperation, consultation, disagreement and negotiation. The settlement-making faculty here is not a matter of isolated individual contemplation, but is a social activity. Individual imagination is certainly involved, but only as an ingredient in a complex social pattern of give and take – of ideas offered, tried, rejected, and improved upon. It is an activity in which specific people engage, and their personalities and habits of interaction with those around them change the activity's character and outcome.

It might be better, therefore, to think not so much of an individual thinker, but of a Christian *community* engaged in active settlement: a community with some existing habits of practice and belief, some existing patterns of commitments, some remembered history; a community working out how to order its life in its present context, how to relate to new challenges and questions. Imagine, for instance, a Christian congregation faced for the first time with a member who has an intersex condition – someone who is biologically not straightforwardly classifiable as male or female. If the life of this congregation is in part ordered by practices that assign clearly-defined and different roles to men and women, the presence of someone who can't easily be assigned to either group may possibly set off a chain reaction of rethinking and reordering that could end up reshaping the whole life of the community. The community will be engaged in active settling to the extent that it tries to make sense of its life in the light of this new challenge that it faces, and in the light of all that it is committed to and all that it has inherited. And that settling is likely to be a social process, a complex mess of cooperation, argument, negotiation, politics.[1]

The character of theological reasoning

The skills involved in being a theological reasoner are analogous to those involved in being a good builder of railway layouts. Reasoning involves a practised familiarity with the materials that need to be taken into account while settling. It involves knowing well how those materials can and do connect. It involves a sense for how much 'give' there might be in any specific connection. What tremors through a whole settlement are going to be set off by a change here? Which connections will that change break, and which can bend to accommodate it? What, therefore, is really at stake in that change? To be a good theological reasoner is to be someone adept at tracing the connections, and so at seeing the constraints and the possibilities faced by those seeking settlement.

To put it another way, theological reasoning involves a Christian community taking responsibility for the exposure to challenge of all that it says, does, and thinks. The German theologian Karl Barth, at the very beginning of his massive *Church Dogmatics*, says that theology arises when the Church 'realizes that it must give an account to God for the way in which it speaks'[2] and 'takes up ... the task of criticising and revising its speech about God'.[3] To say that all theology is reasoning through and through is to say that all theology is engaged in this taking of responsibility, this criticizing and revising. To say that what matters is not the quantity but the quality and kind of reasoning is to say that what matters is how that task of critique and revision is carried out. On what basis is the speech and action of the Church properly criticized and revised – and how does that criticism and revision then proceed? What kind of exposure to challenge does the Church face?

A Christian community might, for instance, claim to be obedient to Scripture in certain ways. If people in that community come to realize that, in what it says, does and thinks, it is implicitly claiming that Scripture says x, they discover a very specific way in which their community is exposed to challenge. It is exposed to the possibility that more assiduous reading of Scripture will show that it does not, in fact, quite say x.

I don't at this stage want to discuss the precise forms of exposure that drive theological reasoning. Different Christian communities will understand their exposure to challenge in other ways – and the whole of the rest of this book could be thought of as an attempt to trace some of the forms of exposure that are central to Christian theology, and to trace the practices of 'criticism and revision' that respond to them. I am more interested at this point in the *form* that all such taking of responsibility shares.

If theological reasoning involves a Christian community taking responsibility for the exposure to challenge of all that it does, says, and thinks, for instance, then it must also involve taking responsibility for discovering how all those things interconnect. The explicit, clearly stated exposure to challenge of the community's action, speech, and thought may be rather limited – but it may turn out, on more careful investigation, that there are deeper connections, increasing the ways in which any given aspect of the church's life is exposed. A church decides not to buy fair-trade coffee for its refreshments after services, for instance, because the catering committee felt the taste was not good enough – but it turns out that this issue is not only connected to the church's vision of how to provide a warm and hospitable welcome, but is also connected to questions about justice and financial responsibility. Or it turns out that the church's habits in regard to the proper length of sermons are related to deep patterns of thinking about the convicting work of the Spirit in bringing people to repentance. Or it turns out that the church's policy on the ministry of women is related to deep questions about the shape of its operative Christology. Each of these connections increases the ways in which the action, speech, and thought of this community is exposed to question. To take responsibility for exploring such exposure is to take responsibility for exploring these connections.

Such theological reasoning is not, however, simply about exposure, challenge, and criticism. It is also about what Barth calls 'revision': the imagination and proposal of ways forward, new forms of action, speech and thought – new ways of settling the pieces that this community has been given, including the new demands that it faces. This means that theological reasoning involves not simply a commitment to tracing commitments and exposures that already exist, but a work of constructive imagination. It involves glimpsing a way that things might be able to hang together differently, and making a proposal for how the layout of all this community's pieces might be remade, in some way that this community can acknowledge to be good.

In other words, theological reasoning involves both *unsettling* (tracing the community's exposure to question, and seeing where those questions lead), and *settling* (imagining new layouts, and seeing to what extent they are possible).

The process of unsettling can be very unsettling indeed. I said earlier that 'nothing can tell you in advance how thoroughgoing the reworking of your existing layout will need to be as you face any particular inconsistency' – and acknowledging that your current way of putting things is exposed to a question that it cannot immediately answer can trigger anything from a minor correction to a wholesale rethinking. Think of both the examples I gave earlier – of a theology student trying to discover how to settle with a claim about the authorship of Isaiah, or a Christian community trying to understand how to relate to someone with an intersex condition. In each case, one can imagine that the challenge might trigger a whole chain reaction of rethinking and altered practice – a whole process of unsettling and resettling – at least if the student or some members of the community are taking seriously the nature of the connections that hold their current settlement together, and are willing to follow the implications of this challenge along those various connections. And in each case, this process might lead to a new settlement emerging: to the development of a new way of imagining how things hang together, and what their connections and exposures can be.

Writing as reasoning

Something of this settling-and-unsettling nature of theological reasoning can be seen in a very practical way when one writes an essay or a paper. For most of us, the difference between an adequate and a great essay is made at the revision stage. Before that, you might have managed to get quite a lot of relevant material down on paper, and given a plausible shape to it; it might make a more-or-less connected whole. In other words, you have something like a settlement – an arrangement of material that is meant to be more-or-less complete (that is, it includes all the relevant pieces – or, at least, as many of those pieces as is reasonable in an essay of this length and level), and an arrangement that is meant to have some coherence to it (that is, so to arrange the pieces that each is connected into a structure that includes all of them). But then you look at what you have written, and ask how cogent all the connections are that hold this layout together – whether this bit really goes with that bit, whether this claim really flows from that claim, whether here you have tried to slide past an idea that you didn't really get, or whether there you have simply asserted something that really ought to have been argued for, whether you have simply stacked one claim upon another without showing effectively how they do in fact link up with one another.

At first, the whole thing might be rather muddy – to the extent that it is hard to say exactly what is wrong with it, except that it is not very clear and well ordered. But as one revises and polishes, giving as much clarity and precision as one can to what one has written, it can become easier to see what the real problems are – the real inconsistencies or breaks in the argument. And, as with the train track, it is not always possible to know in advance how fundamental a revision will be called for by any particular problem that one identifies.

Eventually, one may end up with an essay that is a clear, coherent, orderly argument or presentation – something with an introduction and a conclusion, and a body of writing between the two that actually leads from the former to the latter. One might be tempted to say that the finished presentation is an example of theological reasoning – but actually it is the process of composition and revision (and revision and revision and revision) in pursuit of such a finished presentation that is the real example of theological reasoning. The finished presentation is simply the trace or product of that reasoning – and hopefully a prompt for theological reasoning by others.

Of course, a finished presentation is unlikely to be 'finished' in the sense that everything is settled, all questions answered, and no further lines of enquiry have been exposed. There will almost certainly be questions left open, ideas you have not been able to get clear, material you are aware could have been worked in better to the overall structure. There will, in other words, be a residue of unsettled material (and it is normally best to acknowledge this, and to be as clear about it as you can, rather than trying to pull the wool over your own or your readers' eyes). There is *always* going to be such unsettled material outstanding in any large-scale attempt at settlement; nobody ever finishes settling. And yet that unsettled material retains its power to unsettle. It has the potential to drive further work, further thinking, the unpicking and restitching of one's settlement – and who knows the size of the transformation that these unsettled questions have the power to trigger?

The writing of an essay or paper like this is not a bad model for theological reasoning more generally. Reason involves what one might think of as an ascetic journey, or a spiritual discipline. On the one hand, it involves stepping out in faith, trusting that you have something to say – or that if you do not, you will be able to discover, by means of diligent attentiveness, something to say. But it also involves the willingness to expose your ideas and claims to rigorous testing, and so to expose yourself to the possibility of discovering that you have been wrong. Theological reasoning can therefore be a painful process, in which things in which you have invested time and energy, things that are dear to you, have to be left behind.

One might even say that theological reasoning is a kind of journey of discipleship, or something akin to it: a willingness to follow the implications of the gospel wherever they lead, to trace their connections into any and all areas of practice and thought, to allow them to unsettle and resettle your community's and your own ways of making sense – and to allow your understanding of the Christian gospel itself to be deepened and transformed in the process. The diligence involved in making connections and testing them, the diligence involved in seeking clarity and good order, even the diligence involved in revising an essay over and over again – at their best, these forms of diligence are simply ways of seeking greater accountability (for the Church and for oneself) in what you do, say and think in response to the Christian gospel.[4]

Who reasons?

As in my example above of the student learning about Isaiah, the word 'reason' can conjure up a picture of something done in solitude – by the student with her books, sitting in a secluded corner of a library, perhaps. That might lead one to think that becoming a theologian is a matter of becoming an individual expert: one who has wrestled his or her settlement into order by dint of heroic intellectual struggles in private, and is now ready to pronounce his or her findings to a wider public. In some theologies – some theological settlements – that might be exactly the vision of the theologian that is promoted, but we should certainly not take that for granted. In different theological settlements, the nature of the practice of reasoning itself will be seen in different ways.

In some, the reasoning activity that is most central to theology will be a matter of the shared deliberations of a local Christian community, seeking discernment for the ordering of their life in a changing world; in others, it will be centred on debates between church leaders gathered in councils, setting the boundaries within which they believe the life of their church will flourish most faithfully; in others, it might take place most obviously in the seminars, conferences, journals and books of an academic discipline, in which a restless intellectual conversation is carried on.

In other words, to know what it means for theology to be a form of reason involves asking questions about who reasons, and about those for whom they reason; and it involves questions about the relationships between the deliberations of individual believers, local communities, church leaders, and academic disciplines.

As will have been clear already, I've assumed in this chapter that theological reasoning is first of all the corporate deliberation and argument of the Church – without trying at this point to specify too closely the scale I have in mind when I say 'Church', or where I take the boundaries of the Church to be. (And yes, that does mean that what I have said is not 'neutral'; it will work better for some theological settlements than for others.) The primary kind of settling I have in mind is the process by which the members of the Church deliberate together about the right ordering of their life together: about how the Church can be faithful to its calling in the situation in which it finds itself; about how it can do justice to the gospel, to the various responsibilities given to it, to what it has inherited, and to the challenges it now faces. It is the process by which the members of the Church seek to know how to go on together *as* a Christian Church.

If that corporate settling has priority, then the individual theologian's activity of settling – the process by which he or she tries to make sense for herself of all that she has learnt – is secondary. It is not unimportant, but it matters primarily insofar as it affects, or serves, or participates in the broader, more corporate process of settling of the Church. The individual Christian theologian who makes some claim about the sense that can be made of things is not thereby finishing the theological task, but is setting it going: she is making a *proposal* for how the Church and its members should order their life together in the world, and launching that proposal into the life of the Church to see what becomes of it.[5] As such, her work is inherently experimental: she does not deliver an authoritative ruling that others are required to obey, but makes a claim that others will test.

One of the problems sometimes faced by academic theology – especially theology studied in a university setting – is that there is little practical connection between the reasoning activity that takes place in the classroom or library and the reasoning activity of the Church. Worries about theology being too much a matter of human reason sometimes come down to this: the worry that the processes of theological settlement have lost their moorings in the Christian community, and have become a free-floating activity with no real routes by which they can make a difference to the ordering of the Church's life. It can be the worry that the motor that drives theological development has ceased to be the attempt to do justice to all the demands and commitments that shape the Church's life, and has instead become the desire for intellectual resolution amongst academics. By losing the wherewithal to take serious responsibility for the Church's life, academic theology has become *ir*responsible.

If becoming a good theological reasoner involves a practised familiarity with the materials for settlement, and with the actual and potential connections between them, it also involves an awareness of the connection between the individual theological reasoner and the community or communities with whom and for whom he or she reasons. It involves understanding how these communities take responsibility for the exposure, connection, and development of their own lives, and of the place that the individual theologian can play in that process. To understand theological reasoning means understanding the shape of the community in and for which it takes place.

Who is listening?

The question about the community or communities for whom the theological reasoner reasons – about the audience to whom she offers reasons – is actually a deeply controversial one. By some accounts, it is *the* controversy that has shaped modern theology – and one influential way of mapping the bewildering variety of forms of theology over the past two hundred years or so is to look at how different theologies answer that question.[6]

What I have written in this chapter so far has taken Christian theology to be a practice of reasoning by which the Church seeks to understand better how to order its own life and how to live its life in the wider world. I have, therefore, presented theological reasoning as a form of reasoning addressed primarily to the Church. It might, however, also be understood as a practice of reasoning by which the Church seeks to understand how to address the wider world.[7] A good deal of modern Western theology can be categorized according to whether it offers its reasons primarily to the Church, or primarily to the wider world. So, there are theologies that address their reasons solely to members of the Christian community – and to them only insofar as they are already faithful members of that community. For instance, in answer to the question, 'Why do you believe in the bodily resurrection of Christ?', the reason offered might ultimately be 'Because the Bible tells me so!' or 'Because the creeds tell me so!' or by pointing in some other way to the commitments and sources that shape Christian life. There might still be robust, rigorous, detailed and extended argument about what Christians should do, say and think – argument that cites and examines evidence, and that is capable of changing minds – but it will be argument that takes certain basic sources or authorities for the Church's life for granted – and it will be argument that has weight for people only insofar as they adhere to those sources or authorities.

On the other hand, there are theologies in which the reasoning is entirely and solely aimed at that strange abstract creature sometimes known as 'any reasonable human being', and in which there turns out to be no independent room for the specific claims, habits, sources and authorities of the Christian tradition (or indeed any other tradition). The Christian community's claims will only count as true or proper to the extent that they are translations of claims that could equally well have been made without reference to Christian sources or authorities.

It would be hard, in fact, to use the name 'Christian theology' for something that wholly met this description, because the Christian tradition would, strictly speaking, be entirely dispensable – except as a useful cover under which to convey philosophical content to a particular community. But one would only need to move a little way away from this extreme to find a position that was much more recognizable as a form of Christian theology. There are, after all, plenty of theologies that try to begin with reasons addressed to 'any reasonable human being', and that are supposed to be convincing regardless of the particular community or tradition that the addressee might inhabit – but which claim that there are good generally accessible reasons to attend to specific Christian sources and authorities. So, in answer to the question, 'Why do you believe in the bodily resurrection of Christ?', a theologian focused on providing reasons for any reasonable human being might say 'Because I have examined all the available historical evidence, using the standards of historical argument that I would expect any historian to use, Christian or secular, and I have concluded that this is the most probable interpretation of that evidence'. Such an answer is intended to have weight with any listener who is willing to weigh the historical evidence fairly, and abide by widely accepted standards of historical reasoning.

Most modern theology involves a more complex negotiation between reasons offered solely to the Christian community entirely on its own terms, and reasons offered to other constituencies. It is worth noting, though, that the tension between a 'reasons for any reasonable human being' kind of theology and a 'community reasons only' kind is not a tension between 'rational' and 'irrational' (nor between 'liberal' and 'conservative' or 'radical' and 'orthodox'). All these forms of theology can involve analysis and debate, the assiduous marshalling of evidence, the testing of one's claims against the data that is relevant to them, and the possibility of having one's mind changed by the force of the better argument.

Nevertheless, the worry that theology is irrational, and the opposite worry that theology gives inappropriate sway to human reason, does sometimes rely upon the assumption that rationality really only means the offering of reasons to 'any reasonable human being' – and that the offering of reasons that are only telling for some specific community is not really reasoning at all. But that is an assumption that, in the broadest sense of the word, often has an implicit *politics* behind it. That is, it often rests upon a picture of society as consisting of a neutral public sphere (the realm of arguments open to 'any reasonable human being'), within which there sit various private religious spheres (each the realm of arguments that make sense only to members of a specific tradition). The demand for reasons addressed to 'any reasonable human being' goes with the belief that properly public discourse can only be conducted in terms sterilized of commitment to particular communities or traditions, if peaceable order is to be given to a society with multiple such particular communities and traditions. Yet this picture of how secularity and religion relate is, to say the least, controversial – especially its portrayal of the secular public sphere as itself neutral and traditionless, and its claim that it is possible to address people in the abstract as 'any reasonable human beings', rather than as members of this or that specific culture, formed by this or that specific history.[8]

Worries about the rationality of theology – either the worry that there is too little of it, or that there is too much of it – are therefore tangled up with questions about how particular religious communities negotiate their place in a secular world. They are tangled up with questions about the supposed neutrality or openness of the public sphere, and with questions about the ability of religious participants in the public sphere to speak in their own voices in public. They are tangled up with questions about how peaceful order is maintained in religiously plural societies (and that's why there is a chapter on 'Public reason' later in this section: reason and politics are inseparable). For the purposes of this introductory chapter, however, the point to take away is much simpler. Theology is not written for no one in particular. If a theology offers reasons at all, it is worth asking to whom they are offered – or to whom the author takes himself or herself to be offering those reasons. And even though many of the writing exercises that are set for students of theology are framed as if you were to write for nobody in particular, it is worth asking for whom you are in fact writing, and what difference the identification of the audience makes. For whom will your reasons be telling, and why? To whom are you responsible, in your reasoning? After all, theological reasoning does not live on pages in books hidden away in libraries: those are only the traces of theological arguments. Theological reasoning lives in the giving and receiving of reasons designed to sway or inform or challenge or encourage, and such giving and receiving always takes place, if it takes place at all, between *people*.

What prompts reasoning?

One of the definitions of 'theology' given by the *Oxford English Dictionary* is 'a system of theoretical principles; an (impractical or rigid) ideology'. The worry that theology might be all too much a matter of 'human reason' sometimes comes down to this: that the theological reasoner is too intent upon finding an *intellectual* settlement (a coherent intellectual scheme in which there are no leftover pieces), and too little upon finding a *habitable* settlement, in which a Christian community can live with integrity. The worry is either that the theologian will be too willing to do violence to the commitments and constraints of the community's life for the sake of his or her system, or that he or she will devote time and energy to questions that, from the point of view of habitability, reek of idle speculation. Here, 'idle speculation' would be a matter of providing answers to questions which only arise out of the desire to make the theologian's intellectual system neater, but which make no difference to the life of the community that the theologian's reasoning is supposedly serving. They are questions in which nothing is really at stake.

Theological reasoning might perhaps be thought of instead as something like a matter of solving problems with the habitability of an existing settlement – and the primary form of coherence or neatness that it seeks is therefore that of renewed habitability. That is not to say that simple intellectual coherence is unimportant: for a settlement to be habitable for people who think, and who seek integrity and honesty in their speech, some kind of intellectual coherence is going to be important. But intellectual coherence in and for itself is not itself the goal.

Theological reasoning might, even better, be thought of as responding to challenges that face a Christian community – as it encounters some form of suffering or of need or of outcry to which it does not yet know how to respond. It is not the comfort of the reasoners that is in question – their ability to rest easily in their settlement because it has no rough edges or awkward seams rubbing against their skin – but their ability to respond, to be responsible. Its goal is the development of new ways of living that answer to the cries of others.

Part of what makes a good theological reasoner is, therefore, a practised eye for what is really at stake in a given theological argument. What real problem in the life of Christian communities in the world prompted this argument? For whom is that problem real and pressing, and why? Who cares – and, if nobody cares, why *should* they care? If this question were to be left unanswered, or we were simply to admit our ignorance on the matter, what difference would it make?

Of course, to insist upon such questions will not mean that one gets to avoid knotty metaphysical questions. The history of Christian theology is, in part, a history of people finding that the strangest things *did* matter: that there were real questions about Christian life in the world at stake in arguments about the relationship between the Father and the Son in the life of the Trinity, or about the proper shape of claims about Christ's divinity or humanity, or in claims about the operations of grace on the human will, and so on. Nevertheless, there is no theological claim or conclusion so deeply rooted in the life of the Church that it is not in danger of being pulled free from that mooring and becoming a free-floating intellectual game.

This warning should itself come with a warning, however. Theological reasoning can sometimes be a matter not of problem-solving, nor of idle speculation, but of delight.[9] The boundary between delight and idle speculation is a very hazy one, and easy to slip across, but there is certainly a place for theology as a contemplative exploration of the richness and interconnection of the faith a community has inherited: such delight is, after all, one of the ways in which the theological reasoner deepens his familiarity with the materials available for settlement, and with the connections possible between them. Nevertheless, the ideas that the theological reasoner delights in exploring and connecting are ideas that have their place in the life of the Church, and in the life of discipleship – and the theologian's delighted exploration of those ideas is therefore at the same time an exploration of possible forms of Christian life in the world. Even in delight, theological reasoners should not lose track of what is at stake. Theological reasoning is above all an active pursuit of settlement, an ongoing, iterative, unpredictable social negotiation in pursuit of responsible habitability – and the rest of this book is an attempt to delve deeper into the forms of responsibility, and the forms of negotiation, that this reasoning properly involves.

Looking ahead

The chapters in this section explore various aspects of the practice of theological reason.

Brad Kallenberg describes some of the different forms that theological reasoning has taken in the history of the Church. His chapter shows how far from the mark we would be if we imagined this history to be made up of individual thinkers developing ideas while sitting in their studies or libraries reading books. The history of theological reasoning is not simply a drama of ideas: it is a drama of communities and practices, of experiments in corporate life, of conversations and interactions.

Nicholas Adams' chapter looks more closely at one aspect of this history of theological reasoning: arguing. He shows, again, that arguing is not one single activity, rightly practised in only one way. Theological reasoners have conducted arguments in different ways; they have taken themselves to be doing different kinds of thing when they argue. Adams' chapter itself argues that we should attend to the different shapes and practices of argument – the different logics in play – when we encounter the theological arguments of others, and when we engage in argument for ourselves.

Karen Kilby focuses on another aspect of theological reasoning: the attempt to achieve clarity. She shows that different theological reasoners have hoped for different kinds of clarity, and have worked towards them in different ways. In order to understand the kind of clarity available in theological reasoning, we need to ask what it is that we are trying to be clear about – and that means that theological clarity, which involves clarity about God, might be rather different from other kinds. Kilby nevertheless argues (clearly!) that theological reasoners can and should aim at clarity – even if it will sometimes be clarity about what we can't understand and why.

Simon Oliver explores theological reasoners' engagement with philosophy. In line with earlier chapters, he shows that 'philosophy' is not one thing; it is an activity that has varied in form from context to context and generation to generation. Oliver stresses the ways in which philosophy has, in different ways at different times, been a corporate and practical discipline – a search together for wise ways of living. He then looks at various different ways in which theologians, who are themselves engaged in a search together for wise ways of living, have engaged with philosophy, and the different things they have hoped for – and suggests some questions theological reasoners today might have in mind when they read philosophy.

This section finishes with Chad Pecknold's investigation of the relationship between theological reasons and the public sphere, or public reason. His chapter displays some of the characteristics described above: it is not a general account written by nobody in particular, but a specific argument written by a particular theologian at an identifiable moment in history. Pecknold is a Catholic theologian involved in debates about his tradition's place and role in the public sphere in the United States, and his chapter offers quite a sharp argument from that specific context. That argument displays the kinds of thinking and questioning in which theological reasoners in other contexts, or working within other traditions, might need to engage.

Notes

1 On this topic, see S. Cornwall, *Sex and Uncertainty in the Body of Christ: Intersex Conditions and Christian Theology*, London / Oakeville, CT: Equinox, 2010.

2 He includes in the Church's 'speaking' its 'specific action as a fellowship, ... proclamation by preaching and the administration of the sacraments, ... worship, ... internal and external mission including works of love amongst the sick, the weak and those in jeopardy'. K. Barth, *Church Dogmatics* I/1, trans. G.W. Bromiley and T.F. Torrance, Edinburgh: T&T Clark, 1975, p. 3.

3 Ibid.

4 I elaborate this point a little in *Vulnerable Learning: Toward a Theology of Higher Education*, Cambridge: Grove, 2005, and a lot in *A Theology of Higher Education*, Oxford: Oxford University Press, 2012.

5 This means, incidentally, that the question of whether the individual theologian thinks of himself or herself as a Christian believer is not the most important question to ask. What does matter is the ability of the individual theologian to make proposals about the life of the church that make sense to the members of that church – proposals that do justice to the deep commitments and habits of thought and action of that church. That certainly requires empathetic and imaginative understanding of the life of the church, and to do it well will almost certainly involve some kind of immersion in the life of the church – but it is not hard to imagine someone committing to the pursuit of that kind of understanding, and to making a contribution thereby to the life of the church, whilst still considering themselves an observer rather than a member.

6 See H. Frei, *Types of Christian Theology*, ed. G. Hunsinger and W.C. Placher, New Haven, CT: Yale University Press, 1992, and my discussion of it in *Christ, Providence and History: Hans W. Frei's Public Theology*, London: Continuum, 2004, ch. 8.

7 And that might include its own members, insofar as they are citizens of the world as well as members of the Church.

8 Most famously, perhaps, these ideas were criticized by John Milbank, in *Theology and Social Theory: Beyond Secular Reason*, Oxford: Blackwell, 1990, which begins: 'Once there was no secular. And the secular was not latent, waiting to fill more space with the steam of the "purely human", when the pressure of the sacred was relaxed' (p. 9).

9 Rowan Williams refers to this as the 'celebratory' mode of theology (rather than the 'critical' or 'communicative'), in *On Christian Theology*, Oxford: Blackwell, 2000, p. xiv.

3

SOME PRACTICES OF THEOLOGICAL REASONING, OR, HOW TO WORK WELL WITH WORDS

Brad J. Kallenberg

If anyone is in Christ, it's a whole new world.

(St Paul, 2 Cor. 5:17)

I used to enjoy going on very long runs. Over the years I encountered a surprisingly wide range of animals as I ran: bobcat, eagle, osprey, armadillo, crocodile, wild turkey, owl, coyote, rattlesnake, tarantula, deer, and falcon. Twice I met a bear. But the strangest encounter of all happened on a fire road in the foothills of the San Bernardino Mountains. Coming round the corner I was suddenly faced with a wandering flock of sheep – in urban Southern California! I had never met sheep before and wondered what they would make of me. They were largely unconcerned.

Philosopher and theologian Herbert McCabe asks us to consider the similarities and the differences between the 'world' of sheep and the 'world' of human beings by comparing our respective responses to the presence of a predator, say a wolf.[1] As far as a sheep is concerned, a wolf is dangerous. As far as a human, alone in the wild, is concerned a wolf is also dangerous. 'Danger' is the meaning that the wolf presents to both the sheep and the runner. Because we share this meaning, both the sheep and I would react in similar ways: pulse quickens, nostrils flare, eyes widen and we both flee to avoid the danger posed by the wolf. When we run, we can both be said to act for the same reason.

Acting *for* a reason is one way to describe the world of meanings shared by mammals. In large measure, this kind of 'world' is one that can be described from the outside. A biologist can describe the similarities between the sheep's perception of *Canis lupus* and the human's perception. These similar bodily responses in the presence of a growling wolf are part and parcel of what it means to say that the sheep and the human act 'for the same reason'.

However, human beings also inhabit a 'world' of a higher order than that which we share with other mammals. While both the sheep and I act for a reason, unlike the sheep, I, as a human, can also be said to 'have' a reason for acting. Having reasons means that the wolf becomes significant to humans in ways not available to the sheep. How a sheep reacts to danger is largely (if not entirely) determined by genetics. And while the human has similar genetically determined reactions, the wolf holds added significance to humans because humans share a linguistic world. As a speaker and reader of say, English, I understand that *Canis lupus* is one of the small number of meat eaters that hunts in daylight and hunts in a pack. So while both the sheep and I run *for* a reason (to escape the sharp fangs of the wolf), I do not run directly away from the wolf but at an odd angle because I also *have* a reason the sheep knows nothing about, namely I suspect the unseen presence of the rest of the pack. The sheep cannot conceive facts from books. It can only react to what it perceives here and now. When the rest of the wolf pack becomes perceivable, it will be too late for the poor sheep.

Language users share a higher-order world of meaning than animals can conceive. But language users, being bodily critters themselves, are able to imagine something of what it is like to be a sheep. In fact, in an important sense, human beings can only inhabit this higher-order world of meaning because we are critters who already inhabit the lower-order world of bodies. Now consider: St Paul says that 'if anyone is in Christ: it is a whole new world!' Taken at face value, Paul seems to be saying that there may be an even higher-order world of meaning that eclipses both linguistic and animal worlds and yet remains somehow entangled with them. These interconnections give warrant to one theologian's rough and ready definition of theology as 'the task of working with words in the light of faith'.[2]

Working with words

Our language contains a variety of 'tools' for getting things done ('Shut the door!' 'Will you marry me?' 'I christen thee John.' 'Did you hear the joke about ... ').[3] And the tools themselves are of our making. I do not mean that you or I make up words, but rather that all language speakers, over these many, many centuries, have in the ongoing acts of speaking molded the means by which we communicate. This fact sets us apart: Animals communicate by means that are genetically determined; humans communicate in media of their own making.[4]

Because speaking and being human are deeply intertwined, it is easy to overlook how deeply ingressed language is in us and we in language. Consider an easy word such as 'chair'. Speakers of English know what 'chair' means and show that they do know by using the word appropriately on all the right occasions. This we do without any effort. Conversely, fluency with 'chair' also results in our effortlessly *not* using the word on all the wrong occasions. So, we do not use the word 'chair' when talking about the smell of cheese or the direction of inflation or the imminence of rain. In fact, there are countless ways we do not use the word 'chair' and innumerable ways that we do. How in the world do we keep them straight and manage to do so without paying attention? Part of the answer may be uncovered by watching the way young children learn to speak.

Children begin speaking about the same time they become mobile. First they roll, then they skootch, next comes the army crawl and then ... they're off! In no time they are pulling themselves into standing position and hand-over-hand shuffling from

the decision to let Gentiles into the Church without also requiring them to adopt Jewish ways seems like just the sort of thing Jesus had in mind in his John 17 prayer. But at the time, the decision recorded in Acts 15 was as dicey as it was hard won.

A powerful illustration of theology-as-politics comes from one congregation's response to food shortage in the fourth century.[27] In the year 369 CE, the region surrounding the town of Caesarea [Turkey] – 100 miles from anywhere – was devastated by famine. An extremely dry winter was followed by a spring without rain. The local pastor of the church in Caesarea, a man named Basil (one of the three famous 'Cappadocian Fathers') reported that the sky – 'shut up, naked and cloudless' – has left the fields 'little more than withered clods, unpleasant, sterile, and unfruitful, cracked and pierced to the depths by the hot sun'.[28] The hot spring and summer was followed by another tough winter that made travel from the land-locked town physically impossible. Those who could afford to do so began hoarding grain, while the commoners became 'walking cadavers' as they slowly starved.

Today people are hardened to the horrors of death by starvation because the images are shown so frequently on television. But imagine being a pastor whose job it is to care for these walking cadavers and their swollen-bellied children. There is evidence that the poor were desperate enough to sell their own children as slaves to the rich, thus ensuring nutrition for the child as well as food for the rest of the family for a few more weeks. For their part, the rich had the gall to haggle over the purchase price even though their own act of hoarding grain was making the scarcity problem worse.[29] It was under these conditions that Basil went to work.

The son of a nobleman and therefore at one time independently wealthy, Basil cashed in his own inheritance, bought grain from the hoarders and set up a famine relief center on what used to be the family's summer estate. He organized soup kitchens, built dormitories, constructed a hospital – one of the first, if not the very first, mercy hospitals on record – and hired bona fide physicians and nurses to attend the sick. Basil's *ptochotropheion* (literally, 'Patron House for the Poor') was large enough to create a small economy of its own, enabling the poor as they recovered first to be trained and then actually to serve in various trades.[30] This *ptochotropheion* was the first of several. The sheer scale of these complexes earned them the nickname Basil's Cities.

Basil's activities during this period encompassed a variety of reasoning practices. As we shall see below, Basil was one of the contributors to the doctrine of the Trinity that would be made official in 381 CE. So, obviously Basil excelled at theoretical reasoning. As a pastor/ethicist Basil engaged in practical reasoning classically understood – especially in his homilies, letters, conversations and other verbal strategies he employed to persuade the rich to donate foodstuffs. But also at every turn, Basil was engaged in a distinct sort of practical reasoning called design.[31] Design involves deriving satisfactory responses to problems whose answer cannot simply be 'Googled' by linking 'right means' to 'right aims'. Placement of buildings, layout of each building (whether dormitory or hospital or kitchen), logistics of food acquisition and distribution, procurement of doctors and medicines, organizing day to day care for the sick as well as a jobs-training program as each recovered were all instances of 'right means'. Nothing surprising in this list. The surprise comes under 'right aim'. Basil's city had Christ as its aim. What does it mean for design reasoning to have Christ as its 'aim'?

When Jesus announced to the skeptics 'The kingdom of God is in your midst',[32] he was referring to himself as the first-order instantiation of the new kind of human friendship that he was inaugurating. At that moment, Jesus was the kingdom; later there were a dozen, then 500, then 3,000, and so on.[33] It is not an accident that Basil's *ptochotropheion* was apparently nicknamed *basileia* (Basil's City) because the New Testament phrase for kingdom of God was *basileia theou*. When Christians pray the 'Lord's Prayer', they ask for God's kingdom (*basileia*) to come in the same breath that they ask God to provide bread. In Basil's mind, Jesus' kingdom shows up when bread is provided to the poor of God. Thus, Basil's City was *christomorphic*, which is to say shaped like Christ's kingdom.

Basil's city was christomorphic not only by reason of its mechanical functioning (famine relief) but also by reason of its physical location. Ancient Jewish Law required lepers to live 'outside the city'.[34] That's why Jesus met and healed the ten lepers outside the city wall.[35] Because Jesus befriended the sick and unclean 'outside the city', that is where the author of Hebrews tells us we should go too.[36] 'Outside the city' is where Christ can always be found. Christ went outside the city to suffer and die for the people. And that is the logic behind Basil's intention to build his complexes outside the walled enclaves of the wealthy and often stingy city-dwellers. Like Christ, Basil's complexes made all the difference for the poorest of the poor. Rather than being objects of pity, because of Basil's theology-as-politics the poor were blessed: 'Blessed are you poor (*ptochoi*), for yours is the kingdom (*basiliea*) of God.'[37] By both function and placement, Basil's theological project was community formation of the most revolutionary kind.

Theology-as-conversation

Theology-as-conversation is not something entirely distinct from theology-as-witness or theology-as-politics but rather an aspect of both. In the present age of blogging and texting and tweeting, words seem to have suffered devaluing by inflation. However, for the theologian, words are precious. We've already seen how deeply connected words are with bodily life. Sometimes our bodily living together actually effects a change in the meaning of the words we use. It is the theologian's task to work out the implications of these changes by means of ongoing conversations.

I mentioned above that the predominately Jewish early church restructured common life to include non-Jews. Any non-Jew was welcome who joined in activities such as the prayerful worshiping of Jesus as God[38] and recounting the Good News about Jesus and the reciting of the Shema: 'Hear, O Israel! The LORD is our God, the LORD is one!'[39]

If we understand 'recounting the Good News' to include telling stories like Jesus' prayer in Gethsemane, then the three activities (1) praying to Jesus as God, (2) retelling the story of Jesus' own prayers, and (3) recitation of the oneness of YHWH, constitute a theological headache! It would seem easy to keep any two of the three: (a) one could worship Jesus as God and confess that Jesus himself prayed, so long as one admitted a plurality of gods (for no one prays to oneself!); or (b) one could worship Jesus as the one God, but abandon the notion that Jesus himself prayed;[40] or (c) one could recount tales of Jesus' own prayer life and recite the singularity of

God but thereby infer that Jesus himself must hold a rank somewhat lower than full-fledged divinity.

Most early Christian congregations refused to surrender any of these three practices because together the three activities constituted their identity as Christ-followers (an identity for which many willingly died). These three practices are evident in the opening pages of Acts; the conceptual tension between them was not noticed until some time later. Over the first three centuries of the Church, believers tried to 'settle' things by 'rearranging the tracks' (to borrow Mike Higton's image from chapter 2). And I'll leave it to the reader to ferret out all the details of the drama as it finally came to a head in the fourth century. However, a couple of details about the *manner* of the 'settling' will shed light on the practice of theological reasoning.

There is a huge conceptual difference between the 'settlement' known as the Nicene Creed (325 CE) and the one that was adopted at Constantinople some fifty-six years later (381 CE). Both have to do with the status of the Lord Jesus Christ. After positive assertions of what Christians believe, namely that the Lord Jesus Christ is of the same, identical substance (*homoousia*; *homo* + *ousia* = 'same substance' or *consubstantial*) as God the Father, the Nicene Creed goes on to explicitly outlaw certain ways of saying things.

> But, those who say, Once he was not, or he was not before his generation, or he came to be out of nothing, or who assert that he, the Son of God, is of a different *hypostasis* or *ousia*, or that he is a creature, or changeable, or mutable, the Catholic and Apostolic Church anathematizes them.[41]

The important point for us is the proscription against asserting 'that he, the Son of God, is of a different *hypostasis* or *ousia*'.[42] Obviously, if the Lord Jesus Christ is of identical God-stuff as the Almighty Creator, he cannot be said to be of a different substance (*ousia*)! But Nicaea also prevented Christians from saying the Lord Jesus Christ is of a different *hypostasis*. But now observe: the Constantinopolitan Creed affirms consubstantiality (one *ousia*) but *drops* the proscription against saying Jesus was a different hypostasis. In other words, after 381 it was indeed orthodox to say both that the Lord Jesus Christ was of the same substance (*ousia*) and a different *hypostasis*.[43] In fact, the very construction *proscribed* by Nicaea became *normative* for Christian doctrine after 381: one *ousia*, three *hypostases*, or roughly, 'one substance, three persons'.[44] How did the council of Constantinople ever pull it off, this reversal?

Virtually all the heavy lifting for the semantic transformation of *hypostasis* was done, surprisingly, in a series of hand-written letters. Some of the letters are known by the addressee, such as 'To Ablabius'. Others are simply indicated by number, such as *Letter 38* and *Letter 236* – which tell us something about how many letters theologians wrote, if not also how many attempts it takes to achieve a satisfactory 'settlement'. These letters seem to be preparatory work for longer presentations in group settings.[45] Thus despite the strict synonymy on which Athanasius insisted ('*hypostasis* is *ousia* and has no other meaning apart from *ousia* itself'[46]), Basil (or perhaps Basil's brother, Gregory, the authorship is uncertain) instead proposes in *Letter 236* that the two be understood as semantically distinct.[47]

Although this example of doctrinal development makes for thick conceptual weeds, it does remind us again that theology is not something done by oneself in the closed space between the ears. Not only were these councils triggered by years of intractable bodily practices of worshiping, telling and reciting, but the main players were themselves not social recluses: the very Basil who oversaw the construction of *ptochotropheion* is up to his neck in letter writing about the meaning of *ousia* and *hypostasis*. Nor ought we to conclude that theology is primarily a matter of inventing new concepts.[48] Rather the point is that the best theological language evolves from lengthy and ongoing conversation.

So important is conversation to theology that the practice of theological discussion slowly evolved its own ground rules. These ground rules enabled all parties both to squeeze the very most out of a discussion *and* to keep the conversation going. Thomas Aquinas' thirteenth-century work, *Summa Theologica*, is a good example of these ground rules. Each entry begins with a question followed by a concise summary of what former thinkers had said about the question. Then comes Thomas's own proposal, followed by a defense of the claim, and then finally his answer to the objections of the former voices. This style of theological conversation is called *quaestiones disputatae* (disputed questions). But its goal is not so much to explicate a final position (although some treat it this way) as to invite further conversation.

Theology as working on oneself

Human beings do not naturally run marathons or speak in front of large crowds. Nevertheless, humans are gifted with the sort of nature that can be trained to do things we ordinarily shy away from. It is in this light we may understand how some of the self-imposed 'excesses' of earlier Christians are integral to theological reasoning.

Consider Anselm. Contemporary soteriology cannot move forward without first tackling Anselm's *Cur Deus Homo?* (*Why the God-Man?*). And philosophers of religion are still today debating the merits of Anselm's (so-called) 'ontological proof' in the opening pages of *Proslogion*. Yet many of these same scholars are often surprised to learn of the rigor of Anselm's self-mortification.

Anselm himself recalls his life as a thirty-something theologian at the Bec monastery.[49] He writes that the years between 1063 and 1070 were marked by the study of Scripture and devoted friendships. But these years were also marked by hallucinations! How so? In addition to regular religious fasts, Anselm lived in a self-imposed state of semi-starvation. In addition, Anselm was perpetually sleep-deprived, because the only time for private meditation, writing, and prayer was in the small hours of the morning. Collective worship began well before sunrise and was repeated eight more times, the last around midnight. Semi-starvation and sleep deprivation are surely the biological contributors to Anselm's visions. But Anselm undertook his asceticism intentionally, as a training regimen for knowing God.[50] Today many Western theologians are apt to lament Anselm's regimen, thinking that if he had gotten more sleep and better nutrition he would have done better theology. But Anselm saw his daily grind as crucial to doing theology. And his stance is in continuity with generations of Christian discipleship stretching back to the desert fathers. Perhaps you have heard some of the spectacular tales: one fellow lived atop a small platform (one meter square, forty-five feet high) for four decades; some mixed ashes with their food; others lived without sunshine, beat themselves black and blue, or had themselves lashed to a stake in a mosquito-infested swamp. But why?

There is a simple answer: the early Christian ascetics understood themselves to be martyrs-in-training.[51] In an age where Christianity was illegal ('Deny Jesus or die!'), these brave souls volunteered for severe training now in order not to deny Christ later.

But what has this got to do with Anselm? By his day, Christianity had been the official religion of the Empire for at least five hundred years. Anselm's era was one in which popes crowned emperors rather than flee them! So why the need for self-mortification? If Simeon the Stylite was a martyr-in-training, Anselm considered himself to be a theologian-in-training. Like an athlete or a musician, Anselm knew that excellence would come only as a function of bodily discipline. (Once again we see the inescapable connection between words and bodies.)

Nor was Anselm unique in this view. Six hundred years earlier Augustine had written in his commentary on Psalms that 'We ought not love fullness in this world.'[52] The idea was that privation and pain school one to long for God single-mindedly with one's whole body. For Anselm, it went without saying that the quality of one's knowledge of God was a function of the quality of one's character. And as character (*ethos*, long 'e') was the sum of one's habits (*ethos*, short 'e'), theologians of the age ordered their activities with due diligence. These examples could be multiplied.[53] Today the notion that the quality of one's knowledge is a function of one's character seems ludicrous to most of us. Why is that? What happened? What separates our thinking from that of our theological forebears? One answer, the short version, is that during the long eighteenth-century Enlightenment, we began to forget how to read the Bible canonically.[54] For example, the study of the Bible seems to have been reduced to merely the application of historical critical methodology. Please do not misunderstand me. Historical criticism is enormously helpful to theology.[55] However, historical criticism cannot be the sum of biblical theology because it inverts the position of reader and text. Historical criticism asks the question of correspondence: how well does the biblical text correspond to facts that are known through non-biblical sources? This strategy, in effect, places the reader over the text to render judgment on it. However, good theology also requires one to be under the text, as it were. Theology is not so much us interrogating the text on questions of history as it is allowing the text to interrogate us. Thus Augustine, in a letter to Jerome (d. 420), wrote

> it is from those books alone of the Scriptures, which are now called canonical, that I have learned to pay them such honor and respect as to believe most firmly that not one of their authors has erred in writing anything at all. If I do find anything in those books which seems contrary to the truth, I decide that either the text is corrupt, or the translator did not follow what was really said, *or that I failed to understand it*.[56]

If these examples sound odd to our ears, we probably ought to conclude that it is we and not they who are the oddballs! An integral part of theological reasoning has always been a planning of one's daily grind so as to achieve (eventually, hopefully) the kind of character capable of doing good theology. Consider this sensible piece of advice: if a burglar is breaking into the house, it is too late to *start* lifting weights! Anselm's example urges us to begin 'lifting weights' today. But note this: theological weight training is not restricted to brainwork – like learning to read your Greek New Testament. As much as brainwork is valuable, Anselm would have us pay close attention to what we do with the rest of our bodies. Even children are taught this.

Remember the children's song, 'Frère Jacques'? Brother John is a monk who is dozing during prayer.

> Are you sleeping?
> Are you sleeping?
> Brother John?
> Brother John?
> Soon it will be morning,
> Soon it will be morning,
> Ding, ding, dong,
> Ding, ding, dong.

Pre-dawn prayer (*matins* or *lauds*) was only slightly more difficult than midnight (*compline*) prayers. Nine times a day monks gathered to pray the book of Psalms. And because matins and compline were done in total darkness, it was not uncommon for monks to have memorized the entire book of Psalms! One begins to get the significance of Gavin D'Costa's point that we are to do theology on our knees, perhaps literally.[57] Of course prayer is only one of the ways bodies were made adequate for theological reasoning. The point is this: good theology requires a working on oneself.[58] It is no wonder that, prior to the Enlightenment, theologians were almost always deemed to be *saints* as well as scholars.

Theology as disclosure modeling

Thus far I've recounted four of the (perhaps many) reasoning practices that contribute to the theologian's task. Theology-as-witness is not a simple phrase-by-phrase same-saying, but the deliberate attempt to *show*, as well as to say, the Gospel by means of an intentional alignment of one's bodily life with the form of Jesus' narrative. Theology-as-politics extends that alignment from individual biography to the shape of a community such that together our corporate form of living becomes a plausibility structure for the Gospel. Theology-as-conversation highlights the teamwork and interchange permeating one's work with words.[59] And theology-as-working-on-oneself gestures to the way that decisions about one's daily grind (when to get out of bed, what to eat, and so on) are themselves profoundly theological decisions. In each of these cases, I've tried to show that bodies are connected with the words that are the stock and trade of theologians. We are now ready to glimpse the practice of theological reasoning as an instance of disclosure modeling.[60]

Aquinas gives us a toehold into the notion of disclosure models in his notion of 'analogy'. The tricky bit for us thoroughly Modern Millies to grasp is that not all examples of the English word 'analogy' fit under Thomas's use of *analogia*. For

Figure 3.1

example, the easiest kind of analogy to understand is proportionality. In geometry, one says that two triangles are 'similar' if the lengths of their respective sides are proportional. Is this what Aquinas means by saying theological language is analogical? No. God is not 'similar' to us – albeit bigger, stronger, faster.[61] Aquinas, like Augustine before him, explicitly *denies* that theological language employs proportionality to depict what God is like.[62] It would seem that Aquinas leaves theologians forever tongue-tied when it comes to speaking about the very object of faith, namely God. However, there is another way to understand *analogia*. If scale models can be constructed from 'sideways on',[63] then, in contrast, theology strives for disclosure models by means of growth terms. Let us tackle each in turn.

A *disclosure model* shows or gestures toward something that cannot be stated explicitly.[64] For example, if a math teacher begins drawing a series of regular polygons on the chalkboard: triangle, square, pentagon, and so on (see Figure 3.1), the student fairly quickly sees the circle as the geometric object towards which the series tends. But notice how this has happened: every polygon has a finite number of straight sides. A circle has, by definition, no straight side; in fact a circle has no 'side' at all! Nevertheless, the circle is truly disclosed by a series of polygons, even though the circle is not itself a polygon.

The notion of *growth terms* trades on the fact – a fact we tend to forget – that very few words are merely labels. A significant percentage of words require growth of the speaker if the speaker is to employ them well. For example, 'love' is a growth term.[65] Teenagers imagine that they *know* what love is and on this thin understanding youngsters marry. The teenager is not wrong to use the word 'love'. But thirty years and many hardships later the no-longer-teenage couple will have grown into a deeper fluency with the word 'love'. The teenagers are right to say 'God is love'. But the middle-aged couple is *more* right, for together they read 1 John 4:8 with deeper understanding. It is not that the word 'love' has changed meaning over the course of time, but that the human speakers have grown.

Every practice employs growth terms. Every skilled practitioner can give examples: for the engineer the motor that begins to smell is under too much 'stress'; for the physician a certain 'laceration' suggests a suicide attempt rather than an accident; for the symphony conductor the bass notes are 'too heavy', and so on. Regardless of the field, the presence of growth terms, as well as the tacit knowledge that growth terms are tied to,[66] points to the undeniable fact that to speak well 'inside' of a skill-based practice will require ongoing transformation of the speaker. Theology is no different. Theology done well is a self-involving, self-transforming enterprise. Theology, in addition to all we've seen above, is the employment of (self-demanding) growth terms to effect always provisional disclosure models of God.

With the concept of growth terms we have come full circle, back to the entry point of this chapter: the linguistic philosophy of Fr. Herbert McCabe. We've also reached a place where we can better appreciate the image of 'settling' employed by Mike Higton (chapter 2) to describe reasoning. Like any particular arrangement of the toy train tracks, a disclosure model is necessarily always provisional and context-bound. When one discovers a piece of toy train track under the sofa, one must begin the 'settling' process all over again. While it is certainly the case that a 'settlement' in theology may be a highly structured architectonic system, it must also be acknowledged that theological reasoning may also take the form of parables and stories. Before concluding, let me recount a disclosure model that also involves toy train tracks. This disclosure comes from a surprising source: Catholic novelist Graham Greene.

In 1948 Graham Greene spins a tale of a conversation between two strangers pleasantly surprised by each other's company during a long, frigid, dark December train ride across Britain. The unnamed narrator identifies himself as agnostic. While he has some sympathy for the intuition that God exists, the recent horrors of the Second World War drive him to declare 'intellectually I am revolted at the whole notion of such a God. ... When you think what God – if there is a God – allows. It is not merely the physical agonies, but think of the corruption, even of children ... '[67] His companion, David Martin, who is a religious believer (Catholic in particular), is empathetic but gently objects that the human view is so limited that there can be nothing like an explanation on these matters. The best we can do, David says, is 'catch hints', even if such hints 'mean nothing at all to a human being *other than the man who catches them*'.[68]

So what is required to catch a theological hint? Hints are unlike scientific evidence – objective, repeatable, universally accessible, unambiguous. Catching hints is more like trying to figure out another's look or read another's intentions: 'What did she mean by doing this? What did he mean when he said that?' In the case of God, David suggests, hints of God may be manifest when events turn out as human actors do *not* intend.

As they talk, the narrator begins to suspect that his companion is one of those very rare persons – he has only met one other – who might be described as 'completely happy'. So his ears perk up when David begins to recount the horrifying childhood tale of his own near-corruption at the hands of an ugly, one-eyed baker named Blacker. Blacker – renowned as a free thinker, a skeptic, and an atheist – intentionally plotted to corrupt the then ten-year-old David. The point of the scheme was to procure a Eucharistic wafer so that Blacker might find out for himself 'what your God tastes like'.[69] The bait was an electric train set.

Over a period of several days Blacker patiently cultivated David's fondness for the toy. When David's fondness reached addictive proportions, Blacker made the offer:

> He said, 'You serve at Mass, don't you? It would be easy for you to get at one of those things. I tell you what I'll do – I'd swap this electric train set for one of your wafers – consecrated, mind. It's got to be consecrated.'[70]

David-the-acolyte carries the plan off flawlessly, tucking the consecrated wafer under his tongue and later, in secret, twists it into a bit of newspaper (pregnantly entitled *The Universe*) and stuffs it into his pocket for safekeeping. As he readies himself for bed, he empties his pockets and is instantly 'haunted by the presence of God on the chair'.[71]

As night deepens, Blacker appears ominously outside David's bedroom window with both the promise of the train set *and* the threat of a straight razor – presumably for slitting David's throat should he back out of their bargain.

> 'Give it me,' he said. 'Quick. You shall have the train in the morning.'
> I shook my head. He said 'I've got the bleeder here and the key. You'd better toss it down.'
> 'Go away,' I said, but could hardly speak for fear.
> 'I'll bleed you first and then I'll have it just the same.'[72]

How can a ten-year-old possibly resist the psychological duress of such emotionally charged bullying with clear intent to harm? If we freeze the story at this instant, Blacker has the upper hand. Like the Cyclops of old, this one-eyed baker was very clever with his hands, having made a mechanism of this boy. David was but a cog in a machine that inexorably cranks out intended effects. David was *bound* to hand over the prize. How could he do otherwise? The reader winces because the outcome seems inevitable. Or is it?

> 'I'll bleed you first and then I'll have it just the same.'
> 'Oh no you won't,' I said. I went to the chair and picked it – Him – up. There was only one place where he was safe. I couldn't separate the Host from the paper. So I swallowed both. The newsprint stuck like a prune skin to the back of my throat ...[73]

In a flash, the inevitability of unspeakable evil is foiled. Ours is the kind of universe in which persons who are most susceptible become pawns of 'irresistible' evil, because they are least able to resist evil. Yet, incomprehensibly, it is one of the children who effects a transformation of evil's 'inevitable' success into utter defeat. So startling is the reversal that in retrospect it is evil's defeat, rather than its success, that seems not merely good but in some deep sense *inevitable*. David continues,

> Then something happened which seems to me now more terrible than his [Blacker's] desire to corrupt or my thoughtless act: he began to weep – the tears ran lopsidedly out of the one good eye and his shoulders shook. I only saw his face for a moment before he bent his head and strode off, the bald turnip head shaking, into the dark. When I think of it now, it's almost as if I had seen that Thing weeping for its inevitable defeat. It had tried to use me as a weapon, and now I had broken in its hands and it wept its hopeless tears through one of Blacker's eyes.[74]

It is one thing to hope that an enemy's weapon breaks before it can be used. (Thus the Psalmist prays that 'their sword shall enter their own heart, and their bows shall be broken'.[75]) But sometimes *people* are used as weapons against others. And when those humans-as-weapons break for no apparent reason, and even more so when they are *redeemed* by means of their inexplicable breaking, a trace of something Wonderful remains for the one who can catch the hint.

Conclusion: On knowing when to stop talking

In this chapter, we have examined five complementary practices of theological reasoning. These five are not meant to be exhaustive, nor are they well defined and self-contained. If taken together we can see that to work well with words, the theologian must bear witness, envision and inhabit a politic, invite conversation, undertake a training regimen and construct disclosure models. Along the way I have sampled quotations from the enormous variety of word-workings from past theologians: sermons, biblical commentaries, formal 'orations', systematic treatments (like Aquinas' *Summa*), journal articles, 'apologies', theological books, personal correspondence and novels. I've tried to make the case that working well with words involves all these genres if for no other reason than that theology is a team sport.

I conclude with a reminder that working well with words may sometimes require us not to say anything at all. In our scientific age, theologians are frequently duped into thinking that theology is about explaining what we believe. Because our words are connected to our bodies, we do well always to remember that 'created beings ... find it impossible to speak adequately concerning things ineffable'.[76] Augustine reminds us that the goal of theological reasoning is not explanation. Rather the goal of theology, the criterion of our working well with words, is that we always and only speak in a manner worthy of the Gospel.

> We believe that the Father, Son, and Holy Spirit are one God, maker and ruler of every creature, and that the 'Father' is not the 'Son', nor 'Holy Spirit' 'Father' or 'Son'; but a Trinity of mutually related persons, and a unity of equal essence. So let us attempt to understand this truth, praying that he who we wish to understand would help us in doing so, so that we can set out [in words] whatever we thus understand with such careful reverence that nothing unworthy is said (even if we sometimes say one thing instead of another). ... But we must never allow any error to lead us astray in such a way that we say something about the Trinity which relates to the creature rather than the Creator, or results from wild speculation.[77]

And this means that, in the end, the theologian must grow until he or she knows when it is time to stop talking.

Notes

1 McCabe uses this sort of illustration in several places. For example, H. McCabe, *Law, Love and Language*, New York, NY: Continuum, 2004, ch. 3; 'Soul, Life, Machines and Language', in B. Davies (ed.) *Faith within Reason*, London and New York: Continuum, 2007, pp. 123–49.
2 J.H. Yoder, *Preface to Theology: Christology and Theological Method*, Grand Rapids, MI: Brazos Press, 2007, p. 41. This theme has become the title of a recent book: S. Hauerwas, *Working with Words: On Learning to Speak Christian*, Eugene, OR: Cascade Books, 2011.
3 L. Wittgenstein, *Philosophical Investigations*, ed. G.E.M. Anscombe and R. Rhees, trans. G.E.M. Anscombe, New York, NY: Macmillan, 1953, § 23.
4 McCabe, *Law, Love and Language*, pp. 76–77.

5 L. Wittgenstein, *The Blue and Brown Books*, New York, NY: Harper and Brothers, 1958, p. 24.

6 The memorable phrase is W.V.O. Quine's. Cited in Richard Rorty, 'Hesse and Davidson on Metaphor', in *Objectivity, Relativism, and Truth: Philosophical Papers, Vol. 1*, Cambridge: Cambridge University Press, 1991, p. 166 n. 17.

7 Of course, today the word 'God' more often shows up in coarse language. Thus the comedian's quip that he grew up thinking his own name was 'Jesus Christ' ('Jesus Christ, stop hitting your brother!'). Surely we live in a culture in which learning to use the word 'God' well is very difficult for children. These children grow into adults who are equally difficult to evangelize.

8 Theologians are not content to describe the world-of-meaning from 'sideways on', as it were, like the social scientist does. It is not that theologians are shy to employ social scientific disciplines. But at the end of the day the theologian herself is inside the world of meaning she studies. See K. Barth, 'The Strange New World within the Bible', in *The Word of God and the Word of Man*, ed. Douglas Horton, New York, NY: Harper & Row, 1957, pp. 28–50.

9 What 'under' and 'in step' (Gal. 5:25) mean, of course, are themselves theological questions. But such restrictions are not optional to the would-be theologian, for in abandoning them one ceases to be a theologian.

10 See McCabe, *Law, Love and Language*, pp. 26, 33–38, 44, 54, 60, 61, 113.

11 For example, Mark 9:32.

12 For example, the picture of a suffering servant did not fit the cultural expectation of a militant Messiah.

13 Compare Acts 2:37 with Acts 17:32.

14 2 Kings 4:8–37.

15 The fascinating evolution of the concept of 'resurrection' is detailed by R. Martin-Achard, 'Resurrection (OT)' and G.W.E. Nickelsburg, 'Resurrection (Early Judaism & Christianity)', in *Anchor Bible Dictionary*, ed. D.N. Freedman, New York, NY: Doubleday, 1992.

16 1 Thess. 1:5.

17 The Greek term *apodeixis* was used in secular society to describe the method of 'carding' a person who wanted entrance into the Temple of Isis, which only admitted priests who had previously been initiated into cultic secrets. The test was simple: the person was given a script of hieroglyphics and asked to translate – a *skill* that only cult members could do. So Paul is saying that his message is proved or demonstrated (*apodeixis*) by supernatural knowhow (*dunamis*) of ordinary daily living. See 1 Cor. 2:1–5. See the entry on *apodeixis* in J.H. Moulton and G. Milligan, *The Vocabulary of the Greek Testament Illustrated from the Papyri and Other Non-Literary Sources*, Grand Rapids, MI: Wm. B. Eerdmans Publishing Company, 1930.

18 Acts 21:10–14.

19 See Acts 9:25 and 2 Cor. 11:33.

20 1 Thess. 1:5.

21 I owe this exegetical insight to Glen Stassen.

22 Thus Thessalonian believers who saw what sort of men Paul's party proved to be themselves became imitators of Paul, and thereby imitators of the Lord Jesus, in such a manner that the Thessalonian believers became examples for novice Christians across all of Macedonia and Achaia! 1 Thess. 1:5–8.

23 Aristides, 'The Apology of Aristides the Philosopher', in *The Ante-Nicene Fathers (First Series). Original Supplement to the American Edition*, vol. 10, ed. A. Menzies, Grand Rapids, MI: Wm. B. Eerdmans Publishing Company, 1965, pp. 276–78.

24 The biblical warrant for the notion that lives display the message can be found in 1 Tim. 3:15 where Paul says 'I am writing these things to you ... so that you may know how people ought to conduct themselves in God's household, that is, the church of the living God, the pillar and bulwark of the truth.' The Greek grammar indicates without a doubt that it is the church that is the pillar and bulwark of the truth and not the other way around. The term 'pillar' (*stylos*) was the ancient equivalent of a showcase. See U. Wilckens entry in G. Kittel and G. Friedrich (eds) *Theological Dictionary of the New Testament*, vol. 7,

Grand Rapids, MI: Wm. B. Eerdmans Publishing Company, 1971, p. 733. For further discussion see B.J. Kallenberg, 'The Technological Evangelist', in *God and Gadgets: Following Jesus in a Technological World*, Eugene, OR: Cascade Books, 2010, pp. 43–81.

25 Phil. 1:27. Moulton and Milligan in *The Vocabulary of the Greek Testament*, citing Dibelius, observe that *politeuomai* ought to be understood as virtually synonymous with 'walk' (*peripateo*). A related idea shows up in Gal. 5:25, 'y'all keep in step (*stoicheo*) with the Spirit.' Here the idea seems to be a complex coordinated activity, like a marching band that wheels and turns and spells out 'Ohio' – but always doing so in step to a single rhythm.

26 Phil. 4:2.

27 Thanks to Adam Sheridan for alerting me to 'Basil's Cities'. For a more complete discussion see my *By Design: Ethics, Theology and the Practice of Engineering*, Eugene, OR: Cascade Books, 2013.

28 St Basil, 'In Time of Famine and Drought (*Homila Dicta Tempore Famis Et Siccitatis; Hom 8*)', in S.R. Holman, *The Hungry Are Dying: Beggars and Bishops in Roman Cappadocia*, New York and Oxford: Oxford University Press, 2001, p. 184.

29 Holman, *The Hungry Are Dying*, p. 69.

30 Holman, *The Hungry Are Dying*, p. 74.

31 In the thirteenth century, Hugh of St Victor distinguished mechanical reasoning from theoretical reasoning, practical reasoning and logic/math. All four operations are redeemed in Christ. For further explanation see ch. 10 of Kallenberg, *By Design*.

32 Luke 17:21.

33 1 Cor. 15:6; Acts 2:41.

34 Num. 5:1–4.

35 Luke 17:12.

36 Heb. 13:13.

37 Luke 6:20.

38 There are nine explicit attestations of divinity to Jesus in the Greek New Testament: Rom. 9:5; Jn. 1:1, 18, 20:28; Titus 2:13; 2 Pet. 1:1, 1 Jn. 5:20, Heb. 1:8–9, and the variant reading of Gal. 2:20. Other possible attestations include Acts 20:28, Col. 2:2 and 1 Tim. 6:16.

39 Deut. 6:4.

40 The identification of Jesus as God alone takes various heretical forms of modalism such as patripassianism.

41 J.H. Leith (ed.), *Creeds of the Church: A Reader in Christian Doctrine from the Bible to the Present*, 3rd edn, Louisville, KY: Westminster John Knox Press, 1982, pp. 30–31.

42 *E ex heteras hupostaseos e ousias phaskontas einai.*

43 In point of historical fact, twenty years before the Council of Constantinople, the ambiguity was pushed to the extreme at the Synod of Alexandria (362 CE) which said that *either* formula was acceptable for describing Jesus' status relative to the Creator – one *ousia* and one *hypostasis* OR one *ousia* but three different *hypostases* – so long as the heresy of Arianism was avoided. Arianism was popularized by the sing-song jingle: 'There was a time when the Son was not.'

44 On the one hand, the Constantinopolitan Creed risked bi-theism insofar as it conflicted with Athanasius' (who died a decade before the council) insistence that the two terms were strictly *synonyms*. On the other hand, the Constantinopolitan Creed also risked falling into subordinationism because the pagan philosopher Plotinus had already used *hypostasis* as the label for a lesser mode of existence. Plotinus says that each successive emanation from 'The One' was properly called a '*hypostasis*' while being itself, *ousia*, is properly attributed to 'the One'.

45 For example, Gregory of Nazianzus, 'Third Theological Oration Concerning the Son', in *The Trinitarian Controversy*, ed. W.G. Rusch, Philadelphia, PA: Fortress Press, 1980. Gregory wrote some forty-five 'orations', some for a specific public reading but some also for primarily written circulation. See G.A. Kennedy, *Greek Rhetoric under Christian Emperors*, Princeton, NJ: Princeton University Press, 1983, pp. 215–40.

46 See Athanasius' 'Letter to the Bishops of Egypt and Libya', cited in J. Zizioulas, *Being as Communion: Studies in Personhood and the Church*, Crestwood, NY: St. Vladimir's Seminary Press, 1985, p. 36 n. 23.

47 Full translated texts of the Cappadocian correspondence can be accessed at www.ccel.org/ccel/schaff/npnf208.ix.i.html (accessed 25 October 2013).

48 Of course, occasionally new words are invented: *trinitas* and *synderesis* being among the most important. Tertullian (second century) appears to be the first to use the word *trinitas*. The term *synderesis* appears first in Jerome (fourth century). Although it seems to be a copyist error for the Greek word *suneidesis* ('co-knowledge'), the term plays a crucial role in Aquinas' account of practical reason. See *Summa Theologiae* I.79.12. See also H. McCabe, 'Aquinas on Good Sense', *New Blackfriars* 67.796, 1986, pp. 419–31.

49 For a fuller treatment of the relation of Anselm's asceticism and his theology see B.J. Kallenberg, 'Praying for Understanding: Reading Anselm through Wittgenstein', *Modern Theology* 20.4, 2004, pp. 527–46.

50 In the early days of the Christian Church, asceticism was taken to be the training that readied one for the literal seeing of God: for martyrdom. See M.A. Tilley, 'The Ascetic Body and the (Un)Making of the World of the Martyr', *Journal of the American Academy of Religion* 59.3, 1991, pp. 467–79.

51 Ibid.

52 St Augustine, *Exposition on the Book of Psalms*, ed. A. Cleveland Coxe, *Nicene and Post-Nicene Fathers (First Series)*, vol. 8, Grand Rapids, MI: Wm. B. Eerdmans Publishing Company, 1989, p. 259.

53 For further study see G. D'Costa, 'On Cultivating the Disciplined Habits of a Love Affair or on How to Do Theology on Your Knees', *New Blackfriars* 79.925, 1998, pp. 116–35. A similar emphasis on bodily training ran through ancient philosophical thought. See P. Hadot, *Philosophy as a Way of Life*, ed. A.I. Davidson, trans. M. Chase, Oxford: Blackwell, 1995.

54 This enormous claim is central to H. Frei, *The Eclipse of Biblical Narrative: A Study in Eighteenth- and Nineteenth-Century Hermeneutics*, New Haven, CT: Yale University Press, 1974.

55 To cite one poignant example, evidence of the Ancient Near Eastern 'Myth of Omphalos' in the Hebrew Bible unmasks Solomon's ulterior motive in dedicating the newly finished temple, namely, he is trying to tether YHWH to a physical location. Cp. S. Terrien, 'The Omphalos Myth and Hebrew Religion', *Vetus Testamentum* 20.3, 1970, pp. 315–38; 'The Metaphor of the Rock in Biblical Theology', in T. Linafelt and T.K. Beal (eds) *God in the Fray: A Tribute to Walter Brueggemann*, Minneapolis, MN: Fortress Press, 1998, pp. 157–71; with W. Brueggemann, 'The Royal Consciousness', in *The Prophetic Imagination*, Philadelphia, PA: Fortress Press, 1978, pp. 28–43.

56 St Augustine, 'To Jerome', in *Letters*, vol. 1 (1–82), ed. R.J. Deferrari, Washington, DC: The Catholic University of America Press, 1951, p. 392. Emphasis added. For more on Augustine's seeing himself under or even in the biblical text, see S. Hauerwas with D. Burrell, 'From System to Story: An Alternative Pattern for Rationality in Ethics', in *Truthfulness and Tragedy*, Notre Dame, IN: University of Notre Dame Press, 1977, pp. 15–39.

57 D'Costa, 'How to Do Theology on Your Knees'.

58 'Work on oneself' is the title of theologian and philosopher Fergus Kerr's recent book. Both he and I are borrowing from L. Wittgenstein, *Culture and Value*, ed. G.H. von Wright and H. Nyman, trans. P. Winch, 2nd edn, Oxford: Blackwell, 1980, 24e.

59 Once again we must be careful. For medieval theologians like Anselm, *contemplatio* was an achievement that could only be reached after one had progressed sufficiently in *meditatio* and *cogitatio*, the last of which was often bound up in the teaching and arguing with students, which is to say a *shared* enterprise.

60 Technically speaking, disclosure modeling is a subset of 'design,' a topic at the heart of my own work. See B.J. Kallenberg, 'Dynamical Similarity and the Problem of Evil', in *God, Grace and Creation: The Annual Publication of the College Theology Society 2009, vol. 55*, ed. P.J. Rossi, Maryknoll, NY: Orbis Books, 2010, pp. 163–83; *By Design*; 'Rethinking Fideism through the Lens of Wittgenstein's Engineering Outlook', *International Journal for the Philosophy of Religion* 71.1, 2012, pp. 55–73.

61 It must be noted that Duns Scotus does tend toward this way of thinking. For criticism of what has become called the 'univocity of being', see the writings of Catherine Pickstock and David Burrell, esp. D.B. Burrell, 'Creator/Creatures Relation: "The Distinction" Vs. "Onto-Theology"', *Faith and Philosophy* 25.2, 2008, pp. 177–89; C. Pickstock, *After Writing: On the Liturgical Consummation of Philosophy*, Oxford, UK & Malden, MA: Blackwell, 1998.

62 Aquinas makes a distinction between proportion and proportionateness (*proportionalitatem*). I owe this insight to Michael Cox. See St Thomas Aquinas, 'Liber IV Distinctio XLIX Quaestio II', in *Scriptum Super Sententiis*. See also St Augustine, 'Sermon 117,' in *Part III – Sermons, vol. 4: Sermons 94a–147a*, ed. John E. Rotelle, Brooklyn, NY: New City Press, 1990, pp. 209–23.

63 The term 'sideways on' is borrowed from philosopher John McDowell who criticizes the modern attempt to try to do serious reflection while standing nowhere in particular. See, e.g. J. McDowell, 'Non-Cognitivism and Rule-Following', *The Monist* 62.3, 1979, pp. 141–62.

64 The term is Ramsey's. See I.T. Ramsey, *Models and Mystery*, London: Oxford University Press, 1964; 'Talking of God: Models Ancient and Modern', in J.H. Gill (ed.) *Christian Empiricism*, London: Sheldon Press, 1974, pp. 120–40.

65 See especially, McCabe, *Law, Love and Language*, pp. 68–103.

66 Tacit knowledge is important in every social practice. For an entertaining introduction to tacit knowledge in engineering, perhaps the most technical of fields, see M.B. Crawford, *Shop Class as Soulcraft*, New York, NY: Penguin, 2009, esp. ch. 7.

67 G. Greene, 'A Hint of an Explanation', in *Twenty-One Stories*, New York, NY: Viking Press, 1962, pp. 136–37.

68 Greene, 'A Hint', p. 137. Emphasis added.

69 Greene, 'A Hint', p. 143.

70 Ibid.

71 Greene, 'A Hint', p. 147.

72 Greene, 'A Hint', p. 148.

73 Ibid.

74 Greene, 'A Hint', p. 149.

75 Ps. 37:15.

76 Athanasius: 'For all created beings ... find it impossible to speak adequately concerning things ineffable.' Cited in A.I.C. Heron, *The Holy Spirit*, Philadelphia, PA: Westminster Press, 1983, p. 79.

77 *de Trinitate* IX.i.1, cited in A.E. McGrath (ed.) *The Christian Theology Reader*, Oxford: Blackwell, 1995, p. 100.

4

ARGUING AS A THEOLOGICAL PRACTICE

Nicholas Adams

To consider Christian theological practices of arguing is to consider everything else as well. It is to consider the community and its patterns of relations between persons; it is to consider philosophy and its patterns of rules for drawing inferences; it is to consider the formation of doctrine and the deliberative councils that produce and rethink it; it is to consider Christian ethics and the unending sphere of contention in which it is located; it is to consider the Bible and the perennial disagreements over its interpretation; it is to consider the university which is a house for argumentation; it is to consider the media and the challenges which radio, television, and the internet pose to practices of argumentation.

As a bullet list, arguing relates to the following topics:

- doctrine
- Christian ethics
- Church history
- philosophical theology
- biblical interpretation
- theology in the media.

That might seem daunting enough, for reader and writer alike. But our situation is actually much worse. Arguing may, in fact, be pointless.

The potential pointlessness of arguing can be demonstrated in two ways. The first is to consider the contemporary Western context of much theology, and the expectations of public speech embodied in its public media. The second is to consider more narrowly the hopes and dreams of seventeenth-century philosophers (who forged many of our philosophical rules for arguing) and to note how these hopes and dreams evaporated in a dramatic way in the twentieth century. (They did not evaporate for everyone in the same way, however, and this produces a kind of double life for arguing in theology, as I will show.)

Opinion's triumph over truth

First, some observations about the world around us. Those reading this volume live in an environment dominated by the internet and to a lesser extent by television and the press. Opinion is more powerful than truth, and the most powerful thing one can be is an opinion-former. What one might call 'argumentative time' has changed as its media have changed. What is possible in a long written piece (for example, Augustine's *City of God*) is not possible in a radio interview, in a blog, or in the 140-character limit of a Twitter posting.

Understanding the media of argumentation is complex, not least because what people say (for instance about the importance of truth) often seems to be contradicted by what people do (for instance spending more time and money managing perceptions than pursuing truth). The existence of communication departments, of public relations firms or even just of advertising shows that the art of rhetoric is as significant now as it was in Augustine's time (Augustine originally trained as a rhetorician).

Now, as then, these practices of opinion-shaping are accompanied by another tendency: the quest for truth. This quest is dominated in the popular imagination by natural science and this domination is a big problem for theology, which is not a natural science, as we shall see in the later discussion about authority. The quest for truth is marked by doubt about popular conceptions (which often turn out to be wrong), by the formulation of hypotheses (which need to be tested), and by results (that are published and evaluated by a community of inquiry). This quest for truth appears in a multitude of guises in modern society, from scholarly journals, to investigative journalism, to websites which test consumer products and report on their performance.

It remains the case, however, now as in former times, that the key to influence is how readily one's views are received (and perhaps understood) and not the depth of one's investigation or the subtlety of one's argument. The best advice one can give to young theologians who want to get noticed is, 'give it a good title, fill it with strong contrasts and submit it to a journal with a big circulation'. The quest for truth is not much of a quest unless it is accompanied (with apologies to Augustine) by the *libido opinionem figurandi* – the desire to shape opinion.

It is often said in politics: 'If you are explaining you are losing'. This remarkably lucid *bon mot* contains within it a wealth of wisdom about arguing. It captures the insight that it is vital to take and hold the initiative in any debate. It strongly implies that you should force your opponent to explain his or her views. It offers a rationale for the terse advice (allegedly by the great Oxford theologian Benjamin Jowett) 'never explain, never apologise'. And it casts light on why most scholars are not successful in their own lifetimes, and why they are especially unsuccessful in the world of politics: scholarship is a world of explanation. It also explains why the best television drama has very little direct exposition, or why such exposition (if necessary) is often embedded in dramatic action such as a blazing row or pillow talk. The art of persuasion is, to a significant extent, the art of *not* explaining.

A final observation about the world around us concerns denominations and religious traditions. The Christian tradition is a fractured tradition. The East–West Schism of 1054 divided Christendom into Greek and Latin traditions. The Reformation of the sixteenth century divided the Latin tradition into Catholic and Protestant traditions. The Clarendon Code in England in the early 1660s formally identified Baptists, Congregationalists, Presbyterians, and Quakers as 'non-conformists' and excluded them from public office. And so on. There is a dour Scottish saying, tinged with melancholy: 'only rotten wood doesn't split'.

The separations of the churches have from time to time been accompanied by attempts to move closer together. Some have been bilateral, such as the Anglican–Roman Catholic International Commission (ARCIC), which was set up in the wake of the Second Vatican Council (1962–65). Others have been multilateral, such as the World Council of Churches (established in 1948), which includes nearly all the major denominations with the exception of the Roman Catholic Church. Listing the different denominations of Christianity would take a long paragraph. Listing the bodies formed for their collaboration would be many times longer. Another phenomenon accompanies the fact of fissure within the 'one holy catholic and apostolic church' as the Nicene Creed of 325 (itself an agent of fissure: the Council of Nicea excluded the Arians) puts it. There are also many non-Christian religious traditions with which Christianity has engaged in various ways, in various countries, at various times. The most important of these, historically, are Judaism and Islam. Christianity grew up at the same time as rabbinic Judaism (the Mishnah dates to about 200 CE, making it roughly contemporary with the works of Irenaeus, Clement, and Origen), and the two traditions often defined themselves in opposition to each other. Islam grew up in the seventh century CE, and its major intellectual developments in the tenth, eleventh, and twelfth centuries had a massive impact on the great Christian theologians of the thirteenth. Al Farabi, Ibn Sina (also known as Avicenna) and Ibn Rushd (also known as Averroes) produced a body of knowledge that wove Aristotelian philosophy into its theology in a way that strongly shaped and influenced the theological development of Aquinas, Scotus, and Ockham. This chapter could with profit be devoted entirely to the arguing that went on between the Muslims and the Christians (not to mention the giant contribution of the Jewish Aristotelian philosopher Maimonides in the same period), or to the Dominicans and Franciscans. It won't. But it is important to note that the Christian tradition is fractured, and is constantly produced in relation to other religious traditions, and a lot of arguing takes place because of that. These conclude my brief remarks about the world around us.

Philosophy without authorities

Second, we should consider the hopes and dreams of the seventeenth century. These can usefully be placed in a wider context. There have perhaps been five major developments in the practices of Christian arguing. This is not a generally accepted division, and it is offered here as a provisional scheme. These developments might be named as follows:

- patristic councils
- medieval Aristotelianism
- the Protestant Reformation
- the rise of modern philosophy
- the post-modern turn.

A more historically oriented discussion could with profit devote its discussion entirely to reporting on the differences in the theological practices of arguing displayed in these five periods. Our interest is in the fourth period – the seventeenth century – because of its connection with the possible pointlessness of arguing.

The significant philosophers of the seventeenth century, for our purposes, are Descartes, Spinoza, and Leibniz. They produced their philosophies in the wake of the Thirty Years War (1616–48), a period in which the disagreements produced in the Protestant Reformation a century before became more intense and more violent. Descartes and his contemporaries saw that practices of arguing among Christians followed denominational lines. To say that Catholics and Protestants were unconvinced by each other's arguments would be an understatement. This situation called for a proper diagnosis. Descartes' analysis was that the problems lay in philosophical method. The methods of what we now call 'Scholastic Aristotelianism' (a generalization which covers a long period from 1200–1650) were judged to be in disrepair and unsuitable for producing reasoned debate. There are many elements to this. The main problem, for Descartes, was the fundamental role played by appeal to authorities. If one reads Aquinas' *Summa Theologiae* or Scotus' *Ordinatio*, one sees very quickly that the structure depends on a kind of collision between authorities (e.g. between Aristotle and Scripture) and then an adjudication by the theological reasoner. The structure of arguing by the Scholastic Aristotelians was a confrontation of respected authorities, and a reasoning through of the issues in the light of this confrontation. That method was generative and successful for hundreds of years. Descartes judged it to be defective because of a major post-Reformation development: different denominations appealed to different authorities. Scholastic Aristotelianism depended on appeal to the same authorities, and involved disagreements on how to interpret them or adjudicate their differences. Once disputes arose over which authorities one might appeal to, that method became a problem. The scholastic method took for granted who the authorities were. It could not decide which authorities counted as authorities.

Descartes produced a philosophical method that did not appeal to authorities, and in doing so he produced what we now understand as modern philosophy. Ridding philosophy of appeal to authorities was a big project. The main challenge was to produce a method that tackled the problem of what an argument takes for granted, and what it aims to decide. Every argument takes certain things for granted, and places other things in doubt. Descartes produced a new method for handling these different things. The most precious quality of this method, for Descartes, was clarity. There should be clarity about an argument's basic terms: they must be clearly defined. There should be clarity about what an argument takes for granted: its premises (or 'axioms') must be clearly stated. There should be clarity about an argument's reasoning: its inferences must be demonstrated in the same watertight way as geometrical proofs. One of the most elegant products of this method, which displays its clarity in an exemplary fashion, is Spinoza's *Ethics*, which proceeds exactly in this way, with a presentation of definitions, axioms, and geometrical proofs. The main structure of a philosophical argument, after Descartes, is a pattern of axioms and hypotheses. Axioms articulate what is taken for granted; hypotheses formulate what is placed in doubt, and what is tested. The refinement of this method by

Spinoza and Leibniz laid the pattern for much modern philosophy up to our own day. It did not only shape philosophy: the pattern of testing hypotheses in natural science is also a child of this way of thinking. Newtonian mechanics, for example, does not proceed by appeal to authorities (as Renaissance investigation had, for example), but tests hypotheses.

The so-called debate between science and religion, or science and theology, is a good example of the practice of arguing. This debate has become rather complex in recent years and includes such questions as whether God exists, how the world is to be explained, whether evolutionary theory is in competition with the doctrine of creation, and so forth. One fruitful way to approach this debate, which also has the surprising effect of not getting directly involved in it, is to see it the way Descartes saw Scholastic Aristotelianism. Theology proceeds by appeal to authorities. Science proceeds by the construction and testing of hypotheses. This is a gross over-simplification, but it is not false. (It is an over-simplification in part because the various genres of public writing by scientists are often not natural science, and the mass-readership responses to them by theologians are often not theology.) Scientific objections to theology often rest on a refusal to acknowledge theology's authorities. Theological replies often point out that this is a strange objection, given that the unfolding of a tradition (and the settling of debates within it) is an enterprise rather different from the formation and testing of hypotheses. Darwin's *Origin of Species* is not an authority for biologists in the way that *Genesis* is an authority for theologians. Not noticing this leads to a variety of confusions.

Descartes and his immediate successors were impressed with the power that this new method gave to the practices of arguing, including theological arguing. Proofs for the existence of God became more refined, and many of the classical arguments (e.g. Anselm's so-called 'ontological argument' of 1077, or Aquinas' 'five ways' arguments of c.1265 – which include the so-called 'cosmological argument') were reworked by Descartes and Leibniz, using the new technology afforded by the geometrical method. The turn away from authorities and towards the geometrical relation of axioms to hypotheses in philosophy in the seventeenth century led, in time, to immense confidence in practices of arguing during the Enlightenment of the eighteenth century in Britain, France, and Germany. Theological practices of argumentation, which focused on authorities, were supplemented (and in some cases superseded) by practices of geometrical argumentation, which focused on axioms and hypotheses. What we now call 'philosophy of religion' is to a significant extent the product of this supplementation and supersession.

This confidence came under sustained assault by Nietzsche, especially in his late works of 1886–88. Nietzsche argued forcefully that what is dressed up by theology and science alike as argument is a masked exercise of power and a means of social control. Claims about 'truth' are, he argued, actually bids to take or maintain control. Nietzsche's arguments followed those of Marx who, in 1845, famously referred to the arguments of those in power as '*die ganze alte Scheiße*' (all the old crap). Together they prompted a revolution in thinking about the relation of power and argument, and initiated a historically unstoppable movement towards mistrust in argumentation, especially the argumentation of those who control material, economic or political means. Our current cultural situation is a product of the distrust articulated by Marx and Nietzsche.

The theologian John Milbank urged (argued?) almost exactly 100 years after Nietzsche's rejection of argumentation that theology cannot (and should not try to) argue against its opponents. This is, he suggested, because the bases of all arguments are (as many philosophers in the late twentieth century claimed) insecure and 'baseless'. Instead of trying to argue, on the basis of agreed premises, there can only be a competition between different stories, whose grounds are always baseless. The theological task is not to defeat by argument, but to 'out-narrate' other stories. Theological accounts, and those of their rivals, are alike baseless.[1]

It is for these reasons, or arguments, or perhaps merely opinions, that arguing might well be pointless. The hopes and dreams for argumentation held in the seventeenth century produced a powerful intellectual technology for handling axioms and hypotheses according to a geometrical method, but two factors spoiled these dreams for theology. First, theology rightly proceeds by appeal to traditions. If it does not, it is not theology. Second, the axioms of any chain of theological reasoning are (from a Cartesian point of view) baseless. This sounds drastic, and a bad thing for theology. But it is swiftly demonstrated, and is vital to any theology that is alive and healthy. Any axiom of theological reasoning can be questioned, and none can be secured against criticism. It is axiomatic for most schools of theology that the Bible is authoritative, that Jesus is Lord, that God is triune. Each of these axioms rests on an implicit appeal to authority, whether of the Church, of tradition, of memory, or the Holy Spirit. To think theologically is to value the Church, and tradition, and memory and – in the case of the Holy Spirit – to acknowledge its divinity. Any rejection of these axiomatic claims as baseless cannot be countered by argument. The person who says, 'The Bible is not authoritative *for me*' does not stand in need of correction by argument. What they say is almost certainly true. The person who says, 'The Bible is not authoritative *per se*' is just confused. To be an authority is always to be an authority for someone. Not to be an authority is always not to be an authority for someone (or anyone).

The geometrical method of testing hypotheses on the basis of axioms would only be a secure basis for argumentation if the axioms themselves were a secure basis. As Leibniz so brilliantly observed, any chain of reasoning that contains a hypothesis is itself hypothetical all the way down. The only axioms that cannot be converted into hypotheses are self-evident ones, or analytically true ones. Theological axioms are not of this kind. It is true that in the period of the late eighteenth century and early nineteenth century attempts were made by philosophers to find a 'ground' of philosophy. These attempts failed. Arguably the greatest work on the philosophy of religion, Hegel's *Lectures on the Philosophy of Religion* of the 1820s, proceeded on the basis of what people actually take to be true in their religious lives; it did not attempt (and explicitly refused to attempt) to prove its truth.[2] Anyone who accepts the failure to identify secure grounds is, in some sense, a post-modern thinker – although there are many incompatible varieties of such post-modern thinking.

It is obvious from even a cursory investigation of thinking and arguing in contemporary Western cultures that we are a mixture of modern and post-modern thinking. I do not mean that some of us are modern and some of us are post-modern. I mean that we are all both, to greater or lesser extents. Out and out rationalists, who think that the bases of our thinking can be secured against criticism, were once common in the eighteenth century but are now exceedingly rare. Radically post-modern thinkers, who reject any notion of truth, were rather common in the later twentieth century, but they too are rather rare these days. Ours are times of ecological crisis, financial collapse, and widespread flood and famine. It is a curious and despicable person who shrugs his shoulders in the face of others' desperate suffering, and says that we can't be sure of anything. We can be sure that the gap between rich and poor is widening in the North, and that thousands of children are dying of starvation in the South. Suffering, at least, is real.

To engage in the Christian practice of arguing is to notice and respond to signs of others' suffering. If the Christian practice of arguing is in the service of those who address suffering, then it is clearly not pointless. To deny this is not clever and post-modern, but stupid and decadent. It is not even new. In Marx's words, it is the same old crap, which oppresses the poor and the weak. From this point onwards, this chapter will outline an alternative to the geometrical method of the first modern philosophers, as an aid to responding to suffering. It has taken a while to get to this point. This is because of what I take to be a widespread suspicion about arguing, whether on Marxian, Nietzschean or post-modern grounds. To an extent one can properly share these suspicions, and it is important to traverse this ground, even in the brief way this chapter has done so far. But at a certain point, enough is enough, and it is time to inquire into what good arguing is. Suffering is real. It calls for response.

Suffering and problem-solving

Arguing has multiple purposes that are not reducible to each other. At its most basic, arguing is a form of problem-solving and, as I have already suggested, the most fundamental problem is that of suffering. Problems like suffering do not primarily require explanation. They call for transformation (and where transformation is unavailable, and even where it is available, for companionship). The only reason one might wish to understand suffering is in order to lessen it. Even if it defies understanding, the imperative to address it remains. What reasons are there for thinking one should address another's suffering? If one has to ask this question, it is probably best to stop reading now, because the one who asks this is in deep spiritual trouble; nothing that follows will help.

A taxonomy will be offered here, whose purpose is to classify different kinds of arguing. This will then provide a framework for a little more detail on each of these different kinds.

The first distinction is between describing and arguing.

Describing, or ontology (to use Aristotelian language) or world-disclosure (to use Heidegger's wonderful phrase), is about saying what kind of world is before us. It is the use of existing categories, the transformation of inadequate categories, and the formation of new categories. To describe is to say what there is. A good deal of theology is description, is ontology, is world-disclosure. The use of words like 'creation', 'grace', 'sin' and 'redemption' describes the kinds of things there are in the world, and already says what we should do about them, in the light of what God has done and is doing about them. Such description is 'practical ontology', if you like: they are descriptions to live by. The being of creation, grace, sin and redemption calls for the action of prayer, praise, repentance and gratitude. Description and ethics (or 'is' and 'ought') are utterly entangled. There have been philosophers who denied this. They were wrong. Description, for Christians, is also bound up with petition: with asking. Most services of worship are a complex mixture of describing, asking, and performing the responses to such description and petition. Milbank's combative image of 'out-narrating' one's opponents is essentially a descriptive, ontological, world-disclosive approach.

Arguing, or logic, or problem-solving, is about correcting mistakes, overcoming obstacles to action, trying to live together, forming the minds of the young, and a whole range of other related activities. It is about a lot of different, but often related, forms of articulate action. Description may reveal that we should act. Arguing may be needed to refine and correct such description, to draw inferences correctly, and to determine what form that action should take.

The second set of distinctions lies within the notion of arguing.

These can be named and divided in a number of ways. I offer here three sets of three, which in slightly different ways articulate the same tripartite division:

- demonstrative, grammatical, reparative
- proof, clarification, transformation
- agreement, understanding, healing.

There may be other forms of arguing, but these three capture the most important forms that are encountered in theological argumentation. Each set of three is a version of the same basic insight.

By demonstrative argumentation I mean the attempt to prove something, or the attempt to reach agreement with someone else. There are various forms that demonstrative argumentation might take. The classic *quaestio* approach of the high middle ages, such as one finds in Aquinas' *Summa Theologiae* or in Scotus' *Ordinatio*, is to take a question (e.g. 'Whether the existence of God can be proven'), marshal arguments for and against, and then to reason through the competing possibilities to reach a conclusion. It is the model for much contemporary philosophical theology. The later geometrical method, favoured by Spinoza in his *Ethics*, begins with definitions, presents axioms, and proceeds to draw inferences. It is the model for contemporary formal logic. The much later approach of 'immanent critique', elaborated by Adorno in the twentieth century, considers a cluster of arguments made by a rival, and proceeds to show how they break down when their internal inconsistencies or contradictions are identified. This method attempts as far as possible not to introduce axioms or considerations that are foreign to the arguments that are placed in question. Instead, the critique is powered by showing that the arguments fail on their own ground and in their own terms.

In passing, it is worth mentioning 'deconstruction'. This is not so much a formal and explicit method of demonstrative argumentation, as a vague term covering a variety of methods of criticism refined by Foucault and Derrida. References to deconstructive argument normally mean a process of taking a cluster of arguments and revealing their dependence on a set of assumptions which are not explicitly articulated in those arguments, and then calling those assumptions into question or explicitly rejecting them, or showing that certain assumptions reflect the interests and power of a particular sector in society – especially in cases where the arguments are allegedly 'rational' and present themselves as 'universally' persuasive. To 'deconstruct' an argument is to undermine its apparent neutrality or impartiality. The most arresting examples of deconstructive argument are those which show that the assumptions in play in 'rational' discussion actually express unexamined normative commitments whose effect is to exclude significant groups from full participation in discussion. Much feminist argument has rightly exposed the ways in which certain kinds of rational argument implicitly refuse to take the body seriously as a source of reasons or of meanings. An argument which says, 'a physical bond between persons cannot be a source of reasons which guide their actions' exemplifies this very clearly, and stands in need of correction.

By grammatical argumentation I mean the attempt to clarify something, or to reach understanding with someone else about something's meaning. This mode of argumentation is not so much concerned to prove something, as to make sense of it. It might well result in forms of agreement, but its principal orientation is understanding rather than agreement. There are various forms which grammatical argument might take. Augustine's formula 'I believe that I might understand', refined in Anselm's formula that his *Proslogion* project is 'faith seeking understanding', is a classic version. The aim of argumentation here is to deepen understanding of what we, or you, believe. In demonstrative argumentation the aim is to believe something, we might say. In grammatical argumentation we (or you) already believe something, but we seek deeper understanding of what that means. The later developments of Leibniz display aspects of this grammatical mode of argumentation, as in his 'Principles of Nature and Grace, according to Reason', which examines basic theological topics through the lens of recent models of argumentation. This can also be seen in forms of (especially Roman Catholic) theology in the later twentieth century in the wake of Wittgenstein's philosophy, which attempt explicitly 'grammatical' investigations of theological speech and action, such as Nicholas Lash's *Believing Three Ways in One God*.[3]

It is not always obvious whether an argument is demonstrative or grammatical. There has been considerable debate by scholars concerning Anselm's so-called 'ontological argument' and Aquinas' 'five ways' arguments. Anselm has been taken, by Barth, and Aquinas has been taken, by Cornelius Ernst, to be engaged in grammatical endeavours: they do not aim to prove the existence of God so much as to clarify what it means to assert God's existence.[4] The contrary view, however, has been more common. Brian Davies has offered a strong contrary reading of Anselm which emphasizes his demonstrative ambitions, and Denys Turner has contradicted Ernst's reading of Aquinas' five ways, in an insistence that Aquinas is actually trying to prove something. These disagreements are difficult to adjudicate, as the distinction between demonstrative and grammatical argument is a relatively recent development, and in any case it is quite possible that a particular argument might display features of both kinds of approach.[5]

By reparative argument I mean the attempt to transform debate, and to heal wounds in a tradition's ways of thinking and acting. This kind of argumentation is not common, and its arguments are generally doomed to be a minority voice in a tradition for a long time, until they are accepted by later generations. This is because reparative arguments are very difficult to understand. They are difficult to understand because they offer an alternative way of viewing a problem, and this alternative is radically unfamiliar to its readers who – if they understand and accept it – will find their own thinking and acting transformed by it. Reparative reasoning generally proceeds by rethinking the basic categories in play, in a fundamental way. There are many examples. Aquinas' rethinking of Augustinian theology in the light of categories from Aristotelian philosophy; Descartes' rethinking of Scholastic Aristotelianism in the light of categories from geometry; Kant's rethinking of rationalism and empiricism in the light of new 'transcendental' categories; Hegel's rethinking of the idea of conceptuality in the light of historical categories; Peirce's rethinking of the tasks of philosophy in the light of what he calls 'thirdness'; Collingwood's rethinking of the tasks of philosophy in the light of what he calls 'the logic of question and answer'; Wittgenstein's rethinking of the tasks of philosophy in the light of grammatical categories. In each case, radical proposals are put forward in the face of traditions that are perceived to be becoming stagnant and repetitive. In many cases, the trigger for repair is the insight that current argumentative options rest upon false oppositions. Rather than make a case for one side of such an opposition, as everyone else currently is, the philosopher offers an account in which the source of the false opposition is repaired, and a quite different settlement appears.

Some classic examples may help explain this unfamiliar taxonomy. Aquinas' account of analogical speech about God confronted a false opposition between univocal and equivocal speech. He drew on Aristotle's notion of 'paronymous' speech in *Categories* in his (Aquinas') account of analogy, which cannot be reduced to one or other of the false alternatives. Descartes' response to the tribal oppositions of 'Catholic' and 'Protestant' logics of argumentation was to produce an alternative logic, based on geometry, which could not be reduced to either of the false alternatives, and which was intended to repair the failure of traditions to be able to argue meaningfully. Hegel's account of 'the concept' is a repair of the false opposition in philosophy between 'being' and 'thinking'. His account of 'Spirit' is a repair of the false opposition between individual and community, and of what he sees (very controversially) as the false opposition between God and humanity (which is a consequence, he thinks, of the false opposition between 'being' and 'thinking'). Descartes' and Hegel's reparative argumentation are interesting cases, compared with those of Aquinas and Wittgenstein. Whereas the projects of Aquinas and Wittgenstein have proven generative and welcome, Descartes is largely understood in theology to have made the original problem worse: his remedies caused more damage than they healed. Hegel's proposals, on the other hand, have a strange double life. They are extremely well-known (his *Phenomenology of Spirit* is a classic text in the history of philosophy) but are a source of almost universal puzzlement. This is because much of the philosophical tradition continues to presuppose an opposition between 'being' and 'thinking'. There are objects, 'out there', and there is my thinking, 'in here'. The philosophical task is to show how they are related. Hegel thinks this is wrong-headed. To contemplate objects is to contemplate thinking, and to contemplate thinking is to contemplate objects. Hegel's proposal to overcome what he sees as the false opposition between God and humanity is greeted by almost universal dismay by theologians. This is because he is taken to be saying either that God is really a way of talking about human self-consciousness, or that 'humanity' is really a way of talking about God's self-consciousness. Hegel himself would be puzzled by this, because such an interpretation is still locked in a false opposition between God and humanity! This is not the place to explore these fascinating issues.[6] It will suffice to say two things: first, Hegel is still in his doom, as a minority voice. Second, this is likely to continue until his account of Anselm's ontological argument finds its way into the textbooks. Hegel takes Anselm to be engaged neither in demonstrative nor in grammatical argumentation. He argues that Anselm's account is (in my terms) 'reparative'. Anselm's 'concept' of God overcomes the false opposition between 'thinking God' and 'God's being'. Anselm's account of God is a performance in which being and thinking are harmoniously and indivisibly one. To a philosophical tradition stuck (as Hegel would see it) in the false opposition of thinking and being, this account of Anselm is just puzzling and bizarre.[7]

Some more modern examples of reparative argumentation may offer further illumination. One of the areas where arguing is obviously central to the practice of theology is Christian ethics, which is the discipline devoted to exploring descriptions to live by, or more narrowly to determining how Christians should act. It is a relatively recent development (around two hundred years old) to distinguish different disciplines within theology, such as Church history, the study of the Bible, the study of doctrine and the study of Christian ethics. For most of Christian history theology encompasses all of these, and earlier theologians would probably not have considered them distinct disciplines. The development of the modern university in Germany produced a transformation in the organization of different 'faculties'. The existence of Christian ethics, as a distinct discipline, is the product of this administrative settlement.[8] One of the unforeseen effects of this settlement was the development of the idea that there is such a thing as 'ethics', which enquires into topics such as freedom, punishment, virtue, duty, responsibility, rights, and so on. In the face of this discipline, Christian ethics becomes a sub-discipline within ethics, as well as a sub-discipline within theology. It becomes possible to conceive of Christian ethics as a branch of theological argumentation, in which case it is about the distinctively 'ethical' dimension of doctrinal, historical, and biblical scholarship. It also becomes possible to conceive of Christian ethics as a branch of ethics, in which case it is about distinctively 'Christian' approaches to questions of freedom, punishment, virtue, duty, responsibility, rights and so forth. In the first case the emphasis is on what to *do*. In the second, the emphasis is on *what* to do. There have been attempts to refuse this division of intellectual labour, as in Barth's insistence that 'ethics is dogmatics'.[9] A more radical – and reparative – response can be seen in the work of three contemporary figures: Stanley Hauerwas, Oliver O'Donovan, and John Milbank. These thinkers have different projects, with different concerns, but they share a couple of overriding concerns. The first is that to fight battles about ethics is simultaneously to fight battles about the discipline of Christian ethics. The second is related. To investigate possible courses of action, one has at the same time to investigate the basic categories in which possible courses of action are described. Descriptions often express implicit commitments to action (they contain 'descriptions to live by'), and that means that to argue about action is also to argue about description. It is for these reasons that they say some odd-looking and apparently rather extreme things. Hauerwas insists that 'justice' is a bad idea for Christians; O'Donovan calls into question the notion that a society can be 'pluralist'; Milbank insists that to think theologically is to operate with a rival ontology that stands in conscious opposition to secularist ontologies.[10] The effects of these forms of argument are extreme: indeed they are radical. But the basic insight that they embody is probably one that their fiercest opponents would not contest: to investigate phenomena is also to investigate the categories for describing phenomena. These forms of argumentation are reparative, in my scheme, because they are deeper than merely demonstrative or grammatical. They aim to do more than merely argue for various courses of action in the world, more than merely seek to understand forms of Christian action. They see practices of Christian self-understanding as damaged, and they aim to heal them.

A lot of ground has been traversed quickly. We have confronted the problem posed by a world oriented to 'opinion' rather than 'truth' (Plato's problem is still with us). We have confronted the failed aspirations of the seventeenth century: there is no pure logic that can replace appeals to authorities, and some theologians even think that because we appeal to authorities, and operate with rival ontologies, we should talk more of 'narrative' than 'argument'. We have considered a taxonomy of argumentation which seeks to distinguish different argumentative interests and strategies.

It remains for us to confront the other major problem outlined in the introduction: the fact that traditions are fractured both externally (there are different religious traditions such as Judaism, Christianity, Islam and many others) and internally (within Christianity there are as many denominations as there are world religions).

Fractured traditions

At one level, we already have a way of considering this. Theological argumentation, unlike geometry, involves appealing to authorities like the Bible and the great theologians of the tradition. We can begin by noticing, as Descartes noticed, that different traditions appeal to different authorities, and that this has a fundamental effect on how they argue with each other. If you and I are arguing, and my case rests on appeal to texts and figures which are not authoritative for you, it is probably wise for us to acknowledge this.[11] What next?

At this point, and on this question, there are currently two rival proposals. The first is associated with figures like John Rawls and Jürgen Habermas and their students. They disagree on many of the details, but they agree on at least one thing: there must be 'public reasons' to which appeal can be made. The main quality displayed by public reasons is that they do not rely on appeals to particular traditions and their authorities. Public reasons need to appeal to criteria that are shared. To use language from the late eighteenth century, they need to be 'universal'. The philosophical task is thus energetically to seek the universal or at least the shared, and produce a public sphere or square in which only public reasons count.[12] The second proposal is widely distributed across a range of thinkers in a variety of traditions. They too disagree on many of the details, but again they agree on at least one thing: any appeal that will 'count' for a member of a particular tradition will refer to what is genuinely (and perhaps peculiarly) authoritative in that tradition. If there are 'public reasons' these will be the making public of reasons that are at home in particular traditions.[13] This debate often reproduces many of the Cartesian problems we have already considered, and sets up a dubious (probably false) opposition between 'reason' and 'tradition'. Any attempt to resolve this opposition on the side of 'reason' (Rawls, Habermas and others) or to resolve this on the side of 'tradition' (their opponents) brings the argument to an abrupt impasse.

False oppositions call for reparative argument, rather than demonstrative or grammatical approaches. There are reparative dimensions to both sides of the 'public reasons' argument. Habermas has made what he sees as significant concessions to traditions by focusing on what is shared, rather than what is universal. Some advocates of traditions investigate the basic categories in play in these debates at the same time as they investigate the social phenomena that produce the apparent crisis in the spheres of political and legal judgement. Governments and courts have to produce laws and judgements whose authority citizens from different traditions can and must acknowledge. Investigating shared ground and investigating the basic categories in which the discussion is couched is valuable work.

Further reparative moves are possible. Two in particular are worth considering for those seeking to learn how to engage in Christian arguing. The first is to repair the false opposition between traditions. It is a remarkable and unfortunate feature of the arguments of Rawls and Habermas that they think of traditions as simply different from each other, and they think of difference as a problem. This false opposition can be overcome by pointing out that traditions are often different from each other because of (rather than despite) their engagements with each other. Their self-understandings are often produced by a desire to differentiate themselves from others, and to see difference as a good thing. It is not true that Judaism, Christianity, and Islam grew up separately and now, under modern conditions, find themselves living in the same cities in the same states, with a new and urgent need to relate to each other in the public sphere. This is nonsense. The traditions grew up in relation to each other, and partly define themselves according to that relation to each other. Those relations have often been painful, violent, and unjust. This means that the search for shared ground is not a search for things that just happen to be shared. The traditions already share each other, one might say, and have the scars to prove it. Allied to this is the unwarranted presupposition that traditions are stable, and that the task is to determine what features of these stable traditions can most fruitfully be brought together. This too is nonsense. Traditions change. Judaism was changed by Christianity, and then by Islam. Christianity was changed by Islam, and then by encounter with a whole range of traditions; it was changed by Judaism in a profound way in the twentieth century. Islam was changed by European modernity: fundamentalist Islam is a modern rejection of Islamic traditions, and its habits were probably learned from forms of Christian modernity that rejected Christian traditions. The traditions continue to change. That means that attempts to produce political and legal settlements will not only be a matter of bringing traditions together in the public square. It will also be a matter of those traditions adapting to life together in various ways, as one sees in the lives of Coptic Christians in Egypt, or Turkish Muslims in Germany, or European Jews in the USA.

The first reparative move is thus to see the traditions as already in relation to each other, and always adapting to changing circumstances. Traditions are neither separate from another, nor are they stable. Traditions are entangled and alive.

Comparative logic

The second reparative move is to think not just about ontology but also logic. This sounds rather grand, but it is simple in conception. Traditions differ from each other in different ways. They may appeal to different authorities (the Talmud, the Church Fathers, the tradition of Fiqh). They may describe the world, themselves and each other in different categories (law and tradition, nature and grace, obedience and submission). These are ontological matters: they are differences at the level of considering what kinds of thing there are. Ontological differences call for ontological investigations. But there are also differences in logic. These are more resistant to investigation because the study of logic is highly specialized.

What is meant by 'logic'? A logic is a system of rules for drawing inferences. Less formally, a logic is a pattern of habits for coming to conclusions. To think is to make connections between things. A logic is an ordering of those connections according to rules. Those rules can be made explicit, as in the work of Aristotle and his many and varied successors. They can be further clarified through diagrams, as in the work of C.S. Peirce.[14] By and large they are left implicit, as in the work of most of the rest of us. Those trained in the analytical tradition often behave as if there is one logic, operative throughout history. This may be because modern analytical logic is immensely powerful, and it is possible to cast many arguments from the past or from different traditions, in its own terms. It is not true that there is one logic, however. There are many logics. To be a scholar of medieval philosophy is sometimes to be a comparative logician. A skilled comparative logician can often make an educated guess who the author of a classic text is, by noting the particular logics at work. Comparative logic is possible because there are different logics and they can be compared. The logics of Aristotle, of Augustine, of Anselm, of Aquinas, of Spinoza, or Hegel are different from one another. Some of the earlier logics can be recast in the terms of the later logics. It is an interesting challenge to try the reverse procedure. There can be different logics within the same religious tradition. There are also different logics across different traditions. This can be difficult to see if one does not travel outside one's own cultural context or one's own discipline. Engineering in Beijing is much like engineering in Boston. Philosophy of religion in Munich is much like philosophy of religion in Cambridge. This is because engineers in Beijing may have been trained at MIT, and philosophers of religion in Cambridge may have been trained at Ludwig-Maximilian Universität in Munich. But legal reasoning in Al-Azhar in Cairo is radically different from legal reasoning in the Inner Temple in London. As soon as one shows an interest in history and geography, comparative logic is on the horizon, even if only in an elementary way.

The current debate about 'public reason' is not characterized by energetic investigations into comparative logic. It needs to be. This is unlikely in the near future because we are not training our theologians in comparative logic. We teach them doctrine, ethics, Scripture, history, philosophy. If we teach them logic, it is analytic logic. This is certainly better than no logic at all. But we do not teach them classical Aristotelian logic, or Scholastic Aristotelian logic. We most certainly do not teach them comparative logic in the period between 1100 and 1300, comparing the logics of different Jewish, Christian, and Islamic masters. Were a university to create a masters programme in comparative logic, it is not obvious that it would be immediately over-subscribed. It might have enormous long-term benefits for religious traditions seeking to live together peaceably, however. The most important step, however, is to cease teaching philosophy as an 'option' in theology, and to make it compulsory.

It is possible nevertheless to pursue some worthwhile logical investigations, even if they fall short of the sophistication and power that comparative logic might offer. I want now to revisit the question of appeals to authorities, but to do so in a more formal way. The framework for this is a contrast between thinking in terms of twos and thinking in terms of threes.[15]

The easiest example is the meaning of words. We normally consider that words have meanings. This is a sensible approach. It is an example of thinking in terms of twos. The 'two' in question here is (1) words and (2) meanings. This is a respectable and worthwhile way of thinking. But suppose I pick a word like 'realist'. Suppose I say that Aquinas is a 'realist'. What does 'realist' mean? It could mean that Aquinas is not a naïve fantasist about the challenges posed by human sin. He is a 'realist' about what people are like. It could mean that Aquinas thinks that universals refer to beings in the world. He is not a 'nominalist' about universals. We can continue to think in terms of twos. We can say words have multiple meanings. The two in question here is (1) words and (2) multiple meanings. Again, this is a respectable and worthwhile way of thinking. It is, after all, how we normally (and rightly) think.

But suppose we change the frame and notice that the reason words have multiple meanings is that words take their meanings from their contexts. We are now thinking in terms of threes. The three in question here is (1) words having (2) meanings in (3) contexts. We could even adopt an extreme pedagogical stance and say, 'words don't have meanings; words have meanings for people'. The three in question here is (1) words and their (2) meanings for (3) particular persons.

Once we acquire this new habit of thinking in threes, the question of authorities can be recast. Take the case of the Bible. We can say 'The Bible is authoritative'. That is to think in twos. We can also say 'The Bible is authoritative for Christians'. That is to think in threes. Twos and threes produce different questions. When thinking in twos, we can ask, 'Is the Bible authoritative?' And that will invite a yes/no kind of answer. When thinking in threes, we can ask, 'For whom is the Bible authoritative?' That will invite not a binary yes/no answer, but a triadic answer: 'The Bible is authoritative for Christians'.

Thinking in threes can produce a further level of sophistication. We can say, 'The Bible is authoritative for Christians but not for atheists'. This can be turned into a piece of formal logic:

A is B for X
A is not B for Y.

In this case A is the Bible, B is authoritative, X is Christians and Y is atheists.

We can say, 'the Bible is meaningful for Christians but nonsense for atheists'.

A is P for X

A is Q for Y.

If this way of thinking becomes second nature, we can recast the relation of axioms and hypotheses that we considered in an earlier section. It is an axiom for Christians that Jesus is fully man and fully God. It is not an axiom for Muslims. For Muslims it is at best a hypothesis. Let us say that I am a Christian and you are a Muslim.

What is an axiom for me is a hypothesis for you.

This is a very sophisticated way of thinking. Let us take that example and think in terms of twos again. 'Is Jesus fully man and fully God?' This is a question which invites a binary yes/no answer. We can make it even more emphatic. 'Is it true that Jesus is fully man and fully God?'

This question can be given binary answers. Yes it is true. No it is not true. To think in twos is to acknowledge that either it is true or it isn't true. This is a perfectly respectable and proper way to think. Clearly it is true or it isn't. It is nonsense to say 'It is true for me, but not true for you'. There is no 'for me' or 'for you' in matters of truth.

But the question can be given a three or triadic answer:

'I take it as an axiom that it is true. You take it as a hypothesis to be investigated.'

Or

'I take it as an axiom that it is true. You take it as an axiom that it is not true.'

Where the binary answer was focused on its truth, the triadic question is focused on how it is taken. It is important to notice that binary and triadic approaches are not in competition. We think in binary ways most of the time, and that is proper. But the triadic thinking changes both the question and the tone of the discussion. How does it change the question? In the binary case, there is opposition which will not be overcome. Yes it is true. No it is not true. There is an element of confrontation here. In the triadic case, there is difference which is acknowledged, in a non-confrontational way. It is also important to notice that the question of truth is not excluded in the triadic case. There is no suggestion that truth does not matter, or is relativized in any way. It remains firmly on the table in an explicit way.

What advantages does this have? Basically, it introduces a new set of questions and – crucially – new possibilities for investigation. In a world of binaries, our investigations will be into whether things are true or not. These are good investigations. We should undertake them seriously. In a world of triads, our investigations will be into how you and I understand things, as we attempt to discover how and on what we differ. These are also good investigations, and they are difficult to imagine when we think only in twos. In binary thinking we are curious about the world, and rightly so. In triadic thinking we are curious about each other, and this transforms our relationship to one another. This is a great good. It is not yet comparative logic, but it is on the right path.

If these remarks about axioms and hypotheses in relation to thirds are persuasive, they nonetheless need to be refined along at least one further axis. Axioms (or presuppositions or assumptions) are not best thought of as blocks of knowledge or chunks of propositional content. Just as it is common to observe that beliefs in Christian ethics are products of formation, of education and (in short) of a life, so it is vital to acknowledge that in logic such things as axioms and assumptions are condensed or sedimented forms of a community's history of engagements, debates, and social settlements. Similarly the logics that bring these sedimented forms to life and put them to work are not best thought of as abstract rules that exist independently of those communities that follow them. Logics are (to misquote Heidegger) paths through the wood. They are ways through terrain that have been worn smooth by use. To take an interest in logics is at the same time to confront that terrain and this is best done by thinking about the histories that produced them, and the forms of social life that continue to sustain them.

This chapter has been about arguing. It is worth asking what lessons can be learned in the light of the discussion outlined here. In the briefest terms, theologians can learn to raise the level of debate. Theologians and others can learn to have higher quality disagreements. We can end with seven concrete proposals for theological formation in relation to arguing.

1 Be prepared to argue when confronted with others' suffering. Suffering is the sign of a problem, and addressing problems will very likely require argument.
2 Be realistic about the dominance of opinion in our societies and vigorously pursue questions of truth. Learn how to make the most of modern mass media.
3 Acknowledge that many forms of argumentation depend on the insistence, stemming from the seventeenth century in France, that valid arguments should not appeal to authorities. Be explicit that Christian arguments do rest on appeals to authorities, including the Bible, Christian traditions, and (very often) the wisdom of the community's elders.
4 Distinguish between demonstrative, grammatical, and reparative arguments.
5 When considering how traditions should interact in public, treat traditions as unstable, as already related to each other and as continually adapting to new circumstances.
6 Investigate ontologies.
7 Investigate logics.

Notes

1 J. Milbank, *Theology and Social Theory*, Oxford: Blackwell, 1990.
2 G.W.F. Hegel, *Lectures on the Philosophy of Religion*, vol. 1, ed. P. Hodgson, Oxford: Oxford University Press, 2008.

3 N. Lash, *Believing Three Ways in One God: A Reading of the Apostles' Creed*, Notre Dame, IN: University of Notre Dame Press, 1993.

4 K. Barth, *Fides Quaerens Intellectum: Anselm's Proof of the Existence of God in the Context of His Theological Scheme*, London: Pickwick, 1975; C. Ernst, 'Metaphor and Sacra Doctrina', in F. Kerr and T. Radcliffe (eds) *Multiple Echo: Explorations in Theology*, Eugene, OR: Wipf and Stock, 2007, pp. 57–75.

5 B. Davies, 'Anselm and the Ontological Argument', in B. Davies and B. Leftow (eds) *The Cambridge Companion to Anselm*, Cambridge: Cambridge University Press, 2004, pp. 157–78; D. Turner, *Faith, Reason and the Existence of God*, Cambridge: Cambridge University Press, 2004, pp.193–225.

6 See N. Adams, *The Eclipse of Grace: Divine and Human Action in Hegel*, Oxford: Wiley-Blackwell, 2013.

7 See N. Adams, 'Faith and Reason', in N. Adams, N. Boyle, L. Disley (eds) *The Impact of Idealism Volume 4: Religion*, Cambridge: Cambridge University Press, 2013, pp. 194–218.

8 See F.D.E. Schleiermacher, *Brief Outline of Theology as a Field of Study*, trans. T. Tice, Louisville, KY: Westminster John Knox Press, 2011.

9 K. Barth, *Church Dogmatics* II.2, ed. G.W. Bromiley and T.F. Torrance, Edinburgh: T&T Clark, 1957, p. 518.

10 S. Hauerwas, *After Christendom? How the Church Is to Behave If Freedom, Justice, and a Christian Nation Are Bad Ideas*, Nashville, TN: Abingdon Press, 1999; O. O'Donovan, 'Reflections on Pluralism', in *The Princeton Seminary Bulletin* 29.1, 2008, pp. 54–66; Milbank, *Theology and Social Theory*.

11 See N. Adams, 'Long-Term Disagreement: Philosophical Models in Scriptural Reasoning and Receptive Ecumenism', *Modern Theology* 29.4, 2013, pp. 154–71.

12 See N. Adams, 'Interreligious Engagement in the Public Sphere', in D. Cheetham, D. Pratt, and D. Thomas (eds) *Understanding Inter-Religious Relations*, Oxford: Oxford University Press, 2013, pp. 281–305.

13 See J. Stout, *Democracy and Tradition*, Princeton, NJ: Princeton University Press, 2005.

14 See P. Ochs, *Peirce, Pragmatism and the Logic of Scripture*, Cambridge: Cambridge University Press, 1998.

15 See P. Ochs, 'From Two to Three: To Know is also To Know the Context of Knowing', in S. Kepnes and B.B. Koshul (eds) *Scripture, Reason and the Contemporary Islam–West Encounter: Studying the 'Other', Understanding the 'Self'*, New York, NY: Palgrave Macmillan, 2007, pp. 177–200.

5

SEEKING CLARITY

Karen Kilby

Readers of Augustine's *De Trinitate* usually come to realize that the doctrine of the Trinity is more confusing than ever they had imagined. They realize this, not because Augustine presents them with an especially clever or convoluted explanation of how to understand three-and-oneness or of the deep meanings of technical Trinitarian terms: rather, it is because Augustine is so very persistent in returning time after time to how confused he himself is – so persistent in raising again and again questions which he cannot, or cannot immediately, answer. Augustine, the reader quickly discovers, has thought of more difficulties with the doctrine of the Trinity than any sceptic. What kind of three are the three in the Trinity, if they are not three Gods? What do we actually mean by 'Persons'? And how can the One who is sent not be less than the One who sends? And why is the Holy Spirit not also called a Son if the Holy Spirit also comes forth from the Father? Why does the Holy Spirit have no distinctive name, since 'Holy' and 'Spirit' both also are said of Father and of Son? And if Christ is 'the power of God and the wisdom of God', does that mean that the Father himself is not wise, but only attains wisdom through the Son? The questions come thick and fast.

What Augustine quite dramatically indicates is that the search for clarity, at its best, begins in confusion. Or rather, it begins in *honesty* about confusion, in the willingness to acknowledge what one does not understand, the willingness to consider and explore rather than suppress a difficulty, the willingness to articulate and examine a muddle rather than nervously to push it under a carpet. And it is important to understand that what this in fact means is that the search for clarity begins in faith, in real conviction, in a very distinctive kind of confidence. It is not in spite of his Christian conviction that Augustine can confess so freely everything about the Trinity which he does not understand, but precisely because of it. This is something that shines through very powerfully in *De Trinitate*: Augustine shows an enormous freedom to be puzzled, and exhibits no anxiety whatsoever that if he perhaps probes too far or asks too many questions, the reality under discussion might fall apart, that it might somehow disappear or prove itself unworthy of belief.

Where there is an instinct to suppress uncertainties, confusions, and questions about faith, on the other hand, this may well be an indication of a fear that on some level faith cannot stand up to questioning, that it might dissolve before one's eyes if one allowed oneself to think too closely about how confusing it is. Fragility in the faith of an individual or a community, in other words, is likely to be accompanied by rigidity as well, by an anxiety, a guard kept against raising too many questions, against acknowledging too much confusion. And clearly where such a fragility and such a rigidity reign, there can be little possibility of a genuine search for clarity, though there may well be a good deal of effort to achieve tidiness, completeness, or intellectual closure, to describe a position where the answer to all questions can already be known in advance.

In some ways the style of Thomas Aquinas, the great thirteenth-century theologian, could not be more different from that of Augustine, and yet in him too one can find a search for clarity which begins in something which looks rather like an acknowledgement of confusion, and in him too one can sense a kind of calm conviction – in the truth of God, and in the truth of the faith which he has received – lying behind both the search for clarity and the willingness to dwell with confusion. At every stage Thomas's thought proceeds through the posing of questions, questions to which he never attempts his own answer before he has given voice to a range of difficulties and articulated a series of competing positions. Can God's existence be demonstrated? Is it self-evident? Can a created intellect see the essence of God? Does God know evil things? Does God know singulars? Could God make the past not to have been? Could God create a better universe than this one? Might the universe have always existed? Is there one supreme evil which is the cause of all other evils?

One might be tempted to dismiss the recurring pattern of questioning, always followed by the laying out and weighing up of alternative answers, as merely the formal structure into which Thomas pours his theology – and it is certainly true that readers have to accustom themselves to the systematic division of Thomas's text into questions, articles, objections, replies to objections, and so on. But this posing of questions, and this consideration of rival visions, is in fact not merely a surface feature of Aquinas' thought – it is what shapes and drives it forward. There is a fundamental conviction behind Aquinas' theology, a conviction that the faith which he has received is in its very depths coherent, that ultimately it hangs together and makes sense, and that a patient consideration of all the various voices within scripture and tradition, and of all the available sources of human wisdom, will ultimately serve to illuminate this coherence.

Again, one can see something of this same calm faith exhibited in the work of the great twentieth-century Catholic theologian Karl Rahner, whose trademark essays nearly always begin with some problem, some difficulty, in the faith of the Church as it is currently understood. Rahner's goal is almost always to find a new clarity, and a new simplicity of thought, but his starting point is precisely what is *not* clear, what baffles, what troubles. How can it be, for instance, that God wills the salvation of all (2 Tim.), that faith in Christ and membership of the Church are intrinsically necessary for salvation, and yet there have been and are so many people for whom faith in Christ and membership of the Church are not an option? Or again, in a world of ever-expanding knowledge, who could ever know enough to be in a position to give a genuine intellectual justification of their faith? How could one ever master the competing schools of philosophy, the wisdom to be gleaned from psychology and sociology, the achievements of science, the rival claims and visions of the world religions, the discoveries of historical criticism of the Bible, who could ever master and digest everything that is relevant in all this so as to be in a position to say that all things considered, Christian belief is genuinely a rational and responsible option? Or again, how can a Catholic affirm, as a Catholic must, that there are exactly seven sacraments and no more, without feeling that there is something arbitrary, something 'random', to use the helpful terminology of the teenagers of today, in this number?

The pattern of Rahner's theology is not to suspend belief until difficult questions can be answered, so that for instance we could *only* believe in God's universal salvific will if we can explain to ourselves how it works, or we can *only* accept that Christian faith is rational if we can overcome intellectual pluralism, or Catholics can *only* believe in seven sacraments if they can first give some justification for why there are exactly seven. Even as he probes the difficulties, he never calls into question the fundamental convictions of the faith: he is a Catholic theologian who does not experiment with being anything else. But he *does* probe the difficulties. Rahner offers his own answers to all the questions set out in the previous paragraph, but only after first ensuring that the problem, the difficulty, the tension, is fully felt. There is a kind of therapy involved in his theology: a problem needs to be brought to the surface, it needs to be fully felt, before one can begin to look for a solution. You cannot seek clarity if you will not first acknowledge and give voice to confusion. And the willingness to do this – to acknowledge one's confusion, to examine it and express it – is itself, I am suggesting, an expression of the confidence of faith. This is true whether in Augustine, or in Aquinas, or in Rahner, or in a student of theology today. Clarity does not come if one is not willing first to acknowledge one's confusion, and both the search for the one, and the willingness to acknowledge the other, can be understood as themselves expressions of faith.

But surely, one might be inclined to say at this stage, there must be a limit to the degree to which difficulties can be resolved and confusions clarified. For Christian theology focuses on the God whose self-description is the baffling 'I am who am', whose name is to be honoured by not being pronounced, the God of whom Isaiah writes 'For as the heavens are higher than the earth, so are my ways higher than your ways, and my thoughts than your thoughts' (Isa. 55:9). Jesus speaks constantly in parable and paradox, and is depicted in the gospels as slipping away at the moment he is recognized. And the classic doctrines of Christianity, as articulated at Nicaea and Chalcedon, have very much the look of paradox: God is one and three, Christ fully human and fully divine. To put it very simply, then, if grappling with mystery is at the heart of theology, to what extent can seeking clarity really be its goal?

We can make a start by noting that the idea of clarity is one which itself tends to vary according to the context in which it is used. There is not a *single* understanding of what it is to be 'clear'. The pursuit of clarity will be different for the mathematician, for instance, than it is for a literary critic, and it would make little sense for either to attempt to evaluate or to rewrite the work of the other according to an ideal derived from their own field. The mathematician who tries to reduce an essay of the literary critic to a series of absolutely precise definitions, claims and proofs is engaged in something a little ridiculous, and will either fail completely or lose much of the value in the original essay. In general, then, a sensitivity is required to context, purpose, and style of thought when we inquire into questions of clarity. But then we must go a step further. For if God is not one more thing amongst others, a 'something' alongside and fundamentally similar to all the other 'somethings' in the universe, then arguably theology, with its focus on God, cannot be just one more intellectual discipline amongst others, focused on its particular 'something'. And so it becomes necessary to keep open the possibility that clarity may mean something quite *fundamentally* different in theology from what it means elsewhere.

One might put this point somewhat abstractly as follows. Theology is classically, after Anselm, described as *fides quaerens intellectum*, 'faith seeking understanding'. But both the nature of its 'seeking' and the nature of the 'understanding' it hopes to attain will take something of their character from the nature and content of the 'faith' from which it starts. It is not just any old seeking that faith engages in, nor any old type of understanding that faith seeks, but a form of seeking and a kind of understanding which must be in keeping with what it is in itself – a faith in something radically beyond our control or comprehension. This is the sort of point one finds made repeatedly in the writings of Karl Barth: theology cannot find ready-made, from some other sphere of intellectual life, a general concept of intellectual responsibility and respectability, of what it is to be 'rational', and simply adopt it. It has to allow its own subject matter, God as he reveals himself to us, to determine not only its content but also its method and the standards to which it holds itself.

There can be no question, then, of the theologian beginning from some already given, universal ideal of clarity and trying to determine whether or how ideas about God match up to it. The issue must rather be, what is the type of clarity appropriate to this particular enterprise, to talk about God, about Christ, about revelation, about the transcendent? Of course it is also necessary to add (and this is not always made as clear by thinkers like Barth as it ought to be) that were there *no* continuity between clarity as understood in other contexts and the clarity sought in theology, little would be gained by using the word. The vital point, however, is that we must be willing to discover from the heart of the faith itself in what ways the clarity to be sought in theology is and is not continuous with other concepts of clarity.

The dominant kind of philosophy in the English-speaking world values a particular style of rigorous clarity very highly, and recently, in a movement known as 'analytic theology', a number of philosophers have been turning their attention beyond the traditional topics of philosophy of religion to central questions in Christian theology – beyond questions of the existence of God and the problem of evil, for instance, to the doctrine of the Trinity and the two natures of Christ. A certain mutual suspicion, or at least unease, is often felt between these new 'analytic theologians' and the more usual kind of Christian theologians. One way of articulating this unease, at least as it occurs on the side of the traditional theologians, is precisely in terms of the nature of the clarity that is the goal. The philosophers come to theology deeply schooled in a particular standard and style of clarity, and they try to raise and answer theological questions in a way that meets with its demands. The result can seem odd, somehow unfitting to the subject matter. Brian Leftow, for instance, offers an essay on the Trinity whose main focus is the model that a time-travelling Rockette can provide. After quoting from the Athanasian creed (' ... the Father is God, the Son is God and the Holy Spirit is God. And yet they are not three Gods, but one God') he comments 'Such odd arithmetic demands explaining'[1]. Leftow's analysis is extensive and careful, and includes a substantial excursus onto the possibility of time travel itself. And the time-travelling Rockette has much to offer: she can be one and multiple at the same time; she can dance in perfect unison with herself; she can even, in a certain sense, carry on a conversation. On one level this is very clever; a precise intellectual problem is identified and a precise resolution to it offered. On another level, though, something seems out of kilter; the thinking that produces a resolution to the problem is somehow too detached from the subject matter itself. It seems to be a case of puzzle seeking solution rather than faith seeking understanding. An intellectual difficulty, arising out of the doctrine of the Trinity, has been identified in such a way that it can be cut loose from the doctrine, from everything else that faith in God involves, and be addressed as a self-standing puzzle. Clarity has been achieved at the price of too detached and too narrow a focus.

It is not hard to imagine discomfort coming from the other direction as well, though. Is not the appeal to mystery a very easy refuge? What is to stop the theologian from using mystery as a fig leaf for intellectual laziness and sloppiness, a trump card to defeat an opponent? Indeed, sometimes the invocation of mystery would seem extraordinarily useful not only to the intellectually lazy or irresponsible, but also to those who have control and don't care that it should be questioned too much: if the Church, for instance, is a mystery, then perhaps this means it should not be subject to the kinds of analysis that are appropriate for ordinary human institutions, and in this way those who occupy its current structures might find themselves rather conveniently insulated from criticism.

If mystery is inescapable in theology, and yet not every invocation of it is necessarily legitimate, is it possible to find a simple rule to determine when the appeal to mystery is acceptable and when it is not? I do not know of one. But it is possible, through experience of Christian faith and experience of the Christian theological tradition, to develop a sense for the question, a capacity for discernment. And one can perhaps also identify some rules of thumb.

First, it seems reasonable to suppose that that which is presented as fundamentally mysterious in Scripture should retain something of this quality in theology – even to the point that we might be suspicious of approaches to theology where this is lost. In this sense, one might argue that Anselm's formula suggesting that we understand God to be 'that than which nothing greater can be conceived' is actually more satisfactory, more theologically adequate, than what are supposed to be modern restatements, modern clarifications of his position in terms of God as 'perfect being' or 'maximally great'. If one is going to try to identify in a single formula the God whose baffling reply to Moses' query, 'Who shall I say sent me?' is 'Tell them "I am" sent you', it is better that the formula should have something of the elusive and indirect to it, as Anselm's does and the modern restatements do not.

Second, in an area where we meet persistent paradox in the theological tradition – the relation of the divine and human in Jesus, for instance – it is natural to be tolerant of a contemporary thinker who renews the element of paradox, even if in a new idiom. In Karl Barth's discussion of Trinitarian terminology in §9 of the *Church Dogmatics*, for instance, one can see a combination of careful intellectual work, seeking a certain improvement in clarity, with a very straightforward admission of the mysteriousness of the subject matter. Barth proposes that we replace the traditional terminology of three 'Persons' in God with a new technical term, three *Seinsweise* (ways of being). He defends his suggestion in some detail, arguing on the one hand that an altered intellectual context means that the term 'Person' has acquired a set of associations which serve to confuse rather than illuminate talk of the Trinity; and on the other hand that what positive content the theological tradition had wished the word 'Person' to carry is actually equally or better conveyed by the term *Seinsweise*. But he is very clear that the changes he proposes do not allow him to sidestep or resolve all the difficulties the tradition has always faced:

> The great central difficulties which have always beset the doctrine of the Trinity at this point apply to us too. We, too, are unable to say how an essence can produce itself and then be in a twofold way its own product. We, too, are unable to say how an essence's relation of origin can also be the essence itself and indeed how three such relations can be the essence and yet not be the same as each other but indissolubly distinct from one another. We, too, are unable to say how an essence's relation of origin can also be its permanent mode of being and, moreover, how the same essence, standing in two different and opposed relations of origin, can subsist simultaneously and with equal truth and reality in the two different corresponding modes of being. We, too, are unable to say how in this case 3 can really be 1 and 1 can really be 3.[2]

So where the biblical witness itself seems to insist on mystery we would be suspicious of a theology that fails on some level to preserve this. And where the theological tradition has consistently dealt in paradox we would not be surprised to see contemporary theologians continue to do so. The situation is somewhat different, however, if a thinker introduces *new* elements of paradox or mystery into their theological vision. If someone introduces paradox where there is no strong precedent, so to speak, there are at least grounds for caution. Hans Urs von Balthasar, for instance, suggests, without any very clear explanation, two things: first, that 'man' and 'woman' are equal, and second, that man has primacy. Should we accept this as just another of those paradoxes of which theology is full? Not necessarily. While Christian thought has certainly been marked, over the centuries, by a good deal of unreflective sexism, there is no strong precedent for taking the relationship between men and women, or between masculinity and femininity, as close to the heart of the gospel, or as any kind of central Christian mystery. Contemporary Christians, it is true, face certain difficulties in reconciling particular verses from the Pauline corpus with the convictions of our time about the equality of men and women, and the difficulties need to be dealt with in one way or another. To turn them into a mystery, however, where no mystery has until now been perceived in the tradition, might be just a case of evasion or obfuscation. At the very least one can say that the burden of proof is on the side of the one proposing a new 'mystery'.[3]

So I have suggested that theology cannot measure itself against some prior, general concept of clarity, and more particularly that whatever clarity means in theology, it cannot be the elimination of all elements of mystery and paradox. I have also suggested that while the question of what counts as legitimate appeal to mystery in theology is difficult, one can at least take a starting point in Scripture and some guidance from tradition. It is possible to have a sense, from an immersion in Christian faith and practice, or from a familiarity with the Christian theological tradition, in what sphere mystery and paradox are to be expected, and when on the other hand the invocation of mystery should be approached with more caution.

What is worth considering next is how these two key themes I have been exploring – clarity and mystery – are related to each other. It might seem natural to presume that, in one way or another, they are opposed. One might say, for instance, that while to some degree theology can allow itself to pursue clarity, it is only free to do so in limited areas, and the search must come to an end when the theologian runs up against an element of mystery. Or one might suppose that while all theologians are forced to grant that God *is in some way* mysterious, to the degree that they are successful in their work, they hope to make God just a little *less* mysterious: they will make inroads, however modest, against the divine unknowability, even if they cannot hope to abolish it altogether.

But it is also possible to take a rather different view: to suppose that, at least at times, to the degree that theology is successful, God will become *more* mysterious, more ungraspable. A very important kind of theological clarity, in other words, might be clarity about just how unknowable God is. Perhaps clarity and mystery need not be opposed.

There is sometimes a tendency to identify a distinct strand within the Christian tradition which makes the mystery of God, the unknowability of God, its special focus – a strand of mystical theology, or apophatic theology, or negative theology. But it is not clear that this strand ought to be separated off too sharply from the mainstream of the tradition, or that its proponents ought to be thought of as doing something so very different from what other theologians do. One can find an emphasis on the unknowability of God, for instance, not only in the so-called 'pseudo-Dionysius', who is usually seen as standing at the origin of this tradition of the apophatic in theology, or in the author of the *Cloud of Unknowing*, but also in someone who is at the centre of the medieval tradition such as Thomas Aquinas. Aquinas, with the laconic but programmatic comment that 'we cannot know what God is, but rather what He is not' introduces at a decisive moment in his *Summa Theologiae* a discussion of divine simplicity.[4] And divine simplicity as he presents it turns out to mean, not that we can imagine God to be somehow very uncomplicated, but rather that all the ways in which we might try to imagine and get a handle on God – all of which in one way or another involve an element of 'composition' – must be ruled out.

What holds for Aquinas – that the search for clarity, and the deepening of mystery, can go together – also holds for some more recent thinkers. We will briefly consider two examples: Karl Rahner, who makes reflection on God as mystery absolutely central to his thought, and Kathryn Tanner, who hardly mentions the word. In both cases, nevertheless, we find the same pattern: that an advance in clarity leads not to a diminution of a sense of the mystery of faith, but to its intensification.

In one of his most striking and at times beautiful essays, 'The Concept of Mystery in Catholic Theology',[5] Rahner starts once again from a problem. In the Catholicism of the time (Rahner was writing in 1959) the presumption was that the Catholic faith includes a number of mysteries, and this meant, essentially, a number of truths, of true propositions, which Catholics knew from revelation must be believed but which they could not for the moment (in this life) understand. It was a fundamentally negative concept of mystery – we are in the unfortunate position of being unable to understand certain things – and a fundamentally plural one – it just so happens that there are quite a *number* of these things that we cannot understand. This was a vision which carried with it the danger of making faith itself seem arbitrary, a matter of believing a disconnected set of truths merely on the basis of authority. Being a good Catholic, it might be thought, had to do with being prepared to swallow whatever number of incomprehensible things one was told to swallow.

Rahner argues for the possibility of a radical shift, so that there is only *one* mystery, and the *one* mystery is not a lack in our knowledge but something fundamentally positive: all the genuine mysteries of the faith, Rahner maintains, point to a single mystery, and this mystery is God in God's turning towards and giving himself to the world. And the fact that God is a mystery is not something provisional, temporary, some gap in our knowledge to be cleared up at a later stage. God's incomprehensibility will remain even in the beatific vision, Rahner writes, when we contemplate God 'face to face'; we must not think of this incomprehensibility as something that will be 'a sort of regrettably permanent limitation of our blessed comprehension of God' but 'as the very substance of our vision and the very object of our blissful love'.[6]

Rahner also suggests that this one mystery is something to which we are already now in relationship. The realm of our reason, of our control, of our capacity to know and grasp individual objects, is already sustained, he holds, by our relatedness to something we cannot grasp and know, that cannot be for us one more object among others. We are always already related to God, in other words, not just as one more thing in the world which just happens to be much bigger and more powerful than the others, but as ungraspable, incomprehensible mystery. So we read in his essay

> Man is he who is always confronted with the holy mystery, even where he is dealing with what is within hand's reach, comprehensible and amenable to conceptual framework. … the holy mystery is not something upon which man may 'also' stumble, if he is lucky and takes an interest in something besides the definable objects within the horizon of his consciousness. Man always lives by the holy mystery, even where he is not conscious of it. The lucidity of his consciousness derives from the incomprehensibility of this mystery. The proximity of his environment is constituted by the distant aloofness of the mystery: the freedom of his mastery of things comes from his being mastered by the Holy which is itself unmastered.[7]

It is not, then, that our general capacity to understand the world must contain a few 'gaps' to allow for the mysteries of faith, but rather that everything we do understand is surrounded, embraced, upheld, by a fundamental relationship in which we find ourselves to that which we cannot understand. Mystery is what is most fundamental; the realm of what we can grasp and understand, only secondary.

There is not space here to offer a full explanation of how all the parts of Rahner's thought fit together, but what I have described may be enough at least to give a taste for the kind of approach to mystery Rahner proposes. On the one hand, in his radical revision of the common Catholic view of the relation of mystery to reason, Rahner is attempting a fundamental simplification and clarification of theology – he is trying to bring all of the apparently disparate elements of the Christian faith into focus around a single centre, a centre which is itself intimately linked to experience. But on the other hand, if he is right, even though in one sense he has proposed a reduction – the many mysteries are all drawn into a single centre – most fundamentally mystery in Rahner's theology is not diminished but intensified. He is not trying to explain God a bit more than others have managed to, but to make it more clear that God is essentially not explicable. His theology, if it is successful, does not push back the bounds of what is unknown – not even a little bit – but makes his readers aware of mystery as a deeper, and a more inescapable, phenomenon than they had realized.

While Rahner explores at length the notion of mystery, and in fact adopts 'Holy Mystery' as a preferred way of referring to God, Kathryn Tanner[8] has no explicit focus on this concept. And yet we can see in one of her seminal works, *God and Creation in Christian Theology*, just this pattern where theological clarification comes with not a diminution but an intensification of the unknowability, the ungraspability, of the subject matter of theology.

Tanner's focus is on how Christians can think about God's activity and created activity (our own, in particular) in relation to each other. What is the relationship between divine sovereignty and our freedom? Between God's grace and human free will? Her proposal is that for most of its tradition Christianity has had a particular way of speaking about these things, a particular 'grammar' governing the way God and creation are talked about, but that this grammar, this fundamental pattern of speaking, was lost at some point in the modern period, and Christians have been confused over these issues ever since. A key aspect of this grammar is that it is non-contrastive – that one never sets God's agency and creative agency in opposition to one another. You must never, in other words, speak of God in such a way that the more God does, the less the creature does, or vice versa. And this means that you must not talk of human freedom as though it is incompatible with divine causality, as if we can only be free if God draws back.

This is a very large thesis, and again there is not the space here to enter into an extended exploration of it, nor an evaluation of whether Tanner is right. But for our purposes what matters is that if she *is* right, what her analysis brings is both great clarity and an intensification of mystery. There is clarity, because she gives us a very simple account of common underlying patterns in otherwise very different theological works, a simple set of rules for speaking in a coherently Christian way about God and the world, and a simple diagnosis of why so much Christian theology in more recent times runs into difficulties. But on the other hand, Tanner's approach gives us no help whatsoever in getting a handle on God, or how God works in the world. Any attempt actually to make intelligible God's agency in the world will be an attempt somehow to place it – God is acting here but not there, at one point rather than some others. Perhaps God gets things going at the beginning and sets up the pattern but then does not intervene. Perhaps God invisibly influences things at the quantum mechanical level without violating any physical laws. Perhaps God offers grace if we ask but does not interfere with our decision to accept it or not. All such proposals would give us some way of concretely integrating a vision of God's activity with our general understanding of how things and indeed we ourselves work. But all of them, in saying that God acts *here* whereas over *there* it is only a created being which acts, violate the non-contrastive principle Tanner articulates. So at the same time as she brings clarity to the issue of how to relate God and creation, divine and human agency, she moves it right beyond any chance of our grasping it. To say that divine and created agency cannot be contrasted is not to offer an explanation of how they go together, then, but instead a rule which defeats all possible explanations.

But, a reader might ask, what is the point? What is the point of doing theology if all one can do is become clearer about not knowing? Why bother? Why not just remain quiet? The answer has to be, in one sense, there is no point. If one thinks of theology as an end in itself, as a self-standing intellectual enterprise, and if what it is about is becoming clearer about unknowability, then perhaps there would be no purpose to it. But if one understands theology as a reflection that is rooted in practice, in a relationship to faith, in a relationship, indeed, to God, then it is not quite so hard to see the point. For the resistance against idolatry, against the temptation to turn God into something like us, into something that can be grasped and controlled, something that can be given a place within our broader view of the world – this resistance is absolutely vital to faith, and in this, it would seem, a theology that would become clearer about mystery has a helpful role to play.

Thus far we have touched on the search for clarity as rooted in the capacity to acknowledge confusion, and on the search for clarity in relation to the elusive, mysterious and often paradoxical nature of the Christian faith. One last issue needs to be considered, and that is the presence – or lack – of clarity in theological *writing* itself. Anyone who has been a student of theology will know well that lucidity is unfortunately not something always or easily to be found in the writings of the theologians. One can spend a good deal of time, as a student, baffled – baffled not by the central mysteries of the Christian faith, that is, but by the sheer difficulty of understanding what the theologians are trying to say. Why can theological writing itself not be more clear?

Some of the things which make theology so difficult are also some of the things which make it so fascinating. The theologian works in a very long intellectual tradition, and needs to engage, not just with a few ideas that have come to prominence in the last few years, but with a whole range of disputes, debates, and decisions which have made their mark on this tradition – and also, of course, with the ancient and extraordinarily varied texts which lie behind it all. So a theologian may be as interested as any other contemporary intellectual in the leading ideas of her own time, and all the jargon that goes with them, but at the same time working out her thought in relation to a much larger canvas, drawing as a kind of shorthand on an immense range of technical vocabulary that has built up over eighteen or nineteen centuries. The result is fascinating if it can be understood, but is not always, especially from the point of view of the newcomer to the subject, a model of clarity.

For the student, however, when it comes to writing, the most useful maxim to keep in mind is, I think, Jesus' instruction to 'turn the other cheek'. You may have to read difficult, sometimes jargon-laden writings, but you should aim to write with as much clarity and simplicity as you can muster. Few things are worse than work produced by someone who, impressed by writings that he or she cannot quite understand, seeks to be equally impressive by writing something that others will not quite be able to understand. And, on the other hand, the effort to write clearly and simply is a key component of the effort to *think* honestly and seriously, which is in turn at the heart of the theological task.

So how does one seek clarity in the task of writing itself? In many ways the advice in theology is the same as in any other discipline. Wherever possible, choose shorter words and simpler language: if you must introduce a technical term, make sure to explain it. Read and reread your work, and if you are not quite sure what you mean, don't let it stand. One of the biggest dangers is to think one is writing for a sophisticated audience (i.e. the teacher), and so to think it is not really necessary to lay things out fully. Write as if for a reader like yourself, but like yourself before you learned about this particular subject, and explain things the way you would have liked them to have been explained to you.

It is often harder to seek simplicity and clarity in theological writing than to attempt sophistication, but it is almost always the more honest, the more fruitful, and the more faithful path.

Notes

1 B. Leftow, 'A Latin Trinity', *Faith and Philosophy* 21.3, 2004, pp. 304–33: p. 304.
2 Karl Barth, *Church Dogmatics* I/1, trans. G.W. Bromiley and T.F. Torrance, Edinburgh: T&T Clark, 1975, p. 367.
3 Balthasar is not alone in the twentieth century in wanting to affirm both equality and male primacy – indeed one can find something like this position in Karl Barth. I choose Balthasar here partly because he seems to be peculiarly unconcerned to offer any resolution to the apparent conflict between equality and primacy, and partly because his construal of 'man' and 'woman' and their relationship to one another is quite central to his thought. Cf. chapter 6 of my *Hans Urs von Balthasar: A (Very) Critical Introduction*, Grand Rapids, MI: Eerdmans, 2012, for a discussion of this.
4 Aquinas, *Summa Theologiae*, 1a. 3, prologue, in *Summa Theologiae 2 (1a. 2–11): Existence and Nature of God*, trans. T. McDermott OP, Cambridge: Cambridge University Press, 2006, p. 19.
5 In Karl Rahner, *Theological Investigations* 4, New York, NY: Crossroad, 1973.
6 Karl Rahner, 'The Concept of Mystery in Catholic Theology', in *Theological Investigations* 4, p. 41.
7 'The Concept of Mystery', p. 54.
8 K. Tanner, *God and Creation in Christian Theology: Tyranny or Empowerment?* Oxford: Basil Blackwell, 1988.

6

READING PHILOSOPHY

Simon Oliver

We often think that theology and philosophy have a natural association. As theologians, we expect to read texts and discuss questions that fall within the ambit of philosophy. For example, most students will engage with philosophy of religion in its various guises. Such works might focus on specific questions concerning the existence of God or the problem of evil. A philosophical approach to religion might also include fundamental issues of existence and knowledge in relation to God, or the science of interpretation that we call hermeneutics. However, when we consider the activity of 'reading philosophy', what is it that we are invited to read? There are countless philosophical traditions that produce very different texts, from the dialogues of Plato to the lectures of Hegel, the treatises of Plotinus to the laconic notes of Wittgenstein. Each tradition has its own priorities, methods, and questions that have countless theological implications. Likewise, theology has implications for the way in which we understand the nature and scope of philosophy.

The practice of philosophical enquiry and the kinds of philosophical texts that we might read have changed significantly over the course of our intellectual history. Therefore, in this chapter I intend to take a broadly historical approach to the topic of 'reading philosophy'. We will explore the different ways in which the philosophical task has been understood and discover some examples of how one might read philosophy in its various forms. Initially, I will focus on the period prior to Christianity and the ancient Greek understanding of philosophy as a way of life. This influenced the kinds of text that emerged from the teachings of various philosophers; over time, they came to form the basis of philosophical schools such as Platonism and Stoicism. These Greek texts proved critical to the formation of Christian teaching, so I will next examine the reading of philosophy by the Christian theologians of the first six centuries. Given that they possessed the treasures of Christ's revelation witnessed in Scripture, why did Christianity's first theologians bother reading pagan philosophy? This will lead us into a discussion of the relationship between reason, which is often associated with philosophy, and faith, which is often associated with theology. How does the reading of philosophy aid the life of faith? This will lead us to consider the way in which philosophy was read in the Middle Ages. I will suggest that philosophy is not read in order to scrutinize theology; neither is it read in order to provide theology with rational foundations. Instead, philosophy is read in order to provide the tools to clarify the meaning and implications of the revealed things of faith. Philosophy is read *with* theology in order to aid the life of faith. We will then examine a significant change in the way philosophy is practised, written and read in the modern period, using René Descartes (1596–1650) as an example. Here, we find very different philosophical texts that are read in new ways. Finally, we will briefly examine the priorities of twentieth-century philosophy, exploring the way in which the reading of these texts by theologians continues to be crucial to the theological task. Throughout this chapter, there will be three governing questions concerning 'reading philosophy': *What* are we reading? *How* should we read it? *Why* should we read it?

Reading ancient philosophy

When you think of a philosopher, what kind of character comes to mind? It may be an image akin to Rodin's famous sculpture *The Thinker*, cast in 1902. A man sits alone in deep contemplation, his chin resting on his hand. The figure is almost enclosed; the body envelops a thought. This image reflects the view that a philosopher is a lone and thoughtful figure who is captivated by abstract ideas concerning our most fundamental and perplexing problems.

This image of the lone thinker engrossed in abstract thoughts may be an appropriate way of imagining modern philosophy, but it fails to capture important aspects of the philosophy that influenced Christian thought in the ancient world. In particular, philosophy in ancient Greece was concerned not simply with 'thinking' in the abstract sense, but with an entire way of life. A philosopher – literally, of course, a lover of wisdom – was a particular kind of person who aspired to certain excellences or virtues. The philosopher lived 'the examined life' in which the practices of daily living were continuously scrutinized in order to achieve calmness and peace for the soul. This pursuit of a striking and strange form of life was undertaken within a number of philosophical schools that emerged from around the fourth century BC. Perhaps the most famous of these was the Academy founded by Plato (c.429 BC–c.347 BC) that included Aristotle (384 BC–322 BC) amongst its pupils. To begin with, the Academy was little more than a private discussion group, but it evolved into an organized school for the instruction of students who desired wisdom. Importantly, philosophy in antiquity was concerned as much with the kind of person one should be and how one should live as it was with knowledge and experience. In other words, practical questions concerning how to live and act were knit together with speculative questions about existence and truth. In order to perceive truth, one had to live a certain kind of ordered and focused life. Importantly, philosophy was a pursuit that was undertaken communally by means of conversation and discussion.

The conversational character of ancient philosophy meant that it was primarily an oral rather than a written tradition. This is not altogether surprising because the invention of the printing press that gave such prominence to written texts was many centuries away. This is why handwritten copies of texts, which required huge amounts of time and skill for their production, were so rare and precious in the ancient and medieval worlds. A scroll or a book was something of enormous value. Many students would hear, rather than read, a text. Owning their own copy was almost unthinkable, so texts were often committed to memory. However, there are other reasons for the importance of the spoken word and the centrality of such arts as rhetoric and persuasion to the discipline of philosophy. Many of these can be seen in Plato's dialogue *Phaedrus*. At the beginning of the *Phaedrus*, Socrates, Plato's teacher and the principal character in many of his dialogues, is taking a walk outside the walls of Athens. He is in conversation with Phaedrus, who has been listening to a speech about the nature of love delivered by a famous Athenian rhetorician known as Lysias. Socrates expresses his great desire to hear Lysias' speech and, suspecting that Phaedrus has a copy hidden under his cloak, Socrates persuades him to perform the speech. What is the significance of Phaedrus possessing a *written* copy of Lysias' speech? To write down a speech implies that it can be repeated endlessly *as the same speech*; it can be read over and over again. The speech has, as it were, been 'captured'. Once written down, the speech becomes a document to be passed on; the knowledge it contains can be bought and sold. But when Phaedrus reads Lysias' speech, is Socrates hearing Lysias or merely a copy or echo of Lysias? Plato's dialogue suggests that there is far more to a speech and the learning that it conveys than merely the written words. The context of the speech, including its time and location, the immediate purpose of the speech and the characters of its hearers, are all crucial to the speech's meaning. Plato sees that the context in which wisdom is conveyed is crucial to a proper understanding and the attainment of a perfect state of being and knowledge which all philosophers seek. Towards the end of the dialogue, this leads Plato to suggest that the spoken word is of greater value than the written word. Why? Because the written word implies that wisdom or knowledge can be fixed, captured, and endlessly traded. But wisdom, for Plato and his teacher Socrates, is drawn out of a student by conversation in which circumstance and context – the very form of life – are crucial. The spoken word is fluid and fleeting. It does not pretend to capture wisdom, but seeks it through the performance and movement of rhetoric. To make this point more simply, think of one of the most famous speeches of the twentieth century: Martin Luther King's 'I have a dream' speech, so iconic of the American civil rights movement. Imagine the difference between *reading* this speech on the internet today, and the experience of an African American standing at the steps of the Lincoln memorial in Washington, DC *listening* to King's oration on that August day in 1963. Surely to understand the real power and persuasiveness of Martin Luther King's speech, one must remember its original context and the mode of its delivery, not simply words typed on a page or appearing on a computer screen.

This is why rhetoric, persuasion and, therefore, conversation are so important in the *practise* of ancient Greek philosophy. When we read such philosophy, we must therefore remember that such documents were not intended to be read privately and individually. The treatises of ancient philosophy are frequently the edited notes of students or dictations to a scribe. They were written so that they might be read aloud with all the nuances of the original delivery. The principal means of conducting philosophy was oral discourse. The French classical scholar Pierre Hadot outlines the importance of this way of conveying the philosophical life:

> This relationship between the written and spoken word thus explains certain
> aspects of the works of antiquity. Quite often the work proceeds by the

association of ideas, without systematic rigor. The work retains the starts and stops, the hesitations, and the repetitions of spoken discourse. Or else, after re-reading what he has written, the author introduces a somewhat forced systematization by adding transitions, introductions, or conclusions to different parts of the work.[1]

This helps us to understand why reading ancient philosophy is often so challenging. The pages of Plato and Aristotle will rarely contain the neat orderings of modern textbooks. These philosophical works are the written record of what was originally a shared *conversation* in the pursuit of wisdom and truth. In fact, the practice of reading privately and silently was relatively unknown in the ancient world. Texts would have been read aloud, communally.[2] Reading was an activity not simply of the mind, but also of the voice and the body.[3]

So to learn philosophy in the ancient world was to be inaugurated into a particular school of thought whose aim was not simply to convey knowledge, but to train students in certain spiritual practices and forms of life that enabled the philosopher to see differently, beyond the immediate appearances of things. This was a training in how to look at the world in order to discern its meaning. Each school had its authorities and masters. Strict curricula were established whereby students would study authoritative works in a particular order, enabling apprentice philosophers to develop in a rational manner towards spiritual maturity.

While the principal means for the conduct of philosophy remained oral discussion, from the third century BC a tradition of writing commentaries on authoritative works became increasingly popular. The so-called 'commentarial tradition' remained prominent throughout antiquity and the medieval period, up to the sixteenth century. We therefore have two kinds of text to read: the primary authoritative texts of the masters of ancient philosophy, and commentaries on those texts that are provided for the guidance of student philosophers. Just like the religious and biblical traditions of Judaism and Christianity, ancient philosophy had its authoritative texts combined with commentaries on, or expositions of, those texts. It might therefore be best to understand philosophy in antiquity not simply as a set of abstract philosophical questions, but as a way of life in which conversation with a whole tradition of thought and practice features very prominently.

So how are we to read these texts and enter the conversation of ancient philosophy? It is important to preserve something of the strangeness of the texts and the unfamiliarity of the world from which they emerge. As twenty-first century readers, there will always be a temptation to domesticate such philosophy and to read the texts through the lens of modern assumptions and priorities. So there are perhaps two key challenges of which we should be aware in our practice of reading. The first challenge is our tendency to assume that human knowledge and wisdom progress smoothly through time. We tend to think that what comes later in our intellectual history is more advanced, more correct, wiser or simply better than what belongs to the dim and distant past. Of course it is the case that since the seventeenth century we have witnessed remarkable developments in human understanding, particularly with regard to nature's processes. Our technological abilities bring immeasurable human goods (advances in medicine) as well as potentially devastating costs (climate change or weapons of modern warfare). But despite all this 'progress', it is not clear that we are wiser or better people. For Plato, philosophy is not principally concerned with uncovering more and more facts about the world. As we have seen, it is really about discerning the nature of wisdom and the character of the good life. In these spheres, which are at once both philosophical and theological, we have far more to learn from the philosophers of antiquity than we might imagine. At the very least, the strangeness of the texts – and many are weird and difficult – should unsettle our modern imagination and help us to see things differently. So in order truly to read a text of ancient philosophy, one must allow the text to interrogate us, as readers, rather than understand ourselves simply as interrogators of the text.

The second challenge that confronts us in reading ancient philosophy concerns our tendency to impose priorities, questions, categories or meanings that are alien to the text. For example, it is very tempting when reading a dialogue by Plato to think that the dramatic details are mere decoration behind which lie arguments which might be expressed in bare propositional terms. As we have seen with the *Phaedrus*, the genre of the text and the setting of the dialogue are crucial aspects of Plato's argument that are integral to the way in which he conceives philosophy's task. The text needs to be read as drama, literature, *and* philosophy; for Plato, these form an integrated whole which work to persuade us (rather than compel us) to assent to the argument and vision being proposed. When you are reading a dialogue by Plato, it may be revealing to find some friends with whom you can read the text so that, as when reading a play, each person can take a different part and the conversational character of the discourse can come to life.

Another example of the imposition of questions and priorities that, on careful inspection, are not wholly consistent with a text of ancient philosophy can be found in some readings of Aristotle's great work *Metaphysics*. This text was probably compiled by an editor in the first century AD, around four hundred years after its various chapters and books were written. That same editor gave the title 'Metaphysics' to this work. For Aristotle, these writings and lectures are concerned with what he called 'first philosophy'. This encompassed wisdom, theology (in the sense of the study of ultimate origins and purposes) and 'being' in its most general or abstract sense. Aristotle is not concerned with *particular* things – *this* table, *that* horse, *the* cosmos – but with being *in general*. In other words, this 'first philosophy' encompassed everything including *theos*, or 'God'. Book 12 of the *Metaphysics* is one of the most famous and studied texts in ancient philosophy. It is particularly important for theologians because it apparently offers a significant proof for the existence of God. Put very simply, Aristotle seems to argue that the universe exhibits motion (by which he means any kind of change) and this motion must have an ultimate source or cause that is itself beyond motion. Modern philosophy of religion places discussions of the proofs of God's existence at the very heart of its debates, so there is a temptation to assume that proving the existence of God is Aristotle's primary concern in this central book of his *Metaphysics*. Many modern commentaries and discussions of Book 12 take this approach; they assume that proving God's existence by means of what is now labelled a 'cosmological argument' is Aristotle's principal concern. But is the text all about proving that God exists? Take a look at the opening lines: 'Our enquiry is concerned with substance; for it is the principles and causes of substances that we are investigating.' Aristotle goes on to discuss what he means by substance, and the different kinds of substance that he includes within his cosmology. Amongst these is what he calls 'non-sensible and eternal substance', which is God. But Aristotle's principal concern is not to set out a proof of God's existence in the formal logical sense. Rather, he is articulating a systematic cosmology that includes a particular view of an ultimate, eternal, and unmoved origin. To read Book 12 of the *Metaphysics* as if it were just a proof of God's existence would result in a failure to capture the full extent of Aristotle's purpose and argument.[4] So, presented with texts of ancient philosophy, it is perhaps important to heed one straightforward recommendation which is nevertheless sometimes easier said than done: read the text, the whole text and, to begin with, nothing but the text!

Reading philosophy in the early Church

For the first Christian theologians, the question was not simply *how* to read philosophy, but *why* read philosophy? It was not self-evident that philosophy should be treated as trustworthy or valuable because philosophers were pagan thinkers. By contrast, Christians had received knowledge of a wholly different order in the form of God's revelation in Jesus Christ. Writing at the end of the second century, the North African theologian Tertullian famously asked 'what indeed has Athens to do with Jerusalem?'[5] His question concerns the encounter between two very different traditions of enquiry and literature. 'Athens' refers to the philosophers of ancient Greece, chief amongst them Plato and his followers. These speculative thinkers analyse fundamental problems of existence and meaning through rhetorical argument. By contrast, 'Jerusalem' refers to the Hebraic tradition that we find in the Jewish law and the Hebrew Bible. This literature is not concerned with the carefully fashioned terminology of Greek rhetoric or logical analysis, but with meaning and truth as discerned in narrative, poetry, and drama. In short, for the early Christian theologians the tradition of Jerusalem tells the story of a people, the Israelites, from whom was brought the Messiah, Jesus the Christ. His life, death, and resurrection, told in the narratives and letters of the New Testament, is God's revelation that is now proclaimed through the liturgy of the Church under the guidance and inspiration of the Holy Spirit. Although he used the tools of Stoic philosophy in his treatises, the implication of Tertullian's rhetorical question is that the Church, being the recipient of the revelation of divine wisdom in the incarnate Word of God, should be wary of the wisdom of pagans represented by philosophy. Philosophers were regarded as the forerunners of heretics, not the forerunners of Christians.

At first glance this attitude is understandable. If one opens a book of the Old Testament, whether it be the saga of Genesis, the prophecy of Isaiah or the poetry of the Psalms, it will be very different to what usually passes for philosophy. Yet the historical record shows us that there never was a pure and pristine 'theology', Jewish or Christian, which did not in some way engage with other intellectual traditions, including the philosophical learning to be found in ancient Greece.[6] This is particularly evident in the writings of Greek-speaking Jews who obviously combine Athens and Jerusalem in their lives and work. The primary example is Philo, a first century

Greek (or 'Hellenic') Jewish writer from Alexandria in Egypt. Philo merges the thought of Plato and the Stoic philosophers with Jewish narrative and scriptural exegesis. The theologians of the early Church, including Justin Martyr (c.100–c.165) and Clement of Alexandria (c.150–c.215), and those writing later in antiquity such as the Cappadocian Fathers (writing in the late fourth century), Cyril of Alexandria (d.444) and Augustine of Hippo (354–430), were educated in the thought of the ancient Greeks and deployed their methods and terminology to make clear the meaning and implications of Christian *doctrina*, or teaching. The Church Fathers had two favourite images for the use of philosophy by Christian theology. The first concerns the story of Jesus changing water into wine at a wedding in Cana (John 2:1–11). Christian theology turns the water of pagan philosophy into the rich wine of divine truth. The second concerns the Israelites taking treasures from their Egyptian captors as they fled into the wilderness (Exod. 12:33–36). Like the Israelites who put the treasures of the Egyptians to a higher use in the service of the one God, so Christian theology can take the treasures of ancient philosophy and put this learning to a higher use in clarifying the revelation of God in Jesus Christ.

So why did the theologians of the early Church perceive value in the philosophical teachings of pagans? We can highlight two reasons. First, ancient Greek philosophy as taught particularly by Plato and Aristotle and later, from around the third century AD, by the tradition known as Neoplatonism, had discerned the fundamental importance of a transcendent 'One'. Other ancient schools, including the various paganisms of the Romans, saw the origins of the universe and the fate of human lives to lie in the fickle and capricious behaviour of a plurality of gods. Not only did Plato and Aristotle make the discipline of philosophy more formal and critical, they also discerned the importance of a single source of existence and, therefore, truth. For Plato, this lay in the Form of the Good that, we are told in his dialogue the *Republic*, lies beyond being. For Aristotle, the final end of all things and the source of motion in the universe lay in a divine first unmoved mover who is fully actual. Seeing a single source of being and truth presents a philosophical problem that is very prominent in ancient thought: what is the relationship between that *one* transcendent source, and the *many* changeable things we see in the universe? How can temporal plurality come from eternal unity? The question of the relationship between unity and plurality lies particularly at the heart of Platonic philosophy, yet its discernment of unity as the divine source of all things clearly resonates with the key insight of the Hebrew scriptures: there is only one God. The monotheism of Judaism and Christianity is anticipated in the thought of the finest ancient philosophers.

A second reason why theologians of the ancient Church valued philosophical learning lies in their understanding of the relationship between faith and reason, and hence their view of theology's relationship to philosophy. We tend to think of theology as concerned with matters of faith and religious practice. It deals with God's revelation in Christ mediated through the Scriptures and expounded in Church teaching and Christian life. On the other hand, philosophy is concerned with reason and finds its source in critical human thought. However, for many of the Church's first theologians there was no fundamental discontinuity between the spheres of faith and reason. While God revealed himself most particularly in Christ, nevertheless we could also explore the things of God via philosophical reason as they are disclosed in creation. After all, the reason exhibited in philosophy was understood to participate in the *Logos* or 'reason' through which all things were made (John 1). That same *Logos*, or reason, was made known in the incarnation of the Son, the Word made flesh. So there is no discrete sphere of reason that belongs only to philosophy. Likewise, 'revelation' was not understood as a wholly separate stock of knowledge which suddenly arrives from nowhere in a way that is completely disconnected from the way that we think about reality philosophically. Revelation always has to have *something* to do with our reason, otherwise how could we recognize revelation and make sense of it?

While the early centuries of the Church are an attempt to come to terms with the meaning and implications of the life, death, and resurrection of Jesus Christ, in philosophical learning theologians found the tools and concepts that would allow them to make sense of the event of Christ. Therefore, Christian theology always involved a reading of philosophy alongside a reading of its authoritative scriptural texts. Theology and philosophy, and faith and reason, were always intertwined yet distinct. At the same time, philosophy was consummated in its service of the God-focused reason of the Church. Philosophy was made *more* compelling and rational when it was put to theological ends. Hence we arrive at a broad consensus within both the ancient and medieval Church: philosophy acts as a handmaid to theology, not because of any deficiency or lack of clarity within God's revelation, but because of the sinful weakness of human minds.

It is for these reasons that the early Christians used a number of Greek philosophical texts for understanding the faith they had received from the apostles. For example, the categories used by the Cappadocian Fathers in articulating their Trinitarian doctrine of God were drawn from Greek philosophy. Augustine of Hippo (354–430), perhaps the greatest theologian of the West, was deeply influenced by his reading of the pagan Neoplatonist philosophers Plotinus (205–70) and Porphyry of Tyre (c.234–c.305) as well as by the Roman philosopher and statesman Cicero (106 BC–43 BC) and his dialogue *Hortensius*. While he was competent in reading Greek, Augustine more frequently read texts that had been translated into Latin. The works of Plotinus and Porphyry were available in Latin translation by Marius Victorinus (fourth century). Some of Plato's works were available to Augustine in Greek, but only a portion of the *Timaeus* had been translated into Latin and Augustine shows little sign of having studied Plato's works. Nevertheless, the deep influence of Plato's philosophy, and that of the Neoplatonists whose thought became dominant in antiquity, can be found throughout his writings. The reading of philosophy in this period was therefore not a straightforward affair, being a combination of engagement with translated texts and an oral tradition of teaching and learning. However, reading philosophy was clearly part and parcel of being a Christian theologian and teacher.

Reading philosophy the medieval way

Around the sixth century, as the world of antiquity faded into the period we label the Middle Ages, the reading of philosophy by Christian theologians, particularly those in the Latin speaking West, at first became less and less significant. Crises in

Christian belief surrounding the doctrine of God and the nature of Christ had been negotiated. The Councils of the Church had established a settled Christian teaching, making fulsome use of the philosophical texts and traditions at their disposal. Although a Christianized Neoplatonism remained prevalent, particularly in the Greek-speaking East under the influence of Pseudo-Dionysius (late fifth to sixth century) and Maximus the Confessor (c.580–662), the texts of Plato fell into obscurity and the works of Aristotle were largely unknown except for Latin translations of, and commentaries on, two works: the *Categories* and *On Interpretation*. It was not until the twelfth century that Greek philosophy was read in earnest once again by Christian thinkers of the West. The scholars of the Islamic world had received and translated Aristotle's works from Greek into Arabic. They also wrote commentaries on these works, enabling Greek philosophy, particularly Aristotle's *Physics* and *Metaphysics*, to be taught effectively to students. Michael the Scot (1175–c.1232), an influential philosopher and mathematician, had acquired a knowledge of Arabic and was able to translate Aristotle's works from Arabic into Latin. These works were reintroduced into the Latin West throughout the thirteenth century, spawning a range of commentaries by Christian thinkers. The most influential exponent of Aristotle's ideas was Thomas Aquinas (c.1225–74), the Italian Dominican friar who spent significant portions of his life teaching at the new University of Paris. He was introduced to Aristotle by his teacher and confrère, the German theologian Albert the Great (c.1193–1280). Aquinas simply refers to Aristotle as 'the Philosopher' and makes extensive use of Aristotle's works in composing his most influential treatises, notably the *Summa Contra Gentiles* (summary of theology against unbelievers) and the voluminous introduction to theology for beginners, the *Summa Theologiae* (summary of theology).

Although Aquinas is sometimes described as an Aristotelian, he is not an uncritical reader of Aristotle's works. Aquinas was educated within the context of an alternative and more prevalent philosophical school, Neoplatonism, and wrote commentaries on a number of texts in that tradition. He is therefore chiefly known as a synthesizer of the broadly Platonic and Aristotelian philosophical systems, all in the service of expounding the Church's *sacra doctrina*, or 'holy teaching'.

How does Aquinas read Aristotle, and what can we learn from this reading? We should remember that for a large part of his career Aquinas was not reading Aristotle directly; he was reading a translation of a translation of Aristotle. Reading texts in translation, let alone a translation of a translation, always presents a challenge in preserving the authenticity and integrity of philosophical works. Nevertheless, Aquinas engages in a very detailed reading and interpretation of a number of Aristotle's texts. We witness his reading at first hand in the twelve commentaries he wrote on Aristotelian works, some of them brief but many very detailed and extensive. Aquinas shows that Aristotle's works are well ordered, yet they require critical interpretation. By 'critical', one does not simply mean that Aquinas sought to disagree with, or criticize, Aristotle. Rather, a critical approach is a discerning and interpretative approach to the text: what is crucial and what is less significant? How does one line of enquiry lead to and illuminate the next? How do the various categories and concepts illuminate one another? Can we discern a coherent and singular philosophical vision? What is the philosopher's purpose as revealed in the text?

Aquinas wrote commentaries on Aristotle principally as lectures for his students. Printed books were still centuries away, so this was the most effective way of conveying a body of knowledge to a wider audience. Aquinas' students would 'read' Aristotle by listening to their master expound the key works and very often they would commit lengthy passages of Aristotle to memory. This reveals a very important characteristic of the reading of philosophy in both the Middle Ages and antiquity: one reads *as part of a tradition* of reading and interpretation. This means that one had to be taught *how* to read. It was not simply a matter of hearing Aristotle read aloud, nor even of 'reading the text for oneself' if one was lucky enough to have access to the manuscript. Quite the contrary: reading was a public rather than a private matter which was undertaken in conversation with one's teacher, fellow students and a whole tradition of interpretation which could be accessed through readers and commentators of previous generations. Neither was reading philosophy a matter of being given a stock of facts or concepts which one then deployed at will. A student had to be taken by the hand and led *through* a text, rather in the way that a tour guide might show a visitor around a city. The guide or teacher points to the text's significant 'landmarks', relating those concepts and ideas to each other and to the history of the text's interpretation. It is almost as if one had to 'enter' the text in order to inhabit its viewpoints and witness its trajectory. In a way, when we read novels today we adopt this style of reading; we step into the imaginary world portrayed by the author through the characters and the setting of the narrative. The best novels draw us in, almost turning the reader into one of the novel's characters. For Aquinas, to read Aristotle was a little like reading literature. He leads his students – including us – *into* the text to inhabit the Aristotelian vision, to try to see the world as Aristotle sees it and to walk around within that world.

This reminds me of some advice I received from one of my first teachers of philosophy and theology, himself a lifelong reader of Thomas Aquinas. He told his students not to 'try to get Plato or Aristotle into our heads' because our small minds would not cope. Rather, we should 'try to get inside the heads of Plato and Aristotle'. How? By *entering* their texts as readers in order to try to see the world differently with the eyes of Plato or Aristotle.

The way that Aquinas uses Aristotle in his own writings is also very revealing. In a number of works, Aquinas arranges his material more or less according to the format of a seminar in the University of Paris. A general theme would be identified, for example, the eternity of God. Questions would be posed relating to that theme, for example, does being eternal belong to God alone? To begin with, Aquinas weighs up one side of the argument, for example that eternity does not belong to God alone. He offers a number of points in favour of this view. Then he offers an alternative view and provides a 'response' to the question. He often utilizes a number of sources and authorities in articulating a response, including Aristotle 'the Philosopher'. After the response, he replies one by one to the initial points made when the question was first posed. Throughout his writing, Aquinas places great weight on Aristotle's philosophy and makes very careful use of his concepts and teachings. However, Aristotle is just one of a number of sources at his disposal including, for example, the Church Fathers, Pseudo-Dionysius and occasionally (although sometimes in order to oppose them) the Islamic philosophers and readers of Aristotle, the Persian Avicenna (980–1037) and the Spanish scholar Averroes (1126–98). Of course, the supreme and focal authority for Aquinas is always Scripture. What is crucial, however, is that these various texts are read alongside each other, with Scripture as the governing heart of the discussion. Aquinas places them into con- versation. As a Master of Theology he initiates his students *into* this conversation through a reading of authoritative theological and philosophical texts. It was as if 'reading philosophy' had its own broader intellectual ritual or liturgy. Importantly, it was also conversational in character, just like philosophy in ancient Greece. The conversation did not simply take place within Aquinas' classroom; reading philoso- phy was also part of a conversation with a tradition of voices stretching back cen- turies. When we read philosophy publically, together, in conversation, rather than privately in our heads in a library, we are recovering something of the practice of reading philosophy in antiquity and the Middle Ages.

Nevertheless, to be called 'a philosopher' in the high Middle Ages was not a compliment. Philosophers were pagan thinkers, even though '*the* Philosopher', Aristotle, had, according to Aquinas, achieved great things. The ultimate purpose of reading philosophy was not to become a philosopher and then stop. Rather, philo- sophy was read in order to acquire an ancient wisdom that could provide Christian theology with a handmaid for the clarification of sacred teaching. The crucial point is that philosophy was deployed in order to *think with* the Christian tradition of reason as it is revealed in Christ who is the incarnation of 'divine reason'. It was not the job of philosophy to scrutinize religious teachings or doctrine from a supposed neutral standpoint, but to clarify those teachings. When a conflict arose between a teaching of Aristotelian philosophy and the deliverances of revealed Christian truth, it was clear that the latter was to interpret and place the former, not vice versa. Perhaps the clearest example of a conflict of this kind concerned Aristotle's teaching on creation. According to Aristotle, the universe is of endless time; it has always existed, although its motion finds its fundamental cause in the 'first unmoved mover' who is beyond change. This was at odds with the teaching of the Jewish, Christian, and Islamic theological traditions that God created 'out of nothing' or *ex nihilo*. This idea was contrary to Greek philosophy that claimed that 'from nothing, nothing comes'. For Aquinas, Aristotle's position was quite defensible. However, the Church's teaching was to be preferred because it was based on the witness of Scrip- ture, the teaching of the tradition, and wider doctrinal concerns regarding the nature of God's grace and freedom. Still, Aristotle's thought could be used, even if nega- tively, to outline more precisely the distinctive meaning and implications of doc- trines such as creation *ex nihilo*. To reiterate, philosophy was not principally used polemically to scrutinize the deliverances of faith and neither was it deployed to provide faith with rational foundations. Philosophy was to think 'in parallel' with faith, as Aquinas puts it in one of his early treatises. In the process, it is philosophy which is re-orientated and consummated according to a theological horizon.[7]

Reading philosophy the modern way

The fortunes of Aristotle's philosophy took a significant turn for the worse in the generation immediately after Aquinas. In 1277, just two years after Aquinas' death, the Bishop of Paris condemned a raft of Aristotelian teachings as contrary to the Christian faith. Yet the utility, power, and comprehensive rigour of Aristotle's philosophy meant that his works recovered their influence and came to dominate the schools and universities of the late Middle Ages and the Renaissance. Plato's texts were also introduced to a much wider readership through translations into Latin by the Italian humanist Marsilio Ficino (1433–99). To learn about nature, politics, ethics, and metaphysics, one read (and probably wrote a commentary on) Aristotle. Meanwhile, Plato's *Timaeus* was to have a significant impact on the character of early modern science because of his use of mathematics to understand nature, while his *Republic* influenced political theory. Philosophy was read for reasons that were not immediately connected to the priorities of the Church and the needs of theology.

The proliferation of Aristotelian learning was no doubt encouraged by the invention of the printing press in the late fifteenth century. At the same time, one cannot underestimate the effect of printed books on the practice of reading, including the reading of philosophy. While printing enhanced the transmission of learning to a previously unimaginable extent, it also made possible the *private* ownership of texts. At the same time, this allowed the private reading of texts. Thus far, we have seen the way in which reading philosophy was a public, communal, and conversational practice undertaken in the context of a much wider tradition of interpretation and communal learning. Following the advent of private collections of printed books, a reader could sit alone with a text, scrutinizing the text and coming to her own interpretative conclusions. It seemed that no training or initiation in *how* to read the text was required. The text was not encountered and received collectively, but privately by individuals. The reading of philosophy had become a very 'interior' or private exercise.

How is this more individualistic approach to reading philosophy reflected in modern philosophy's texts? René Descartes's *Meditations on First Philosophy*, published in Latin in 1641, is often regarded as a paradigmatic text of modern philosophy. The subtitle is revealing: 'in which the existence of God and the immortality of the soul are demonstrated'. This philosophy might be read not in order to understand better the Christian theological tradition and the revealed things of faith, but so as to provide a rational foundation for religious belief. The very fact that religious belief was deemed in need of a rational foundation from an autonomous philosophy already implied that religious belief was in itself a-rational or, worse still, irrational.

Descartes describes retreating alone to a room in order to question his every belief and search for an absolutely indubitable foundation for human knowledge. Eventually, that foundation is provided by his conviction that 'I am, I exist'. This was later expressed in his famous *cogito ergo sum*: I think, therefore I am. There was one thing Descartes could not doubt simply because he was doubting: his own existence. If there is doubt, something is doing the doubting, this 'I' which is, according to Descartes, a *res cogitans*, a 'thinking thing'. This is the foundation of his epistemology, or theory of knowledge. It also provides the basis for his proof that God exists.

When I first read Descartes's text as a student, it struck me as very strange and artificial, almost 'experimental'; philosophy seemed to be disconnected from the communal and complex way people actually think and live. Descartes is fully aware that he is undertaking a specific and technical exercise of doubt; he commends it to his readers as something that might be undertaken at some time in their lives. However, the sense of the individual philosopher thinking in complete isolation stands in striking contrast to the picture we receive from ancient philosophy of the philosopher as part of a conversational school of thought. It seems that in modernity philosophy is not so much a way of life as a technical exercise in individual thinking. It suggests an image akin to Rodin's sculpture *The Thinker*, with which we began this chapter.

The eventual demise of the Aristotelian worldview in the seventeenth century, often associated with Descartes's writings, is also regarded as the beginning of that characteristic period in our intellectual and cultural history that we label 'modernity'. As well as developments in natural philosophy that heralded a radical break from that proposed in Aristotle's *Physics*, new priorities emerged for philosophy, particularly in relation to theology. The reading of philosophy was now undertaken not in order to 'think with' theology and provide a handmaid for the exposition of sacred teaching. Instead, philosophy had turned to face and scrutinize theology. It was to provide either a rational foundation for religious belief, as in Descartes, or critically to examine religious claims according to the standards of an independent reason, as in figures such as David Hume (1711–76) and Immanuel Kant (1724–1804). Hume famously critiqued miracles in his *An Enquiry Concerning Human Understanding* (1748) and the design argument for God's existence in his posthumously published *Dialogues Concerning Natural Religion* (1779). Kant's *Religion within the Bounds of Mere Reason* (1793), one of the most influential texts in philosophy of religion, is an attempt to reduce religion to its most basic rational foundations.

In modernity, philosophy came to be associated less and less with communal practices of reading and conversational thinking. Neither was it associated with schools and traditions of thought; this is part of modernity's suspicion of tradition as a source of intellectual authority. One way of describing this shift in philosophical priorities suggests that certain strands of philosophy became increasingly abstracted from traditions and histories of thought, and evermore focused on the establishment of a single category of ahistorical reason that is accessible to all.[8] Philosophy was apparently seeking to establish its own rational foundations devoid of any reference to theology or transcendence. It is during this period that philosophy comes not only to stare into the face of theology to lend its rationalist credentials or pronounce the life of faith to be lacking reason. It also comes to stare into a mirror. One of philosophy's concerns is itself: given the increasingly separate natural sciences, the new social and human sciences, and a theological discourse which seemed to be concerned with an evermore autonomous stock of knowledge called 'revelation' which lies beyond reason, philosophy was left once again with two pressing questions: what is philosophy, and how is it undertaken?

In the late nineteenth and twentieth centuries, two very different answers to those questions emerged. One answer regarded philosophy as a set of canonical questions or issues that are to be pursued by making language as simple and transparent as possible. At its most straightforward and basic, the language to be deployed was that of symbolic logic, although so-called 'ordinary language philosophy' emerged in the later twentieth century to revive the use of everyday language in philosophical enquiry. This approach to philosophy was not concerned with history or tradition, but with a set of increasingly abstract and often narrow metaphysical problems requiring logical resolution. This school, which is nevertheless notoriously difficult to define with any precision, continues to dominate philosophy in the Anglophone world and has become known as 'analytic philosophy'. It is associated particularly with figures such as Ludwig Wittgenstein (1889–1951), Bertrand Russell (1872–1970), Gottlob Frege (1848–1925) and G.E. Moore (1873–1958).

A range of alternative answers to the question of the nature of philosophy emerged from the tradition of European philosophy that came after Immanuel Kant (1724–1804). It is associated with figures such as Søren Kierkegaard (1813–55), his nemesis G.F. Hegel (1770–1831), the German poet and philosopher Friedrich Nietzsche (1844–1900), the phenomenological school of philosophy founded by Edmund Husserl (1859–1938) and influenced by Martin Heidegger (1889–1976), so-called post-structuralist philosophers such as Jacques Derrida (1930–2004), and those focused on hermeneutics (the science of interpretation) such as Hans-Georg Gadamer (1900–2002). Originally, the term 'continental philosophy' simply defined everything that was not regarded as analytic philosophy. In the broadest terms, 'continental philosophy' is concerned with the history and cultural context of philosophy and human enquiry. It avoids any simple empirical approach to philosophical enquiry and scrutinizes the way in which we experience and interpret reality, regarding this not as a fixed and stable given, but as malleable and context-driven. Unlike analytic philosophy, continental philosophy tends to be much more sceptical concerning the power of modern science adequately to grasp the full reality of the world. On some accounts, a distinction can be drawn between analytic and continental philosophy with reference to the concept of 'reason'. Analytic philosophy has been seen as committed to a view of reason that is often associated with the Enlightenment: reason is ahistorical, objective, and accessible to all. By contrast, continental philosophy has apparently regarded reason as contextual and driven by traditions and practices of thought. It does not provide an independent ground by which to judge other discourses in purely dispassionate fashion.

Much that passes for 'philosophy of religion' in religion departments in the UK and America belongs more to the analytic school of philosophy; it structures its discourse around abstract metaphysical problems (proofs of God's existence, the evidential force of religious experience, the problem of evil) rather than figures and traditions of thought in their context. However, an increasing number of philosophers regard the distinction between continental and analytic philosophy to be unhelpful and increasingly meaningless. Nevertheless, both approaches have something to teach us about 'reading philosophy'. The analytic approach is often commended for its clarity and succinctness of expression. Meanwhile, the continental tradition pays more attention to the historical circumstances in which philosophy and theology are undertaken. Perhaps most importantly, it sometimes adopts a method that has been labelled 'genealogy' and is particularly associated with Nietzsche and the French philosopher Michel Foucault (1926–84). Put simply, this approach claims that, like people and their families, concepts such as 'God', 'society' or 'being' *have histories* or 'genealogies'. In other words, concepts do not have a uniform meaning throughout our intellectual tradition. They arise in different contexts and take on subtly different meanings. Those changing contexts and meanings can be traced 'genealogically'. For theologians, this is crucial because the concepts we employ – God, evil, revelation, creation, love, reason – are used in very different ways throughout the tradition. To read and write theology responsibly, we have to be acutely aware of the ever-changing meanings and contexts of the concepts we use.

So when reading philosophy (particularly modern and late modern philosophy) it may help to be aware that philosophers will have a range of views concerning the nature, scope, and aims of philosophy. It is therefore particularly important to keep some key questions to the fore when reading such philosophy: Why was this text written? In what context was it written, and for whom? What does it assume about the nature and task of philosophy? Is there an implicit theological perspective underlying the text?

Reading philosophy today

In the nineteenth century, the German philosopher Friedrich Nietzsche announced the death of God. In the early twentieth century, a philosophical school named 'Logical Positivism' announced the end of theology and metaphysics because their subject matters – God, for example – were not empirically verifiable and were therefore meaningless. Despite these attempts by modern philosophy to inoculate itself against theology, even the most cursory glance at the practice of philosophy in recent decades reveals that the disciplines of theology and philosophy continue to be ineluctably intertwined.[9] Reading philosophy is an undertaking proper to any theologian, for in philosophical enquiry we find the 'stretching' of the human soul towards ultimate questions of transcendence which belong also within the ambit of theology. In this chapter, we have seen *how* the practice of reading philosophy has changed as the discipline of philosophy has developed. We have referred to some very different understandings of *what* constitutes philosophy. We have also examined *why* theologians have read philosophy. Perhaps the most important lesson to be learned from the reading of philosophy as it was undertaken by the earliest Christian theologians is that philosophy is a way of life focused on conversation. Here, the reading of philosophy blends with theology because, as humans engage together in a philosophical conversation concerning truth, meaning and purpose, the claim emerges from Christian theology that God has entered that conversation decisively and corporeally in the incarnation of the *Logos*. At the point of God's address in Christ, philosophy finds itself addressed. God speaks *into* human philosophy and history. In order to read that conversation rightly, we might ask a properly Platonic and Aristotelian question: What kind of habits and forms of life are required for theologians who seek to become good and able readers of philosophy in all its complex historical guises? Certainly patience to enter into the text, to inhabit the world of the philosopher who authored the text through attentiveness to context and history. Certainly humility to allow the text to speak for itself and scrutinize the reader. Also, love. Ancient philosophy spoke fulsomely of *eros*; it is a virtue one associates rather less readily with modern philosophy. The 'lover of wisdom' was Socrates' defining characteristic. Such love began not with the proud parading of a stock of knowledge or the clever techniques associated with the Sophists, but with what became known as a 'learned ignorance'. As a philosopher, Socrates was first aware that, while others thought they were knowledgeable but in fact were not, he was aware of his own ignorance and was driven by that lack and the associated desire for understanding. Yet Socrates also understood that he was not an active enquirer beginning from scratch within a passive universe; he had been the subject of an address. Through the visible reality we inhabit, he had been spoken to by beauty, truth, and goodness.[10] The good reader of philosophy knows her own lack of knowledge, receives an address, and enters an ancient and complex philosophical conversation that eventually has to deal with the outlandish theological claim that God himself has addressed creation in his own incarnate *Logos*.

Notes

1 P. Hadot, *Philosophy as a Way of Life: Spiritual Exercises from Socrates to Foucault*, trans. M. Chase, Oxford: Blackwell, 1995, p. 62. See also P. Hadot, *What is Ancient Philosophy?*, trans. M. Chase, Cambridge, MA: Harvard University Press, 2002.

2 For an excellent account of the practical ways in which texts were read in the ancient and mediaeval worlds, see P.M. Candler Jr., *Theology, Rhetoric and Manuduction, or Reading Scripture Together on the Path to God*, Grand Rapids, MI / London: Wm. B. Eerdmans Publishing Company/ SCM Press, 2007, especially pp. 1–20.

3 See D.W. Frese and K.O. O'Keefe (eds) *The Book and the Body*, Notre Dame, IN: University of Notre Dame Press, 1997, cited in Candler, *Theology, Rhetoric, Manuduction*, p. 6.

4 For a close and attentive reading of Aristotle, *Metaphysics* Λ, see H.S. Lang, 'The Structure and Subject of *Metaphysics* Λ' in *Phronesis* 38.3, 1993, pp. 257–80.

5 Tertullian, *De Praescriptione Haereticorum* (On Prescription Against Heretics), trans. P. Holmes, in A. Roberts and J. Donaldson (eds) *Ante-Nicene Fathers*, vol. 3, Peabody, MA: Hendrickson Publishers, 1995, ch. 7, quotation appearing on p. 246.

6 Acts 16:9 tells of Paul's calling in a dream to 'cross over' to the Greek province of Macedonia from the city of Troas in Asia Minor (modern day Turkey). This 'crossing over' is taken as a metaphor for the journey of revealed faith into Europe and the encounter with Greek philosophical learning. See Pope Benedict XVI, 'Faith, Reason and the University – Memories and Reflections', a lecture delivered at the University of Regensburg, 12 September 2006: 'The encounter between the Biblical message and Greek thought did not happen by chance. The vision of Saint Paul, who saw the roads to Asia barred and in a dream saw a Macedonian man plead with him: "Come over to Macedonia and help us!" (cf. Acts 16:6–10) – this vision can be interpreted as a "distillation" of the intrinsic necessity of a rapprochement between Biblical faith and Greek inquiry.'

7 See S. Oliver, 'The Parallel Journey of Faith and Reason: another look via Aquinas's *De Veritate*' in S. Oliver, K. Kilby, and T. O'Loughlin (eds) *Faithful Reading: New Essays in Theology in Honour of Fergus Kerr*, London: Continuum, 2012, pp. 113–30.

8 A. MacIntyre, *After Virtue: A Study in Moral Theory*, 3rd edn, Notre Dame, IN: University of Notre Dame Press, 2007, and *Whose Justice? Which Rationality?*, London: Duckworth, 1996.

9 To take just one small example, we might note the intense interest in St Paul amongst contemporary continental philosophers. See J.D. Caputo and L.M. Alcoff (eds) *St Paul among the Philosophers*, Bloomington and Indianapolis: Indiana University Press, 2009.

10 See Plato's dialogue *Apology* in which Socrates discovers that he is the wisest person because he is aware of his own ignorance. See also S. Oliver, 'Wisdom and Belief in Theology and Philosophy', in M. McGhee and J. Cornwell (eds) *Philosophers and God: At the Frontiers of Faith and Reason*, London: Continuum, 2009, pp. 231–46.

7
PUBLIC REASON

C.C. Pecknold

It is often assumed that theology has no place in the public sphere. All reasons are permitted in a liberal democracy, but 'religious reasons' are not among those that can gain widely shared assent, and so these are ruled out of court. Theological reasons are deemed 'private', partial, and thus they do not concern the public, the political, the universal, or the common good. On one level, this is an entirely theoretical exclusion, since 'religious reasons' most certainly animate many major public debates about moral goods (e.g. debates about abortion, euthanasia, poverty, marriage, sex, religious freedom, human rights). Yet this exclusionary principle seems to be necessary, we are told by advocates of political liberalism, because ours is a uniquely pluralist situation, and since 'religion' is divisive it cannot serve the common good and peace that the state is charged with securing. Most judges will not allow 'religious reasons' to influence their decisions, and theological reasons are never admitted into the debates of national political cultures without serious prudential reservations. Public arguments might well be difficult to settle through the democratic process, and such arguments may be deeply informed by people knowledgeable about a wide array of temporal matters, but theology should not be one of them. It seems, then, that public reason seeks the help of all kinds of reasons, except for theological reasons. Why?

There are various reasons, not least our mythical assumption that religious reasons are divisive and thus contrary to the common good.[1] There is also the idea that ours is a uniquely pluralist situation that calls for new measures with respect to 'public reason'. Because there were so many competing theological voices in the early modern period, and because we now have the problem of 'religious diversity', including theistic and atheistic claims about the nature of reality, we assume that we have arrived at a historically unique moment in which that which counts as 'public' can no longer count as 'religious' precisely because of our new pluralist arrangement. Such an objection can be defused by returning to older voices, and by showing that our context is not more but less pluralist, and that modern liberal orders have not excluded religious reasons from the public, but have made liberalism itself into a shared religious framework.

In the first part, I will examine Augustine's exemplary philosophical, legal, and theological critiques of the Roman Republic – the *res publica*, 'public thing' or 'public reality', or what we might call 'public affairs'. Rather than present his critique abstractly, I will examine his response to a concrete moral problem – namely that of honour and justice in taking life – which will help us to compare his approach to a similar case in our own time. In the second part I examine the invention of the modern secular idea of 'public reason'. We will see that it involved turning away from the idea that public affairs should be understood in relation to that which is transcendently and objectively true and good, and instead focused on new ideas of collective consent. The third part of the chapter demonstrates how these new ideas about the *res publica* have shaped all discussions of 'theology and public reason' in the twentieth century, especially in debates surrounding the work of the political philosopher John Rawls. I will ask whether contemporary constructions of 'public reason' continue to detach us from claims about what is transcendently and objectively true and good – about reality (*res*). In the final part, I will suggest that modern secular public reason seeks to be comprehensive in precisely the way that theology seeks to be comprehensive. Both theology and secular public reason seek to provide human beings with a way of understanding how the world hangs together. That secular public reason does not recognize any transcendent accounts of reality does not, however, mean that it does not make world-comprehensive claims. Theologians might offer 'public reason' an important check, then, on precisely the transcendence-aversion that liberal orders seem committed to. On the one hand, theology might help public reason to identify and resist forms of totalitarianism that threaten when human beings construct systems of power divorced from our capacity to know the truth – including the totalitarian tendencies of modern secular public reason itself. On the other, theology might exemplify for the world another mode of public reason – one that can admit more reasons in relation to the source of reason itself.

Augustine: Arguing for life in public

A fourth-century African bishop can help us to deflate the claim that our situation is uniquely pluralist. Like Plato and Aristotle, St Augustine was aware that there were many competing accounts of the nature of reality. In *The City of God* Augustine displays his own grasp of the plurality of Roman beliefs. He considers all the major philosophical schools. The Stoics, the Sophists, and the Sceptics all have comprehensive doctrines embodied in their various ways of life (it never occurs to Augustine that these comprehensive doctrines would be simply matters of private opinion).[2] In his analysis of the many competing views he surveys, Augustine offers profound analyses of all the ways in which competing accounts of the good life function as what we would today call 'religions'. While some of Augustine's discussions are theoretical, his opening arguments with Roman readers begin with concrete and practical concerns.

Take the example of his argument with Rome about suicide. Many Romans believed that, in certain circumstances in which a person's honour was at stake, suicide was reasonable and morally justified. Augustine attends to several suicides in Book One, and pays special attention to the suicide of Lucretia.[3] This is particularly important since Lucretia's suicide, as every Roman reader knew, was the instigation for the Republican uprising that finally ousted the kings and founded the Roman

Republic. Lucretia's suicide was not seen by Roman readers as an 'intrinsically evil act', but as a noble act – an act which defended a person's honour and dignity. It is partly because of the influence of Augustine's public arguments that we no longer think of suicide as noble. His argument, however, is not simply theological, but he weaves a complex cord of publicly accessible reasoning that is philosophical, moral, and theological.

Augustine's philosophical argument is interspersed throughout his analysis of suicide in Book One. He tells us that his case is constrained between questions of virtue, or 'the order of right living' on the one hand, and 'reasoned argument' on the other.[4] So he often goes back and forth, between virtue and intellect, between life and thought, between goodness and truth, between moral, philosophical and theological argumentation. His philosophical argument is essentially that suicide is irrational. Drawing partly upon Stoic reasoning, Augustine argues that suicide is an act that is ruled by the emotions – by either a sense of shame or dishonour – and readily sees that 'any man of compassion would be ready to excuse the emotions which lead them to do this'.[5] But that's just the problem: suicide is a flight from rationality itself. It allows the emotions to rule tyrannically over the body rather than to find the proper harmony for the well-ordered life conformed to truth. He gives the example of Judas.

> We rightly abominate the act of Judas, and the judgment of truth is that when he hanged himself he did not atone for the guilt of his detestable betrayal but rather increased it, since he despaired of God's mercy and in a fit of self-destructive remorse left himself no chance of a saving repentance.[6]

One can see here how the philosophical argument arises out of reflection on a biblical narrative, but it does not begin or end there. 'How much less right has anyone to indulge in self-slaughter when he can find in himself no fault to justify such a punishment!'[7] It is irrational especially because suicide, self-destruction, as a response to unspeakable violations, does not decrease but exponentially increases the injustice. Indeed, the punishment owing to the violator is irrationally inflicted on the violated.

In the main, Augustine's moral argument follows this theme that suicide does not atone for any evil act, but only increases injustice. But one of the most interesting aspects of his moral argument is the inclusion of a legal argument, drawn from Roman law (but implying an appeal to natural law). 'I appeal to Roman laws and Roman judges. To execute a criminal without trial was, according to you, a punishable offence.'[8] Augustine interestingly argues that Lucretia's suicide (and by extension every suicide) is, in fact, illegal because under Roman law no capital punishment can be imposed in the Republic without a just trial. The 'outraged Lucretia' acted illegally as judge on behalf of 'highly extolled Lucretia'.[9] The illegality of the act reinforces the argument that an honour suicide contravenes a moral law, as well as a law of reason.

Importantly, his theological argument comes by way of contrast with that which is illegal, immoral, and irrational: 'such has not been the behaviour of Christian women'.[10] What is interesting is that he begins his theological argument by pointing to the forms of life that Christians are actually living in the face of the same kinds of tragic violence and suffering. It is important that he first identifies a people who live a publicly identifiable form of life before turning to the theological reasons they have for living this way. These women follow the God of Abraham, Isaac, and Jacob. That God simply does not permit suicide, because that God is the source of what is reasonable and good. The God of Israel commands his people not to kill because murder does not conform to God's goodness communicated to us in his creation. Augustine interprets the sixth commandment in light of the greatest commandment of Christ, to love the Lord your God with all your heart, soul and mind, and to love your neighbour as yourself.[11] Reading the Old and New Testaments together, Augustine reasons that if we are not to kill our neighbours then surely we are not to kill ourselves. This juxtaposition of God's law with the preceding reflections on Roman law is highly suggestive of a correlation between divine and human law, but more than this, it suggests that attentiveness to God's law will not contradict Roman law, but will make it more coherent, more just. Moreover, Augustine suggests that each strand of argument is stronger because each coheres with the other. If history is any indication, Augustine's arguments, whether immediately effective or not, con-tributed to a shift that dramatically reversed how society viewed the moral good of suicide.

Can you imagine how surprised Augustine would be if he were transported to our own time, and then told that our 'secular age' was now too pluralistic to hear his theological arguments? What does that tell us about the kind of pluralism we embrace as late moderns? It should tell us that the kind of pluralism we embrace is actually an 'exclusionary' pluralism – which is to say that we are not nearly as pluralist as we think we are. Or we are at least not as pluralist as Augustine's Roman readers. It certainly never occurred to Augustine that his public arguments concerning suicide should exclude theological reasons – even if he fully expected theological disagreements to arise in public discourse, and even if he thought these needed to be publicly addressed just as much as philosophical, moral, and legal disagreements.

So far we have only spoken in the most general way about the place of theology in Augustine's public reasoning. But by Book Ten of *The City of God*, Augustine brings his Roman readers to precisely the theological heart of his very public argument. He opens with a philosophical truism: 'that all men desire happiness is a truism for all who are in any degree able to use their reason' (X. 1). Augustine has already made his argument, from Platonic sources ('the philosophers with whom we should debate'), for the existence of God. And he reminds his readers that no one can attain this happiness 'unless he has adhered, with the purity of chaste love, to that unique and supreme Good, which is the changeless God' (X.1). The problem with the Roman people is that, out of their desire to be attached to the object of their hap-piness, they give the wrong kind of worship (an argument which occupies him through much of Books Eight to Ten).

Throughout *The City of God*, Augustine argues with Roman readers about the nature of the Republic, drawing on Cicero's definition of a republic as founded in the idea of justice as 'to each his due' (*suum cuique*). But how do we know what is due to people? How do we know the proper order of things? What is just is that which is properly ordered; that which is honourable is that which is just. Augustine argues that proper order, and thus the justice which constitutes a republic, can only be achieved by that community of persons who render what is due to God, since all things, after all, owe their very existence to the Creator. Here he asks about 'the kind of worship which we owe' to God. He assesses the words for worship that he finds most accessible to his Roman readers, namely *latreia* and *religio*. But as he notes, 'we have no right to affirm with confidence that "religion" is confined to the worship of God ... [since it also] refers to an attitude of respect in relations between a man and his neighbour.'[12] That is to say that *religio* is that which attaches us to one another justly, and does so by attaching us through our worship of the one true God. The honour paid by Lucretia to her gods was a distorted attempt to make her own life a sacrifice to cleanse herself from a grave injustice. But Augustine insists that we cannot offer such a sacrifice for ourselves, and that the true God does not want these kinds of sacrifices.

Many of the Roman people were claiming, in the wake of the tragic sack of Rome, that Christianity was harmful to the Republic. Romans should exclude Christianity, and return to the gods of the Republic. In a sense, Augustine knows that many of his readers are hostile to Christianity. But that does not lead him to soften his theological argument, but encourages him to treat it more forcefully in public. Addressing the sacrifice which is at the heart of Rome's own civil religion, he is able to contrast the inadequacy of their own implicit theology with

> the sacrifice of Christians, who are 'many, making up one body in Christ'. This is the sacrifice which the Church continually celebrates in the sacrament of the altar, a sacrament well-known to the faithful where it is shown to the Church that she herself is offered in the offering which she presents to God.[13]

Thus Augustine is able to make a public argument for the Eucharist as the one true sacrifice that renders true justice, in which we can participate. Lucretia's sacrifice, however, renders no justice, indeed, increases the injustice – and this is the same for Rome's desire to return to their civil religion.

This line of argumentation reaches a climax in Book Nineteen of *The City of God* where Augustine concludes that, on Cicero's own definition, Rome cannot be a republic without true justice – Rome is thus not a true republic until it renders justice to God, which it can only do through Christ, who is the one true sacrifice, reconciling us to God, and thus conforming us to the true, the good, and the beautiful. The contrast is stark – Lucretia's suicide, or the Eucharist.[14] It is certainly not an argument that he expects all Romans will accept. He knows that many Romans will have different ideas about what is good and true; and they will seek to order their communities differently, in the light of those ideas. From his theological vantage point, however, these differing forms of community can be arranged into a hierarchy according to their common objects of love. The higher their objects of love, the higher the kind of republic they are. This allows for diverse political arrangements, but does not back off from the strongest claim, namely that the Church is the highest kind of 'public thing' because it is ordered to the love of the triune God – and there is no higher object of love than Love Itself, than Truth Itself, than Being Itself. This is a claim that Augustine makes in public, deploying a combination of philosophical, moral, and theological arguments. He uses arguments built on reasons he takes to be accessible to all people, arguments based on the specific customs of the people he's talking to, and arguments based on the revelation to which he holds fast as a Christian.

Augustine's work inspired a hierarchical view of societies that manifests itself in medieval thinking about the ordering of public goods – and the polities that would enable virtue to flourish and would inhibit vice. In the next section we will contrast the medieval Catholic imagination of Thomas Aquinas with that of the late medieval William of Ockham, and the early modern Protestant imagination of Martin Luther, for an analysis of how we have come to see 'public reason' in light of inner–outer, private–public distinctions which contribute to a new understanding of the relationship between theology and public reason which would have been foreign to Augustine.

Inventing 'public reason'

The prophet Isaiah writes, 'Come, let us reason together' (Isa. 1:8). And Thomas Aquinas observes that it is the light of reason, evidenced especially by our socio-linguistic capacity, which distinguishes us from all other animals. We are dependent rational animals, linguistic, social, and political. This is so, Thomas says, because no one's individual reason is sufficient 'to provide for life unassisted'. We need one another to speak and reason together. Aquinas would say that 'public reason' is essential to our nature as social and political persons.

> It is not possible for one man to arrive at a knowledge of all these things by his own individual reason. It is therefore necessary for man to live in a multitude so that each one may assist his fellows, and different men may be occupied in seeking, by their reason, to make different discoveries … one in this and another in that.[15]

Yet, wherever there is a multitude, there must be an agency to care for the common good, lest each person look after his or her own interests alone.

St Thomas says in *De regno* that while kingship is the most beneficial form of government, democracy is the least harmful; and in his *Summa* he prefers some sort of mixed constitution.[16] Nevertheless, when Aquinas is giving advice to the king of Cyprus, his counsel is on kingship. Like Augustine, what Aquinas is keen to convey to the king of Cyprus is that kings are finally accountable to God. And also like Augustine, Thomas tries to dissuade the ruler from the love of human glory, and to raise his vision to the glory of God, who alone can bring true power, virtue, and happiness. God is the true end of our desire to be happy, and thus it is communion with God that can be the only 'fitting reward for a king'.[17] Put differently, Thomas tells the king of Cyprus that the highest honour he can seek is to be made a saint ('a citizen with the Saints and a kinsman of God').[18] What is most striking about St Thomas' account is that he commends the king not only to wisdom and virtue, but also commends the king to holiness as a 'more excellent way', for only God's way is befitting the dignity of kingship.

Thomas certainly respects the kind of relative autonomy that a king enjoys as an agent of the commonweal whose job it is virtuously to direct all things to 'those ends attainable by human power'. But he also recognizes that this is only an intermediate end, and thus is 'subject to him to whom pertain the care of the ultimate end, and [must] be directed by his rule'.[19] And here we can see tucked into St Thomas' letter to the king of Cyprus the crux of the medieval theo-political arrangement: 'kings must be subject to priests ... all the kings of the *Populus Christianus* are to be subject [to the successor of St Peter, the Vicar of Christ, the Roman Pontiff] as to our Lord Jesus Christ Himself.'[20] In this way, Aquinas develops the hierarchical vision of medieval society that Augustine advocated nearly nine hundred years before.

The entire medieval arrangement follows Augustine quite closely, even in these reflections on the place of papal sovereignty. Popes are sovereign over all kings only with respect to all ends attainable by divine power alone. Neither Augustine nor Thomas, of course, insist that kings can be forced to render justice to God, only that the failure to do so would not be fitting. Their hierarchical vision recommends a non-coercive theocracy – but once a king is Christian (as all kings were in medieval Europe, at least from the time of Charlemagne onwards), the arrangements between human and divine power within an ecclesial culture become more complex, for such kings now recognize a power which transcends their own. The investiture controversies are an indication of this new complexity.[21] Kings sought to take control over the Church, especially through the appointment (investiture) of bishops; and bishops considered kings lower in rank than deacons. Such conflicts established a pattern of conflict between temporal and spiritual power that was internal rather than external to the Church. Despite these medieval conflicts about the relationship between temporal and spiritual power, both pope and king shared the view that an agency was required to care for common goods, and that not only virtue but also holiness was integral to this agency.

Here we might speculate that medieval public reason actually required a much more complex account of what sort of reasons – natural or revealed – were required in light of which ends are under consideration. If a judgement is required that touches the power and ends proper to the Church, then it was simply taken for granted that theological reasons would be given priority. Obviously, the negotiation was not always easy, and it did not mean that conflicts would not arise in learning to navigate between different kinds of judgements that serve a common good. This was easier for a more hierarchical vision of the society as a 'community of communities', in which small communities were ordered to different natural ends, but none of these ends were thought to be truly good or rational if they excluded or stood in contradiction to the supernatural end of the beatific vision, the end of the happiness that was commonly desired by all. Such a complex view of medieval public reason was, however, dependent upon a philosophically realist, participationist, and theo-centric view of nature. Aquinas can commend wisdom and virtue to the king of Cyprus, and there is an agreement about what those words mean. Similarly, he can even commend him to the more excellent way of holiness, and that is also a reasonable counsel. But such counsel does not last into the late medieval period.

A wedge might be seen to begin with the thought of William of Ockham. Like Aquinas, Ockham was also interested in giving advice to kings about the use of their power to restrain wickedness and to do the good. But where Thomas added a recommendation of holiness to wisdom and virtue, William had no interest in commending holiness to the king. He begins to make a distinction between the 'internal' and 'external' realms. In the internal realm, we find the intention to love God given to us by God; that is the realm of holiness and salvation. For St Thomas, holiness involved both the interior act of the will, and the exterior acts of the will. But for Ockham, external acts (habits of action, life in public in the broadest sense) are not intrinsically connected to internal acts. Holiness, for Ockham, belongs solely to the interior realm – whereas kings deal with that which is extrinsic and temporal, and thus they rule over an external realm. This view is most readily apparent in Ockham's heretical view of papal power, which he bifurcates into a spiritual power (which the pope rarely exercises) and his temporal human power (how popes normally exercise their power). To the extent that the pope has external power – power to order public life – it is a power that cannot really be spiritual. The public realm is not the proper realm of holiness. This allows him to recommend the limitation of papal power precisely because he regards papal power to be just as corruptible as kingly power, and perhaps more so – because the externalizing of spiritual power can mask internal corruption. Ockham's intrinsic/extrinsic distinctions give him a very pessimistic view of papal power; he believes that the authentic Christian will want to divest themselves of external power (and material possession). He therefore wants to check papal power seriously – in part by strengthening conciliar power, as well as by a new attentiveness to the Catholic faithful as an organic source of ecclesial power. But in checking these ecclesial powers in this way, Ockham also changes the nature of kingship. On the one hand he extends greater powers to kings than previous theologians were happy to do. But on the other hand, Ockham could no longer commend a king to a more excellent way. He sets up a wall between the internal and external realms that makes 'reason exchange' between the papal and the political almost impossible.

With William of Ockham, then, we begin to see the emergence of a public realm in which claims about holiness and the love of God aren't native – in which theology strictly speaking doesn't belong. Instead, the kinds of arguments and reasons that belong in public are more pragmatic, even utilitarian: the power and virtue of the ruler are not seen in terms of how they are ordered to transcendent ends, but solely in terms of what is presently necessary and useful to secure the state.[22]

It is a long walk from Ockham to Martin Luther, let alone to liberal democratic polities, but it is most likely that Luther's critique of the papal power would have looked different if it were not for William of Ockham's intrinsic–extrinsic distinction in his analysis of the will. Not surprisingly, the inner–outer distinction is crucial for Luther too. Luther will also teach that spiritual power attends to that which is interior, and the temporal power attends to that which is exterior. That arrangement was giving way to a more dualistic way of thinking. Thus Luther's *Landskirke* (or notion of a state church) is not so much the organic unity of the medieval arrangement as it is a profoundly bifurcated unity.

John Neville Figgis once wrote that 'it was the function of Luther … to transfer to the State most of the prerogatives that had belonged in the Middle Ages to the Church'.[23] That is a harsh judgement, and there is much that complicates that picture, yet the overwhelming impression is that we can see a trajectory forming from Ockham to Luther. Theology could increasingly be thought of as a private, internal matter, and 'public reason' was something else entirely.

William Cavanaugh has argued that this has, in fact, been the central project of the modern nation-state from the beginning: to construct religion as something private and interior, and to exclude any definition of religion as inherently public, as authoritative with regard to how we order our common life.[24] What could the practice of Christian theology look like in the wake of such novel constructions? Do such trends doom theology to the private? Without breaking back into medieval arrangements – which is impossible – how can theology be practised in a bifurcated world that has put up walls against its hearing?

Theology and public reason

The twentieth-century political philosopher John Rawls is famous for stating that 'religious reasons' should normally be excluded from the public sphere. This has been necessary, according to Rawls, ever since the Reformation and the so-called 'wars of religion' set Europe on fire. A new arrangement – liberalism – provided a new order for the ages (*novus ordo saeculorum*).[25] The new social contracts that emerged – first with Thomas Hobbes and John Locke, then with Jean-Jacques Rousseau and the French, and also the American revolutionaries – set out to provide the world with a new kind of power that would save us from our intractable metaphysical and theological differences.[26] A memory of that higher good – a common good that transcended politics – remained in a diminished form, often through the concept of civil society, and also civil religion. Yet since God had been excluded from the public square, what could provide us with that justly ordered society that Cicero had once commended?

What is needed, Rawls reasoned, is an account of justice that everyone can agree with, and an 'overlapping consensus' about what counts as 'public reason'. To arrive at a truly fair, impartial account of justice in a pluralistic world, Rawls would have us all put on a hypothetical 'veil of ignorance' – asking what kind of principles of justice we would affirm if we knew nothing of our own particular status, social position, range of resources, or religious tradition. Such a veil would enable each of us to inhabit an 'original position' from which we can freely arrive at a concept of justice as fairness without theology (or any 'comprehensive doctrine') getting in the way. In this way, every person would commit themselves to the equality of rights, liberties, and opportunities for all people. It is from such representative persons that a proper account of the principles of justice will arise, and it is from such representative persons that we will know what counts as 'reasonable'.[27]

Rawls does not say that those who do not accept this procedure for arriving at public justice are irrational, only that their reasons are not public. This is perfectly acceptable according to Rawls because 'not all reasons are public reasons, as there are the nonpublic reasons of churches and universities and of many other associations in civil society'.[28] Clearly, a great deal depends on what is meant by 'public'. Rawls argues that public reason is 'public' in three ways: as the reason of the public, as serving the good of public justice, and as a reflection of a democratic society's conception of political justice.[29] But notice the tautological definition of public reason provided here: what counts as public reason is whatever serves the wishes of the public, and the public is the community governed by public reason. In fact, Rawls reveals the tendency of liberal democratic thought to exclude the whole idea of transcendent checks on power, reason, truth, justice, the good, and especially on what counts as public; it works by excluding religion from public life (since it is interior, nonpublic). However, confining religious beliefs to the nonpublic is really only possible with the help of state coercion and intellectual persuasion.[30] The coerciveness of liberalism is not always in plain sight, but it often comes into view whenever Rawls mentions the relation of citizens to their laws. Rawls takes public reason to be that reason exercised by 'equal citizens who, as a collective body, exercise final political and coercive power over one another in enacting laws and in amending their constitution'.[31] The representatives who exercise that 'final political and coercive power' decide what counts as public; and above all, the judicial branch decides what counts as public reason.

In some respects, Rawls is treating an ancient problem of how to relate the One and the Many in a modern way. 'Public reason', for Rawls, must be one, whereas nonpublic reasons are many. Nonpublic reasons (theology) belong to the 'background culture' that serves, like a blank sheet of paper, as contrast for the writing of a 'public political culture'.[32] As we have noticed above, Rawls is very careful not to call these nonpublic reasons 'private', since he knows very well that these nonpublic reasons are undeniably present in the social imagination. But it is difficult to imagine how 'nonpublic' does not mean private for Rawls, when it is only the 'public political culture' (and its legitimate exercise of coercive force) that determines the common good.

Many have noted that Rawls has developed his view to be more inclusive of 'religious reasons', precisely in response to criticisms that he was weak on 'religion'. But Rawls has not developed as much as he claims. As he has responded to religious critics, he has merely become more skilled at concealing the ways in which he thinks liberalism excludes 'the tradition of the Church' from political public reason. It is his deeply cherished belief that the great accomplishment of secularization has been the separation of Church and state, which he largely interprets as the triumph of the public over the nonpublic.

Earlier in this chapter I suggested that our contemporary situation is not nearly as 'pluralist' as it describes itself to be. As my treatment of Rawls should indicate, 'public reason' in modern liberal democracies is positively exclusionary.[33] It is an irony of history that John Locke, the founder of the classical liberal tradition, excluded the 'non-religious' (atheists) from the public square, while contemporary liberals seek to exclude the religious. Of course, the other person that Locke thought needed to be excluded was the Catholic.

Why does the father of liberalism exclude Catholics and atheists? There is one very good reason to exclude them: Locke believes that their inclusion poses a threat. The Catholic poses a threat because they follow the transcendent dictates of a 'foreign potentate' whose commands trump those of the social contract, and the atheist poses a threat because, Locke thinks, they have no basis for the moral convictions necessary to make for good citizens. Rather, what Locke wants, as much as Rawls, is to shape a particular kind of citizen for a particular kind of egalitarian and homogenous society (a kind of unity that might appear as functionally 'religious').

Any allegiances that threaten liberal democratic orders must be excluded, through force if necessary, but that force will always be justified by framing the narratives of legitimate discourse and belief. 'Democratic values', then, function like the creed of a newly formed church, a mystical body that stands as the one true religion of liberalism. This is largely why we are willing to die for 'democratic values', or more worryingly, why we are willing to kill for them.[34] Rawls embraces political liberalism, more or less, as the one true religion – and what counts as public reason is only that which is ordered to this *religio*.

Democratic thinkers like Rawls all seek to protect liberal democratic discourse from one ultimate threat. The monumental fear that constitutes the identity of modern liberal democracies is the spectre of absolutism or totalitarianism, which in Rawlsian terms appears as any comprehensive doctrine. Like Locke, most proponents of liberal democratic orders fear especially allegiances which materially transcend democracy itself. Locke excluded Catholics, Rawls excludes 'religious reasons', but the fear is the same. As Patrick Deneen writes, in liberal democratic orders 'each seeks to protect the sphere of democratic politics from ultimate disruption … each fears, above all, the "absolutist" who would, in turn, threaten an "absolute" commitment to democratic values.'[35]

What I think this reveals is that 'public reason' entails a kind of absolute devotion to democracy as an inviolable project – what Augustine called *religio*. Just as Augustine could identify a kind of idolatrous worship at the heart of Roman political culture, so can we begin to see something like 'political worship' at the heart of liberal democratic ideas about progress, self-transformation, even self-deification through human association. As Deneen convincingly argues, this shows us that liberal democracy is 'a secular faith aimed at human transformation into democratized divinity itself'.[36]

There have been interesting philosophical and theological attempts to move beyond the 'public reason' of Rawlsian-style liberalism in light of such criticisms. The Princeton philosopher of religion Jeffrey Stout, for example, has issued a pragmatic argument for getting beyond the religious exclusivism of liberal democratic discourse. In his influential book, *Democracy and Tradition*, Stout critiques the liberalism of philosophers like John Rawls and Richard Rorty, both of whom exclude religious reasons from political argument. Rorty excludes religion because he thinks it is a 'conversation stopper' and Rawls excludes religion because, as we have seen, it is 'nonpublic' and thus merely part of the background culture against which 'public reason' operates. Stout argues that the way Rawls restricts the role religious reasons can play in public is actually undemocratic, and is an 'extremely counterintuitive' move which 'seems so contrary to the spirit of free expression that breathes life into democratic culture'.[37] Stout rejects the Rawlsian search for 'a common justificatory basis of principles' which all 'reasonable citizens' can accept. What he proposes instead is reframing the question about religion's role in the terms of an 'expressive freedom' (the freedom to express any and every cultural–linguistic particularity in political argument) which can transform political arrangements through conversation, through a democratic exchange of reasoning across difference towards an 'ever evolving end'. However, the question remains: who counts as a reasonable citizen? For Stout, there is a simple democratic answer to this: anyone who 'participates responsibly in [this] process of discursive reasoning'.[38] In this light, then, it would be possible to imagine Christian theology as a practice of public reason. As long as the theologian were ready to participate responsibly in the kind of reasoning processes Stout describes, he or she could indeed make theological claims in public, like Augustine arguing about suicide. But doesn't that simply shift the question of what counts as reasonable to what counts as responsible participation in the right kind of reasoning processes? Giving theology 'a place at the table' might be just another version of domesticating theology so that it conforms to the ends of a given democratic polity. What if our understandings of 'responsible participation' and of 'reasoning processes' themselves need challenging, or are oppressive or exclusionary?

The tensions in Stout's account are quite apparent when, for example, he simultaneously claims that democracy does not necessarily exclude theological voices and that it will be 'imprudent in most contexts' to make this reasoning explicit.[39] Stout says that it is practically unwise to use theological presuppositions 'in an argument intended to persuade a religiously diverse population'.[40] But elsewhere he says:

> I would encourage religiously committed citizens [to express] their premises in as much depth and detail as they see fit when trading reasons with the rest of us on issues of concern to the body politic. If they are discouraged from speaking up this way, we will remain ignorant of the real reasons that many of our fellow citizens have for reaching some of the ethical and political conclusions they do.[41]

Perhaps Stout has really done nothing other than to dwell in the paradox that Rawls otherwise thought was resolvable in political liberalism. What Stout reveals, just as much as the more exclusive liberalism of Rawls, is that democracy is intimately bound to the exclusive nature of liberalism, which is in turn bound to the exclusionary origins of the early modern nation-state itself.[42] In this way, even a theorist of liberalism who invites theology into the 'exchange of public reasons' does so in a way which seeks to keep the power carefully balanced in favour of democratic reasoning processes as intrinsically and practically unifying, and the practice of theology as part of a larger whole that it must serve. If we follow Stout, it seems that liberal democratic reasoning is a benevolent king who permits theology to speak within his courts. But what about coercion and conflict?

Arguing for life in public (reprise)

In this final part of this chapter, we have to ask ourselves about what the relationship between theology and public reason actually looks like in the liberal democratic cultures of late modernity. As I write these words, Catholic Christianity and 'public reason' are at loggerheads in America over a controversial new plan that would provide universal health care coverage through all private insurance companies – including coverage of sterilization, contraceptives, and abortifacient drugs which have been determined to be an issue of women's health, and thus fundamental to the public good. Such 'preventive services', however, violate the Catholic Church's teaching on the sanctity of human life, and thus a profound conflict has arisen between competing visions of the Good. It is likely that a kind of ad hoc procedural compromise will be found that temporally 'patches' the real fissure between Catholic and liberal visions of the Good. But regardless of what temporary solutions may or may not be found, many will have avoided what is most fundamental to the conflict. So let us examine it now, comparing the Catholic and liberal views of theology and public reason on this particular issue.

Like Augustine, the Catholic Church believes that all acts should be ordered to their proper end. To place artificial obstacles in the way of the unitive and procreative ends of the sexual act is to flee from the rationality inscribed in our nature. On philosophical grounds, the Church believes that contraception is irrational – contrary to the givens of nature. The Church also believes that the decision not to exempt the Catholic Church from this requirement to provide, through its insurers, this contraception coverage is illegal. This legal argument is the one that has received the most attention because it is the only argument that liberal democracies are readily willing to entertain (*pace* Stout). Having excluded metaphysical, moral, and theological disagreement from the exchange of public reasons, liberal orders insist on procedural solutions based on the constitution – thus making legal arguments the main way in which the Church is allowed to state publicly its comprehensive doctrines and forms of life – having the effect of always making conflict between comprehensive orders legal and procedural, excluding from public discourse the moral, metaphysical, and theological disagreement. In order to 'use the peace of the earthly city' for the sake of the Church, Catholics naturally must appeal to the laws of the land, but it is not easy to do so for one simple reason: the constitution is rooted in a liberal tradition designed to protect individual rather than group rights – individual freedom rather than the freedom of a community to order its life a different way, and so group exemptions are actually fraught with difficulty for this tradition. Communal (or common to a group) theological reasons are not really admissible into the public square. Yet Augustine would have insisted that the problem here is not simply that American culture is being irrational and immoral with respect to contraceptive acts or the lives of the unborn. Augustine would also press the theological problem, which is an idolatrous view of sacrifice for the sake of freedom.

There is a deep disagreement here about the goods pursued by our society. For the Catholic theologian, the claim that all human life is sacred by virtue of it being created by God, and imbued with *imago Dei*, is a theologically comprehensive doctrine which is inclined to view the medical prevention of the *imago Dei* as nothing less than the intention to prevent the sacred from entering the secular. On the other side, for the liberal public reasoner, naming artificial sterilization, contraception, and abortificient drugs as moral goods is a way of securing one of the most important aims of modern democratic life: individual freedom as a freedom from interference. For the liberal, the Catholic 'comprehensive doctrine' obviously needs to be ruled out because it conflicts with this kind of negative freedom. But as Augustine might say, a negative freedom, especially when it is freedom from that which transcends us, and which gives us life, is no freedom at all. Yet political liberalism is built on precisely this negative freedom – freedom from the Christian past, freedom from the Church, freedom that is exclusive even of God.

The anthropology of the 'enlightenment' tradition holds that human beings are naturally free, which means that they are autonomous, independent choosers whose choices are really only limited by the harm they might cause to others. Of course, the most important choice is the choice to enter into this social contract, in which the state acts as an agent that protects individual freedom. To protect and to serve this anthropology, however, requires the state to exercise extraordinary coercive powers, providing procedures for protecting individual rights at the same time as it attempts to regulate the harm that individual activities might cause. There might be plenty of room for a plurality of 'private' visions of the good, but the one intolerable thing is any other comprehensive vision of the good life. In his *Letter Concerning Toleration*, Locke wrote that toleration could not be extended to any faith whose allegiances transcended the nation.[43] Yet Catholic allegiances – all Christian allegiances – can and must transcend the nation.

Christianity is a universal call to participate in the holy presence of Christ's Body – a real presence in the world – and to be made holy through that participation we call Church. It involves a different anthropology, one that claims to be more rooted in the nature of reality as it is given, and also one that is capable of receiving Jesus Christ – capable of an obedience that makes free. Humans are most free, according to the Church, not when they are most autonomous and independent, but when they are received into the Body of Christ. But even before they are received into the most excellent way of Christ, they are 'dependent rational animals' who need the virtues – habitually embodied in community, culture, law and religion – if they are to flourish and order things rightly and justly.[44] In brief, all human beings are called to a greater freedom than the liberal anthropology offers – human beings deserve more than immunity rights, they have a dignity which demands to be ordered to human flourishing, to virtue, to the highest Good, to wisdom. And just as with Thomas Aquinas' kingly friend from Cyprus, in our democratic cultures the human person also has a dignity that commends her to a more excellent way, to holiness, to communion with God. In this way, Catholic Christianity has always been concerned about everyone, whether they believe in Jesus Christ or not. Catholic Christianity entails a comprehensive vision of what it means for human beings, Christian or not, to be virtuous, and to be ordered to the ends of virtue. It is the very public nature of the Catholic Church that makes it odious to the rival comprehensive vision of the Good offered by liberal orders.

Conclusion: Public reason in the courtyard of the Gentiles

The problem that this account leaves us with is severe. Theology can be bound up within itself, or it can accommodate itself to norms external to itself, norms that are finally corrosive of the very truths that theologians want to discuss in public. Yet the problem is not new. The Apostle Paul frequently noted that he suffered, that he was mistreated, but that 'in spite of great opposition' he had courage from God to give reasons for the same hope to which the Apostle Peter bore witness, even to the point of death (1 Thess. 2:2, 1 Pet. 3:15). St Paul also notes that while the reasons that he gives are demanding, he always sought to be gentle, and joyful, and to give reasons 'which abound in love' (1 Thess. 3:12). The practice of Christian theology must recover a strong sense of working from this 'courage from God' to make theological reasoning hearable in bifurcated secular cultures that have built up a wall against God.

1 Eroding obstacles to hearing. Theological argumentation cannot proceed in public without having first listened long enough to public conversations to know exactly where the obstacles to being heard reside. As we have seen, often the obstacles are in the political and legal frameworks, and thus there is a need for theologians to engage in conversations with political philosophers and legal thinkers about the sustainability of an order that excludes conversation about God. Here theologians need constantly to refuse the idea that 'reason', 'argument', 'debate', 'openness', 'pluralism', 'freedom', all belong to secularity rather than religion.

2 Making public reason local and embodied. Part of the problem for theologians is that 'public reason' has increasingly become all-encompassing, comprehensively competitive with the comprehensive claims of theological reasoning. Theoretical conversations about the rules of engagement often neglect the fact that 'public reason' is always embodied locally, and often operates in ways that elude the public philosophy. In universities, in newspapers, in social networks, there is something akin to an exchange of public reason that does not strictly follow the bifurcations of a secularizing cult or culture. It is often the case that engaging deeply in a local conversation can have surprisingly extensive effects.

3 Bring public reason nearer to the question of God. The essential problem for theology is that an increasing number of human beings have, as Charles Taylor notes in A Secular Age[45], found it increasingly difficult to believe in God. Yet they cannot stop talking about God and religion in ways that are recognizably false in the eyes of theologians. We need to find ways of asking clear, simple, and direct questions about God that challenge facile public conceptions, expose wherever possible false theologies disguised as true philosophies, and heighten the quality of debates about true and false religion. This requires:

4 The courtyard of the Gentiles. Ancient Israel practised what it called 'the courtyard of the Gentiles', in which all the nations could draw nearer to the one God, nearer to the holy of holies, especially through conversation with God's people. Christian theologians need to recover such a space, and such a practice: to find new venues for conversing not only inter-religiously, but also with agnostic and atheistic people who do not know God, but would like to talk about an Unknown God.

5 Holy teaching, holy lives. Most of all, theologians who are committed to such an exchange of reasons in the courtyard of the Gentiles need to share the Apostle Paul's sense that while the teaching is demanding – requiring the same complex modes of argumentation that we saw in Augustine – it should also be rooted in a form of life that is gentle, patient, joyful, and abounding in love. In short, the giving of 'reasons for hope' depends on a particular form of life that will often be counter-cultural, yet will give a visible witness to the truth conformed to the Christ the King, marked by wisdom, virtue, and holiness. It is only by arguing like 'a citizen with the Saints and a kinsman of God'[46] that theology will bear witness to the reasons which are most truly common to all.

Notes

1 No one has unmasked the fictions that religion is divisive and that we need a state that can save us better than William Cavanaugh in his path-breaking book *The Myth of Religious Violence: Secular Ideology and the Roots of Modern Conflict*, Oxford: Oxford University Press, 2009.

2 Cf. P. Hadot, *Philosophy as a Way of Life: Spiritual Exercises from Socrates to Foucault*, trans. M. Chase, Oxford: Blackwell, 1995.

3 Augustine, *The City of God*, trans. H. Bettenson, London: Penguin Books, 2003, I.19. Lucretia was an exemplar of Roman virtue, and her life is seen as integral to the foundation myths of the Roman Republic. Livy's *History of Rome* (I.16) recounts the famous story known to all Romans, namely the story of the king's son ingratiating himself to Lucretia one night, and then raping her, thus 'stealing her honor' to serve his own lust to dominate. Lucretia's subsequent suicide – to defend her honor – instigates the Republican revolution that banished monarchial rule from Rome, making Lucretia a kind of hero of the Republic precisely through her noble suicide. Augustine's moral critique of suicide, thus, is never far from his political critique of Rome itself.

4 Augustine, *The City of God* I.16.

5 Augustine, *The City of God* I.17.

6 Ibid.

7 Ibid.

8 Augustine, *The City of God* I.19.

9 Ibid.

10 Ibid.

11 Augustine, *The City of God* I.20.

12 Augustine, *City* X.1.

13 Augustine, *City* X.6.

14 Cf. William Cavanaugh's study of torture in Pinochet's Chile as a kind of 'counter-liturgy' to the Eucharist, in *Torture and Eucharist: Theology, Politics and the Body of Christ*, Oxford: Blackwell, 1998.

15 Thomas Aquinas, *De regno ad regem Cypri*, trans. G.B. Phelan and I.T. Eschmann, Toronto: Pontifical Institute of Medieval Studies, 1949, I.1; http://dhspriory.org/thomas/DeRegno. htm

16 Thomas Aquinas, *Summa Theologiae* I-II, q. 105 art. 1, in *Summa Theologiae 29: The Old Law (1a2ae. 95–105)*, trans. D. Bourke, Cambridge: Cambridge University Press, 2006, pp. 266–274.

17 Thomas Aquinas, *De regno* I.9.

18 Ibid.

19 Thomas Aquinas, *De regno* I.15.

20 Ibid.

21 See M. Miller, *Power and the Holy in the Age of the Investiture Conflict: A Brief History with Documents*, Bedford: St Martin's Press, 2005.

22 S. McGrade, *The Political Thought of William Ockham*, Cambridge: Cambridge University Press, 2002.

23 J.N. Figgis, *Studies of Political Thought from Gerson to Grotius*, Cambridge: Cambridge University Press, 2011, p. 71.

24 See Cavanaugh, *Myth of Religious Violence*.

25 See R. Beiner, *Civil Religion: A Dialogue in the History of Political Philosophy*, Cambridge: Cambridge University Press, 2010.

26 See C.C. Pecknold, *Christianity and Politics: A Brief Guide to the History*, Eugene, OR: Cascade, 2010.

27 See J. Rawls, *A Theory of Justice*, Cambridge, MA: Harvard University Press, 2005.

28 J. Rawls, *Political Liberalism*, expanded edn, New York, NY: Columbia University Press, 2005, p. 213.

29 Ibid.
30 For contrasting accounts, see R. Plant, *Politics, Theology, and History*, Cambridge: Cambridge University Press, 2001, and S. Macedo, *Diversity and Distrust: Civic Education in a Multicultural Democracy*, Cambridge, MA: Harvard University Press, 2003.
31 Rawls, *Political Liberalism*, p. 214.
32 Rawls, *Political Liberalism*, p. 220.
33 A. Marx, *Faith in Nation: Exclusionary Origins of Nationalism*, Oxford: Oxford University Press, 2005, has argued that modern liberal democracies have been exclusionary from the beginning.
34 See W. Cavanaugh, *Migrations of the Holy: God, State and the Political Meaning of the Church*, Grand Rapids, MI: Wm. B. Eerdmans Publishing Company, 2011.
35 Patrick Deneen, *Democratic Faith*, Princeton, NJ: Princeton University Press, 2005, p. 30.
36 Deneen, *Democratic Faith*, p. 83.
37 J. Stout, *Democracy and Tradition*, Princeton, NJ: Princeton University Press, 2004, p. 68.
38 Stout, *Democracy and Tradition*, p. 82.
39 Stout, *Democracy and Tradition*, p. 98.
40 Stout, *Democracy and Tradition*, p. 99.
41 Stout, *Democracy and Tradition*, p. 64.
42 Marx, *Faith in Nation*.
43 J. Locke, *A Letter Concerning Toleration*, Amherst, NY: Prometheus Books, 1990, pp. 47ff.
44 A. MacIntyre, *Dependent Rational Animals: Why Human Beings Need the Virtues*, Chicago, IL: Open Court, 2001.
45 C. Taylor, *A Secular Age*, Cambridge, MA: Harvard University Press, 2007.
46 Thomas Aquinas, *De regno* I.9.

Part II
SCRIPTURE

8
SCRIPTURE

Jim Fodor

Scripture has always been central to the life of the Church; it is one of the defining features of Christian faith. As Frances Young says, 'The Bible is the one thing held in common among all those who claim the name Christian.'[1] This set of holy writings is continuously listened to, read, studied, debated, and commented on, even as it is also treasured, celebrated, processed, and prayed in regular weekly worship. Scripture is the lifeblood or 'soul' of Christian faith.[2] It should therefore come as no surprise that the practice of theology accords Scripture a central place, commensurate with its centrality to the life of faith.

Part of the work that will be taken up in the chapters that follow is (1) to trace some key historical, philosophical, and cultural developments that have shaped contemporary approaches to and understandings of Scripture; (2) to point out how the authoritative status of Scripture crucially shapes the practice of theology; (3) to explore the ways in which Scripture tends to challenge, 'unsettle', and critique established frameworks and patterns of human relating; and (4) to examine the distinction between literal and figurative readings of Scripture and explore several ramifications it has for one of the fundamental rules of reading Scripture; namely, the instruction to follow 'the way the words go'.

Before we can turn to these questions, however, this introductory chapter explores three important preliminary matters: (1) the relation of Jewish and Christian scriptures, (2) the centrality of hearing in Christian engagement with Scripture, and (3) the relationship of Scripture to time.

Jewish and Christian scriptures

The Muslim sacred text, the Qur'an, famously describes both Jews and Christians as 'people of the book' (*Ahl al-Kitab*, Qur'an 3:19). Of course, the book to which the Qur'an makes reference is not necessarily a physical book in the modern sense of the term – a codex[3] – but rather sets of sacred writings, preserved in various forms, and taken by the Jewish and Christian communities respectively to be God's authoritative word. How faithfully these communities actually follow their sacred writings is a matter of ongoing dispute – including within the Qur'an and within these Jewish and Christian sacred writings themselves – but they are certainly 'people of the book' in the sense that they are communities gathered around sacred texts regarded as capable of imparting the wisdom of God to the faithful in each generation.

This is made visible in the central role the sacred texts play in study, prayer, and worship. In Jewish synagogues, for example, pride of place is given to the Ark of the Covenant, which houses the sacred scrolls of Torah. During worship the Torah scrolls are removed, elevated, and processed to be reverently touched or kissed by the faithful, before being returned and set upon the altar, where they are unrolled and read aloud in worship. Similarly, in many Christian churches the elevated Gospel-book is processed, often with incense and a cross, with the congregation rising to stand and hear the sacred text read out loud in worship. And for Jews, Christians, and Muslims alike, the sacred text is not simply read out loud or recited when the community gathers for worship; it is also explained, expounded, and applied to present life in a sermon or homily, often by authorized interpreters.

No sooner have we said this, however, than differences start to emerge. There are, for a start, differences *within* each tradition – differences in the interpretation of what these texts mean, and what their ramifications for life today might be. This is an inherent feature of a religious community gathered around a text: sacred writings are contested writings. That they are contested, however, should not be taken immediately or even primarily as a sign that their authoritative status is in question, or that these texts are simply at the mercy of certain individuals or groups vying for power by claiming the texts for themselves. Rather, the meaning and implications of the scriptures are debated precisely because they are expected to speak to the whole of life in each generation – yielding wisdom in relation to questions and contexts that differ from those faced by earlier generations – and because Scripture itself is not a single, uniform text but comprises a plurality and diversity of texts. Scripture is a library, so to speak: a set of texts that sit next to one another in an internally tensive relation.

Disputes about the meaning of Scripture, therefore, should not always be regarded as signs of breakdown; they are often symptoms of the presence of a healthy, vibrant community, alive to the importance of differences within Scripture, and the need to attend to those differences patiently rather than to collapse them into a premature harmony.[4] Indeed, Scripture's authoritative status is upheld precisely *in* the contesting – and in that sense the careful 'preserving' – of these differences. It attends to the ways the words actually go, rather than the ways we would have them go.

There is a deep tendency in Christian interpretation, however, precisely because Scripture is regarded as God's authoritative Word, for interrogation of Scripture's differences to be motivated by the desire to explain them away or cancel them out – to be impatient with them, and so to be inattentive to Scripture's complexity, for the sake of seeing the whole text coherent and unified.

Such a problematic tendency to explain away or cancel out differences is also visible when we turn from differences *within* each tradition, and focus instead on differences *between* traditions. And the problem with this tendency becomes particularly clear if we focus on the relationship between Jewish and Christian scriptures.

Judaism is the womb in which Christianity was conceived and given birth. This means that for the first Christians their sacred writings were in fact exactly those of the Jews – what Christians later named the 'Old Testament' or the 'Old Covenant'. To be sure, over time Christians also recognized as sacred and authoritative other writings, which they described as the 'New Testament'. The challenge Christians have faced throughout their history, then, of how to deal with a dual canon, also calls for the 'preservation' of differences – not only within its own authoritative Scripture but also between its own canonical set of texts and the canon of Jewish sacred texts from which it issues; and to do so without advocating, consciously or unwittingly, a form of supersessionism. Supersessionism is the conviction that a religious dispensation remains valid until the coming of one that succeeds it. Once the new dispensation arrives, it renders the previous one obsolete and redundant – fit only to be ignored, suppressed or eradicated. A Christian reading that avoids supersessionism is, by contrast, one that is carried out in respectful awareness of, and serious engagement with, Jewish readings.

The next section illustrates the kind of awareness and engagement that is possible by examining a particular set of scriptural texts. The texts chosen will also help to open up the second main theme of this chapter, because it is a theme explored (albeit in differing ways) by both Jews and Christians: the hearing of Scripture as God's word.

A Jewish hearing of the Shema

There is perhaps no scriptural text more central to Judaism than Deut. 6:4–9, known by its Jewish name, the Shema.[5]

> Hear, O Israel: The LORD our God is one LORD; and you shall love the LORD your God with all your heart, and with all your soul, and with all your might. And these words which I command you this day shall be upon your heart; and you shall teach them diligently to your children, and shall talk of them when you sit in your house, and when you walk by the way, and when you lie down, and when you rise. And you shall bind them as a sign upon your hand, and they shall be as frontlets between your eyes. And you shall write them on the doorposts of your house and on your gates. [RSV]

What the people of Israel are charged with in this passage seems obvious enough. In Michael Fishbane's words, they are called

> to affirm God in one's life, through mind and heart and deed, through teaching and interpretation everywhere; and to cultivate a mindfulness of this duty through signs and symbols, so that one will always be reminded of the sanctity of the body and its actions – in the home (as the domain of one's family and future generations) and in the city (as the domain of society and the sphere of interpersonal values).[6]

As clear an injunction as Deut. 6:4–9 may seem, however, it nonetheless supports a wider set of meanings when 'framed' or 'contextualized' in conjunction with other texts of the Jewish scriptures – and this illustrates the differences of reading that can exist *within* a tradition.

If one situates the Shema textually in the narrative framework of Deuteronomy (i.e. setting it within 'the world of the text') where Moses is addressing the children of Israel in Moab, as the Israelites are about to cross the Jordan into the promised land, then the command, 'Hear, O Israel ... ' will convey one set of meanings. In this context, the words act as a sort of preface to Moses's longer exposition of the fundamental covenantal relationship between Yahweh and the people of Israel, and what stands front and center is the prominence of the Ten Commandments and the reminder of the undivided allegiance that Israel owes to Yahweh as their deliverer. A pronounced stress falls on the exclusivity of Israel's worship (i.e. the LORD *alone*, not the LORD plus some other deities) and on the oneness of Yahweh (i.e. the LORD is *one*, which means that God is without a consort or helper).

If one assumes as normative the ancient historical context of origin as portrayed by the text, then the passage yields this kind of meaning. However, this is not the only context in which these texts are read. For neither the ancient Israelites nor later Jews read Deuteronomy by itself in isolation from all five 'books of Moses', nor from the wider context of the Hebrew Bible. Thus, when one frames the Shema within the larger literary environment of the Jewish canon of sacred writings, and keeps in mind how the hearing of these texts might have been received at later junctures in Israel's history, then the very same passage seems to take on different resonances. It grows in significance and meaning as it is used and reused, read and re-read over time in varying contexts.

How might the Shema have been heard and received, for example, in the late period of the monarchy, when Israel is no longer portrayed as living under the shadow of Sinai or wandering in the desert but instead as settled in the land, established alongside other peoples with their own gods and defining cultures? One could plausibly read the Shema in a later period of Israel's history, say the time of Josiah's reform, as setting forth a programmatic agenda for amendment and covenantal renewal predicated on a close connection between Deut. 6:4 (the oneness and exclusivity of God) and the regulations about the place of worship in Deut. 12:1–14 (the injunction not to worship the LORD as do others in the land, but to 'look only to the site that the LORD your God will choose amidst all your tribes as His habitation, to establish his name there' – v. 5). Read in this way, the meaning of the Shema will be compatible with, yet importantly different from, what it conveyed in the context of Moses's first delivering the Law to the people. In the earlier setting, the exclusivity and oneness of God receives pronounced emphasis; in the later setting, stress is more on the indivisible unity of the *one* God for the *one* chosen people, dwelling together in *one* land and worshipping at *one* site.

These are, of course, but two of the many hearings of the Shema that stretch over the course of Israel's very long history, both in the biblical and post-biblical periods, right up to the current Jewish observances of the Shema in post-Shoah Judaism after the creation of the modern state of Israel. It is not only Jews, however, who have heard and interpreted the Shema.

A Christian hearing of the Shema

Without question, the Shema continues up to the present as the fundamental articulation of the responsibilities of Jewish observance, a summary description of

Jewish identity and self-understanding. Christians, however, have heard this text as the Word of God addressed to the Church, throughout the course of its own distinctive and no less varied history. After all, Deuteronomy falls within the Christian canon too. How might Christians hear Deut. 6:4–9 as their own word from the LORD, addressing them as a people, as a church, while at the same time 'preserving' – i.e. hearing, respecting, and being challenged by – the different ways in which Jews continue to hear, pray, and practice the Shema within their own communities of faith?

Walter Moberly notes that, 'Christian use [of the Shema] has predominantly had two concerns: on the one hand, the oneness of God in 6:4, and on the other hand, love for God in verse 5'.[7] Clearly the pressure to affirm the oneness of God is felt rather differently by Christians than it is by Jews. Whereas Jews, living for much of their history as a minority in a majority culture, are confronted with the challenge of affirming God's oneness against the backdrop of wider polytheistic cultures, Christians face the challenge of showing how an affirmation of the oneness and unity of God is compatible with a Trinitarian understanding of God. Hence, at certain junctures in Christian history the Shema rises to prominence in defining moments of theological construction and polemical debate.

In the fourth century, for example, the Shema played a significant role in the Arian controversy, which concerned the divinity of Jesus. In this context, Deut. 6:4 was refracted through certain New Testament passages, specifically 1 Cor. 8:5–6:

> For although there may be so-called gods in heaven or on earth – as indeed there are many "gods" and many "lords" – yet for us there is one God, the Father, from whom are all things and for whom we exist, and one Lord, Jesus Christ, through whom are all things and through whom we exist. (RSV)

Clearly this is an explicitly Christian re-reading or re-articulation of the Shema that in some sense includes Jesus in the affirmation. While a Jewish reading of this passage may have had as its prime purpose the inhibiting of idolatry, the church fathers' governing interest was to show how the affirmation of God's oneness is not antithetical to but is compatible with – indeed, includes – the affirmation of Jesus' divinity.

There are obviously very significant differences between these Jewish and Christian readings of the Shema. There is no need to discount, ignore, elide, harmonize or erase these differences. It is simply not adequate to think that, deep down, all scriptures teach the same truths; they do not. Sometimes, as in the matter of Jesus' divinity, they teach truths that are incompatible. But they also often convey teachings that have a much more complex relation to one another than either straightforward agreement or direct opposition – as with the different meanings given to God's unity in these various readings. These differences can be preserved, and in some sense intensified or clarified, if they are kept in play. That is, it is possible to keep the different texts and different readings 'in conversation', allowing them to 'feed off' one another and challenge one another.

Of course, it would be irresponsible to leave the impression that 'preserving' differences in reading scriptures is a benign, easy, and friendly affair. Deep and bitter polemics have characterized Jewish–Christian disagreements about how properly to read shared scriptures, and the history of those disagreements over centuries is anything but a bright and happy story. Yet for all that, the differences can become productive if attended to patiently.

Reading together?

We can illustrate this further if we attend to the ways in which, for both Jews and Christians, the Shema has been heard in the context of a wider network of texts as speaking about a daily pattern of prayer and worship as the primary avenue through which God's word is received.

Walter Moberly explains that "'The Shema" is really shorthand for the name of the historic Jewish practice of daily prayer, the *Qěrî'at-Shěma'*, which is classically composed of Deut. 6:4–9; 11:13–21; and Num. 15:37–41, together with certain blessings.'[8] For a rough Christian equivalent, we might look not to Christian use of the Shema, but to the Lord's Prayer. While Matthew's so-called Sermon on the Mount (Matt. 6:9–14; cf. Luke 11:2–4) is the scriptural setting of this most defining of Christian prayers, it is more often encountered by Christians liturgically in relation to other scriptural passages, in ways that bring it into very close proximity to the Shema. As a rough analogy, one might say that praying 'The Lord's Prayer' is for Christians what praying 'The Shema' is for Jews.[9]

Both Jews and Christians have thought about the daily rhythm of praying and of receiving Scripture as they hear the story of God providing the people of Israel with manna in the desert (Exod. 16), with the accent falling on the importance of gathering in the mornings only what food (manna) is necessary for the day. In these interpretations, in both traditions, the satiating of the people's hunger is transmuted figuratively from material food to spiritual sustenance. In Exodus 16, God's provision of manna is a response to the people's complaint, and the *giving* is also a kind of *testing*: grace, in other words, is also a kind of judgment. Although entirely gratuitous, God's providence is also searching and formative. As well as providing the people of Israel with literal food, it trains them in the daily discipline of gathering the manna, and teaches them to become a people who live by divine instruction. Deut. 8:2–4 therefore says,

> And you shall remember all the way which the LORD your God has led you these forty years in the wilderness, that he might humble you, testing you to know what was in your heart, whether you would keep his commandments, or not. And he humbled you and let you hunger and fed you with manna … that he might make you know that man does not live by bread alone, but that man lives by everything that proceeds out of the mouth of the LORD.

These words about bread and the mouth of the LORD are also found in the gospels on Jesus' lips, not surprisingly within a similar context of testing (Matt. 4:4; Luke 4:4). Here too reference to God's providential feeding of the people in the wilderness receives pride of place. In John's gospel, the people look to Jesus for a sign that God is with them – in a 'complaint' rather like those of the children of Israel of old. The crowds say to Jesus,

Our fathers ate the manna in the wilderness; as it is written, 'He gave them bread from heaven to eat.' Jesus then said to them, 'Truly, truly I say to you, it was not Moses who gave you the bread from heaven; my Father gives you the true bread from heaven. For the bread of God is that which comes down from heaven, and gives life to the world.' They said to him, 'Lord, give us this bread always.' (John 6:31–34)

In astonishment, the people are then met with Jesus' self-declaration: 'I am the bread of life. He who comes to me shall not hunger, and he who believes in me shall never thirst' (John 6:35; RSV).

Once again, the difference between Jewish and Christian interpretations is clear, especially in relation to this affirmation about Jesus. There is, nevertheless, a more complex commonality as well. One can discern in both Jewish and Christian inter-pretations an understanding that the petitions in the Shema and the Lord's Prayer for spiritual food and instruction in the law, for signs of grace and of judgment, are daily occurrences: as much for those who recite the Shema 'when they rise' (Deut. 6:7) as for those who in the morning pray the Lord's Prayer, 'give us this day our daily bread' (Matt. 6:11).

Hearing Scripture

Jews and Christians also share, despite their deep and sometimes incommensurable differences, a recognition that the Word of God comes primarily by hearing rather than by seeing. God's word is address before it is text. Indeed, God's word is received in worship and praise; it is first and foremost uttered, prayed, and recited.

One of the questions that we wish to examine in this whole section of the book is: Where and how does Scripture show up in the life of faith? A quick yet accurate response would be: 'Everywhere!' and 'In an astonishing variety of ways!' Scripture turns up in every kind of place imaginable and in all sorts of circumstances – some familiar and expected, others curious and unpredictable. In contemporary Western societies where universal education (at least up to a secondary level) is taken more or less for granted, Scripture predominantly turns up in the material shape of a book: a set of printed pages in codex form (though this is rapidly changing as new electronic modes of delivery become common).

Those who engaged directly with Scripture in book form were, however, for most of the Church's history, a relatively small group: a learned, scribal or clerical class. Ordinary lay Christians were instead exposed to their Scriptures through carved stone and stained glass, through mosaics, tapestries, paintings, hymns, prayer books, and passion plays – and, especially, through preaching and liturgy. After all, even had books been easily produced and readily available to all, which they were not, most people would not have been able to read them on their own because they were illiterate in our modern sense of that term.

From the vantage of our contemporary culture, being deprived of an opportunity to engage directly with the pages of Scripture as a book strikes us as a distinct disadvantage. It precludes the individual believer from being able to follow the words of Scripture independently, working their way through the text and discerning a meaning for themselves. But what we take for granted as an unquestioned boon of modern life – the prerogative of making up one's own mind, of self-determination within relatively egalitarian social structures – also serves to conceal our own blind spots.

One of these blind spots is our tendency to think of the transmission of Scripture primarily as the reproduction of a static, material object – the book. We may well miss, therefore, a host of other structures, processes, and objects through which the Scriptures are embedded and transmitted in our culture – in 'low' or 'popular' as well as in 'high' culture. Biblical motifs, symbols, imagery and allusions to its central stories pervade the world of cartoons and marketing campaigns, TV ads and movies, just as they do the world of high culture on display in museums in the form of tapestries, carvings, paintings, sculptures, and so on.[10] In focusing narrowly on the book, we may miss many other ways in which Christians constantly find themselves, within virtually every facet of daily life, engaging with Scripture.[11]

We also tend to regard reading as by nature a visual and cognitive process, an activity primarily of the eyes and brain rather than of the ears and body. For most people educated in the modern West the normative figure of a reader – whether of Scripture or any other text – is that of a solitary individual silently poring over a book. However, a different picture was suggested by our brief exploration of the Shema and of the Lord's Prayer. Before it is seen silently in private, Scripture is heard communally, in public worship ('Hear, O Israel … !').

The unmistakable auditory primacy of the communal reception of the Word of God has profound implications for understanding better the Church's relation with its sacred texts. To hear means that we are spoken to or called, which establishes the possibility of dialogue; hearing implies response. This does not only have ramifications for those who prayerfully receive the Word but for those who preach it as well.[12] It is, after all, the preacher's task to give faithful voice to the text in worship, to communicate to the congregation not her own words but the Word of God. As Frances Young says,

> The Bible is the one thing held in common among all those who claim the name Christian. In every century, in every place, in every church of whatever tradition, the homily or sermon has been the principal locus of theological exploration. Whether generated by the lectionary, or part of a sequence on a particular biblical book, or emerging from the demands of a particular occasion or situation, always the discernment of God's word for the moment is rooted in the reading of scripture, and scripture inspires discernment of God's way of addressing present contingencies. In other words, theology grows out of engagement with scripture in such a way as to create meaning for the particular people gathered together for liturgy. The reading of the Bible fosters a sense of identity and community, which issues in a particular way of life, which may challenge societal norms.[13]

In order to be true to this calling, the preacher must first be apprenticed in the art of assiduous listening – in silence, in meditation and prayer – to Christ who dwells within by the power of the Holy Spirit, and to Scripture, the Word of God inscribed in the letters of the text.[14] Paying attention to the details of actual Christian practice thus affords a fundamental insight regarding the customary way Christians engage Scripture: it is one of address, dialogue, conversation, discourse. What is set in motion by the preaching of the Word – both as presupposition and as expectation – is a kind of call and response, a dialectic between the reader and the auditor, between the preacher and the congregation.

Listening to the Word of God, hearkening to the 'voice' of the text, also conjures up musical images or associations. Reading the Scripture out loud in public worship sets off resonances or reverberations in ways that introduce to the listeners the necessary rhythms, motifs, and melodies by which they are enabled to join in meaningfully with its performance. One can think of Scripture as being like a musical score that is meant to be 'played' – or a script of a play meant to be 'acted out' on a stage – rather than as a text meant to be read silently and alone with the expectation that all that is required of the reader is to give notional assent to the information it contains.[15]

Musicians and actors, of course, spend long hours in acquiring and honing specialized skills. But even the most ordinary of persons learns skills that, although seemingly mundane and unremarkable, are nonetheless no less sophisticated when it comes to the virtues of listening and attunement. Learning to receive and respond to the words of another in ordinary conversation is predominantly an auditory skill requiring careful attention and long apprenticeship in good habits of hearing. Indeed, hearing the Word of God might be likened to entering a conversation which is already in progress. To be sure, joining an ongoing conversation is no easy task, given that one must acquire an understanding of what has transpired before one arrived on the scene, while at the same time gathering an appreciation of the present dynamics and relations among the interlocutors, even as one imaginatively anticipates how the current dialogue might shape future conversations. This is a complex and intricate task that happens on multiple levels at once and in a manner that implicates and engages the readers' orientations to the past, the present and the future – yet it is perfectly achievable.

The time of the text

Historical criticism

One of the challenges faced when entering into a conversation as deep, as long and as broad as that of the Christian tradition, is learning how to respect the 'pastness' of Scripture (i.e. to appreciate how very strange and distant the world of the text is from our own time and place) while at the same time recognizing the need to assimilate the world of Scripture into one's own life (i.e. to hear it as a direct, personal address, as God's word and not simply as an ancient artifact of enduring cultural value).[16] Here we come to another area of interest in rightly understanding Scripture: the need to preserve a creative tension between the indispensable value of historical-critical methodologies in reading ancient texts, including Scripture, and the need to honor Scripture as a living text currently animating the lives of believers and their communities of faith. Too much stress on one or the other courts distortion; pursuing one to the exclusion of the other virtually guarantees it.[17]

The historical-critical method is a set of academic tools developed by modern scholarship to help understand more fully and precisely the nature of ancient texts (sources, origins, composition, transmission, and so on) and how they were used in past centuries. The primary aim is often to uncover what the text would have meant in the contexts of its original production and reception, and to refrain from reading into it meanings that come from another time (namely, the time of later interpreters). This is often expressed technically as the distinction between exegesis (a disciplined mode of reading by which meaning is 'led out of' the text) and eisegesis (the undisciplined and idiosyncratic mode of reading by which one imposes or 'reads into' the text one's own preferred meaning).

In reading historical-critical accounts of the biblical texts, one often comes across the distinction between 'what the text meant' (meaning) and 'what it means' (significance). Often the historical-critical approach to Scripture is unfairly accused (in part because of its interest in 'objectivity') of focusing so much on the former that it fails to address the latter – Scripture's present meaning and significance. But this may be more a matter of mistaking a difference in emphasis for a principled difference in kind. Philosophical and hermeneutical approaches to Scripture, equally scholarly and methodologically rigorous, complement historical-critical approaches by showing how classic, foundational texts like the Bible can transcend their origins and conditions of early use. For example, literary theory effectively shows how authors have very little control over the text once it becomes inscribed (written or 'published'). Writing, which seems to ascribe a certain permanence or 'fixity' to the text, does not thereby result in an invariant 'determinacy' of meaning, as texts invariably take on new meanings never imagined at the time of writing. Indeed, one of the invaluable insights of reader-response or reader-reception theory is the way it reveals how, as different questions are asked of them, texts take on different meanings (indirectly supporting the idea that Scripture has, even on a textual level, not just a past but a future as well).

One lesson that needs to be learned, then, is that rigorous historical-critical approaches to Scripture are not inherently opposed to theological understandings of Scripture nor are they hostile in principle to placing sacred texts in their 'native' liturgical environments. There is another important lesson here, however – namely, that just as there is no one final, 'once for all' meaning of Scripture so too there can be no single, overarching and all-sufficient method by which to understand Scripture. To phrase this more positively, there is merit in adopting approaches to Scripture that put a premium on respecting differences – by retaining them in creative, dynamic, and dialectically interactive tension – rather than collapsing them into an easy and flaccid, because 'forced', unity.

One virtue of keeping several critical methodologies in play is that the very 'dialogue' of methods, like human interchange, tends to keep the conversation honest insofar as no one approach, just as no one interlocutor, dominates. True dialogue precludes monologue. More important perhaps than each voice having an equal say, the dialogical model of multiple disciplinary methods promotes mutual (and hopefully constructive) interruption that honors difference by leaving room for it, by allowing it to do its work in mutual correction and in a reciprocal expansion and deepening of understanding. Keeping the historical-critical method in concert with literary theory, structuralist, and post-structuralist analysis, reader-response theory, and so on, facilitates a fruitful interaction that generates fresh insights and new meanings that could not be achieved by pursuing any one methodology on its own.

For example, literary theory advances indispensable insights regarding key elements in the process of reading and its history. Biblical scholars of the nineteenth and twentieth centuries devoted a lot of time to investigating the author's biography, historical circumstances, and influences. The danger of these author-focused interpretations is that they tend to confine the significance of the author's text to the past, cutting it off and leaving it stranded in an era long vanished, unable to say anything to the present. Structuralism, on the other hand, sets authorial intention to one side and focuses on the text itself – where meaning is seen to be inscribed in the very structure of linguistic works, such that what the text means invariably 'occurs' quite apart from human motives or goals or intentions. The danger of such approaches is that meaning seems somehow to happen 'automatically', on its own, so to say – making both author and reader redundant. Similarly, reader-oriented criticism (reader-response or reader-reception theory) focuses attention on the reader's inevitable contribution to the meaning of the text. Texts unavoidably take on new meanings as the circumstances in which they are received change and in accordance with the questions readers bring to and ask of the text. The danger of reader-oriented interpretations is the implication that the reader may be seen as commanding such a principal role that they can make the text mean virtually anything they like.

Each of these three approaches – with interests in the author, the text, and the reader respectively – have proven strengths and virtues, without which our understanding of the meaning of Scripture would remain impoverished. While each critical approach contributes invaluable insight into how texts – including the texts of Scripture – are constructed, received and appropriated, at the same time each calls out for qualification and adjustment in light of the others. For it is simply not possible to privilege the author, text or reader as the single and sufficient criterion for establishing meaning, insofar as the creation of meaning is possible only through the interaction of all three.

Keeping time with Scripture

Scripture has often been referred to as a 'timeless' text, but it is probably more accurate to speak of it as a truly 'time-full' set of texts that asks of its readers a readiness to follow its temporal movements – i.e. to keep time with Scripture.[18] For apart from the willingness of the faithful in each generation to learn how to 'tell' the time of the text, or 'keep' time with it by performing it, Scripture would not speak to every age.

Earlier we spoke of the preacher's first and foremost responsibility as that of learning to become a good 'listener' to the text before she can be a faithful expositor of God's word to her audience. This is true of the reader/listener as well, insofar as the reception of a sermon is inseparable from its delivery. The preacher ponders the text 'out loud' with the congregation, the joint effect of which is to draw the preacher/reader/listener into the text in ways that enable 'a transformation of outlook, and, potentially, of behaviour'.[19]

Christians therefore learn how to tell time – and thus how to 'keep' time – by listening to Scripture in prayer and worship, which is Scripture's 'native' environment. But Christians also learn to tell time in the academy study and critical interrogation of Scripture. Study of the history and literary structure of the Bible in the university, however, reveals that much more is in play than linear, chronological concepts of time. By bringing academic readings of Scripture into conversation with liturgical modes of reading, something of the density and complex overlapping and interweaving of various temporal modes comes to light.

Scripture is unmistakably a product of its time, having been shaped by a specific culture and history and language of its authors and its first audience, but also by the diverse contexts of its reception and use throughout history. The challenge, then, is to coordinate – to synchronize – the temporality of the text with the temporality of its hearers and readers in ways that expect, and thus allow for, discordances and tensions as well as harmonies and unities. The task of reading Scripture faithfully is not so much to leave biblical time behind or to set it aside, but to engage fully with its rhythms and movements, experience its temporal flows, interruptions, subversions, contradictions and cross currents. The kind of unity exhibited by Scripture, then, is no easy whole but what might be called a 'dissonant concordance' or a 'concordant dissonance'.[20]

Recognizing that the unity of what is read can only be 'worked out' in time is crucial. Indeed, it takes time because any sense of the whole cannot be achieved merely by a single passing through the texts of Scripture. In that regard, reading Scripture is not like reading a single book, a novel say. The fact that Christians read their sacred texts in the shape of a final canon should not mislead one in thinking that Scripture is therefore a text 'settled' once and for all rather than a text that continually calls out for settlement. Indeed, one might say that the regular, disciplined reading of Scripture accords with the way we read our lives; namely, as a continual striving to achieve an always provisional – because only temporarily and partially suitable – unity and coherence. Making an initial pass through the text, taking it 'as it is', and then reading it again, invariably alerts the reader to 'deeper movements or rhythms within it'[21] not noticed the first time. Exposure on subsequent readings to deeper levels of meaning, which often correlate with becoming alert to more subtle temporal registers of the text, can be unnerving and disorienting. The reader finds that because of this disorienting effect, she needs time to recover her footing and regain her bearings before she can resume her reading.

Reading Scripture is thus a 'time-full' undertaking. Scripture always invites its own re-reading; it is *lectio continua*. Participating in the continuous hearing of Scripture in prayer and worship, a form of *lectio continua*, is thus to enter richly into the various rhythms and movements of the text. Readers so schooled by Scripture come to recognize that there can be no adequate reading of this foundational text which ignores 'the time of the text itself, its own movement'.[22]

Whatever unity that obtains between text and reader cannot be a static homogeneity but more that of a continuous, diachronic textual dynamic that follows the flows and rhythms of the text in order that 'the time of the text becomes recognizably continuous with' the time of its readers. The kind of 'fusion of the horizon' of the reader with the horizon of the text, however, is not best conceived in terms of a territorial take-over or usurpation of one time by another, the past by the present, say. Rather, it is better conceived as a process played out over time by which the various temporal registers of the text interweave and inter-animate with the multiple temporalities of the reader/listener. Whatever unity or fusion that is achieved is one that must each time be worked out and worked through continuously. What is a given in Scripture is truly God's word, but it is the nature of this gift to have been given in time – which means, like the manna given to the children of Israel in the wilderness, it must be gathered daily, again and again.

Rules for reading Scripture

In summary, we can set out a rough and ready list of rules for reading Scripture.

1   Be attentive to where and how Scripture shows up in the life of faith, and always be prepared for surprises and the unexpected. Although traditionally the Scriptures have been copied, preserved, transmitted and consumed in the form of a book, be alert to the various other forms in which Scripture is instantiated. Text means more than black marks on a page. Correlatively, because diverse reading practices overlap and are analogically related, look for cross-fertilizations – in particular, be attentive not only to the intellectual or cognitive dimensions of Scripture's meaning but its affective and aesthetic dimensions as well.

2   When reading Scripture, read more with your ears than with your eyes. God's word is address before it is text. Scripture is heard before it is read, and that hearing happens for Christians primarily in contexts of worship and prayer. The Jewish Shema, 'Hear, O Israel' and the Christian 'Our Father' illustrate this, suggesting indirectly that the meaning of Scripture is a communally established event, not a private undertaking, fashioned in the dialectic between addresser and addressee, issuing a summons and receiving a response, giving and returning, etc.

3   Reading Scripture invariably calls for judgment, not only about what is the appropriate way to read contingent upon what type or kind of text is being read but in the sense that reading is always a matter of reasoning or settling, of being made alert to what might be fitting, what might be called for, in the present situation. Reading is, in a way, to expose oneself to grace and to judgment at once. To read is to be judged to the extent that Scripture tends to 'unsettle' established frameworks and customary patterns of human relating that often hide inequity, oppression, and injustice.

4   Reading Scripture is a 'time-full' activity, which requires an apprenticeship of sorts in the habits of attention that makes one a capable listener or 'hearer of the Word'. The Word of God is fundamentally an act of communication, an address, which by its very form invites and expects a response. In accordance with its nature, right readers of Scripture must adjust to the rhythms and temporal patterns of that address as embodied in the written words of the sacred texts and take the time necessary to 'work with' the multiple temporal modalities

of Scripture. Faithful Christian readers are those who accept the discipline of Scripture in this way.

5 Scripture's holiness is not so much contained in the material artifact of the text itself as in its people, in its faithful readers who enact and perform Scripture in their daily lives. Hence to read Scripture as a holy book do not look for qualities that somehow inhere in the text itself, that set it apart from all other texts, in isolation from its interpretation or performance. Rather, the holiness of Scripture is found in the lives of those who are its faithful readers, those who are enabled to enact the texts in their lives.

6 Sacred writings are contested writings – which means that the disputes and disagreements over their meaning are not always, or even primarily, the result of an impasse or impediment in discernment as much as they are a consequence of the fact that Scripture is more a library than it is a single book in the modern sense. To the extent that Scripture comprises diverse literary forms, written over vast periods of time, by multiple authors, means that tension-filled relations will invariably exist. But tension is healthy and creative; it is a provocation and not an impediment to meaning. There is no one, pre-set pathway through Scripture – which means that there will be many ways in which one can 'work through' the text.

7 Learn to read Scripture hospitably. Read Scripture in ways that preserve textual differences rather than seek to erase them for the sake of reaching a premature and 'forced' harmony. Often this strategy hides a covert form of supercessionism, as has too often been the case of Christian readings of Jewish Scripture. Learn to read disputatiously and respectfully rather than oppositionally and adversarially, always keen to preserve and if possible deepen the quality of the differences discerned between the reading habits of your own religious tradition and the reading habits of those in other religious traditions.

Looking ahead

The chapters in this section will explore various aspects of the practice of the theological use of Scripture.

The opening chapter, 'Scripture, devotion, and discipleship', outlines three fundamental approaches to Scripture. A first approach 'pivots on the past' and assumes that the normative basis for Scripture's meaning can only be determined if the historical origins of the text can be established. A second approach 'pivots on the present' and focuses on Scripture's use within current ecclesial contexts. A third approach pivots neither on the past nor the present but begins somewhere in the middle of the Church's history of Scripture reading, which means that it exhibits a much more complex temporality. Our exploration of Scripture's meaning must somehow engage all three temporal modes – past, present, and future. The practice of *lectio divina* is offered as an extended example illustrating how the Church today might be challenged, reinvigorated and called into question by reclaiming some of its past Scripture reading practices. The chapter opens up a wider and more diverse set of reading practices – some devotional, some scholarly – all of which challenge theologians to strive to make sense of the many *overlaps*, the *tensions* and the *clashes* between different reading practices.

Kevin Vanhoozer's chapter, 'Scripture and theology: On "proving" doctrine biblically', sets forth a fourfold typology, each quadrant of which recognizes an essential aspect of what Scripture is; namely, principles, images, testimony and data. Vanhoozer makes the case that there is a reciprocal relation between one's view of God and one's use of Scripture. He argues that for Christians Scripture is the out-working or 'play' of the divine drama, which means that any theology that is 'in accordance with the Scriptures' (1 Cor. 15:3) must 'follow the way the words go', must be enacted or performed as actors would follow the director's instructions and the words of the play script. Understanding or 'proving' doctrine, therefore, means looking to Scripture as offering dramatic direction for the Church so that readers of God's word might faithfully and fittingly participate in God's drama of redemption.

The chapter by Bill Cavanaugh, 'Scripture and politics', focuses on how reading Scripture for many people in today's world, especially those living in conditions of economic disadvantage and political oppression, begins with a strong desire to know the truth of what God is speaking to them now. The strength of this desire arises out of the urgency of their immediate situation. For them, the point of reading the Bible is primarily to involve themselves in the ongoing story of God's salvation of the world, and not just to study it dispassionately as an ancient story. This relative emphasis on the personal and political does not eschew critical, scholarly modes of reading the scriptural texts; in fact, it embraces them by asking how the Bible invariably shapes political judgements. Ideological agendas are not absent but only disguised or hidden in biblical scholarship that advances itself as objective or scientific. Cavanaugh alerts readers to the ways in which political considerations are intrinsic to Scripture and not ancillary, opening up the Bible to political readings but also opening up other texts and practices to being analysed, challenged, and critiqued from a biblical point of view.

Gerard Loughlin's chapter, 'The literal sense and the senses of Scripture', examines the long and evolving history of what constitutes a literal reading of Scripture. Loughlin contends that 'to read for the literal sense is to follow the letter of the text, the way the words go'. Contrary to common judgment, the literal and the figurative do not stand in antithetical relation to one another. They are not mutually exclusive but organically related; the metaphorical or figurative builds on, or grows out of, the literal. One way to appreciate the intimate relation between literal and figurative is to retrace the development of that distinction from how it was first understood by ancient and medieval Christian readers to how it is now deployed by modern readers of Scripture. Patristic and medieval Christians tended to assume that Scripture held or supported multiple meanings, literal and figurative, but with the advent of modernity these ideas were radically altered or rejected. Loughlin shows that it is possible to retrieve them, and that, rightly understood, the literal sense is figurative, perhaps the most figurative sense of all.

Notes

1 F. Young, 'From Pondering Scripture to the First Principles of Christian Theology', in *God's Presence: A Contemporary Recapitulation of Early Christianity*, Cambridge: Cambridge University Press, 2013, pp. 7–43: p. 11.

2 The phrase 'Scripture as the Soul of Theology' comes from Pope Leo XIII's encyclical *Providentissimus Deus*, which was then borrowed by *Dei Verbum*, the Dogmatic Constitution on Divine Revelation from Vatican II (par. 24). It also serves as a title to the eminent Catholic biblical scholar Joseph Fitzmyer's book: *Scripture, The Soul of Theology*, Mahwah, NJ: Paulist Press, 1994.

3 A codex is a collection of pages stitched together along one side. It replaced earlier rolls of papyrus and wax tablets. Among its advantages, it could be opened at once to any point in the text, it permitted writing on both sides of the leaf, and it could contain long texts.

4 The importance of 'keeping the text in play' is explored more extensively in M. Higton and R. Muers, *The Text in Play: Experiments in Reading Scripture*, Eugene, OR: Cascade Books, 2013.

5 In what follows, I am indebted to the work of Walter Moberly, *Old Testament Theology: Reading the Hebrew Bible as Christian Scripture*, Grand Rapids, MI: Baker Academic, 2013, especially Chapter 1, 'A Love Supreme' and Chapter 3, 'Daily Bread'.

6 M. Fishbane, *Sacred Attunement: A Jewish Theology*, Chicago, IL: Chicago University Press, 2008, p. 45.

7 Moberly, *Old Testament Theology*, p. 12.

8 Moberly, *Old Testament Theology*, p. 7, n. 1.

9 The subtleties and complexities by which this connection is established are helpfully clarified in Walter Moberly's chapter 3 'Daily Bread', in *Old Testament Theology*, pp. 75–105.

10 See M.L. Budde, *The (Magic) Kingdom of God: Christianity and Global Culture Industries*, Boulder, CO: Westview Press, 1997.

11 'Reading' is a term used generically of this wide array of engagements. The seemingly endless ways in which various reading practices overlap and are analogically related in relation to Scripture is explored in the next chapter of this book, especially the section 'Varieties of reading'.

12 In what follows, I am indebted to the insights of Frances Young, in 'Pondering Scripture'.

13 F. Young, 'Pondering Scripture', p. 11.

14 See C. Harrison, *The Art of Listening in the Early Church*, Oxford: Oxford University Press, 2013. Harrison notes that 'It would not be a wild overestimate to suggest that around two-thirds of the early Christian texts which we now read were originally spoken, rather than written, and were intended for hearers, rather than readers. They sounded, resonated, and impressed themselves upon the mind and memory through the ear rather than the eye' (p. 1).

15 A seminal essay by Nicholas Lash, 'Performing the Scriptures', in *Theology on the Way to Emmaus*, London: SCM Press, 1986, pp. 37–46, is one in what has now become a long line of studies that explores the theological potential of the analogy between reading Scripture and performing a drama or a musical score.

16 Paul Ricoeur refers to the process of establishing a critical distance from the text being studied as one of 'distanciation'. This is a necessary moment in the interpretive process, but one that on its own is insufficient to complete the hermeneutical arc. A complementary and equally necessary moment is to 're-connect' with the text, to enact what Hans-Georg Gadamer refers to as a 'fusion of horizons' – the horizon of the reader with that of the text.

17 This is not to suggest that the only legitimate way to read Scripture is from the perspective of faith. Scripture can also legitimately be read as a document within the university using methods and techniques that one would use to read any other text, classic or otherwise. Indeed, to presume a simple demarcation between these two approaches is to offer a naïve and misleading picture of the present situation. Churchly readings of scripture and scholarly readings are not antithetical.

18 I am indebted to Rowan Williams' important essay for many of the insights that follow. See R. Williams, 'The Discipline of Scripture', in *On Christian Theology*, Oxford: Blackwell, 2000, pp. 44–59.

19 Young, 'Pondering Scripture', p. 19.

20 The expressions are Paul Ricoeur's. See *Time and Narrative*, vol. 3, trans. K. Blamey and D. Pellauer, Chicago, IL: University of Chicago Press, 1988, pp. 137–41.

21 R. Williams, 'The Discipline of Scripture', p. 45.

22 R. Williams, 'The Discipline of Scripture', p. 47.

9
SCRIPTURE, DEVOTION, AND DISCIPLESHIP

Jim Fodor and Mike Higton

Introduction

If you are studying Christian theology, you will find that Scripture is talked about in your classes, and in the literature you are asked to read, in a wide variety of see-mingly incompatible ways. It is not just that different claims are made about the meaning of specific verses or about the likely history behind specific passages. Rather, you will find that you encounter thoroughly different kinds of discussion in different contexts.

Pivoting on the past

For instance, you are very likely to encounter some forms of reading that pivot on the past. In other words, a good deal of the study of Scripture amongst modern theologians and historians starts by asking about a text's historical origins, and its reception amongst the communities who first read or heard it. If it treats the reception of the text in other times and places at all, such scholarship tends to situate it in relation to that original history – and it tends to say that more recent readings should be judged according to how well they capture the original meanings of the text.

To speak very broadly, reading that pivots on the past can wear two different faces. It can appear in the form of a debunking: a demonstration that some recent reading is questionable once we know the true history of the text. Take Psalm 2, for instance. Because verse 7 says, 'I will tell of the decree of the Lord: He said to me, "You are my son; today I have begotten you"', the Psalm has been read by many Christians as a prophetic reference to Christ. Yet when the historical critic David Clines puts the text back into its original context, he finds it depicting the king of Judah, claiming Judah's God as his backer and so presenting himself as that God's 'son', faced with a real or imaginary coalition of vassal kingdoms, and laughing them to scorn before threatening them with violence should they not honour him. Clines points out just how deeply problematic this makes the text.

> [I]t is not just that the ideology of the psalm is in conflict with mine (and that of people I approve of): it is in conflict also with other streams of

thought in its own culture – in ways that make its ideology questionable. In a word, while Israel is very happy to have been liberated itself, this psalm does not want anyone else to be liberated ... *[T]he text is an act of bad faith* ... [1]

Christian readings which take this Psalm as a template for their thinking about Christ begin to look rather suspect when seen against that background.

Alternatively, reading that pivots on the past can appear as a bringing alive of the text: a reinvigorating of present reading by attention to some fresh detail of that history. For instance, consider N.T. Wright's discussion of 1 Thessalonians 4:16–17:

> For the Lord himself, with a cry of command, with the archangel's call and with the sound of God's trumpet, will descend from heaven, and the dead in Christ will rise first. Then we who are alive, who are left, will be caught up in the clouds together with them to meet the Lord in the air; and so we will be with the Lord for ever.

Wright's reading draws on the historical background to some of the vocabulary used to make fresh sense of these verses:

> When the emperor visited a colony or province, the citizens of the country would go to meet him at some distance from the city. It would be disrespectful to have him actually arrive at the gates as though his subjects couldn't be bothered to greet him properly. When they met him, they wouldn't then stay out in the open country: they would escort him royally into the city itself. When Paul speaks of 'meeting' the Lord 'in the air', the point is ... that, having gone out to meet their returning Lord, they will escort him royally into his domain, that is, back to the place they have come from. Even when we realize that this is highly charged metaphor, not literal description, the meaning is ... that one is expecting the emperor to come from the mother city to give the colony its full dignity, to rescue it if need be, to subdue local enemies and put everything to rights.[2]

Being introduced to these kinds of modern biblical scholarship, whether they lean towards debunking or revitalizing, can often involve being invited to participate in an ongoing story with a very familiar shape. We are all used to stories of academic progress – stories in which scientists or historians discover or uncover or decode what to their predecessors was a mystery. The story of modern biblical scholarship that pivots on the past is often told like this. Try reading, for instance, Stephen Neill and N.T. Wright's *The Interpretation of the New Testament 1861–1986*.[3] It is quite an exciting read: a story of investigators pushing back the boundaries of knowledge, of discoveries in the desert, of mysteries uncovered and codes cracked.

There is often another kind of storyline in the background, however, one that goes back to the Reformation and beyond. This is the storyline that starts with the original purity or vitality of the New Testament church, then traces its slow fall into centuries of obscurity, error, and confusion, awaiting some return to the sources of the faith that will make possible a purifying renewal or reformation. Modern biblical scholarship that pivots on the past is sometimes presented as the continuation of precisely this kind of reforming work.

Pivoting on the present

Alongside all these forms of scholarship, however, you will also encounter readings that pivot on the present. That is, you will encounter forms of the study of Scripture that start with Scripture as a book that is read in the church today. Sometimes (though rather more rarely than one might expect) that will involve detailed empirical description of current practice in a variety of particular churches. More commonly, such scholarship will pivot around more or less idealized descriptions of what contemporary reading could be or should be. Of course, such scholarship is not simply interested in describing present practice: it will go on to explore the assumptions that are being made by this reading, to ask what questions it raises and what implications it has, to explore how it relates to the past and how it might develop in the future – but present Christian practice, real or imagined, is the touchstone of the discussion.

The focus in such scholarship often falls on the distinctiveness of Christian reading of Scripture: its difference from other ways of reading texts. In particular, you will find discussions of the difference between such Christian reading and patterns of reading that have developed in the modern world, including the patterns of reading funded by the kind of scholarship that pivots on the past.

For scholarship that pivots on the present, the focus often falls on reading as *devout* – as an ingredient in the life of discipleship, contributing to the growth in holiness of the communities and individuals who practise it. Ellen Davis and Richard Hays write, for instance that

> Scriptural interpretation is properly an ecclesial activity whose goal is to participate in the reality of which the text speaks by bending the knee to worship the God revealed in Jesus Christ. Through Scripture the Church receives the good news of the inbreaking kingdom of God and, in turn, proclaims the message of reconciliation. Scripture is like a musical score that must be played or sung in order to be understood; therefore, the Church interprets Scripture by forming communities of prayer, service and faithful witness. The Psalms, for example, are 'scores' awaiting performance by the community of faith. They school us in prayer and form in us the capacities for praise, penitence, reflection, patient endurance and resistance to evil.[4]

You will also find scholarship that pivots on the present in a more critical form – as the exposure of problematic power dynamics or of forms of exclusion that shape the ways the text is used today. Michael Prior, for instance, traces the ways in which white South Africans in the middle of the twentieth century read their history through the lens of the narrative of Israel's Exodus and arrival in the Promised Land, in such a way as to promote 'the unity of Afrikaners, on the one hand, and their separation from the black peoples, on the other.'[5] Such reading of the Bible was one of the supporting pillars of apartheid.

Beginning in the middle

To complicate matters, you will also encounter – perhaps even more than you encounter scholarship that explicitly pivots on the present – forms of scholarship that begin somewhere in the middle of the history of Christian reading of the Bible. That is, you will find scholars who begin with some example of the way in which Scripture has been read in the history of the Church (Patristic figural interpretation, or medieval *lectio divina*, or Reformation commentaries, for instance). Such theologians look at how the text was read in that context, seeing how it drew upon and transformed older traditions of reading, but also asking how the Church's reading today looks against this backdrop, and how it might be called into question and be reinvigorated by it.

This kind of scholarship tends to have more in common with the kind that pivots on the present rather than with the kind that pivots on the past. It tends to be no less interested in the distinctiveness of these examples of Christian reading, and no less interested in the patterns of corporate and individual devotion of which they were a part – and the implications for the Church's present practice are often very firmly in view. It sometimes shares something of the narrative shape of scholarship that pivots on the past, however. It suggests that the Church today has lost the distinctiveness and devoutness of the reading practices that it once had, and that this turn to examples from its history will fund a recovery – a reformation or renewal.

Henri de Lubac, for instance, in his great multi-volume work on *Medieval Exegesis*, writes in his Preface about his reasons for spending so long delving into a past era's ways of reading the Bible. He says

> I have always been of the naive belief ... that in the witness they give to their faith, no less than in the witness they expect from us in return, all the Christian generations enjoy a oneness and solidarity. It is some portion of this witness ... that I seek to grasp and comprehend. ... It ought to be a joy for the historian to unearth some inkling of humanity from a far-distant past. It ought to be a still greater joy if he succeeds in restoring in its freshness some ancient form of the life of the mind, a form whose beauty has been lost, even if he has no hope of kindling it to life again other than as an aspect of memory. How much greater would the joy of the Christian be if he succeeded in conveying a part of this heritage to the present generation, commending it to its understanding, to its esteem, and to its admiration, without hiding from it the weaknesses and decrepit elements that mark it.[6]

Varieties of reading

Scripture

One way to think about the difference between these various approaches is to say that they are focused on different objects of study. Scholarship that pivots on the past is, at least in some of its forms, interested in a set of historical events – the writing and reception in specific historical contexts of the texts later gathered together as Christian Scripture. When a copy of the Bible appears in a classroom where such scholarship is being pursued, it appears as a translation and edition of some of the evidence for that real object of study.

Scholarship that pivots on the present, however, is interested in the book found in multiple forms and editions and languages in churches today, and when a copy of the Bible appears in a classroom where such scholarship is being pursued, it appears as an example of one of those editions, one taken out of its home context for the sake of study.

In this chapter, our focus falls on the study of Scripture that pivots on the present. Our object of study is Scripture as a text lived with by a community in the context of various practices. That is, the object of our study is not simply a text in the abstract – a string of characters or sequence of information. It is a text that is embodied in particular physical objects, and is encountered by the senses. It is heard; it is read aloud or in silence; it is encountered in the midst of numerous liturgical practices or rituals, in the midst of numerous patterns of devotion. In various contexts around the world, it is paraded, studied, distributed, chanted, annotated, elevated, smuggled, danced with, bequeathed, copied, highlighted, performed, translated, sung, kissed, hidden, illuminated, and proclaimed. The object of our study is the object that is involved in all these practices and processes – and to study it without attending to them would be like studying a particular human being without paying attention to her biography.

It is worth taking some time to ask yourself in what contexts, and in the midst of what practices, you encounter the Christian Bible today. In what contexts, and in the midst of what practices, did you first encounter it? When we asked a group of scholars this in Cambridge some time ago, we found that some had first encountered the Bible in short passages heard in the midst of a liturgy, some as the text of songs sung in church, some as an object danced with and venerated, some as a focus of intense small-group study, and so on.

Reading

Amongst the practices within which Scripture is encountered are practices of reading. In the world we live in, reading tends to be thought of largely as a process that employs eyes and minds. It is inward, silent, and solitary – the mind decoding visual symbols on pages or screens. It is almost a disembodied process – or, at the very least, we tend to think most readily about the mind and what is happening in it, and relegate any thoughts about the physicality of the process to a minor, secondary place. If I ask, 'Have you read the latest Dan Brown?', I'm not likely to be thinking about whether you have felt the book, hefted it in your hand and smelt it; I'm not likely to be interested in the posture you adopted or the space in which you did so; I'm not likely to be interested in the rhythm of your breathing or the moving of your fingers.

We think of reading, on the whole, as a process by which meaning, or ideas, or a story, are gleaned from a text – a gathering, sorting, and storing of some kind of information, taken from the page or from the screen. The mind mows across the surface of the text, harvesting thoughts.

We teach young children to read, and hope to get them to the point where they can read silently, to themselves ('in their own heads'), suppressing any mumbling or any moving of their lips. And that kind of teaching is clearly important; it is a necessary precondition for increasing the speed and efficiency of reading, for enabling the child to take off as a solo reader. Quite a lot of the reading in which we engage is, however, a matter of hasty consumption. We live in a world of texting and tweeting, Facebook status updates, and blog comments. We can navigate a world characterized by the ever more pervasive spread of the written word only because we can read quickly and superficially, skimming off the meanings we need almost at a glance. Reading is a quick skill of eyes and mind.

This remarkable and virtually complete disappearance of the body in reading (or at least in our ways of thinking about reading) is a relatively recent development. Unlike the speed of light, readers and reading habits are hardly constant at all times and places. Reading is not a single universal experience.

The philosopher Ludwig Wittgenstein can help us here. He examined our normal notion of reading, and noted that we commonly assume that 'reading is a quite particular process' and that when we read 'something special is going on, something highly characteristic', which we generally think of as a distinctive kind of conscious experience.[7] Of course, reading may involve many other ancillary behaviours, activities, and sensations, but 'the one real criterion for anybody's reading is the conscious act of reading' – or at least this is what we are inclined to think.[8]

One misleading step leads to another. From the assumption that an act of reading is genuine only if it involves a certain kind of conscious experience for the reader – because reading is a silent, inward, primarily mental process – we are then hood-winked into thinking that what is going on during reading is a matter of deriving something called meaning from the words inscribed on the page. Meaning is construed as somehow inhering in the printed words – it is something waiting to be harvested from the words. We end up leaning towards some sort of 'container' theory of meaning: the words printed on the page somehow 'hold' or 'contain' meaning, and what the activity of reading does is enable the reader to gain access to and experience that meaning.

This psychologized account of reading is, according to Wittgenstein, deeply beguiling. It misleads not only because it presumes that reading must be an essentially mental operation but because it assumes that reading names one thing: a single, characteristic experience that is more or less invariant to all people at all times and places. This is a common mistake – but it is still a mistake.

The approach suggested by Wittgenstein, if we want to get beyond this simplistic and misleading picture, is to attend to the grammar of the word 'read' – to examine how variously we use the term, in different ways on different occasions and in different social settings. Consider just a few of the many ways in which we are said 'to read' – only a few of which involve texts or text in the ordinary sense of that word:

- A blind person 'reads' a Braille text or 'reads' the contours of the path by sweeping her cane back and forth over its surface.

- A customs officer 'reads' the faces and gestures of the people being interrogated at international border crossings.
- A person 'reads' a road map to determine which is the best route to take.
- A person tells the time by 'reading' the position of the hands on the dial of a watch.
- A church-goer 'reads' a wall-painting, a fresco or a stained-glass window.
- A cabinet-maker 'reads' the grain in the wood before cutting it, or before applying a plane to its surface, or sanding it to a smooth finish.
- An experienced canoeist 'reads' the currents of the river, thus finding the most efficient channel of flowing water into which to steer the canoe.
- A seasoned farmer or a sailor 'reads' the sky in search of possible signs of change in the weather.
- An ice hockey player 'reads' the play as it is developing, and anticipates – in order successfully to intercept – a pass from an attacking player to a team-mate.
- A surfer 'reads' the wave so as to be able to catch and ride it all the way to shore.

'Reading' in short, names not one single mental activity but a large number of differing practices or processes, related by family resemblances but hardly possessing a single essence. If we want to capture some of the rough unity between these processes, we have to reach for very general and imprecise descriptions, rather than for a precise definition.

In each of these activities there is something that is read. In each of them there is some practice or activity that is shaped by the reading – that responds in some way to what is being read. In most of them that practice or activity is a matter of skills acquired over time through training, exercise, practice and apprenticeship – and reading involves a carefully trained responsiveness, a living sensitivity to the details of the thing being read. We could only say what it means to read *well* in each of these cases, however, if we paid close attention to the nature and goals of the wider practice within which this reading takes place, and the forms of attentiveness and responsiveness that feed those goals.

All this matters when we come to consider the reading of Scripture. We are not, you will recall, talking about the reading of a text in the abstract – a sequence of characters or bits of information. We are talking about the reading of a variety of actual objects used in the life of the Church and the life of individual Christians – whether it is a heavy lectern Bible, a well-thumbed and heavily highlighted pocket Bible, the screen of a smartphone displaying a Bible app, or any one of hundreds of other possibilities. These objects are handled within a whole host of reading practices, activities or performances. Each of those activities has its own specificity, and whatever the resemblances there might be between them there is no way of asking what it means to read 'well' in each case without attending to the details of the particular activity in question.

What does it mean to read Scripture well, if the reading in question is the choral singing of Psalms in a cathedral evensong? The first and most obvious answers will have to do with the quality of singing – precision of rhythm and tone, the blend of voices, the practised inhabitation of the resonances of the cathedral space. If we broaden our view, however, we might start thinking about the ways in which that singing forms part of a liturgy that allows the congregation to hear the scriptures and be caught up in prayers provided for them. The singing of the Psalms is not part of a concert-hall performance, but of a form of corporate prayer: they are sung on behalf of the congregation, and the congregation are invited to find themselves in the words – time and time again. The beauty of the singing is (or should be) ordered to this higher end.

Or consider the kind of reading involved when a student is faced with a short extract – a gobbet – of New Testament Greek in an exam, and is asked to translate it. Here, the reading involves bringing to bear a set of recently-learned skills in the declining of nouns and the conjugating of verbs, and the ability to access a mental dictionary of relevant vocabulary. To read well in this context is to demonstrate to an examiner that one has understood the vocabulary, grammar, and syntax of the Greek, and shown some skill in representing what one has found in reasonably natural English.

Or consider the kind of reading involved in the preaching of a forty-minute exegetical sermon, or in an Ignatian retreat, or in a television documentary on the Bible's hidden secrets, or in choosing a text to write in a Get Well card, or in opening a copy of the Bible at a random page to seek divine guidance, or in writing a volume of the *International Critical Commentary*.

These are all practices that are shaped by some kind of engagement with the words of the Bible. They are all practices that we could try to describe carefully and richly, and for which we could try to discern the goals in view, and what it might mean to read well within this practice.

The kind of reading well that is associated with scholarship that pivots on the past – the careful sifting of historical evidence in order to provide a plausible and cautious reconstruction of the history behind the text – will in this context appear simply as one family of reading performances, guided by one family of goals, within which 'reading well' takes one particular family of forms. It will be an open question whether and how any of the other practices of biblical reading relate to this historical-critical reading – whether and how reading well within any of these other practices relies upon or makes reference to or contributes to the performances of reading well conducted by historical critics.

For scholarship that pivots on the present, this is an important discipline: to begin with *description* of the practices of reading in the contemporary Church (or in some past period of the Church's life) and to ask what is involved in reading well in those practices, what assumptions about the nature of Scripture are involved, what questions are posed – without assuming that there is just one kind of activity properly called reading, and without assuming that all attempts to read the text are to be judged according to the canons of that one activity.

Reasoning

Amongst the many practices of reading that surround Scripture, there are practices of reasoning. If you look back to the chapters in the first main section of this book, you will find descriptions of a whole wide range of reasoning practices. Some of those reasoning practices are shaped in telling ways by attention to the words of the

Bible. Similarly, many of the practices of reading that we have been thinking about in this chapter so far involve forms of activity that, in the light of those earlier chapters, we can plausibly call practices of reasoning – practices of active settling in relation to the words of the text.

Even a practice as apparently simple as reading the Bible out loud – perhaps in a church service – involves patterns of reasoning. In order to read well, without stumbling, and capturing something of the phrasing of the text, one needs to be engaged in a complex practice of construal – seeing (or hearing) a shape within which the words ahead fall, anticipating the ways that the text might turn next. There is a practice of active settling, in the sense discussed in chapter 2, involved even here.

There are many different practices of reasoning with Scripture, however, that operate on a larger canvas – that are involved in the practices by which a pattern of life is settled or unsettled, or by which a community's or individual's settlement with the scriptural text is explored or tested. Many a sermon, for instance, might be thought of as a move in an ongoing practice of settling – and have the implicit message, 'Given the ways in which we have settled with Scripture so far, what difference should reading this particular passage make to us?' Or consider the communal discussion of Scripture in a Bible study group, or in an academic seminar. By 'reasoning with Scripture', we mean any practice of reasoning which is responsive to the words of Scripture, to the patterns and shapes of those words that can be registered within those practices.

There is no one practice of reading Scripture, no one practice of reasoning with Scripture. But neither are these practices discrete, each one parcelled away in its own isolated cupboard. Practices overlap and interact; they shade into one another, influence one another, interrupt one another. Most readers of Scripture are involved in a whole tangle of differing practices of reading and reasoning – and, perhaps, in the overlap of the multiple communities that sustain those differing practices.

From the point of view of scholarship that pivots on the present, questions about the proper use of Scripture will often be questions about these overlaps and interactions. What difference does or should it make to engagement in the practice of preaching a sermon if one is also engaged in the practice of reasoning with Scripture in an academic seminar? What difference does or should it make to engage in personal devotional reading of Scripture with the aid of published Bible notes if one is also translating gobbets of New Testament Greek while revising for exams? What difference does it make if one's church community puts on Ignatian retreats focused on the imaginative inhabitation of scriptural narratives, if the same church also encourages its leaders to train in courses where they are expected to buy, and to make use of, historical-critical commentaries?

From the point of view of scholarship that pivots on the present, questions about the relationship between devotional and critical reading, or between religious and secular, are in the first place questions about the relationship between differing (but overlapping) practices. They can't be answered in the abstract, by considering the proper form of the one mental activity called 'reading', or the one proper way of discerning the meaning of a historical text. Rather, as the previous subsection suggested, any good answer is going to begin with description – with careful, rich attention to the specificities of the practices of reading involved, attention that asks what is involved in reading well in those practices, what assumptions about the nature of Scripture are actually involved, and what questions about the cogency and truthfulness of the reading are appropriate to these specific practices.

Reading for devotion and discipleship

Some of the scriptural reading practices that one can find amongst Christian communities and individuals have as their goal growth in holiness, or a journey deeper into a life of God, or the development of Christlikeness – the shaping of life together and individually before God. And in at least some of the contexts where these practices take place, the patterns of reading are not seen as *extrinsic* to that goal, as if one could equally well achieve the goal by other means, but as *intrinsic*. It might be thought, for instance, that to be a disciple is to follow Christ well, and that part of what this means for Christian readers is that they should follow the scriptural witness to Christ well. To be a good disciple, it might therefore be thought, inherently involves reading well or being part of a community that reads well (even if it doesn't necessarily involve the skills we normally think of as literacy).

This is not, then, simply a matter of readers gleaning – or mowing – information from the text, in an effectively disembodied intellectual process. It is something quite different. This kind of reading has been characterized by Paul Griffiths as 'religious reading'.[9] To read religiously is, he says, to read 'as a lover reads, with a tensile attentiveness that wishes to linger, to prolong, to savor, and has no interest at all in the quick orgasm of consumption'.[10] It is reading in which

> the work read is understood as a stable and vastly rich resource, one that yields meaning, suggestions (or imperatives) for action, matter for aesthetic wonder, and much else. It is a treasure-house, an ocean, a mine: the deeper religious readers dig, the more ardently they fish, the more single-mindedly they seek gold, the greater will be their reward. The basic metaphors here are those of discovery, uncovering, retrieval, opening up: religious readers read what is there to be read, and what is there to be read always precedes, exceeds, and in the end supersedes its readers. There can, according to those metaphors, be no final act of reading in which everything is uncovered, in which the mine of gold has yielded all its treasure or the fish pool has been emptied of fish. Reading, for religious readers, ends only with death, and perhaps not then: it is a continuous, ever-repeated act.[11]

Such reading is, he suggests, best understood as a form of training for discipleship – and it is a form of training that is comprehensive, unsurpassable, and central. It is comprehensive because, for the religious reader, everything falls within the compass of this training. It is unsurpassable because there is no moving on from it to some higher or deeper curriculum. And it is central because it is held to give the reader's life its most basic orientation – it helps establish the goal or good that guides and shapes all the reader's practices.

Religious reading, devout reading, reading for discipleship, is reading that is pursued because it is believed that it reshapes the reader; it orients the reader towards

God. It shapes the reader's vision of the good, the goal, towards which not only this reading practice but all their practices are ultimately ordered. It trains the mind to focus on that goal, awakens the affections to yearn towards it, and strengthens the will to pursue it. It is reading understood as a spiritual discipline.

To call this reading 'spiritual' should not, however, obscure the extent to which recent theologians have seen it as, in multiple ways, a *bodily* form of reading. You will find discussion of the literal body of the reader – the physical practices of meditative reading, which involve attention to breathing, posture, silence, the taking of slow time over the business of reading. You will find attention to the corporate body within which this reading takes place – to reading as a communal activity, which need not assume the literacy of all involved, and which is intended to build up the life of the body. You will find attention to the bodily metaphors that are used to describe the practice of reading – the caressing and ingestion of the text, the text taken in as medicine that chases disease from the body. And you will find attention to the relation of reading to the Body of Christ – to the ingestion of the text as the taking in of Christ's body in a way that echoes the Eucharist, and to the text as food that helps the reader grow into Christlikeness.

Lectio divina: *Retrieving a medieval reading practice*

Discussions of religious reading amongst theologians today often refer back to practices of reading sustained in medieval monasteries. (This is an example of biblical scholarship 'beginning in the middle' of the history of Christian reading, as mentioned above.) You will find many theologians discussing various forms that prayerful, meditative reading took in monastic settings – the text read out to the eating monks over a silent meal; the practices of meditative memorization; the exploration of the multiple senses that a passage might yield when heard again and again in this context (see chapter 12 by Gerard Loughlin). You will also find many theologians advocating the retrieval of at least some aspects of these medieval reading practices in the present – and that will often be promoted by means of a strong contrast with forms of biblical reading associated with biblical scholarship that pivots on the past.

Although *lectio* came to full fruition in medieval times, and although it has undergone many changes over the centuries, it has nonetheless been a persistent tradition throughout Christian history, and one of the more distinctive and enduring modes of engaging Scripture. It is a spiritual discipline that combines reading the Word of God with practices of meditation and the life of prayer.

Lectio has frequently been understood as a dialogue. The reader listens attentively to God's voice in Scripture, and responds in prayer. Cyprian of Carthage, in a letter to his friend Donatus in the year 256, said, 'Be constant as well in prayer as in reading [*lectio*]; now speak with God, now let God speak with you, let Him instruct you in His precepts, let Him direct you.'[12] Advocates of *lectio* recognized, of course, that the dialogue could never be symmetrical. For while we are fully and unreservedly transparent to God, God is not so transparent to us. 'For our knowledge is imperfect ... For now we see in a mirror dimly, but then face to face. Now I know in part; then I shall understand fully, even as I have been understood' (1 Cor. 13:9–12

RSV). *Lectio*, was, however, understood as prayerful reading that cultivates an ever deeper friendship with God.

Writing in the fifth century, John Cassian envisioned *lectio* as a kind of 'ascending dialogue' that lifts the reader to ever higher levels of being, understanding, and delight.

> But as our mind is increasingly renewed by this study, the face of Scripture will also begin to be renewed, and the beauty of a more sacred under-standing will somehow grow with the person who is making progress. For its form is also adapted to the capacity of human intelligence, and it will appear as earthly to carnal persons and as divine to spiritual persons, such that those to whom it previously seemed wrapped in thick clouds will be unable to grasp its subtlety or endure its splendor. ... [A]ll the heavenly commands are shaped for the whole human race according to the measure of our condition.[13]

By means of *lectio divina* both reader and Scripture become mutually attuned: Scripture is so framed that it yields fruit appropriate to the situation of the person reading, and the reader in turn is slowly changed in ways that allow her to appreciate ever more fully the beauty and splendour of the face of Scripture. In Gregory the Great's memorable formula, Scripture is likened to a river, at once shallow enough for lambs to wade and deep enough for elephants to swim.[14]

Another way of speaking about *lectio divina* is to say that Scripture presents itself to us as a mirror – but Scripture is understood to be an *active* mirror; not a purely passive text lying before the human intellect, but a living, active, purifying Word in dialogue with the evolving Christian.[15] Henri de Lubac articulates well the nature of this personal, dialogical interaction between Word and reader. In the scriptural mirror,

> we learn to know our nature and our destiny; in it we also see the different stages through which we have passed since creation, the beautiful and the ugly features of our internal face. It shows us the truth of our being by pointing it out in its relation to the Creator. It is a living mirror, a living and efficacious Word, a sword penetrating at the juncture of soul and spirit, which makes our secret thoughts appear and reveals to us our heart. It tea-ches us to read in the book of experience and makes us, so to speak, our own exegesis. ... It is the Scripture that measures us, and which scrutinizes us, and which makes the fountains of living water spring forth in us ...[16]

As the reader reads Scripture, Scripture in turn 'reads' the reader – i.e. questions, examines, challenges, and interrogates them. It is the 'living' Word of God, able to respond to the life of the specific reader, searching out all the inner recesses of the reader's heart (Heb. 4:2–13).

Another common metaphor for *lectio divina* is that of drinking – but the images used are not simply of the immediate quenching of thirst. Cassian, for example, describes *lectio* as a process of stocking the cool cellars of memory, and then drawing up what has been stored for refreshment and delight.

> If, then, these things have been diligently listened to, stored in the recesses of the mind, and sealed by deep silence, afterward, like certain sweet-smelling wines ... brought forth from the vessel of your breast with a strong aroma, they will bubble up like an unceasing fountain out of the springs of experience and the watercourses of virtue, and they will pour forth continual streams as it were from the abyss of your heart.[17]

Advocates of *lectio* see it as a mode of encounter with the superabundant fullness of the Word that might only gradually yield clarity and understanding. What is initially 'taken in' from Scripture is something deep, something we delight in and feel, before we can receive it intellectually. Intellectual understanding emerges slowly:

> the successive books of Holy Scripture must be diligently committed to memory and ceaselessly reviewed. ... [for] ... the things that we have not been able to understand because our mind was busy at the time, things that we have gone through repeatedly and are laboring to memorize, we shall see more clearly afterward ... , especially when we are silently meditating at night. Thus, while we are at rest and as it were immersed in the stupor of sleep, there will be revealed an understanding of hidden meanings that we did not grasp even slightly when we were awake.[18]

Prolonged practice and continuous immersion in the practice of *lectio* results in the melding and merging of the words of Scripture with the reader's own words and experience. The Psalms in particular are read as though they were directed personally to the reader even as the faithful reader personally lifts up his prayer in response. In the words of Cassian,

> taking into himself then all the dispositions of the Psalms, he will begin to repeat them and to treat them in his profound compunction of heart not as if they were composed by the prophet but as if they were his own utterances and his own prayer. Certainly he will consider that they are directed to his own person, and he will recognize that their words were not only achieved by and in the prophet in times past but that they were daily borne out and fulfilled in him.[19]

The practice *lectio*, then, is understood as a means of reinscribing, or re-authoring, Scripture's voice in one's own prayerful utterances in response to the Word's address, and in thankful, lived application of Word in the world.

Religious reading and criticism

One of the tasks of Christian theology, then, is the tracing of practices of devout reading – paying attention to the embodied specificity of each reading practice, its goals, and its appropriate standards of excellence. And these reading practices do not exist in isolation from one another – so you will also find a great deal of theological discussion that is driven by the overlaps, the tensions, and the clashes between different reading practices.

In particular, you will find a lot of theological discussion asking how practices of religious reading, of the kind described in the previous section, can relate to practices of critical reading as they have been developed in the modern academic world and beyond. That is, you will find a lot of theological discussion asking how practices of religious reading relate to practices of reading that pivot on the past, especially of the debunking kind, and also to practices dedicated to the uncovering of the power dynamics and the forms of exclusion that shape the present.

There is no abstract answer to this question of the relationship between reading practices. The investigation has to begin (or ought to begin – though quite often it does not) with detailed attention to the specifics of the particular practices in question, asking what questions they do and don't ask, what assumptions they involve, what has to be true of the texts and of their background in order to make sense, and to what challenges they are therefore exposed. We are going to finish our chapter, therefore, not with a single neat answer as to the relationship between religious reading and critical reading, but with one example, that we hope might act as an illustration and a prompt.[20]

Earlier in this chapter, we mentioned in passing the reading of Psalm 2.

> Why do the nations conspire,
> and the peoples plot in vain?
> The kings of the earth set themselves,
> and the rulers take counsel together,
> against the Lord and his anointed, saying,
> 'Let us burst their bonds asunder,
> and cast their cords from us.'
> He who sits in the heavens laughs;
> the Lord has them in derision.
> Then he will speak to them in his wrath,
> and terrify them in his fury, saying,
> 'I have set my king on Zion, my holy hill.'
> I will tell of the decree of the Lord:
> He said to me, 'You are my son;
> today I have begotten you.
> Ask of me, and I will make the nations your heritage,
> and the ends of the earth your possession.
> You shall break them with a rod of iron,
> and dash them in pieces like a potter's vessel.'
> Now therefore, O kings, be wise;
> be warned, O rulers of the earth.
> Serve the Lord with fear,
> with trembling kiss his feet,
> or he will be angry, and you will perish in the way;
> for his wrath is quickly kindled.
> Happy are all who take refuge in him.

We noted that the very same words that have been read by many Christians as prophetic of Christ (as the true king of Zion, of whom the Lord says 'you are my son') are read by the historical critic David Clines as depicting the king of Judah scorning the desire for political freedom of a coalition of vassal kingdoms, threatening them with violence should they not abase themselves to him.

Imagine, now, a particular practice of devout reading of this Psalm. Imagine someone hearing it in a service of choral evensong in an English cathedral. Sitting in hard wooden seats, beneath stone pillars leaping to a distant roof, the congregant hears the Psalm as a stately, formal chant performed by a robed choir. She might follow the words in the Psalter at the back of the Prayer Book on the wooden shelf in front of her, or settle back in her seat and let her thoughts be carried upwards by the voices of the choir. Scripture here is not primarily something written but something heard – a pattern of sounds heard over and over again as the church's years roll by.

The rhythm and solemnity of the chant invites her to hear the words of the Psalm not as an urgent imprecation caught up in a specific historical drama, but as something more like a timeless pattern of words for reflection. Not quite timeless, however: this chanting of the Psalm occurs in a liturgy that also involves readings from the Old and New Testaments set alongside one another, bracketed by canticles in which Christ's coming is presented as the fulfilment of Israel's hopes. The Psalm's words are set, by the liturgy, in the context of this narrative of salvation – the narrative of God's providential work in Israel and its consummation in Jesus.

In such a context, how might a devout and meditative 'reader' (a hearer, in this case) understand the Psalm, as their thoughts wander through it in the midst of this liturgy? Hearing the Psalm's striking image of kingship, participants in this liturgy might well hear it as words about the Christ who is, for them, the one in whom the kingly line of Israel has come to its fulfilment. And when they hear the Psalm's language about the king of Israel being God's son, they might well hear it in the light of their belief that Jesus is the one in whom that relationship of divine sonship has its deepest and fullest expression. Participants in this liturgy will be likely to hear this Psalm in the light of the liturgy's structural embodiment of the idea that in Jesus God has taken up, transformed, and fulfilled the history of which this Psalm is an expression.

We might ask all sorts of questions about this way of reading or hearing the Psalm. One of the sets of questions we might ask, however, is how such a devout reading of the Psalm relates to the critical reading of historical scholars. Suppose the congregant were to have come to this service of evensong by walking across the road from the nearby Department of Theology and Religion, where she had sat in a seminar discussing the work of David Clines and in particular his essay on this very Psalm. What does it mean for her to move between these two contexts, and hear the words of the Psalm in both?

In part, we might simply answer that the two forms of reading have little to do with one another. The Psalm as heard in the cathedral is not heard in the context of its historical emergence, in the cut and thrust of the political dramas that lie behind it. That context has been shorn away, and it is heard now in a context more vertical (remember those soaring pillars, and the stone tracery of the roof high above) than horizontal (the complex storytelling that is the meat and drink of the history seminar).

That won't quite do, however, because the liturgy *does* place this Psalm in a story – in the midst of a history. The liturgy assumes, at the very least, that Jesus emerged from the historical background of which this Psalm is a part, and that he makes sense against that background and helps us make sense of it. By weaving together the various scriptural texts that it includes, it invites us to read the story of Jesus as a commentary upon the text of this Psalm, and the text of this Psalm as a commentary upon the story of Jesus. The congregant who has moved from seminar to cathedral might therefore appropriately find herself asking, as she sits listening to the choir, how this Psalm's vision of kingship relates to the transformation of ideas of kingship in Jesus' ministry – a question that might also be asked, albeit in a very different form, in the seminar room.

The devout reader, as she sits meditatively in the cathedral, can pursue this reflection – can make sense of the Psalm's presence in this liturgical setting, and explore the avenues of thought about her faith that it makes possible – without necessarily denying (or worrying about) the core tenets of the seminar room. That is, she can make sense of the Psalm devoutly and liturgically without denying that it can also be made sense of, and made sense of differently, in the seminar room – that it did indeed emerge in a particular historical setting centuries before Jesus, and can be made sense of in that context without any nagging remainder that would demand a different kind of reading. That is, she might not be troubled about the juxtaposition of these two contexts, these two patterns of reading, at the general methodological level.

She might, however, find herself thinking about the particular substance of Clines' analysis of the Psalm, and wondering whether that has any bearing on her devout meditations. His identification of the patterns of violence and repression present in this Psalm might persuade her to ask herself whether any such patterns have lodged themselves in her faith – in the pictures she has of Jesus' kingly rule.[21] Are her images of Jesus' rule, formed by participation in countless services like this, shaped by the narrative of a king who will *get* his enemies in the end? Do her images of Jesus as King have a whiff of the tyrant about them? Do they encourage her to fantasize about the imperious, irresistible overthrow in the end of those who have not followed Jesus? Those are questions that it is worth this devout reader asking – not as questions that overthrow her practice of religious reading, or require her to leave the cathedral as a matter of conscience, but as questions that she might properly ask of herself precisely *because* she is devout, and is seeking after holiness. They might well be 'edifying' questions: not in the sense that they are nice, pious, and heart-warming, but in the deeper sense that they are interrogative, disturbing, and potentially transformative.

So here is a particular example of how religious and critical reading might interact, in complex but potentially fruitful ways. It is not a template for a general answer, as if this was the way in which historical criticism in general will contribute to devout reading in general, but it does illustrate our more general claim – that exploring the specific connections between particular practices of reading is a proper and important task for theology, and that it properly begins in detailed description.

Conclusion

As you develop your skills as a theologian, and begin to explore more widely and deeply the roles that the reading of Scripture can play in theology, keep the following rules of thumb in mind.

Don't assume that it is obvious what kind of object the word 'Bible' or 'Scripture' means. The identification of that object can differ from reading practice to reading practice.

Don't assume that 'reading' names one simple activity, primarily inward and intellectual. Recognize that it is a name for a whole host of loosely related practices shaped by engagement with the words of a text.

Look at the specifics of the reading practices in which believers and scholars are engaged. Attend to them not simply as methods or patterns of ideas, but as bodily, corporate practices.

Ask, of each practice, what standards of excellence are internal to it – what it means to read well in this specific practice. And ask what broader vision of the good is being pursued by those who are engaged in this practice, in part by means of this practice.

Ask what questions are raised by this practice – what assumptions it makes about the nature of Scripture, what claims about history it involves, what kinds of thing it takes for granted. But also pay attention to the questions it doesn't pose, the assumptions it doesn't involve, even though they matter to other practices of reading.

Attend to the overlaps between different practices of reading, where those overlaps genuinely emerge from your attention to the specifics of each practice. Look closely, and let careful, rich description of those practices animate your analysis. And then ask, so what? What follows from the fact of this overlap? What challenges and opportunities does it create? Reading practices are not static, fixed by long usage into immovable ruts – they have histories, they evolve, and some of the energy for that evolution is generated precisely at the overlaps, the places where one reading rubs against another.

Notes

1 David J.A. Clines, 'Psalm 2 and the MLF (Moabite Liberation Front)', in *Interested Parties: The Ideology of Writers and Readers of the Hebrew Bible*, Sheffield: Sheffield Academic Press, 1995, p. 180, emphasis mine. We will come back to this example at the end of the chapter.
2 N.T. Wright, *Surprised by Hope*, London: SPCK, 2007, p. 145.
3 Oxford: OUP, 1988.
4 E.F. Davis and R.B. Hays, 'Learning to Read the Bible Again', *Christian Century*, April 20, 2004, pp. 23–4; http://www.religion-online.org/showarticle.asp?title=3047
5 Michael Prior, *The Bible and Colonialism: A Moral Critique*, Sheffield: Sheffield Academic Press, 1997, p. 92.
6 H. de Lubac, *Medieval Exegesis 1: The Four Senses of Scripture*, trans. M. Sebanc, Grand Rapids, MI: William B. Eerdmans Publishing Company, 1998, p. xxi.

7 L. Wittgenstein, *Philosophical Investigations*, trans. by G.E.M. Anscombe, Oxford: Basil Blackwell, 1953, §165.

8 Wittgenstein, *Philosophical Investigations*, §159.

9 P.J. Griffiths, *Religious Reading: The Place of Reading in the Practice of Religion*, New York and Oxford: Oxford University Press, 1999.

10 Griffiths, *Religious Reading*, p. ix.

11 Griffiths, *Religious Reading*, p. 16.

12 St Cyprian of Carthage, Epistle 1.15, in A. Roberts and J. Donaldson (eds) *Ante-Nicene Fathers*, Grand Rapids, MI: William B. Eerdmans Publishing Company, 1981, pp. 279–80.

13 *John Cassian: The Conferences*, trans. B. Ramsey, O.P., Ancient Christian Writers 57, Mahwah, NJ: Paulist Press, 1997, p. 515.

14 Gregory the Great, *Morals on the Book of Job*, dedicatory letter 'Ad Leandrum', 4 vols, trans. J. Bliss, Oxford: J.H. Parker, 1844–50.

15 For more on this 'mirroring' relationship that constitutes the reading/praying of Scripture in *lectio divina*, see L. Ayers, 'The Soul and the Reading of Scripture: A Note on Henri de Lubac', *Scottish Journal of Theology*, 61.02, 2008, pp. 173–90. The idea of an 'active' mirror is, of course, something of a mixed metaphor on the order of another familiar scriptural mixed metaphor: 'living stones'. See 1 Pet. 2:4.

16 H. de Lubac, *Medieval Exegesis 2: The Four Senses of Scripture*, trans. E.M. Macierowski, Grand Rapids, MI: William B. Eerdmans Publishing Company, 2000, p. 142.

17 *John Cassian: The Conferences*, 14.13.5; p. 518.

18 *John Cassian: The Conferences*, 14.10.4; pp. 514–15.

19 *John Cassian: The Conferences*, 2.11.4, p. 384.

20 This example is explored further in M. Higton and R. Muers, *The Text in Play: Experiments in Reading Scripture*, Eugene, OR: Cascade, 2012, ch. 7.

21 See the chapter by Jenny Daggers on the deeply problematic character of some biblical texts; namely, their patriarchy and gender injustice; see also the chapter by Rachel Muers on reading questionable traditions.

10
SCRIPTURE AND THEOLOGY
On 'proving' doctrine biblically

Kevin J. Vanhoozer

Introduction: Why scripture belongs to theology

Scripture is as vital an ingredient to the practice of Christian theology as are the stars to nautical navigation, or a play script to dramatic performance. Scripture is the 'soul' of theology, the script of the play or 'theodrama' in which the Church has been summoned to participate.[1] As such, Scripture is the key resource for speaking well of what God has done and is doing in and through the person and work of Jesus Christ, the core subject matter about which faith seeks even greater understanding. In particular, Christian theology attempts to articulate the meaning and significance of Jesus' death and resurrection 'according to the Scriptures' (1 Cor. 15:3–5).

Understanding 'according to the Scriptures' – being 'biblical' in that sense – is part and parcel of being 'Christian'. Theologians must show how Scripture authorizes their proposals about God and everything else in relation to God. Even more importantly, theologians must help disciples conform their lives – their heads, hearts, and hands – to what Scripture shows God to be doing to renew all things in and through Jesus Christ. Scripture's role in theology is not simply a matter of providing raw material for systems of doctrine but rather of forming a people able rightly to participate in God's missionary outreach to the world. The aim of theology is to inculcate right theodramatic practice, the ability to participate fittingly in the dramatic subject matter of the Scriptures.

Christian theology is the disciplined intellectual effort to refine the dross of mere opinion about God into the gold of knowledge, gold mined largely from scriptural shafts. It is the attempt to understand the gospel – God's drama of redemption – that new state of affairs 'in Christ' in which the Church has been caught up. It is also the disciplined effort to train disciples to make judgments and decisions that conform to the wisdom of God displayed in the person and work of Jesus Christ, the climax of the drama of redemption. Theology studies Scripture – the authoritative transcript of what God has said and done – in order to help the Church understand its own role in God's drama of redemption, the story of God's making all things new (2 Cor. 5:17). We can see where the biblical plot is heading by looking at the drama's end, that future point where Christ will be 'all in all' (Eph. 1:23; cf. 1 Cor. 15:28): 'And the one who was seated on the throne said, "See, I am making all things new." Also he said, "Write this, for these words are trustworthy and true"' (Rev. 21:5).

'Scripture' says more than 'Bible'. One can read the Bible as literature or study it as a document of the university, but to call it 'Scripture' is to acknowledge its authoritative use in the Church. It is the Church's holy transcript and script, a record of what God has done for the world and of what the Church ought to do in grateful response. To speak of 'Scripture' is to indicate that the Bible is more than raw material to be worked or processed; rather, 'Scripture' indicates that the theologian will hearken to the authority of the biblical text, respecting 'the way the words go' – the diverse literary forms, canonical context, and Christological content – and following the signs and signposts to the reality to which they point.

Practicing Christian theology demands that we give an account of what Scripture is, what it is for, and how to read it. To the extent that these accounts involve God, we find ourselves having to articulate theology's first principles – a 'first theology,' as it were. For we can only speak of the God of Jesus Christ on the basis of the Scriptures, and the biblical texts are 'Scripture' – an authoritative guide for the Church, its designated community of interpreters – by virtue of their distinct relationship to God and his purpose. Not surprisingly then, theologians have accorded special status to Scripture as the Word of God for most of Church history. The tendency in much modern theology, by contrast, has been to view Scripture as an expression of human experience of God. But even this proves the general rule: one's view of God affects one's view of Scripture (and vice versa). Scripture and theology are joined at the hip.

Biblical authority in theory and practice

We begin with some preliminary distinctions. First, we must distinguish *viewing* from *using* Scripture. It is one thing to hold a high view of Scripture (e.g. a theory of its verbal inspiration, namely, the idea that the Spirit of God guided the prophets' and apostles' choice of words such that what they wrote was God's word as well as human discourse), quite another to know how, where, and when to use Scripture to establish a theological proposal. There is no more necessary correlation between a person's having a high view and subsequent right use of Scripture than there is between a person's being in awe of calculus and her ability to solve differential equations. Professing a high doctrine of Scripture is one thing, knowing how to use Scripture to formulate doctrine something else.

A second distinction, between *interpreting* and *using* Scripture, is equally important. It is one thing exegetically to determine what a text originally meant, quite another to say what it entails for the Church today. Though some theologians take translation to be the best picture of the relation between Scripture and theology, others insist that theology does more than restate what the Bible says when it deploys Scripture in an argument. It is one thing to translate Scripture, another to use it to authorize a theological proposal. David Kelsey's *Proving Doctrine: The Uses of Scripture in Recent Theology*[2] is the most comprehensive analysis of our subject to date. Kelsey proposes some helpful diagnostic questions: What aspect of Scripture is authoritative and why? What role does Scripture play in the argument and how does it authorize a given theological proposal? More systematically, we can distinguish questions about (1) *text*: how does a theologian view Scripture? (2) *context*: how does a theologian use Scripture to argue for or authorize a doctrinal proposal? (3) *pretext*: on what basis does a theologian decide to view and use Scripture? Kelsey also examines seven cases of theologians who argue from biblical texts to Christian doctrine and effectively shows that they appeal to Scripture's authority in several different ways: as teaching, as symbol, as historical information, as myth, etc.

There is no higher court of appeal than God's word, which is why many Christian theologians wrap themselves in the cloak of biblical authority. The real problem of 'Scripture and theology' only arises, however, when interpreters disagree about what God is saying. Whose reading or use of Scripture counts, and why? This was the burning issue in what, according to Mark Noll, was perhaps the first real crisis over biblical authority in the United States: the Civil War. The issue was slavery, the discussion was political, and the stakes were the highest possible. To the Reverend Henry Ward Beecher, in the North, slavery was a conspicuous evil that the Bible clearly condemned and for which the whole nation had to repent. By contrast, to James Henley Thornwell, in the South, slavery was an institution that the Bible indicated was a 'good and merciful' way of organizing labor 'which Providence has given us'.[3]

Individuals and denominations alike split over this contentious issue. It was all too tempting to turn Scripture into the ultimate piece of propaganda, either for or against slavery: 'In the uncertain days of late 1860 and early 1861, the pulpits of the United States were transformed into instruments of political ideology.'[4] The pro-slavery view initially had an easier time of it, as many biblical passages (e.g. Lev. 25:44–46) appeared, often implicitly but sometimes explicitly, to condone slavery. Even in the New Testament, the apostle Paul says 'Servants, obey your masters in all things' (Col. 3:22). Southern preachers were quick to point out that Jesus never explicitly condemned the practice of slavery. The anti-slavery northern preachers made the case for abolition not by citing chapter and verse but by appealing, with Jonathan Blanchard, to the Bible's general principles, like justice and righteousness, and central symbols, like the image of God. The conflict was to some extent between those who appealed to particular texts and those who appealed to the broad sweep of the biblical message. Harriet Beecher Stowe showed the dead-end of appealing to particular verses in her *Uncle Tom's Cabin*. In one telling passage, passengers on a steamboat carrying slaves down the Ohio River throw biblical passages at one another: one quotes Genesis 9:25 ('Cursed be Canaan: a servant of servants shall he be') while another retorts with the Golden Rule, as if citing Scripture were itself a kind of argument (though, as we shall see below, that is too simplistic a picture). Noll's verdict on this stand-off is deeply ironic: 'It was left to those consummate theologians, the Reverend Doctors Ulysses S. Grant and William Sherman, to decide what in fact the Bible actually meant.'[5]

The use and abuse of Scripture in theology

What does it mean to be biblical in one's theology, to demonstrate a particular doctrine to be biblical? It should already be apparent that this is no idle, or easy, query. Why does it matter? All Christians agree that God is the ultimate authority whose rightful say-so derives from his being the author and originator of all things, visible and invisible. If Scripture has authority, then, it is because it is somehow related to God's revelatory and redemptive activity. For many theologians, the Bible is not merely a description of what God is doing in the world but a vehicle of God's own communicative action, a 'living and active' divine word (Heb. 4:12).

The Bible is authoritative for theology because it is more than a human record of religious experience. It is ultimately God's word and divine address, the varied verbal means that God has chosen to communicate his covenant purpose for Israel and the Church. Only speech renders behavior unambiguous: we would not know God or what God was up to in the world unless we had actual words from God. And this is precisely what Scripture claims to be: divine discourse, where discourse is what someone (God) says about something (the covenant; Jesus Christ) to someone (the covenant community) in some way (the various forms of biblical literature).

Theologians differ regarding the nature and extent of the domains over which the Bible exercises authority. Some claim that Scripture's authority extends to all areas of human life and thought, including science; others maintain that its authority is limited to matters of faith and practice. Kelsey notes that there is no single way to use Scripture in the course of making theological arguments. In some arguments, the conclusion follows logically from the premises. 'God is love' (1 Jn. 4:8) is a good example. Here the theological conclusion is identical with the biblical premise upon which it is based, reinforcing the idea that theology is simply a 'translation' of Scripture's message. Most theological arguments, however, are not so straightforward.

Kelsey draws on Stephen Toulmin's *The Uses of Argument*[6] and his analysis of what it is to make a case for something. To make a case for something is to give grounds for one's claims. Consider the following theological claim: 'God has endowed all men and women with certain inalienable rights.' Among the grounds given to support this claim are biblical texts that speak of God creating human beings in his image (Gen. 1:26–27) and forbidding murder because humans bear this image (Gen. 9:6). Just as important as these biblical *data*, however, are the *warrants* that authorize the move from data to conclusion, and the *backing* that supports the warrant. For example, one warrant for the claim that God has endowed men and women with certain inalienable rights is that Genesis is divinely inspired and affords us insight into God's intention for the created order.

A particular conclusion may be authorized in different ways, however, raising the question whether Scripture is best used as data, warrant, and/or backing. Paul Tillich is a case in point. According to Kelsey, Tillich views Scripture as authoritative because it both expresses and occasions religious experience. Specifically, Tillich appeals to the Gospels not as accurate factual records according to modern methods of historiography, but primarily as symbolic expressions of the disciples' experience of Jesus as the revelation of God.[7] The picture of Jesus Christ symbolically discloses what Tillich calls 'the power of new being' (i.e. the courage to affirm life despite experiences of existential anguish). Tillich justifies this use of Scripture by providing an account of the way religious symbols function in general, and his backing for this warrant is not a biblical text but an appeal to the phenomenology of religious experience. Clearly, he is using Scripture, yet the backing and warrant of his argument seem to rely more on existentialist philosophy than Scripture itself. At best, Scripture for Tillich is illustrative rather than constitutive of the symbolic disclosure of the power of new being. Given the 'mixed parentage' of Tillich's argument, then, it is difficult to discern whether or not, in what way, and to what extent his proposal – that Jesus Christ is the power of new being – is 'biblical'.

As concerns the use of Scripture in theology, it is often easier to identify bad rather than good practice, ways in which some *wrongly* handle the word of truth (cf. 2 Tim. 2:15): 'There never has been an evil cause in the world that has not become more evil if it has been possible to argue it on biblical grounds.'[8] P.T. Forsyth concurs: 'There is nothing you cannot prove from parts of the Bible.'[9] Jesus' words in John 15:6 were apparently thought to provide a warrant for the medieval practice of burning heretics. While negative examples can be instructive, it is better to learn to avoid abusing the Scriptures in the first place. As with logical fallacies, so with vicious uses of Scripture: one has a better chance of avoiding them when one learns how to identify them. The good news is that Scripture itself identifies prideful habits of its wrongful use; it says that God desires mercy and steadfast love, not ritual sacrifice or formulaic pieties (Mt. 7:21; 9:13). In Forsyth's words: 'the Bible cures the wounds the Bible makes. It pulls down the errors it was misused to build.'[10]

'Lead us not into temptation' is an apt petition for those of us inclined to use Scripture for our own purposes and agendas. This is not the place to provide a comprehensive encyclopedia of biblical malpractice. Nor do I wish to point an accusatory finger at one theological party only. N.T. Wright has catalogued misreadings of the theological 'right' (e.g. the materialist 'health and wealth' understanding of biblical promises) and the 'left' (e.g. the cultural relativist claim that the strange old world of the Bible cannot be taken seriously in the modern world).[11] A brief representative sampling of typical fallacies that occur when theologians too hastily press Scripture into theological service will nevertheless help us to identify common errors – interpretive *vices* – that many need to unlearn. This is the first step towards acquiring interpretive virtues, such as honesty, attentiveness, humility, and obedience.[12]

A first set of abuses occurs on the lexical level. Some theologians who have a high view of the Bible as the Word of God develop doctrine from word studies alone. *Ekklesia* is a compound word ('called out of'), but the authors of the New Testament probably did not have the etymology of the term in mind when they used it. It is not the etymologies but the discourse that is authoritative: what the authors were saying/doing with their words. Word studies are helpful to a point, but it is important to keep in mind the difference between words and concepts. The same word can carry different meanings, and the same concept can be expressed by a variety of verbal means. For example, even if *monogenes* in John 3:16 means 'one and only' rather than 'only begotten', there may be other, less direct, grounds on which to ground the Nicene–Constantinopolitan Creed's claim that the Son was eternally begotten ('begotten of the Father before all worlds'). Dictionaries and concordances are helpful servants but terrible masters of divinity.

A second set of abuses occurs on the literary and canonical levels. One particularly pernicious mistake on the *literary* level is that of assigning the wrong kind of truth claim to a text by misidentifying its genre. For example, reading Genesis 1 as if it were science or, conversely, reading historical narrative as if it were myth are only two of the most egregious examples of how words can be made violently to go against their textual grain. Theologians use Scripture against the *canonical* grain when they (a) ignore or reject passages of Scripture that challenge what they are saying or present an opposing viewpoint or (b) exaggerate certain biblical teachings and exclude others.[13]

Perhaps the most infamous theological practice as concerns the use of Scripture is 'proof-texting'. On this view, an isolated verse of the Bible serves as a datum that directly underwrites a theological conclusion. The more such verses or supports one can find, the better: one verse, one vote. For example, Arians argue against the deity of the Son by claiming the Son to be a creature, albeit the highest one, citing Colossians 1:15 in support: 'He is the image of the invisible God, the firstborn of all creation.' The picture of theology as an inductive science holds both lay and professional theologians captive. It is all too tempting to lift texts out of their historical and literary contexts. Moreover, it is often far from self-evident how the biblical texts in question actually bear on the theological matter under discussion.

Charting the uses of Scripture in theology

How then do theologians derive and establish doctrine from Scripture? It would be wrong to treat biblical texts as if they were premises and propositions in a proof of Euclidean geometry. Scripture is not a collection of freestanding axioms but a library of different kinds of literature in which the parts make sense only in light of the whole. We may nevertheless speak of proving doctrine in the sense of testing and establishing it as a faithful and reliable rendering of what Scripture says. Doctrine then proves itself true by directing disciples rightly to participate in the drama of redemption – what the Father is doing in Christ through the Spirit to renew the world – that is the ultimate subject matter of Scripture.

Kelsey concludes from his analysis of the diverse ways theologians use Scripture that the kind of authority one accords Scripture is tied up with one's decision as to what Christianity is all about, which itself derives from a sense of how God is involved with Scripture. In other words, a theologian's use of Scripture follows from her prior insight – or 'imaginative judgment', to use Kelsey's term – regarding the essence of Christianity and the mode of God's presence in the Church. Theologians 'construe' Scripture – see it *as* this or that (e.g. as doctrine or story or symbol) – on the basis of how they think God is relating to the people of God via the text. B.B. Warfield holds the teaching of the Bible to be its authoritative aspect because he construes God's presence in terms of revelation and salvation in terms of believing certain things.[14] By contrast, Elisabeth Schüssler Fiorenza locates the authoritative aspect of Scripture only in those texts that transcend and criticize their patriarchal culture because she construes God's presence primarily in terms of justice – delivering from social oppression – rather than truth.[15] Call it 'Kelsey's Rule': one's view and use of Scripture is ineluctably tied up with one's view of God (and vice versa).

To this point we have distinguished between (1) the theory and practice of biblical authority and (2) interpreting vs. using Scripture. It is important that we do not confuse holding a high view of Scripture with obeying it, a mere profession of Scripture with its actual practice, or deploying the Bible to shore up our own agendas and ideologies with submitting them to the scrutiny of the Scriptures. A final distinction is in order before we turn to the task of charting the various theological uses of Scripture. Let us distinguish *biblical* data, warrants, and backing from their *extrabiblical* counterparts. This distinction complicates our initial query – 'What does it mean to be biblical?' – for even biblical authors use extrabiblical data (e.g. Lk. 1:1–4). Merely quoting Scripture is no guarantee of correct doctrine, as the aforementioned example of the Arians makes clear. The real issue concerns the categories and conceptual framework – the *systems* – that govern one's use of Scripture. Note well: the concept of the 'Trinity' is, strictly speaking, unbiblical (in the sense that the actual term is not in Scripture), though arguably it accords with the text. We come, then, to a parting of the methodological ways in which one uses Scripture in theology: does Scripture rule the way in which one deploys extrabiblical categories, or does a conceptual framework gleaned from somewhere else than Scripture govern one's view of God and what Christianity is all about? Theology that is 'in accordance with the Scriptures' (1 Cor. 15:3) is careful to let the biblical testimony to the economy of redemption (i.e. the outworking or 'play' of the divine drama) rather than some other system of thought (i.e. metaphysical speculation or general human experience) govern one's thinking about God.

We begin our charting exercise by considering positions that construe the Bible's authority as either primarily doctrinal (i.e. propositional) or narrative. The two poles of our first axis, then, are *statements* and *stories*.

Proposition / statement————————————————narrative / story

Thomas Aquinas construes Scripture as divinely revealed knowledge necessary for human salvation. Theology is a science unto itself whose special object is divinely revealed truth: the *sacra doctrina* found in the articles of faith found in *sacra pagina*.[16] Many contemporary Evangelicals follow in the wake of Aquinas and Warfield, construing Scripture as propositional revelation and viewing the information conveyed as its authoritative aspect. Modern critics of this approach, noting the advances in science and history, worry that it fails sufficiently to take extrabiblical knowledge into account. Others object that the propositional approach turns Scripture into an epistemic criterion rather than a means of grace, thus encouraging a biblical variation on a foundationalist (modernist!) theme.[17] Still others (e.g. N.T. Wright) resist its tacit suggestion that the abstract set of propositional truths distilled from the text has more authority than the text of Scripture itself, thus implying that God gave us the wrong kind of book. This concern for the Bible's original form takes us to the other side of the spectrum.

The Bible is largely narrative in nature, but only in the late twentieth century did this fact take on theological significance. It was Karl Barth who viewed Christology – the attempt to answer Jesus' question 'Who do you say that I am?' – as oriented not to questions of substance and metaphysics but to history and narrative. Theology is a matter of faith seeking understanding, and Scripture is narrative; hence, knowing how to follow a story is as important as knowing how to follow a logical argument. According to Kelsey, Barth construes Scripture's authority in terms of its ability to 'render an agent' in narrative. Scripture's authority for theology lies in its narrative renderings of the character and identity of Jesus Christ, and thus the nature of God. To say 'God is love' is, for Barth, not to make a metaphysical claim so much as it is to describe a pattern of personal action: 'In this is love, not that we loved God but that he loved us and sent his Son to be the atoning sacrifice for our sins' (1 Jn. 4:10).

The best theological practice is to do justice to *all* the various forms of biblical discourse. That means acknowledging the role of statements and stories alike. It is not necessary to deny the propositional component to Scripture in order to acknowledge the authority of biblical narrative; one only has to remember that statements must be read in the context of the broader story. What kind of authority might a story exercise in addition to rendering personal identity? N.T. Wright thinks that stories do more than illustrate truths or reveal a person's character. The gospel story does not merely describe the way in which God is renewing creation in and through Jesus Christ, but is itself an *active ingredient* in the process. Wright believes, with Kelsey, that biblical authority is ultimately a matter of *shaping Christian identity*. Specifically, we use Scripture 'in order to be refreshed in our memory and understanding of the story within which we ourselves are actors, to be reminded where it has come from and where it is going to, and hence what our own part within it ought to be'.[18] Wright compares the situation of the Church to that of an acting company trying to perform a Shakespeare play whose fifth act had been lost. Scripture gives an authoritative account of the first four acts, and it is incumbent upon the Church to continue the drama of redemption in a way that befits the script/story/Scriptures.[19]

Though 'proposition' and 'narrative' cover a multitude of uses, we need another axis fully to do justice to the various ways in which theologians actually engage Scripture. Narratives divide into histories and stories, propositions into lower-level data and higher-level principles. Let us therefore take as our second axis (vertical rather than horizontal) the difference between the earthly and literal on the one hand and the heavenly (i.e. ideal) and figurative on the other. At the one end of this vertical spectrum (i.e. 'from below'), theologians take biblical statements and stories as empirical data about 'what we have heard, what we have seen with our eyes, what we have looked at and touched with our hands' (1 Jn. 1:1). At the other end (i.e. 'from above'), theologians use the propositions and narratives as expressing something about the mysteries of faith or even being itself. The following chart thus combines the two axes, allowing us to place a particular theologian's use of Scripture not simply along a single spectrum but rather in one of four quadrants (I–IV) on a comprehensive grid (see Figure 10.1) that allows us to position all of the theologians in Kelsey's case studies as well as others that he does not discuss.

The chart represents both positive (i.e. virtuous) and pathological (i.e. vicious) uses of Scripture. Here is the key principle: *follow the way the biblical words go*. This means appealing to propositions as propositions, images as images, stories as stories, etc. It is therefore incumbent upon theologians to discern what kind of discourse they are dealing with in a given biblical passage. It is also crucial to recognize that the Bible is made up of a variety of forms of discourse (Heb. 1:1). The circle in the

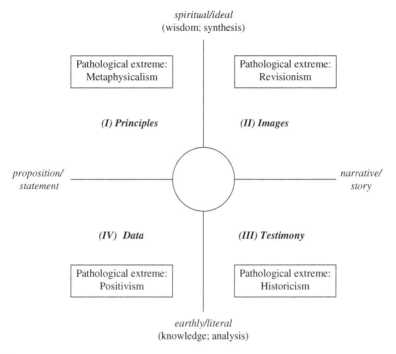

spiritual/ideal
(wisdom; synthesis)

Pathological extreme:
Metaphysicalism

Pathological extreme:
Revisionism

(I) Principles

(II) Images

proposition/
statement

narrative/
story

(IV) Data

(III) Testimony

Pathological extreme:
Positivism

Pathological extreme:
Historicism

earthly/literal
(knowledge; analysis)

Figure 10.1

middle of the chart in Figure 10.1 represents the set of right uses of Scripture. To be biblical is to be sensitive to the variety of biblical discourse, acknowledging statements as statements and stories as stories. Being biblical means avoiding the trap of thinking that *all* of Scripture should be used in one way only (e.g. as propositional information). The rectangles represent various pathological (i.e. monological) extremes. Good theological practice depends on having interpretive ears attuned to the diverse voices speaking in the Scriptures.

Quadrant I features theologians who view biblical propositions as expressing not empirical data but higher, theoretical or timeless truths that may be systematized, perhaps with a little help from philosophy. For example, on one telling of the history of doctrine, classical theists read the name of God revealed in Exodus 3:14 ('I am who I am') for all its philosophical worth and discovered the so-called 'metaphysics of Exodus'. 'I am who I am' became 'the one who is' – an epithet that enabled scholastic theologians to ascribe any number of properties (e.g. simplicity; impassibility) to God as perfect being. Theologians in this first quadrant rightly recognize that Christianity is a matter of divine revelation interpreting divine redemption: God has acted and spoken, especially in the person of Jesus Christ, making himself known in intelligible statements. The tendency in this first quadrant, then, is to focus on divine revelation as propositional truth. The accompanying danger – call it the pathological extreme – is the temptation to let the categories of some extratextual philosophy (i.e. metaphysics) coordinate and govern these biblical truths.

Theologians in the second quadrant (II) take as their authoritative aspect in Scripture not its propositional *principles* but its storied *images* (e.g. symbols; metaphors; types). These various forms of figurative speech are the means by which the biblical authors express (and then lead their readers to experience) the revelatory and redemptive significance of the event of Jesus Christ. For example, a number of patristic and medieval theologians read the Song of Songs not as an erotic poem or a marital love song but rather as a typological or allegorical picture of the mutual love of Christ and the Church. Theologians rightly practice biblical authority when they let Scripture not only inform their minds but also transform the desires of their hearts. The pathological extreme in this quadrant (i.e. liberal revisionism) is the temptation to dislodge the biblical images from their canonical context and appropriate them to some extratextual framework. This is Kelsey's worry about Paul Tillich. In taking the gospel stories as myth, Tillich makes the history of Jesus Christ 'logically dispensable': what counts is the image rather than the reality of Jesus' death and resurrection, an image that Tillich puts at the service of his existentialist philosophy.

Theologians in the next quadrant (III) also see narrative as the authoritative aspect of Scripture, but tend to construe it more as *testimony* to revelation in history than as symbol or myth. Irenaeus' ancient Rule of Faith, that summary of the Bible's storyline that connects the God of Israel to the Father of Jesus Christ, is a prime example. In the twentieth century, Wolfhart Pannenberg emphasized the apocalyptic nature of Jesus' history: the New Testament testimony to his death and resurrection is not simply a record of a past event but a preview of the end of history itself. For Herman Bavinck, similarly, Scripture is no mere record of revelation in history from which it is detached but, on the contrary, it is part and parcel of the history of revelation of which it is an organic part. Theologians in this quadrant rightly hear the bass rhythm of redemptive history that undergirds the melody of theology and the songs of faith. The core of Christian theology is the message of a historical narrative: the good news that God has found a way to us in Jesus Christ. Here the pathological extreme is the tendency to treat history as naturalistic rather than redemptive, and to use Scripture as evidence for the history of religion (i.e. historicism) rather than testimony to redemptive history.

The focus in the final quadrant (IV) is again on propositions, though here the tendency is to take them as conveying various kinds of empirical information (data) rather than timeless metaphysical truths (though these crop up as well). Here it may be helpful to recall the distinction between *fides qua creditur* (i.e. 'the faith that believes' – the subjective faith that trusts in God) and *fides quae creditur* (i.e. 'the faith believed' – the content that Christians confess). Understanding the faith – the task of theology – involves setting forth the substance of what Christians believe, on the basis of Scripture, about any number of topics in relation to God: the origins of life; the nature and destiny of human beings; the problem of evil, etc. Without some propositional content, Christian theology would be reduced to a vague sentiment of good will, an organism with no backbone. The pathological extreme in this quadrant, sometimes associated with fundamentalism, is a kind of positivism in which discrete packets of biblical data are affirmed in isolation from the broad narrative sweep of Scripture and without regard for the results of modern learning, including biblical scholarship.

As a rough approximation, we might say that the pathologies in the upper quadrants (I and II) make the Bible subservient to some *external* framework (i.e. some -*ism*), while the two in the lower quadrants (III and IV) fail sufficiently to recognize the Bible's own *internal* framework (i.e. the unified narrative of redemptive history). Yet each of the quadrants also represents a legitimate theological use of Scripture, for each recognizes an aspect of what Scripture *is* (e.g. principles, images, testimony, data). Theologies are in accordance with the Scripture when they are attuned to these different forms of discourse, for Christian theology is a matter not of informing the head but of transforming one's whole being – one's heart, mind, soul, and strength. Doing theology is not simply a matter of organizing information but of becoming the kind of person who can rightly participate in God's ongoing mission in the world – what we have termed the 'theodrama'. The goal is to become what C. S. Lewis calls 'little Christs'.[20] The various discourses in the Bible are an important means for the formation of Christian character and wisdom. Christian theologians need to develop canonical competence: the ability to follow the way the various words point to Jesus Christ and enable us to participate as witnesses to his work and as members of his family, the Church. For theology's ultimate aim is to cultivate persons with holy wisdom: disciples who have the ability to articulate, and advance, the reconciling action of the evangelical drama (2 Cor. 5:18–19).

Between biblicism and christocentrism

One particular strategy for using Scripture in theology deserves special mention. 'Biblicism' raises the question of whether the Bible is fundamentally about Jesus Christ or something else, and whether the Bible can be rightly used as a general knowledge handbook that tells us how the heavens go rather than being a special covenant book that tells us how to go to heaven. According to Christian Smith, 'biblicism' names a theory and practice of biblical authority that emphasizes the infallibility, self-evident meaning, internal consistency, and universal applicability of the Bible. For biblicists, Scripture speaks authoritatively on any number of topics, from economics and politics to dieting and dating. Smith, a sociologist, presents numerous examples of books by biblicists that purport to help people find biblical solutions to various problems of daily living.[21]

The main problem with biblicism, says Smith, is that it is practically impossible. It fails as an account of authority for the simple yet indisputable reason that the same biblical texts yield very different results: 'Even among presumably well-intentioned readers – including many evangelical biblicists – the Bible, after their very best efforts to understand it, says and teaches very different things about most significant topics.'[22] As William Blake poetically puts it: 'Both read the Bible day and night/But thou read'st black where I read white.'[23] In short: biblicism as a practice of biblical authority founders on the problem of pervasive interpretive pluralism, namely, the phenomenon that even those who agree *that* the Bible speaks authoritatively on all doctrinal and ethical matters cannot agree on *what* the Bible actually says.

William Newton Clarke's 1905 Yale Divinity School lectures, published as *The Use of the Scriptures in Theology*,[24] addressed this very problem early in the twentieth century, navigating a narrow way between modern biblical criticism and a biblicism that maintained verbal inspiration. Clarke accepts the results of critical biblical studies, arguing that we use the Bible rightly only when we use it 'for just what it is'. Biblicists mistakenly try to make the Bible into something it is not: an answer book from heaven. Clarke's view of what Scripture is clearly affects the way he thinks theologians ought to use it. For example, he considers the practice of using Scripture as equal throughout to be theologically distorting: 'It is the prime need of theology to distinguish the Christian element in the Scriptures from everything else that lies beside it there.'[25] Only by assuming the equal authority of the law, the Psalms, the prophets, Paul, and Jesus could we defend the practice of proof-texting. Clarke here anticipates the problem of biblicism and pervasive interpretive pluralism a century before Smith: 'No man ever exactly reproduced the Bible in theology, or stopped making theology when he had reached the end of his biblical material.'[26]

The way forward for Clarke is to identify and isolate 'the Christian element' in Scripture and to give it pride of place as the nugget of theological gold amidst the historical and cultural dross. As to the non-Christian elements in the Bible, well, Clarke denies that they bear authority. What is 'the Christian element' in Scripture? Clarke responds by pointing to revelation of God in Christ: 'That is Christian which enters into or accords with the view of divine realities which Jesus Christ revealed.'[27] Specifically, Jesus makes known the gracious, loving character of God. This is the Christian element in Scripture, and any doctrine or conception of God that does not correspond to Christ's view of God must be banished from theology. It follows for Clarke that just because something is *biblical* does not mean that it is *Christian*. On the contrary, Christ's understanding of God functions as a critical principle that enables Clarke to separate the Christian sheep from the sub-Christian, cultural goats as he walks through biblical pastures.

The key question for Scripture and theology is no longer 'Where is it written' but 'does it accord with Christ's view of God?' Clarke shrugs aside the objection that this criterion is too vague. The Bible may not always be clear, but apparently Christ is. Clarke goes on to reject the doctrines of propitiation and imputed righteousness – the idea that Jesus, by dying on the cross, takes the wrath of God due sinners onto himself and ascribes his innocence to sinners who place their faith in him – on the grounds that Jesus 'had no place for the idea that God holds himself aloof from the sinful'.[28] Furthermore, the Jewish hope in a Davidic king is according to Clarke a *pre-Christian* element, thus the expectation that Jesus will return is not Christian teaching but a pre-Christian idea that influenced the apostles. In Clarke's hands, the Christian principle – Jesus' doctrine of God – becomes a tool with which to sift out the historically transient from the genuinely transcendent. Broadly speaking, then, Scripture informs theology not by direct and authoritative statements on specific topics but by reforming our doctrine of God: 'We must transfer our faith from the book that reveals God in Christ, to God in Christ whom the book reveals – from the telescope to the sun.'[29]

Smith's constructive proposal is remarkably similar to Clarke's: both see Scripture as authoritative for theology by virtue of its focus on Jesus Christ as the key to understanding God, humanity, and God's relationship to humanity. Smith and Clarke represent a tendency, identified especially with Karl Barth, to use Scripture in theology *christocentrically*. Instead of expecting Scripture to speak directly to every theological issue, as in biblicism, christocentrism is the practice of using Scripture indirectly, approaching issues through the single lens of the gospel of Christ: 'We only, always, and everywhere read scripture in view of its real subject matter: Jesus Christ.'[30] Smith observes that working with such a 'canon within the canon' is inevitable – we always read some biblical texts in light of others – though he insists that the right canon-defining canon 'must only and always be Jesus Christ'.[31] How do we come to know Jesus Christ? Here Smith replies that it is less a matter of picking and choosing biblical texts than it is appealing to 'the real and living person and work of Jesus Christ' who makes himself available through the Lord's Supper and in the communion of saints through the Holy Spirit.

The christocentric approaches of Clarke and Smith provide a helpful material corrective to Kelsey's formal notion of construing Scripture inasmuch as they remind us of the importance of attending not only to the wording of the text but also to its subject matter. A theologian's use of the Bible depends not only on his or her imaginative construal of the way in which God is present to the community via Scripture, then, but also on the manner in which Jesus Christ is seen to be present in Scripture and thus in the community. However, christocentrism as a practice of interpreting and using Scripture for theology is just as likely to fall prey to pervasive interpretive pluralism as biblicism is. As Jaroslav Pelikan demonstrates in his *Jesus Through the Centuries*, each age answers Jesus' question 'Who do you say that I am?' in its own way.[32] The problem, then, is that of normative specification: whose Jesus, and which Christology, should serve as our template for 'the Christian element'? Should theologians defer to the Jesus as depicted in the Gospels or the historically reconstructed construct of the Jesus Seminar? It is all too tempting to project our own values – medieval asceticism, Victorian morality, or postmodern tolerance – onto the figure of Jesus, as well as onto God. The problem becomes particularly acute when one is tempted to play off Jesus' statements about the love and mercy of God (Jn. 14:23; Lk. 6:35–36) with others that stress divine wrath and judgment (Mt. 10:34–38; 23–25).

A way forward may be to distinguish a naive biblicism that attempts to bring biblical data (and biblical data alone) directly to bear on various issues, and a critically biblicist christocentrism that regards the Bible not as the sole source of knowledge for life but rather as the supreme norm for speaking well of Jesus Christ. We cannot rightly say who Christ is for us apart from the authorized depictions of his person and work in the Scriptures: 'all talk of Christ is sustained first and last by its attention to the scriptural text.'[33] Unless theology can show where in Scripture an idea or claim may be found and how it is grounded, it lacks Christian adequacy. More pointedly: unless we acknowledge an authoritative Scripture, the confession 'Jesus is Lord and Savior' will be either meaningless or else prey to pervasive interpretive pluralism. Barth himself was well aware of the need for an exegetical foundation to his christocentric approach: '[Theology] can know the Word of God only at second hand, only in the mirror and echo of the biblical witnesses.'[34] We therefore turn to examine several virtuous practices of using Scripture that view theology itself as a form of discipleship which follows the way the biblical words go on the grounds that Scripture is itself the risen Christ's own commissioned testimony, the written means of his self-proclamation as Lord and Savior.[35]

Biblical thinking: The canonical pedagogy of reason and imagination

Jesus Christ is both Word of God (Jn. 1:14) and a speaker in his own right. Most importantly for our purposes, Jesus came proclaiming, doing theology by identifying himself with the long-awaited kingdom of God promised in the Hebrew Scriptures. According to Luke's gospel, he begins his public ministry by reading from Isaiah – 'The Spirit of the Lord is upon me, because he has anointed me to bring good news to the poor' (Isa. 61:1) – only to draw the astounding conclusion 'Today this Scripture has been fulfilled in your hearing' (Lk. 4:16–21). Christian theology arguably begins with this 'Big Bang': Jesus' use of Israel's Scripture to interpret his person and work. Using Scripture to identify God and his salvific purposes is arguably Christian theology's oldest practice, one inaugurated by Jesus himself.[36] Jesus' use of Scripture to identify himself therefore represents the paradigmatic pattern for the Christian theologian's use of Scripture in general.

Of course, not everyone agreed with Jesus' use of Scripture. Luke's temptation narrative depicts the devil using Scripture theologically too, in this case to challenge Jesus' interpretation of his messianic vocation. The devil quotes Psalm 91:11–12, a sober reminder that merely quoting Scripture falls short of what is required: 'If you are the Son of God, throw yourself down from here, for it is written, "He will command his angels concerning you, to protect you"' (Lk. 4: 9–10). Jesus replies with another quotation, this time from Deuteronomy 6:16: 'It is said, "Do not put the Lord your God to the test"' (Lk. 4:12). Case closed – but how? Why does Jesus' proof-texting trump the devil's? Before answering, it is important to see that what Jesus is doing with Scripture is no isolated case.

Each of the Gospels identifies Jesus as the Christ largely by drawing on Old Testament texts in ways that show how Jesus Christ is the fulfillment or completion of the way the prophets' words run.[37] For example, Mark draws upon four primary Old Testament backgrounds in order to identify Jesus as the Christ: the Righteous Sufferer of the Psalms; the Servant of Isaiah 40–55; the Son of Man of Daniel 7; the Shepherd of Zechariah 9–14. The apostle Paul uses Scripture in similar fashion. He appeals in Romans 15:7–12 to four Old Testament texts, from different genres, in order to argue that the gospel is for Gentiles as well as Jews, a theological claim that would have been heard as startling if not scandalous in the context of Roman-occupied ancient Israel. The salient point is that Jesus, the Evangelists, and Paul used Scripture to do distinctly Christian theology – a 'proof-texting' of a higher order that wove Old Testament texts into elements in a pattern of biblical or canonical reasoning, a pattern of which Christ is the key.

The practice of Jesus and the apostles only makes sense on the presupposition that the Old Testament was God's own law and promise fulfilled in Jesus Christ. The right use of Scripture in theology ultimately depends on one's grasp of its nature (i.e. ontology) and purpose (i.e. teleology). What the Bible *is* and what it *does* takes precedence over what theologians say about and do with the Bible, for theology is the intelligent creaturely response to God's own teaching about God in and through Scripture. John Webster argues that both Scripture and its use in theology are elements in the domain of the Word of God, 'the sphere of reality in which Christ glorified is present and speaks with unrivaled clarity'.[38] For Webster, the use of Scripture in theology is a thoroughly theological phenomenon in which the Holy Spirit illumines the Word by renewing hearts and minds. The practice of using Scripture in theology participates in the triune economy of revelation and redemption (i.e. God's self-communication in Son and Spirit for the salvation of the world), as does Scripture itself.

The Bible is the creaturely medium for what is ultimately a divine communicative act whose end is knowledge of, and communion with, the triune God. Using Scripture to formulate doctrine – direction for discipleship – is thus intended to be a teaching moment in the divine pedagogy: 'Study to show thyself approved unto God ... rightly dividing the word of truth' (2 Tim. 2:15; KJV). God desires creatures to use their own natures and capacities to their full extent. The various exegetical disciplinary practices, viewed theologically, are 'elements in created reason's work in the economy of the Spirit'.[39] Webster's emphasis on the ontology and teleology adds a normative element to Kelsey's descriptive account of the uses of Scripture: we use Scripture rightly when we respect its nature and purpose as a vital element in the economy of God's revelatory and redemptive grace, the primary means by which the risen Christ instructs and rules his Church. 'Then beginning with Moses and all the prophets, he interpreted to them the things about himself in all the scriptures' (Lk. 24:27). This insight into the true subject matter of the Scriptures lies at the heart of Barth's christocentric approach, as it does in others that see patterns and parallels connecting the people, things, and events in the Old Testament ('types') to their fulfillment in the person and history of Jesus Christ (the 'antitype').

Theology lives and moves and has its being in discerning, and thinking through, such patterns. Biblical thinking involves biblical reasoning and imagining: 'The principal task of theological reason is figuring out the literal sense, that is, what the text says.'[40] To follow the way *these* words go – data, principles, images, and testimony alike – is to perform exegetical service in the domain of the Word of God. This calls for literary sensitivity, so that we do not mistake metaphor for literal description or apocalyptic symbols for historical reportage. Exegetical reasoning presupposes biblical literacy: theologians must be careful not to derive from the text information that it was not designed to give. Webster calls for a further level of biblical thinking, however, a dogmatic reasoning that conceptually elaborates in contemporary idiom what it has learned by following the biblical words: 'Dogmatics is the schematic and analytic presentation of the matter of the gospel.'[41] We think biblically when our creaturely intelligence follows, and displays, the divine intelligence that animates the history of Jesus that alone makes sense of the histories of Israel and the Church.

To practice this kind of biblical thinking requires us not only to reason but also to imagine the world Scripture imagines. To do theology is to use Scripture to form our hearts and minds to see and act in the world depicted by Scripture, and to accept it as the real world: 'Theology is the name we give to the effort of our minds to grasp the world conjured up by God and construed by Scripture.'[42] This requires discipline, perhaps even mortification. To follow the way the words go so as to attain understanding of their subject matter is, in the final analysis, the act of a disciple. Here it is no longer a matter of using Scripture for our own purposes but rather of 'according to' the Scriptures, of being used *by* Scripture for its own purpose, namely, to mediate the knowledge and love of God.

To think biblically is less about mining Scripture for isolated propositional truths than it is indwelling Scripture as a unified narrative with rich patterns (e.g. judgment and mercy) and interwoven images (e.g. sacrificial lambs) that come into greater focus as they are seen to center on Jesus Christ. We think biblically when we take our bearings from and participate in the great drama of redemption in which we are summoned to be actors. Scripture both informs and forms us; it not only conveys information about God and the gospel but also shows us how to process it. The apostles do more than convey information: they teach us how to make canonical associations and how to think in economic terms (i.e. in terms of the one drama of redemption that links the histories of Adam, Israel, and the Church with that of Jesus Christ). We can only speak well of God by learning the deep patterns of canonical association.[43] Theology's ultimate vocation is to minister understanding and nurture faith, following (and thinking) after the canonical Scriptures, pedagogues that aim to repair human knowledge and love of God.

How might we describe this practice of biblical thinking we have been considering? Perhaps we need to stop talking of 'using' the Bible and speak instead of *receiving* Scripture. C.S. Lewis distinguishes 'using' and 'receiving' texts.[44] We *use* texts when we put them to work on our own projects; we *receive* texts when we exert our reason and imagination on behalf of the author's pattern. The *user* is a poor reader who wants only to do something with the content. By contrast, the *recipient* is an ideal reader, desiring to understand and be molded by the subject matter. Christian theologians must decide whether they want to be users or recipients of Scripture: 'Choose this day whom you will serve' (Joshua 24:15).

Conclusion: Proving doctrine or getting wisdom?

How can we speak well of God? To think biblically is to think of God as the one who sends his word to Israel and ultimately reveals himself in the person and work of Jesus Christ. But who do we say that he is, and how? This was precisely the problem confronting John the Baptist. After hearing various reports about Jesus, John sent two of his followers to ask Jesus point blank whether or not he was the Messiah: 'Are you the one who is to come, or are we to wait for another?' (Lk. 7:19). Jesus replies: 'Go and tell John what you have seen and heard' (Lk. 7:22), namely, that because of Jesus the blind see, the deaf hear, the lame walk, the dead are raised, and the poor hear good news. Jesus' answer is indirect; taken by itself, it does not seem to be an adequate basis on which to construct a Christology. However, one who is scripturally literate cannot help but notice that Jesus uses a number of phrases from the prophet Isaiah (29:18–19; 35:5–6; 61:1) that describe what God will do to renew and transform the created order on the day of salvation.

'Tell them what you have seen and heard.' Witnessing lies at the heart of the theologian's task: to report what she has seen and heard of God in the history of Jesus attested in the Scriptures, to say what this history means in canonical context, and to think through its presuppositions and implications. Doing theology in accordance with the Scriptures is a matter of conceptually elaborating the words and works of God as these form part of a coherent narrative: the triune economy that makes up the drama and history of redemption. This is the larger interpretive framework behind the apparently piecemeal appeals to the Old Testament by various New Testament authors, and Jesus himself. Thinking with this redemptive-historical context in mind puts an entirely different spin on proof-texting.

There is a kind of proof-texting that, at its worst, is an abuse of biblical authority, an illegitimate short cut to developing doctrine. It is illegitimate because it *uses* the text, forcing it to bend to the theologian's agenda in flagrant disregard of its historical, literary, and canonical contexts. Call it illiterate proof-texting. Jesus' use of Scripture is different. His use of Old Testament texts is an example of biblical thinking *par excellence*, the canonical practice of viewing biblical things, persons, and events in terms of a unified narrative and progressive redemptive history that culminates in Jesus' own person and work.[45] Jesus' words were not always meant to function as isolated propositional truths but rather as tips of a typological iceberg. And this is precisely the force of his rebuttal to the devil's use of Scripture mentioned above. Jesus' proof-texts function as theological short hand, implicitly invoking not independent bits of information but a single history of redemption. At its best, proof-texting is a kind of canonical competence – the ability to discern meaningful connections across the testaments and between books.[46]

Today, as throughout history, the temptation to use Scripture to promote one's own theological agenda is great. The user you will always have with you. In this chapter I have gestured towards a better practice, a practice of receiving God's word, where Scripture forms the theological imagination, one's mind and heart, and directs theological reason better to understand, and love, God and the gospel.

In sum: theologians ought not to use Scripture simply to build systems of doctrine. To be sure, there *is* a unified truth – a collection of true teachings about God, the world, and ourselves – that can be gleaned by studying the diverse human writings that serve as the creaturely media of God's word. Yet the overarching purpose of Scripture is not to serve as raw material for systems of theology but to serve as a charter and guide for the Church and its performance as the body of Christ in the ongoing drama of redemption. The best theological uses of Scripture are those that minister understanding of what the Father is doing in Christ through the Spirit to make all things new. The doctrine we discern in the Bible ultimately offers dramatic direction for the Church: in coming to understanding what God has done in Christ – God's drama – we come also to understand what we must say and do to participate in that theodrama in ways that are both faithful (i.e. in accordance with the biblical representation of the truth, goodness, and beauty of God's creative and saving work) and fitting (i.e. appropriate to the present context).

Scripture's ultimate theological purpose is to inform and form wise witnesses and right worshipers, disciples who can make judgments that correspond to canonical patterns, do the truth, and embody faith, hope, and love – disciples in whom the word of Christ dwells richly (Col. 3:16). The proper end of the theological study of Scripture is not simply communication – the sharing of information – but communion, the sharing of the saints in the light, life, and love of God.

Notes

1 A 'drama' is a play that is to be acted out. In speaking of 'theodrama' I am referring to the play of redemption that God has acted out in the histories of Israel and Jesus Christ.

2 D. Kelsey, *Proving Doctrine: The Uses of Scripture in Recent Theology*, Philadelphia, PA: Trinity Press International, 1999.

3 Cited in M.A. Noll, *The Civil War as a Theological Crisis*, Chapel Hill, NC: University of North Carolina Press, 2006, p. 2.

4 Noll, *Civil War*, p. 1.

5 Noll, *Civil War*, p. 50.

6 S. Toulmin, *The Uses of Argument*, Cambridge: Cambridge University Press, 1964.

7 Kelsey, *Proving Doctrine*, pp. 64–73.

8 K. Stendahl, 'Ancient Scripture in the Modern World', in F.E. Greenspahn (ed.) *Scripture in the Jewish and Christian Traditions: Authority, Interpretation, Relevance*, Nashville, TN: Abingdon Press, 1982, p. 205.

9 P.T. Forsyth, 'The Efficiency and Sufficiency of the Bible', *The Biblical Review* 2, 1917, p. 10.

10 Ibid.

11 N.T. Wright, *Scripture and the Authority of God: How to Read the Bible Today*, New York, NY: HarperOne, 2011, ch. 7.

12 An interpretive virtue is a habit of reading that is conducive to achieving the good intrinsic to the practice of interpretation, namely, *understanding*. See R.S. Briggs, *The Virtuous Reader: Old Testament Narrative and Interpretive Virtue*, Grand Rapids, MI: Baker, 2010, pp. 21–22.

13 For further examples of bad practice, see M.T. Brauch, *Abusing Scripture: The Consequences of Misreading the Bible*, Downer's Grove, IL: InterVarsity Press, 2009.

14 B.B. Warfield, *The Inspiration and Authority of the Bible*, Philadelphia, PA: Presbyterian and Reformed, 1948.

15 E.S. Fiorenza, *The Power of the Word: Scripture and the Rhetoric of Empire*, Philadelphia, PA: Fortress Press, 2007.

16 *Summa Theologiae* I.1.8, in *Summa Theologiae 1: Christian Theology*, trans. T. Gilby OP, Cambridge: Cambridge University Press, 2006, pp. 28–32.

17 So W.J. Abraham, *Canon as Criterion in Christian Theology: from the Fathers to Feminism*, Oxford: Clarendon Press, 1998.

18 Wright, *Scripture and the Authority of God*, p. 116.

19 N.T. Wright, 'How can the Bible be Authoritative?' in *Vox Evangelica* 21, 1991, pp. 7–32.

20 'The Church exists for nothing else but to draw men into Christ, to make them little Christs. If they are not doing that, all the cathedrals, clergy, missions, sermons, even the Bible itself, are simply a waste of time. God became Man for no other purpose.' C.S. Lewis, *Mere Christianity*, New York, NY: Touchstone, 1996, p. 171.

21 C. Smith, *The Bible Made Impossible: Why Biblicism Is Not a Truly Evangelical Reading of Scripture*, Grand Rapids, MI: Brazos, 2011, ch. 1.

22 Smith, *Bible Made Impossible*, pp. viii–ix.

23 W. Blake, 'The Everlasting Gospel', in D.H.S. Nicholson and A.H.E. Lee (eds), *The Oxford Book of English and Mystical Verse*, Oxford: The Clarendon Press, 1917; http://www.bartleby.com/236/58.html

24 New York, NY: Charles Scribner's Sons, 1905.

25 Clarke, *Use*, p. 18.

26 Clarke, *Use*, p. 44.

27 Clarke, *Use*, p. 56.

28 Clarke, *Use*, p. 101.

29 Clarke, *Use*, p. 170.

30 Smith, *Bible Made Impossible*, p. 98.

31 Smith, *Bible Made Impossible*, p. 116.

32 J. Pelikan, *Jesus Through the Centuries: His Place in the History of Culture*, New Haven, CT: Yale University Press, 1999.

33 A. Paddison, *Scripture: A Very Theological Proposal*, London: T&T Clark, 2009, p. 65.

34 K. Barth, *Evangelical Theology*, Grand Rapids, MI: Eerdmans, 1963, p. 31.

35 See J. Webster, *The Domain of the Word*, London: T&T Clark, 2012, ch. 2: 'Resurrection and Scripture'.

36 For further development of this issue, see S. Moyise, *Evoking Scripture: Seeing the Old Testament in the New*, London: T&T Clark, 2008, and W.C. Kaiser, K. Berding, D.L. Bock et al., *Three Views on the New Testament Use of the Old Testament*, Grand Rapids, MI: Zondervan, 2007.

37 See, for example, K.S. O'Brien, *The Use of Scripture in the Markan Passion Narrative*, London: T&T Clark, 2010.

38 J. Webster, 'Preface' to *The Domain of the Word*, p. viii.

39 J. Webster, 'Illumination', *Journal of Reformed Theology* 5, 2011, p. 339.

40 J. Webster, 'Biblical Reasoning', *Anglican Theological Review* 90, 2008, p. 749.

41 J. Webster, 'Biblical Reasoning', p. 750.

42 L.T. Johnson, 'Imagining the World Scripture Imagines', in L.G. Jones and J.J. Buckley (eds) *Theology and Scriptural Imagination*, Oxford: Blackwell, 1998, p. 4.

43 See K.J. Vanhoozer, 'Love's Wisdom: The Authority of Scripture's Form and Content for Faith's Understanding and Theological Judgment', *Journal of Reformed Theology* 5, 2011, pp. 247–75.

44 C.S. Lewis, *Experiment in Criticism*, Cambridge: Cambridge University Press, 1961, pp. 88–89.

45 See D.J. Treier, 'Proof Text,' in K.J. Vanhoozer (ed.) *Dictionary for Theological Interpretation of Scripture*, Grand Rapids, MI: Baker, 2005, p. 623.

46 Similarly, proof texts in later theological works, such as Calvin's *Institutes*, function 'as shorthand references to the more extended exegetical bases for doctrinal claims that could be found in his commentaries' (R.M. Allen and S.R. Swain, 'In Defense of Proof-Texting', *Journal of the Evangelical Theological Society* 54.3, 2011, p. 602).

11
SCRIPTURE AND POLITICS
William T. Cavanaugh

'The point isn't that they would just *say* the Virgin was a communist. She *was* a communist.'[1] So contends Laureano, one of the Solentiname *campesinos* commenting on the Song of Mary, or Magnificat, in Luke's Gospel (1:46–55). In 1965, the Nicaraguan poet-priest Ernesto Cardenal founded a Christian community of poor fishermen and farmers on the islands of Solentiname in Lake Managua, which lasted until the military destroyed the community in 1977. Cardenal recorded some of the people's roundtable reflections on the Bible in the book *The Gospel in Solentiname*. In the book, voices from the community vary. Some, like Laureano, push for a definite identification of the biblical characters with particular contemporary actors or programs. Others resist such readings, and speak in more general terms of God's love for the poor and opposition to injustice. Most of the voices in the book, however, seem to assume that the Bible has something to say directly to the way that contemporary Nicaraguan society is run.

My students in the United States tend either to approve of such readings, because they assume that deriving meaning from the Scriptures – like all other types of meaning – is an act of personal preference, or to dislike such readings, because they are 'political' readings, not 'religious' ones. As we discuss the matter, however, it becomes clear that the Solentiname readings are challenging to both types of students. For the first group, it becomes apparent that the Solentiname community is not interested in personal preference; they want to know the truth of what God is speaking to them now. The second group is challenged to examine the very distinction between 'religion' and 'politics'. It is perhaps not written into the very nature of things, but is a contingent way that society in the United States is organized. If this is true, then my students too are doing a political reading of the Bible, despite their preference to think that 'political' reading is what other people do.

But to say that the Bible shapes political judgments for anyone who takes the Bible seriously only invites a series of much more difficult questions about how such judgments are properly made. If it is important that Christians make political judgments that are consistent with the Christian Scriptures, how do we draw lines from the Bible to our political commitments? If the Virgin Mary was not a communist, was she Conservative or Labor, Republican or Democrat? How do we read the Bible without simply reading our own political prejudices into the text?

These are not easy questions to answer, and there is no simple formula for how to apply the Bible to political life. Nevertheless, if we are not simply to succumb to cynicism and assume that all interpretation is a matter of justifying our own previous political commitments, we need to identify some good practices, in the form of considerations that any interpreter or community of interpretation should keep in mind when approaching the Bible for political guidance. In what follows, I will ask and attempt to answer some basic questions about what texts to use, how to interpret them, and who should do the interpreting. In each section I offer some suggestions for good practices and comment briefly on the virtues necessary to sustain those practices.

Is the Bible a political text?

To embark consciously on a political reading of the Bible is already to intuit that the categories of religion and politics are not always as neatly separable as we sometimes suppose. If this is the case, then we may begin our search for good practices in reading Scripture politically with a recognition that, although the Bible has a special authority for Christians, the Bible is not *essentially* different from the texts that one may study in a political science class. That is, the Bible is concerned with addressing many of the same concerns that at least some political theory addresses: What are human beings like? What is the goal of human life? Who is sovereign? What is the basis of human law? How are communities of people to be organized? Political theory typically begins with some view of the human person and the human predicament, then offers a political system as a way of solving that predicament. The Bible also offers an account of the human person and the human predicament, then offers an account of salvation that at least in part depends on the recognition of sovereignty (God's), law, and community. To accustom oneself to the practice of using the Bible for political discernment, it helps to see that the Bible is not up to something that is essentially alien from what goes on in what we think of as normal channels of political theorizing. But this comparison works in both directions; to see the Bible as 'political', it helps to see political theory as 'religious'. As the German jurist Carl Schmitt has written

> All significant concepts of the modern theory of the state are secularized theological concepts not only because of their historical development – in which they were transferred from theology to the theory of the state, whereby, for example, the omnipotent God became the omnipotent lawgiver – but also because of their systematic structure, the recognition of which is necessary for a sociological consideration of these concepts. The exception in jurisprudence is analogous to the miracle in theology.[2]

It is important to pay attention to the ways in which political theories present other gods, other creation stories, other visions of the human person, and other visions of salvation under the guise of a supposedly secular science that is essentially distinct from the religious.

In my undergraduate political theology course, we begin by comparing the opening creation account in Genesis with that found in the *Leviathan* of Thomas Hobbes. *Leviathan*, published in 1651, is commonly studied in political theory classes as the first text in the modern science of the political. Although much of the book concerns the contours of a Christian commonwealth, Hobbes' approach is different from medieval political theory because he founds his commonwealth not on revelation but on supposedly empirical observation of the human person. Hobbes begins not – as in medieval political theory – with an account of the laws that God has handed down in revelation, but with a putative 'state of nature' that predates human society. Nature, says Hobbes, has made humans ('men') equal.

> From this equality of ability, ariseth equality of hope in attaining of our ends. And therefore if any two men desire the same thing, which nevertheless they cannot both enjoy, they become enemies; and in the way to their end, which is principally their own conservation, and sometimes their delectation only, endeavor to destroy, or subdue one another.[3]

The result is the 'war, as is of every man, against every man'.[4] The solution to this predicament is the creation by contract of Leviathan, the 'mortal god', the state, which will, by threat and use of violence, restrain the greater violence of all against all. The state is enacted by contract when each person subordinates his own will to that of the sovereign power.

Structurally, Hobbes' account is very similar to Genesis. Both give an account of human nature and the human predicament. Both appeal to a sovereign god to save us from that predicament. And both enact a society – Israel or the commonwealth – to embody the purposes of the sovereign. The differences between the two accounts are not so much in the form as in the content. For Hobbes, the god is mortal. In Hobbes, the view of human nature is pessimistic; because there is no fall, violence is simply the way things are, not a falling away from an essentially good creation. In Hobbes, humans are essentially individuals; in Genesis, individualism is the consequence of the fall. Because of these differences, the kinds of politics that *Leviathan* and Genesis envision are quite radically different. Because of the similarities, however, we can see both texts as equally 'political' and 'religious', and the comparison of the kinds of politics envisioned can be between apples and apples, as it were, and not between apples and oranges.

It is good practice, then, to be attentive to the ways that the Bible is not *essentially* different from the texts that we normally consider 'political'. This leveling of the playing field not only opens the Bible up to political readings, but also opens other texts and practices to being analyzed from a biblical point of view. The biblical theme of idolatry, for example, suddenly takes on a particular contemporary relevance. We cannot assume that pledging allegiance to God and pledging allegiance to a flag are *essentially* different endeavors. Indeed, the Bible never tires of identifying ways that reverence toward created realities is in direct competition with worship of the one true God. People have a tendency to treat all sorts of things as gods, even – as Paul says – their own bellies (Phil. 3:19). As we might guess from this example, the Bible does not assume that one must explicitly regard created things as gods in order for a practice to qualify as idolatry. Paul obviously does not think that the people in question believe that a deity resides somewhere south of their own rib cage. The problem is rather that 'their minds are set on earthly things' (Phil. 3:19). The same point is made in Colossians 3:5: 'That is why you must kill everything in you that is earthly: sexual vice, impurity, uncontrolled passion, evil desires and especially greed, which is the same thing as worshipping a false god.' Idolatry in the Bible is not so much a metaphysical error as a moral problem; it is not about what people believe but how they behave. The problem is betrayal, not stupidity.[5] When the Israelites ask for a king in 1 Samuel 8, God responds that they have thereby abandoned God's reign over them to serve other gods (1 Sam. 8:7–8). No indication is given that the Israelites intended to worship the king like a deity. The problem is the tacit transfer of trust from God to the earthly king.

If this is the case, then we should be alert to the ways in which contemporary political loyalties can be idolatrous as well, even if we would regard the explicit worship of a political ruler to be ludicrous. If idolatry is not simply a metaphysical error, but a moral failing, then those who would read Scripture politically must cultivate the virtue of faith, which includes a critical attitude toward one's own tendencies to substitute faith and trust in other things for faith and trust in God.

Which biblical texts should be given priority?

Once we have decided that the Bible is not off limits for political readings, we are left with a bewildering variety of texts upon which our attention could be focused. A typical approach to political readings of the Bible is to single out a few texts as being 'the political texts' and then build a political theology out of a reading of just these few texts, without much regard for the rest of the Scriptures that surround these passages. It is common, for example, to go directly to the episode of Caesar's coin (Mk. 12:13–17, with parallels in Matthew and Luke) and to Paul's brief discourse on the governing powers in Romans 13:1–7 ('Let every person be subject to the governing authorities ... '), to find the New Testament's position on politics. American Christians often find in these two passages a generally favorable view of government, a clear obligation to respect the governing authorities, and a neat division of the things of God from the things of Caesar that bears a remarkable resemblance to the American separation of Church and state. Thus comforted by the sheer familiarity of the biblical approach to politics, the reader is freed to carry on politically as usual.

But why single out these two texts for special treatment as 'political' texts? Instead of reading Romans 13, why not Revelation 13, in which the Roman governing authorities are portrayed as demonic? Or we could look to Daniel 7:1–7, on which the author of Revelation draws, where the Seleucid Greek dynasty is depicted as a beast, devouring and trampling on its victims. Why not regard as normative Jesus' denunciation of the Gentile rulers as 'tyrants' (Mk. 10:42), or Peter and the apostles' trenchant dictum 'We must obey God rather than any human authority' (Acts 5:29)?

The choice of isolated texts of either kind will never suffice for a proper political theology. We must begin to expand the focus by looking to the surrounding texts for clues to their full meaning. Romans 13, for example, should not be read in isolation from Romans 12. There we find Paul admonishing the church 'Do not be conformed to this world ... ' (12:2) and 'Bless those who persecute you ... ' (12:14). Christians are told 'Do not repay anyone evil for evil ... ' (12:17); they are forbidden to take revenge, for 'Vengeance is mine, I will repay, says the Lord' (12:19). Christians are to overcome evil with good, feeding their enemies and giving them something to drink (12:20). All of this puts Paul's comments on the governing authorities in the next few verses of chapter 13 in a different light. Those authorities have been instituted to execute God's wrath on evildoers (13:4). Given Paul's prohibition in chapter 12 on Christian participation in the punishment of evil, Paul seems to reject the idea that Christians could actually participate in government's violent function, at least as government was constituted in Paul's time. In the light of chapter 12, Paul's brief comments in chapter 13 seem less a blanket endorsement of governing authorities and more a quite limited claim that Christians should not resist them – because God punishes evil through them – but neither should Christians participate in this work. In Romans 13, governing authorities – by which Paul means the same Roman imperial idolaters that executed Jesus and will soon kill Paul himself – hold a purely negative function of maintaining order by punishing vice; no mention is made of any positive role, such as the nurturing of virtue.

The more we expand the focus to the surrounding texts, the more we will need to consider the context of the entire narrative of salvation history. We must seek to build a political theology out of the whole of Scripture, insofar as this is possible. Oliver O'Donovan is one thinker who has attempted to do just that, in his book *The Desire of the Nations*[6] and other writings; another example is John Howard Yoder's acclaimed book *The Politics of Jesus*.[7] Though the content of their political theologies differs considerably, both assume that if Scripture is normative for Christians, if Scripture is in some significant sense the Word of God, and if God is one, then Christians must do their best to discern a coherent political theology in the pages of the Bible, taken as a unified whole. O'Donovan traces the notion of kingship and the kingdom of God through the Old and New Testaments to build a political theology based on the analogy of God's rule with human rule. Yoder locates the key to God's rule in the cross of Christ, finding in Israel and the Church an alternative political community based on a reversal of the world's definition of power.

This type of approach to Scripture as a whole both participates in and bucks important trends in biblical scholarship. On the one hand, it participates in the general trend among biblical scholars over the last several decades to highlight the Jewishness of Jesus and therefore the potential continuities between the two canonical testaments. Yoder's approach, for example, rejects the assumption that Jesus' pacifist ethic stands diametrically opposed to the violence of the Old Testament, and argues that Old and New are in continuity, for both assume that life is God's to give and take; killing is not under human authority.[8] On the other hand, however, taking Scripture as a whole bucks the tendency in biblical scholarship to emphasize diversity within the Bible, to identify and focus on various ideological agendas within the Scriptures that stand at cross-purposes to one another. O'Donovan is quite conscious of bucking this trend, and while acknowledging the diversity present within the text, he contends that the Christian is obligated to seek the Word of God in the text. The Christian interpreter cannot simply impose a New Testament grid on the Old, discarding elements that refuse to fit.

[The interpreter's] claim is more modest: in the midst of the ambiguities he claims to see a line of continuity relating Jesus and the Christian faith to the history of the Jewish people, and it is that continuity which he sets out to trace.[9]

The virtues called for in such an approach include the ability to be open to be challenged by texts that one has not already 'mastered', and in particular to be open to the Jewish experience of Scripture, which broadens the horizons of a Christian reading.

What is the attitude of the Scriptures toward the political status quo?

O'Donovan's basic approach is sound: a Christian political theology should be based upon the story of God's dealings with Israel, which come to a fulfillment in Christ, and that story is best told by looking at the way the entire canon hangs together. Nevertheless, O'Donovan has been criticized for favoring an 'official history' of Israel, which privileges Davidic kingship over more critical voices found within the text. O'Donovan writes: 'Nor can theologians do justice to [the Old Testament] as a history by constructing a subversive counter-history, a history beneath the surface which defies and challenges the official history of Israel.'[10] O'Donovan's point is to reject postmodernist approaches that prioritize suspicion and constantly seek to unmask the biblical writings as the ideological justification of a powerful elite. To prioritize suspicion is to abandon hope that God could actually reveal Godself in history. But although O'Donovan recognizes critical voices in the text itself, he tends to demote them to the position of a secondary, prophetic critique of the main storyline of the 'Zion–Davidic' theology of First Temple Israel. O'Donovan recognizes the juxtaposition of pro-monarchy (1 Sam. 9, 10) and anti-monarchy (1 Sam. 8) texts, but claims that 'in the end nobody opposed the monarchy'.[11] O'Donovan privileges the Psalms and their emphasis on kingship and largely neglects the Pentateuch, especially Deuteronomy, in which the law emerges in defiance of kingship as the unifying political principle of Israelite life. Gordon McConville argues that it is the Deuteronomic critique of monarchy that should be given priority, 'not only because it is part of the story (and not a disposition of the suspicious reader), but also because – canonically – the critique comes first, rather than coming along after as a reactive movement'.[12] The position of the Pentateuch in the Bible indicates its priority. It establishes a divine law-centered polity in opposition to ancient Near Eastern ideas of divine kingship and is not simply a dissenting reaction to Davidic kingship, which comes later in the story as the biblical text tells it.

The point of all this is not just to mount a critique of O'Donovan's emphasis on kingship but to raise the larger issue of how the biblical text is to be handled with regard to the political status quo. Certainly scriptural passages have been used to promote loyalty to the powers that be. Romans 13 most notoriously has been used to drum up Christian support for the Nazi regime, apartheid in South Africa, and oppressive governments in Latin America.[13] Such uses are widely shunned in scholarly circles, but on what basis? Should critical texts in general be given priority within the Scriptures? Is there an overall preference in the Bible for or against those who hold power within any given political system?

Certainly one can find a preferential option for the poor and downtrodden in the many biblical texts that condemn the powerful (e.g. Amos 5:10–12) or mandate a special care for the meek and downtrodden (e.g. Mt. 25:31–46).[14] More basically, however, there is a logic to the way the entire biblical narrative is constructed that lends itself to a critique of the status quo. The story the Bible tells is a salvation history, the history of humankind's rescue from peril. The conclusion toward which the story works is a 'new heaven and a new earth' (2 Peter 3:13, Rev. 21:1). Clearly there is something wrong with the old order; the status quo is always under judgment. A good creation is fallen; the Israelites await a Messiah to restore things to the way they ought to be. Christians identify that Messiah as Jesus of Nazareth, but even after his life and death and resurrection and ascension, we await the final consummation of the Kingdom of God in his Second Coming. Christ has triumphed and we now know that the story will end well, but we do not know when or exactly how, and in the meantime we are never satisfied with the status quo, but always 'straining forward to what lies ahead' (Phil. 3:13).

This eschatological dimension to the biblical story is most apparent, perhaps, in the prophetic materials that offer blistering promises of future punishment for the human powers that be (e.g. Jer. 5:26–29) and promises of justice and peace under the coming anointed one (e.g. Is. 11:1–10). But already in the very foundations of the biblical narrative in Genesis we see a revolutionary principle embedded. The point can be grasped by comparing the story of creation and fall in Genesis with the Babylonian creation myth *Enuma Elish*.[15] In the Babylonian account, creation occurs from a war amongst the gods. The earth is made from the body of the slain goddess Tiamat. There is no fall in the *Enuma Elish*; violence is simply part of the way things are. In Genesis 1–2, by contrast, creation unfolds in an orderly and peaceful way, and God sees that it is very good. What remains is to explain why things are so messed up. Chapter 3 lays the blame at the feet of human beings and their disobedience to the commands of God. God is therefore not the source of evil. Human choice brings about evil, as witnessed in the first murder in chapter 4. By 6:11 we are told that 'the earth was filled with violence'. In both accounts the end result is apparently the same: a world in which violence seems to prevail. In fact, however, it makes all the difference in the world that the world in Genesis is fallen. In the *Enuma Elish*, things are messed up from the start; the gods are violent, so violence is just the way things are. In Genesis, on the other hand, violence is not just the way things are, but a deviation from a more original goodness. Already, then, there is a revolutionary principle embedded in the text: the way things are is not the way things are supposed to be. More than this: the way things are in empirical fact is not the way things really are in their essence. That is, despite the violence and disorder that seem to reign in the world, creation is good, because it is made by a good God, who really reigns. The point is not to turn a blind eye to evil, or pretend it is not there. The point is to undo the despair that comes with thinking that evil is inevitable, that violence is just the way things are. In addition to dissatisfaction with the status quo, Genesis carries within it a principled hope.

As a result, neither the world as it has always been nor the world as it is as a result of the fall should be used as an excuse for buttressing the status quo. The subjugation of women, for example, has long founded justification in Western culture on God's words to the woman in Genesis 3:16: 'your desire shall be for your husband, and he shall rule over you.' To take these words as God's command, however, is to miss the point that God here is laying out the consequences of human sin. It makes all the difference in the world that these words appear in chapter 3 and not chapter 1 of Genesis. The equal status of women in the image of God in Gen. 1:27 makes clear that the subjugation of women in 3:16 is not part of the way God intended the good creation to be, but is rather a consequence of human disobedience and the disorder in human society that is produced by sin. To excuse injustice by appealing to its inevitability in a fallen world is to turn Genesis upside down. The whole point of a fall account is to undo the inevitability of evil, because it makes clear that sin is a departure from the norm established by God for God's good creation.

Near the end of the film *The Mission*, representatives of Spanish and Portuguese governments are called into the office of Cardinal Altamirano who was sent from Rome to judge the question of the removal of the Jesuit missions from territory newly acquired by the Portuguese from the Spanish. After the Cardinal rules in favor of removing the missions, a slaughter of Guarani Indians and their Jesuit defenders takes place, a slaughter which the Portuguese representative laments, but regards as unavoidable: 'We must work in the world, and the world is thus.' Recognizing his own guilt in the matter, Cardinal Altamirano responds 'No, Senhor Hortar, thus have we made it. Thus have *I* made it.' The Cardinal's attitude represents the biblical point of view. We can never justify our actions by claiming simply that the world is thus and we have to act within those constraints. This supposed 'realism' is, Genesis makes plain, not realist at all. What is really real is a good creation made by a good God. It is we, not God, who make the world an unjust place filled with violence.

A further principle for interpreting the Bible politically follows immediately from this same realization: if the Bible is revolutionary, the true revolutionary is not us but God. The account of the fall makes plain that the presence of evil in the world is the result of human action. For this very reason, not only should we not accept evil as inevitable, but we must not put our faith in human action alone to heal it. History is the history of salvation because we need a savior to save us from ourselves. Genesis 3 identifies the denial of this fact as the primordial sin. The serpent's temptation is to deny our creaturely limits: 'for God knows that when you eat of it your eyes will be opened, and you will be like God' (Gen. 3:5). Human history is littered with the casualties of political projects of self-salvation. Revolutionaries, like God, want to change the world, but human revolutionaries, as Gerhard Lohfink points out, have one problem: they are short on time. If the inert masses are to be roused within one's own short lifetime, there must be tremendous upheavals, for which violence is required. Only violence could change the whole world in one blow. But as Lohfink says, God is the only revolutionary with time. God wishes to change the whole world and radically so, but without taking away freedom by resorting to violent coercion. So God elects to change the world nonviolently by choosing a community of people to witness to the salvation of the world, a chosen people where salvation begins small, 'where the world becomes what it is supposed to be according to God's plan'.[16] People are to be drawn into this people's story only by attraction, not by force.

The scriptural challenge to the status quo requires that the interpreter cultivate the virtue of courage, the ability to confront the powers that be with God's plan to change the world. This means first and foremost the ability to see how one benefits from the status quo; challenges to the status quo must begin at home. As Lohfink's comments suggest, however, the courage to act must be accompanied by the virtue of hope that the story is ultimately a comedy, not a tragedy. We hope and trust that God is in charge of history and we are not.

What contexts should political interpretation consider?

Political theology is often closely identified with the notion of *contextuality*, specifically the idea that any interpretation of Scripture must take into account the social and political context within which the interpreter lives. Poor and oppressed people, for example, should not be bound to supposedly 'scientific' forms of scriptural interpretation that seek to reveal the meaning of the text for all contexts by recovering the original intent of the author. Such supposedly scientific methods of Scripture study, often identified as 'historical-critical' scholarship, arose in Europe in the nineteenth century as a way of studying the scriptural texts independent of one's faith commitment, or lack thereof. Methods were devised to study the historical contexts in which the Bible was written, to compare biblical texts to other ancient texts, and uncover patterns which reveal how the texts were written, edited, and compiled according to the experiences and interests of the ancient authors, editors, and communities. What mattered was not the experience of the contemporary interpreter, but rather the historical context that shaped the original intent of the ancients. Historical-critical methods were considered to be neutral and scientific, and therefore – ideally, anyway – free of the political or religious agendas of the contemporary interpreter.

Contextual approaches to political theology tend to be suspicious of historical-critical scriptural study. To begin, Scripture study is never as 'scientific' as some practitioners claim; if it were, there would be more consensus among the guild of scholars, but there is little. This fact leads to the suspicion that ideological agendas are not absent but only hidden from view in such scholarship. First-world bourgeois scholarship has tended to render a first-world bourgeois Jesus who is a spiritual teacher uninterested in political liberation. Beyond claims of bias, however, the contextual approach tends to reject unbiased scholarship as a goal to be pursued in the first place. The point of reading the Bible is not just to study dispassionately an ancient story but to involve oneself in the ongoing story of God's salvation of the world. If the Bible is the Word of God, then God's voice should not be locked in the past. God should be able to speak anew to people in new contexts as part of God's ongoing revolutionary plan to liberate and save. And God ought to be able to speak to ordinary people – biblical interpretation should not be the exclusive preserve of an elite of academic practitioners. For all these reasons, many contextual theologies reject the idea that the original intent of the biblical text, even if it can be confidently isolated, should determine the way that the text is read.

Before we leap to the conclusion that there are no limits to the way that contemporary people read the Bible in light of their own experiences, however, we should consider the gains that can be made by careful study of the original context of any given text. Part of the task of reading the Bible politically is to allow it to criticize the present, to give us a fulcrum from which to gain leverage on our own context and our own myopias. A consideration of the past can prevent reading in the context of the present from becoming an exercise in limiting God to the confines of our own experiences. As Christopher Rowland puts it,

> the knowledge of that past story is an important antidote to the kind of unrestrained fantasy which then binds the text as firmly to the world of the immediate present and its context as historical-critical exegesis bound it to the ancient world.[17]

Let us take for example the episode of Caesar's coin (Mk. 12:13–17) to which I earlier referred. A contemporary American reader has no trouble interpreting this passage in her own context; Jesus' admonition to 'Give to the emperor the things that are the emperor's, and to God the things that are God's' fits snugly into the American separation of Church and state. When we ask historical questions of the text, however, the distance between the ancient and modern contexts begins to question the reader's confidence that Jesus can be understood as endorsing our current political arrangements in any straightforward way. Jesus asks for a denarius and, looking it over, asks 'Whose head is this, and whose title?' Jesus' questioners simply reply 'The emperor's', but historical scholarship indicates that the image would have been of Tiberius, who ruled AD 14–37, and the title probably read *Tiberius Caesar divi Augusti filius Augustus*, or 'Tiberius Caesar, son of the divine Augustus'.[18] This historical fact makes a significant difference for the interpretation of the passage. The fact that Caesar was being proclaimed a son of god complicates the notion that Jesus the Son of God was content to divvy up responsibility for the governance of the world between God and Caesar in some amicable division of labor. The first commandment insists that God is a jealous God; it is highly unlikely that, for any Jew, the pagan cult of the emperor as god would rest easily beside worship of the God of Moses. Indeed, if one considers God's words to Moses in Ex. 19:5 – 'the whole earth is mine' – it is hard to see what is left for the emperor once one has given to God what is God's. To say that Jesus did not endorse American-style liberal government is not necessarily to imply that modern followers of Jesus cannot do so in good faith; it is to imply rather that we should not regard our own nation's political arrangements as God-given and inevitable. Much more needs to be said and done to arrive at a worthy interpretation of this passage, and it is highly doubtful that historical-critical scholarship alone will render the mind of Jesus on the proper way to arrange political institutions. But this example suggests that understanding the historical contexts surrounding biblical texts can prevent people from being bound to the limited horizons of their own cultural contexts.

The best political exegesis is a constant back and forth between the ancient and the contemporary contexts. Latin American exegetes, for example, talk about the way that, among the poor, the exodus story of liberation from the oppressive power of Pharaoh becomes their own story of liberation from oppression. They do not view the exodus story as simply an ancient tale but as a story of how God operates in history and continues to operate today to set God's people free. While learning from the historical context, what is most important is not the meaning of the text for its authors, but the meaning it bears for its readers, a community of interpretation that moves through time. To see the modern military dictator as the new Pharaoh is not to commit anachronism but to make the text come alive in one's own context.

Not all contexts are equal, however. Paul Althaus was doing contextual political theology when he argued that the importance of peoplehood in the Old Testament was being realized in Nazi Germany. Context-specific political theologies, in other words, are not good in and of themselves. Contextual theologians tend to emphasize the privileged position of the experience of the poor and oppressed as a basis for sound exegesis. If it is true that the biblical God is a revolutionary in the sense I explored in the previous section, then it is the experience of longing for change in the status quo that provides an important key to the political meaning of the biblical text. All poor people are not necessarily sophisticated and insightful interpreters; it is rather that their very presence as oppressed makes clear where God's revolution is most urgently called forth. All interpreters of Scripture must cultivate the virtues necessary to listen patiently across time and space to the contexts of others. For privileged interpreters, it is especially important to listen to the experience of the poor, so that God's call for justice can be discerned.

Who decides what is a valid political interpretation of Scripture?

So was the Virgin Mary a communist? If we take historical scholarship seriously, the answer is 'no'. Karl Marx had yet to appear on the world stage, and the historical figure of Mary, the mother of Jesus, would most likely have found many of Marx's ideas alien. As already indicated, to hear Mary say that God has 'brought down the powerful from their thrones, and lifted up the lowly' (Lk. 1:52) is not irrelevant to the present context. Nevertheless, understanding the original context of the biblical text puts a check on the direct reading of one context onto another. However, not many people have extensive knowledge of historical scholarship. What other checks on fantastical and potentially dangerous political interpretation are there?

It would be a mistake to read this chapter as a series of principles and techniques for the individual interpreter to arrive at a proper analysis of the text. Biblical interpretation is never done alone; one is always in conversation, acknowledged or not, with other past and present interpreters. This recognition is especially important in political theology, since politics is always about the common action of members of a group. The interpretations of the peasant community of Solentiname appear at first to be rather freewheeling affairs, but it is extremely significant that they take place in communities that are not like some first-world support groups, where each person is invited to express his or her opinion and the others are expected to refrain from judgment. The members of the Solentiname circles seem free to experiment with different interpretations, but they do not hold back from judging each other's words. They often disagree, sometimes vehemently. They are after truth, not self-expression. It is also interesting to note how Fr Ernesto Cardenal conducts the sessions; he encourages the participants to unlock the significance of the Scriptures for their own lives as Nicaraguan peasants suffering under an unjust and corrupt regime, but he frequently intervenes to guide the discussion, often with critical questions or historical background to the texts being examined. It is clear that, as the ordained member of the community, Cardenal exercises a kind of gentle authority.

'Question Authority' is a popular slogan in the US; 'Says Who?' is the proper smart aleck's reply. Authority is a dirty word for many because it is conflated with power, the mere exertion of one will against another. Political theology is often misunderstood as the fight against authority, but one must always ask what is left when the fight has been won. Are not all proper political communities oriented around the authority of some truth about human life? It is the search for truth that keeps politics from being the mere pursuit of self-interest, the scourge of modern democracy. Authority well exercised is simply service to the truth.

Authority appears in different modes in Christian political interpretation of Scripture. First, the reading of Scripture takes place preeminently within the Church's liturgy. In many Christian communities, the Scripture readings are set by an official lectionary, not by the choice of the presider. Scripture is heard in the context of the gathering of the community. The preacher authoritatively interprets the Word in the same context, and hears about it after the service if he or she has done it poorly. The context of liturgy makes clear that the Bible is the Church's book, not a set of tarot cards for the individual diviner.

Second, political interpretation of Scripture takes place within a tradition of interpretation stretching back to the patristic era. One does not begin from scratch, but offers political interpretations within the ongoing argument that is Church tradition. One need not always agree with Augustine, Aquinas, Luther, Dorothy Day, et al. – they don't always agree with each other, of course – but one needs to be conscious of the fact that the Church includes both the living and those who have gone before us marked with the sign of hope. Tradition, as G.K. Chesterton said, is the 'democracy of the dead'.

Third, the living in every ecclesial community have decision-making procedures for getting at the truth of a given matter. Bishops, as shepherds of the flock, are charged with keeping the sheep from straying. But the poor and the meek exercise an important kind of authority as well, in keeping the Church true to the revolutionary implications of the salvation history into which the God of Jesus Christ has called us. Indeed, it is often necessary for the meek to remind the bishops of the difference between authority and mere power. In all these dimensions of authority, the main point for our purposes is that Christian political discernment of Scripture should not be an exercise of individual power, but should always be checked by the truth as witnessed by the Church, on earth and in heaven, as a whole, guided by the Holy Spirit. Paul's church had prophets, but it also had those charged with distinguishing true spirits from false ones; Paul's church had those who spoke in tongues, but it also had those charged with interpretation of tongues; and they all participated of the same Spirit (1 Cor 12:4–11).

As Paul makes clear in I Corinthians 13, none of this communal discernment is effective without the virtue of love. As anyone who has lived in community knows, it takes a great deal of patient love even to want to find a common way forward. If politics is about building a common life, it cannot be based in suspicion and hostility – as so much of what passes for politics is today – or the negotiation of mutual self-interest or even mere tolerance for one another. The discernment of a true common life requires some measure of love.

Conclusion

In this chapter I have tried to display some important practices and virtues for the application of Scripture to political questions. Perhaps the last word of the chapter ought to be 'humility'. Politics is a dangerous game; people kill and people die. A Christian must allow the Scriptures to guide our politics, but the Bible should never be wielded. We should rather humbly submit to the Word of God, and to the image of God found in others.

Notes

1 E. Cardenal, *The Gospel in Solentiname*, trans. D.D. Walsh, Maryknoll, NY: Orbis Books, 1976.
2 C. Schmitt, *Political Theology: Four Chapters on the Concept of Sovereignty*, trans. G. Schwab, Cambridge, MA: MIT Press, 1985, p. 36. Schmitt is a controversial figure because he was, for a time, a favored jurist of the Nazi party, before running afoul of party functionaries in the 1930s. Nevertheless, he is now considered a key figure in the development of twentieth-century political theology simply for his recognition of the theological stakes in all forms of modern politics.
3 T. Hobbes, *Leviathan*, New York, NY: Collier Books, 1962, pp. 98–99.
4 Hobbes, *Leviathan*, p. 100.
5 On this point, see M. Halbertal and A. Margalit, *Idolatry*, Cambridge, MA: Harvard University Press, 1998, pp. 24, 108–9.
6 O. O'Donovan, *The Desire of the Nations: Rediscovering the Roots of Political Theology*, Cambridge: Cambridge University Press, 1996.
7 J.H. Yoder, *The Politics of Jesus: Vicit Agnus Noster*, 2nd edn, Grand Rapids, MI: Wm. B. Eerdmans Publishing Company, 1994.
8 See the chapter 'God Will Fight for Us' in Yoder, *Politics*, pp. 76–88.
9 O'Donovan, quoted in C. Bartholomew *et al.* (eds) *A Royal Priesthood? The Use of the Bible Ethically and Politically*, Grand Rapids, MI: Zondervan, 2002, p. 20.
10 O'Donovan, *Desire of the Nations*, p. 28.
11 O'Donovan, *Desire of the Nations*, p. 53. O'Donovan claims that even 1 Sam. 8:7 – where God says that the Israelite desire for a king is a rejection of God as king over them – is not a rejection of human kingship as such, but only a rejection of the concentration of all God's kingly powers in one figure (p. 52). This, he claims, is comparable to the modern preference for a 'separation of powers' in constitutional law.
12 J.G. McConville, 'Law and Monarchy in the Old Testament' in *A Royal Priesthood?*, p. 73.
13 N. Elliott, *Liberating Paul: The Justice of God and Politics of the Apostle*, Maryknoll, NY: Orbis Books, 1994, pp. 13–14.
14 A compendium of such passages can be found in R.J. Sider (ed.) *Cry Justice: The Bible on Hunger and Poverty*, New York, NY: Paulist Press, 1980.
15 A translation of the text can be found online at www.sacred-texts.com/ane/enuma.htm.
16 G. Lohfink, *Does God Need the Church?: Toward a Theology of the People of God*, trans. L.M. Maloney, Collegeville, MN: Liturgical Press, 1999, p. 27.

17 C. Rowland, 'The Foundation and Form of Liberation Exegesis', in W.T. Cavanaugh, J.W. Bailey, and C. Hovey (eds) *An Eerdmans Reader in Contemporary Political Theology*, Grand Rapids, MI: Wm. B. Eerdmans, 2012, p. 15.
18 R.E. Brown, J.A. Fitzmyer, and R.E. Murphy (eds) *The New Jerome Biblical Commentary*, Englewood Cliffs, NJ: Prentice Hall, 1990, p. 621.

12

THE LITERAL SENSE AND THE SENSES OF SCRIPTURE

Gerard Loughlin

St Augustine of Hippo (354–430) famously said that he knew what 'time' was until someone asked him about it. For then, on enquiry, the meaning of time slipped away, its nature becoming ever more perplexing and unreal.[1] Augustine admitted to such ignorance in his *Confessions* of 397–98, and his subsequent meditation on temporality occurs in the course of reflecting on the story of the world's beginning in the book of Genesis. 'Let me hear and understand' – he beseeches God – 'the meaning of the words: In the beginning you made heaven and earth.'[2] He implores to know their meaning – not their literal meaning, but just their meaning. If Moses were still around, Augustine would 'lay hold of him ... and beg and beseech him to explain those words'. We might have given up thinking that Moses wrote Genesis, and we might suppose that the meaning of the text is its 'literal sense'. But we might also have to admit, as does Augustine of time, that we know what the *literal sense* means until someone asks us to explain it.

The word 'literal' means according to the letter, from the Latin for the latter, *littera*. So to read for the literal sense is to follow the letter of the text, the way the words go; and following the words is literal reading, which surely is just what reading is. For what else do we do when we read, if not follow the letters on the page or the screen, on whatever it is we are reading? We always begin with the literal sense. It is the foundation of reading. It is the base on which the sense of the text is built, and the idea of this – as it were – literal foundation was also an assumption of those ancient and medieval Christian writers who long pondered the senses of Scripture, and with whom much of this chapter is concerned.

Origen, in the second century, was one of the first to offer this view of the literal as foundational, and the foundational as the record of history. 'Let us see the reports that are related about [the ark], ... so that, when we have laid such foundations, we may be able to rise from the text of the history to the ... sense of spiritual understanding.'[3] This image of the literal-historical as the foundation for all other meanings in Scripture became foundational in the tradition, a constant and uninterrupted usage in ancient and medieval authors. And from the first, the historical was the meaning of the literal. But history is another seemingly straightforward but on inspection puzzling category, and it too, like literality, has a history. But before further considering this puzzling category we should briefly outline the other, spiritual senses that Origen supposed resting upon the foundation of history.[4]

Multiple meanings

Today, many are familiar with a distinction between the literal and metaphorical senses of a text. The literal is the obvious, straightforward sense, the plain, undisputed meaning; while the metaphorical is a more contentious, less agreed sense, because it is an interpretation of the first, taking things and events, and the relationships between them, as standing for something else. Thus, at the literal level, Noah might have built an ark, but when the ark is taken as a metaphor it can become almost anything; it can become the ark of salvation, the Church. The ark becomes a metaphor, a word on the move; it becomes a figure for something other than itself, and in a sense becomes that other thing through figuring it.

All ancient and medieval Christian readers understood the distinction between the literal and the figural, and when they wrote they assumed the difference between the historical and spiritual senses of a text. The spiritual was so named because it concerned not what had happened, but the meaning of that happening for Christian life in the present, at the moment of reading. The text became a teaching about the pursuit of God through love of neighbour.

A metaphorical or figural reading of the literal sense was also known as an allegorical interpretation, and it was in thinking about this kind of interpretation that there developed a complex, sometimes contradictory, set of views about different allegorisms, different ways of interpreting the figural, and different ways of dealing with the dilemmas that such interpretations raised. Allegory – an other (*allos*) speaking (*agoria*); speaking an other sense – is a grammatical term, used by St Paul (Gal. 4:24), but originating in non-Christian contexts before it became subject to Christian use and development. And in that development, allegory (*allegoria*) became more than a trope, a figure of speech; it became the practice of so reading the Scriptures that they everywhere disclosed the Christian mystery (*mysterium*).

'Allegory exists when the present sacraments of Christ and the Church are signed by means of mystical words or things.'[5] And it was in detailing how the mystical words or things could sign Christ, the Church and Christian hope, that different authors produced different accounts of the allegorical. Some adduced more and some fewer senses, and some contradicted themselves as to the number. But in the course of time – a course that is exhaustively explored by Henri de Lubac (1896–1991) in his magisterial and monumental *Exégèsis médiévale* (1959–64) – the Church more or less settled on three allegorical senses in addition to the literal, giving Scripture four senses that matched the four gospels of the canon. By the thirteenth century Thomas Aquinas (1225–74) could confidently assert that these senses were: 'the historical or literal, the allegorical, the tropological or moral, and the anagogical'.[6]

As already suggested, these senses were ways of reading Scripture so as to produce more than one meaning. Thus the allegorical sense was concerned with Christ, with showing how the Old Testament bespeaks the New. The third sense – the second allegorical practice – came into play when it was needful to show how 'the things done in Christ and in those who prefigured him are signs of what we should carry out'.[7] This was the moral or tropological sense, which took this name because 'allegory' was already taken. Tropology might as easily have been called allegory, or allegory called tropology, since tropology is simply the science of *tropes*, figures of speech or turns of phrase.[8] Medieval *tropologia* is speech that is – as de Lubac has it – turned around or that turns something else around. It is 'a "turned" or "turning" manner of speech"'.[9] Finally there is anagogy (*anagógia*), which concerns the things that are to come; heavenly matters to which we must ascend. It is named for the Greek *anagógé*, taken to mean a climb rather than a journey. This fourth sense – which again names an interpretative practice – refers to both the things of heaven and the means by which they may be known; it names the eschatological mysteries and the manner of their contemplation.[10]

But now we turn back to the words of Scripture, to the literal sense, and to the claims that it is history and the foundation of everything else. For if God had not created the world and got caught up in its story there would be nothing to expound, no path for our ascent.

Figuring literalism

Though once foundational, the literal sense is hardly this in the modern period. This is not because it has disappeared, but because there is nothing built upon it. If it is a foundation it is that of a ruin, of a building long gone. There is a story to be told about how the senses of Scripture were reduced to just the literal, and how it then became purely historical. The identification of the literal with the historical is ancient, as is also scepticism about the historicity of the Scriptures, or parts of them. But what is new in the modern period is a determination by some to maintain the frankly incredible as the meaning of a text, and to suppose that this incredible history is the only sense that the text can have. This is modern literalism. This chapter cannot rehearse how such a situation has arisen,[11] but will instead consider the nature of the literal sense in days when it was but the first of several senses, the means to get at the symbolic or figurative. For then these were the senses that really mattered, that addressed the present and foretold the future. And our exploration of the literal sense will begin to show how it too is figurative, perhaps the most figurative sense of all.

What does it mean to read the Bible literally? How easy is such a practice? As we shall see, it is more difficult than might be thought. Almost any part of the Bible will show this difficulty, but one might as well start at its beginning, with the story of the start of all things, since this has become one of the most contested sites for the claim of the literal, for taking the Bible at its word. As is well known, Genesis – the book of beginnings – narrates the birth of the world twice over, and famously claims that God made the world in six days, resting on the seventh (Genesis 2:2). God makes Adam out of earth, and Eve out of Adam (Genesis 2:7, 21–22). The story seems straightforward enough, until we try to read it as history, which, as we have seen, is what most take literal reading to be. The story is of course extremely telegraphic, fragmentary. We have to fill in a lot of details in order to imagine a coherent, continuous narrative. But there are limits to this.

The creation is measured in days, but days depend on the earth revolving on its axis and around the sun, and the sun is not created until the fourth day. God made all the world's vegetation on one day, all the fish in the sea on another, and all the land animals, including man and woman, on a third; and yet we know that life on earth evolved over millions of years. What are these 'days' in the beginning, that seem independent of the very things that make a day, and are not the same length as the days those things now make. This is to state the problems in a modern way, drawing on modern knowledge. But the problems were known much earlier, expressed in more ancient ways.

Augustine pondered the story of creation on several occasions, and most famously in the last three books of the *Confessions*. But there he doesn't get very far into the text, being constantly distracted by the problems it poses. He had fared better in earlier expositions, in his commentary written against Manichean interpretations, and in his *Unfinished Literal Commentary on Genesis* (composed 393–95 and revised in 426), where he had got as far as Genesis 1:26. Then in 401 Augustine began writing on *The Literal Meaning of Genesis*, which he completed in 415, and in which he made it to the end of Genesis 3. But before completing the commentary, in 413, he began work on *The City of God*, which he completed in 426, and in this text too he dwelt upon the meaning of Genesis, providing us with some of his last thoughts on the subject. So it is to this work that we turn rather than the earlier commentaries, though we will have cause to mention them again along the way.

In the second part of *The City of God*, Augustine follows the Bible in telling the story of the world from its creation to the coming of Christ. But he is easily distracted from the narrative, turning away to consider various issues of interpretation or philosophy and theology. And yet, as we shall see, this is consistent with his approach to reading the Bible, for the Bible is always pointing beyond itself, being as much about present lives in the Church as about past ones in history.

Augustine notes that 'the days known to us have no evening other than by the setting of the sun, nor morning other than by its rising.'[12] What then are these Genesis days, and how was light made on the first day, before the sun, which was made on the fourth day (Genesis 1:14–19)? Augustine sees the problems but might be thought to dodge them by saying that though we cannot 'understand how it was' – which is to say, how the story makes any literal sense – nevertheless we must 'believe it without hesitation'. But Augustine rarely resists trying to make sense of things, and immediately begins to speculate as to what this light before light, before the sun, might have been. Maybe it came from another source, from 'the upper part of the world', or from the place where the sun would be put, or perhaps it was from the 'holy city' of the 'angels and blessed spirits'. Any one of these things – the existence of which is covered by the fact that God made the heavens and the earth – might be what is meant by the 'light' created on the first day (Genesis 1:3). But is this to read 'light' literally? It is certainly an attempt to give it an historical reference, but it is to do so by the very means by which we get from the literal to the allegorical. It is to treat 'light' as standing in for something else, for a particular source of radiation. It is to treat it as symbolic, and so to lose the literal sense in the very attempt at its preservation. The historical has become allegorical.

But Augustine is still worried by thought of sunless days, and so offers yet another, more wonderful reading of the 'days' of creation.[13] Noting that night is not mentioned in measuring these days, but rather evening and morning, Augustine likens the rising and setting of the sun to the dawning of our darkling knowledge, for compared to 'the Creator's knowledge, the knowledge of the creature is like a kind of evening light'. To know things, and to know them in the 'light of God's wisdom', and in praise of God, is to know them in daylight. Each day is the dawning of such knowledge, of the things named for that day. When the creature praises and loves God in the 'knowledge of itself, that is the first day'. 'When it does so in the knowledge of the earth, the sea, and of all the things that spring from the earth and have their roots in it, that is the third day.' And so on. The days are entirely symbolic. They are not durations but intelligences, and indeed prayers. Their light is the light of God, informing the minds of those who sing God's praise. They have, as we might say, an existential rather than historical reference.

God rested on the seventh day (Gen. 2:2). Taken literally, that would seem to imply an exhausted God, tired out by the labour of making the world. But this would be to understand the story in a 'childish' way, Augustine notes. 'Rather, God's rest signifies the rest of those who rest in God, just as the joy of a house means the joy of those who rejoice in the house.'[14] God's resting is a figure of speech, in which the effect is transferred to its cause. Our resting becomes God's. But does this mean we have moved from a literal to a symbolic meaning, or does this figure of speech belong to the literal?

Faced with the opening stories in Genesis, Augustine makes some feint toward a literal sense, but very quickly turns to symbolic readings, which save the text and clearly interest him much more. For Augustine is convinced that the stories have a purpose, and that purpose is our edification. Nevertheless, he does want to find a historical meaning if at all possible. We can see this when he comes to relate the story of Noah and his ark (Gen. 6). Augustine is clearly aware that the story must seem fanciful, if not preposterous. He rehearses the sceptical questions of others. Could there have been a flood so great as to cover all the land, including the highest mountains, which are above the clouds from which rain comes? And surely the ark would have been too small for all the animals it had to contain? And how could anyone have built such a large vessel? And would there not have been a need for more animals than those decreed, in order to feed the animals that live off the flesh of others?[15] And why did God have to preserve the animals in this way? Could God not have simply created them again, as he had at the first? No doubt some of these questions were also Augustine's, and against them all he insists that no one should think the story of the flood 'unhistorical', its language 'merely figurative'.[16] He goes to some lengths to establish the plausibility and so the historicity of the story.

If mountains can get as high as they do, why not also the waters that covered them? After all, water is lighter than earth, and so can rise higher.[17] This is not for us a convincing response, and we would have to allow that Augustine's 'adversaries' have the better case. But as to the size of the ark, it was larger than the objectors think, 900 x 150 cubits when all three floors are taken into account, and Mosaic cubits – Moses being the author of Genesis – may have been up to six times bigger than Augustinian ones. No one really knows the size of the ark. It was large enough. As for its building, that took a hundred years, and so was not impossible, and once afloat it was 'steered by divine providence rather than by human prudence, lest it incur shipwreck'.[18] As for the carnivorous animals aboard the ark, they may have become vegetarian for the duration of the voyage, as it is not unknown for such animals to eat 'vegetables and fruit, especially figs and chestnuts'.[19] As to why God chose this laborious method to repopulate the earth, rather than creating land animals anew, as initially, this is not really answered by Augustine, other than by saying that a 'most sacred mystery was being enacted'.[20] But in fact there is a reason, and it is entirely literary.

Augustine insists upon the historicity of the flood story, despite all evidence to the contrary. He rejects the view that the story has only a symbolic meaning.[21] And yet it is the symbolic meaning that most interests him, since of course it is the symbolic that saves the story from being merely antiquarian. '[W]e are to believe that the writing of this account had a wise purpose; that the events recorded are historical; that they have a symbolic meaning also, and that the symbolic meaning is intended to prefigure the Church.'[22] The historical makes the symbolic possible; but it is because of the symbolic meaning that the historical came to pass, for the sake of the 'most sacred mystery that was here being enacted'.[23] The historical – or literal – is the means by which God's wise purpose is brought to pass. This is why God chose to save the animals by gathering them, two by two, aboard the ark, so that they could be symbols for future readers. For the ark, without doubt, is a symbol of the 'City of God on pilgrimage in this world: that is, of the Church which is saved through the wood upon which hung "the Mediator between God and men, the man Christ Jesus"'.[24]

Augustine explains that everything about the ark, its dimensions and structure, symbolizes the body of Christ. The door in its side is the wound in his, pierced by a spear (Jn. 19:34). It is the means by which we enter into salvation, for out of the wound there flowed the sacraments of the Church. 'Again, when it was commanded that square wood be used, this signifies the stability of the lives of the saints; for in whatever direction you turn that which is square, it will remain stable. And all the other details mentioned in connection with the building of the ark are signs of things in the Church.'[25] Augustine has no difficulty in finding churchly equivalents for the ark's details, including its three storeys, which bespeak married chastity in the bottom storey, widowed chastity above, and virginity on top. And what controls such interpretations is not, as we might think, that they cohere with the text, but that they can be 'reconciled with the harmony of the Catholic faith'.[26]

The *Unfinished Literal Commentary on Genesis* opens with a summary of the Catholic faith, since it is this that must measure any literal reading of the text, guarding against wayward, heretical interpretations. And such a guard is needed because the text is so difficult to construe, its literal meaning so uncertain. The story of the world's making, along with the mysteries of the world that is made, are best 'discussed by asking questions [rather] than by making affirmations'.[27] This observation and injunction starts Augustine's commentary, and it is one that Augustine follows throughout, as also – and as we have seen – in his later musings on the Scriptures. It is a remarkably tentative, cautious approach for an author given to strong views, and it is an approach that modern critical readings can only confirm, and should emulate more than they do.

Behind Augustine's insistence on retaining the literal, historical sense of Scripture is Paul's admonition that 'the letter kills, but the Spirit gives life' (2 Cor. 3:6). This might have been understood as requiring Christians to abandon the literal in favour of spiritual or figural readings of the text. It was certainly used as encouragement to such readings, but Augustine and his predecessors took the verse to mean that the letter taken alone kills, but the letter as means to the spiritual is vivifying. Indeed the spiritual depends on the literal, which is, as we have already noted, the foundation for the figures it supports. For these Christian readers it was the Jews who made the mistake of reading no further than the literal sense. 'The Jews' – Origen explains with regard to the Book of Judges – 'read these things "as histories of things done and gone" whilst we, for whom they had been written, apply them to ourselves'.[28] Origen does not deny the historicity of Judges, but rather points out that 'things done and gone' have more significance for the Church than the merely historical.

Henri de Lubac, in discussing the literal sense of Scripture, is concerned to establish that the patristic authors always had a concern for the historical sense, and he is somewhat reluctant to allow that on occasion they did admit defeat in this regard. Thus notoriously Origen denied historical reference to several passages, and not surprisingly to much of the story of creation. 'Now what man of intelligence will believe that the first and the second and the third day, and the evening and the morning existed without the sun and moon and stars?'[29] More surprisingly, he also doubted stories in the New Testament, such as that the devil took Jesus to the top of a high mountain and showed him the kingdoms of the earth (Matt. 4:8).[30] The astute reader 'will detect thousands of other passages like this in the gospels, which will convince him that events which did not take place at all are woven into the records of what literally did happen'.[31] It is a perhaps alarming principle that the Scripture mixes fiction with fact, but such fictions were never thought to be untruthful, only unhistorical. Origen supposed that the absurdity of such stories pointed to their figural nature, to the demand that they be read allegorically.[32] They convey the mysteries of faith.

De Lubac will admit that the 'Latin Middle Ages have, like the age before it, and even more than it, made an often intemperate use of allegorism, for which they have brought into play some quite questionable methods'.[33] But he will not allow that it was an allegorism that sucked out 'the letter, the historical tissue'.[34] 'For the Middle Ages', de Lubac insists, 'the "historical sense is solid" and "the solidity of the history is not violated" by the expression of the spiritual sense.'[35] De Lubac can seem oversensitive on this point, and he may have been more concerned with honouring the historical than were those about whom he writes, for he is anxious to insist on the literal in a way that they were not. They valued the figurative, and thought that it saved the text from being about mere happenings, about which there could always be questions, doubts. Augustine's own questions about the literal sense, and eagerness to get on to the symbolic, are testimony of this. Moreover, allegory distinguished Christian from Jewish reading, and made it possible to convert the entire Bible to the Christian outlook. Yes, it told of things from before Christ, but those things – rightly interpreted – told of Christ. In 'the Old Testament is concealed the New, and in the New Testament is revealed the Old'.[36] De Lubac, on the other hand, is writing after the fall of such reading, writing for people who have grown suspicious of flights of fancy, as they may often seem, and who value the historical as history, and not as a means to something else. De Lubac is trying to save the historical in order to save allegory.[37]

Significant things

Augustine's reading of Noah's ark opens an ambiguity in thinking of the literal sense as historical reference. Does the sense reside at the level of the text, or at the level of the events that the text narrates? It would seem that it has to be both, for the text picks out some things and not others, and orders them through its telling of them, but they themselves are already ordered by divine providence. God is the author of the story because God was first the author of the events that the story tells. We can further explore this view through considering Thomas Aquinas's account of the literal sense.

Andrew Louth once noted that many people seem to have a 'fundamental distaste for, or even revulsion against, the whole business of allegory'. They think that 'there is something dishonest about allegory'. For by allegory 'you can make any text mean anything you like'.[38] Louth was writing in 1983. But ten years later, and Frances Young was arguing that the time was right for a return to allegory, for the context of biblical studies had 'dramatically changed'.[39] People had a new appreciation for the literary quality of the biblical texts, and for how the interests of those who read them affect the meaning of what they read. However, the context may have changed less radically than Young thought, for almost twenty years later and we find Hans Boersma and Matthew Levering making a similar observation on the waning of historical-critical approaches to the Bible and an increased enthusiasm for its spiritual sense.[40] The return of allegory is still arriving. Its exponents still have to contend with the fear that allegory – the spiritual sense – is unconstrainable, that it takes away from the certainty for which the fearful yearn. And such concerns have always attended the opening of the text to more than one sense.

'Allow a variety of readings to one passage, and you produce confusion and deception, and sap the foundations of argument; examples of the stock fallacies, not reasoned discourse, follow from the medley of meanings.'[41] This is Thomas Aquinas writing in the thirteenth century. But it is Thomas stating the position that he proceeds to reject. For he is quite certain that God is the author of Scripture and that since God 'comprehends everything all at once in his understanding, it comes not amiss, as St Augustine observes, if many meanings are present even in the literal sense of one passage of Scripture'.[42] As he observes, Thomas is following Augustine, but Thomas brings a determined precision to his account of the literal and the spiritual senses, and to his attempt to avoid the dangers of the spiritual sense that he so succinctly states.

Thomas makes a sharp distinction between the text and the things to which the text refers, and it is these things that God adapts in order to convey meanings beyond the literal. 'In every branch of knowledge words have meaning, but what is special here is that the things meant by the words also themselves mean something.'

> That first meaning whereby the words signify things belongs to the sense first-mentioned, namely the historical or literal. That meaning, however, whereby the things signified by the words in their turn also signify other things is called the spiritual sense; it is based on and presupposes the literal sense.[43]

The literal and figurative senses are divided between text and thing, *littera* and *res*. It is not the text that refers to Church (allegory), morals (tropology), and heaven (anagogy), but the things to which the text refers, for they too are signs. Genesis refers to the ark, but it is the ark that refers us to Christ and the life of the Church. This distinction between word and thing is long established in the tradition. 'The actions speak,' Augustine affirmed. 'The deeds, if you understand them, are words.'[44] But we might wonder why either Augustine or Thomas bothered with the distinction. For if things are signs they are akin to words, and so not outside but inside textuality, like the spiritual senses they convey.[45] God may be able to move things around as we do words,[46] but the meanings that God thereby enables are disclosed only in texts such as those written by someone like Thomas, in his commentaries on the books of Scripture.[47]

Moreover, what about those textual signs that have no historical referents, but are indeed fables or fictions, 'dreams in the night' as Theodore of Mopsuestia put it?[48] It was supposed that in such cases we go directly to the figurative sense, bypassing the literal-historical, since it does not exist. But in such cases, it is not the thing but the sign (of the non-thing) that has figural meaning, and the passage into history is unnecessary, and if unnecessary in such cases then perhaps unnecessary in all. Whether or not there was an ark, the 'ark' figures the Church.

By making the distinction between the literal sense of words and the spiritual sense of things, Thomas is able to avoid – or so he thinks – the danger of 'confusion and deception' threatened by multiple meanings. For these meanings are in things and not the words. 'Consequently holy Scripture sets up no confusion, since all meanings are based on one, namely the literal sense.' Arguments are to be drawn from the literal sense alone, and nothing serious is lost by not knowing the spiritual sense, 'for nothing necessary for faith is contained under the spiritual sense that is not openly conveyed through the literal sense elsewhere'.[49]

Thus Thomas seeks to allay the fears of those who think that allegory leads to confusion about the plain meaning of Scripture, while also allowing for such plain meaning to open onto richer, spiritual insights. Indeed, Thomas's literal sense is far from plain, for it is where one finds what we might call the metaphorical and which he calls the parabolic. This sense emerges in cases where there is no historical reference, where the figural – the thing figured – is the literal sense.[50] 'When Scripture speaks of the arm of God, the literal sense is not that he has a physical limb, but that he has what it signifies, namely the power of doing and making.' God has no arm, so there is no *thing* that could mean creative power; it is rather the text that means this, and its literal sense is the power of God. 'This example brings out how nothing false can underlie the literal sense of Scripture.'[51]

We might enjoy the ingenuity of Thomas's model – his distinction of the literal and figural along the axis of word and thing – but we might also think it strained or unnecessary. Why not simply say that these senses are effects of reading a text one way – as referring to historical or fictional events – and then another way – as evoking through those events present or future realities? But there are at least two lessons that we can take from Thomas's attempt to free the literal from the figural – free except in the case of the parabolic.

First, and as already indicated, the signifying thing does not escape the letter, the textuality that alone provides the context in which things can come to mean anything at all. God gives meaning to things by bringing them into Scripture, and in finding them there we find them meaningful. It is because Jesus walks into Scripture that he becomes the long awaited Messiah (Luke 4:16–21[52]) and finally the word of God in flesh (John 1:1). But that enfleshment is at the same time an enwording, a clothing in the textuality that gives bodies meaning.

When Jesus reads from the scroll in the synagogue we find that the things he does – bringing good news to the poor, release to the captive, sight to the blind – are not just his actions but God's actions in him. Jesus is God acting in the world. But one does not see this by simply meeting Jesus. One has to meet Jesus in a story, and in and through the Christian practice of reading that story; and Scripture has stories about this. Two disciples were walking to Emmaus, when a man they did not recognize joined them. But then, 'beginning with Moses and all the prophets' (Luke 24:27), he began to recount the Scriptures, and when, later that evening, he broke bread with them, they saw who he was.

Thus Thomas's distinction between word and thing is not so much about separating the figural from the literal as it is about bringing the literal-historical into the realm of meaning, of scriptural textuality, where its significance can unfold. And indeed, Thomas is quite clear that the figural is always within the literal, for 'it comes not amiss ... if many meanings are present even in the literal sense of one passage of Scripture'.[53] This inclusion is especially evident with regard to the parabolic sense, when 'the literal sense is not the figure of speech itself, but the object it figures'.[54] And this leads onto the second point, though it is not a path that Thomas followed: the literal is always already figural, even if it is the first figure. The plain sense is itself the result of a figuration, a set of conventions, which are never entirely fixed, and by which we learn to interpret the words on the page as referring to events beyond them.

One way in which the literal is figurative is in the sense that the history recounted in the Old Testament was understood as a figure – or shadow – of what came after in the New Testament, but an after that is in a sense before, in that it is the reality to which the earlier history points.[55] But this means that the literal sense of the New Testament is already allegorical, being the spiritual sense of the Old Testament. It is historical and allegorical at the same time, and so its second sense is not the allegorical but the tropological, the moral. 'Narrating the mysteries of our redemption, Scripture relates what has been done for us historically so as to signify what is to be done by us morally.'[56]

The Song of Songs is a fascinating site for finding the literal turning figural. From the earliest days of the Church this text was problematic for those who sought the literal sense. For it was impossible to take it at face value, as it seemed to relate a number of erotic encounters and missed opportunities. Thus, apart from one or two expositors,[57] everyone read it allegorically, as about the relationship between Christ and the Church, or between the soul and Christ. Celibate monastics in particular found it an encouragement and wrote endless commentaries upon it.[58]

But in time the allegorical approach became doubtful, and in the nineteenth century a literal interpretation was increasingly favoured. As Stephen Moore argues, this connects with the ascendency of an ever stricter heterosexuality, an ideology obsessed with separating the masculine from the feminine, and so ever more uncomfortable with a text that, read allegorically, turned the male reader into Christ's would-be bride, imploring him for the kisses of his mouth (Song of Songs 1:1).[59] Literalizing the text and returning such verses to an entirely female persona could avert the horror, hide the temptation, of homoerotic yearning. But – as Moore points out with dismayed relish – the desire to return to the literal sense has led to an ever greater 'sexting' of the Song, as Kevin Vanhoozer has called it,[60] though perhaps without realizing how far this has gone in some commentaries, which have found euphemisms in almost every line.[61] Read in such a way – as figured with innuendo – the literal text becomes explicitly pornographic. These readings are startling examples of what Moore calls the New Allegorism, when the literal is turned into its presumed opposite, but a turning that reveals the literal as itself always already figural.[62]

Authoring Scripture

The ancient and medieval authors could move so easily – and eagerly – from the literal to the figural because they were in pursuit of Scripture's spiritual sense, believing Scripture to have a divine author whose intentions were unconstrained by the human writers of the biblical texts. Indeed, just as there could be differences of opinion between the readers of a biblical text, so also between those readers and the text's writer, and so, by implication, between the text's writer and the divine author. But Augustine – for one – saw no harm in this.

> Provided ... that each of us tries as best he can to understand in the Holy Scriptures what the writer meant by them, what harm is there if a reader believes what you, the Light of all truthful minds, show him to be the true meaning? It may not even be the meaning which the writer had in mind, and yet he too saw in them a true meaning, different though it may have been from this.[63]

Discerning the divine mind is a matter of the communal mind, over time; a discerning by the body of Christ. No one person, not even the inspired writer of Scripture, comprehends everything.

It was only later Christian readers who came not so much to doubt the divine authorship as collapse it into that of human intentionality. Of course, it was long held that the Bible's human authors were inspired in their penmanship, but just insofar as meaning became identified with human intentionality, it became increasingly difficult to suppose that human authors had entertained the bewilderingly diverse, seemingly infinite, range of meanings made possible through spiritual exegesis.

More recently – with the advent of what we can recognize as properly modern, historical-critical ways of reading – the only recognized intentionality was that of the Bible's human writers, and then even that began to slip away. For the biblical texts began to be read as not so much the work of authors – the Pentateuch penned by Moses, the Song by Solomon, the Gospels by Matthew, Mark, Luke, and John – as those of compilers or editors. These anonymous individuals had collected and then stitched together what had come down to them, first in a rather haphazard fashion, and then with more design – as scholars moved to seeing them as more like novelists than mere reporters. Thus a certain kind of intentionality returned to the texts, but it was that of their editors, reading communities and canonizers; or, if you will, of the scholars who reconstructed them.[64] And these intentionalities were altogether human, subject to human interests and limitations, and analysable in terms of the cultural and social forces that shaped them.

Other forms of textual interrogation returned something more like a divine intentionality, but one without aid of human authors. Structuralist readings of Scripture would find in it meanings that, though they moved through human amanuenses, were not those intended by them. Structuralism is a kind of figural reading, but one that is less concerned than earlier interpretations with how a biblical text tells of the Church, of morality, or of things to come. (However, just in so far as structuralism supposes that its texts – Amazonian myths or Christian gospels[65] – work to express and alleviate strains and tensions in the cultures that produce them, it practises something akin to that turning of the text to present interests that we see in the eagerness of an Origen or Augustine to explain what a story of the past – say that of the ark – has to say about Christian life in the present.)

It is because Scripture is divinely authored that it can be thought to tell a single story, to have a single meaning or *hypothesis*, despite the variety of its writers, forms, and seemingly contradictory texts.[66] It is also why it can be thought to have so many meanings. Of course it was possible to consider the interests of Scripture's human authors, but just as they had been inspired in the writing of Scripture, so too were its devout readers, who sought to read in the Spirit, discerning what the Spirit had to say now, through the Scripture, about the present and the future.[67] But it has to be understood that divine authorship undercuts intentionality as the measure of textual meaning, for divine intentionality is known only through human reading, 'the crucial locus in which meaning is generated'.[68] As such, divine authorship is formally indistinguishable from the interests of those who read the Scriptures, and so it may always be but 'human discourse writ holy'.[69]

Nevertheless, the Church ventures upon such reading as a community, with each reader ideally listening to the interpretations of others. It is together that the faithful may hear the address of God in the words of Scripture. Such an undertaking cannot be the reading/hearing of a closed, hermetic community, for then it will only echo itself, narcissistically. It must not fear the questing, questioning nature of such an undertaking, seeking to police the possibilities of interpretation. For then it would indeed deny what the tradition has long held – from Jesus and Paul to Augustine and Thomas – that God's authoring of Scripture is fruitful of multiple meanings, and that it is in the learning of these that the truth of Christ is slowly, painfully, joyously disclosed.

So how might we now read for the literal sense of Scripture? Well, we could hardly do better than take our lead from Augustine and adopt an interrogative mode. Such a mode cannot go back behind the forms of questioning that arose in the nineteenth century and continued throughout the twentieth.[70] We cannot unlearn the fictionality of the texts, the degree to which they are interested interpretations of what may or may not have happened. We cannot, therefore, escape the need for honest but *faithful* reading. But we need not think that in doing so we are abandoning earlier practice, for from the first, faithful readers have questioned the historicity of certain stories, and disagreed among themselves as to what was and was not plausible history, just as we will disagree with them, and disagree among ourselves.[71] Indeed, the seeming scepticism of historical-critical approaches can help us to see when we should read for the figurative, spiritual sense.

It is not new to say that discerning the history is an ever renewed undertaking, a communal labour of the body that must always be seeking the unity of Scripture and of Scripture with God's other testament, the world as disclosed through human learning. Worldly knowledge is not less diverse than Scripture, but like Scripture the world may be assumed to have a truth and unity appropriate to being the creation of a God who walked the world in the cool of the day (Genesis 3:8) and in the heat of more troubled, more historical times. Since grace perfects nature, Thomas saw no incompatibility between faith and natural reason.[72] Thus when we read Scripture we should expect it to cohere with the way the world goes. In short, we should be guided by the axiom that 'nothing false can underlie the literal sense of Scripture'.[73] This then means that when a historical reference would result in nonsense, as with talk of God's right arm, or the 'days' of creation, the literal sense is – as Thomas argued – the figurative sense.[74] The literalist, in such cases, fails to grasp the literal sense.

Though many have looked for a return to more allegorical modes of reading – Andrew Louth in the 1980s, Frances Young in the 1990s, Hans Boersma and Matthew Levering in the 2010s – the Church is unlikely to ever go back to the rich, complex, multi-layered forms that such reading took when it was most abundant. But nor can it go back to a naïve literalism, for literalism always turns out to be a disguised allegorism, a figuration of the literal as unlikely history. We should read for the literal sense, but a literal sense that will often turn out to have a spiritual sense as well, or only a spiritual sense, as seems best on occasion. We can hardly do better than align ourselves with Thomas Gilby, and wish for what he – writing in the 1960s – perceived as a trend 'towards giving the literal sense a fuller content, *sensus litteralis plenior*, reinforced with elements from the spiritual senses described by St Thomas'.[75]

Notes

1 Augustine, *Confessions*, trans. R.S. Pine-Coffin, Harmondsworth: Penguin Books, 1961, bk XI, ch. 14, p. 264.
2 Augustine, *Confessions*, bk XI, ch. 3, p. 256; citing Gen. 1:1.
3 Origen quoted in H. de Lubac, *Medieval Exegesis: The Four Senses of Scripture*, trans. M. Sebanc and E.M. Macierowski, Grand Rapids, MI: Wm. B. Eerdmans Publishing Company, 1998–2009, vol. 2, p. 47; see Origen, *Origen, Homilies on Genesis*, trans. R.E. Heine, Washington DC: Catholic University of America Press, 1982, Homily 2.1, p. 72.
4 We should note, however, that others favoured an organic rather than architectural figure for the relationships between the senses, thinking the spiritual meanings to lie within the husk of the literal sense. The reader has to peel open the text in order to find the mysteries within.
5 Amalarius of Metz (died 850) quoted in de Lubac, *Medieval Exegesis*, vol. 2, p. 91.
6 Aquinas, *Summa Theologiae* 1a.1.10 in *Summa Theologiae 1: Christian Theology*, trans. T. Gilby OP, Cambridge: Cambridge University Press, 2006, p. 37.
7 Aquinas, *Summa Theologiae* 1a.1.10, *responsio*, p. 39.

8 Indeed, it is the possible confusion of these terms that occurs in my earlier exposition of Aquinas, where the allegorical becomes the tropological. See G. Loughlin, *Telling God's Story: Bible, Church and Narrative Theology*, 2nd edn, Cambridge: Cambridge University Press, 1999, p. 125. The earlier text should be corrected by the present one; corrected by Aquinas.

9 De Lubac, *Medieval Exegesis*, vol. 2, p. 129.

10 See further de Lubac, *Medieval Exegesis*, vol. 2, pp. 179–87.

11 For this story see Loughlin, *Telling God's Story*, pp. 127–32; and behind this, H. Frei, *The Eclipse of Biblical Narrative: A Study in Eighteenth and Nineteenth Century Hermeneutics*, New Haven: Yale University Press, 1974.

12 Augustine, *The City of God Against the Pagans*, ed. R.W. Dyson, Cambridge: Cambridge University Press, 1998, bk XI, ch. 7, p. 457.

13 Augustine, *City of God*, bk XI, ch. 7, pp. 457–58.

14 Augustine, *City of God*, bk XI, ch. 8, p. 458. Augustine often describes as childish what might be thought the literal reading of a text. Figural readings are adult readings.

15 Augustine, *City of God*, bk XV, ch. 27, pp. 689–92.

16 Augustine, *City of God*, bk XV, ch. 27, p. 689.

17 Augustine, *City of God*, bk XV, ch. 27, pp. 689–90.

18 Augustine, *City of God*, bk XV, ch. 27, p. 690. It may be noted that while Augustine is prepared to allow that past cubits may have been larger than present ones, he is not prepared to allow that present years might be longer measures of time than more ancient ones; a supposition that would reduce the recorded ages of men like Noah – 950 when he died (Genesis 9:29) – to more credible numbers. See bk XV, chs 12–14. Noah needs time in which to build the ark.

19 Augustine, *City of God*, bk XV, ch. 27, p. 692.

20 Augustine, *City of God*, bk XV, ch. 27, p. 691.

21 Augustine, *City of God*, bk XV, ch. 27, p. 692.

22 Augustine, *City of God*, bk XV, ch. 27, pp. 692–93.

23 Augustine, *City of God*, bk XV, ch. 27, p. 691.

24 Augustine, *City of God*, bk XV, ch. 26, p. 687; citing 1 Timothy 2:5.

25 Augustine, *City of God*, bk XV, ch. 26, p. 687. As Augustine notes, these signs are further detailed in his *Reply to Faustus the Manichaean* (*Contra Faustum manichaeum*); see this in P. Schaff (ed.) *The Nicene and Post-Nicene Fathers of the Christian Church*, Grand Rapids, MI: William B. Eerdmans Publishing Company, 1996, vol. IV, pp. 155–345; bk 12.14, p. 188. Augustine's reading of the ark as Christ's body, the Church, was already an established interpretation, offered, for example, by St Cyprian in the third century. See Cyprian, *Epistles* in A.C. Coxe (ed.) *The Ante-Nicene Fathers*, vol. 5, Grand Rapids, MI: William B. Eerdmans Publishing Company, 1995, epistle 75.2, p. 398.

26 Augustine, *City of God*, bk XV, ch. 26, p. 688.

27 Augustine, *Unfinished Literal Commentary on Genesis* in *On Genesis*, trans. E. Hill, ed. J.E. Roelle, The Works of St Augustine 13, Hyde Park NY: New City Press, 2001, 1.1, p. 114.

28 Origen quoted in de Lubac, *Medieval Exegesis*, vol. 2, p. 52; see Origen, *Homilies on Judges*, trans. E.A.D. Lauro, Washington DC: Catholic University of America Press, 2009, Homily 2.5, p. 59.

29 Origen, *On First Principles*, trans. G.W. Butterworth, Gloucester, MA: Peter Smith, 1973 [1966], bk 4, ch. 3, sec. 1, p. 288.

30 Origen, *On First Principles*, bk 4, ch. 3, sec. 1, p. 289.

31 Origen, *On First Principles*, bk 4, ch. 3, sec. 1, pp. 289–90.

32 Origen, *On First Principles*, bk 4, ch. 3, sec. 4, pp. 293–96.

33 De Lubac, *Medieval Exegesis*, vol. 2, p. 56.

34 C. Spicq, *Esquisse d'une Histoire de l'Exégèse Latine au Moyen Age*, Paris: Vrin, 1944, p. 28, note 2.

35 De Lubac, *Medieval Exegesis*, vol. 2, p. 56; quoting Prudentius of Troyes.

36 Augustine, *Instructing Beginners in Faith*, trans. R. Canning, Hyde Park NY: New City Press, 2006, 4.8, p. 70.

37 The second part of de Lubac's *Medieval Exegesis* (vols 3 and 4) is devoted to arguing that the diminishment of the allegorical senses in favour of the literal – which is said to have led

to the modern division between theology and biblical studies – occurred in the fourteenth century and not, as many supposed, in the twelfth. De Lubac sought to save Hugh of St Victor (c.1096–1141) from blame, and instead charged Nicholas of Lyra (c.1270–1349) with mainstreaming a development that can be traced back to Joachim of Fiore (c.1135–1202). For a discussion of this Lubacian plotting of exegetical history, and an attempt to rescue Nicholas from de Lubac's charge, see R. McDermott, 'Henri De Lubac's Genealogy of Modern Exegesis and Nicholas of Lyra's Literal Sense of Scripture', *Modern Theology* 29.1, 2013, pp. 124–56. Nicholas's concern with the literal was literally a concern with the letter on the page.

38 A. Louth, *Discerning the Mystery*, Oxford: Oxford University Press, 1983, p. 97.

39 F. Young, 'Allegory and the Ethics of Reading', in F. Watson (ed.) *The Open Text: New Directions for Biblical Studies?*, London: SCM Press, 1993, pp. 103–20: p. 105.

40 H. Boersma and M. Levering, 'Spiritual Interpretation and Realigned Temporality', *Modern Theology* 28.4, 2012, pp. 587–96: p. 587.

41 Aquinas, *Summa Theologiae* Ia.1.10, p. 37.

42 Aquinas, *Summa Theologiae* Ia.1.10, *responsio*, p. 39.

43 Aquinas, *Summa Theologiae* Ia.1.10, *ad secundum*, pp. 39–41.

44 Augustine quoted in de Lubac, *Medieval Exegesis*, vol. 2, p. 86.

45 It 'is only the way the story is told in the biblical material that makes the events significant in any sense'. Young, 'Allegory', p. 105.

46 See Aquinas, *Summa Theologiae*, Ia, 10, 2.

47 The allegorical distinction (between things and words) is like that between history and historiography, the things that happened and the story that tells them; and without the story the things hardly come into view. There is no history without historiography (of some sort). The distinction is also like that between allegory and typology, the latter having been invented in order to escape the ignominy of allegory while retaining its effects. The figuration of the New Testament in the Old was supposed to be a matter of objective history, accessible – at least in principle – from outside the biblical text.

48 Theodore (c.350–428) is objecting to those – like Origen – whom he thinks turn all of Scripture into a dream rather than history. 'When they start expounding divine Scripture spiritually – "spiritual interpretation" is the name they like to give to their folly – they claim that Adam is not Adam, paradise is not paradise, the serpent not the serpent.' Quoted in P.W. Martens, 'Origen against History? Reconsidering the Critique of Allegory', *Modern Theology* 28.4, 2012, pp. 635–56: p. 638; see Theodore of Mopsuestia, *Commentary on Galatians*, in H.B. Swete, *Theodori Episcopi Mopsuesteni in epistolas B. Pauli commentarii*, Cambridge: Cambridge University Press, 1880, vol. 1, 74.6–75.2.

49 Aquinas, *Summa Theologiae* Ia.1.10, *ad primum*, p. 39. See also Ia.1.9, *ad secundum* (p. 35).

50 These are Origen's mysteries, signalled by the lack of historical reference. They are also evidence of that shifting of the allegorical from thing to text that Christopher Ocker sees in Thomas's notion of the *sensus parabolicus*. See C. Ocker, *Biblical Poetics before Humanism and Reformation*, Cambridge: Cambridge University Press, 2002, pp. 41–42.

51 Aquinas, *Summa Theologiae* Ia.1.10, *ad tertium*, p. 41.

52 The story of Jesus preaching in the Nazareth synagogue, followed by his rejection, is also given in Mark (6:1–6) and Matthew (13:54–58). But only in Luke are we told what Jesus said that at first so pleased (4:22) his hearers: 'The Spirit of the Lord is upon me, because he has anointed me to bring good news to the poor. He has sent me to proclaim release to the captives and recovery of sight to the blind, to let the oppressed go free, to proclaim the year of the Lord's favour. ... Today this Scripture has been fulfilled in your hearing' (4:18–19, 21; quoting Isa. 61:1–2; Lev. 25:10). They reject him only after he has told them that they will, giving the sayings and texts he cites (1 Kings 17:9, 8–16; 2 Kings 5:1–14) a different literal meaning from their normal reference. Jesus applies the texts to himself and his audience. In this story the literal and figural are entangled from the start, and tangled by Jesus.

53 Aquinas, *Summa Theologiae* Ia.1.10, *ad primum*, p. 39.

54 Aquinas, *Summa Theologiae* Ia.1.10, *ad tertium*, p. 41.

55 De Lubac, *Medieval Exegesis*, vol. 2, p. 53.

56 Guerric of Igny (c.1080–1157) quoted in de Lubac, *Medieval Exegesis*, vol. 2, p. 129; see Guerric of Igny, 'Sermon IV for the Feast of the Purification', *Cistercian Studies Quarterly* 3.1 (1968), pp. 104–8: p. 104.

57 Stephen Moore identifies Theodore of Mopsuestia and Jovinian (died 405) as attempting non-allegorical readings of the Song. See S.D. Moore, 'The Song of Songs in the History of Sexuality', in *God's Beauty Parlor and Other Queer Spaces in and around the Bible*, Stanford CA: Stanford University Press, 2001, pp. 21–89, 212–39: p. 74. Such readings may have withered under the glare of the Church, but continuing aspersions against such literal interpretations – offensive to pious ears – testify that for some the Bible turned bawdy in the Song (pp. 74–75).

58 See D. Turner, *Eros and Allegory: Medieval Exegesis of the Song of Songs*, Cistercian Studies 156, Kalamazoo, MI: Cistercian Publications, 1995.

59 Moore, *God's Beauty Parlor*, pp. 80–82.

60 K. Vanhoozer, 'Ascending the Mountain, Singing the Rock: Biblical Interpretation Earthed, Typed and Transfigured', *Modern Theology* 28.4, 2012, pp. 781–803: p. 785.

61 See M.D. Goulder, *The Song of Fourteen Songs*, Journal for the Study of the Old Testament Supplement Series 36, Sheffield: JSOT Press, 1986; M.H. Pope, *Song of Songs: A New Translation with Introduction and Commentary*, Garden City NY: Doubleday, 1977. See also L. Eslinger, 'The Case of an Immodest Lady Wrestler, in Deuteronomy XXV 11–12', *Vetus Testamentum* 31, 1981, pp. 269–81; and R. Boer, *Knockin' on Heaven's Door: The Bible and Popular Culture*, London: Routledge, 1999.

62 Moore, *God's Beauty Parlor*, pp. 82–89.

63 Augustine, *Confessions*, bk XVIII, ch. 18, p. 296.

64 See B. Childs, *Old Testament Theology in a Canonical Context*, London: SCM Press, 1985, and for more recent discussion L.M. McDonald, *The Biblical Canon: Its Origin, Transmission and Authority*, Peabody MA: Hendrikson, 2007, and L.M. McDonald and J.A. Sanders (eds) *The Canon Debate*, Peabody MA: Hendrikson, 2002. See also F. Watson, *Gospel Writing: A Canonical Perspective*, Grand Rapids, MI: William B. Eerdmans Publishing Company, 2013.

65 See C. Lévi-Strauss, *Myth and Meaning*, London: Routledge & Kegan Paul, 1978; E. Leach and D.A. Aycock, *Structuralist Interpretations of Biblical Myth*, Cambridge: Cambridge University Press, 1983.

66 Lewis Ayres notes how Irenaeus of Lyons (died 202) stressed the unity of the text – and of the Old and New Testaments – and did so through adapting classical reading practices, which in non-Christian contexts had not been used to determine a unified meaning across diverse materials. See L. Ayres, '"There's Fire in That Rain": On Reading the Letter and Reading Allegorically', *Modern Theology* 28.4, 2012, pp. 616–34, pp. 621–22. Such practices included correcting punctuation, determining who is speaking at any point, identifying figures of speech and quirks of style, clarifying obscure terms by reference to other parts of the text and relating obscure passages to a perceived overall meaning (pp. 620–21). Ayres proposes that there are intrinsic connections between these practices and the emergence of a revelatory canon (p. 623). It was in and through such practices that the Scripture became Scripture (pp. 626–67). And still today we have to say that it is only the Church's reading – reading in the Spirit – which turns the Bible scriptural, revelatory. See further Loughlin, *Telling God's Story*, pp. 42–51, 116–19.

67 For an earlier account of scriptural inspiration see Loughlin, *Telling God's Story*, pp. 109–19.

68 Young, 'Allegory', p. 108.

69 Vanhoozer, 'Ascending the Mountain', p. 783.

70 See Lubac, *Medieval Exegesis*, vol. 1, pp. xix–xxi. '[T]o be cool toward the scientific knowledge and the mental habits of our own time would not be a help in retrieving the mental habits of times gone by. To take refuge in an exegesis improperly dubbed "mystical" and made up "of human expedients and arrangements" would simply be ridiculous' (xix–xx; quoting Pius XII, *Divino afflante spiritu*, 1943).

71 Aquinas seems to have thought the garden of Eden an actual place, near the Equator; as signalled by the flaming sword of the cherubim set to guard its entrance. *Summa Theologiae*

IIa–IIae.164.2, *ad quintum*, citing Gen 3:24. But Origen wondered who would be 'so silly as to believe that God, after the manner of a farmer, "planted a paradise eastward in Eden" (Gen 2:8), and set in it a visible and palpable "tree of life" (Gen 2:9)'. Origen, *On First Principles*, bk 4, ch. 3, sec. 1, p. 288.

72 Aquinas, *Summa Theologiae* Ia.1.8, *ad secundum*, p. 31.

73 Aquinas, *Summa Theologiae* Ia.1.10, *ad tertium*, p. 41.

74 For Aquinas' rather painful attempt to figure out the days of creation see *Summa Theologiae* Ia. 65–74. The way the world goes now is not the way it went for Thomas, for whom the sun revolved around the earth (Ia.74.3, *ad septimum*).

75 T. Gilby, 'The Senses of Scripture', in *Summa Theologiae* 1: *Christian Theology*, trans. Thomas Gilby OP, Cambridge: Cambridge University Press, 2006, Appendix 12, pp. 140–41, p. 141.

Part III
TRADITION

13
TRADITION

Mike Higton

In this section of the book, we turn our attention to 'tradition', and to the ways in which the practice of Christian theology involves engagement with tradition. The word 'tradition', however, can be used in several different ways.

The most obvious way in which the word 'tradition' is used is to name a pattern of belief and practice that has been preserved over a long period of time, often over many generations, by a particular community or society. In popular usage, the word most easily refers to

1 the exotic customs of a group or community isolated from what we take to be the mainstream of modern life;
2 the oppressive habits of mind and action that drive a community's resistance to the development of progressive and enlightened behaviour; or to
3 patterns of established practice and belief that help protect a community against the onset of various forms of chaos.

In other words, we take 'tradition' to refer to what a community has always done, the presence of the past in its members' lives, which goes largely without saying and almost entirely without question.

In theological contexts, some uses of the word 'tradition' retain this sense of a sacred deposit, carefully preserved and handed down. The decrees of the First Vatican Council in 1870, for instance, speak of 'unwritten traditions, which were received by the apostles from the lips of Christ himself, or came to the apostles by the dictation of the Holy Spirit, and were passed on as it were from hand to hand until they reached us'.[1]

In other theological contexts, however, the word can be used with a different nuance. The word can name an *activity* – the activity of handing on a message. The focus in this case falls less on a static content (even if there is still a consistent message to be handed on), and more on the process by which that message is passed from hand to hand, or generation to generation. The emphasis can even fall on the ingenuity and creativity required to enable this handing on – the translations of the message from medium to medium, the different ways in which it needs to be packaged for different environments, and the different modes of transport by which it has been conveyed.

Tradition and innovation

Theological discussions of tradition often involve, therefore, questions about continuity and change, or preservation and innovation. In some contexts, the two are presented as opposing poles, and the question asked is how the Christian good news can be preserved from change, or protected in a changing environment. Think, for instance, of Revelation 22: 18–19:

> I warn everyone who hears the words of the prophecy of this book: if anyone adds to them, God will add to that person the plagues described in this book; if anyone takes away from the words of the book of this prophecy, God will take away that person's share in the tree of life and in the holy city, which are described in this book.

In other contexts, however, the relationship between continuity and change is more complex. The theologian Karl Rahner, for instance, acknowledged that Christianity involves a consistent saving truth that remains the same throughout history,

> but while remaining the same, it has had and still has a history of its own. This 'sameness' communicates itself to us continually, but never in such a way that we could detach it adequately from its historical forms, in order thus to step out of the constant movement of the flow of history on to the bank of eternity, at least in the matter of our knowledge of truth. We possess this eternal quality of truth in history, and hence can only appropriate it by entrusting ourselves to its further course. If we refuse to take this risk, the formulations of dogma wrongly claimed to be 'perennial' will become unintelligible, like opaque glass which God's light can no longer penetrate.[2]

In other words, the 'same' Christian message, according to Rahner, always appears to us in a form appropriate to a particular place and time. And it is only if the form in which it appears is truly appropriate to that place and time that it can communicate fully in that context. It is only then that God's light can penetrate the glass. That means, however, that if the form appropriate to one place and time is preserved too inflexibly into another place and time, it will become incapable of communicating the message, or letting the same light through. What was clear glass in one context will become opaque in another. The act of 'handing on', for Rahner, has to involve the search for new forms in which to communicate the same Christian message, forms that will be adequate to new contexts.

If something like Rahner's picture is correct, then there is a sense in which all tradition – precisely in order to be tradition, a genuine handing on – will constantly involve innovation. It will involve creative re-tellings of the story that is being passed on. Given that the contexts into which the Christian message is being handed on are constantly changing, any attempt at handing on (any attempt at tradition) will always, therefore, be a proposal for a new way of telling the Christian story. Any such proposal will need to be scrutinized to see whether it is indeed faithful (whether the same message is recognizably being passed on in this re-telling) but it will also need to be scrutinized about whether it is creative enough. Is the message truly being passed on to a new audience, in a new context? Has it been rendered in a form that is genuinely audible in this new place and time?

Continuity and repair

Another way of thinking about tradition as an activity connects back to the discussion of reason in chapter 2. This is a way of thinking about tradition that doesn't allow us quite so easily to talk about an unchanging substance carried within a changing form; it doesn't divide tradition up into substance and form in quite that way, as if the form were a mere 'container' of, and thus neutral with respect to, the content. Chapter 2 described the process of ongoing, iterative, unpredictable 'settling' by which a community might seek to do justice both to what it has inherited, and to what it has discovered in its present context. If we turn back to that image, either we could use the word 'tradition' to refer to the collection of material that is inherited from the past, or we could use it more broadly to refer to the whole history of this ongoing process of settling. (This would, of course, have the consequence of making 'tradition' more or less synonymous with 'the history of Christian reasoning'.)

Think back to the metaphor of the toy train track, and picture someone with a roughly coherent track layout in front of him or her. It is only 'roughly' coherent because it is not completely free from loose ends, or joints with rather too much strain on them – but it is coherent enough that it can be used for a good game of train driving. That person is heir to the process of reasoning (of ongoing, iterative, unpredictable negotiation) that went in to the making of this layout; he or she has inherited not only the raw materials (the pieces of track), but an ordering of those materials into a layout.

Now picture again what happens when something changes. It might be that the strain on one of the joints turns out to be too great as more and more trains are run over it. It might turn out that one of the loose ends, which had seemed so peripheral as to be easy to ignore, turns out to be an awkward hazard as trains are moved around faster. It may be that some new piece is discovered (or perhaps even 'rediscovered' after a long time under the sofa) that demands to be found a space in the network. It may be that something subtly shifts in the context – the carpet at one end of the room slides slowly sideways – so that connections that used to work cease to make any sense.

As we saw in chapter 2, any such change will demand a response, and the response will be to continue the very activity of reasoning that produced the layout that has now been disturbed. The response will be another round of ongoing, iterative, unpredictable negotiation. The change will demand, in other words, that the track-builder enter into and continue the same activity of tradition that generated the track.

It is possible to imagine two quite different strategies that the track-builder might use. One would be to throw up his or her hands in despair, and to attempt to start again from scratch. The existing layout would be dismantled until all that was left was the collection of raw materials, and then a completely fresh layout could be constructed using those materials. The builder in this case would be turning his or her back on the tradition – the ongoing history of negotiation – that had gone before. The analogy here might be to a theologian who thought it possible, or even necessary, to return to the 'raw material' of Scripture (or of religious experience, or of some other preferred source for theology) and to set aside all the ways in which it had hitherto been read, discussed, and handed on by intervening generations – as if that were possible.

The alternative approach is not to start from scratch, but to attempt to repair the existing layout. In this case, the builder begins with what is in front of him or her, and then explores the level and kind of alterations that might be required in order to solve the specific problems that have arisen in that layout. Those alterations might end up being quite small-scale – or they might eventually require rather dramatic reworking. They may in time amount to transformations of the whole layout sufficient to make a casual observer think that the builder had adopted the 'start from scratch' strategy after all. But a reparative approach remains fundamentally different in its approach from a 'start from scratch' approach.

If the analogue of the 'start from scratch' strategy was an approach to theology that tried to step back behind the history of settling activity, the analogue of the reparative strategy would be an approach to theology that explicitly situates itself within a particular community and that community's history. It might, for instance, be a theology that acknowledges in its approach to Scripture that all its ways of reading have been ineradicably shaped by the reading of past generations, and that even the form of the texts it now reads has been shaped by that history. That does not mean that such theology will simply regard itself as stuck with any or every aspect of that inherited settlement, though, because any component of that settlement can be examined, and this community may learn to think differently about that component as a result. But the practitioners of reparative approaches to theology do not believe themselves capable of starting again, with a completely blank sheet of paper.

All the tools and the skills that theologians use to repair problems – the making of a clarification or distinction here, the imagining of a new institutional form or the envisioning of a new way to tell an old story there – don't come from nowhere. Theologians are not restricted to the repetition of things they already know, or of moves they have already made, but the creativity available to them is not an ability to create new things out of nothing. It is an ability to improvise upon what they have already received.

To switch metaphors, repair of a settlement can be compared to the process of repairing the raft on which one is floating. All the materials available to plug the leaks, and the tools that one can use to manipulate those materials, have to be taken from the material of the raft itself.

Tradition and irreformability

When repairing the raft, however, it is probably important not to untie the rope holding the main structure together, simply in order to improvise a fender around the edges. Any attempt at repair therefore involves taking some view of the structure of the raft – or, if not of the whole raft, at least of the parts of the raft surrounding one's attempted repair. Similarly, to seek a new settlement within a tradition, in response to problems or changed circumstances, involves taking some view of the structure of that tradition. Repair or the pursuit of a new settlement cannot take place if every part of what one has inherited is regarded as equally important, and equally inviolable. Only if one is able to construe the tradition as having some kind of articulated structure, with more peripheral and less peripheral elements, shallower and deeper reasons, will it be possible to propose developments or alterations, and participate in the dynamic of tradition.

The picture I painted in the previous section was of tradition as a process of ongoing settlement, driven by a reparative rather than a 'start from scratch' strategy. Within any given iteration of reparative activity, one cannot know in advance how deep the reconstruction might need to go – how wide-ranging and thoroughgoing the changes might be that cascade from the initial alterations one makes. You begin by wondering whether, for purely pragmatic reasons, it makes sense to switch from hymn books to a digital projector, and end up re-examining the whole way in which your community thinks about literacy, which leads into a reconsideration of the practices of communal and individual reading of Scripture that you advocate, which then leads into questions about your community's operative understanding of Scripture's authority – and so on. It is not that communities can or do remake the whole of Christian faith every time they make an apparently simple decision, but it is true that communities can't necessarily see in advance how far the rippling effects of one butterfly-flap of discussion might spread through their practice and belief.

For some Christian communities, it is possible for it to emerge through the ongoing process of renegotiation that some particular beliefs or practices have such centrality and stability that they can be corporately recognized as immovable – as givens around which other elements of the tradition can be rearranged, but which cannot themselves be moved. Every time someone has tried untying this rope in order to repair some other part of the raft, the whole raft has started to drift apart, and the rope has been hastily retied. After the first few occasions on which this has happened, we begin to realize just how central to the structure this rope is. It begins to become clearer and clearer that, whatever one does to remake the raft, one should not untie that rope.

To use a different metaphor, these elements are a little like the save points in a computer game. Once one has reached them, one knows one will never need to go back behind them – one may always, if the way ahead becomes obscure, return to this point and find a new way forward.

Christians think about these matters differently. In some Christian contexts, it is primarily the Scriptures that are thought of this way. Yes, there was a complex process of development behind their emergence. Yes, there was an equally complex process of discernment behind the recognition of their authority. But once they had emerged, and once their authority had been recognized, they became fixed points – the bedrock upon which the rest of the tradition was built (insofar as it was built well), and the ultimate reference point in any new attempt at repair.

In other Christian contexts, the great ecumenical councils also play a similar role: they represent fixed points in the Church's communal discernment of authoritative truth, and can have unstinting reliance placed upon them.

In still other Christian contexts, there are institutional structures put in place for the official recognition of the Church's corporate ongoing discernment of such fixed points, and their naming as infallible reference points for all future development.

For still other Christian contexts, there might be other elements of the tradition that appear to have this kind of centrality: the confession 'Jesus is Lord', or baptism in the name of the Father, the Son, and the Holy Spirit, or some other set of beliefs or practices or commitments.

You will, as you study theology, almost certainly come across debates between theologians who think about these matters differently. For some, the ongoing, iterative, unpredictable negotiations involved in the process of tradition can only be saved from their tendency to wander off into error or chaos if there are God-given, rock-solid anchors, revealed through the Spirit's ongoing work, holding the whole process in place. For others, these anchors cannot be exempted from possible reconsideration without dulling the potentially disruptive and transformative power of the Scriptures or of God's Spirit – and even if some deep elements of the Christian life have such weight and importance that an extraordinarily high burden of proof would be required from any who wanted to revise or reformulate them, still those elements remain reformable in principle.

These are different ways of construing the structure of the tradition – identifying what is deeper (and how deep it runs) and what is shallower; discerning what possibilities of reconstruction there might be, as the ongoing work of settlement continues.

Mapping traditions

I have started to shift towards a third use of the word 'tradition'. If the first usage named the original content that was passed down by a community, and the second named the activity of passing on, the third names the community in which the passing on takes place – a community stretched out in time, engaged together in the long process of settling. One fruitful way to think of a tradition in this third sense is as a sustained corporate conversation – a community discussing or arguing about its proper development.

Such conversations provide the context for theological work – and whether it is acknowledged or not, nearly all theology is written in and for specific traditions. That does not mean that all theologians are acting as spokespersons for their traditions. It means, however, that wittingly or unwittingly – and even if they wrongly take themselves to be writing for any rational human being – theologians always draw upon resources and pursue forms of argument that are only going to be quickly recognizable to a particular community of practice and discourse. They speak most directly to some specific community because they have, through various forms of apprenticeship, become acclimatized to that community's patterns of conversation.

It is a mistake, however, to speak as if there were a single, monolithic Christian tradition, or as if there were a neat set of discrete Christian traditions lying alongside one another – each one a coherent and evolving process of settlement, with clear boundaries. Our picture needs to be much messier and more complex than that.

Any attempt to identify 'a tradition' can only be an identification for some particular purpose. For some purposes, as when we talk about the whole Body of Christ gathered under Christ as its one head, there might be a certain degree of plausibility in speaking about 'the Christian tradition'; in another context, as when we are focusing on characteristic patterns of worship, it might make more sense to speak about 'the Anglican tradition' or 'the Russian Orthodox tradition'; in another context, as when our focus is more on recognizable intellectual styles, it might make sense to talk about 'the Barthian tradition' or 'the tradition of open evangelicalism'; in still other contexts one might need to talk instead about specific local traditions. None of these identifications provides the single natural scale at which the word 'tradition' in this third sense really belongs, because any such identification is an inevitably artificial classification for the sake of some broader intellectual project.

One could think of a map of traditions and sub-traditions as taking the form of a fractal – that is, as an image in which the large-scale structure holding together various components in a recognizable pattern is repeated as a whole at ever-smaller scales in each of those components. To get an idea of what such a map might look like, imagine harvesting data from Facebook and from Twitter and other online social networks to identify relationships between people in the Church. The picture that emerged would not consist of monolithic and isolated blobs of community, each consisting of a web of uniformly and densely interconnected people only very sparsely connected to people in other blobs. The map would, rather, be much more of a mess than this, and identifying traditions would be a matter of identifying relatively tighter tangles in an insane cat's cradle of connections. How many traditions one saw would depend on how far one sat from the screen.

Any given theologian is unavoidably entangled in multiple traditions, at whatever scale one chooses to look – a messy patchwork of overlaps and inclusions, of frayed edges and patches. This inevitably complicates the picture I painted earlier: a tradition is not an isolated raft, and the process of a tradition's development cannot be confined to materials drawn from that one context. Just as there can be no return to the sources of a tradition that is not shaped by the history of that tradition, so there are no developments in any tradition that are not affected by the whole complex surrounding the patchwork of traditions. The work of settling and of repair within one tradition might involve the adoption of a distinction from another; the improvisation of an institutional structure inspired by models found in another; the acceptance of a reading of a key text from another – or any of a thousand kinds of border crossing and borrowing. No tradition can be understood in isolation – even at the broadest level where we are thinking about the Christian tradition alongside the traditions of other religions: we can only make sense of their histories when we see them together.

Working with tradition

Any real attempt at settlement or repair – any active participation in the process of tradition – is always ultimately a proposal to a particular community (however fuzzy-edged, internally complex and hard to delimit that community might be). It is a contribution to a conversation, and (as with contributing to any conversation), it is likely to be more fruitful as a contribution the more it has been shaped by familiarity with the way that conversation has been going.

Engagement with tradition is therefore a key component of theological work. It involves learning the tenor and flow of a community's conversation over time, learning to recognize key voices within it, becoming familiar enough with it to be able to construe its structure, and recognize its fixed points. It involves becoming familiar with the variety of voices in play, and with their ongoing arguments – and it involves learning what is at stake in those arguments. It involves learning to anticipate the kinds of question that might be asked by this community of any proposal that one wishes to make.

The community with which one needs to engage can exist at very different scales. If one is simply making pragmatic proposals for the clearing up of a little local difficulty, the conversation that one is entering will probably be correspondingly small, and the acquisition of the necessary familiarity with its rhythms and constraints might be quite informal and undemanding (though anyone who has had to negotiate the use of the bathroom in a shared student house will know how rapidly the labour involved might escalate). As soon as one starts asking questions about deeper matters, however, the community with which one needs to engage begins to expand – and it expands in both space and time. It expands in space, because the community of people with a stake in the matter one is discussing, the community who might question or critique one's proposals, and whose responses one needs to learn to some extent to anticipate, quickly grows. It expands in time, however, because one is proposing a rearrangement of a carefully evolved settlement, and one therefore needs to learn about the emergence of that settlement, the nature of the decisions that have underpinned it, the nature of the connections joining it to other elements of the Christian life, the nature of the issues that are at stake in the current structure. One needs, in other words, a deepening familiarity with the extended history of conversation that one is seeking to join.

Just as when one is trying to understand the participants in the Church's contemporary conversation, when one is trying to understand the history of Christian conversation on any matter it is important to do justice to the other participants. One will not understand the structure of the tradition within which one stands, or understand what might be at stake in any proposed reformulation, revision or extension of that tradition, until one begins to learn what was at stake for earlier participants: why they argued as they did, what tools and skills they drew on for the sake of their work, what was the tenor and tendency of their conversations. Even if one is reading the Christian tradition for the sake of a debate today, one needs to learn to read each part of it in its own integrity, in the light of its own context and questions – even if that means losing sight for a time of the connections with one's own concerns. There is, in other words, a proper demand for an appreciation of the tradition *as history*.

The other side of the equation, however, is put well by Karl Barth.

> [T]he theology of past periods, classical and less classical, also plays a part and demands a hearing. It demands a hearing as surely as it occupies a place

with us in the context of the Church ... We have to remember the communion of saints, bearing and being borne by each other, asking and being
asked, having to take mutual responsibility for and among the sinners gathered together in Christ. As regards theology also, we cannot be in the
Church without taking as much responsibility for the theology of the past,
as for the theology of our present. Augustine, Thomas Aquinas, Luther,
Schleiermacher, and all the rest are not dead but living. They still speak and
demand a hearing as living voices, as surely as we know that they and we
belong together in the Church. They made in their time the same contribution to the task of the Church that is required of us today. As we make our
contribution, they join in with theirs, and we cannot play our part today
without allowing them to play theirs. Our responsibility is not only to God,
to ourselves, to the men of today, to other living theologians, but to them.
There is no past in the Church, so there is no past in theology.[3]

'There is no past in the Church,' Barth says. The voices from the past, which we
need to understand in their own historical integrity – which means, in part, in their
difference from us – are part of the one conversation of the Body of Christ. We
listen to their specificity and difference in order to hear more clearly what contribution they might make to that ongoing conversation – what challenge to our
proposals, what questions of our current settlements. Engagement with tradition is
not an antiquarian pastime, therefore, because to engage with tradition is to enter
into the cut and thrust of the one conversation of the Church.

Looking ahead

The chapters in this section of the book explore various ways in which theologians
engage with tradition – how they learn the shape and flow of the Christian community's
conversation well enough to join in.

Jason Byassee's chapter explores what it means for theology to be done in service
of a community that worships. Given that much of this section concentrates on
engagement with the Christian tradition as represented in its texts, this chapter is an
important reminder that those texts are not the whole story – because they come
from and reflect back upon the life of a community that is engaged in praise, in
baptizing and celebrating the Eucharist, in blessing and praying. The goal of theology,
he suggests, is not simply to think correctly, it is to worship more truly and deeply.

Morwenna Ludlow's chapter asks how and why theologians devote their time to
reading and re-reading classic texts – texts (other than Scripture) that have played
important roles in shaping a Christian community or communities over some considerable period of time in ways that are largely thought to be positive, and which go
on being fruitful for that community's thinking or practice as its members continue
re-reading them. She describes the practice of reading such classic texts as an ascetic
discipline, effortful and attentive, but open to surprises.

John Bradbury provides a guide to theological engagement with two very specific
kinds of classic texts: formal creeds and confessions, documents accepted as
authoritative summaries of belief by some Christian communities. He explores the

many different roles that the classic creeds (the Apostles' Creed and the Nicene Creed, for instance) have played in shaping the whole theological enterprise, and the different ways in which the authority of such creeds – and of the more recent formal confessions of faith produced by some churches – has been understood in theology since the Reformation. He also describes what it might mean for a particular church to find itself in a position where a new formal statement of belief – a new confession – is needed to rule out decisively some pressing form of corruption.

Rachel Muers tackles a question that has been in the background of all of the chapters in this section. What are theologians to do with the fact that many of the texts that have shaped their tradition are, to one extent or another, problematic – and some of them are deeply damaging? She describes how theological readers can identify and expose the ways in which a text is wrong, and can search in that text and in the wider tradition of which it is a part for resources to overcome that wrong – not in order to exonerate the author in question, but in order to participate in the ongoing practice of seeking justice.

Stephen Plant's chapter explores what it means for theologians to spend a good deal of their time reading texts written fairly recently by other theologians – texts of modern theology. He shows that 'modern' theology is not just theology that has been written recently, but theology that engages with deep questions that have come to the fore in the modern period. The point of engaging with the modern theologians is not that they are authorities whose ideas we are meant to repeat, but that they provide a kind of apprenticeship that trains new theologians to explore and answer these questions for themselves.

With Paul Murray's chapter, we return to the life of the Church as the context for the practice of Christian theology. He shows how theology follows up problems that arise in the life of the Church – including mismatches that arise between the Church's ideas about itself and its actual practice. It is an activity, therefore, that requires both attentiveness to the Church's traditions of thinking, and attentiveness to the actual lived reality of the Church's life in the world. He finishes by asking what it means to do theology in a context of divided churches – multiple Christian traditions in some degree of conflict with one another – and advocates the practice of 'receptive ecumenism' as an appropriate and fruitful way forward.

Notes

1 N. Tanner, *Decrees of the Ecumenical Councils*, London: Sheed and Ward; Washington DC: Georgetown University Press, 1990, Session 3, ch. 2, §5.
2 K. Rahner, 'The Historicity of Theology', trans. G. Harrison, in *Theological Investigations IX: Writings of 1965–1967, 1*, New York: Herder and Herder, 1972, pp. 64–82: p. 71.
3 K. Barth, *Protestant Theology in the Nineteenth Century: Its Background and History*, London: SCM Press, 1972, p. 17.

14
THEOLOGY AND WORSHIP

Jason Byassee

The church where I serve as pastor has recently started a midweek Eucharistic service. This is nothing earth-shattering, it is the sort of thing churches do all the time – gather for prayer, mutual support, and praise. What is of interest is its very ordinariness.

This gathering is as spare as we Methodists get. No music, no offering, not much in the way of trappings at all. Just twenty or so people at the end of their work day, in the middle of their week, gathering in twilight to praise. We gather in the loveliest room here at our church – a high ceilinged, airy space where we can see our town's greatest mountain through the stately windows, and we bathe in the numinous light of that hour of the day. I have occasionally used the second-century prayer, 'Oh Gladsome Light, pure brightness of the ever-living Father in heaven, oh Jesus Christ, holy and blessed. Now as we come to the setting of the sun, and our eyes behold the vesper light, we praise thy name oh Father, Son, and Holy Spirit.' But more often I have prayed extemporaneously.

The form of the Eucharist is based on our Methodist Church's roots in the Church of England, which are in turn based on some of the most ancient liturgies of the church universal. The opening prayer glances at God's omniscience ('Almighty God, to you all hearts are open, all desires known, and from you no secrets are hid') and our calling to perfect love ('cleanse the thoughts of our hearts … that we may perfectly love you'). Then we pray a blessing over the reading and preaching of the word ('Open our hearts and minds … that we may receive with joy what you say to us today'). I read scripture and preach a (mercifully) short homily, often with responses of objection or agreement from the small congregation. Then we pray for our needs and the needs of others. These prayers are often why they have come. Their hearts are heavy, and they need help lifting them up to God. Next, the Eucharist offers that help: 'Lift up your hearts!' I command with the ancient words, and they all throw their hearts up in the air ('We lift them up to the Lord'). Then with the ancient liturgy I recount God's saving work in the Old and New Testaments. We pray with the seraphim in Isaiah and the elders in Revelation, 'Holy Holy Holy Lord, God of power and might' – sometimes I even sing that and they sing back. I ask that the bread and wine be transformed for us into the body and blood of Christ. They process up and I tell them, 'The body of Christ, broken for you. This is the body of Christ, the bread of heaven.' Another worshipper holds the cup, 'The blood of Christ, the cup of salvation.' They eat and drink, we pray, sometimes I make an announcement or two with service opportunities later in the week, and we all return to our lives.

It's all strikingly ordinary. Or if it strikes you at all, it's because your senses have been trained to notice the radical nature of the everyday. Christianity is always a matter of 'traditioned innovation', with an emphasis on both words.[1] It's never simply traditional – keeping the way we've always done things frozen in amber, as if for viewers in a museum. Nor is it simply innovative, making things up as we go along. It's always a matter of reaching back into our tradition to pull out what's old for a new day. Arguably there is no innovation anywhere, inside or outside the Church, without rich tradition; and likewise no tradition kept alive without some form of innovation. Jaroslav Pelikan, the great Orthodox scholar, liked to contrast tradition, which he called the 'living faith of the dead', with traditionalism, the 'dead faith of the living'. Creativity always depends on memory.[2]

I'm struck as I preside over this worship how close to the origins of the Church we are. 'Do this in remembrance of me', Jesus commands, and the Church always has, since well before there was a New Testament. One can see quickly how other forms of human creativity have been encouraged through such simple worship. Someone who has actual musical talent or training hears my feeble singing and offers something more intricate, or more rousing, for next time. Someone else writes a hymn we can all sing. Someone offers to portray Jesus in a picture, someone else to adorn our simple table with a cloth, or to throw pottery for our plate and cup, or to bake our bread or make our wine. Someone else offers to adorn the space. Others propose mission opportunities in which we can serve with our own hands. Others ask questions – how can we say Jesus is God when the Old Testament insists there is only one? How can we portray the unportrayable one in a picture when one of the Ten Commandments says not to do so? Should we leave all these crumbs on the floor? What do we do with the extra? Can we use food more indigenous to the people we're preaching to? Say, rice and tea in some places? Chips and beer for students?

The people of God who gather are never quite the same as they were in the previous gathering, even if the roll call is identical. We're different than we were last week. And hopefully we've brought friends. Or we come with new talents or new concerns and so bring new things to worship. Those who gather regularly will notice slight differences. Theology tries to name those differences, to test them against tradition and the needs of the community currently, to speak well of them within and beyond the church.

In short, a vast amount of material and intellectual creativity spring from this simple Eucharist and return to that Eucharist with more gifts to offer God and neighbor.

Christian faith has always been a practice as much as it is a list of beliefs – a practice born in baptism, Eucharist, preaching, service to the world. But this has often been forgotten in theology as we have concentrated on other appropriate topics, such as doctrine, especially when it needs clarifying in response to a challenge. Thinking about Christian faith is essential. We cannot understand God the way we can a computer or a fly swatter or a yo-yo. We cannot take God apart and put him back together, satisfied we know how the parts fit. But we can wonder about how what we know about God fits together. How does what we learn from the Bible fit with what we can reason out intellectually? How does what we learn from the Church's tradition mesh with our lived experience? Thinking in this sense is a wondering about the coherence, rationality, and beauty of the God we're always already worshiping. We cannot practice such simple prayers as our church conducts without hard questions coming up, demanding answers that in turn spark new questions. It's the God of the universe we're talking about here, fleshed in Jesus, poured out on the world in the Holy Spirit in mercy and grace, all one God – how does that work exactly? Theology as a practice is born of such simple, wide-ranging questions. Yet the danger for those who are called to work in such areas is living in our heads alone. Academic theologians, like all sorts of other academics, can treat their practice like an intellectual curiosity, rather than the lifebread of a hungry community. I think here of the way the young Dietrich Bonhoeffer viewed the vocation of a theologian as simply one profession among many he might choose from to satisfy his ambitions. He entered theology with no sense that his calling was to produce words of hope from beneath a tyrannical jackboot, though his rather bourgeois view of the vocation of theologian would later change spectacularly. Or of such theological movements as Radical Orthodoxy in the US and UK over the last twenty years, full of bracing and brilliant work, but with very little sense that a church like mine is waiting to hear a word from the Lord for them today, rather than a discourse on ever more obscure continental philosophers. Theology can act like its own master, rather than the servant of the Church.

Theology is a servant of the Church or it is a waste of time, it quite literally disgraces itself. The Church, in turn, is the cradle of theology, the place from which theological inquiry and examination and enhancement is born. We only contemplate God for the sake of a worshiping community. That community, in turn, looks to the office of theology to determine whether its prayers are in line with what the Christian community has long thought and practiced and ought to now. *Lex orandi, lex credendi* is the Latin name for this venerable principle: the law of prayer is the law of belief, and vice-versa. This principle is most often spoken of with enthusiasm in Roman Catholic or Anglican circles, in part because the idea (if not the words) is often attributed to Prosper of Aquitaine, a western patristic thinker. To caricature a bit, Catholics are often eager to appeal to Church tradition as a rationale for practices such as veneration of Mary that more Reformed Christians tend to find questionable. In Anglican settings the principle offers a kind of broad guideline for a theology without a single founding intellect. If the Lutherans have Luther, the Reformed Calvin or Zwingli, the Church of England has the law of prayer, most emblematically in the Book of Common Prayer. The principle is less often enunciated in evangelical traditions like my own, though it could stand as a resource for us too. Theology draws from and leads to prayer; prayer is guided and normed by theology. There is the possibility of a virtuous circle here. There are also problems – how can theology be culled, pruned, for greater faithfulness, if worship is its only stricture? From a much different vantage, what does God do when our worship is insufficiently faithful? When the church offers songs that reduce God to one who meets my sentimental needs, for example, rather than the consuming fire of Israel?

This chapter will offer some historic touchstones for understanding *lex orandi, lex credendi*, with an eye to enriching Christian worship and evangelizing Christian theology itself. It will engage the work of St Basil the Great, St Augustine, and St John Damascene, before summing up with the work of the contemporary theologian Geoffrey Wainwright and concluding with a glance back at worship. I hope this engagement shows as much as it tells. We are working on tradition in two senses. One, tradition is the content of faith as it has been passed on through the ages. Two, tradition is a verb – it is the act of handing on faith from one generation to the next. It changes as it stays the same – as saints and visionaries have long insisted will be true of the vision of God that awaits his people. This chapter's hope is that our churches will drink deeply at the well of the faith handed on to the apostles, lived into for a new day, and that those who practice theology in churches, universities, seminaries and elsewhere will see the *telos* (goal or objective) of their work the more faithful worship of the Christian community. Jesus himself prayed for worshipers who would worship 'in Spirit and in truth' (Jn. 4:24). One of the Trinity asked another that a third would gather a people for true worship. *Lex orandi, lex credendi* is not a Protestant or Catholic or evangelical thing. It is born in a prayer of Jesus. No part of the Church should be bashful about reclaiming this ancient Christian treasure for a new day.

St Basil: Who saves? Whom do you glorify?

One early significant argument for *lex orandi* is the Cappadocian father St Basil, often called 'the great' in the Church. Basil, with his younger brother Gregory of Nyssa and their friend Gregory of Nazianzus (the three are usually referred to by the title 'Cappadocian fathers')[3] and their slightly older colleague across the Mediterranean Sea, Athanasius of Alexandria, articulated and honed many of the arguments that came to be understood as Trinitarian orthodoxy. Although the fourth century defenders of the Council of Nicaea (AD 325) and its insistence on the Son's status as one who is *homoousion* (one substance) with the Father often insisted they were simply defending what the Church had always taught, recent scholarship has shown they were doing something much more interesting. They were innovating, in a way (as their critics charged – innovation was not the prized category then that it is in modernity!), but they were doing so in concert with scripture and tradition for the sake of a new day.[4] More polemical modern scholarship has suggested that the ancient controversies over the nature of the Trinity were simply a power grab. Other recent scholarship has suggested, on the contrary, that those arguing in favor of Nicaea actually had powerful arguments in their favor, while not denying the influence of politics in the Church.[5]

Basil's great text 'On the Holy Spirit' was written in 375 as a defense of a liturgical practice: 'Lately while I pray with the people, we sometimes finish the doxology to God the Father with the form "Glory to the Father *with* the Son, *together with* the Holy Spirit".'[6] Basil's opponents charge that this doxology is an innovation against their preferred form, 'Glory to the Father *through* the Son *in* the Holy Spirit'. While Basil himself claims to be content with either form of the doxology, and one might ask, 'What's all the fuss about prepositions?', his opponents charge him with illegitimately elevating the Holy Spirit to a rank equal to that of God the Father. These arguments are taking place after the Council of Nicaea in 325, so all parties have no choice but to agree, in principle, that the Son is divine. Nevertheless those who are concerned about the perceived polytheism of Nicaea, or perhaps about its Sabellianism (the belief that the three are really simply one God appearing in different guises) are here fighting a sort of rearguard action by trying to argue that the Spirit is a ministering servant of God, not to be elevated to the rank of divine equality. In deference to those whom he's trying to win over, Basil does not here insist that the Holy Spirit is God, *homoousion* with the Father and Son, the way his successors would do. He lays out the biblical logic for such a case in hopes that his hearers will draw that conclusion on their own.[7]

Basil works hard to apply to the Holy Spirit arguments that have long been made for the Son's divinity.[8] Just as the terms 'Father' and 'Son' logically imply one another, so too with the term 'Spirit': no one can live without their spirit. God must then be inseparable from his Spirit.[9] In both cases Basil, like other pro-Nicenes, tries to sheer off misinterpretations of our frail language (e.g. that a son would be younger, generated sexually by, or deserving of less dignity than a father) and draw out grammatical implications more in keeping with arguments for the Spirit's equal divinity. In fact, he and other pro-Nicenes are creating a clear distinction where there was not one before: one between God and creation. If descriptions of a Father, a Son, a Spirit, then angels, other creatures and so on once suggested a descending order of rank with no clear division between God and creatures, pro-Nicene polemicists insisted on just such a hard distinction, with the Spirit on 'God's' side of the demarcation. Even for angels, 'Holiness is not part of their essence; it is accomplished in them through communion with the Spirit.'[10] Basil is on his way to arguments his later colleagues would make clearer: that divine action is always cooperatively executed by the three persons, with no distinction in gradation or time or place as there would be with creatures cooperating. God is not circumscribed by time or place. The Spirit is regularly described in scripture as doing things that are only God's prerogative: only by the Holy Spirit can anyone confess Jesus as Lord, only by the Spirit is anyone made holy, he resurrects Jesus from the dead and eventually will raise us, he inspires scripture, he fills us as God fills his temple in the Old Testament.[11] Either we rank such a one with the Father and the Son as one God, or we must claim there are three distinct entities doing divine work. The options are either Trinitarian monotheism or idolatry.

Another key argument for those in favor of the Trinity in the fourth century was an essentially liturgical one. In whose name are we baptized? The seemingly simple question implies more profound ones: who do we trust to save us? And to whom do we offer glory in our worship? In both cases the answer has to be God, Father, Son, and Spirit. On the basis of such crystal clear texts as Matthew 28:19, the 'Great Commission',[12] the Church has always baptized in the Trinitarian name. And on the basis of other clear triadic texts the Church has always worshipped the Father, the Son, and the Spirit, one God. 'What makes us Christians?' Basil asks. 'How are we saved? Obviously through the regenerating grace of baptism.' And in whose name are Christians always baptized? He waxes poetic and eloquent on this point: 'If baptism is the beginning of my life, and the day of my regeneration is the first of days, it is obvious that the words spoken when I received the grace of adoption are more honourable than any spoken since.'[13] The name we trust to save us must be a divine name, or our salvation falls apart, and we commit the idolatry of trusting a creature. Basil's opponents are, in one way, correct; the Church has often followed biblical language in offering praise *to* the Father, *through* the Son, *in* the Spirit. But that is simply an accurate representation of the order through which God's benefits come to us in salvation. Biblical descriptions of the Son's being 'less' than the Father are taken by pro-Nicenes as indications of his self-emptying, incarnation, and saving work among us. So too descriptions of the Spirit as third in Trinitarian formulae do not indicate a lesser rank. They indicate God's saving presence among us: 'Therefore we use both phrases, expressing His unique dignity by one, and His grace to us by the other.'[14]

In one way these arguments are enormously complex, so naturally they took hundreds of years for the Church to sort out. Theology is like philosophy in that it must lead to coherence, logic, elegance, and Basil's makes clearer sense of the biblical witness and worshiping life of the Church than did his opponents. Basil's arguments won out because they made simple what was otherwise confusing: our worship applies pressure to our theology, offers correction to it, and makes us perfect, joining us to God. Either the two historic doxologies refer to the Trinity in equally appropriate ways, one naming the persons' equal majesty and dignity, the other referring to the Trinity's self-outpouring among us in Christ and by the Spirit, or one of the doxologies is blasphemous and should be eliminated. His opponents have rationale for one doxology, but none for the other. They fail to tell the story of salvation as well as Basil does. Our baptism – that is, the moment when God joins us to his saving works – either saves us by joining us in the Spirit to the unity the Son shares with the Father or it doesn't save us at all. Basil is aware that to some people these arguments seem overly subtle, trifling, and pedantic ('a battle over an *iota*', as Edward Gibbon famously dismissed the fourth-century debate between *homoousions* and *homoiousions* in the fourth century). But Basil counters,

> Those who are idle in the pursuit of righteousness count theological terminology as secondary, together with attempts to search out the hidden meaning in this phrase or that syllable, but those conscious of the goal of our calling realize that we are to become like God, as far as this is possible for human nature. But we cannot become like God unless we have knowledge of Him, and without lessons there will be no knowledge. Instruction begins with the proper use of speech, and syllables and words are the elements of speech. Therefore to scrutinize syllables is not a superfluous task.[15]

Words either successfully join us to God or number us among the idolators. Nothing less is at stake in our worship. It is the primary site in which we learn to talk about God.

One final important argument in *On the Holy Spirit* must be named for our purposes. Basil places a great importance on the unwritten tradition of the Church – practices and beliefs that come down to us from our predecessors that are not recorded in scripture. He situates his opponents rhetorically as only believing what can be proven by chapter and verse (and of being hypocritical at that – he points out practices of theirs that are not strictly biblical). 'For instance,' he writes, 'Where is the written teaching that we should sign with the sign of the Cross those who, trusting in the Name of our Lord Jesus Christ, are to be enrolled as catechumens?'[16] He goes on to list several catechetical practices not directly commanded in scripture: facing the East during prayer, specific words in the liturgy, blessing oil and water, baptizing with three immersions, the renunciation of Satan before baptism, and more. These are practices handed on in the Church but not written down in scripture. Basil argues that the apostles must have handed them down orally so they would not be exposed, trampled on, misunderstood by outsiders. Here again worship has a corrective effect on our beliefs, and not just worship that is directly mandated in written scripture, chapter and verse. It may take time and space for argument to recognize the corrective pressure of worship on our talk about God. That time and space is the office of a theologian – whose thinking, reading, writing, and above all conversation with others draws out the implications of (or offers challenges to) the Church's worship.

Some Christian arguments have taken this claim for the equal validity of unwritten tradition with written scripture as carte blanche for whatever worship practice in the Church of any ancient provenance having validity – if it's not in scripture and we do it, well, it must have been passed down, unwritten. Protestants have long complained that Catholic practices around veneration of Mary or the pope's authority are based on scriptural silence and relatively recent innovation; whereas Protestants are often in the position of Basil's opponents, claiming a sort of *sola scriptura* that is all but impossible to practice. For our purposes it is important to note that Basil offers some further strictures for determining whether a practice of worship is to be trusted. He claims to have examined his preferred doxology and to have found it to be of an 'early date', and to have come from patristic sources known 'for the precision of their knowledge'. In the Church earlier doesn't necessarily mean better – Arius predates Athanasius and so is 'closer' to the apostles in time, but in another, in terms of logic, he could not be farther from them or his opponent. Basil, discussing Origen's place in traditions over the Spirit, acknowledges that 'his notions ... are not always sound'. Yet on the Spirit he offers some truth: 'See how the powerful force of tradition often compels men to express themselves in terms contrary to their own opinions.'[17] In other words, scripture's pressure moves even Origen to some correct claims on the Spirit. Basil brings up Gregory Thaumaturgos, whose holiness he assumes his audience will respect, whatever their opinion on the question at hand: 'Shall we not number with the apostles and prophets a man who walked in the same Spirit?' He mentions martyrs who went to their deaths with Trinitarian praise on their lips. And he accuses his opponents of being people of ambition, 'jostling for high positions', each trying to 'thrust himself into high office'. Clearly some of this is just classical ancient rhetoric, 'heretics' had their martyrs and saints as well. Yet a greater point stands – correct theology and holy living go hand in hand. As we seek to make use of *lex orandi* in our theology, we too should use Gregory's guidelines: early provenance is important, scriptural use predominant, God's generation of holiness among us is supreme.

St Augustine: Receive what you are

For St Augustine, theology happens after the fact of worship, in an act of praise seeking understanding.[18] Christians are those people who are constantly offering praise to God. Having offered such praise, some among us look back over the scriptures and the gestures in worship and claims we have made about God and the world to try and wrestle as full a sense from them as we limited human beings can. The goal is not to understand God – an idol can be understood; the Creator cannot. The goal is to have our intellect catch up with the offering of praise we have always already just offered. It is to learn to wonder in the right way, to marvel at God, his scriptures, his creation, and our own transfiguration from sinners into saints.

A teacher, whether in the Church or elsewhere, faces a tall task. To use the language from Cicero on which Augustine was intellectually reared and which he himself taught, a teacher must strive to instruct, to delight, and to move her or his audience toward a certain form of life.[19] For Augustine it is Christ who is working through his Church to instruct, delight and move all of humanity toward himself. The theologian takes part in this divine wooing of creation back to God.

The Church must first instruct those whom it seeks to join its ranks. This is no easy task – Augustine himself was convinced by the Manichees for many years that their faith was intellectually superior to Catholic Christianity. So a catechist must be prepared to give the entire narrative of world history, from the opening chapters of Genesis until now. She or he must be able to show the unity of the Old and New Testaments, and the way the gems – the highlights of each story – are elegantly placed in a gold setting of love. Charity (love) is what ties the entire Christian story together, and since catechesis is meant to introduce a person to an entire new world, to a new set of relationships, a new family, a new history, and a new future, the teacher must be able to point all those things out. But this task is not narrowly intellectual. Augustine tells a certain Deogratias that the chief ingredient for a successful catechist is her or his joy.[20] The teacher's delight will be contagious. He or she must learn anew the things they teach to someone who has not heard them before, like a tour guide discovering anew the beauty of the place in the first-time vision of the guest. But this is not simply a matter of imagining oneself in another's position. When a new person joins the Church, the two are bound together in one body, both of their 'we' changes. As Augustine exudes in one sermon, 'I do not want to be saved without you!'[21] This teaching is also a rhetorical task. The teacher must oscillate between clear and open teaching of the faith and that which is hidden, concealed, and difficult. For God has set up a structure for human learning. We would despise what's easily learned and despair of what we cannot learn. So God reveals his treasures slowly, increasing delight as we move from unknowing, to beginning to glimpse, to something more like full knowledge. Intellectual knowledge is a step on the way to delight. It also requires the virtue of patience as God works on us over time. We are the secondary agents in theology; God is always the primary agent.

We might think here of Augustine's own experience of learning the Christian faith from Ambrose, told in his great *Confessions*. He did not attend worship in Milan at first to become a Christian. On the contrary, his Manichaean brethren had helped him attain good employment, and he was convinced the Church's views of God were unacceptably and primitively physical. Yet he'd heard of Ambrose's reputation as a master practitioner of rhetoric, and sure enough, as he listened some of the truth of his teaching leaked through. Ambrose also showed Augustine 'courtesy':

'My heart warmed to him … as a man who showed me kindness.' The two never became close, but Ambrose's brilliance and willingness to attend to the young Augustine, even a little, were key in his conversion. In one example, Ambrose preached to those enrolled for baptism in Milan about Elijah.[22] His hearers were fasting for forty days during Lent to prepare for baptism, as the prophet once had. As a result, Elijah was able to raise a dead child, to call down fire from heaven, and eventually to be swept up into heaven himself. Likewise the catechumens would be raised to new life in baptism, would draw down the fire of the Holy Spirit, and would be drawn in baptism into the heavenly mysteries. This is how patristic biblical teaching worked: it drew on both Testaments, it drew on the experience of those listening, and drew on the natural order, tying each together in a whole that is at least intellectually satisfying, and at best aesthetically delightful, moving, life-saving. Ambrose certainly showed Augustine how to teach – *after* he showed him courtesy, and gave him a model for an intellectual life in the Church.

Once someone like Augustine decides to submit his name for baptism (no small step), the patristic church had an enormously sophisticated system of catechesis and mystagogy by which to hand over the faith to them in its fullness. People often decided to become Christian because of fear of judgment, or because of a dream, or the experience of a miracle. The church's catechesis tried to take those experiences and direct catechumens' attention to the scriptures as well. And this was a task that involved the whole body of the one being taught. Unlike other intellectual options on offer in this world, Christianity affirmed the human body. It is a resistant and stubborn animal and needs teaching, but it can be bent to the will's desire and formed in the practices of holiness. And the body is beautiful as a creature of a gracious God. Augustine is capable of upsetting Gnostic or Manichaean condemnations of the body by simply praising its beauty. More importantly for our purposes, Augustine saw the deep connections between the outer and inner person, between confession with one's lips and the motions of the heart: 'You will believe what you hear yourself saying, and your lips will repeat what you believe.'[23]

At one point in the process of catechesis, catechumens would submit to a rite called 'the scrutiny'.[24] They would enter the church bowed down low or even prostrate themselves, signaling the humility that is the antidote to our pride. Then they would strip off their outer cloaks and stand on a sackcloth of goatskin, stomping on it. The description itself is visceral, dramatic – a humbled person, naked, stomping on an animal skin. But why a goatskin? First, it was held that the loincloths Adam and Eve wore when they fled the garden were made from goatskins. The catechumen was then lamenting the fall and longing for humanity's restoration. Second, the rite works to instil in us a fear of winding up as one of the goats on Christ's left at the judgment (Mt. 25:31–46). Augustine, in his preaching on this step of conversion, reminded his hearers that they renounced Satan, whom they 'rebuked in the name of the earth-shaking all-powerful Trinity, you were not clothed in goatskin-sackcloth; however your feet mystically stood on it. The vices and hides of goats must be trampled on.'[25] That's quite a lot of teaching from one goat hide! But notice its elements: the catechumens had a physical experience to remember, teaching about it drew on the full breadth of history from Genesis to the judgment, and new believers were urged to live up to the high calling of their baptism – a process begun by God through the Church in something so visceral as an animal skin. Catechesis in North Africa was like Augustine's preaching generally: he strained every word, wringing every ounce of meaning out of it for the sake of the holiness and love of God of those listening.

William Harmless, whose account of Augustine and the catechumenate I am following closely here, speaks well when he says Augustine's way of wondering is 'easier to intuit than to analyze'. It is a theology of the poet rather than that of, say, the metaphysician or even the biblical interpreter that Augustine often is elsewhere. Christians have long spoken of multiple layers of biblical exegesis – most commonly of the literal, the allegorical, the tropological and the anagogical, in the Middle Ages' mature four-fold description.[26] Augustine speaks here of multiple levels of exegesis too, but not as though they are properties 'in' a text. He rather marvels at a biblical text in relationship to something happening in the life of the Church now and often also to something in the natural order. The Bible, creation, and the conversion of the Church from Christ to Christ, from God's humanity to God's divinity, are the wide-open fields of play for this way of wondering. A venerable churchly word for such wonder is 'contemplation', pondering the depths of biblical meaning and seeing ever more of the infinitely glorious God reflected there. The goal here is the constant conversion of those for whom theology is being done: as Harmless quotes Augustine, 'the community did not simply celebrate Pasch [Easter], rather, "we enact Pasch"'.[27]

For example, Augustine can tell the entire gospel in startling detail through a description of the bread of the Lord's Supper as the body of Christ. The Church is also the body of Christ, of course, so Augustine can charge his hearers to 'Be what you see, and receive what you are.' Bread began as seeds, nurtured by rain, ripened into kernels, which were gathered, threshed, winnowed, gathered into a granary, milled, prepared, and baked into bread. Each detail corresponds to a detail in the church: hearers were created and brought to the threshing floor by the oxen (preachers). They were then set aside as hearers, then in Lent they were milled and sifted by fasts and exorcism. At baptism they were moistened and joined in a doughy lump. Then they were baked in the fire of the Holy Spirit. Here Augustine has taken an image so routine as to be easily overlooked not just by any church member but by any bread-eating person. And he has shown how each detail corresponds with the change being wrought in the hearers. From now on, any mention of bread, whether in church or out, should register in a different key for the hearers. For bread is only *there* at all as an image of what God is doing in the world, in the scriptures, in us, in Christ. Bread is no longer 'just' bread (indeed, no thing is any longer 'just' itself). It is part of the economy of salvation. Theology trains us to pay attention to the routine, to see remarkable depths stretched out before us precisely there, where an untrained eye would fail to stop short and luxuriate. What else might we wonder about in a similar way?

To step back briefly into contemporary church life, I once heard the distinguished American author Barbara Brown Taylor preach about baptism. She spoke of witnessing the great South African Archbishop Desmond Tutu preach about baptism. She saw him do something she'd never seen before – showing anew that innovation and tradition are twins. She described Tutu opening the baptismal font and blowing on the water. This is not only an echo of ancient Christian teaching that water should be 'living', moving, and not stagnant. It's also an echo of God's own Spirit hovering over the water in Genesis. It reminds us of God who blows life into human beings and the Holy Spirit into believers (Gen. 2:7, Acts 2:4). It reminds us of Jesus commanding his followers to receive the Spirit after his resurrection and blowing in their faces (Jn. 20:22). In Augustine's day, preachers would hiss in the faces of those approaching for baptism. It was a way of rebuking Satan, exorcizing demons, disrespecting the evil in us all (one pagan law forbade people, presumably Christians, from hissing at images of the emperor!). Having heard Taylor on this point, intrigued by her delight, I speak often of it in my own preaching on baptism. The image is strengthened by coming from Tutu, himself a man of heroic virtue whose ministry bore profound fruit. For all that it wouldn't be helpful or interesting if it failed to make a biblical point, one rooted also in the ongoing liturgy and preaching of the Church. Having heard it, water and air are now different. They're marked with Christological and ecclesial particularity. They're not only there to slake thirst and offer warmth, deeply good as those things are. They're there to save us.

The point of Augustine's preaching is not simply to delight us as hearers, important as that is, nor simply that we be instructed about the nature of things. It intends us to be moved, changed, into a different sort of person. Harmless speaks of Augustine offering a 'crossweave' of doctrinal and moral teaching in his catechetical instruction. Augustine wants his hearers feeding Christ in his poor. He wants an 'us' that works to mend the social order from one of selfishness and destructiveness to one of peace, grace, and feasting. For one often accused, even lampooned, as a 'neo-Platonist', and so supposedly unconcerned with material realities in the world, Augustine can't think long about bread without also thinking of those whose bellies are currently empty. Those who gather up surpluses steal from Christ, who intends our goods to go to his poor. Those who have received stupendous mercy from a generous God are necessarily also those who offer mercy and generosity to others, and Augustine is not hesitant to use language both threatening and beautiful on this point: 'Let the hungry Christ be fed; let the thirsty Christ be given drink; let the naked Christ be clothed; let the foreign-born Christ be sheltered; let the ill Christ be visited.'[28]

This way of reading scripture is normally spoken of as 'mystagogy', and the fourth and fifth century as great eras of mystagogy in the Church. That is, of wondering after the fact at what God is doing in our midst in scripture, creation, and in our own transformation. Mystagogy is a supreme example of *lex orandi, lex credendi*. At a basic level, every church (or whatever other human institution) needs a process by which to integrate new people, including instruction, opening of particular delights, introduction to a place for that person to serve and thrive. In the Church we're all striving to be born again through the womb of preparation. Like the Israelites in the wilderness we fast, pray, worry, wonder, and are provided for by God. After that Lenten journey we pass through the water of baptism, like our forebears through the Red Sea of old (ever wonder why it's red?). And now as we struggle with the life of discipleship we are like Moses, presiding over the battle of the Israelites with the Amalekites – while our arms are raised in prayer we thrive, when they fall from that cruciform posture we suffer defeat (Ex. 17:8–13). This is quite unlike most forms of interpretation encouraged in modernity (though by no means is it incommensurate with it). Yet for that it is not less rigorous – it simply trades in delight rather than discovery of ever more remote layers of pre-history, and so has to notice the response of the hearers as well as the words on the page. It works to shape a people's imagination. It offers a way of wondering that informs the whole of life. It informs not only what we believe, and what we pray, but who we are, on the way to what we're becoming, namely, children of God.

St John of Damascus: Do we worship matter?

One of the perennial difficulties in Christian theology is what value to give to the created order. On the one hand, we find texts in John's gospel and elsewhere that describe the 'world' in quite negative terms – as something to avoid, or at least whose contamination the Church should shun (e.g. Jn. 15:18–21). On the other hand, we have a God in the Bible who creates, sustains, and dies to save the 'world'. In our times, concerns over the environment add moral urgency to this theological topic. Some more fundamentalist Christians might be content to let the world burn (presumably because they assume they won't be in it when it happens, having been raptured). Yet we shouldn't pillory fundamentalists simply for having the courage of their convictions – Christianity as a whole has a world-denying component to it, one that can tip over into hatred of the world, the body, the self. Indeed it often has done precisely that. Meanwhile, others' desire to care for creation makes them sound little different than liberal politicians.

In the ancient church a concern arose that is adjacent to our own, though not the same. The church had a long tradition of visual portrayals of Jesus and the saints in 'icons' – images intended for veneration in the liturgy. Even now Orthodox Christians will light candles in front of, kiss, and bow before icons in worship. But in the seventh and eighth centuries some Christians decided these traditions were illegitimate. Doesn't the second commandment outlaw visual portrayals of God, let alone Christian worship of images?[29] (Ex. 20:4–6). These gained authority by the ascent of Islam, with its clear denunciation of all image-making and veneration as idolatrous. Emperors came to power and called councils that denounced icons. What did Christians in favor of such veneration have to say for themselves?

One such Christian is now remembered as St John of Damascus, or Yuhanna Al Demasqi, whose name and home make clear he was an Arab Christian. His monastery near Jerusalem, Mar Saba, was outside the reach of Roman imperial authorities, but interestingly in the territory of the very Muslims who were keen on wiping out idolatrous images. From that monastery he penned a brief and influential defense of icon veneration, the argument of which hinged on the incarnation. John's work is a key chapter in the history of *lex orandi*, and more than that it demonstrates the best way to read this tradition. If an argument for *lex orandi* depends upon and requires the incarnation, the word made flesh, for it to work, it deserves a greater hearing in the Church than one that does not.

John cheerfully acknowledges scripture's frequent denunciation of idolatry. These are present because of the biblical Israelites' proneness to idolatry and indeed also because of our own.[30] Put an image in front of us creatures and we tend to worship it. Scripture is appropriately vigilant against this tendency. We Christians further know that we cannot ever pretend to depict God. The divine nature in itself is uncircumscribed, unimaginably beyond us, unable to be imagined, let alone drawn in a picture.

If the story ended there, our Muslim neighbors would be right, let God never be drawn, and we would do well, like ancient and modern iconoclasts, to smash images of God to make their idolatrous nature plain. Yet that is not the end of the story. Formerly, God was without a body, and could not be depicted visually. But now that God is in the flesh, in his incarnation, he can be depicted. The incarnation has changed the story dramatically, irreversibly, so that John can now exclaim

> I do not worship matter; I worship the Creator of matter who became matter for my sake, who worked out my salvation through matter. Never will I cease honoring the matter which wrought my salvation.[31]

John acclaims the God who 'clothed Himself in the royal purple of my flesh', who 'leads us through matter to the invisible God'.[32] The Seventh Ecumenical Council crowned John's and others' arguments canonically with a claim that Christians not only can depict God and honor those depictions – they indeed must do so.[33] If they fail to draw pictures of God they will undo and undercut the incarnation, the staggering claim that God became flesh in order to save and glorify all who are also flesh.

John's argument has a number of implications. One is that we should not only depict and honor images of Jesus, we should also depict and honor images of the saints. If God has indeed visited humanity in the flesh, bound himself in flesh to the Church, and made members of his body holy, then those members also deserve our veneration. Not our adoration – John is careful to distinguish between *latreia*, that adoration due only to God; and *doulia* or *proskinesis*, often translated 'veneration', which we offer to the human nature of Christ and to his members, the saints. But Christians do indeed owe veneration to those whom God has joined in flesh and made holy. John quotes another author to this effect: 'If you love God, you will be eager to honor his servants also.'[34] John elaborates, 'I bow before the images of Christ, the incarnate God; of our Lady, the Theotokos and Mother of the Son of God; and of the saints, who are God's friends.' Such claims will feel awkward and unfamiliar to some Reformed and evangelical Christians, and more at home to Orthodox and Catholic ones. Worship in Orthodox churches is a visual, olfactory, even sensual affair, with believers bowing before and kissing images of Christ and the saints. The honor they offer there is transferred to the one whose flesh is there depicted, and indeed a sensual, world-affirming faith can follow.

For our purposes another corollary of John's argument is that all matter is, in some sense, honored, glorified, shown to be beloved of God. If God became matter, all matter is divinely visited, hallowed, worthy of our affection. 'Behold the glorification of matter!' John exclaims against his polemical opponents. 'Do not despise matter', he elaborates, 'for it is not despicable. God has made nothing despicable', He who 'in his love for mankind stooped down' to our level.[35] For the defenders of icons, their veneration is the natural outworking of a doctrine of creation and of the incarnation. God delights in matter enough to have created it and maintained it in being despite human sin, he binds himself to us in love by his election of Israel and assumption of flesh. Far from despising matter, God adores it and raises it toward the level of his own dignity. John points out the shocking implications of this in a number of places – pagans and Jews both are horrified by dead bodies; Christians, on the contrary, build churches on top of graves and honor relics.[36] Far from despising geographical places we make pilgrimage to them, especially those of special import in the history of salvation. For there 'God, who alone is holy, has rested', so they are holy 'not by nature, but by adoption'. Finally, John concludes, we must offer to one another our 'veneration', for 'we are God's inheritance, and were made according to His image, and so we are subject to each other, thus fulfilling the law of love.'[37] John quotes an earlier father, Gregory Nazianzus, speaking in the voice of the recently baptized, insisting on his dignity: 'I have been transformed into Christ by baptism; you must worship me!'[38] Or to be more specific to St John – you must venerate me, and adore only God.

Eastern Orthodoxy has not always lived up to the implications of this radically world-affirming view of the incarnation any more than any other church has. We have often refused to recognize in one another the dignity of our having the flesh that God took, glorified, and loves. But the resources are there for such a lavishly world-loving view of our faith. And for the purposes of this chapter the implications of *lex orandi* are clear: John argues we must venerate images in our worship, a church council crowned that argument, it is up to us to figure out how to live into that high demand, at once liturgical and ethical: honor and revere the flesh God assumed, still has, cherishes, and will one day make transparent to the fullness of the divine presence it already bears.

At the risk of sounding like the preacher I am, let me note that Desmond Tutu has often preached that anytime we see another human being we ought to genuflect – an appropriate gesture for those made in the image of God. One can imagine white racists in South Africa hearing this and scoffing. One can also imagine black South Africans refusing to bow to those who've asked them to bow and abused them when they did not. I love the language in *Christianity Today*'s Christian Vision project of the Church needing to be a 'counter-culture for the common good'. We'll often be over-against the world and our neighbors, but it is for the good of those neighbors and that world that we're over-against – especially in our effort to offer a beauty that terrifies and converts, such as in the works of the Church's iconographers and their depictions of the saints.

Geoffrey Wainwright: Some criteria

Having introduced three figures from the first millennia of the Church's tradition of thought on *lex orandi* – St Basil the Great, St Augustine, and St John of Damascus – it may help to introduce at least one from the more recent millennium. Geoffrey Wainwright is a Protestant who has written with deep sympathy about the Catholic church. Indeed his book *Doxology* speaks of theology as a task that has its end in worship. Wainwright helpfully describes the conflict between churches over *lex orandi, lex credendi*, and then offers some criteria by which we might distinguish more from less faithful uses of it. He does so knowing he's a bit of an oddity – very few Protestant theologians tend to weigh in on the topic (he confesses that for a magisterially-sized book like his he could find 'no more than a handful' of such Protestant sources).[39] For Protestants the weight has been placed decidedly on the *lex credendi* side of the ledger – doctrine corrects worship, rather than the reverse. If a practice of worship is out of step with biblical teaching, then uproot it, smash it, correct it, change it. Reformed iconoclasts were responsible agents in this tradition when they destroyed images and statues in the Reformation.[40] Wainwright shows how the Roman Catholic Church has often taken *lex orandi, lex credendi* as a means of conferring authority on its own magisterial office. He cites Pope Pius XII: 'In regard to the liturgy, it is a zeal both unwise and misguided that would go back to the ancient rites and customs and repudiate the new regulations which under God's wise Providence have been introduced to meet altered conditions.'[41] What in the church fathers was an argument from the worship of the entire church comes here to mean that whatever the Vatican authorizes should be taken as authoritative. No wonder Protestants have shunned the doctrine.

Yet it was not always so in Catholic thought. *Lex orandi* was re-championed first among sixteenth and seventeenth century liturgists within Roman Catholicism. Then and subsequently it has served as a *corrective* to the liturgy, not just an imprimatur upon it. One champion of *lex orandi* critiqued his own tradition by saying there is 'much that is idle, profane, and foreign to true religion' in Catholic practice; another insisted that 'not every devotion of Catholics is a Catholic devotion'.[42] This corrective function of doctrine *within* Catholic thought and practice has a long tradition in the Church. St Cyprian already insisted in the third century that custom without truth is simply old error! So how do we know which innovations in church life are simply intrusions of human sin and which are genuine guidance of the Holy Spirit?[43]

Wainwright revisits the text of Prosper of Aquitaine from which *lex orandi* originates. Prosper was a disciple of St Augustine and a defender of his late-career anti-Pelagian arguments. For Prosper, grace is always a matter of Christ's prior action upon us, so that no faithful human action in response to God is possible independently or antecedently to that work of grace. Any human work is enabled by God's grace and never independent of it. Prosper cites in his favor the pastoral practice of praying for those throughout the world who are now without faith: 'When the presidents of the holy congregations perform their duties, they plead the cause of the human race before the divine clemency and, joined by the sighs of the whole church, they beg and pray, "that grace may be given to unbelievers ... "'.[44] Apostolic precedent is important to Prosper, but neither papal teaching nor apostolic injunction *add* anything to the argument from the Church's worship. The fact that the Church prays this prayer, and God answers it with people's conversions, is the strength of the argument.

Wainwright goes on to offer three suggestions for the use of *lex credendi* in our day – in his context, as an ecumenist, he does so in hopes that a reunited Church may use this tradition anew. First, he suggests that the Church grant more weight to places where the Triune God has acted in our history. For worship is primarily an act of the Trinity, one based on divine initiative rather than creaturely, that sweeps up human response into it. In matters of doctrinal dispute then, 'Most weight will be given to ideas and practices which go back to Jesus', the Triune God's incarnation among us.[45] Another test for liturgy will be the degree to which a practice approaches universality in the Church's worship. St Vincent of Lerins famously insisted that what is catholic is that which has been believed 'always, everywhere, and by everyone'. That criterion may be unreachable, and may indeed have been unattainable already in St Vincent's fifth century, but it remains a helpful ecumenical goal. Finally Wainwright points to the 'ethical component of holiness'. Does a practice produce holy people? On these grounds Wainwright grants some space for Quaker practices of worship, despite his own heavy sacramentalism and Quakers' minimalist Trinitarianism, for they have borne fruit in the world.

These are good suggestions. Yet the breadth of the suggestions shows that *lex orandi, lex credendi* is not the sharpest tool for distinguishing between faithful practices and those that are not. We might rather think of the saying as an aspiration. We should want our prayer to influence and change our theology, just as we want our theology to lead to and empower more faithful prayer. The two sides to the saying put weight on one another and create what we hope will be a fruitful tension. This is not a paradox or a dialectic that seeks resolution. It is an appropriate tension to keep before the eyes of the Church in every act of prayer, in every act of theology. Is what we're doing faithful to the mind of the Church, fleshed in Jesus, witnessed to in the scriptures, continuing in his body in all places now? And as we do theology we must constantly ask, how does this serve the worshipping body of Jesus during this time between his first coming and his second? This does not only mean that theology must be accessible in some sense to the proverbial person in the pews, though there is that.[46] It also means that theology must be in service to the Church as a gathering of Christ's body or it must be deemed to be something other than Christian theology.[47]

This chapter has tried to describe the mutually corrective functions of theology and worship in the life of the Church. Worship brings pressure to bear on our speech about God, as St Basil argued in the fourth century Trinitarian debates. If the Church has always praised the Trinity as God, has always baptized in the triune name, how can that One not be divine? St Augustine's goal is for theology to be a rhetorical art in which the Triune God woos us back to right delight in him by catechesis and life-long worship. St John Damascene tries to defend his church's robust, world-affirming faith and practice of veneration of icons, and so of all humanity, by distinguishing it from the adoration offered to God alone. And Geoffrey Wainwright helps us talk across lines of ecclesial fracture about how to use *lex orandi* to discriminate practices that will make for the churches' (Church's?) wholeness from those that will bring further fracturing. Worship shows the Church's theologians what is true about God in a way that may be just beyond us, such that we struggle to catch up with what God is saying. In turn the theological office is partly one of correction to practices of worship that may step out of line with God's intention for us all.[48] We all have plenty of work to do. But the force of *lex orandi* is toward worship. Theology exists in service of the Church's worship rather than the other way around.

Back to worship

Think again with me of that evening Eucharistic service I mentioned. Theology belongs to that table. It takes its cues from and leads back to breaking that bread, pouring that wine, distributing the divine nature to those present, so they may in turn be the divine presence in the world, challenging injustice, inviting to mercy, proclaiming the day of the Lord's favor. The Church has been right to invent, found, and support institutions of learning meant to prepare pastors and other leaders for those difficult sets of tasks. Yet those institutions, from the church to the seminary and the university, must in turn be open to correction from that table, the scriptures resting upon it, the people gathered there to adore, feast, and receive blessing. Is our way of doing this, of celebrating this mystery, faithful to who God is? In recent memory the decision in some parts of the Church to invite women not only in front of the table but also behind it as leaders, as what they see as a faithful expression of those scriptures, our memory, and that sacramental practice, is a major revision. It bears the burden of proof to show how that revision is faithful rather than an innovation that does not bear holiness into the world. It does so by showing this to be the work of the Holy Spirit, one that deepens our marvelling at Christ, his Church, and his scriptures, one that turns on the incarnate nature of God. The Church – the presence of God in the world now – is not impervious to change, slow as that change may be for our tastes sometimes. She is, we hope, impervious to any other leading than that of our incarnate Lord.

The Eucharistic service focuses *lex orandi* in another way. Theology is a word about God, conducted in the third person. But it is also a word addressed to God in prayer.[49] This is always preceded by a word from God in creation, election, incarnation, scripture. The purpose of theology is praise, worship, joining with Christ to his Father. 'Receive what you are,' Augustine instructed. The final goal of theology is not to think correctly – that's a necessary but insufficient step. It is to *be* differently – namely the people God created and redeems us into being, a body for him in the world.

Notes

1 'Traditioned innovation' is language coined at Duke Divinity School's Leadership Education: www.faithandleadership.com. It is echoed in David Ford's language of 'Creative retrieval' in his *The Future of Christian Theology*, Oxford: Wiley-Blackwell, 2011.

2 I'm grateful here for Sam Wells' discussion in his *Transforming Fate into Destiny*, Eugene, OR: Cascade, 1998, and to J. Fodor and S. Hauerwas, 'Performing Faith: The Peaceable Rhetoric of God's Church', in W. Jost and W. Olmstead (eds) *Rhetorical Invention and Religious Inquiry: New Perspectives*, New Haven, CT: Yale University Press, 2000, pp. 382–414.

3 Although even that is subjective – iconography tends to image Basil with Gregory Nazianzen and St John Chrysostom as exemplars of the ascetic, the theological teacher, and the pastoral lives, respectively. The great modern scholar of the ancient church, Jaroslav Pelikan, tended to include Basil and Gregory's sister Macrina among the luminaries. See his *Christianity and Classical Culture: The Metamorphosis of Natural Theology in the Christian Encounter with Hellenism*, New Haven, CT: Yale University Press, 1993.

4 See, for example, L. Ayres, *Nicaea and its Legacy*, Oxford: Oxford University Press, 2004.

5 See also R. Williams, *Arius: Heresy and Tradition*, Grand Rapids, MI: William B. Eerdmans Publishing Company, 2002; J. Behr, *The Formation of Christian Theology*, 2 vols, Crestwood, NY: St Vladimir's Seminary Press, 2001–4.

6 St Basil the Great, *On the Holy Spirit*, trans. D. Anderson, 3rd edn, Crestwood, NY: St Vladimir's Seminary Press, 1997, p. 17. This is a good text to attend to not least because

it is short, punchy, and its English translation is accessible, even vibrant (contrary to its introduction, extolling 'dry and logical' Cappadocian theology! [p. 12]).

7 St Basil here seems to me to be laying out a Christian case for the necessity of innovation in order to maintain continuity in ways very similar to those John Henry Cardinal Newman would develop in the nineteenth century. See here Rowan Williams' essay, 'Newman's *Arians* and the Question of Method in Doctrinal History', in I. Ker and A.G. Hill (eds) *Newman after a Hundred Years*, Oxford: Clarendon, 1990, pp. 263–85.

8 Ayres, *Nicaea and its Legacy*, p. 212.

9 Basil, *On the Holy Spirit*, p. 67.

10 Basil, *On the Holy Spirit*, p. 63.

11 Basil, *On the Holy Spirit*, p. 74.

12 'Go, therefore, and make disciples of all nations, baptizing them in the name of the Father, and of the Son, and of the Holy Spirit' (RSV).

13 Basil, *On the Holy Spirit*, pp. 46–47.

14 Basil, *On the Holy Spirit*, p. 36.

15 Basil, *On the Holy Spirit*, p. 16.

16 Basil, *On the Holy Spirit*, p. 99.

17 Basil, *On the Holy Spirit*, p. 109.

18 I argue this at length in my book *Praise Seeking Understanding*, Grand Rapids, MI: William B. Eerdmans Publishing Company, 2007.

19 See here D. Cunningham (ed.) *To Teach, to Delight, and to Move: Theological Education in a Post-Christian World*, Eugene, OR: Cascade, 2004.

20 The book I follow throughout this section is W. Harmless, *Augustine and the Catechumenate*, Collegeville, MN: Pueblo Books, 1995 (here p. 134).

21 Sermon 17.2, quoted in Harmless, *Augustine and the Catechumenate*, p. 188.

22 This comes from Harmless, *Augustine and the Catechumenate*, p. 95.

23 *De Symbolo ad catechumenos* 1.1, quoted in Harmless, *Augustine and the Catechumenate*, p. 276.

24 Harmless notes that while some form of the exsufflation (hissing in another's face) was common in churches throughout the world, this particular moment in the rite seems to have been unique to North African churches. See also 'It Happened One Saturday Night: Ritual and Conversion in Augustine's North Africa', *Journal of the American Academy of Religion* 58.4, 1990, pp. 589–616.

25 Harmless, *Augustine and the Catechumenate*, pp. 263 and 273.

26 A standard illustration of the *quadriga*, or four-fold medieval approach to biblical interpretation, is of the richly biblical word, 'Jerusalem'. On the literal level it is a city on a map locatable in Palestine. Allegorically speaking it is the Church. Tropologically, it is the kingdom for which Christians hope. Anagogically it is heaven. In pre-modern imaginations Jerusalem can 'be' each of these things at once.

27 Harmless, *Augustine and the Catechumenate*, p. 301, quoting sermon 223I.1.

28 Harmless, *Augustine and the Catechumenate*, p. 327, quoting sermon 236.3.

29 On this topic see also the related chapter in this volume by Richard Viladesau, 'Engagement with the arts'.

30 St John of Damascus, *On the Divine Images*, trans. D. Anderson, Crestwood, NY: St Vladimir's Seminary Press, 1997, p. 18.

31 John of Damascus, *On the Divine Images*, p. 23.

32 John of Damascus, *On the Divine Images*, pp. 16 and 67.

33 The Seventh Ecumenical Council is the coronation of Orthodoxy in the eastern churches, but has never been as widely received or respected in the western churches.

34 John of Damascus, *On the Divine Images*, p. 42, quoting one Leo of Cyprus, whose book bears the disgraceful title, *Against the Jews*.

35 John of Damascus, *On the Divine Images*, pp. 24, 25, and 35.

36 On this point see P. Brown, *The Cult of the Saints: Its Rise and Function in Latin Christianity*, Chicago, IL: University of Chicago Press, 1982; John of Damascus, *On the Divine Images*, p. 58.

37 John of Damascus, *On the Divine Images*, p. 87.

38 John of Damascus, *On the Divine Images*, p. 102.

39 G. Wainwright, *Doxology*, Oxford: Oxford University Press, 1980, p. 219.

40 See here E. Duffy, *The Stripping of the Altars: Traditional Religion in England, 1400–1580*, New Haven, CT: Yale University Press, 2005.

41 Wainwright, *Doxology*, p. 223.

42 Wainwright, *Doxology*, pp. 220 and 221.

43 In a helpful essay, Rowan Williams casts doubt on the *lex orandi* tradition, pointing out that one ancient liturgical practice in the fourth century was to identify the seraphim of Isaiah 6 with the Son and the Holy Spirit, and to praise Christ with biblical and traditional language of angelology. Pro-Nicene authors took this to be a subordinationist tradition and so ruled it out. Yet that tradition was more ancient than those that came after. Clearly *lex orandi, lex credendi* needs some nuancing.

44 Wainwright, *Doxology*, p. 225. It is significant that Pelagian polemicists would have used a practice like this – prayer for unbelievers – to argue for human freedom over against grace that, for them, takes away human initiative. Why would the church pray for conversions, they would ask, if God has already decided human destiny from before all eternity?

45 The reference 'back', if taken historically, could suggest a primitivism that might be objectionable. A logical reference might be better – practices should find their roots in Christology, not necessarily in what we can surmise the incarnate Jesus might have been thinking.

46 Naturally theology will not always be easily explainable to the simple, pious believer. Some will be conducted over technical terms, or at a philosophical plane, and will be accessible by only a few. Nevertheless that must be able to be broken down and re-presented to the saints or it runs the risk of Gnosticism – the heresy of thinking the whole of the Church is only there for a special few in the intelligentsia.

47 The goal here is not to impugn other traditions and their theology. It is to say that Christians will have richer conversations with Jews and Muslims, for example, when each group delves most deeply and faithfully into the riches of its tradition for the sake of genuine difference, rather than eliding differences in pursuit of a superficial conversation. Scriptural Reasoning (www.scripturalreasoning.org/) is a tradition that thinks through such conversations with profundity and humility.

48 See here Mike Higton's chapter on 'Reason' in this volume, with its helpful description of how arguments reach settlements, tenuously, and then subsequently become unsettled. I think on these lines of Herbert McCabe's description of Christian theology, that we don't know what Christians will believe in the twenty-fourth century, but we know they won't be Arians or Nestorians. The history of doctrine closes off some options as deadly. But there remains a vast amount of freedom for the Church to walk through. Actually closing off deadly options enhances and deepens that freedom.

49 I am taking these categories from Geoffrey Wainwright's lectures on worship at Duke Divinity School.

15
READING CLASSIC TEXTS

Morwenna Ludlow

What is a 'classic text'?

There is clearly much more to be said about classic texts than that they have not, for the most part at least, been regarded as Scripture.[1] This chapter therefore begins by discussing some other answers to the question. This is not simply for the purpose of defining terms, but because these answers reveal much about the way in which Christians have, in fact, gone about the practice of reading classic texts and, no less importantly, the process whereby certain texts have become classic.

The concept of a 'classic' Christian text usually implies orthodoxy and a perceived coherence with Scripture. Indeed, a classic text might derive its authority largely or partly from being an interpretation of Scripture (to take two very different examples: Bernard of Clairvaux's *Sermons on the Song of Songs* or Karl Barth's *Commentary on Romans*). But it is worth noting that what is orthodox for one Christian tradition might not be orthodox for another and that many a text will cohere with a specific interpretation of Scripture that might not be a universal one. (Not all Christians will accept the allegorical method of interpretation that Bernard uses to read the *Song of Songs*, nor the particular mystical theology that forms and is formed by it.) Thus, while there is a fairly broad consensus between Christians about the contents of the biblical canon – give or take a few books – there is by no means a similar consensus about a list of Christian 'classic texts'.

On the other hand, not all orthodox Christian texts can be regarded as classic texts – a little-read treatise seems not to qualify. By a 'classic', one seems to mean a text that has played an important role in the (or a) Christian tradition. In other words, an understanding of reception – and thus of practice – is built into the notion of a 'classic'. There are both stronger and weaker examples of this kind of reception. Most strongly, there are texts that have become foundation documents for Christianity or for a particular Christian tradition. For example, the version of the Nicene Creed received at Constantinople in 381 has been read by Christians as normative for the way in which they understand the relationship of Jesus Christ to God the Father. It is not only normative as a formula of words around which like-minded Christians could unite, but also as a rule by which to read Scripture (thus the members of the Council of Chalcedon in 451 clearly understood their role as reading the Bible through the Niceno-Constantinopolitan Creed and providing further clarification where it seemed ambiguous). Furthermore, some creeds became classic texts for certain groups because they excluded other Christian communities, whether unintentionally or intentionally. For example, the fathers who formulated Chalcedon clearly intended to exclude some views and individuals, but it is highly unlikely that they intended the Creed to lead to schism as it did (because various eastern church communities thought its definition stressed the unity of Christ too little or too much). Other formulas of faith were specifically conceived to define a certain community over against another – some of the confessions drawn up in the Reformation fit this pattern, for example, although whether any particular confession should be read mainly as a rejection of certain other church communities or as an attempt to retrieve or return to what is crucially important about Christianity is an arguable point.

Other classic texts have become normative for a particular Christian tradition not because they were formulated to exclude opponents, but because they were drawn up for a limited group who saw themselves as having a particular role: for example, the monastic rules of Basil or Benedict have become classic texts for those communities following them and have come to be read as if they were founding documents of a particular kind of Christian tradition. Besides creeds, confessions and rules there are other classic texts of a more strictly theological nature that have been so influential on a particular tradition and so intimately bound up with its identity that they might be read as (partially) defining it: for example, the sermons of Gregory Nazianzus and John Chrysostom, Aquinas' *Summa Theologica*, the writings of Luther, or Calvin's *Institutes*.

More weakly, one might suggest that a classic text is not necessarily one that has founded a particular Christian tradition, but is one that has stood the test of time. For example one might point to the way that Augustine's *Confessions*, or his *City of God* have proved themselves as great theological works over many centuries. Like the idea of a founding document, the notion of standing the test of time relies on the notion of reception – readers continue to read *The City of God* with excitement 1,500 years after it was written. The idea of durability also excludes books which are wildly popular for a short time but then sink into oblivion, but it also perhaps tacitly acknowledges that there could have been some other classic texts that are now lost.

The notion of reception is more explicit in the idea that a classic text has not only stood the test of time but has been accepted by a substantial number of people as classic. This does not, of course, mean that all Christians or even a majority need to accept a text for it to become a classic – theological disagreements and problems of literacy levels make this too high a bar to clear. But it seems that a certain weight of theological opinion needs to lie behind a classic text. That does not necessarily mean, incidentally, that a theologian agrees with everything in a classic text in order to regard it as a classic: a Protestant could easily regard Aquinas' *Summa* as a classic text without agreeing with everything in it; modern Reformed churches can regard Calvin's *Institutes* as a classic text whilst having a lively critical approach to its reading, interpretation, and application.

Finally, the notion of a classic text seems to imply that it has stood the test of time and has been received positively by many people because of its inherent qualities. That is, it is not coincidence that such a text has been received so positively; rather, it has been received positively because it has proved to be fruitful. It has, for example, founded a lasting Christian community who continue to identify themselves by it, or it is complex and bears frequent re-reading which reveals new aspects of it, or it has stimulated further creative theological thought, or it has inspired certain kinds of moral action or reflection. As we shall see, a theological classic is often regarded as having the capacity to speak meaningfully to readers today – although that will not necessarily mean that one can apply it directly to modern problems in a simple way. The advice that 'you will know them by their fruits' (Mt. 7:20) could as easily apply to Christian texts as individual persons – although the difficulties of discerning a 'good fruit' remain the same.

Thus, I am arguing that a classic text in Christian theology is a non-Scriptural text which has been received by a Christian community or communities as a broadly orthodox expression of its faith and which has played and continues to play an important role in the development of a Christian tradition or traditions – that is, it has been fruitful either in terms of practice or theory.

I would however emphasize a few further cautions. First, as I have implied, a text accepted as 'classic' by one tradition will not necessarily be accepted as such by another: thus a Lutheran and a Greek Orthodox believer will probably have different opinions about the writings of both Luther and Gregory Nazianzus. Many Christians will be completely ignorant of texts which are classic for certain Christian traditions: for example, few Western Christians know the *Doctrine of Addai* which has immense importance for Syriac Christianity, tracing its origins back to King Agbar who, it has said, welcomed the disciple Addai (Thaddeus) into his kingdom.

Second, although I have suggested that a text needs to have stood the test of time to a certain extent, that does not mean that a text which is classic now has always been a classic. Throughout Christian history there has been a rich and fruitful process of the rediscovery of certain texts which have been overlooked (or, at least, overlooked by some traditions) but which have later (re)gained a classic status. Notable (but very different) examples include the Western European rediscovery of Origen by Renaissance scholars; the re-reading of classic texts of the English civil war (such as Winstanley's *The New Law of Righteousness*) in the light of twentieth-century interests in Marxism and liberation theology; and Christian feminists' retrieval of women's voices in neglected or rediscovered texts, such as the *Book of Margery Kempe*. The whole *ressourcement* movement of the twentieth century, under the influence of scholars such as Étienne Gilson, Jean Daniélou, and Henri de Lubac, sought to get back to the sources of the Christian tradition by making texts by Greek and lesser-read Latin church fathers more readily available; it was hugely influential on the shape of Catholic and other theology more generally. Currently, there is a movement in Evangelical Protestant circles – especially in North America – to renew both scholarly and lay interest in the early church fathers, after their neglect as 'classic texts' in comparison with the texts of the Bible and the Reformation.[2]

Finally, one should be flexible about what we mean by a text: classic texts are not just books. The most obvious examples of this point are sermons: in late antiquity, for instance, these were often preached, taken down by scribes as they were preached, then published afterwards with varying degrees of editing. Even those classic sermons that were preached from a written text and then published afterwards must be read with an appreciation that their classic status came about in a context and form that was not original to their first public airing. Some other classic 'texts' blur the boundaries between orality and textuality in even more striking ways: thus, one could regard certain liturgies (for example, that of St Basil) or catechisms as 'classic texts' in that they have been received as classic over many centuries and by many people as foundational to a certain tradition and have proved to be spiritually fruitful – even though very many people never actually read them.

Ways of reading a classic text

In this section I will outline a descriptive account of various ways in which classic texts can and have been read, before moving in the next section to some more pre-scriptive suggestions as to what a good theological reading of a classic text might consist of. I will not focus on classic texts that can be regarded as authoritative in a fairly straightforward way – texts such as the founding texts of a particular tradition (creeds, confessions, rules) which I touched on in the previous section and which will be the subject of the next chapter. Although there will always be problems with their interpretation and although people will share different assumptions about how they relate to Christian tradition, nevertheless such texts are generally accepted as having the authority to govern, limit or inform what people believe or do: that is what makes them the kind of texts they are. Thus, the Nicene Creed is read as lim-iting the ways in which it is possible to speak of the relationship between the Father and the Son (limiting them, that is, to ways that confess that they share the same essence/substance/being). The *Rule* of Saint Basil is read by those religious living under it by setting out for them a pattern of work and prayer and giving advice for a harmonious community life.

The texts addressed in this section are those to which appeal is made in order to authorize and inform theological proposals more indirectly. The various ways in which such appeals are made, I suggest, reflect the text's function for the reader without implying that its value or effect can be reduced only to one function. A reader might appeal to a text for one or more of the following reasons: because she believes it conveys authoritative theological ideas; because it has the potential to help her solve a taxing theological, philosophical or ethical problem; because it inspires her at an intellectual, spiritual or emotional level; because it is an illuminating example of a particular literary form. In order to clarify my argument I will use as illustrations some readings of Augustine's *Confessions* – a classic text which has proved itself fruitful in very many ways, spiritual, theological, philosophical, literary and more. As Henry Chadwick writes:

> Augustine's *Confessions* will always rank among the greater masterpieces of western literature. … the work has a perennial power to speak, even though written virtually sixteen centuries ago and certainly a book rooted in anti-quity. The contemporary reader today may find much of it so 'modern' that at times it is a shock to discover how very ancient are the presuppositions and the particular context in which the author wrote.[3]

Margaret Miles, even though reading Augustine from rather a different perspective from Chadwick's, concurs with the way in which the text strikes today's readers as both ancient and modern: 'The *Confessions* of St Augustine, [is] provocative to modern readers for its insistently contemporary flavor, yet [is] difficult to translate into the language with which *we* explore the self'.[4] A classic, for sure, then – but one that has perplexed its readers as much as it has attracted them: why does Augustine conclude the story of his early life, academic quests and conversion with three books of philosophical theology on such difficult themes as time, eternity, and creation? To what extent can the *Confessions* be regarded as an autobiography? Why does Augustine spend so much time on outlining his former life, revolted by it as he appears to be in retrospect? What precisely are the 'confessions' of the title? What is the function of the prayers that punctuate the text? What is the role of the other characters, especially Augustine's mother and close friends, named and unnamed?

This provocative book then, is an excellent example of the wide variety of ways in which a classic text can be read. Some might argue that it is almost too good an example: hardly any other Christian book from its time raises questions about reading and interpretation quite so insistently. It might almost be described as an exercise in the reading of classic texts:

> the story of these books [*Confessions* 1–9] can be read as the story of Augustine picking up and setting down a series of different books, from Cicero's *Hortensius* forward, until he picks up a volume of Paul's letters and, with God's grace, can read it in the right way. The biographical story of the *Confessions* is, thus, importantly a bibliographical story.[5]

However, Augustine's hermeneutical self-awareness helps rather than hinders my task, because it provokes many of his readers to reflect on how they read him: it enables me not just to discuss various readings, but to discuss readers who reflect on how they read. Furthermore, the fact that the *Confessions* has provoked an unusually broad range of readings also suits my purpose which is to map out that range. I do not suggest that they will all be applicable to all classic texts. Nevertheless, I have a lingering suspicion that what makes a classic text classic is precisely its capacity to be read, fruitfully, in more than one way.

A source of authority

Sometimes a text's orthodoxy and authoritative status is presumed when it is cited in support of a theological opinion. For example, *The Catechism of the Catholic Church* appeals to Augustine's *Confessions* at least ten times, on subjects as diverse as humanity's desire for God as the source of their happiness, God's transcendence over creation, the celebration of the Eucharist for those who have died and the concepts of natural law and chastity.[6] In this context, there is no detailed reading of the text: it is cited in footnotes (alongside the Bible and other sources, including other works by Augustine), its authoritative status on these topics being presumed. Of course, more detailed appeal has been made to Augustine's text over the centuries, especially with regard to free will, grace, and predestination. When Pelagius heard the words 'grant what you command and command what you will' he was reportedly shocked.[7] After Pelagius was condemned, Augustine's text became an authoritative witness against him. Importantly, however, theologians did not just appeal to the *Confessions'* assertions regarding the priority of divine grace (for such authoritative statements they tended to refer to Augustine's later anti-Pelagian writings). Rather, Augustine's experience as narrated in the *Confessions* was held to be a perfect illustration of the doctrine of grace (as Augustine doubtless intended!). No less importantly, Augustine's reading of Paul in the *Confessions* became foundational for much of later Western Christianity.[8]

Problem-solving

A rather different approach can be seen in, for example, James Wetzel's grappling with Augustine's treatment of free will and predestination.[9] Wetzel does not offer a line-by-line exegesis, but he does offer a fairly deep engagement with *Confessions* Book 8 (Augustine's reading of Romans 7 and 9), Book 2 (Augustine's theft of the pears read alongside the biblical narratives of the Fall [Gen. 2–3] and the prodigal son [Lk. 15]) and Book 7 (Augustine's earlier, 'Platonic', mystical vision). Wetzel clearly respects and wants to learn from Augustine the theologian. He accepts that the interpretation of this text has been crucial in Western theology, precisely because Augustine's concept of predestination has had both its passionate advocates and opponents. But Wetzel neither rejects nor whole-heartedly accepts what Augustine has to say: rather, Augustine's theology is carefully judged against Scripture and by the criterion of coherence (Wetzel's argument relies partly on the idea that had Augustine followed his theological ideas through consistently, he would have avoided the more objectionable aspects of his theology of predestination). Most importantly, though, Wetzel is brave enough to look Augustine straight in the eye. Having admitted that he will not 'be trying to uphold Augustine's doctrine [of predestination] in quite the manner he espoused it', he states:

> I begin my defence, then, with an eye towards the most unsavoury parts of Augustine's doctrine. These will turn out to be every bit as unpalatable as his judicious critics have imagined. Nevertheless, the centre holds, and in the main, I take my inspiration from there. In conclusion, I return to the antithesis between free will and predestination and reconsider the wisdom of Augustine's critics. When his doctrine is viewed from the centre of his vision, it can be seen to accommodate much of the wisdom taken traditionally to oppose it. Augustine was right to be uncompromising, but wrong to be unaccommodating. There is room in his inspiration for a wide diversity of temperament, talent, and insight. In respect of this, I offer an unpolemical defence of predestination.[10]

Such a treatment of Augustine, therefore, respects him as a theological authority, but does not regard him as having the authority to have the final word on a matter: rather his theology is used as a foundation for further discussion. That is, Augustine does not merely open the debate with an intelligent question, but he has done a lot of the work on the way to answering it.

A similar approach can sometimes be found with respect to Augustine's philosophical ideas – although here Augustine is often respected more for his brilliance and the acuteness of his arguments than for his orthodoxy and interpretation of Scripture. Thus, for example, the analytic philosopher John Lucas seriously engages with *Confessions* Book 11, particularly with regard to Augustine's definition of time as the extension of mind and the problem of the ever shrinking present.[11] Again, Augustine is not presumed to have the last word, but neither is he used merely as a jumping-off point: both the questions he raised and the solutions he proposed are taken seriously.

In both cases, then, writers appeal to this classic text because its author is recognized as a great thinker: Wetzel and Lucas, in different ways, show themselves willing to learn from the way in which Augustine tackled a problem that remains as pressing and difficult in our day as it was then. Wetzel and Lucas each return to Augustine as a means of restarting their own discussions, not because they are unaware of all the historical water that has passed under the bridge since Augustine's discussion, but precisely because of the way in which Augustine's views have been appealed to as authoritative in the meantime and have formed Western sensibilities about the human experience of sin and time. Wetzel and Lucas disagree with regard to the criteria by which Augustine should continue to be regarded as authoritative, but they subject him to some specific criteria in order to pursue their aim, which is to seek answers to some pressing questions.

Inspiration

Classic theological texts are sometimes used not as the source of an authoritative statement of belief, nor as a way towards finding an answer to a particularly knotty problem, but rather as an inspiration towards doing theology in a particular way (especially, a new way).[12] This inspiration could be directed in an intellectual direction – for example, a text might encourage a reader to think about a particular topic in a new, interesting and fruitful way, even if she rejects some or all of the author's specific conclusions. The traditional way of expressing this in academic theological terms is to say that a classic text inspires a fruitful method. Alternatively, the inspiration might be directed in a more ethical, emotional or spiritual direction, inspiring the reader not so much to think differently, but to *be* differently. The traditional way of expressing this theologically is to say that a reader can be changed, or transformed, by a text. As we shall see from a focus on the analyses of Charles Mathewes and David Burrell it is not clear that these two can be entirely separated. Furthermore, it is notable that the ancient description of a text as anagogical – something that leads the reader up to something – can apply to both these kinds of inspiration and indeed often seems to unite the two.

Charles Mathewes reads Augustine's *Confessions* as revealing Augustine's perspective on 'the nature of religious belief and faithful life':[13]

> For [Augustine] faithful life is a project of resisting our always premature attempts at conclusion, in order better to see the project of 'inquiry into God' as an infinite undertaking, in community with others, organized centrally around reading and inhabiting the thought world of the Scriptures. The

> *Confessions* turns out to be a story of Augustine learning to ask questions in
> the right way and to accept the dynamic of questioning as an energy moving
> him toward God.[14]

Mathewes distinguishes this approach from three others. First, from one which sees
'questioning ... as a mode of seeking knowledge in the form of answers',[15] which
encourages us to see ourselves as 'problem solvers rather than ... as beings with a
capacity for contemplation and wonder' and in fact reduces the role of questioning
to a mere preliminary to knowledge.[16] If, as Mathewes asserts, this kind of questioning aimed at specific answers is not Augustine's task in the *Confessions*, then, by
implication, we his readers should not be reading the text to find answers to our
questions. (Thus Mathewes is in effect rejecting my first and perhaps also my second
way of reading a classic text.) Second, Mathewes distinguishes Augustine's mode of
questioning from one aimed at '"simple piety", unquestioning faith': faith for
Augustine is not the end of a process of questioning, but the beginning.[17] Finally,
Mathewes distinguishes Augustine's method of questioning in the *Confessions* from
scepticism that withholds assent to the truth.[18] Mathewes reads Augustine's text –
especially the narrative of *Confessions* Book 5 – as identifying a problem with such a
stance: it can lead to cynicism or it can become an anaesthetic allowing one to evade
the urgency of decision.

Rejecting these three models of questioning, Mathewes turns to the last four
books of the *Confessions* to understand what questioning is. For Augustine, questioning
'blossoms into exegesis' and exegesis is not 'seeking closure' but rather a basic mode
of 'being-in-the-world'.[19] Mathewes reads Augustine's account of the vision at Ostia
in Book 9 as indicating that 'understanding' – and thus 'questioning' – are eschatological
concepts:

> History is not a series of failed attempts at reaching union with the divine;
> it is one long lesson in (because one long act of *ascesis* for) what that union
> will one day, at the end of days, be revealed to be ... Life is lived in quest-
> ing, seeking after God, beseeching God for more profound insight, ever
> deepening (at once affective and intellectual) understanding; but this dee-
> pening understanding is always equally a revelation of ever deepening mystery.
> ... The 'enduring' of the 'continuing tension' of such questioning is in fact
> not merely something one suffers regretfully; it is, rather, a mark of being
> alive. To come to see the joyous endlessness of such questioning, and to
> begin to inhabit it, is to pass from death into life.[20]

The main aim of Mathewes' reading of the *Confessions* is descriptive: to understand
the text better and, thereby, to 'rethink our typical fixation on religious belief as a
final end'.[21] But Mathewes' constant emphasis on Augustine's readers as 'we'/'us'
strongly suggests another aim too – to argue that the new way of life that Augustine
comes to at the end of the *Confessions* is a life Augustine wishes 'us' his readers to
share: 'understanding the *Confessions* as a liberation of questioning ultimately entails
a radical reshaping of *our* eschatological expectations and through them an alteration
in *our* understanding of the nature and meaning of time and eternity'.[22]

Mathewes' reading of the *Confessions* begins with an epistemological focus (questioning as finding answers to things) and concludes with a highly theological perspective on questioning as a way of being-in-the-world. Furthermore, he moves from Augustine's grappling with his situation through his texts to our grappling with our situation through Augustine's text. There is a similar movement from the narrowly epistemological to the theological and from Augustine's to the reader's perspective in David Burrell's (rather earlier) reading of the *Confessions*.[23] Like Mathewes, Burrell steers away from the attempt to read Augustine as providing a definitive answer and stresses the importance of paying attention to the way in which Augustine asks the questions he asks.[24] Indeed, Burrell argues that readers should pay attention to the historical and intellectual background to the *Confessions* because this affected the way in which Augustine asked his questions.[25] But this is not simply a matter of historical criticism; rather:

> the manner in which [Augustine] comes to grips with questions shows us how much the question is his question. If we respect this fact, we will be less and less tempted to take home what he says as an 'answer'. For what Augustine says, he has worked out in response to his question. Yet in compensation we will have learned a little better how to meet our questions, by participating in his attempt to formulate his. In this manner, reading becomes exercising, as learning passes over from learning about to learning how.[26]

Burrell's analysis depends in particular on a reading of *Confessions* books 7 and 8 that identifies Augustine's emphasis on intellect and grace and will with a developing conceptualization of understanding as insight and grace and discipline.[27] He argues, that is, that in the *Confessions* Augustine comes to a new understanding of 'understanding':

> Understanding what something is demands more than insight or vision; it will also require an appropriate discipline so that we can articulate what we understand in a word which faithfully expresses our present situation. In things that matter, there is no knowing short of becoming, no articulation short of a faithful expression of where it is that one is. ... Hence, understanding cannot escape self-understanding.[28]

However, Burrell is rather more insistent on the transformative aim of his analysis of the *Confessions*: while Mathewes' prior aim seems to be to understand Augustine/the *Confessions*, whilst recognizing that this has potentially transformative consequences for the reader, Burrell's stated *aim* is 'not to swell the bulk of Augustiniana but rather to assist anyone who would engage himself in a work as engaging as the *Confessions* with some hope of advancing his theological understanding'.[29] That this is not merely an intellectual exercise is evident from the emphasis throughout on understanding as insight, grace, and discipline – 'learning how', rather than 'learning about'.[30] Burrell insists, for example, that any historical understanding of Augustine's conceptual frameworks should force the reader to reassess her own.[31] However, Burrell is much more insistent than Mathewes that this insight should be put into practice in some way by the reader: 'The inspiration comes from Augustine; we can only hope to bring our human quest for understanding to term by engaging our all-too-human selves upon it … In matters religious, understanding demands that we attempt to live what we are trying to speak.'[32] To put it another way, Burrell reads Augustine's *Confessions* as an attempt 'to assist human understanding along the way' and he sees his task as Augustine's interpreter not just to clarify what Augustine thought, but to help Augustine's text fulfil its purpose.[33]

Different theologians will have different opinions as to how such a reading of a classic text is compatible with a text's use to support a theological claim, as outlined above. It is clear, for example, that Burrell and Mathewes, although rejecting a reading of the *Confessions* which plunders it for dogmatic answers, nevertheless do see it as a warrant for a certain kind of approach to theological hermeneutics – and, as I have argued, to a certain kind of vision of theology as a way of life. Further-more, it would not be hard to probe below the surface to find some doctrinal claims still lurking: for example, claims about Augustine's concept of grace and his reading of Paul. A much more radical approach to reading the *Confessions* can be found in various interpretations that have been influenced by recent post-modern and post-structuralist theorists.[34] Some of these, of course, are self-professedly *not* theological, but for others the case is not so clear. For example, a recent volume *Seducing Augustine* asserts that 'Augustine's *Confessions* turn us aside from the straight and narrow path of revealed truth … '.[35] Rather than seeking theological certainty from Augustine, or even a valid theological method, the co-authors' model for the effect of the text is seduction: 'There are many ways to read Augustine's *Confessions*, but if we want to read it for seduction, then we must stop looking for revelations'.[36] Given Augustine's own description of the way he felt he was seduced both by his passions and his intellect in his early life, seduction is a common trope when scholars write about the *Confessions*. However, is there a danger that his readers are being seduced too – particularly given the fact that he was trained in rhetoric, the ancient art of persuasion? Mathewes alludes to this possibility briefly,[37] but *Seducing Augustine* raises the problem most forcefully. The authors point out that when he was a young man Augustine made up 'shameful deeds' he had not committed in order to impress his friends: 'Augustine misled his audience when he was sixteen – unremarkably perhaps. We might pause to ask whether he is doing it still.'[38] This is not just a question about historical errors. What if Augustine in fact leads his readers astray in a more profound sense? What is the difference between a text being transformative (or 'anagogical') and it being merely cleverly persuasive or perniciously seductive? Burrell's and Mathewes' answer to this question would seemingly be to judge Augustine against the criterion of Scripture; but as they implicitly acknowledge, Westerners' reading of Scripture (at least of Romans and Genesis) has been conditioned by the *Confessions*. This problem of circularity is one that affects the reading of many classic texts. Another solution might be to attend to the work more as a piece of literature, and it is to this reading that we will now turn.

The classic text as a literary text

Both Burrell and Mathewes pay attention to the importance of literary form;[39] the book *Seducing Augustine* uses a wide variety of literary methods to read the *Confessions*.

Here, however, I wish to examine briefly a paper that puts a literary analysis of the work in central place. Frances Young argues that in order to understand the *Confessions* one needs to steer carefully away from the anachronistic application of categories like autobiography: the problem is not the term 'autobiography' in itself, but rather the assumptions that it might be assumed to carry with it, in particular the idea that the importance of ancient autobiographers 'lies in their telling how it was for them – uncovering their experience, their feelings'.[40] In a rigorous scholarly challenge to this assumption Young sets Augustine's *Confessions* alongside Gregory of Nazianzus' so-called autobiographical poems and argues that in fact a far more urgent concern of ancient Christian autobiographers was the creation of a narrative of their life which was 'typological'. That is, by retelling his life with close reference to key stories from the Bible, the autobiographer was not only trying to make sense of it, but was also presenting it to the reader as a moral or spiritual tale: its purpose was 'to provide a didactic "type" or exemplar from which others will benefit by coming to an understanding of their own lives'.[41]

Fascinatingly, however, Young chooses to end on another note – one which echoes our earlier themes and one which is, as she implies, perhaps unexpected in the context of a literary exposition that could have been pursued by a classicist not a theologian:

> Finally, I would hint that we have much to learn from this. For our own Christian consciousness, our own telling of our own story, might likewise with profit be shaped by scripture and by tales of the saints. By conforming to 'type' we might discern in our lives the workings of God's grace. In fact, if I dared, I could give an account of my own life, with Samuel, Jeremiah and Paul, Augustine, Gregory and John Wesley, in terms of a mother dedicating a child before birth, of miraculous rescue from death, of strange providential coincidences, of trial and testing through suffering, of Damascus Road, call and commitment. But this is not the place to pursue that further.

Classic texts are often *complex* texts. As such they merit study on their own terms and for their own sake. But Frances Young's surprising conclusion suggests that even that approach can be fruitful theologically. Perhaps some readings are fruitful theologically precisely because they are readings done for their own sake, because of the sheer attention paid to the text?

How best to read classic texts?

Whilst the last section attempted to outline some examples of how classic texts have been read, in this section I want to move from a descriptive to a prescriptive mode: how *should* a classic theological text be read? In other words – setting this question in the broader context of the practice of theology – is there a praxis of reading classic theological texts and what might guide this praxis?

One approach might be to judge one's reading of a classic text according to the foundations of Christian faith – for example, Scripture and tradition, and perhaps also reason and experience. The problem is that, as we have seen, a classic text can be seen as one of the elements that has formed tradition, the interpretation of Scripture and even the development of reason and experience. Better than insisting that readings of classic texts are judged by any one of these criteria in a simplistic way, therefore, might be an approach that recognizes the complex and potentially circular relationship between these aspects.

A second approach might be to stress that all reading is interpretation and therefore active, not merely receptive. However, this will be more obvious with some kinds of reading than others: for example, readers of founding documents often claim or aspire to a relatively interpretation-free reading; a reader of a classic text who is hoping that it will transform her, on the other hand, may be hoping that her reading will be a highly interpretational exercise. One issue that continually pursues the theological reader of any classic text, therefore, is the question of the limits of interpretation: how does one mediate between the responsibility to be faithful to a text and the desire to open it up to new readings or applications? How to adjudicate between responsibility and freedom? To put it in terms we have quoted before, how to preserve a text's 'perennial power to speak', whilst endeavouring to understand its 'presuppositions' and particular 'context'? How to retain its 'insistently contemporary flavour' along with a sense of the difficulty of 'translating' it into the language of modern debate?[42] One can caricature this as an argument between opponents who accuse each other of 'being too conservative' or 'going too far', but in fact most readers negotiate between readings which are too closed and ones which are too open, even if they may not be aware of what they are doing.

However, the problem with construing the debate in terms of 'too open/radical' or 'too closed/conservative' readings is that it tacitly implies there is a golden mean between the two: some perfect interpretation that avoids the pitfalls at either end. But the question of where the mean lies is notoriously liable to be judged according to personal perspective. Another way of getting a purchase on the question of how to acknowledge the need for structure whilst also allowing for a degree of openness, is to think of reading classic Christian texts as a discipline or a kind of *ascesis*. This is to understand *ascesis* not in the narrow historical sense, but to think of the Christian life in general as *ascesis* in theological terms – specifically, in terms that accept the complementarity of the intellectual and the practical and acknowledge the need for both human discipline and divine grace.[43] The advantage of this approach is that there is complementarity not opposition between the intellectual and the practical and between discipline and grace. In the practice of reading a classic text, therefore, it might be more constructive to try to combine these qualities in such a way that they are fruitful, rather than trying to find a supposedly perfect position between two opposing poles of the 'open' and the 'closed'. I will conclude by suggesting briefly what a reading that achieves this balance might look like.

First, as I have shown, some of the most provocative readings of Augustine's *Confessions* conclude that readings of that classic text should engage all aspects of the human – heart as well as mind, will as well as intellect. This coheres well with an understanding of Christian *ascesis* as an activity that directs the whole person towards God.

Second, I suggest that a disciplined practice of reading might include the following aspects (all of which relate to traditional elements of the discipline of ascetic life):

- A commitment to *regular* reading, because one needs to return to a text and to read a variety of texts in order to get the most out of them.
- *Effortful* reading, because most classic texts do not offer up their fruits as the result of a quick skim. The effort might involve intellectual training (e.g. the learning of a new language or a new philosophical technique) or emotional preparation (e.g. the facing up to a text which is uncomfortable or distressing to the reader) or spiritual discipline (e.g. developing the modesty to accept that one might not have fully understood an apparently 'simple' text).
- Reading that is *attentive* or *free from distraction*. By this I do not mean a reading that is withdrawn from the rest of Christian tradition, nor one that is isolated from everyday life, but rather a reading that is keenly focused on the text. Although this is not always possible, there is much to be said for a reading, such as Young's, that is *not* done for the sake of some other theological purpose, but which takes a text seriously as a text to be understood for its own sake.
- Reading that is *outward, as well as inward-looking*. That is, a reading that is not bound by one's own psychological needs but that is attentive to, for example, teachers or the members of one's community.

Third, a reading that is open to grace will be open to surprises. At an intellectual level, it will allow its own presuppositions to be challenged. At an emotional or spiritual level it will allow the reader to be challenged by the text, to be open to being changed by the text (without abandoning a critical approach to the text). It might leave open the question of what the end of reading the text is or be alive to the possibility that a reading of the text ostensibly for its own sake might yield unanticipated insights.

Finally, to adapt an insight taught by many teachers of the ascetic life, the best way to read a classic text is to watch how other people have done it and to try it oneself – and to let the two processes of learning from others and active personal engagement refresh each other constantly.

Notes

1 There are some classic Christian texts which seem at one point to have been read as part of the New Testament canon, even though they were not accepted into the final canon: for example, the *Epistle of Clement* or the *Didache*.

2 See, for example, the Baker Academic series *Evangelical Ressourcement: Ancient Sources for the Church's Future*, especially D.H. Williams, *Evangelicals and Tradition*, Grand Rapids, MI: Baker, 2005.

3 H. Chadwick, 'Introduction' to his translation of Saint Augustine, *Confessions*, Oxford World's Classics, Oxford: Oxford University Press, 1991, p. ix.

4 M. Miles, 'Infancy, Parenting, and Nourishment in Augustine's *Confessions*', *Journal of the American Academy of Religion* 50.3, 1982, pp. 349–64: p. 349.

5 C.T. Mathewes, 'The Liberation of Questioning in Augustine's *Confessions*', *Journal of the American Academy of Religion* 70.3, 2002, pp. 539–60: p. 552.

6 *The Catechism of the Catholic Church*, Citta del Vaticano: Libreria Editrice Vaticana, 1993, digital English translation available at www.vatican.va/archive/ENG0015/_INDEX.HTM (accessed 22 December 2011), sections 1.1.1.1; 1.2.1 (Art. 1, para. 4); 2.2.1 (Art. 3, para. 5); 3.1.3 (Art. 3, para. 1); 3.2.2 (Art. 6, para. 2).

7 *Confessions* 10.29 (40). See Chadwick's note to his translation of Augustine, *Confessions*, pp. 202–3.

8 See, for example, J. Wetzel, 'Snares of Truth: Augustine on Free Will and Predestination', in R. Dodaro and G. Lawless (eds) *Augustine and His Critics*, London: Routledge, 2000, pp. 121–41: p. 139, n. 20: 'The Paul of western Christianity is arguably Augustine's invention'. Paula Fredricksen's reading of the *Confessions* involves an unpicking of Augustine's rereading of Paul: see, for example, her 'Paul and Augustine: Conversion Narratives, Orthodox Traditions, and the Retrospective Self', *Journal of Theological Studies* n.s. 37.3, 1986, pp. 3–34. See also J. Riches, 'Readings of Augustine on Paul: Their Impact on Critical Studies of Paul', *Society of Biblical Literature Seminar Papers* 37, 1998, pp. 943–67.

9 Wetzel, 'Snares of Truth', esp. pp. 130–38.

10 Wetzel, 'Snares of Truth', p. 126.

11 J.R. Lucas, *A Treatise on Time and Space*, London: Methuen, 1973, pp. 14 and 20–25.

12 For the term 'inspiration' see, e.g. D. Burrell, 'Reading "The Confessions" of Augustine: An Exercise in Theological Understanding', *Journal of Religion*, 50.4, 1970, p. 350. This article is studied in more detail below. See also Wetzel, 'Snares of Truth', p. 126, although his inspiration is more doctrinal than methodological.

13 Mathewes, 'The Liberation of Questioning', p. 539.

14 Mathewes, 'The Liberation of Questioning', extract from abstract.

15 Mathewes, 'The Liberation of Questioning', p. 544.

16 Mathewes, 'The Liberation of Questioning', p. 545.

17 Mathewes, 'The Liberation of Questioning', p. 547.

18 Mathewes, 'The Liberation of Questioning', p. 548. Mathewes also identifies this scepticism with the kind of apophaticism that is merely scepticism 'in a theological gown'.

19 Mathewes, 'The Liberation of Questioning', pp. 549–50.

20 Mathewes, 'The Liberation of Questioning', pp. 551 and 552.

21 Mathewes, 'The Liberation of Questioning', p. 557.

22 Mathewes, 'The Liberation of Questioning', p. 555 (my emphasis); cf. p. 549: 'Just what is it that we are doing or trying to do when we live our lives, as Augustine manifestly wants us to do, in unleashing our desire to ask questions?'

23 Burrell, 'Reading "The Confessions"', pp. 327–51.

24 Burrell, 'Reading "The Confessions"', p. 329.

25 Burrell, 'Reading "The Confessions"', p. 328: such scholarship 'can bring us to a sharp appreciation of the schemes which dominated Augustine's shaping of the work. These schemes provide the material rules of inference which license some implications and restrict others. To identify them is to explain why questions are posed in the terms in which they are, and why certain issues are taken up and others dropped.'

26 Burrell, 'Reading "The Confessions"', pp. 329–30.

27 Burrell, 'Reading "The Confessions"', pp. 339–40.

28 Burrell, 'Reading "The Confessions"', p. 333.

29 Burrell, 'Reading "The Confessions"', p. 327.

30 Burrell, 'Reading "The Confessions"', p. 330.

31 Mathewes, 'The Liberation of Questioning', p. 544. Burrell, 'Reading "The Confessions"', p. 328: The questions about Augustine's and the reader's intellectual frameworks are 'correlative': 'How does [Augustine] use the schemata offered to him? And a correlative question: what do the obstacles I feel in approaching the text tell me about what is going on in the unfolding of Augustine's exposition, or in myself?'

32 Burrell, 'Reading "The Confessions"', p. 350. It should be noted that the contrast I draw here between Mathewes and Burrell relates not to their theological stances in general, but merely to these two specific articles (whose perspective may have been affected by, for example, the context in which and the purpose for which they were originally composed).

33 Burrell, 'Reading "The Confessions"', pp. 334 and 336.
34 Very influential in this respect is G. Bennington and J. Derrida, *Jacques Derrida*, Chicago / London: University of Chicago Press, 1993, which consists of a study by Bennington, 'Derridabase', with a reflection, 'Circumfession', by Jacques Derrida, as a running footnote. See also, J.D. Caputo, and M.J. Scanlon, *Augustine and Postmodernism: Confessions and Circumfession*, Bloomington, IN: Indiana University Press, 2005.
35 V. Burrus, M. Jordan, and K. MacKendrick, *Seducing Augustine: Bodies, Desires, Confessions*, New York: Fordham University Press, 2010, p. 13. The authors come from a variety of academic backgrounds: Burrus from early church history, Mark Jordan from theological ethics and Karmen MacKendrick from philosophy.
36 Burrus, Jordan, and MacKendrick, *Seducing Augustine*, p. 30.
37 Mathewes, 'The Liberation of Questioning', p. 551, on the narrative of the vision at Ostia in *Confessions* book 9: 'perhaps we are too seduced by the immanence [and imminence] of Augustine's recounting to remember that it is, after all, a *re*-counting'. The danger of being taken in by Augustine's narrative is also a theme in Fredriksen, 'Paul and Augustine'.
38 Burrus, Jordan, and MacKendrick, *Seducing Augustine*, p. 12.
39 Burrell, 'Reading "The Confessions"', pp. 330–34; Mathewes, 'The Liberation of Questioning', p. 541 (on understanding the 'interrogative voice').
40 F. Young, 'The *Confessions* of St. Augustine: What is the Genre of this Work?', 1998 St. Augustine Lecture, Villanova University, *Augustinian Studies* 30.1, 1999, p. 16.
41 Young, 'The *Confessions* of St. Augustine', p. 15.
42 See the quotations from Chadwick and Miles above.
43 It is notable that both Burrell and Mathewes seem to refer to this kind of idea in their use, respectively, of the terms 'discipline' and 'ascesis'.

16

USING CREEDS AND CONFESSIONS

John Bradbury

Christian theology only exists because there are communities of faith that collectively embody certain beliefs and practices. Whilst an individual who engages with the practice of theology may or may not consider herself a member of a church, it is nevertheless the embodied practices and beliefs of the churches with which she is concerned.

Most theology in universities is done by individuals, and frequently happens through engagement with key individual figures from both past and present who have themselves engaged with the beliefs and practices of the Church. However, not all theology is done by individuals; the Church does theology corporately too, and seeks to understand its practices and its beliefs, and to find appropriate ways of using language to make those beliefs and practices known. There are various means by which this has happened throughout the history of the Church, but two of the most significant are in the formulation of creeds and confessions of faith.

Creeds and confessions

For many Christians, creeds are a regular part of their worshipping life. In the Orthodox, Catholic, and Anglican traditions, for instance, the saying of a creed together forms a necessary part of an act of Eucharistic worship, and saying creeds together will happen at times in Lutheran, Reformed, and Methodist worship too. For many Christians, if you ask them what they believe, the words of the creeds may come to mind: 'I believe … ' Creeds are, at the most basic level, statements of the content of Christian belief.

Confessions of faith fulfil this function too. They are less likely to be encountered in worship (and are often very much longer than creeds!), but they too seek to set out 'the sum and substance' of the Christian faith. Confessions come in varying forms. Some are sets of propositional statements; others come in the form of catechisms – often a series of questions and answers designed to help members of the Church understand the content of their faith.

Both creeds and confessions stand in a relationship to Scripture, although this relationship is understood somewhat differently in different traditions. Creeds and confessions are often understood as an attempt to summarize the significant things that the Church believes are contained within Scripture. For some traditions (particularly the Orthodox and the Roman Catholic), creeds also function as the lens through which Scripture is to be interpreted – as setting out rules for the proper reading of Scripture, or boundaries on acceptable interpretation. These traditions might understand Scripture and the tradition of the Church as being like two sides of the same coin, each of which is necessary to understand the other. In the traditions that stem from the Reformation, Scripture tends to be treated as the sole source for defining the official teaching of the Church, but creeds and confessions are attempts to summarize that teaching, and are useful guides to reading to the extent that they show how the Church has summarized the teaching of Scripture in the past.

Different traditions of the Church accept different lists of creeds and confessions as being authoritative statements of the faith. For most traditions the creeds of the early Church have particular significance. For the Orthodox churches the so-called Nicene Creed in the version accepted at the First Council of Constantinople in AD 381 (properly the 'Niceno-Constantinopolitan Creed') is a centrally authoritative statement of the faith, and is understood as functioning as a lynchpin of the teaching of the first seven ecumenical councils that the Eastern Orthodox church accepts as authoritative. Alongside this, in the Western church (including the Roman Catholic, Lutheran, Reformed and Anglican traditions) the so-called Apostles' Creed traditionally acts as a summary of the faith as used by candidates for Baptism, and the Athanasian Creed is a more technical summary of those things that are necessary to believe for salvation.

These credal statements can be understood as the Church itself articulating its faith. While they may have initially emerged from the writings of individuals, they are authoritative by virtue of their acceptance by the Church as a whole, normally by a decision of an ecumenical council of the Church.

In addition to these creeds, we must also mention the Chalcedonian definition. At Nicaea the credal statement confessed that Christ was *homoousios* (of one substance) with the Father, in response to the claims of the Arians that Christ was 'only' the first born, and therefore secondary to the Father. This led to further debates about the nature of Christ, and about whether and in what way he could be said to be both divine and human. This dispute was settled by the Council of Chalcedon's definition of Christ as fully human and fully divine. The definition was not a new creed, but it is a statement that serves a function within theology rather like that of a creed. It defines the way Christians should speak of Christ (as having two natures, in one person).

The function of creeds

Creeds can be understood in various different ways. Firstly, they may be seen as an attempt to delineate the boundary around orthodox belief – and this can be understood both positively and negatively. For example, when the Nicene Creed says that Christ is *homoousios* (of one substance) with the Father, it makes a positive statement. It is, however, a brief and abstract statement, and invites further elaboration. The exploration of the consequences and outworking of this statement can be thought of as taking place within a space the boundary of which is defined by the statement. One of the practices of theology is to explore that space. There is also a negative side to credal statements, however, because the boundary also marks out what is outside that space. In fact, the original version of the Nicene Creed was partnered with a very clear negative statement of that which the Church does not believe. This is called an 'anathema': a statement of that which is outside the boundaries of orthodox faith. In the case of Nicaea that anathema reads:

> As for those who say that 'there was when he was not,' and 'before being born he was not,' and 'he came into existence out of nothing', or who declare that the Son of God is of a different substance or nature, or is subject to alteration or change – the catholic and apostolic church condemns these.[1]

Creeds and confessions mark out not only orthodoxy (right teaching) but also heresy (false teaching).

One of the ways in which creeds do mark out a positive space for exploration is by marking out the significant topics of the Christian faith. We sometimes refer to these as 'doctrinal loci': the key areas and aspects of faith that make up the Christian faith. If we examine the Apostles Creed we can see how this functions:

> I believe in God, the Father almighty,
> creator of the heavens and earth.
> I believe in Jesus Christ, his only Son, our Lord,
> who was conceived by the Holy Spirit,
> born of the Virgin Mary,
> he suffered under Pontius Pilate,
> was crucified, dead and buried;
> he descended to hell,
> on the third day he rose again;
> he ascended into the heavens,
> he is seated at the right hand of God the Father almighty,
> and he will come again to judge the living and the dead.
> I believe in the Holy Spirit,
> the holy catholic church,
> the communion of saints,
> the forgiveness of sins,
> the resurrection of the flesh,
> and eternal life.[2]

We note that this creed comes in three parts. They are often understood as reflecting the three persons of the Trinity, although we also need to note that classically theologians have always understood that the work of any one person of the Trinity is equally the work of the whole of the Godhead. In the first part, belief is confessed in God the Father and in the divine creation of the world. The second part deals with the person and work of Jesus Christ, and the third part the Holy Spirit, and under this the Church, forgiveness, and eschatology. From this, we can begin to list the headings under which we do theology. Theology concerns the Godhead, One God – Father, Son, and Holy Spirit (following the three parts of the creed). It also concerns creation, Christology (the person of Christ), soteriology (the work of Christ), pneumatology (the doctrine of the Spirit), ecclesiology (the doctrine of the Church), and eschatology (the theology of the future Kingdom). All theology works with these categories (along with others). Even when theology is reflecting upon topics well outside of the credal statements (or even topics that were not imaginable in the first few centuries of the Church) these loci come into play. For example, we might want to think theologically about the environment and global warming. Clearly the creeds do not say anything directly addressing this topic. However, it is with reference to the things that we do confess in the creeds that we begin to work. So we might ponder what is implicit in the confession of the divine creation of the world, and the work of the Spirit within creation, and what this has to say about how we understand our environment. We might then move on to reflect upon the ethical demands that might be reasonably understood to be a Christian theological approach to the environment. Even when reflecting upon something seemingly far removed from the early creeds, the loci of theology that they define are key to the way in which theology addresses the question.

These credal loci not only give us the conceptual headings under which theology will begin thinking, but also stand in relationship to one another. When we are specifically attempting this task we might be rightly understood to be doing 'systematic theology'. This is an attempt to think through each aspect of the Christian faith in relationship to all the other aspects. Very often we therefore find that works of systematic theology are shaped roughly in the same way that the creeds are shaped. Sometimes the creeds are even taken as the starting point for the development of a systematic theology. One classic example might be John Calvin's first edition of his *Institutes of the Christian Religion* from 1536.[3] Calvin's work is sub-headed: 'Embracing almost the whole sum of piety, and whatever is necessary to know of the doctrine of salvation', which gives a clear indication that this is an attempt to speak of the whole of the Christian faith. A significant part of the *Institutes* is formed by a commentary upon the Apostles' Creed, which gives the shape to Calvin's work. Many other theologians, of varying traditions, have written commentaries upon the early creeds. Other examples of more recent times include Karl Barth[4] and the Roman Catholic theologian Hans Küng[5] both of whom have written relatively short commentaries upon the Apostles' Creed. The Scottish Reformed theologian T.F. Torrance has written a book length exposition of the key theological elements of the theology of the Nicene Creed.[6]

The shape of the early creeds not only forms one of the foundational sources for Christian theology in the sense that theologians use them as the basis for commentary. They also offer something of a shape for the whole of the theological enterprise when it is seeking to be systematic and exhaustive. We often find, therefore, that these credal loci give shape to whole systematic theologies. The German theologian

Wolfhart Pannenberg has written a three volume systematic theology. The first volume deals with God, the question of revelation and the Trinity, the second volume deals with creation, humanity, Christology and Salvation, and the third volume deals with the Spirit, the Church, and the Kingdom.[7] Roughly speaking one can see that nearly two millennia after the creeds began to be formed, their pattern can be discerned in a late-twentieth-century multi-volume work of theology.

Creeds do not simply offer a set of headings with which theologians work, of course. They also contain substantive claims about God – such as the claim that Christ is of one substance with the Father from the Nicene Creed, or the Chalcedonian definition's statement that Christ has a human and a divine nature in one person.

The theologian George Lindbeck has addressed the question of the nature of the truth claims that Christian doctrine makes.[8] He points out that the kinds of doctrines that are contained within the creeds can be understood as functioning in various different ways. Some people understand doctrines as containing straightforward propositional claims that make true statements about the objective reality of God. The statement 'Jesus is of one substance with the Father' is true because Jesus is properly said to be of a substance, and is truly of one substance with the Father. The doctrine provides the correct vocabulary for describing reality, and the true way of deploying that vocabulary to make true statements, and any other way of saying it is inadequate or untrue.

A second way of understanding doctrine is to see it as giving expression to the deep shape of religious feeling or experience: the doctrines point to these feelings or religious experiences, and it is those experiences themselves that are significant, not the particular doctrinal formulations. 'Jesus is of one substance with the Father' is, for this way of thinking, one way of expressing the core Christian experience, that it is through encountering Jesus that we experience the fullness of relation to the divine. Ultimately it is these religious sensibilities that doctrines are attempting to express that matter, and doctrinal statements can be reformulated as long as the new formulations remain true to that experience.

Lindbeck, however, proposes a third way of thinking about doctrine, proposing an alternative model that he calls a 'cultural-linguistic model'.[9] He develops the idea that doctrines function rather as grammar functions within language. Doctrines do not themselves point directly to objective reality; they provide rules that guide how the Church talks (and how it practises more generally). When guided and shaped by those rules, the Church can indeed truly refer to or conform to the objective reality of God – but it is the life of the Church shaped by doctrinal rules, not doctrinal statements in the abstract, that does the referring.

As part of his exploration of this account of doctrine, Lindbeck examines the key doctrines set down at Nicaea and Chalcedon. In doing so he points out that there is a difference between the doctrines themselves and the terminology and language in which they are expressed. Lindbeck suggests that the precise terminology that the doctrines are expressed with (the language of 'substance', 'person' and so on, borrowed from Hellenistic culture) are simply the means by which the doctrine is expressed in one culture. The terms themselves are not intrinsic to the way the doctrines work. He suggests that the same doctrines – the same rules for guiding Christian speech and practice – might be expressed in other ways, and illustrates this by suggesting that there are at least three 'regulative principles' at work within the credal for-mulations. The first is the monotheistic rule, that Christians should worship only one God; the second is that they should take 'Jesus' to refer to a specific, real human being; the third is roughly speaking that they should let this Jesus be definitive for their understanding of God.[10] The precise vocabulary in which these rules are actu-ally stated is drawn from the cultural and linguistic framework of the context in which the theologian is working. One of the tasks of the theologian, then, is to practise the translation of the deep rules encoded in doctrines into new contexts and situations, and to relate those deep rules to the reality of the contexts themselves.

Rowan Williams has offered a fascinating account of the theological process by which the Nicene Creed itself was formed. He examines the debate between Arius, who maintained that Christ was the first-born of God, and those who argued for the position enshrined at Nicaea, that Christ is 'of one substance with the Father'. Williams points out that the prevailing context in which the debate was happening was very different from that within which the Scriptures had emerged. He states that

> There is a sense in which Nicaea and its aftermath represents a recognition by the Church at large that *theology* is not only legitimate but necessary. The loyal and uncritical repetition of formulae is seen to be inadequate as a means of securing continuity at anything more than a formal level.[11]

What he is suggesting is that Arius was ultimately the conservative figure in the debate, utilizing old categories whose meaning had shifted through time. Repetition of those categories led to a situation in which he was apparently saying the same thing as the tradition he had inherited, but in which it had taken on a different meaning. Williams goes on to suggest that the constructive task of theology is to engage in the process that Athanasius was engaged in: 'the contemporary task of critically appropriating once again the heritage of doctrinal history'.[12]

To take an example of how a more recent theologian has worked with a classical formulation, we can briefly examine the way Dietrich Bonhoeffer uses the logic of the Chalcedonian Christological definition in his *Ethics*. The definition, as we saw, states that Jesus is fully divine and fully human, with these two natures being united 'without confusion, without change, without division and without separation'.[13] Bonhoeffer appropriates the logic of this Chalcedonian definition to shape his prac-tice of theology as he writes about ethics. He was not seeking to make a point about Christ himself, but rather drew on what the definition said about Christ to make a point about the way in which Christians are called to live within the world. He wrote his *Ethics* in the context of the National Socialist regime in Germany, where he was part of the 'Confessing Church', which had resisted Hitler's attempts to appropriate the church for his own nationalistic purposes. Bonhoeffer engaged with the question of ethics in part to explore the question of what resistance might mean theologically, and in part to begin to think about how humanity and the Church needed to live in the period after National Socialism. We only have parts of his argument, because the *Ethics* was left unfinished when Bonhoeffer was killed by the Nazi regime shortly before the end of the Second World War.

Bonhoeffer begins by making a radical claim that those who are engaging with ethical questions must give up the very question that they are seeking to ask, 'How can I be good?'[14] Instead of this question, Bonhoeffer states that we must seek after the 'will of God'. The next stage of his argument follows from the presumption that God is supremely revealed in Jesus Christ (following the logic of the Nicene Creed where Jesus is confessed as 'of one substance' with the Father). The source of ethics is not rooted in human beings, rather it is rooted in 'the reality of God that is revealed in Jesus Christ'.[15] The question of ethics, therefore, is how we participate in God's reality and how that reality becomes manifest within the life of the world. Bonhoeffer picks up on the meaning of the Chalcedonian definition, and even mirrors some of its language as he moves to make his point:

> In Christ we are invited to participate in the reality of God and the reality of the world at the same time, the one not without the other. The reality of God is disclosed only as it places me completely into the reality of the world. But I find the reality of the world always already borne, accepted, and reconciled in the reality of God. That is the mystery of the revelation of God in the human being Jesus Christ ... What matters is *participating in the reality of God and the world in Jesus Christ today*.[16]

Bonhoeffer is taking the logic of the Chalcedonian definition and using it to help him address the question of ethics. Because Christ is fully human and fully divine and to be Christian is to participate in Christ, to be Christian is to be both fully worldly (human) and fully participating in God (in Christ). Bonhoeffer, in a passage shortly prior to this one, mirrored even more of the language of the Chalcedonian definition, using the word 'indivisible' when speaking of the whole of God's reality revealed in Christ, both worldly and divine.

In this example from Bonhoeffer we see at work something of what Lindbeck refers to as doctrine functioning as a form of grammar. It is the full relatedness of the human and the divine in Christ which Bonhoeffer uses to speak of the full relatedness of the world and God, such that Christian ethics can never be understood as either a flight from the reality of life in the world, or as a set of principles or human ideas that emerge from elsewhere than God revealed in Christ in the midst of the world. The Chalcedonian definition provides the doctrinal shape within which Bonhoeffer is able to address an entirely different set of issues.

The practice of theology is never simply the repetition of ancient formulae. Rather it involves taking the deep logic within those formulae and using that logic to address questions of how the reality of God is spoken of in the present context, exploring how that deep logic helps us address other questions of concern within our contemporary life in the world.

The nature of confessions

Confessions of faith emerged at the time of the Reformation, and stand in a slightly different relationship to the life of the Church than creeds. The Reformation cry of *sola scriptura* (Scripture alone), led to the understanding that the doctrine of the Church can only be determined by reference to Scripture itself. Scripture is understood as interpreted by reference to itself, rather than any other hermeneutical scheme, and the creeds of the ecumenical councils are not themselves understood as a necessary lens through which Scripture must be read, or automatically as the best summary of the teaching of Scripture. This means that the creeds fall into a slightly different category for the Reformation traditions from the one that they occupy in many other traditions.

Many of the Reformation churches nevertheless produced their own statements of faith. Confessions act as a summary of the content of the gospel, frequently stating directly that they are summaries of the doctrine that is contained within Scripture. The Lutheran and Reformed strands of the Reformation (the former emerging from the Reformation inaugurated by Luther within modern-day Germany, the latter from the Swiss Reformation and Zwingli in Zurich and Calvin in Geneva) relate to confessions of faith somewhat differently. For the Lutheran tradition the Augsburg Confession has ended up holding a position alongside the early creeds and is understood as a 'symbol' of the faith with the same authority as the early creeds. The term 'symbol' in this context suggests something that states authoritatively and permanently the Christian faith. For the Reformed, on the other hand, confessions of faith are more often understood as being particular to a specific time and place.

Historically, two confessions that are particularly important within the Reformed world are the Heidelberg Catechism (commonly in use in Continental European Reformed churches) and the Westminster Confession (commonly used in English speaking Reformed churches). Reformed churches have a tendency to formulate new confessions of faith in new situations. For example, when two Reformed churches merge to form one new united church, often a new confession of faith will be adopted to inaugurate the new united church (the United Reformed Church in the United Kingdom would be one such example). Other situations give rise to new confessions within the Reformed tradition too – for example when the surrounding culture is understood to have shifted so drastically that a new confession of faith is required to state the gospel in terms which speak to that new cultural situation (as when a new confession of faith was adopted by the Presbyterian Church in the United States of America in 1976), or at times even when political events are perceived as warranting a new confession of faith (as with the Presbyterian–Reformed Church of Cuba after the Socialist Revolution).[17]

Not all traditions accept confessions or creeds as having any kind of authority. For example, the Disciples of Christ (Churches of Christ) have never accepted the authority of creeds or confessions but rather only the authority of Scripture itself. This tradition, which emerged in the nineteenth century, was reacting against a situation in which subscription to a creed or confession was being used to determine admittance to the Lord's Supper. They argued that only the confession of Jesus Christ as Lord and Saviour was required, not subscription to any particular formulation of the content of the faith. Scripture alone was that which was authoritative, not any attempt to 'summarize' it.

The Lutheran and Reformed traditions are the two that are most commonly thought of as 'confessional' traditions. They both relate somewhat differently to the early creeds of the Church. The Augsburg Confession states in its first article that:

> We unanimously hold and teach, in accordance with the decree of the Council of Nicaea, that there is one divine essence, which is called and which is truly God, and that there are three persons in this one divine essence, equal in power and alike eternal: God the Father, God the Son, God the Holy Spirit.[18]

Here we see that Nicaea is upheld as authoritative. The position in many of the Reformed confessions is somewhat different. Frequently we find that the teachings of the councils of the Church are only accepted in a way that is clearly subordinate to Scripture. A typical example is found in the Second Helvetic Confession that was adopted in 1566 in Zurich. It sets out first of all the primary place Scripture has. When going on to speak of the early Church Fathers in Chapter Two, it states that 'we modestly dissent from them when they are found to set down things differing from, or altogether contrary to, the Scriptures', and goes on to say that 'in the same order also we place the decrees and canons of councils.'[19] Councils, and therefore the creeds adopted by them, are authoritative only insofar as they are understood as being supported by Scripture.

Confessions of faith in the Reformed tradition are therefore frequently called a 'subordinate standard'; subordinate to Scripture. However, the language and formulations of the creeds, particularly concerning the Trinity and the person of Christ are frequently adopted. The Second Helvetic Confession, whilst having subordinated the position of the creeds to Scripture, goes on, for example, to state that God is

> in person inseparably and without confusion distinguished as Father, Son and Holy Spirit so, as the Father has begotten the Son from eternity, the Son is begotten by an ineffable generation, and the Holy Spirit truly proceeds from them both, and the same from eternity and is to be worshipped with both.[20]

The language and expression of the Nicene creeds is taken over here quite directly, so that although the creeds adopted in the early ecumenical councils are only regarded as authoritative to the extent that they can be supported by Scripture, they are clearly considered to be so supported, and therefore can be repeated in this confession of faith.

Creeds, confessions, and ecumenism

One of the practices of theology that engages frequently with creeds and confessions is ecumenical dialogue. One of the challenges confronting ecumenical dialogue is the fact that different traditions at times have confessed different things about the same issues, and at times have issued anathemas against those in other traditions who do not confess their faith in the same terms.

Ecumenical dialogue works with these differing confessions and accompanying anathemas to see what forms of reconciliation might be possible. One example of this is the dialogue that there has been within Europe between the Lutheran and Reformed traditions, which ultimately led them to recognize one another as churches, and to share full pulpit and table fellowship (i.e. to share the Eucharist together) and recognize each other's ministries. This happened in 1973 when the Leuenberg agreement was signed and then adopted by Lutheran and Reformed churches across Europe. Later, the Methodist church also signed.

One of the key issues that had to be resolved before this was possible concerned the understanding of the Eucharist. The Lutheran and Reformed traditions had developed different understandings of the Eucharist at the time of the Reformation. In 1529, Luther and Zwingli had debated the matter at what has become known as the Colloquy of Marburg. In essence, Luther had argued that Christ was really present in the bread and wine (This *is* the body of Christ), whereas Zwingli had argued that Christ was represented in the bread and wine (This *signifies* the body of Christ). Essentially, Zwingli was arguing that the word 'is' was functioning in the same way as it does when we say that 'Jesus is the vine': Jesus is not literally a vine; it is a metaphor. It took from 1529 to 1973 before this disagreement was resolved in the Leuenberg declaration.[21] Behind this debate was a Christological issue: could the body of Christ be everywhere (omnipresent) because it was divine, or was it truly a human body and therefore could only be in one place, seated at the right hand of the Father (and hence not in multiple places on the altar)?

The position of the Lutheran tradition can be seen in the Augsburg Confession, which in paragraph 10 states that:

> It is taught among us that the true body and blood of Christ are really present in the Supper of our Lord under the form of bread and wine and are there distributed and received. The contrary doctrine is therefore rejected.[22]

We can contrast with this what the Second Helvetic Confession states about the presence of Christ in the Eucharist:

> We do not, therefore, so join the body of the Lord and his blood with the bread and wine as to say that the bread itself is the body of Christ except in a sacramental way.[23]

During the twentieth century these two divergent views came together. The process of this began in the 1930s in Germany, where some Lutheran and Reformed Christians worked together to resist the attempts Hitler was making to bring the churches into the service of the National Socialist state. At the time a confessional statement, the *Barmen Declaration*, was signed. Following this joint declaration (and also the fact that in the nineteenth century some Reformed and Lutheran churches had been united within Germany) there was a desire to overcome remaining differences and fully accept the sacraments of one another's traditions. A further meeting in Halle (the Second meeting of the Fourth Confessing Synod of the Evangelical Church of the Old Prussian Union) declared that it was possible for the two traditions to celebrate the Lord's Supper together, and began to use the language of 'Personal Presence'.[24] This ultimately, following many years of dialogues and conversations across Europe, laid the basis of the Leuenberg Agreement, which brought the Lutherans and the Reformed into full fellowship, and both sides declared that:

In the Lord's Supper the risen Jesus Christ imparts himself in his body and blood, given up for all, through his word of promise with bread and wine. He thus gives himself unreservedly to all who receive the bread and wine; faith receives the Lord's Supper for salvation, unfaith for judgment.

We cannot separate communion with Jesus Christ in his body and blood from the act of eating and drinking. To be concerned about the manner of Christ's presence in the Lord's Supper in abstraction from this act is to run the risk of obscuring the meaning of the Lord's Supper.

Where such a consensus exists between the churches, the condemnations pronounced by the Reformation confessions are inapplicable to the doctrinal position of these churches.[25]

It is interesting to note the way in which the practice of ecumenical dialogue has taken two seemingly contradictory positions, and found within them a common way of expressing the nature of the Eucharist; by speaking of Christ's giving of himself in the whole act of communion, while shifting away from attempting to define precisely *how* that happens.

Not only does this illustrate one of the practices of Christian theology (ecumenical dialogue), but the results of the dialogue in and of themselves begin to constitute what might be called a new confessional statement which then becomes one of the sources for the practice of Christian theology by individual theologians. An example of how ecumenical statements have been taken up in this way comes to us from Michael Welker's work on the nature of the Eucharist, *What Happens in Holy Communion?* He uses the results of this ecumenical process as a source from which he is able to develop his particular understanding of the nature of the Eucharist. His personal conclusion about the proper way of understanding the presence of Christ in the Eucharist draws on these ecumenical 'confessions', using them as a source of authority:

In this process the whole Christ is present: the pre-Easter Jesus whom we remember, the Crucified One whom we proclaim, the Risen One to whom we bear witness, and the Human One whom we expect and await. In the celebration of the Supper, the gathered community is permeated and surrounded by Christ, by the entire richness of his life. The notion of Christ's 'real presence' is better suited than that of Christ's personal presence to provide a framework for the difficult task of understanding this complex of relations.[26]

What Welker is doing, in effect, is taking the content of ecumenical dialogues as the source of the Church's teaching, and exploring the theological logic embedded within that content. He then offers a particular interpretation of that language, developing it more fully than the wording of the ecumenical texts themselves. So the historical confessional texts form authoritative statements of the different traditions, which are then explored theologically through the practice of ecumenical dialogue, which itself gives rise to ecumenical statements, which then themselves function as confessional texts that individual theologians can use in their practice of theology.

New confessions

Whilst ecumenical texts frequently function like confessions of faith, there are also moments in the life of the Church when new confessions of faith are required in specific contexts. In these moments, we see another set of interrelationships between the practice of individual theologians and the Church's corporate practice of theology. There were two moments in the twentieth century when churches used the adoption of confessional texts to respond to particular situations. The Barmen Declaration (to which we have already referred) was adopted by a Synod of what was known as the Confessing Church in Germany in 1934. It was a theological response to the way the German Christian movement, which had taken control of much of the church, was accommodating the demands of Hitler's National Socialist State.[27] The other instance concerned apartheid in South Africa, which was effectively declared a heresy in a process that led to the adoption of the Belhar Confession.[28] Both situations have become known as situations of *status confessionis* – of confessional status. This means that something emerged in those situations that the Church came to believe required a decision that was integral to the confession of the gospel – something that had to be 'confessed' and believed. The confessions produced in these situations mark out, as earlier creeds and confessions do, the boundaries of the faith and the consequences of that faith.

The Barmen Declaration serves as a useful illustration both of the formation of texts such as this, and also of the way in which they then serve the work of individual theologians. The Barmen Declaration arose as a response to the church situation in Germany in the early days of the National Socialist State. The key presenting issue was the introduction of the 'Arian Paragraph' within Germany, which prohibited Jews from holding public office. As German ministers of the church are civil servants, this restricted the ability of the church to determine its own ministry. In the case of the Barmen Declaration, as is usual in the formation of confessional texts, the drafting was done by a small committee. The key drafting of the text was done by Karl Barth. The Barmen Declaration consists of six key articles. Each article begins with citations from Scripture, then makes a positive theological statement, and then contains a statement of that which is rejected. In this sense it follows the pattern we have seen in other Reformation confessions, of a positive statement of faith, and then an anathema. The theological logic of the whole declaration stems from the first paragraph, which reads:

> 'I am the Way and the Truth and the Life; no one comes to the Father except through me.' (Jn.14:6)
>
> 'Truly, truly I say to you, he who does not enter the sheepfold through the door but climbs in somewhere else, he is a thief and a robber. I am the Door; if anyone enters through me, he will be saved.' (Jn. 10:1, 9)
>
> Jesus Christ, as he is attested to us in Holy Scripture, is the one Word of God which we have to hear, and which we have to trust and obey in life and in death.
>
> We reject the false doctrine that the Church could and should recognise as a source of its proclamation, beyond and besides this one Word of God, yet other events, powers, historic figures, and truths as God's revelation.[29]

What this statement is particularly reacting against is a form of 'natural theology': the notion that God reveals Godself within human history and life in the world, independently of God's revelation in Christ. Karl Barth himself offers a commentary on this article in his *Church Dogmatics* and places the confessional statement in its historical content. He suggests that it is reacting to a new form of natural theology which arose in the

> demand to recognise in the political events of the year 1933, and especially in the form of the God-sent Adolf Hitler, a source of specific new revelation of God, which, demanding obedience and trust, took its place beside the revelation attested in Holy Scripture, claiming that it should be acknowledged by Christian proclamation and theology as equally binding and obligatory.[30]

We see here a complex relationship between the act of adopting confessions of faith and the role of the individual theologian within this process. The *Barmen Declaration* is authoritative because it has been adopted by the churches (many Reformed and United churches in Germany and throughout the world have adopted the Barmen Confession as one of their authoritative confessional statements). It is not authoritative because Karl Barth wrote it, however great a theologian one might consider him to be. It is authoritative, rather, because the churches recognized it as warranting confessional status (*status confessionis*). Moreover, because it has authority through the act of the churches adopting it as a confessional standard, Barth is then able to use it as a source for his own personal theological engagement as he reflects on the place of natural theology.

The Barmen Declaration has become a significant source for the practice of theology in various ways. Much as the early creeds have become a basis for theological commentary, there are examples of Barmen being used in this way too. One such comes from the German Lutheran theologian Eberhard Jüngel, who offers commentary on various paragraphs of Barmen as the basis for a constructive theology of the State.[31] The South African theologian John de Gruchy has also drawn upon Barmen in his theological work concerning apartheid in South Africa. He draws upon the first article of Barmen to offer a set of theological reflections that ultimately are concerned with the injustice of the apartheid system. He follows the logic of the Barmen Declaration, which moves from the first article quoted above through to a proclamation of the Lordship of Christ. He offers the following development of this line of thought:

> For Gentile Christians the fact that Jesus the *Jew* is Lord should mean a total openness toward and solidarity with the Jewish brothers and sisters of Jesus. For Christians the fact that Jesus is *Lord* should mean a rejection of all ideologies that dehumanize and destroy any sister or brother of Jesus, whether Jew or Arab, black or white.[32]

What de Gruchy is doing here is taking an authoritative teaching of the Church as accepted in the Barmen Declaration, and drawing from it the theological principle at work, and engaging that within a new context; in this case South Africa and the apartheid system. As we noted above in the observation of Rowan Williams, the simple repetition of credal or confessional formulae is not the primary task of theology.

The primary task rather is to engage the theological issues at stake within credal and confessional theology, and through that engagement to continue to state and restate the fundamental truth of the gospel. We see de Gruchy doing just that with the Barmen Declaration. He puts the matter this way:

> Barmen as both a confessing word and event has functioned as a 'liberating symbol' within the church struggle in South Africa and continues to do so. But Barmen cannot simply be repeated in a different context. To idolize Barmen is to deny its message. In each situation the church struggle is at once the same and yet different. The confession remains 'Jesus is Lord', but the concrete implications differ.[33]

De Gruchy here is illustrating well much of what we have been thinking about in this examination of creeds and confessions. The practice of theology includes the Church itself as it engages with the expression of its faith in the formulation of creeds and confessions. The individual theologian then appropriates those creeds and confessions, and they shape (to differing degrees and in different ways) both the content and the form of his or her theological practice. The individual theologian in her practice of theology interrogates credal and confessional statements and engages their theological content, and inner theological logic, and brings that to bear on the question at hand. This question may be one of the interrelationship of one part of theology to another, as in the construction of a systematic theology. Alternatively it may be the interrelationship between the content of the faith as contained within credal and confessional statements and concrete political situations of life in the world, as in the case of Nazi Germany or apartheid South Africa. Alternatively, it may be that the content of the faith as expressed in creeds and confessions is brought into relationship with particular themes, academic disciplines, or almost any subject imaginable, such as science, art, environmentalism, the law and so on.

The practice of theology relies upon credal and confessional statements in the sense that they provide the theological substance that has emerged from the Church's ongoing engagement with Scripture and with its own tradition. They can also act the other way around by providing the interpretative lens through which Scripture and the tradition of the Church can be appropriated. The practice of the individual theologian may concern itself at times with the construction of new confessional texts, as we have seen in the case of ecumenical dialogues and the agreements that result from them, or with Karl Barth at Barmen. The individual theologian may also be engaged with commentary upon earlier credal and confessional statements. Even when creeds and confessions are not self-consciously being engaged by the individual theologian, they are still shaping the practice of theology by defining the loci of the theological endeavour, and by acting as summaries of the collective memory of the tradition of the Church.

Notes

1 In A.E. McGrath, *The Christian Theology Reader*, 3rd edn, Oxford: Blackwell, 2007, p. 10.
2 In McGrath, *Christian Theology Reader*, p. 11.

3 J. Calvin, *Institutes of the Christian Religion, 1536 edition*, trans. F.L. Battles, Grand Rapids, MI: William B. Eerdmans Publishing Company, 1986.

4 K. Barth, *Dogmatics in Outline*, trans. G.T. Thomson, London: SCM Press, 2001.

5 H. Küng, *Credo: The Apostles' Creed Explained for Today*, trans. J. Bowden, London: SCM Press, 1993.

6 T.F. Torrance, *The Trinitarian Faith*, Edinburgh: T&T Clark, 1998.

7 W. Pannenberg, *Systematic Theology*, 3 vols., trans. G.W. Bromiley, Grand Rapids, MI: William B. Eerdmans Publishing Company, 1991–98.

8 G. Lindbeck, *The Nature of Doctrine: Religion and Theology in a Postliberal Age*, London: SPCK, 1984.

9 Lindbeck, *Nature*, pp. 32–41.

10 Lindbeck, *Nature*, pp. 92–96.

11 R. Williams, *Arius*, London: SCM Press, 2001, p. 236.

12 Williams, *Arius*, p. 244.

13 McGrath, *Christian Theology Reader*, p. 282.

14 D. Bonhoeffer, *Ethics*, trans. R. Krauss, C. West, and D. Stott, Minneapolis, MN: Fortress Press, 2005, p. 31.

15 Bonhoeffer, *Ethics*, p. 49.

16 Bonhoeffer, *Ethics*, p. 55.

17 For the text of these confessional statements, along with others from the latter part of the twentieth century, see L. Vischer (ed.) *Reformed Witness Today: A Collection of Confessions and Statements of Faith Issued by Reformed Churches*, Bern: Evangelische Arbeitsstelle Oekumene, 1982.

18 J.H. Leith (ed.) *Creeds of the Churches: A Reader in Christian Doctrine from the Bible to the Present*, New York: Anchor Books, 1963, p. 67.

19 A.C. Cochrane, *Reformed Confessions of the Sixteenth Century*, Louisville, KY: Westminster John Knox Press, 2003, pp. 226–27.

20 Cochrane, *Reformed Confessions*, p. 228.

21 For a historical account of this see D. MacCulloch, *Reformation: Europe's House Divided*, London: Penguin Books, 2004, pp. 171–73.

22 Leith, *Creeds*, p. 71.

23 Cochrane, *Reformed Confessions*, p. 287.

24 M. Welker, *What Happens in Holy Communion?*, Grand Rapids, MI: William B. Eerdmans Publishing Company, 2000, pp. 91–92.

25 *Agreement between Reformation Churches in Europe (Leuenberg Agreement)*, Frankfurt am Main: Verlag Otto Lembeck, 1993, p. 40.

26 Welker, *Communion*, p. 100.

27 For a historical account of the Synod at Barmen, see K. Scholder, *The Churches and the Third Reich, 2: The Year of Disillusionment, 1934, Barmen and Rome*, trans. J. Bowden, London: SCM Press, 1985, pp. 122–72.

28 For an excellent account of the formation of the confession and its theological implications see: P.J. Naudé, *Neither Calendar nor Clock: Perspectives on the Belhar Confession*, Grand Rapids, MI: William B. Eerdmans Publishing Company, 2010.

29 Cited in E. Jüngel, *Christ, Justice and Peace: Toward a Theology of the State*, trans. D.B. Hamil and A.J. Torrance, Edinburgh: T&T Clark, 1992, p. xxii.

30 K. Barth, *Church Dogmatics II/1: The Doctrine of God*, trans. G.W. Bromiley et al., London: T&T Clark, 2009, p. 173.

31 E. Jüngel, *Christ, Justice and Peace*.

32 J.W. de Gruchy, *Bonhoeffer and South Africa: Theology in Dialogue*, Grand Rapids, MI: William B. Eerdmans Publishing Company, 1984, p. 128.

33 De Gruchy, *Bonhoeffer and South Africa*, pp. 130–31.

17
READING QUESTIONABLE TRADITIONS

Rachel Muers

Introduction: difficult conversations

As this section of the book makes clear, Christian theology works with and within traditions. In practical terms, this means that doing Christian theology involves reading and working with texts (and other materials) from the Christian past. What we do will be recognizably Christian theology if, and only if, it is recognizably in conversation with Christianity's past. The conversation with tradition is, of course, generally recognized as a conversation in which critical questions can and should be asked. Theology develops, at least in part, through the process of question and argument. To that extent at least, tradition is always questionable. As discussed elsewhere in this volume, carefully articulated disagreement, the interrogation of assumptions, acknowledgement of the participants' different contexts and how they provoke different claims, and other features of any good argument about an important topic, all properly form part of theology's conversation with tradition.

However, staying with the analogy of a conversation, we can all think of circumstances in which we would find ourselves unable to continue a conversation on easy or peaceable terms, treating a conversation partner as a fellow participant in the search for truth – even if he or she were saying important things. What if the conversation partner, in the course of presenting his or her ideas, consistently defends practices or attitudes that you find deeply abhorrent ? What if the conversation partner appears not to be prepared to talk to *you* – on peaceable terms, or at all? Or what if the conversation partner consistently attacks, misrepresents, or advocates violence against your friends and neighbours? And – what if you then find yourself stuck in a room with that person and unable to avoid hearing, at least occasionally, what he or she says?

Anyone who reads or works with the texts of Christian history confronts this problem. You do not need to be anti-Christian, or an advocate of radical reform to Christian theology, to recognize the manifold ethical and political *wrongness* in Christian tradition – both in the history of Christianity itself and in the texts that bear witness to and shape that history. Especially since the middle of the twentieth century, numerous readers of Christian tradition have drawn attention to theologically-justified sexism, racism, anti-Judaism and colonialism – to name but a few of the most prominent examples (some of which are dealt with at more length elsewhere in this book). These are, or should be, of concern to everyone who tries to work with and within Christian tradition – not just to those who identify themselves with groups who have suffered Christian history's wrongs.

So how can or should theologians make use of traditions that include 'texts of terror', practices of exclusion, problematic ideologies, collusion with horrendous evil, and the rest? And what is involved in Christian theologians doing justice to their questionable inheritance – working with and within tradition? Are we forced to ignore or explain away the ethical and political problems we find in the texts we read, in order to continue working faithfully within a tradition? Or should we be expunging certain texts from our 'lived traditions' altogether, ceasing to read or converse with them? If we can reject utterly some recent versions of 'Christianity' – as, for example, Christians worldwide rejected the pro-apartheid churches and theologies of late twentieth-century South Africa – could we ever do the same with older texts that are more deeply embedded within the tradition, but that carry equally problematic ethical implications? And if so, how would we deal with their multiple and ongoing effects within Christian traditions and communities?

Before exploring these questions, I want to draw attention to a wider issue that arises when we start to look at tradition in this way. Doing theology is, we often say, an activity that involves and engages the whole of a person's life – emotions, experiences, and lived relationships, as well as intellectual and religious formation. That is easy to say, but difficult to handle. It means, for example, that theology is not a very safe 'conversation', and the risks are not the same for everyone and are not evenly distributed. It means, moreover, that theologians have to learn to handle the affective dimension of their work – how the texts we read may evoke deep emotional responses in us. When you study Christian tradition, you may find yourself looking at texts that you simply *cannot* go on reading, let alone draw into a productive conversation. Or you may find yourself in an uneasy negotiation between your deep love for a text and your deep discomfort with some of its assumptions or claims – an uneasy negotiation perhaps comparable to conversations I remember with a close friend, much older than I, who was consistently and unthinkingly racist.

I suggest that acknowledging the many ways in which texts affect us and others – emotionally, socially, aesthetically, and so forth – is part of good reading and shapes good reading. A 'felt' response to a text is not necessarily something that needs to be confined to an introductory paragraph or an embarrassed footnote. There are some things in theological texts that *should* (for example) horrify or disturb a reader, and there is no loss of rigour in pointing this out and exploring why. At the same time, as we will see, doing theology requires you not only to acknowledge a 'felt' response, but to reflect on it in the wider context of theological work – the context of a God-formed community.

This in turn means that the issue of how to read questionable traditions demands a response that is itself theological and ethical. We will return to this point later.

Dimensions of wrong

To help us to approach a complex area, it is useful to make a few distinctions between kinds and levels of 'wrongness' we might identify in theological texts. First, we might want to distinguish between texts that carry and express an underlying assumption that is ethically problematic, and texts that appear directly to advocate, approve or justify an ethically problematic position. Consider, for example, the judgement that much of Christian tradition is sexist. This judgement could be, and often is, supported by quotations from thinkers who have been recognized as major influences on theological tradition and who argue not only for women's inferiority, but also for their propensity and proximity to evil. Thus, contemporary gender-critical readers of Christian tradition often quote Tertullian, who addressed women thus:

> You are the devil's gateway: you are she who first violated the forbidden tree and broke the law of God. It was you who coaxed your way around him whom the devil had not the force to attack. With what ease you shattered that image of God: man! Because of the death you merited the Son of God had to die![1]

However, even without such direct articulations and rhetorical justifications of sexism, one could easily find texts expressing underlying assumptions about women's proximity to evil. Consider, for example, how Augustine writes in the *Confessions* about his mental struggles at the time of his conversion:

> The nearer the point of time came in which I was to become different, the more it struck me with horror ... Those trifles of all trifles, and vanities of vanities, my one-time mistresses, held me back, plucking at my garment of flesh and murmuring softly: 'Are you sending us away?' ... what were they suggesting to me, O my God? Do you in your mercy keep from the soul of your servant the vileness and uncleanness they were suggesting.[2]

This passage is not mainly about women, and is not intended as a justification of any particular attitude to women – but it reflects and reinforces certain notions about women, and in particular women's sexuality, as a moral threat (to men) that needs to be controlled. To that extent it is, as it were, part of the same problem; but we might respond to it differently if we judge it to be merely an indication of, rather than an argument for, a problematic attitude.

Another distinction worth bearing in mind is between an inter-communal wrong and an external wrong. This is not because either is necessarily worse than the other, but because they may require different theological approaches. There are texts that express, advocate or justify oppression or injustice within the Christian community – such as, we might say, Tertullian's letter to his 'sisters', quoted above. There are other texts that express, advocate or justify oppression or injustice beyond the Christian community – such as expressions of anti-Judaism, or the numerous theological justifications of the Crusades. How might this distinction make a difference? For a start, the first group of texts – expressing internal injustice – may well be read or used, as part of a living tradition and an ongoing conversation, by people who feel themselves to be on the 'receiving end' of the problems reflected in the text (women Christian theologians reading, and seeking to work with, the *Confessions*). The question arises – how can I relate positively to, and be part of a conversation with people who think that about me? Is there space for us both in the same community and the same conversation?

In the case of an external wrong, although of course in many cases the texts will be read by people who identify with their 'victims' (Muslims studying Christianity and reading Christian justifications of the Crusades) the question for the Christian reader is different – how can I identify with, and be part of a conversation with, people who think like that about my neighbours? How can I, as part of this community, make sure that I do not repeat its past mistakes?

Approaching questionable traditions

Exposing the structures of wrong

An important first step for many theologians reading and using problematic traditions is, simply, to acknowledge, expose, and analyse the problem. This is itself a complex task. It is easy enough to pick out the obviously 'wrong' quotations – although even then, taking the theological task forward means we need to analyse their wrongness in some detail. Look, for example, at how Zoe Bennett Moore discusses the passage from Tertullian given earlier:

> [This quotation] demonstrate[s] several important aspects of men's assessment of women's sin ... The story of the Fall, of Adam and Eve in Gen. 3, is interpreted in such a way as to throw the blame on Eve, making women more culpable than men by their very nature. This culpability is connected with cunning wiles, 'coaxing' and the capacity for sexual manipulation ... The evaluation of women as source of sexual sin, as possessing less reason and capacity for responsibility than men, and as needing to be controlled, is widespread historically and geographically. Here it is mapped onto Christian theological themes in a way which shapes subsequent thought and action down to the present day.[3]

Here, Bennett Moore is drawing on a range of scholarship on religion and gender (for example, in the claim about the widespread 'evaluation of women as sources of sexual sin') to inform her account of what is 'wrong' with Tertullian and why. She is locating Tertullian as a reader of Scripture and as a shaper of key theological concepts (such as sin and nature). She is paying close attention to the details of his rhetoric. Most importantly for our purposes, she is reading him as a – highly problematic – voice of living tradition, whose failures matter because in their contribution to ongoing theological reflection they 'shape subsequent thought and action'.

Theological readers of Christian tradition often want to argue – as does Bennett Moore in this example – that there is an ethical problem with the tradition as a whole, or with some major strand of it. It is very important to recognize that this is not necessarily or obviously an anti-Christian move; it is made by many Christian theologians as part of constructive theological projects. To argue the case that the tradition as a whole has a problem, it will be necessary both to expose the ethically problematic character of some texts from the tradition, and to be able to claim that these texts are either representative ('just a few of the hundreds of examples I could have picked') or decisively influential. It will probably also be necessary to demonstrate that the ethical problem is structural and not merely incidental – that it is not simply a matter of some poor choices of words or images, but rather that the way in which these texts understand and relate to God, humanity and the world is itself problematic.

Having done all this, if one is reading within Christian tradition, the exposure of 'wrongness' will be carried out in the conviction that Christianity itself in some way resists the wrong – whether through the texts of the 'established' tradition, through Scripture read against tradition, or through suppressed or marginalized voices that form part of the larger tradition of Christianity.

For an extended example of theological analysis and exposure of pervasive problems with tradition, I take R. Kendall Soulen's account of the theological problem of Christian anti-Judaism. This is the first half of a constructive Christian theology of Israel, and incorporates detailed and critical readings of several theological texts. Soulen begins with a discussion of Justin Martyr and Irenaeus. The justification for the selection of these figures is made clear from the beginning:

> [the] creation of a framework for reading the Christian Bible [i.e. for relating what came to be called the Old and New Testaments] was to a considerable degree the accomplishment of Justin Martyr and especially Irenaeus of Lyons … Irenaeus' achievements provided the basic design for what would become the church's standard canonical narrative.[4]

In other words, these thinkers matter because they taught subsequent Christians how to read the Bible (through what Irenaeus sets out as the 'rule of faith'); and Soulen will then go on to demonstrate the problems that their teaching bequeaths to those subsequent Christians.

What he uncovers, as he reads, is not explicitly anti-Jewish statements, but structures of thought that tend to denigrate the core of (what Christians read as) the Old Testament and to marginalize Judaism. Here is a sample quotation from Irenaeus, with Soulen's comments:

> Near the beginning of *Against Heresies*, Irenaeus offers the following statement of the rule of faith:
> '[The Church believes] in one God, the Father Almighty, Maker of heaven, and earth, and the sea, and all things that are in them; and in one Christ Jesus, the Son of God, who became incarnate for our salvation; and in the holy Spirit, who proclaimed through the prophets the dispensations of God, and the advents, and the birth from a virgin, and the passion, and the resurrection from the dead, and the ascension into heaven in the flesh of the beloved Christ Jesus, our Lord, and His future manifestation from heaven in the glory of the Father "to gather all things in one," and to raise up anew all flesh of the whole human race, in order that Christ Jesus … should execute just judgement towards all.'

... The point to note here is that the rule of faith provides a narrative framework for reading the Scriptures that identifies God as the God of the Hebrew Scriptures (that is, maker of heaven and earth) while all but ignoring the centre of those Scriptures ... Irenaeus sketches out the overarching drama of God's consummating and redemptive purposes for humankind in a way that is almost wholly uninformed by God's history with the Jews.[5]

There are several features of this example that are worth noting. First, Soulen has chosen a text that expresses the heart of Irenaeus' theology – and that is instantly recognizable as coherent with, or influential on, the heart of subsequent Christian theology. This is a tradition that matters, both historically and in the contemporary context – so it is by the same token a tradition that, if it proves to be problematic in some way, is worth worrying about. In fact, if you became concerned, as you read this extract, that Soulen was about to show that Christianity as a whole was problematic and that Christianity would have to change beyond recognition in order to solve the problem – your concern is reasonable.

Second, Soulen is drawing attention to a problem with a text, but he is (implicitly here and explicitly elsewhere in his work) linking it to deeply problematic practices – anti-Jewish policies in Christian and Christian-dominated states, and anti-Jewish actions by Christians. Serious Christian theological reflection on anti-Judaism in tradition began (with a few notable exceptions) after and as a response to the *Shoah*/Holocaust – the mass murder of Jews in 'Christian' Europe. It was, in other words, catastrophic failures by Christian individuals and communities that prompted a consideration of the failures of Christian texts.

Some further comment on this point is necessary. The historical relationship between Christian anti-Judaism and the *Shoah* is the subject of ongoing scholarly debate, and we should beware of simply assuming that the one is a cause of the other. More generally, and more importantly for this chapter, we should *always* beware of making facile assumptions about the relationships between beliefs and practices – especially when we are talking about the deep structures of belief, which may manifest themselves in very different ways in different circumstances. Kathryn Tanner's *The Politics of God* gives an extended demonstration of how difficult it is simply to 'map' theological ideas about creation (for example) onto political practices.[6] It would be simply irresponsible – a failure of the responsibility of a reader, as well as of the particular responsibility to a living past – to assume without historical evidence that a given theological position automatically produces politically or ethically unacceptable actions. Of course, it would be equally irresponsible to deny, or cover up, the role of theology in providing ideological justification and motivation for horrendous wrongs; and it is also important to remember that the text itself – as most obviously in the examples from Tertullian and Augustine discussed above – can *be* 'wrong'.

To return to our discussion of Soulen: third, the quotation he has chosen makes no direct reference to Jews, Judaism or Israel. It is not the piece you would have picked if you had been skimming through patristic texts looking for examples of Christian anti-Judaism. As Soulen explains, it is the absence of Jews, Judaism, and Israel that is the problem. The critical question with which Soulen begins his reading – how do Christian theologians think about Israel? – enables him to see new dimensions of a wide range of texts, observing absences and marginal presences as well as explicit and developed themes. Reading for what or who is missing is a common and important strategy in the ethically critical interpretation of tradition. In many cases, the ethical problem *is* the exclusion, silencing, and enforced invisibility of certain groups, both within and outwith the Christian community. Note also that one does not have to be writing a book or article on an obviously relevant subject (Christianity and Judaism, women in Christian tradition) in order to have, and make use of, this critical attention to absences in texts.

Fourth, in Soulen's description of Irenaeus' rule of faith he identifies a tension within it. The tension is only alluded to here, but it becomes rather important later in Soulen's discussion. He notes that Irenaeus has on the one hand identified God as the God of the Hebrew Scriptures (by calling God the 'maker of heaven and earth'), and on the other hand included almost nothing in the rule of faith that relates to 'the center of those Scriptures'. We learn elsewhere in Soulen's discussion that the first of these moves – identifying God as the maker of heaven and earth, and defending Christian use of the Hebrew Scriptures/Old Testament – is core to Irenaeus' project of opposing Gnosticism. The problem, Soulen is saying (and says at more length later) is that Irenaeus has not carried his own project through far enough. Regardless of whether this is a fair judgement, the key point to note is that Soulen, in reading this core text of Christian tradition, is finding a way to read it against itself. If Soulen is right, the problem is still there and still serious; but he also suggests that the tradition contains the resources to redress the problem – and that Irenaeus himself, as a faithful reader of the traditions and scriptures that preceded him, can give some indication of where these resources might be.

This, however, takes us a few steps beyond 'exposing the wrong'. How can theologians go on reading and working with traditions they take to be problematic?

Participating in the struggle for justice

I suggest that the other side of the inescapability of tradition – the fact that theologians cannot simply stop reading and working with their theological forebears – is the recognition that we are part of the same community as them and are affected in some way by the same problems. This does not mean that historical context is irrelevant, or that we can straightforwardly equate today's issues with those of previous eras. It also does not mean that all of us are affected in the same way by the 'wrongness' reflected in tradition and pervasively present within Christian communities. To take one of my earlier examples, sexism is everybody's problem, but it affects men and women differently (and different men and women differently).

So what does it mean to understand oneself, as a theologian, as part of a living community with authors of the questionable or 'wrong' texts we read – and, more to the point, how might it affect the way we work with these texts? For one thing, it can mean – at least in some cases – that we can keep reading the texts without having to make excuses for the authors, but also without having to pass final and decisive judgement on them. The authors are in the same predicament as us – called towards a vision of full flourishing in right relation with God, humanity, and the world, and caught in structures of sin that impede that flourishing. At the very least, remembering this makes it harder to hold the authors up as hate figures, or to place all the blame for past wrongdoing on the shoulders of one or two individuals.

Beyond this, it may be possible to read our own ethical struggles with and within tradition as part of a larger 'tradition' – a series of theological encounters with, and responses to, ethical and political wrong. We might want to see the practice of theology as, in part, a practice of struggling with 'wrongness' from within the situation of wrong. Both we and the theologians we read are engaged in that struggle – and all of our struggles may have outcomes beyond what we could foresee or intend.

To illustrate this point further, look back to the example given above from R. Kendall Soulen, and consider by contrast how J. Kameron Carter reads Irenaeus in *Race: A Theological Account*. Carter, like Soulen, is trying to diagnose and respond constructively to a pervasive ethical and political problem within theology – in this case, racism in modern Western theology. In brief, Carter takes Soulen's criticism seriously but then looks at the bigger picture of Irenaeus' context and work, and ends up making Irenaeus his ally – albeit not an infallibly reliable one – in an ongoing theological and ethical struggle.

On Carter's reading, Irenaeus' struggle against Gnosticism reflected in *Against Heresies* was ethical and political. Irenaeus was attacking the Gnostics' attempt to set up a hierarchy within which Judaism and Jews were devalued. There is a direct parallel, as Carter sees it, with the struggle against contemporary theological racism undertaken by African-American scholars and others.

> Afro-Christian faith, as was the case with Irenaeus' account of Christian identity forged in the kiln of his engagement with Ptolemaic Gnosticism, embodies an effort to rescue the discourse of theology from being a discourse of death.[7]

Elsewhere, Carter quotes Irenaeus' *Epideixis* as evidence of the latter's deep commitment to affirming the importance of the 'Old Testament' and of Judaism:

> Irenaeus is able in effect to explain the ongoing link between the Old Testament Mosaic Law, which the prophetic writings uphold, and the fourfold Gospel ... to overturn a key pillar of Gnostic theology and exegesis: namely, the inferiority of the God of Israel and the Old Testament Scriptures ...
>
> '... Isaiah, in this fashion, says "He will complete and cut short [his] Word in righteousness; for God will make a concise Word in all the world" [Isa 10:22–23; Rom 9:28]. ... the Lord also, when he was asked, which is the first commandment, said "You shall love the Lord your God with [your] whole heart and [your] whole strength; and the second like it, you shall love your neighbour as yourself ..." And therefore he made "a concise word" in the world.'
>
> ... this cutting short and fulfilling of the Law in another Law should not be read as an early instance of Christian supersessionism, the notion that Christians replace Israel as God's people, that God discards the Jews in favour of Christians. ... While being 'cut short', the Word of God remains identical. That is, there is a deep unity between the Old and New Testaments.[8]

Look closely at what is going on here, and at how it relates to the parallel example I discussed from Soulen. Carter is, like Soulen, examining the heart and the deep structures of Irenaeus' theology – but he is doing so primarily in order to find the resources for a reparative and constructive project, the project of challenging contemporary theological racism. Moreover, Carter is lifting up a theme in Irenaeus' work – the relationship to Israel and Judaism – that has tended to be marginalized or ignored, and is doing so in order to enable the ethical rereading of tradition. He is putting urgent questions about the ethical and political 'wrongness' of past and present Christianity to the traditions he reads, and this is enabling him to see dimensions of the texts that are generally ignored.

Most importantly, Carter acknowledges the tension noted by Soulen, between denigrating Jews and Judaism – 'Christian supersessionism' – and defending the Old Testament. However, rather than seeing this primarily as a tension and problem within Irenaeus' work, Carter locates it as an ongoing issue within Christian theology – one in which Irenaeus himself belongs mainly, as it were, on the right side, although he may easily (Carter implies, with a footnoted reference to Soulen) be used and interpreted for the denigration of Jews and Judaism.

How might we try to resolve the issues between Soulen and Carter in their reading of this enormously influential and – it would seem – ethically ambivalent strand of Christian tradition? One obvious first move would be to evaluate their respective interpretations of the primary texts. Are they giving not only coherent, but also plausible accounts of what Irenaeus says? Do these accounts make plausible and relevant reference to the contexts and purposes of Irenaeus' writing? In other words, is this good intellectual history?

However, starting with these questions might mislead us into thinking that Soulen and Carter are seeking neutral readings of tradition, and that any debate between them could easily be resolved by working out what Irenaeus 'really' said. This is not the point. Both theologians are, we have seen, motivated by deep concerns about the ethical and political implications of certain strands of Christian tradition – and, in particular, about voices, perspectives, and issues that have been consistently excluded from theological consideration. For them, searching for a 'neutral' perspective is likely to repeat the exclusions and failures of the past. If we pretend to adopt a neutral perspective, we are likely to be too naively uncritical of both the text and our own context. We may fail to ask questions about issues to which the text does not directly refer, or fail to see how the text challenges pervasive contemporary assumptions. So, resolving the issues between Soulen and Carter will also involve adopting an ethical stance yourself – placing *yourself* in some sort of relationship to Christian theology's struggles to do justice. At the very least, it will involve understanding the frameworks from within which they pose their ethical questions – learning why and how they ask questions about Christian anti-Judaism, and how that might connect with racism in theology.

The other assumption that you might make, but which should at least be questioned, is that this debate is all about trying to decide whether Irenaeus is 'good' or 'bad'. For constructive projects of Christian theology, this on its own is at best unproductive. Reading within a living tradition shaped by eschatological hope means recognizing that the limitations of the text and the author are limitations that, differently, we as readers share. We have no position of final judgement from which we can either write an author off completely or place him or her on an unassailable pedestal. We will inevitably make provisional judgements of various kinds – about the ethical and political problems that confront us in the texts and in the world, and about where and how the texts speak about them. So – careful and deep analysis of the 'wrongness' or the 'rightness' of texts is useful, not mainly because it lets us stop reading them, but because it develops our sense of how to go on doing ethical theology in the tradition of which they are part.

One loose analogy we might use for this way of reading questionable texts is with the developing tradition of restorative justice. Restorative justice – in its many different forms – is an approach to wrongdoing that focuses on restoring right relationships within a community, rather than simply on punishing an offender or satisfying some rules. Restorative justice practices generally involve the full and public disclosure of the wrong done, and the beginning of a process of change that can reintegrate the offender into the community. In working with tradition, even though past texts and dead authors cannot be 'changed', they can be read and used in ways that do not stop with the attribution of blame. They can be used, for example, to raise questions about, and seek responses to, contemporary structures of sin.

Consider Rowan Williams' response to the long and ignoble tradition of Christian acceptance of slavery (in particular, the enslavement of Africans):

> for hundreds and hundreds of years – in fact for thousands of years – people did not see the evil of slavery. Around them human beings were suffering in terrible ways and yet somehow people did not see, even Christians did not see … [we must ask] what it is that we now are blind to; who is it now whose suffering we cannot see, cannot understand? In some societies it may be women or old people, it may be children. It may be minorities of one kind or another. It may be that in our wealthy countries – it is the case in our wealthy countries – that we do not see the reality of suffering and injustice in so much of the world. And we may not know for a long time just how many things we have not seen. But at least we can begin to pray 'Lord, open our eyes'.[9]

Note that Williams neither denies nor excuses Christian collusion with slavery (although he arguably understates the active participation of Christians in all aspects of the enslavement project); there is at least an opening here for 'full disclosure' of the wrongness in tradition. Note, also, that he acknowledges his own particular location in relation both to the slave trade and to contemporary wrongs. He speaks from 'our wealthy countries', that is, as a material beneficiary both of the history of slavery and of contemporary injustices. This is another useful reminder that the ethical interrogation of tradition forces the theologian to become aware of, and to interrogate, his or her own position and the ethics of what he or she is doing – and that this is an ongoing practice rather than a one-off ground-clearing exercise.

Final thoughts: the limits of conversation

The examples discussed above seem to suggest that, with enough work, all kinds of apparently 'questionable' traditions can be brought into conversation. This conversation should involve the frank acknowledgement – without making glib excuses – of their problematic and questionable character. So far, however, my argument suggests that acknowledging deep ethical and political problems does not mean cutting off conversation. The analogy with restorative justice suggested the possibility of forgiveness and restored relationships – perhaps the constructive reappropriation of traditions, or at least the possibility of continuing to work with a text or author as a genuine conversation partner – on the other side of 'full disclosure'.

However, the analogy with restorative justice should also remind us that forgiveness and the restoration of relationships do not happen automatically, and can pose ethical problems of their own. For example, it is known that ordinary restorative justice processes do not work particularly well in situations where there is a significant power imbalance in the relationship between the victim and the offender – for example, in cases of domestic violence.[10] Forgiveness, in such a situation, might turn out to be a mandate for further abuse. Analogically, it might be very difficult to go on reading and working with a 'powerful' text – a text that is held up as key to the tradition and cited everywhere as an authority – that you experience as excluding or abusing you, especially if you do not find that your theological or church community empowers you to challenge the exclusion or the abuse.

What kinds of relationships to tradition are possible in this situation – a situation of power imbalance, in which the reader is not able to treat the text as a conversation partner? Obviously, as theologians we all select what, and whom, we read; there is an opportunity to avoid extended conversation with the 'abuser', even if there is no opportunity to escape him or her altogether. Another point to bear in mind is that suspicious readings of tradition – readings that explore and enumerate the problems with a text, reading it against itself – can be ways of bringing a 'powerful' text down from its pedestal and back to a level at which critical conversation is possible.

Beyond this, there is of course a real question about whether everything in theological terms is 'forgivable' – whether some texts, actions or even authors must, on ethical and political grounds, be excluded from Christian tradition, or included not as living conversation partners but as examples of bad practice. The argument here would be that, just as there are theological boundaries determining what counts as Christian, there are also ethical boundaries – and the two are intimately connected. There are ways of acting (including ways of writing) that are simply and obviously incompatible with faith in the God of Jesus Christ. So, for example, the World Alliance of Reformed Churches could declare in 1982 that Christian support for apartheid was a 'heresy'; and it is, we might think, legitimate to make similar declarations about past ethical and political failures.

There is, however, a note of caution to be sounded here. Consider the case of a Christian theologian who declares that the anti-Judaism she finds within Christian texts is a heresy – in other words, that it is not really Christian at all. From the theologian's point of view, this is a very important normative claim – it expresses a commitment for the future, declaring what Christian theology, including and especially the theology she herself intends to write, must (or must not) do. However, from other points of view it might well be heard – or misheard – as a descriptive claim. It might sound as if the theologian was saying that anti-Judaism is not very common within Christianity, or not really something for which Christians can be held responsible.

An interesting exchange of views about how to interpret, characterize and deal with ethically 'heretical' texts within Christian tradition can be found in Robert Morgan's review of Susannah Heschel's book on Nazism and Christianity, and Heschel's extended response.[11] Answering Morgan's claim that pro-Nazi theology and biblical interpretation was 'a heresy that deserves more obloquy than Dr Heschel's non-theological perspective can offer',[12] Heschel agrees with his characterization of Nazi theology as 'contrary to [Christian] religion', and suggests why this characterization may not always be helpful.

> 'Heresy' is ... an easy way to divorce the antisemitism of theologians such as [Walter] Grundmann [*a key pro-Nazi scholar*] from the Christian theological world today. That hardly seems a responsible approach ...
>
> There is no logical or necessary reason for Christian theologians to adopt antisemitic positions, in my opinion; doing so runs contrary to their religion ... [but] clearly, there are firm historical and theological bases that Grundmann and others have been able to make use of when they construct a racist version of Christianity. ...
>
> The African-American Protestant theologian Howard Thurman asked in 1949, 'Why is it that Christianity seems impotent to deal radically, and therefore effectively, with the issues of discrimination and injustice on the basis of race, religion and national origin? Is this impotency due to the betrayal of the genius of the religion, or is it due to a basic weakness in the religion itself? The question is searching, for the dramatic demonstration of the impotency of Christianity in dealing with the issue is underscored by its apparent inability to cope with it within its own fellowship.' Thurman's questions ought to be posed by theologians of other religions as well.[13]

Thurman's question, quoted by Heschel – is there an underlying problem with Christianity, or are these ethical failures 'betrayals' of Christianity? – is a useful one for the reader of problematic traditions to bear in mind; but it does not admit of easy answers. In the end, the critical reading of problematic traditions, as of any traditions, is highly unlikely to leave us in a position to characterize 'Christianity' as a whole. Decisions about the boundaries of Christianity – about heresy, in other words – may be unavoidable, but they are also always historically situated, ethically and politically engaged, and hence revisable.

There is still much to be done in working through Christian theology's relationship to the questionable traditions with which it works. The challenge is to find ways of working that do justice *to* the past and *for* the future. At the very least, the encounter with questionable traditions serves to remind theologians of the multiple ethical and political dimensions of their task, and of the many directions of their responsibility.

Notes

1 Tertullian, 'On the Apparel of Women', in *Ante-Nicene Fathers 4: Tertullian, Minucius Felix, Commodian, Origen*, trans. A.C. Coxe, Edinburgh: T&T Clark, 1869, § 1.1.
2 Augustine, *Confessions*, trans. F.J. Sheed, Cambridge: Hackett, 1993, § 8.XI.

3 Z. Bennett Moore, *Introducing Feminist Perspectives on Pastoral Theology*, Sheffield: Sheffield Academic Press, 2002, pp. 92–93.

4 R. K. Soulen, *The God of Israel and Christian Theology*, Minneapolis: Augsburg Fortress, 1996, p. 34.

5 Soulen, *God of Israel*, p. 42, quoting Irenaeus, *Against Heresies* § 1.10.1.

6 K. Tanner, *The Politics of God: Christian Theology and Social Justice*, Minneapolis, MN: Augsburg Fortress, 1992.

7 J.K. Carter, *Race: A Theological Account*, Oxford: Oxford University Press, 2008, p. 36.

8 Carter, *Race*, pp. 26–27.

9 R. Williams, Sermon in Christ Church Cathedral, Zanzibar, 18 February 2007, accessible on rowanwilliams.archbishopofcanterbury.org/articles.php/1588/amazing-grace-sermon-at-zanzibar-cathedral (accessed 19th December 2013).

10 See J. Stubbs, 'Beyond Apology? Domestic Violence and Critical Questions for Restorative Justice', *Criminology and Criminal Justice* 7.2, 2007, pp. 169–87.

11 S. Heschel, *The Aryan Jesus: Christian Theologians and the Bible in Nazi Germany*, Princeton, NJ: Princeton University Press, 2008; reviewed by R. Morgan, 'Susannah Heschel's Aryan Grundmann', *Journal for the Study of the New Testament* 32.4, 2010, pp. 431–94; response in S. Heschel, 'Historiography of Antisemitism versus Anti-Judaism: A Response to Robert Morgan', *Journal for the Study of the New Testament* 33.3, 2011, pp. 257–79.

12 Morgan, 'Heschel's Aryan Grundmann', p. 488.

13 Heschel, 'Historiography', pp. 271, 283–85, quoting H. Thurman, *Jesus and the Disinherited*, New York: Abingdon-Cokesbury, 1949.

18
THE STUDY AND PRACTICE OF MODERN THEOLOGY

Stephen Plant

There are three different ways of using the word 'modern' in relation to theology. First, modern theology can mean the theology done in a definable period of history, say from the seventeenth century to the end of the twentieth century. Second, the word 'modern' can be understood to refer to a phase of intellectual and/or societal development; understood this way modern theology means theology that deals with characteristically modern questions and themes in characteristically modern ways. Third, modern theology can simply mean contemporary theology, the theology we are doing now in contrast, say, to Patristic theology or medieval theology. Each of these three understandings of 'modern theology' might give rise to related but different accounts of what is involved in the study and practice of modern theology. A small number of theologians confine themselves strictly to one of these three understandings; but more often than not two or more of them are mingled together.

In this chapter I want to pay attention to each of these three possible understandings of 'modern theology' without privileging one approach over another. My first step will be to flesh out some of the difficulties in defining what is meant by the terms 'modern' and 'modern theology' and look at how three recent textbooks have tackled these definitional challenges. Next, I will explore modern theology historically as an era in the history of theological ideas before concluding with some suggestions about how theologians today might work with the 'modern' theological themes and questions that we have inherited.

Defining modern theology

It is often a sign of immaturity when a writer begins by defining key terms, but because the word 'modern' and the term 'modern theology' are used in such widely different ways some provisional clarification is unavoidable. The English word 'modern' derives from the late Latin word 'modernus' based on 'modo', meaning 'just now'. From the sixteenth century 'modern' was used in English to mean 'now existing', or 'pertaining to the present or recent times'. 'Modern' was later used to describe an epoch and eventually to describe the opinions and tastes consistent with belonging to that epoch.

To term a period of history 'modern' is to position oneself in relation to it in such a way as to suggest: 'People who belong to this period or think this way belong recognizably to the same world I belong to. I share a number of basic experiences and ideas with people who live and think in this modern way that I don't share with people from earlier periods or with different ways of seeing things.' Perhaps because almost every age wants to think of itself as modern, agreement about exactly when modernity begins is hard to achieve. Take the term 'modern European history': does it begin with the 'end' of the Middle Ages – say, with the victory of Henry Tudor at the battle of Bosworth in 1485? Does it begin with the political 'triumph' of Enlightenment rationalism, say, with the storming of the Bastille in 1789? Or does it begin with the widespread European industrialization of the 1830s? Ask three historians and you may get three different answers. Or take modern art: does it include nineteenth-century Impressionism, or does it begin with the advent of abstract art forms in the early twentieth century? Alas, there are no commonly agreed answers to such definitional questions. Even the entry on 'Modernity' in *The New Fontana Dictionary of Modern Thought*, which one might expect to express a clear view, states resignedly that 'Modernity is sometimes seen as dating from the Enlightenment of seventeenth- and eighteenth-century Europe, sometimes from the development of industrial society in the nineteenth century.'[1] 'Modern' is thus a functional shorthand expression conveying recent times and the views and tastes most common within them, but in practice the word is often used quite loosely. As with many terms used by academics, there is always a danger of hypostasizing what is merely a mental construct. 'Modern' is simply a word we use to make sense of history and our relation to it, a word that tells us as much about ourselves as it tells us about an earlier historical era.

Just as fraught as debates about when modernity began and what make up its peculiar themes are debates about if and when modernity gives way to *post*modernity. Has the modern cultural, intellectual, and theological era already given way, or is it in the process of giving way, to postmodernity? If so, what are the defining characteristics of postmodernism? While Gareth Jones, as we shall see, is prepared to assert that modernity has passed and that a postmodern period began around 1980, few are prepared to be so bold. Kevin Vanhoozer, editor of a recent textbook on postmodern theology, points out that while '"postmodernity" has become a gregarious adjective … those who attempt to define or analyze the concept of postmodernity do so at their own peril'.[2] If rapid change, flexibility, and fluidity of meaning are indeed defining characteristics of a postmodernity, perhaps we should be unsurprised if thinking about postmodernity turns out to be like trying to write on water. Recently, following the period of austerity resulting from the financial crisis of 2007, one theologian who has paid serious attention to postmodernity was already beginning to ask 'is postmodernity over?'[3] In short, few theologians would resist the suggestion that the question of whether modernity has given way to postmodernity be treated as an open one. Modernity has developed, certainly, and it may be appropriate to think of our own time as 'late modernity'. But for all the excitable chatter about postmodernity, I think it safe to say modernity is not through with us yet.

A convenient way to develop our thinking about what the study and practice of modern theology might involve is to take note of the way 'modern theology' is construed by the editors of three recent textbooks dealing with the subject. The editors of these volumes are confronted by the need to make decisions about several definitional questions:

- When does the modern period begin?
- Has modernity ended and if so when did it end?
- Is modern theology an exercise in *historical* theology in which the work of particular theologians of the recent past is described and evaluated?
- Is modern theology, rather, contemporary *systematic* or *dogmatic* theology addressed to questions 'thrown up' by life in the modern era?

In *The Modern Theologians* David F. Ford aims to 'introduce the thought of most leading Christian theologians and movements in theology since the end of World War I (1914–18)'.[4] Immediately we see that Ford focuses on the theology of the twentieth century. This bold decision identifies modern theology with *very* recent and contemporary theology. Second, though Ford takes seriously the need to enter the subject *historically*, he goes on to identify several *issues* to which modern theologians and theological movements have paid particular and distinctive attention. Ford's volume begins with chapters exploring six theologians – three Roman Catholic and three Protestant – who may be regarded as classic modern theologians: Barth, Bonhoeffer, Tillich, de Lubac, Rahner and von Balthasar. From this entry point he explores theological responses to modernity characteristic of Germany, Britain, and the USA. Several trends in modern theology are explored next, including post liberal theology and postmodern theology. Each of the remaining six sections of the book attends to issues 'thrown up' by modernity to which there have been significant theological responses. Three chapters deal with theology and the sciences. Next, two chapters deal with theological engagement with Christian practices such as prayer. The expansion of theology beyond Europe and North America, and also beyond white male theologians, is reflected in several chapters on what Ford terms 'particularizing theology', including chapters on Liberation Theology and Feminist Theology. The boundary-bursting character of modern theology is further developed in a section on global engagements that take note of the ecumenical movement, of Eastern Orthodox theology, and of the astonishing and hugely important growth in Pentecostalism. A penultimate section on 'theology between faiths' is followed by one on modern theology's multiple engagements with modern media, with the visual arts, film and modern music. Ford thus takes 'modern theology' to mean *very* recent theology together with contemporary theology. His approach is a hybrid that incorporates historical description and evaluation of key modern theologians and movements, but also engages with responses by modern theologians to modernity, for example to the geopolitical consequences of globalization. Though there is a chapter on post-modern theology, the architecture of Ford's volume does not suggest, either explicitly or implicitly, that modernity has been superseded by postmodernity.

In *The Blackwell Companion to Modern Theology*, Gareth Jones begins by noting that modernity can be understood either in terms of a period of time or as a distinctively modern set of themes. In contrast to Ford, Jones sets wide time para-meters and is decided in viewing modernity as having now given way to post-modernity. If one thinks of modernity in terms of time, Jones tells us, 'then modern theology is roughly the period 1600–1980, with early modernity arguably evident in the sixteenth century, and late modernity giving way to post modernity in the 1980s'.[5] However, Jones also recognizes that one may view modernity in terms of certain characteristically modern themes or attitudes; understood in this way, one might potentially delve even further into history since texts belonging chronologically in the medieval period (for example Dante's fourteenth-century *Divine Comedy*) may be said to display modern ways of thinking. Jones concludes that his companion volume to modern theology is consequently:

> not simply a companion to a particular period of Christian history, or a particular set of figures, ideas, and challenges. It is also a companion to a way of thinking through the main principles and values of Christianity, its relevance for the world as well as the Church, and the great contribu-tions all kinds of intellectual reflection make to the life of faith seeking understanding.[6]

Like Ford, Jones includes a section – Part IV – dealing with a number of key individual figures in modern theology. Jones, however, includes figures from the nineteenth as well as the twentieth century, and indeed figures that, though their impact on modern theology is undeniably great, might not regard themselves as theologians. Thus there are chapters on Kant, Hegel, Schleiermacher, Barth, Rahner, Bonhoeffer, one on Bultmann and Tillich together, and on von Balthasar.

Part I of Jones's volume explores a number of topics, including biblical studies, philosophy, culture, social theory and history, with which theology has been engaged and through which it has expressed itself in the modern period. Part II examines how modern theologians have typically dealt with the study of earlier per-iods in Christian history, for example with medieval theology. Part III focuses on five themes in Christian theology, roughly in the order they appear in the historic creeds of the Church, beginning with the doctrine of God and ending with the Church and sacraments. A final part engages with key contemporary issues.

Jones differs from Ford with respect to the inclusion of the nineteenth century. Like Ford, however, Jones offers a hybrid approach that includes both historical theology and contemporary doctrinal engagement with modern issues and questions. Jones's suggestion that modernity has been superseded by postmodernity is not implemented in a doctrinaire fashion and the concluding part on contemporary issues is at least a bridge from modern to postmodern theology.

In contrast to the 'hybrid' approaches of Ford and Jones, in a third recent book, *Mapping Modern Theology: A Thematic and Historical Introduction*, Kelly M. Kapic and Bruce L. McCormack decide upon a purely thematic approach:[7]

> Our idea is to organize modern theology along the lines of classical doctrinal topics or themes so that more complete coverage of significant develop-ments in each area of doctrinal construction might be achieved. In this way,

students might be introduced to the problems that have been basic to reflection on all the major doctrines treated by modern theologians.[8]

McCormack's sophisticated opening essay deals openly with the difficulties of defining modernity and of capturing what might characterize theology as modern. He concludes, however, that the modern period has given rise to modern ways of doing theology, concluding that 'Other approaches to Christian theology that do not take seriously the need to take steps like these will be found in the "modern" period, but they will not themselves be "modern"'.[9] Modern theology, in other words, is properly speaking a style of theology rather than a period of theological production. The volume then unfolds by way of a series of essays dealing with doctrinal loci such as the Trinity, the Person of Christ, pneumatology, ecclesiology and eschatology. The question of when the modern period began is not, for Kapic and McCormack, nearly as interesting as the question of what the shared characteristics of a modern theology might be. Most decidedly, their approach is to treat modern theology as an approach to the doctrinal loci that modern theologians share with theologians of earlier periods, but which they engage with in the light of a number of shared modern questions and assumptions. Kapic and McCormack thus share the view, expressed elsewhere by Rowan Williams, that if 'Modernity is a set of questions, preoccupations and anxieties'[10] then modern theology has to do with reflection on, with and through Christian Scriptures about the particular questions, preoccupations and anxieties of modern people.

Modern questions

The next step must be to give a stronger sense of the shape and content of the attitudes, questions, preoccupations and anxieties of modern people. To do this is a demanding task. It not only requires fluency in a very broad range of historical sources, but the ability to organize the history of ideas into patterns that are plausible and illuminating. One of a number of recent writers bold enough to attempt the task is Charles Taylor in Sources of Self: The Making of the Modern Identity.[11] Taylor aims to 'explore various facets of' what he calls 'the "modern identity"'. He continues that:

> To give a good first approximation of what this means would be to say that it involves tracing various strands of our modern notion of what it is to be a human agent, a person, or a self.[12]

For Taylor, it will turn out that the construction of modern identity is closely bound up with what are taken to be the goods to which human lives are directed; selfhood and morality, as he puts it, are intertwined.

Taylor proposes a map of modern identity that he acknowledges to be rather over schematic. He describes three 'domains' of modern selfhood, noting that 'they are continually borrowing from and influenced by each other'. Some modern movements try, indeed, to combine more than one strand – for example Marxism, which he describes as 'a marriage of Enlightenment naturalism and expressivism'.[13] Yet his scheme conveys essential truths. Taylor proposes that the modern notion of self is 'constituted' in three ways. The first is a sense of inwardness. It is not the case, he suggests, that human beings have always conceived of themselves as living with an inner tension between the inner self and the outward self: such an opposition is demonstrably 'in large part a feature of our world, the world of modern Western people'.[14] Christian theology was, in no small measure, responsible for this turn. Augustine of Hippo was not the first to trade on oppositions between spirit and matter, higher and lower, eternal and temporal, but he was among the first to make such distinctions central to self-understanding. Yet Augustine departed significantly from Plato in his belief that 'inward lies the road to God':[15] the good to which human life ought properly to aim is, for Augustine, the contemplation of God to which inner reflection can take us by God's grace. In the early modern period, Descartes gave 'Augustinian inwardness a radical twist and takes it in a quite new direction': instead of the inward turn being towards God as the fulfillment of the good, Descartes 'situates the moral sources within us'.[16] Descartes' interest in scientific method effected a deliberate and radical rejection of a Platonic idea of the good as the goal of human knowledge and life and its replacement by an anthropocentric philosophy and a mechanistic account of the universe. The modern self operates a rational mastery of the world in which the 'hegemony of reason is defined no longer as that of a dominant vision but rather in terms of a directing agency subordinating a functional domain'.[17] In Locke, this modern self is further adapted into what Taylor calls 'the punctual self', who 'gains control through disengagement'. Locke shares Descartes' rejection of a teleological view of human nature in terms both of epistemology and morality. The consequence was that, by about 1800, something like a modern self has been constructed, for whom the inner life of reason and feeling are confined to minds disengaged from the world, that treasure ideals of freedom and dignity.

The next constitutive aspect of modern identity, according to Taylor, derives from modern notions of nature and 'the *affirmation of ordinary life*'.[18] Taylor means by this a restructuring of moral identity such that value is relocated from the sacred, the ideal and the otherworldly to the mundane, to production and reproduction, to art and craft and to family life. Again, religion lies at the fountainhead of this turn, in particular in Protestant rejections of ecclesial hierarchy and of monasticism, and its affirmation of marriage and work. The fusion of disengaged reason and the affirmation of ordinary life led, in turn, Taylor argues, to a 'rationalized Christianity' that became dominant in modern Western technological society. Industriousness and rationality combined, and the amalgam aimed at improvements that would benefit not only oneself, but society as a whole.

A third turn taken in the journey of modern identity, Taylor continues, arose from a growing love of nature associated with a cult of sensibility. In religion Pietism and the evangelical revival (of which Methodism was a lasting product), and in culture and philosophy Romanticism, were characteristic of this modern turn which Taylor calls 'the *voice of nature*'. Its features include a heightened sense of the importance of the exploration and expression of feeling, of personal conviction and commitment beyond coolly rational conviction. Politically, nationalism was its most radical expression. In culture the Romantics and the rapid rise of the novel to a central place in literature characterize it.

Inevitably, my hurried description of Taylor's rich, sometimes rambling, and often illuminating account of modernity raises as many questions as it answers. In the context of this chapter, it serves on the one hand as an example of how the 'identity' of modernity may be attempted and on the other of the challenges involved in describing such a complex phenomenon.

Theological responses to modernity

To build a bridge between Taylor's account of the construction of the modern self and a discussion of theological responses to modernity, it is helpful to glance at Bruce L. McCormack's discussion of what makes theology modern. It comes in his introduction to a collection of essays about the greatest modern theologian, Karl Barth, and forms a backdrop to McCormack's answer to the question of whether Karl Barth may be said to be *Orthodox and Modern*.[19] The question of whether and in what way Barth was a *modern* theologian plainly depends on a judgment about what it means to be 'modern' in the context of theology. McCormack's own view of what constitutes the modern self is that the essential precondition of modern theology

> was the rise of 'historical consciousness' – by which I mean the awareness that all human thinking is conditioned by historical (and cultural) location – that was most basic to the emergence of what we tend to think of as 'modern' theology today.[20]

This 'historical consciousness', McCormack believes, came about at the point at which two strands of thinking came together. The first was Immanuel Kant's thesis that what human beings may know by theoretical reason is limited. The second was the emergence of Romanticism, which favoured the themes of freedom, individuality, and feeling over Kantian rationalism and which, in a period of emerging urbanization and industrialization, expressed nostalgia for a world now lost in which everyone had a sense of belonging. Note that McCormack traverses here similar terrain to Taylor: the rationalism of the disengaged self and the voice of nature represented by Romanticism. It was Romanticism, McCormack tells us, that established the pre-conditions for the rise of nationalism, one of modernity's defining features. He goes on to identify some of the consequences that followed from the development of an historical consciousness. These include

> an acceptance, in principle at the very least, of critical methods for studying the Bible; a recognition of the loss of respect among philosophers for classical metaphysics in all of their (Greek) forms; the recognition of the breakdown of Aristotelian–biblical cosmology.[21]

Further 'negotiable elements', to which only some modern theologians adhere, include a relatively positive stance towards evolutionary science, and (amongst

Protestant theologians) a wary view of natural theology. McCormack's basic thesis is that, in keeping with other modern theologians, Barth accepted Kant's conviction that human knowledge, including knowledge of God, is always limited. Barth further believed that God nonetheless really exists, whole and entire in Godself, apart from and prior to human knowledge of God. Finally, Barth believed that this same God reaches across the epistemological gap, his hiddenness fully present in the gift of his self-revelation in Jesus Christ, and in the witness to him made in Scripture and preaching. For McCormack, therefore (and here he makes a counter-proposal to an earlier interpretive consensus), Barth was *both* orthodox and modern. Orthodoxy, McCormack thinks, is best understood as something dynamic, and orthodox Christian faith best conceived as always in a process of being reinterpreted. Thus, 'what Barth was doing, in the end, was seeking to understand what it means to be orthodox *under the conditions of modernity*'.[22]

Turning momentarily to the analogy of the inter-generational transmission of tradition, it is worth noting what Barth – regarding him for this purpose as a 'representative' modern theologian – says on the one hand about the accountability of the contemporary theologian to the confessional traditions she inherits and, on the other, her freedom to think afresh in the light of contemporary questions. For Barth, theology is in a real sense 'determined', that is, a Christian theologian 'cannot do dogmatics in a vacuum but only as we are influenced by a group of authorities which for inner or outer reasons holds good for the dogmatician concerned'. This 'formal determination' is not, however, a 'straight jacket', but 'offers protection, even if only relative, against Christian caprice and riot'. Theology (Barth uses the word 'dogmatics') regards past theological writings in this sense as authoritative; they provide the rules of theological thinking. However, 'As regards content, [theology] is a free and not a captive science':[23] theologians, that is, are rooted in traditions of past wisdom from which they draw nourishment, but they are called by God to think for themselves.

But with Barth we are getting ahead of ourselves; we should first take in how eighteenth- and nineteenth-century theologians dealt with the shifts in identity that modernity brought about. One of the few studies to deal with theological movements across linguistic and political boundaries is Claude Welch's two-volume study of *Protestant Thought in the Nineteenth Century*.[24] Welch's volumes, though focused on Protestant theology and on the nineteenth century, deal with themes affecting Protestants and Catholics throughout the modern period. Instead of narrating the development of schools and parties in theology, Welch explores 'dominating theological concerns, tendencies, and problems, through which the character of the century as a whole may be more adequately understood'.[25] He thinks it possible to discern 'three interweaving themes, or questions, that appear in shifting focus and fluctuating intensity as major preoccupations of theologians throughout the century, without respect to national boundaries'. For Welch, though one can with some truth maintain that the first of the three themes was the key focus in the first part of the century, the second of the middle part, and the third of the final part, each 'focus of interest is present at all stages of the century's development, since each necessarily involves all the others, and any one of the themes could usefully be used to organize a discussion of the whole century'.[26] It is, moreover, 'strikingly plain' that the problems theologians wrestle with in the twentieth century 'are continuous with those of the nineteenth'.[27] Remarkably, and for my purposes reassuringly, there is a significant degree of correspondence between the questions Taylor proposes give rise to the modern identity, and the questions that Welch identifies as characterizing the identity of modern theology.

The first theme Welch identifies (which corresponds to Taylor's 'inwardness') is the question of the *possibility of theology*. What is the inner rationale of theology? Is knowledge of God really possible? By what methods should theology proceed? Is the Bible reliable and authoritative? Common to the practical problems modern theologians face is how to understand the relation of theology and other academic disciplines: is theology one amongst many *Wissenschaften*?

From the mid nineteenth century a second theme emerged as central for theologians: the problem of Christology. This is clearest in what has come since to be called the quest for the historical Jesus. This was about more than the vexed issue of the historical reliability of the biblical evidence concerning Jesus' life: it concerned genuinely theological questions about the relationship between Jesus' humanity and divinity. This alone, of course, was not a new theological issue; what was new was a modern quality to the answers given. The Christologies proposed had in common that they sought to engage the questions *von unten nach oben*, beginning with the historical figure of Jesus, for example with Jesus as teacher of a new morality. This theme corresponds with what Taylor termed the affirmation of ordinary life. Patience with the metaphysical speculations of medieval and Patristic theology was in short supply as theologians sought to reclaim what Adolf von Harnack called 'the essence of Christianity' from the carapace of doctrinal speculation.

Welch continues that at the turn of the nineteenth and twentieth centuries 'the question of Christianity and culture, or church and society, came to flower'.[28] In different locations and with different theologians, this took different forms. With some it took the form of a social gospel, of muscular religious hands guiding society towards a moral utopia. For others it took the form of *Kulturprotestantismus* arising from a desire to accommodate the Christian faith to culture, to see the sacred in the mundane, in music, in art and in nature. Even where theologians were nervous about Christian capitulation to a sinful world, the emphasis on feeling was a theological echo of Romanticism. This third theme corresponds neatly with Taylor's description of the role of the voice of nature in the formation of modern identity.

The study of modern theologians

One of the ways in which modern questions are explored by contemporary theologians is through the study of the work of modern theologians. To gain insight into what such study is like I suggest the analogy of the relationship between generations within human family life. Nothing in my experience has shed more light on my relationship with my parents than my relationship with my children. Thinking about what habits, tastes, opinions and convictions I am passing on to my children sheds light on what I myself received from my parents. From relatively trivial things such as facial and verbal expressions, through tastes in film and music, to political views, a lot of what I am passing on is inherited from my parents. When it comes to my deepest convictions and beliefs, this process is more intentional; thus, it is because I learned the value of attending church from my parents that I take my children to church hoping that they will appreciate the value of belonging to a church community. This process is not always a smooth one. Tension between parents and children is natural and much of what one inherits is questioned, challenged and changed before it is handed onto the next generation. This is as it should be: part of what it means to 'come of age' is to establish our own identity *over and against* our parents. Nevertheless, even when we renew and reshape what we inherit most radically, our greatest debts, for better and for worse, are to those who have gone immediately before us.

A good deal of what it means to work in modern theology as a field of study is illuminated by seeing it in terms of inter-generational conflict, or of the process of the transmission of traditions within a family. Contemporary theologians, for all the novelty of the questions they address or the creativity that they bring to their work, are always addressing challenges in the light of the questions and insights of the previous generations. What Claude Welch has written of the relationship between nineteenth- and twentieth-century theology, is equally true of the relationship between theology in the twentieth and twenty first centuries, and thus of the modern period as a whole:

> it is at least a defensible thesis that the theological situation of the twentieth century is peculiarly dependent on the development of the nineteenth century. That is, not only do the same problems continue to bedevil and fascinate, but the shapes which those questions still bear are essentially derivative from the forms they were given in the nineteenth century.[29]

In short, in spite of diversity in the answers given by modern theologians, there is a discernible family resemblance between them with respect to the questions they address.

As we saw with David Ford and Gareth Jones's respective treatments of modern theology, there exists a certain current consensus about which theologians in the modern period are 'classic' sources. It is worth noting that that consensus is not permanently fixed; for example, when he died in 1889 Albrecht Ritschl was widely regarded as a key figure in modern theology who had successfully integrated the doctrinal and apologetic concerns of the first part of the nineteenth century (given expression by Schleiermacher) with the historical and communitarian concerns of the second half of the century. But Ritschl is rarely read now, except from the perspective of historical theology. Similarly, in the 1980s, when I first studied theology, the French Jesuit Pierre Teillard de Chardin was in favour while Karl Barth was regarded as a passing fad; today de Chardin is largely a specialist interest while Barth studies, especially in the English speaking world, is a major theological industry.

Comparing the reception histories of several 'classic' modern theologians one sees both irregularities and common patterns. Some theologians achieve prominence in their own lifetime, like Karl Barth. Others, like Dietrich Bonhoeffer, have reputations that are built posthumously. Some theologians make their name in the context of heated controversy, in which friends and enemies take sides: for Barth, the theology of crisis contra von Harnack and the heated exchange with Emil Brunner on natural theology; for Bultmann demythologization and existentialism; for Bonhoeffer, death of God theology and secularization. In the early phase texts written by particular theologians are freely plundered, raided for insights that can provoke or stimulate the contemporary doctrinal engagement with modernity. Slowly, 'schools' of thought begin to solidify around key interpretive questions, and a theologian can find quite different views attributed to him (sadly, until the second half of the twentieth century the contribution of women to modern theology was often hidden). In Stephen R. Haynes's lively narrative of the reception of Bonhoeffer's theology, the variety of interpretations is bewildering. Bonhoeffer is seized upon as progenitor of a radically secularized theology, or as a Marxist theologian, or a pietist evangelical theologian, or a conservative Lutheran theologian, and more.[30] The confusion of such secondary debates then leads to a desire for clarity, and for the sake of clarity, the production of a standard scholarly text on which to base discussion. Again, taking Bonhoeffer as an example, the result of this desire for a firm textual basis for discussion resulted in the production of the seventeen-volume *Dietrich Bonhoeffer Werke*[31] from 1988 to 2005 and subsequently to a sixteen-volume English translation of the complete works. The production of scholarly editions of key texts, and of the publication of less well-known texts, changes the 'feel' of the engagement with the theologian concerned. Instead of raiding his writings for resources for one's own theological reflection, engagement with the text shifts subtly to 'scholastic' debates about what the text means, to its context (both biographical and within the history of ideas), and to its relationship with the development of the author's overall theology; in short, the task becomes exegetical. Beyond that, there is perhaps – and one begins to observe this in Bonhoeffer scholarship – a further shift to thinking with and through textual exegesis towards creative doctrinal proposals resourced by dialogue with classic theological texts. As secondary scholarship burgeons, a buffer sometimes seems to form between a classic modern theological source and the contemporary student, who feels she must master the secondary debates before forming her own opinion about the primary texts. When that happens, the maxim should always be: 'read the primary texts and think about them for yourself'.

The contemporary practice of modern theology

One question thrown up by the study of modern theologians is: what is their authority for contemporary theologians seeking to think about the Christian faith in light of modernity? Modern theologians are important, as we have said, because they belong to the most recent generation to have reflected on God's self-revelation. They teach us because the questions they deal with are, of all questions treated by theologians in the past two millennia, nearest to our own. Yet a careful distinction needs to be made between the value of modern theologians and their authority. To be quite clear, modern theologians should not be treated as an alternate source of authority to the authority of Scripture. Modern theology is to be taken seriously only to the extent that it helps contemporary theology hear the Word of God in the

Bible and think through what that means today. Contemporary theologians should be conscious of their debts to modern theology, but they are not merely free but are obliged to depart from the doctrine of particular modern theologians where their own faithful hearing of God's Word requires it. In this respect I agree with Karl Barth's insistent claim that both responsibility to past theologians, and freedom from them, characterize the calling of the contemporary theologian:

> there comes a point – and no theologian can evade it – at which theology does become dangerous and suspect. This is the point where the twofold question arises: What are you going to say? Not as one who knows the Bible or Thomas or the older Blumhardt, but responsibly and seriously as one who stands by the words that are said: you? And what are you going to say? Not how impressively or how clearly or how well adapted to your hearers and to the present age – these are all secondary concerns – but what?[32]

For contemporary theologians it is inadequate simply to restate or even to refine the theology of the generation immediately preceding them: theological apprentices must eventually find their own ways of responding to God in the context of the modern world.

Notes

1 A. Bullock and S. Trombley (eds) *The New Fontana Dictionary of Modern Thought*, 3rd edn, London: Fontana/Harper Collins, 1999, p. 540.
2 K.J. Vanhoozer, 'Theology and the Condition of Postmodernity: A Report on Knowledge (of God)', in K.J. Vanhoozer (ed.) *The Cambridge Companion to Postmodern Theology*, Cambridge: Cambridge University Press, 2003, p. 3.
3 G. Ward, 'Theology and Postmodernism: Is it all Over?', *Journal of the American Academy of Religion* 80.2 (2012), pp. 466–84.
4 D.F. Ford 'Preface', in D.F. Ford with R. Muers (eds), *The Modern Theologians: An Introduction to Christian Theology since 1918*, 3rd edn, Oxford: Blackwell, 2005, p. viii.
5 G. Jones, 'Preface', in G. Jones (ed.) *The Blackwell Companion to Modern Theology*, Oxford: Blackwell, 2004, pp. xii–xiii.
6 Jones, 'Preface', p. xvi.
7 K.M. Kapic and B.L. McCormack (eds) *Mapping Modern Theology: A Thematic and Historical Introduction*, Ada, MI: Brazos Press, 2012.
8 The citation is from the introduction to the volume, which is written by Bruce L. McCormack, p. 1.
9 Ibid., p.17.
10 R. Williams, 'Preface', in D. Dormer, J. McDonald and J. Caddick (eds), *Anglicanism: The Answer to Modernity*, London: Continuum, 2003, p. viii.
11 C. Taylor, *Sources of Self: The Making of the Modern Identity*, Cambridge: Cambridge University Press, 1989.
12 Taylor, *Sources*, p. 3.
13 Taylor, *Sources*, p. 486.
14 Taylor, *Sources*, p. 111.
15 Taylor, *Sources*, p. 129.
16 Taylor, *Sources*, p. 143.
17 Taylor, *Sources*, p. 149.
18 Taylor, *Sources*, p. 211.

19 B.L. McCormack, *Orthodox and Modern: Studies in the Theology of Karl Barth*, Grand Rapids, MI: Baker Academic, 2008.
20 McCormack, *Orthodox and Modern*, pp. 10–11.
21 McCormack, *Orthodox and Modern*, p. 11.
22 McCormack, *Orthodox and Modern*, p. 17 (McCormack's italics). Note that Barth identifies modernity in theology with a move first made by the philosopher Descartes in his famous axiom 'I think therefore I am' which, he argues, encapsulated a turn from God as *subject* (i.e. acting agent) to the *modern* tendency to locate revelation to the feeling or experience of the human subject, a move Barth takes to be profoundly mistaken.
23 K. Barth, *The Göttingen Dogmatics* 1, Grand Rapids, MI: William B. Eerdmans Publishing Company, 1991, pp. 293–94.
24 C. Welch, *Protestant Thought in the Nineteenth Century, 1: 1799–1870*, New Haven and London: Yale University Press, 1972; *Protestant Thought in the Nineteenth Century, 2: 1870–1914*, New Haven and London: Yale University Press, 1985.
25 Welch, *Protestant Thought 1*, p. 4.
26 Welch, *Protestant Thought 1*, p.5.
27 Ibid.
28 Welch, *Protestant Thought 1*, p. 6.
29 Welch, *Protestant Thought 1*, p. 1.
30 S.R. Haynes, *The Bonhoeffer Phenomenon: Portraits of a Protestant Saint*, Minneapolis, MN: Fortress Press, 2004.
31 Published by Gütersloher Verlagshaus in Munich.
32 Barth, *Göttingen Dogmatics 1*, pp. 5–6.

19
ENGAGING WITH THE CONTEMPORARY CHURCH

Paul D. Murray

My purpose in this chapter is to explore the area of theology that deals most directly with the study of the Church: ecclesiology. I first reflect on the more general task of theology as presented in this book as a whole, before asking what it means for theologians to 'think well of the Church'. I argue that thinking well of the Church requires a bifocal perspective – empirical and doctrinal. I explore how ecclesiology brings these two modes into transformative relation, in order to diagnose the ills and promote the increased flourishing of Christian communion. I then focus on the specific challenges posed by the divided state of the Christian churches, and ask what contribution ecumenical engagement can make to ecclesiology – finishing with an exploration of two examples of such engagement.

Ecclesial engineering

Christianity is something lived before it is something thought. Not only is theology itself a practice; it reasons about a prior practice of faith. It is a process of reasoning about the practices of the Church (as these have responded through two thousand years of Christian history to the practice of God in Christ and the Sprit) and about all the reflections that these practices have generated. It is conducted in light of the live questions, issues, and invitations that these practices continue to raise.

St Anselm's classic description of theology as *fides quærens intellectum*, 'faith seeking understanding', expresses this well. Neither 'faith' nor 'understanding' should be understood in a purely intellectual sense. The lived context for Anselm's own faith and for the questions it provoked was that of monastic life, and the daily routine of prayer, liturgy, meditation, study, teaching, and self-examination that it entailed. Similarly, the understanding that he sought was not only conceptual, doctrinal clarity (as in his asking in *Cur Deus Homo* after the reason at work in the Incarnation) but also increased practical, ethical, and spiritual understanding of what it means to live in the light of this teaching.

St Thomas Aquinas is making a similar point in his *Summa Theologiae* when he says that theology, as the study of God, includes 'all things … relative to God as their origin and end'.[1] This cannot be a merely intellectual exercise; it is not simply a matter of devising an ordered cognitive cosmology and of seeking intellectually satisfying answers to the various questions posed en route. On the contrary, understanding any particular thing in all its specificity in relation to God as source, sustainer, and end involves *both* reverencing it as disclosing some particular aspect of God's infinite glory *and* relating to it accordingly in practice. It is for this reason that such a considerable amount of the *Summa Theologiae* is given over to what we can most naturally describe as theological ethics.

In such classical ways of thinking, it is insufficient to view the Christian theological task simply as providing an ordered account of Christian belief, or a compelling narrative of things in Christian perspective, or an inspiring theological vision. Important as all of these things are as aspects of the theological task, their real importance is in service of closer conformity to Christ in the Spirit, and greater proficiency of creatively faithful Christian performance. In terms of George Lindbeck's influential image of doctrine as the rules by which the Christian game is played, or the grammar governing Christian speech,[2] it is the graced performance and communication of Christian faith that matters most, not proficiency in reciting and manipulating the rules of grammar for their own sake. The latter exist to aid the former rather than *vice versa*.

Recent Christian theology has a sharpened sense of this proper priority of the lived and the practical, thanks to the widespread influence of various liberationist and praxis-oriented approaches to theology. These approaches draw on a variety of critical theoretical tools to help diagnose and address contradictions between theory (doctrine and belief) and practice (Christian life). In this perspective a somewhat less elegant contemporary rendition of St Anselm's understanding of theology as *fides quærens intellectum* might be something along the lines of: theology as critical and constructive reflection on the practice and understanding of faith, and on the questions, issues, and difficulties raised there, with a view to enhancing and renewing the quality of such practice and understanding.

In place, then, of images of theology as variously a primarily descriptive, explanatory, classificatory, poetic, aesthetic, and inspirational discipline, or as a competency- and skills-based utilitarian training exercise (for Christian ministry), this is theology seen as a diagnostic, even therapeutic, exercise. Here theological analysis is understood to be geared towards the rigorous, systematic identification and diagnosis of the various questions, difficulties, and dissonances thrown up by Christian practice and belief (whether historical, conceptual, organizational, social, ethical or practical) and towards their attempted remedy and healing, through the articulation of appropriate constructive responses. This is theology practised as a ministry of medicinal diagnosis and attempted cure of the felt difficulties and disturbances, paralyses and pathologies, tensions and ills, in the habits of understanding and performance at work in the ecclesial body of Christ.

A weakness in this image of theology as General Practitioner medicine for the Church is that it might seem just too *ad hoc*, reactive, and piecemeal to speak adequately of the Christian theological task in the round. Inasmuch as Christian theology is properly focused on understanding the whole truth of things in Christ and the Spirit (on understanding and relating to all things viewed in relation to God as source, sustainer, and end), then theology must properly have a sense of this whole about it and a concern to understand and live each part in relation to this whole. As such, it might be helpful here to switch images from medicine to the world of engineering.

Engineering is a discipline of the whole. It is a discipline that requires a view of how each part of the process or system that is in view relates to the whole. But the whole that is in view is not an abstraction, a purely theoretical system, but a real and highly complex process beset by specific challenges and circumstances, and oriented to specific practical effects (e.g. the successful design and production of turbine generators). It is within such an overarching whole that the specific reasoning processes of engineering are properly situated: from monitoring and quality control, through routine in-process problem solving and personnel management, to front-line research on how aspects of the system can be reconceived and re-ordered in the light of fresh understanding. Even when working on a specific problem, engineering reasoning is geared towards the coherence, efficiency, and productivity of the system as a whole.

The age of grand systematic theology might now be over – if, by that, we mean the illusory, even idolatrous, search for an all-encompassing, and permanently adequate system of Christian theology, as though the inexhaustible mystery of God's grace could be captured in a system of concepts. Counsel and encouragement against such idolatrous aspirations can be found if we remember that both St Thomas's *Summa Theologiae* and Karl Barth's *Church Dogmatics*, arguably the two greatest works of Christian systematic theology of all time, are each left to us quite literally unfinished. But there is, nevertheless, something of abiding significance – as the medical practitioner and engineering analogies each suggest – in the rigorous pursuit of systematic analysis, diagnosis and attempted repair in Christian theology, where the part is engaged and treated in the light of the whole. Such analysis is not 'systematic' theology in any sense that isolates it from the vagaries of Christian practice – a matter merely of manipulating the conceptual furniture of the Church. Rather, this is systematic theology as integrated with, and always in service of, the practice of the Church in a particular time and place. The systematic theologian is here the General Practitioner or the Engineer of the Christian theological task, with the health of the body or the effectiveness of the system as a whole in view and in such fashion as enables each other specialism to be properly located in service of the healing and greater productivity of the whole.

If, however, all theological reasoning fundamentally derives from and relates to the prior practice of the Church, this might appear to make ecclesiology redundant as a specific theological sub-specialism – on the grounds that all theology is properly to be seen as analysing the practice of the Church. Viewed in another way, however, ecclesiology focuses what is true of all theology, and gives it distinctive expression, by attending to the structures, organizational realities, systems of decision-making, and distributions of power and authority in Christian churches.

There is a further question, however, as to what the 'Church' is. Is it simply the sum total of Christians and their social codes and actions? Is ecclesiology, therefore, synonymous with the analysis of any aspect whatsoever of Christian behaviour and action? Or does the Church have some theological specificity beyond this? Is there some theological significance to the organizational and structural dimensions of the Church, and is it the analysis of these dimensions that gives ecclesiology its specific task? Each of these perspectives can be pressed to unhelpful extremes. The first is in danger of suffering from too little Church and viewing ecclesiology proper as redundant. The second is in danger of suffering from too much Church and mistaking the real heart of Christian theology – that is, the creating, forgiving, transforming grace of God in Christ and the Spirit – for the structures and systems that give collective form to Christian responses to this grace.

Also complicating things here is that where there is positive theological appreciation of the organizational and structural dimensions of the Church, it has traditionally been pursued in a purely doctrinal register without any explicit integration with empirical studies of how these dimensions of the Church are actually lived in practice. In contrast, guided both by recent sharpened appreciation for the priority of practice in Christian life and by the development of a now considerable range of empirical approaches to the study of the Church, Nicholas M. Healy's *Church, World, and the Christian Life* influentially articulates the need for a move away from ideal descriptions of the Church abstracted from actual historical, practical existence in the exigencies of particular circumstances.[3] He rejects the deductivist approach once standard in dogmatic and systematic ecclesiology – of first articulating an ideal theorized description of the Church on the basis of historical sources, key theological writings, relevant philosophical analyses and the like, and only then turning to ask how this might be better instantiated in practice – and instead calls for an 'ecclesiological ethnography'. This resonates with other initiatives in the contemporary study of the Church, such as Jeff Astley's emphasis on 'Ordinary Theology',[4] and has become something of a mantra amongst contemporary ecclesiologists.[5]

It is less common, however, to find fully worked out demonstrations of how to pursue genuinely systematic theological analyses of the organizational and structural realities of the Church in a manner that is both doctrinally serious and empirically responsible. The remaining sections of this chapter seek to trace how this might work.

Thinking well of the Church

In the most common-sense meaning of the term the Church is a complex family of human organizations that has endured and evolved for nearly two thousand years, in remarkably diverse historical, cultural, geographical, and political contexts. We need to draw upon modes of investigation suited to analysing these very human organizational dimensions of the Church – even though our convictions about the theological identity of the Church have sometimes meant that it has not come naturally to do so. We need, in other words, modes of understanding that help us engage and understand the living, breathing, empirical reality of the Church as it actually is and not simply as we would have it or imagine it to be.

I referred earlier to Aquinas' understanding of theology as including all particular things taken in relation to God as their origin and end. It has, however, been too common in the tradition to miss the implication here – fully observed by Aquinas himself – that understanding any particular thing in relation to God presupposes that we understand it precisely in its particularity, and that includes the kind of understanding that can be gained by viewing it in natural perspective. James Gustafson coined the counter-intuitive phrase 'theological reductionism' to refer to this tendency to so emphasize the explicitly theological, the doctrinal, as to downplay the human and the natural.[6]

In this regard, given the tendency towards high theologies of the Church in Orthodox and Catholic traditions (for example, as the mystical body of Christ in twentieth-century Catholic theology), it is perhaps no coincidence that sociological and ethnographic approaches to the study of the Church have tended to be pursued first in relation to Protestant contexts, where the propensity is towards theologically lighter accounts of the Church (for example, as the community of disciples).

However, if the *minimum* to be said about the Church is that it is a complex family of human organizations that need to be understood and analysed as such, this is by no means *all* that needs to be said. The explicitly theological understanding of the Church might indeed need to take account of natural perspectives if it is to be true to this empirical reality, but explicit theological analysis remains essential. In specifically ecclesiological terms, this means that the true identity of the human community of the Church is not understood well until it is explicitly set within Christian salvation history, and understood as a graced sharing in the communion of the Trinity – until, that is, the Church is seen as that community brought into being and held in being through the life-giving self-giving unto death of the incarnate Word, and through the power of the Spirit.

In such ways of thinking the identity of the Church can never adequately be understood simply as that human organization enduring through time that provides means for the disciples of Jesus to relate and act together. Rather, the Church is that community – more precisely, that family of variously and imperfectly related communities – that understands itself to exist in relation to the communion of the Trinity in which all that exists is held, and which has been called into being in order to be witness to and sacrament of God's eternal plan for creation as revealed in Word and Spirit.

The point is that, if there is a danger of 'theological reductionism' in exclusively focusing on doctrinal definitions of the Church to the occlusion of the lived, empirical reality of the Church, there is equal danger of a better-known sociological reductionism that fails to take the specifically theological identity of the Church into account. The challenge for an adequate approach to contemporary ecclesiology and the study of the Church is to find a way of holding these two perspectives together. A fully systematic account of ecclesiology needs to find means of integrating the practical and the doctrinal.

So, asking after the living truth of the Church requires us to understand it in both its divine and human dimensions. It requires us to take seriously the divine origination, operation, and ordination of the Church. Equally, it requires us to keep clearly in view that this very Church, understood as having been born from the side of Christ as his Spirit-filled body in the world, exists not in some other realm but precisely here and now in the nit and grit realities of ordinary ecclesial existence; not merely as an inspiring teaching on a page but in the living, breathing – and all too often dis-appointing and frustrating – actuality of real ecclesial communities. We simply do not understand properly what is meant by our theological affirmations about the identity of the Church until we understand what it is to affirm them of the empirical Church we experience.

Nor can it simply be a matter of placing these two tellings of the truth of the Church – the theological and the empirical – alongside each other. The telling of each must be informed by, and fulfilled in, the telling of the other. In Christology we are used to holding these two principles together and are appropriately sensitive to the need to avoid a false dualism between the divinity and humanity of Jesus. Something similar is now needed in the practice of systematic ecclesiology. We need to proceed in ways that make clear *both* that the profound reality of the Church as articulated in a high ecclesiology pertains to the concrete, empirical actuality of the Church – however counter-intuitive this may seem at times – *and* that this concrete, empirical actuality – howsoever far it falls short in practice – is not understood properly until understood as the arena in which the elevated narrative of a high ecclesiology is genuinely being worked out.

Attending to the Church as it is and as it might be

As discussed earlier, the basic task of theology is critical and constructive reflection on the practice and understanding of faith, and on the questions, issues, and diffi-culties raised there, with a view to enhancing and renewing the quality of such practice and understanding. As such, theology is driven by live questions, open issues, felt difficulties, dissonances, even gaping sores pertaining to Christian faith (whether conceptual, organizational, social, ethical, or practical). These problems are then probed, diagnosed, and responded to in as rigorous, disciplined, and creative a fashion as possible, in service of their remedy and healing.

The specific task of systematic ecclesiology is the rigorous, critical, constructive, and intentionally reparative analysis of the Church's forms and practices, its tensions and tears, with a view to enhancing the quality of its life. It does not start out from a concern to articulate an exhaustive theory of the Church but from a concern to pursue with rigour the specific questions and difficulties that arise within the life of the Church.

The ecclesiological task understood in this way could, for instance, include pur-suit of a New Testament studies question such as 'How did St Paul understand his metaphor of the Church as the body of Christ?' Adequate pursuit of an answer involves asking how this particular Pauline metaphor coheres with St Paul's other theological claims and doctrinal commitments, such as what he has to say about the bodily resurrection of Jesus. Equally, it involves asking how St Paul understood the social, relational, even organizational implications of this metaphor for ecclesial existence and how all that was in turn related – either critically or affirmatively – to the prevailing societal norms and patterns of relationship and organization with which he would have been familiar. In other words, pursuit of such a question would display both systematic concern to test for the *internal* coherence of Christian faith and systematic concern for the *extensive* (or external) connections of the

Christian tradition to what we otherwise know of the world, whilst also allowing for the tradition's own distinctiveness.

The concern to explore the tradition's internal coherence could also be taken in a diachronic (Greek: *dia*, through; *chronos*, time) direction, stimulated by questions about the coherence of specific aspects of Christian faith and ecclesiological self-understanding across nearly two thousand years of tradition. To stay with the example just given: how has the notion of the Church as the body of Christ evolved and changed across the course of Christian tradition, from St Paul, through medieval uses, to mid-twentieth-century official Catholic teaching, and beyond? And how have the respective organizational, relational, and ecclesiological implications of this metaphor been understood in these different contexts in terms of the respective distributions of power, mutual accountability, and responsibility that have variously been supported within the Church? The diachronic version of the concern for internal coherence focuses on the question as to how all of this hangs together across time.

Alternatively, the question of internal coherence could be taken in a synchronic (Greek: *syn*, with) direction, stimulated by the concern to ask how the expression given to one specific locus of Christian faith in a given time and context hangs together with the way in which all the other loci of Christian faith are understood there. Karl Barth's great spiralling treatment in the *Church Dogmatics* of each locus of Christian faith in relation to all of the others, returning repeatedly to similar points from a variety of perspectives and vantage points, represents just such an exercise in sustained synchronic questioning. Far from being insulated from the realm of contextual difficulties as an exercise in abstract system building, it was driven throughout by Barth's experience of the near criticism to extinction of an intellectually confident Protestant orthodoxy, fragmented and limping in the face of ceaseless critical and reductive analysis. It was on this specific issue that Barth's own attempted reparative reasoning was focused, where that which was most needed, in his judgement, was precisely to show how the tradition hangs together and presents a collective view far surpassing that to be gained from any more limited perspective on human existence.

On the other hand, the question of extensive or external coherence is raised when we ask how an aspect of Christian faith as articulated or performed in a given context hangs together with what we otherwise take seriously about the world. This has traditionally been played out in investigations of the relationship between philosophical and theological understanding and, more recently, in investigations of the relationship of theology to the natural sciences, the political sciences, economics, the social sciences, critical theory and organizational studies.

Taken together, all of this so far tells us something about how to take a particular question arising within ecclesial practice (e.g. 'In what sense is the Church understood as the body of Christ and what should this mean in practice?') and then to pursue it with systematic rigour, asking both about internal and extensive coherence. At many points such an investigation will have touched directly on the prior lived, practical dimension of Christian faith and ecclesial existence, but it will nevertheless have done so from an overtly theological, doctrinally-laden perspective – asking questions about the Church as the body of Christ and the like. What we have yet to do – linking explicitly now with the need identified in the previous section to view the

Church in dual perspective – is to identify what role might be played in the systematic ecclesiological task by empirical analyses of the concrete Church (e.g. qualitative ethnographic studies of particular congregations and quantitative surveys of members' attitudes). Do such empirical analyses simply show us the practical and organizational out-workings of relevant ecclesiological claims? Do they simply serve to illustrate the characteristic denominational practices and cultures associated with differing formally articulated ecclesiologies? Or do they have a more integral, properly critical, and genuinely theological contribution to make to the transformative task of systematic ecclesiology?

It is helpful here to expand the traditional systematic concerns for internal coherence – both synchronic and diachronic – and extensive coherence by thinking also in terms of the need to ask about the *pragmatic coherence* between articulation (doctrine/theory) and performance (practice) in Christian tradition. By 'pragmatic coherence', I mean the concern to analyse whether a given theological conviction or doctrinal tenet can be seen to hang together with what actually happens in practice. This opens a way genuinely to integrate a concern for the practical, the empirical, the concrete, within the systematic ecclesiological task. My claim is that the specifically theological significance of empirical studies of the Church lies in their providing a means to identify systemic practical discordance between the kinds of ecclesiological claims that churches make about themselves and their lived ecclesial reality. Where it occurs, such systemic discordance raises sharp questions about the adequacy, the living truthfulness, of a church's ecclesiological claims – and those questions open the need and possibility for those claims to be refreshed and renewed. Empirical methods and findings can serve, then, a role of critical accountability in relation to formal, doctrinally-driven ecclesiological concerns.

A useful case in point here might be the possible implication of certain theologies of ordination and clerical distinction in the sexual abuse crisis as this has been manifest within Catholic contexts. Whilst recognizing both that the pathology of sexual abuse is by no means an exclusively clerical phenomenon – the occurrence and extent of sexual abuse in secular, both State-run and private, institutions being every bit as significant – and that specifically clerical sexual abuse is in turn by no means confined to Catholicism, a responsible Catholic response to the crisis must nevertheless engage questions such as: 1) is there anything distinctive about the Catholic sexual abuse crisis? 2) If so, do such distinctive factors disclose any cultural, structural, and procedural weaknesses – pathologies even – within Catholicism that require healing and repair alongside the reparation that needs also to be made to the survivors? 3) Are there any aspects of Catholic ecclesial self-understanding and formal theology that are implicated in such pathologies? And 4) do the relevant patterns of self-understanding and formal theology lend themselves to any reweaving and reconfiguration that might enable the relevant core of Catholic self-understanding to be retained while being rescued from these pathological tendencies?

In this regard, whilst far more thorough empirical testing is needed, there is already some data suggesting that one contributory factor in the sexual abuse crisis – for survivors and perpetrators alike – has been the highly elevated way in which the ordained are understood within formal Catholic theology and more generally regarded throughout Catholic life. This may also have supported a more general ecclesial blindness and deafness to the reality of abuse. Some theologies confuse an appropriate and necessary distinction between lay and ordained with a two-tier caste mentality in which lay and ordained live on differing levels of Christian existence. If this is the case then we are confronted with a very serious performative contradiction at the heart of Catholic theology and practice of order: a theology aimed at promoting the holiness of the ordained would be shown to be complicit in creating the conditions in which the sexual abuse crisis became possible, and in which it could go uninvestigated.

The specifically doctrinal and constructive ecclesiological challenge is then to ask whether the operative webs of Catholic theology can be rewoven in order to take account of and to repair this diagnosed weakness, whilst also continuing to maintain what is core to such webs. As explored more fully in other places, a possible way forward here is to view the essential difference between lay and ordained as consisting not in two essentially different levels of Christian existence, nor in two essentially different types of Christian ministry, but in two essentially different modes of performance of the one and the same Christian existence and ministry: one public, official, and formally representative; the other relatively unofficial and informal, but each intrinsically related and appropriately accountable to the other.[7]

So, engaging with the lived, empirical reality of the Church has a crucial role to play in the overall transformative task of systematic ecclesiology, of promoting critical accountability by exposing wounds *within* specific ecclesial traditions. What, however, about the wounds and divisions *between* the various Christian traditions? What contribution can systematic ecclesiology make in this regard and how does the task of ecumenical ecclesiology need to be construed if it is to deliver on this task?

Serving Christian communion

The modern ecumenical movement stemmed from the experience of the nineteenth-century Protestant missionary traditions, which became aware of a significant performative contradiction between the gospel of reconciliation they were each proclaiming and – acting as powerful counter-witness – the competition over the winning of souls and turf in which they were effectively engaged. As a consequence, from the outset a fundamental ecumenical concern has been to seek for ways to move from mutual hostility and mistrust to recognition and effective collaboration in worship, work, and mission. Following the watershed 1910 Edinburgh World Missionary Conference, this concern issued in the Life and Works movement; which would later constitute one of the key streams flowing into the establishment of the World Council of Churches in 1948.

This was the crucial first phase of ecumenical engagement – first, not only chronologically but also in terms of abiding priority. This *ecumenism of life*, as it is sometimes called, is to ecumenical engagement as oxygen is to physical life: it is the *sine qua non* of all attempted ecumenical healing, without which nothing else is possible; and the churches always need more of it. Equally, no matter how much of it there might be, it alone is never going to be sufficient to solve the ecumenical problem. At its heart the ecumenical problem consists not simply in breaches of affection, shared prayer and witness – all of which occur within each of the Christian traditions and not simply between them – but in the institutional, ministerial, and sacramental divisions which over centuries fomented and cemented such breakdowns.

At the heart of the ecumenical problem is the broken witness the Christian churches give to the world by not being able to live consistently in full and visible structural, sacramental, and ministerial communion. Actions speak louder than words. St Francis is claimed to have told his friars, 'Preach always and when necessary use words'. The first way in which the churches witness to the Gospel – even before they engage in social mission – is by their own lives, their own organizational realities. And here the unpalatable truth is that for as long as the Christian churches are prevented from living in full and visible structural, sacramental, and ministerial communion with each other (which does *not* equate to uniformity), they find themselves in a state of profound contradiction; rent by tears in the ecclesial body of Christ.

It is this realization that in turn drove one of the other key strands of the modern ecumenical movement, also emerging from Edinburgh 1910 and also subsequently feeding into the establishment of the World Council of Churches: the Faith and Order movement. The core concern of Life and Works ecumenism was – and remains – to build shared relationship and practice across formally divided traditions. In contrast, the *ecumenism of truth* or the *ecumenism of dialogue* at issue in the work of Faith and Order focuses on formal doctrinal and ecclesiological causes of division, and asks how they might be healed and overcome; or how they might, at least, come to be understood as legitimate differences rather than as fundamental divisions. Here ecumenism takes a specifically and self-consciously ecclesiological form.

There have at times been tensions at various points between proponents of Life and Works ecumenism and of Faith and Order ecumenism, but there is no necessary opposition between them. Indeed, there is a sense in which Faith and Order ecumenism – the concern for the formal resolution of points of division in order to journey towards full structural, sacramental, and ministerial communion – both follows after and requires Life and Works ecumenism. On the one hand, the development of relationship with and direct personal experience of a separated tradition and its members can itself serve to promote an urgent desire for the overcoming of all that hinders full communion and so release significant energy for the self-consciously ecclesiological work of dialogue. On the other hand, as the many participants in the classical bilateral ecumenical dialogue processes from the late 1960s onwards attest, the patient endeavours of the bilateral dialogues were sustained throughout and only able to make the progress they did on account of the quality of relationship that grew between the respective teams of participants.

Quite remarkable gains were indeed made by this second key phase of ecumenical endeavour, as exemplified by the Anglican–Roman Catholic International Commission (ARCIC); the most influential bilateral ecumenical dialogue in the English-speaking world since its inception in 1967 as an outflow from the Second Vatican Council. The methodology and strategies progressively developed by ARCIC in turn shaped the work of all the other bilateral dialogues. Three in particular were important: 1) demonstrating that some assumed divisions have been built upon misunderstandings and caricatures of one tradition by the other; 2) drawing upon new scholarship to show how the traditions could now more easily say jointly what they previously assumed could only be said in opposition; and 3) establishing that harmony between differing theological webs does not require uniformity of expression but, rather, ease of translation across what can legitimately remain differently articulated webs of practice and belief.

Throughout the first major phase of ARCIC's activity (ARCIC I, 1970–81) and continuing well into the second (ARCIC II, 1983–2005), the application of these and related strategies revealed that one key area of assumed historic division after another was not actually a point of real communion-dividing difference: whether teachings about the Eucharist, or about ordained priestly ministry, or about the relationship between justification and sanctification. Surfing the considerable energy released by Catholicism's formal entry into the ecumenical movement during Vatican II (1962–65), the magnitude of achievement during the first phase of ARCIC's activity fed dizzy expectations about the possible realization of full structural, sacramental, and ministerial communion within a generation. The essential tasks of the dialogue partners were to come to the ecumenical table valuing the other tradition and prepared both to explain one's own tradition in relation to specifics with sufficient clarity and sophistication as to enable the members of the other tradition to understand it aright and affirm it, and to have their own appreciation of the other's tradition similarly refined, all with a view to coming to reconciled understanding.

In contrast, however, to those heady days, the contemporary ecumenical scene seems considerably more sober and constrained. Indeed, on many fronts and despite the undoubted historic achievements, the structural, sacramental, and ministerial reconciliation of the traditions now seems further away than ever; causing many to speak of an ecumenical winter or of an ecumenical cul-de-sac. The great wave of reconciliation through theological clarification appears to have crashed on the beach, dissipating its energy and leaving some of the great dialogue documents as the high water mark of a tide now turned.

This is particularly evident in relation to some of the longer-running dialogue processes where the 'softwood' of relatively easy early gains has now been exhausted, giving way to the 'hardwood' of lasting substantive differences: differences over the ways in which the local churches and the universal Church relate, over decision-making at various levels of Church life, and over the nature of eligibility for ordained ministry. There have also been significantly differing formal discernments between the traditions in relation to the pastoral care of gay and lesbian people and the legitimacy of admitting women into ordained ministry. Here and in related cases we are dealing not with mere mutual misunderstandings and differences of articulation that can be clarified and relatively easily tidied up. Rather, we are dealing with substantive, long-term differences which at the formal level are not going to be resolved for the foreseeable future. It is important to recognize this whilst also recognizing that on the ground *within* the traditions there can be considerable diversity of opinion, with faithful members exploring what possibilities for eventual change might actually lie open.

On account, however, of the ecumenically game-changing nature of these 'hardwood' issues at the formal level a different, third-phase, strategy is required, one aimed less at short-term harmonization and reconciliation (cf. the second-phase dialogues) and more at long-term mutual challenge, development, and growth by bringing the traditions into encounter with each other precisely in their difference. This third-phase strategy needs to be aimed less at asking what it is that another tradition needs to understand better about one's own tradition and to be aimed instead at asking what it is that one's own tradition has to learn and needs to learn from the other traditions. Just such a counter-intuitive third-phase ecumenical strategy has been developed in recent years under the title of Receptive Ecumenism, guided both by theological principle and by pragmatic insight.[8]

The operative theological conviction is that if the call to full, visible communion is indeed a gospel imperative that shares in the reconciling work of the Triune God, then whilst the formal ecumenical journey might now be facing fresh challenges, this should not be mistaken either for arrival at the end of the road, or as an insuperable road block. In Christian understanding God does not manoeuvre us into corners and blind alleys in order to prod us with a stick for sport; rather, God can be trusted to be faithful to God's call and to provide the resources necessary to live that call fruitfully in any given context. Similarly, hope, unlike optimism, is not a form of reality-denial that ignores the reality of apparent roadblocks in order to stay buoyant; on the contrary, hope takes reality seriously in all its problematic aspects and asks how the churches are resourced to live in the face of and through the road blocks in question.

Receptive Ecumenism maintains that whilst the second-phase ecumenical concern to move as directly as possible to the harmonious reconciliation of apparently contradictory theological frameworks has, at least for the time being, now run as far as it can on many fronts – particularly so in the case of the more mature dialogues – this should not be taken as returning us to the first-phase ecumenism where all that is possible is to attend to the quality of relationship, shared prayer, and witness between divided traditions. Abidingly important as such first-phase ecumenism undoubtedly remains, there must also be something more: there must be an appropriate means of continuing to walk towards and to live in anticipation of the reality of full communion.

For Receptive Ecumenism this third way is to take seriously the gospel call to continual renewal and conversion at the heart of Christian life, and to view the churches collectively as each being on a long-term path to ecclesial renewal and growth in the face of the other; as being in a state, as Martin Luther would put it, of *semper reformanda* or, as Vatican II's 'Dogmatic Constitution on the Church', *Lumen Gentium*, put it, of *semper purificanda*. In this perspective, the longer-term ecumenical journey on which the Christian churches are embarked and the recalibration of ecumenical expectation that this promotes, is not a matter of failure and judgement. It is a consequence of the softwood having been passed and the hardwood now being engaged. It is a time of grace for growth towards the goal by the only route possible: that of patient, grace-filled learning of how each is called to grow to a new place where new things become possible. The fig tree is being given the additional year it requires if it is to bear fruit.

Complementing and reinforcing these theological convictions at work in Receptive Ecumenism are some equally important pragmatic insights and principles. Key here is the recognition that during the same period that the churches have come to see the fulfilment of the ecumenical goal as being on a slower track than once envisaged, they have also come to – or have had forced upon them by external circumstances – more sober appraisals of their own respective wounds, difficulties, and needs. Each tradition has specific characteristic difficulties and limitations that are open to view and that can become impossible to ignore but which the tradition in question can be incapable of resolving from its own existing resources. Think, for instance, of the widespread public recognition across the full range of Catholic opinion by the time of the election of Pope Francis that systemic pathologies around excessive centralism and a decadent bureaucracy required address. Seeking to resolve such pathologies using existing internal resources is like a hamster running on a wheel: there might be a sense of movement but no real progress is being made. On the contrary, the existing pathological logic is simply being reinforced. There is, consequently, a need for refreshment and renewal from without, from the alternative logics and ecclesial experiences of other traditions. This in turn is a dynamic process that will take each tradition to new places, in the first place for their own respective health and flourishing, but by so doing also opening up currently unforeseeable fresh possibilities for their relating to each other.

At the heart, then, of Receptive Ecumenism is the assumption that any further formal progress towards the abiding ecumenical goal of full structural and sacramental unity will only be possible if each tradition moves from asking how other traditions need to change and focuses instead on its own difficulties and tensions and consequent need to learn, or receive, from the best discernible practice and associated understanding in other traditions. As with the broader understanding of the ecclesiological task traced earlier, this reflects a move *away* from ideal theorized, purely doctrinally-driven, ecclesiological constructs in ecumenical dialogue and a definite move *towards* taking the lived reality of traditions absolutely seriously, together with the difficulties and problems, tensions and contradictions to be found there.

The general tendency, of course, is to seek to hide such wounds, particularly from those outside the family circle. Consequently, too much ecumenical engagement is a matter of getting the best china tea service out: of showing ourselves somewhat formally in the best possible light to our distant relatives who are coming to visit rather than allowing to come into view the more warts-and-all self-understanding we keep locked behind the closed doors of the intimate family space. In contrast, rather than the ecumenism of the best china tea service, Receptive Ecumenism represents an ecumenism of the wounded hands: of being prepared to show our wounds to each other knowing that we cannot heal or save ourselves; knowing that we need to be ministered to in our need from another's gift and grace; and trusting that as in the Risen Lord, in whose ecclesial body these wounds exist, they can become sites of our redemption, jewels of transformed ecclesial existence.

Case studies in ecumenical engagement

High rhetoric indeed but what might all this look like in practice? Various initiatives in Receptive Ecumenism have taken root and developed in different contexts around the world. Closest to home (for this author at least) in the North East of England is a regional comparative research project in Receptive Ecumenism and the Local

Church that has been running for a number of years now, involving nine of the major Christian denominational groupings of the region. The focus has been on the respective organizational cultures, structures, and processes from regional to congregational levels. The basic intent has been to draw the groupings into a process of mutual self-critical self-examination concerning respective strengths and experienced difficulties in these cultures, structures, and processes and to ask in each case how the specific difficulties and limitations of one might be fruitfully tended to by learning and receiving from what is strong in the others.

To pursue this end three research teams have focused respectively on Governance and Finance, Ministry and Leadership, and Learning and Formation.[9] First, each team conducted a mapping of what is in principle happening within each denominational grouping, drawing upon extant documentation, formal ecclesiological self-understanding and regulations together with some initial interviews. Second, the teams conducted more detailed empirical testings, through structured interviews, questionnaires, focus groups and participant-observation. Third, a series of congregational studies explored how these interrelated issues worked in the round. Fourth, for each denominational grouping all the findings deriving from earlier phases were then integrated into a report that identified strengths and difficulties – and areas of potential receptive learning from the gifts and strengths of one or more of the other groupings. Fifth, these constructive proposals in turn are being subjected to further rigorous testing at the three levels of *internal*, *extensive*, and *pragmatic coherence*; examining whether that denominational grouping's ecclesiological self-understanding can indeed be expanded and rewoven with integrity in order to accommodate the new insight and practice, whilst retaining all that is essential in the host tradition, albeit potentially transposed and reworked. As regards the testing for pragmatic coherence, the key questions are as to whether a given proposal can reasonably be viewed as being timely and fruitful for the community and, with that, whether the necessary resources of time, personnel, will, and money exist to implement it.

To take a very different example from this local initiative, the third major phase of work of the Anglican–Roman Catholic International Commission (ARCIC III) has committed to pursuing its mandated joint focus on the Church local and universal and on ethical discernment in receptive ecumenical mode.[10] This requires a very challenging move *away* from the refined articulation of theorized, doctrinally-driven accounts and *towards* also asking after the lived experience of decision-making in each tradition and the real difficulties and tensions to be found there. In keeping also with the principle of pragmatic coherence briefly indicated earlier, these difficulties and tensions are being used as means of probing and testing the theorized accounts and identifying key areas for potentially fruitful receptive learning from the other.

In proceeding in this way ARCIC III is making no claim to being able to overcome at this point the very deep meta-differences in decision-making structures and processes that pertain *between* Roman Catholicism and Anglicanism. That would be utterly unrealistic. What it is seeking to do instead is to focus honestly on respective difficulties *within* the traditions as these arise in the experience of the concrete Church and to make some kind of progress, albeit doubtless more modest than might once have been hoped for.

Conclusion

Taking its start from an understanding of theology – in keeping with the vision of this *Companion* as a whole – as critical and constructive reflection on the questions and problems arising from the Church's practice and understanding with a view to enhancing the quality of the latter, I have focused on ecclesiology: the task of engaging the dual living truth of the Church as both complex human organization and as the Spirit-filled, charism-endowed body of Christ, witness to and servant of the Gospel, sign and sacrament of the Kingdom.

I have argued that we need to extend the traditional twin systematic theological concern to test for the internal coherence of Christian tradition with itself (both diachronic and synchronic) and to test for its extensive coherence with what we otherwise know of reality, by explicitly testing also for what has been referred to here as the 'pragmatic coherence' of Christian tradition. We need to ask *both* after the degree of performative dissonance between the theology of a tradition and its lived reality *and* after the degree to which this exposes fault-lines that are in need of repair within that theology.

Turning to the fault-lines *between* traditions, I have argued that, whilst second-phase ecumenism might still have important work to do in the context of relatively young ecumenical dialogue processes where misunderstandings and prejudicial attitudes can still prevail, Receptive Ecumenism offers a constructive way ahead where such dialogues seem to have run out of steam. Receptive Ecumenism starts with humble recognition of the wounds, tears, and difficulties in one's own tradition and asks how the particular and different gifts, experiences, and ways of proceeding in the other traditions can speak into and help heal these wounds that elude the capacity of one's own tradition to heal itself.

I have argued that this way of reparative receptive ecumenical learning – this way of refreshment and *ressourcement* by and through the separated other – is the only way in which the currently divided traditions can walk towards full structural, ministerial, sacramental communion and their own healing together. Receptive Ecumenism sets each tradition on an open-ended journey both towards its own healing and greater flourishing and to coming to recognize itself in the other, the other in itself, and each as bound together in the fullness of Christ and the Spirit. This is not a journey of return to any imagined uniformity. It is not a matter of the absorption of the many into a great undifferentiated unity. It is, rather, a journey towards the particularity of each coming to full flourishing and shining in all its particular glory. The wholeness, the full communion, of full catholicity thus understood is like the fully decked, fully illuminated Christmas tree – or like a polyphonous choir singing in harmony – in which each unique ornament, each distinct voice, is needed for the whole. It is in service of such greater ecclesial flourishing in communion and the resulting collective shining of the Church in the world – called to be *Lumen gentium*, light to the nations – that the reparative, critical-constructive task of ecclesial engineering is properly pursued.

Notes

1 *Summa Theologiae* I.1.7, in *Summa Theologiae 1: Christian Theology*, trans. T. Gilby OP, Cambridge: Cambridge University Press, 2006, p. 24.

2 See G.A. Lindbeck, *The Nature of Doctrine: Religion and Theology in a Postliberal Age*, London: SPCK, 1984.

3 See N.M. Healy, *Church, World, and the Christian Life: Practical-Prophetic Ecclesiology*, Cambridge: Cambridge University Press, 2000.

4 See J. Astley, *Ordinary Theology: Listening and Learning in Theology*, Aldershot: Ashgate, 2002.

5 See, for example, Christian Scharen's and Pete Ward's establishing of the Ecclesiology and Ethnography international network and related academic journal: http://ecclesiologyand ethnography.wordpress.com.

6 See J.M. Gustafson, *Treasure in Earthen Vessels: The Church as a Human Community*, New York: Harper, 1961.

7 For further, see P.D. Murray, 'Searching the Living Truth of the Church in Practice: On the Transformative Task of Systematic Ecclesiology', *Modern Theology* 30.2, 2014, pp. 251–81; also 'Discerning the Dynamics of Doctrinal Development in Post-foundationalist Perspective', in S. Oliver, K. Kilby and T. O'Loughlin (eds) *Faithful Reading: New Essays in Theology and Philosophy in Honour of Fergus Kerr*, London & New York: T & T Clark, 2012, particularly pp. 205–15.

8 See P.D. Murray (ed.) *Receptive Ecumenism and the Call to Catholic Learning: Exploring a Way for Contemporary Ecumenism*, Oxford: Oxford University Press, 2008, particularly Murray, 'Receptive Ecumenism and Catholic Learning: Establishing the Agenda', pp. 5–25; and Murray, 'Receptive Ecumenism and Ecclesial Learning: Receiving Gifts for Our Needs', *Louvain Studies* 33.1–2, 2008, pp. 30–45. Also see: www.dur.ac.uk/theology. religion/ccs/projects/receptiveecumenism/.

9 See www.dur.ac.uk/theology.religion/ccs/projects/receptiveecumenism/projects/localchurch/.

10 See the official communiqué released at the end of the inaugural May 2011 meeting: www. anglicancommunion.org/ministry/ecumenical/dialogues/catholic/arcic/docs/pdf/ARCIC_III_ Bose_2011.pdf.

Part IV
EXPERIENCE

20
EXPERIENCE

Jim Fodor

In this final section of the book, we turn our attention to experience, and to the ways in which the practice of Christian theology is shaped by it. The territory covered by the word 'experience' is extraordinarily broad and disparate, and many ambiguities – and sometimes confusions and misunderstandings – surround its use. We therefore begin by looking at some of the characteristic ways in which theologians appeal to experience in their arguments, and then construct a map of six different meanings that the word 'experience' can have in theology, and six different characteristics of thoughtful appeal to experience. Although we start with apparently simple cases, in which 'experience' might be taken to be one distinct source or criterion for theological claims, we move on to the idea that the practice of theology is always and unavoidably experiential, because it is always and unavoidably the practice of particular people living in particular contexts and in particular relationships.

Appealing to experience

Modern theologians[1] invoke experience as part of their argumentation and reflection in a variety of ways and for different purposes.[2] When someone prefaces what they are about to say with the phrase, 'in my experience … ', they may be using this expression as no more than a simple 'linguistic cipher',[3] that is, as a signal of good conversational manners, to indicate a wish to enter the conversation (like raising one's hand in a classroom). It can, however, have a variety of nuances and intricacies. For instance, some interventions that begin with 'in my experience … ' carry a strong emotional valence, a sense of urgency or perhaps even exasperation ('I've been patiently listening to the views of others and now it's my turn!'). Others convey an assurance of authenticity, calling attention to the fact that the opinions expressed are truly those of the speaker ('These are my own views, so please don't confuse them with the views of others or think that I'm simply mouthing conventional opinion'). Others are intentionally timed to add force or credibility at a particular stage in the argument or conversation, or to support a particular interlocutor whose ideas have already been aired ('Hear, hear! I agree with what she just said'). Others – like those prefaced with phrases such as 'personally speaking … ' or 'my experience tells me that … ' – suggest the speaker's preparedness to risk her own reputation ('I would be untrue to my own convictions if I did not say that ... '). Still others assume the force of a counter-appeal: that is, they may implicitly question either the authenticity of one's conversation partners or the normative status of their claims – although because couched in a polite manner the intervention may not always give the appearance of being a challenge.

The ways in which appeals to experience are made often make sense in the light of a cluster of cultural and intellectual attitudes that comprise a distinctively 'modern' sense of experience. Each person takes it that they have a right to describe their experience openly, and to assume that what they say will not simply be ignored or dismissed out of hand but instead will be respected, considered, weighed, and discussed. It is assumed that reports of experience are worth taking seriously – and perhaps, at least in principle, that public discussion of these various experiences will lead to a reconciliation of our accounts, and a shared understanding of the truth.

For many modern Christian inhabitants of the West, such appeals to experience have come to seem appropriate and natural, even obvious. At the risk of over-simplifying, modernity (understood both as a distinct historical epoch and as a philosophical worldview),[4] exhibits the following representative features: 1) a shift away from a God-centered toward a human-centered world; 2) confidence in the autonomy and self-sufficiency of human reason, which displaces Scripture or ecclesiastical structures (popes, bishops and other holders of Church offices) as the chief locus of authority; 3) the ascendancy of the individual, with a pronounced accent on individuals' freedom, equality, and right to self-determination; 4) a stress on human authenticity, self-actualization ('being all you can be'), and a privileging of the 'expressive self' with its emphasis on self-exploration and self-expression; 5) a new historical consciousness highlighting development, progress, and innovation; 6) a penchant for mastery and control via technological, instrumental forms of rationality; and 7) a shift, at least in principle, away from hierarchical structures of authority to more distributive, democratic, and egalitarian social arrangements.

Within this complex modern shift of attitudes and practices, there is a growth in 1) the idea that the self is tasked with establishing true knowledge by doubting all claims until they have been shown by inquiry to be trustworthy; 2) the idea that our reason can challenge any and all forms of authority standing in the way of or threatening to override free inquiry; and 3) the idea that our reason will base its inquiry ultimately on individual observation – on our direct experience.

However, when a person's experience is understood as giving them fairly direct and straightforward access to the world, appeals to experience also come to function as a new kind of authority. To appeal to one's experience is to lay a claim to be able to say how things really are – and therefore, perhaps, to say how things must be for others as well. Invoking one's experience can turn into an insistence that 'my' experience can't be denied, and that it therefore trumps any contrary opinion in the conversation.[5] Indeed, the very possibility of real conversation can get lost, because claiming something as 'my experience' places it beyond question.

Appeals to experience can, therefore, lead to a standoff. Think, for instance, of the protests one often hears that the Church is out of touch with the lives and experience of the present generation, especially the youth. This amounts to saying, 'Since what you say is not my experience, it cannot be authoritative.' At the same time,

Church authorities issue pronouncements and say to the faithful that it is they who are out of touch, and that the Church's experience validates its authority. This amounts to asserting, 'Since what you say is not in keeping with authority, it is not *authentic* experience – because authentic experience would fit with our experience.'[6] Difference and disagreement harden into opposition and what gets lost along the way is the possibility of discourse, conversation, dialogue.

In order to get past such standoffs, we need to look more closely at the different meanings that 'experience' can have, and probe a little more deeply what it means to appeal to our own experience.

Varieties of 'experience'

Sense experience

Perhaps the most obvious use of 'experience' relates to the five senses: seeing, hearing, tasting, touching, and smelling. 'Sense experience' is a phrase we use to refer to a set of bodily processes by means of which humans relate to and acquire first-hand knowledge of themselves and their world. A theologian might refer to experience in this sense because she wants to check what she has learned from others against her own experience – against what she can see with her own eyes and touch with her own hands. (Think of Thomas, hearing about the resurrection from the other apostles, and saying, 'Unless I see the mark of the nails in his hands, and put my finger in the mark of the nails and my hand in his side, I will not believe' – Jn. 20:25.)

Experience in this sense is inescapably tied to bodily life, and we most naturally think of it as the experience of a single body – an individual person. But individual bodies are part of social bodies, and questions abound about the relationship between personal experience and group experience. After all, individuals learn to distinguish experiences, to name them, categorize them, and speak about them, from the people around them. There is clearly therefore at least some sense in which the wider social order 'sets the terms' for personal experience – but how should we understand that relationship? Does an individual's experience give him or her knowledge of the world that is independent of the habits and thought-patterns of the social bodies of which he or she is a part? Or does that wider social order so set the preconditions for individual experience that it determines what an individual can and can't experience? Or – which is more probable – is there some more complex kind of symbiosis?[7]

Experience and knowledge

The second way of thinking about experience is closely related to the first. It concerns the role of experience in distinguishing what we know from what we merely hold as an opinion. As already suggested, a widely-shared assumption in our culture is that genuine knowledge must be open to public scrutiny and verification; it must stand up to examination, to testing, to corroboration – and 'experience' in this epistemological sense has a close affinity with 'experiment'.[8] The conviction at work is that the experiments of multiple people, who hold each other to account on the basis of their findings, are a reliable avenue to truth – to establishing the 'facts'. Indeed, some would go further and argue that testing knowledge claims in this way is not only *one* reliable way of establishing knowledge but it is *the* privileged method or mode of knowing.

One important thing to note here is that this approach to knowledge does not simply rely on each individual experiencing everything for himself or herself. It requires a community of experiencers, communicating about their experience to one another, testing what they hear from each other, and building up together a store of tested and communally owned knowledge.

Affective experience

A third way that 'experience' gets deployed concerns the feelings, emotions, desires, and the overall mood of those doing the experiencing. Far from dismissing these as a set of irrational or at best a-rational responses with no bearing on the truth, we can recognize that emotions and feelings are in fact important indicators of the quality of our engagement with the world; they point to the *significance* for us of what we encounter through our senses, and to the nature of our relationship with it. And just as a theologian might think of testing theological claims against sense experience, so he might think of testing them against affective experience – seeing whether those claims do justice to the way that he experiences the world, or whether they help open up a way of relating to the world that he can inhabit.

Here, too, questions abound. There are questions about the extent to which our patterns of affective experience are simply given, and the extent to which they can be moulded by our formation within particular communities and contexts. And there are questions about the relationship between affective experience and, on the one hand, aesthetics (beauty, delight, harmony, what is 'fitting,' and so on) and, on the other, the shaping of moral sensibilities and of ethical judgments. What role does our affective experience have in our identification of what is beautiful, and of what is good, and what kind of objectivity can those identifications have?

Experience as moral testing

In older uses, 'experience' could mean 'putting to the test' or 'making a trial of', and refer to investigation of a person's moral character through examination or trial. An episode in the Joseph cycle of stories provides a helpful illustration. In Genesis 42:15 the Hebrew term rendered in some English translations as 'experience' carries precisely this sense of 'putting to the test'. Joseph's brothers travel to Egypt to buy food because of a famine in the land of Israel, and come before Joseph, who immediately recognizes them, even though they fail to see in Joseph their own brother (whom they long ago sold into slavery). Rather than revealing his identity to them directly, Joseph instead decides to examine their character. He accuses them of being spies, a charge that they flatly deny. Joseph then responds (in the words of the Wycliffe translation of 1395): 'Now y schal take experience of ʒou' ('Now I shall take experience of you') – or 'By this you shall be put to the test' (Jewish Study Bible, 2004). Joseph means to establish, through trial or ordeal, the trustworthiness of his brothers' words.

This, then, is a fourth distinct use of 'experience' – but we are beginning to move away from the idea of experience as a source or criterion for theological claims, and beginning to focus on how the theologian herself might be formed and tested through her experience.

Experience and know-how

A fifth sense of 'experience' takes us further down this route. The word can be used to name the difference between 'knowing how' and 'knowing that'. The focus of the former is on practical judgment acquired by means of long-practiced familiarity with proven ways of doing things. The 'experienced' person exhibits their 'know-how' in the deftness and confidence with which they deploy reliable, time-tested methods. We speak, for instance, of an experienced teacher, or an experienced musician, or an experienced police officer. To be 'experienced' is nothing less than being able to carry out expertly and effortlessly, as if by second nature, a certain practical know-how. Practice alone will not of course automatically result in 'experienced' persons, as is confirmed by many who invariably grow old *with* experience yet who do not become skilled or wise *in* their experience. A simple amassing of experiences is not sufficient; the goal, rather, is the effective exercise of a certain kind of self-reflectiveness that learns from, and feeds back into, those experiences. 'Experienced' persons have a critical, constructive self-awareness that enables them to adapt and adjust to feedback from past attempts at a practice in order better to realize the goods or excellences intrinsic to those practices or that way of life as a whole.[9]

'Knowing how' and 'knowing that' are qualitatively different albeit related kinds of knowledge. 'Lived experience' is an expression often used in reference to the former; it is gained by those who indwell a form of life, and who learn to negotiate it from 'the inside', so to speak.[10] 'Knowing that' can name an aptitude for theoretical reflection on, or conceptual articulation of, lived experience – whether by people who are living that life or by others who are not yet living it but nonetheless have an understanding or conceptual grasp of it. The point is important because some of those whose lived experience is under study may themselves be ill equipped or unable to articulate with any degree of conceptual clarity their own personal lives or the lives of others in their community. In order to come to a fuller, more complete understanding, *both* types of knowledge/experience are required; 'knowing how' and 'knowing that' are needed; they are complementary rather than antithetical. Someone who 'knows about' a way of life without actually living it may nonetheless be able to bring insights to bear that are simply out of reach or inaccessible from the point of view of someone who inhabits that form of life.

Spiritual experience

A sixth way that 'experience' gets deployed in theology comes with reference to phenomena sometimes described as 'mystical' or 'spiritual'.

This can be tied right back to our first sense of 'experience'. A line of Christian thinkers reaching back at least to the third century and extending to the present – including the likes of Origen of Alexandria, St Bonaventure, Jonathan Edwards, and

Hans Urs von Balthasar – all appeal in one way or another to the concept of the 'spiritual senses'.[11] Their underlying conviction is that there is some meaningful way in which 'contact' with God is possible through these senses. Scripture provides ample warrant for this understanding: believers are enjoined to 'taste and see that the Lord is good' (Ps. 34:9; see also 1 Pet. 2:3); the people of Israel are commanded to 'hear the word of the Lord' (Hos. 4:1); righteous living is said to release a divine fragrance, the 'sweet aroma' of God (2 Cor. 2:15); those 'pure in heart' are promised that they will 'see God' (Matt. 5:8). Debate and discussion continue over what to make of these biblical descriptions. Do they imply peculiar, extraordinary modes of seeing, hearing, smelling, tasting, and touching divine things? Or are they better understood as intensifications or augmentations of what is already present, albeit latent and submerged, in everyday human experience? Are these moments of sudden insight – the appearance of a 'depth' previously obscured by ordinary encounters that only touch the familiar surface of things?[12]

Descriptions of some experiences as mystical or spiritual press the question whether it is appropriate, intelligible and indeed theologically coherent to say, 'I have experienced God.' On the face of it, the claim sounds odd – like a category mistake. According to Christian teaching on the relation between Creator and creation, God is not an object (even a very big object) that exists alongside other objects in the world – or even beyond the world. God, in that sense, is transcendent. Since one cannot experience what by definition transcends phenomena, the claim 'I have experienced God' is, on logical grounds, strictly impossible. But more than logical matters are at stake here. There are also theological reservations about idolatry, because taking God to be an 'object' of human experience risks reducing God to the categories of human understanding or limiting God to material coordinates.

Not surprisingly, therefore, theological language about God and God's presence (or absence) in human life is always carefully and complexly qualified. Christianity teaches, for example, that human life is already 'in' God's presence, and that fleeing or attempting to escape from God is futile (Ps. 139) given that God is closer to us than we are to ourselves. There is therefore a danger of viewing so-called 'mystical' or 'spiritual' experiences as events cut off from the rest of one's life, in which God is somehow supposed to be differently and definitively present. The Christian doctrine of the incarnation, however, invites attention to the entire gamut of human experience as the place where God may be found, as in God's entering in Jesus Christ altogether and without reservation into the realm of human experience. In an attempt to do justice to this theological insight, another approach to the claim, 'I have experienced God', is opened up – what some theologians call 'the mysticism of everyday life'. On these accounts, common, everyday human phenomena – such as love and hope, disappointment and frustration, joy and delight, praise and thanksgiving – should themselves be made sense of in relation to God. Experiencing God cannot be limited to some special cloistered preserve of the 'sacred' or the 'holy' but involves *all* human experience.

And yet it can be theologically fitting to speak of certain experiences of (or 'in') God as profoundly disruptive, unsettling and transformative. St Paul's experience on the Damascus road (Acts 9) is a case in point. From the scriptural record, Paul had many powerful and memorable experiences. But perhaps none outranks this one in importance. What sets it apart is not, however, that it featured unique, extraordinary or supernatural qualities found nowhere else in human experience (e.g. the special divine light, and the voice that only Paul himself could hear). What makes this experience distinctive was that it involved a fundamental re-orientation of his life and being. For what was disclosed to St Paul was the purpose behind all of his experiences. In that regard, experiencing God in this way did not make *a* difference, it made *all* the difference.

It is a mistake – and a fairly common one, unfortunately – to try to isolate the distinctive qualities in experiences that make them uniquely 'religious' as opposed to 'ordinary' or 'everyday'. Some, like Rudolf Otto in *The Idea of the Holy*, thought that what uniquely sets off religious experiences from all the rest is a felt experience of a numinous presence. The numinous, he claimed, evokes feelings of *mysterium* (wholly otherness), *tremendum* (dread, awe), and *fascinans* (fascination). Others, like William James (*Varieties of Religious Experience*), sought to equate what is religious with specific states of human consciousness. For him, these mystical experiences or states of consciousness were ineffable (i.e. they defied human expression; no adequate report of such experiences could be given in human words); they had a certain noetic quality (i.e. they conveyed insight into depths of truth unplumbed by the discursive intellect, and thus were weighted with authority); they were transient (i.e. mystical states were of brief duration); and the person who reported the experience noted a strong sense of passivity (i.e. the mystic felt as if her own will somehow was in abeyance). To be sure, St Paul may well have experienced some or even all of these qualities during his experience on the Damascus road. Yet the account in Acts 9 shows surprisingly little interest in Paul's mental consciousness or interior psychological state. Rather, the passage concerns itself with the sudden, dramatic 'paradigm shift' by which Paul came to reframe the whole of his experience. In the terms used in Chapter 2 of this book, his existing settlement was dramatically unsettled, and he was drawn into a process of comprehensive rearrangement.

The questionability of experience

Close analysis of experience from one end of the spectrum to the other – from its most rudimentary use as 'my sensory experience', in reference to relatively discrete events in the life of a particular human being, to its use in talking about deep patterns of know-how or religious experience characteristic of a whole pattern of life – reveals various ways in which experience is inherently open to question, to investigation and discussion.

Experience as mediated

It is worth paying attention, first of all, to the *media* in which experience is passed on and stored. Think of newspapers, pamphlets, magazines, telegraph messages, radio, TV, movies, web pages, paintings, photographs, sculptures, mosaics, parks, walkways and urban layouts, and so on. Each of these media can carry the tangible products or traces of experience, and in all these ways we *mediate* experiences to one another.

It is, however, not only when we hear or receive the experiences of others that those experiences are mediated. When we consider our own experience, we represent it to ourselves in imagination and memory – we tell ourselves stories, we picture things to ourselves, we arrange and identify and name our experiences. Human experience is very rarely, if ever, 'raw', direct and immediate: all of our experiences – and certainly all our ways of representing and communicating our experience – are filtered, framed, processed, shaped, manipulated, and screened by means of intermediate processes and structures.

One never, therefore, comes across experience directly and immediately. Experience is always framed, articulated, or told in some particular way – and one can investigate and question that way. Recognition of the constructed nature of experience calls for a certain vigilance toward theological arguments that would treat experience as immediate and direct – as a 'given' that simply has to be taken into account as is.

Experience and multiplicity

The mediation of our experience is an ongoing process. We gather and organize the disparate happenings of our lives into a more or less coherent unity, some sense of the whole, some kind of narrative structure – but that process is never complete.[13] We are continually un-stitching and re-stitching the stories we have created or received, and the stories that we stitch together – whether personal or corporate – are never seamless. They all contain numerous gaps, irregularities and loose ends, inviting further repair.

And although we might aim at some sense of continuity and unity, we never inhabit one simple story: we simultaneously belong to several different narratives, inhabiting several worlds of experience at once, at different levels and with varying degrees of invested interest and commitment. How do we understand and integrate the so-called metanarratives (*grand récits*) that dominate our cultural epoch with our personal stories (*petit récits*) in a way that does justice to them all?[14]

Experience as selective

Selection is an important aspect of this mediation. All our experience is selective; only certain events and episodes are noticed, taken in, remembered, recounted, and passed on. What does get remembered and passed on is never complete, and it therefore always possesses an open-endedness that invites new reception.

Invariably, specific social arrangements tend to valorize specific narratives, elevating them to an honorific status even as they demote and devalue other accounts as secondary, trivial or dispensable. Who gets to tell their story? Who contributes to 'the official' story? Or, to ask this question from the side of exclusion: Which stories are deemed not worth listening to? There are many whose stories are marginalized, suppressed, or forgotten – sometimes even actively 'erased' as, for example, the stories of those killed in the uprising in Tiananmen Square in 1989, or who 'disappeared' in Chile during General Pinochet's dictatorship in the 1970s. Whenever these stories are remembered and recounted, the effect is one of complicating and unsettling, if not subverting, 'the approved story' – they are, in Johann Baptist Metz's apt phrase, 'dangerous memories'.[15]

Experience as located

No appeal to experience is made in a vacuum. Such appeals always take place in particular social spaces; they are made by someone, to someone, for some purpose, in the context of existing relationships, activities and communities. Recognizing this should act as a check upon the modern penchant to construe experience as autonomous, self-contained, and private. William James, in his now classic *The Varieties of Religious Experience*, redefined religion in terms of experience – 'immediate personal experience', to be precise – with religion heuristically understood as 'the feelings, acts, and experiences of individual men in their solitude, so far as they apprehend themselves to stand in relation to whatever they may consider divine'.[16] The effect of this definition is to render invisible the social, mediated and linguistic character of appeals to human experience.

Experience as derivative

To speak of the nature of experience as derivative is not to demote its status or denigrate its value but to underscore the importance assigned to receiving and appropriating what has been given – i.e. what has been inherited, received, passed on. To say, 'in my experience … ', is also to say 'according to what I have received'. This is the traditional or derived dimension of experience. Being taught by experience or learning from experience proceeds, of course, in both formal and informal ways. It refers to what one has learned through institutional schooling or education, but also the customs, manners, and habits that one assimilates through family upbringing or broader socialization.[17] These communities bequeath a language to the person, shape their attitudes and capacities for feeling, apprentice them in the use of concepts and rules, and generally habituate them into complex but readily distinguishable forms of life. Seen under this aspect, there can be no experience which can be strictly 'mine' just as there can be no experience that is exclusively that of 'the group'. Acknowledging the derivative nature of all appeals to experience is another way of conceding just how profoundly intertwined are the personal and the social.

Experience as dialectical

The inevitably complex, ongoing and questionable processes of mediation turn our accounts of our experiences into sites of conversation, debate, and contestation – and at times even sharp division. Our stories and their interactions are potentially divisive; they can provoke open conflict and inflict deep wounds, but can also fashion strong bonds of friendship and solidarity.

When appeals to experience are misused or misunderstood, they tend to shut down rather than open up conversations. When they operate well, appeals to experience raise issues rather than settle them. Arguments of all kinds, theological or otherwise, involve a give-and-take, an appeal and a response, a listening and a speaking.

Appeals to experience are but one 'moment' in the dialogue. To be sure, interventions occasioned by such appeals are often interruptive, at times even disruptive. But they are not inherently destructive, nor do they necessarily undermine the integrity of faith or the coherence of tradition. Rightly understood, they constitute a negative moment or phase in the conversation to the extent that they alert everyone to what is absent, what has been left unexpressed: namely, the fact that the speaker's views have not been represented by, or given place within, the self-articulation of the other participants in the conversation. Something is missing; a lacuna needs filling, which the appeal to experience by the speaker is intended to make good. The obverse side of the interventions that come in the form of appeals to experience is what might be called their constructive or 'positive' moments: namely, their ability to raise awareness, to bring to consciousness, to make room for the unexpressed, repressed, unarticulated experiences of the other. To be sure, there are times when these appeals are met with anger, resistance, and counter-appeal. But either way the dialectical thrust or intention of the exchange is in play. If an appeal to experience serves to halt the conversation, collapse the dynamic of the interchange to some kind of stasis or inert state, then the dialectical movement is blocked, the consequence of which is lethal for theological argument and the life of faith.

Experience and the practice of theology

'Experience' does not simply name one source of knowledge to which theologians might choose to attend, and which might then need to be related to other sources (such as Scripture and tradition). Rather, the practice of Christian theology is experiential through and through. It is pursued by people who are in the process of discovering what it means to live in specific times and places as members of God's people (and so as readers of Scripture, in conversation with the tradition). To use the language introduced in Chapter 2, the practice of theology is pursued by people who are involved in the process of settling, drawing on all the materials of their lives corporately and individually.

The practice of theology is always undertaken by people who have bodies – who *are* bodies – immersed in the physical world. And it is always undertaken by people who are members of social bodies: it draws upon the languages and habits of perception sustained in those settings, apart from which experience could never be recognized or named, manifested or known, exchanged or shared, confirmed or challenged.

The practice of theology involves attention to those who are 'experienced': those who are wise and expert in ways that set them apart as respected voices of the community. Their 'know-how' is virtuously displayed in their skills, judgments, dispositions and affections, which they deploy and direct toward the goods and excellences constitutive of Christian life. Such 'know-how' or 'experience' also manifests itself by way of appropriate feelings and emotions, affective responses by those making wise judgments. It cannot be had without some kind of dedicated self-involvement and commitment on the part of the knower to advancing a way of life that makes sense of their identity and sustains them in their purpose. Part of that 'know-how' also involves practical wisdom and moral discernment: an ability to examine and test the truthfulness of the claims of one's interlocutors, and to have yours tested by them in turn. Finally, because wise and 'experienced' persons have cultivated over time the art and discipline of a life well-lived, they will have also acquired certain awarenesses, discriminating forms of attention and finely-tuned sensibilities, with regard to life's mystical and spiritual dimensions. These, too, will inform the 'experienced' person's judgment, and through them the community's, so as to enrich and deepen understanding overall.

Practitioners of theology communicate the results of their settling using multiple media, and in multiple forms – especially by telling stories – and all that communication is unavoidably selective and creative, and shaped by differential social, political, and economic power relations. To think about the practice of theology as 'experience' is to ask who is getting to tell their story, both on a personal and on a collective level, and whose stories are being overlooked, silenced or refused. Every telling is partial, and inevitably invites questioning, disagreement, contestation and sometimes even discord, as every telling gives rise, in its reception, to others – and so on until the end of time. The task is not to break free from the contingencies and particularities of experience in order to arrive at some ideal 'view from nowhere', but rather to enter ever more fully and deeply into, and hence perpetuate, the virtuous cycle of reception, testing, and passing on.

Looking ahead

A conceptual map of the various meanings of 'experience' might be a handy thing to have. But it is important for the theologian to recognize that the map is not the territory. The actual work of understanding how experience shapes theological reflection and argumentation remains to be done, not in the sense that it has yet to receive due attention but in the sense that the theological task is one that is ever new, one that each generation must take up for itself even as it draws upon what has been bequeathed from earlier generations.

It is easy to lose sight of what is perhaps most obvious: namely, that learning how to appeal to experience is itself a practice, the proper exercise of which calls for an induction into and ongoing strengthening and refinement of a set of requisite Christian virtues. There is a certain inevitable circularity here: one only becomes adept at invoking experience as a fundamental category for theological reflection and argument as one acquires experience in doing so from and with those who have shown themselves 'experienced' in the Christian faith.

The chapters in this final section of the book explore particular ways in which experience in some setting has informed, impinged on and indeed transformed the theological task. Of course, *every* chapter in this book emerged from experience, in the sense we have been exploring – but these chapters highlight that fact, and reflect upon it more explicitly.

Garrett Green's chapter, 'Experience in theology', is a winsome, insightful and creative account that interweaves his own personal work in prison ministries with a compelling, able narrative of how modernity has helped transform 'experience' into primarily an epistemological category, one that exalts the empirical and is wary of the emotional. The cost of this transformation, unfortunately, has been rather steep: a negative tension between, if not an outright bifurcation of, head and heart. The challenge for contemporary theology is to forgo any tendency to treat polarities as if they were simple dichotomies – i.e. thinking that would separate the cognitive from the volitional and the affective – and retrieve instead 'the sense of the heart' through a renewed focus on how the Holy Spirit is present in the world today. Because experience is for Green as much a pneumatological matter as it is an epistemological one, the way forward is to articulate – following the lead of Jonathan Edwards – a theological account of Christian affections that accentuates the interruptive, surprising and at times altogether unexpected joyful in-breaking of God in human lives.

Jenny Daggers' chapter, 'Feminist theologies', explores the ways in which women's experience provides an invaluable source or site of theological reflection. She focuses in particular on the experiences of struggle and solidarity, community and collaboration that stir the heart of feminist theologies. Feminist theologies not only collaborate with other groups that strive for justice, struggles that cross lines of race, class, sexuality and (dis)ability within particular social contexts, but they also toil in broader global networks that include both human and non-human elements, struggles like post-colonial and liberation theologies, and ecofeminism, with its commitment to healing the earth in the face of widespread ecological degradation. What feminist theologies seek in all their varied forms is genuine coexistence.

Willie Jennings' chapter, 'Practicing black theologies', uses the Japanese film *The Animatrix* as a provocation to think more deeply about race, theology, and the perceptions of reality that flow out of each. The animated film illustrates the subtle, insidious power of ideology and illusion that sustains what is still a largely 'Euro-centric' theological vision   a vision that tends to deny the ways in which it is sustained by the experience of particular, powerful groups and excludes the experience of others. To break the hold of this vision requires that one be brought 'inside' the matrix to appreciate how the real is constructed and manipulated. But an intellectual awaking is not all that is needed. What is also required is a profound transformation of the habitus of Christian life: our dispositions, attitudes, imaginations, and sensibilities.

Thia Cooper's chapter, 'Liberation theology', opens up for the reader the wide and varied world of emancipatory theology, movements of theological reflection and action committed to the difficult, challenging, long-term task of freeing humanity from oppression in all its forms. Taking as her starting point the 'base ecclesial communities' of Brazil, Cooper explores how powerless and marginalized populations, largely ignored by traditional theologies, developed and refined a distinctive method of theologizing where practice is reflected upon and serves as the grounds for action, and where corporate discernment is key. Finding God in all things applies especially to people. What follows from this central conviction is that each person's experiences are priceless because God can be heard in everyone's voice. From a liberationist perspective, the discussion starts from the margins – with those who have been dismissed, ignored, left without a voice and thus are powerless to act. Liberation theologies operate with a posture of openness and welcoming, especially of the excluded. Community is prioritized to the extent that we come to know God through knowing others.

Susan Abraham's chapter, 'Postcolonial theologies', examines the history and the mutual interaction of postcolonial theory (a form of critical thinking in the academy aimed at decolonizing Western modes of knowing) and postcolonial theology (a constructive enterprise aiming to do theology using the many tools and insights of postcolonial theory in specific postcolonial contexts, like the Indian subcontinent, for example). A key insight of postcolonial theology is that our thinking about God, Christ, the human being and the Church, on the one hand, and our thinking about the ways imperial systems of domination are created and sustained, on the other, are inextricably related. By means of this reciprocally enhanced self-awareness, the assumed normative status ascribed to Western ways of knowing will be relativized, open to correction and healing. At the very least, theologians in the Christian West will be much more chastened when articulating theological notions like freedom, liberation, and religious identity and will learn instead to be open to and embracing of cultural proposals issuing from postcolonial contexts which have either been ignored or are unknown in traditional Western theology.

Richard Viladesau's chapter, 'Engagement with the arts', examines the long and sometimes controversial history of how Christian experience has been shaped through its interaction with the arts. Through most of the Church's history that engagement has been rather more practical and ad hoc than theoretical and systematic; hence, the arts tend to be a rather neglected area of experience in Christian theology, which recent attention, including Viladesau's, seeks to remedy. The iconoclastic controversy of the eighth century evinces a much-debated theological question about whether and to what extent it is appropriate artistically to represent the divine. Does art merely represent, illustrate the divine, serve as an effective teaching or catechetical instrument, or does it in addition mediate, actually render the divine present? Do images and objects of art serve as occasions for religious 'awakening', sites of possible illumination and transformation available in no other way? Might the arts be regarded as independent modes of thinking, a kind of non-conceptual mode of practicing theology? Clearly the fascinating set of questions in Viladesau's chapter expand enormously the range of human experience available to theology, indirectly reminding the reader of just how logocentric (i.e. text- and literary-centered) has been the world of Western intellectual culture and scholarship, including theological scholarship.

Michael DeLashmutt's chapter, 'Theology and popular culture', explores the immensely rich, pervasive and multi-form character of popular culture – the 'atmosphere' that most of us breathe without even being aware that it constitutes our ever-present, pervasive medium. This relatively recent area of theoretical inquiry has provided promising resources to theologians who are more and more situating the subject matter of theology within their own and others' experience of 'the complex inter-relationship between meaning-bearing texts and the meaning-making practices which make up everyday life'. The shift in focus from 'high' to 'low' culture accentuates the quotidian in ways that help draw attention to the ubiquity of popular culture, raising the prospect of discovering the presence of God in every dimension or facet of our world. Directing attention to the popular is at once revealing, because of bringing to light areas that were heretofore thought to be unavailable for theological appropriation, and unsettling, because challenging long-held assumptions about 'inside' and 'outside', acceptable and unacceptable. The tendency is to discount or ignore popular culture, on the assumption that surely it cannot be a key site disclosive of our highest hopes and most cherished ideals. DeLashmutt's chapter helps dispel the force of that prejudice by analyzing misconceptions regarding the relevance of popular culture to the theological enterprise and advancing in their place a vision of the reign of God that is without boundaries.

Notes

1 Here 'modern' is used in an admittedly ambiguous way that conflates the senses of 1) a particular historical epoch or era, 2) a philosophical-cultural outlook, and 3) 'contemporary'– as in current or present use.

2 For what follows, we draw substantially on George Schner's fine typological/grammatical analysis of the role of experience in theology. The final section of his article, which proposes a continuum of possible uses of the appeal to experience within theological arguments, is especially helpful. See G.P. Schner, S.J., 'The Appeal to Experience', *Theological Studies* 53.1, 1992, pp. 40–59.

3 Schner, 'The Appeal to Experience', p. 41.

4 For more on the characteristic traits of modernity, see Stephen Plant's chapter on 'Modern theology', in the Tradition section of this volume. See also Garrett Green's short but helpful survey of the history of modernity's attempt to ground faith in experience in the chapter, 'Experience in theology', especially the subsection, 'Experience as an epistemological issue.'

5 'To assert my opinion as part of the dialectic of an argument is one thing, to presume the assertion is the conclusion of the argument is another.' Schner, 'The Appeal to Experience', pp. 44–45.

6 See G.P. Schner, S.J., 'New Ways of Speaking with Love and Mercy', in P.G. Ziegler and M. Husbands (eds) *Essays Catholic and Critical*, Burlington, VT: Ashgate, 2003, pp. 3–20. As Schner explains, 'the two sides harden into just that – two opposed individuals or groups such that no real conversation, no discourse, can go forward. The two tend to feed off one another and keep the opposition going. The more authority becomes authoritarian, the more experience can be invoked in order to escape the imposition of a heteronomous judgement. Likewise, the more the appeal to experience becomes idiosyncratic, the more it too becomes authoritarian; in the same way, the authoritarian appeal to universal truths becomes equally idiosyncratic. This is the way in which *both* authority *and* experience usurp the role of *discourse* such that the situation becomes intolerable.' Ibid., p. 6.

7 There can be no experience apart from an attendant form of expression. 'The fact is that experience and its expression are as inextricably connected as convex and concave; there is no apprehension of what we have encountered or undergone which is not at the same time mediated in some form of expression … ' J.E. Smith, 'William James' Account of Mysticism: A Critique', in Steven T. Katz (ed.) *Mysticism and Religious Traditions*, Oxford: Oxford University Press, 1983, p. 248.

8 A 'tentative procedure; an operation performed in order to ascertain or illustrate some truth' is one of several definitions of 'experience' in the *Oxford English Dictionary*.

9 This process is akin to the definition of practice offered in the general introduction to this volume (drawing on the work of Alasdair MacIntyre): 'any coherent and complex form of socially established cooperative human activity through which goods internal to that form of activity are realized in the course of trying to achieve those standards of excellence which are appropriate to, and partially definitive of, that form of activity, with the result that human powers to achieve excellence, and human conceptions of the ends and goods involved, are systematically extended.'

10 As Paul Murray puts it in his chapter, 'Engaging with the contemporary Church', 'Christianity is something lived before it is something thought.'

11 A germane passage comes from John Climacus, *The Ladder of Divine Ascent*, trans. by C. Luibheid and N. Russell, New York: Paulist Press, 1982, §. xxx, p. 288: 'When a man's senses are perfectly united to God, then what God has said is somehow mysteriously clarified. But where there is no union of this kind, then it is extremely difficult to speak about God.' This passage from Climacus is noteworthy because it demonstrates the close intimacy, indeed the inseparability between language (the divine Word) and experience (recounted in human words). It is not accidental that in the Western theological tradition the expression 'spiritual senses' refers equally to non-literal modes of interpreting *scripture* and to non-physical human *perception*, underscoring once more how Scripture and Experience are not two independent sources but rather aspects of one complex, multi-dimensional reality of divine self-disclosure.

12 For more on the tradition of 'the spiritual senses', see B.T. Coolman, *Knowing God by Experience: The Spiritual Senses in William of Auxerre*, Washington, DC: The Catholic University of America Press, 2004, and the edited volume by S. Coakley and P.L. Gavrilyuk, *The Spiritual Senses: Perceiving God in Western Christianity*, Cambridge: Cambridge University Press, 2012.

13 Perhaps one of the more extensive accounts of the interrelations between time, narrative and the self can be found in Paul Ricoeur's three volume work, *Time and Narrative*, trans. K. McLaughlin and D. Pellauer, Chicago, IL: The University of Chicago Press, 1984, 1985, 1988. For a helpful overview of the role of narrative in theology, see S. Hauerwas and L.G. Jones (eds) *Why Narrative? Readings in Narrative Theology*, Grand Rapids, MI: William B. Eerdmans Publishing Company, 1989.

14 For more on this, see J.-F. Lyotard, *The Postmodern Condition: A Report on Knowledge*, trans. G. Bennington and B. Massumi, Minneapolis, MN: University of Minnesota Press, 1984.

15 See J.B. Metz, *Faith in History and Society*, trans. D. Smith, New York, NY: Seabury Press, 1980, but also J.B. Metz, *A Passion for God: The Mystical-political Dimension of Christianity*, trans. J.M. Ashley, New York, NY: Paulist Press, 1998.

16 W. James, *The Varieties of Religious Experience*, The Works of William James 15, ed. Frederick H. Burkhardt, Cambridge, MA: Harvard University Press, 1985, p. 34.

17 Describing the appeal to experience as derivative means to point 'to what has shaped my consciousness from both beyond myself and through the structuring operations of consciousness itself, those which are natural and those which are learned.' Schner, 'The Appeal to Experience', p. 48.

21
EXPERIENCE IN THEOLOGY[1]

Garrett Green

How did experience come to be a controversial topic in modern theology? There is a clue in the notion of 'modern' itself, for modernity can be defined by the understanding of experience that first emerged in the 'new science' of seventeenth-century Europe – what we today call 'modern science'. The names of Copernicus, Galileo, and Newton have come to signify a turning point in Western history (and eventually in world history): a new way of orienting ourselves in the world, of understanding what is real and how truth is discovered. The defining feature of modern science is its empirical approach to reality: all knowledge begins with experience; and any claim to know something that ignores experience and tries to begin with 'pure reason' is automatically suspect. And the only kind of experience that counts, according to scientific empiricism, is sense experience, which provides the raw data needed to generate reliable knowledge. Any other kind of experience, especially if it involves the emotions, must be rigorously excluded from the data, for it could lead only to confusion and distortion. The ideal scientific inquirer is disinterested; in seeking the truth about reality he or she strives to exclude everything personal or subjective, especially any experience tinged with emotion. This approach to knowing the world has been enormously successful (just look at the wonder world of science and technology we inhabit today!) – so successful that it has become our model of knowledge in the modern world. One might be tempted to put it more boldly still: the modern world simply *is* that world in which reality is assumed to be identical with the results of empirical science.

But that account is too simple, for people have always known that there is more to life than what the sciences can deliver, and the prime example of that 'more' has been religion. No wonder that 'science and religion' has become a thriving industry in our culture: we feel sure that there are truths to be learned beyond the limits of empirical reason alone, so we go on trying to find a way to secure those truths, all the while assuming that any reliable purchase on reality must follow something like the scientific-empirical method – which means that it must start from some sort of experience.

Experience as an epistemological issue

The most ambitious attempt in modern thought to achieve that goal, to have it both ways, to affirm the epistemology of modern science while acknowledging a legitimate place for religious truth as well, is the critical philosophy of Immanuel Kant. His solution, however, requires a concession that Christians should be unwilling to make, for he proposes to secure the rationality of faith at the price of denying its claim to knowledge. (He also reduces religion to morality, but that is an error more easily remedied.) 'I have ... found it necessary,' Kant famously announces in the preface to the second edition of the *Critique of Pure Reason*, 'to deny *knowledge* in order to make room for *faith*.'[2] Notice that it is not reason but knowledge that he wishes to exclude from religion; but what kind of rationality are we left with after it has renounced knowledge? Kant's answer is what he calls 'practical' reason, according to which we rational beings are permitted – nay, required – to 'postulate' three fundamental notions – freedom, immortality, and God – without actually knowing them. We must simply take them on faith, without claiming to know that they are true; indeed, not to do so would be to act irrationally. What Kant is proposing is a two-tier system of truth, in which modernity will grant an important but carefully circumscribed arena to religion, so long as it knows its place and doesn't get too uppity in its assigned task of keeping watch over our 'values', while those in the know retain primary responsibility for truth.

The modern rift in Christianity between historic credal orthodoxy and the various liberal and modernist alternatives that have emerged since the Enlightenment stems from the refusal of many Christians to accept the Kantian compromise, while others have tried to accommodate the demands of modernity by making certain adjustments to the Church's claim to speak the truth. Until recently the main battles between these two sides focused on matters of doctrine; but lately the raging controversies have centered on moral issues, especially those concerning acceptable sexual behavior and the taking of life. After a surge of ecumenical goodwill in the latter half of the twentieth century, churches are once again falling into schism over conflicting moral teachings.

How Karl Barth sent me to prison: A testimony

Why this thing in my head about prisons? For years – more than I can now recall – the idea of doing prison ministry would surface in my brain from time to time. Odd, since I didn't know anyone who had been in prison, either as an inmate or a volunteer, so where did such a thought come from? My picture of prison life, like everyone else's, came from TV and the movies. One time while I was traveling I visited a church, and during the announcements someone talked about some men in the congregation who were working with inmates. Afterwards I talked with a couple of them in the parking lot (I think they were volunteers with Prison Fellowship), but then I went back home and forgot all about it as I plunged back into work and the general busyness of life.

313

> * * * * *
>
> He breaks the power of canceled sin, he sets the prisoner free ...[3]
> * * * * *
>
> I woke, the dungeon flamed with light;
> My chains fell off, my heart was free,
> I rose, went forth, and followed Thee.[4]

Given the defining role of the scientific paradigm in the modern age, theology has come to view experience as an epistemological issue. Since we moderns have convinced ourselves that truth is always acquired empirically, the theological question of truth has focused on this question: what kind of experience can serve as the raw material, the data, for theological knowledge? And the obvious answer has seemed to be *religious* experience. The paradigmatic text of the modern religious quest is William James's 1902 Gifford Lectures on *The Varieties of Religious Experience*, a book whose title alone, even for people who have never read it, epitomizes the central theological quest of modernity. And it is no accident that its author was not a theologian but a philosopher-psychologist.

> Once in graduate school my professor mentioned (as I recalled it later) that Karl Barth, breaking with the long tradition of treating pride as the cardinal sin, put sloth in its place. I always intended to read that part of the *Church Dogmatics* but never got around to it (!) – until after I retired from teaching and my life began to fall apart. Then I discovered that Barth did not really replace pride with sloth but rather saw them as two sides of the same coin. And 'sloth' (I always pictured that creature hanging from a tree limb) doesn't really do justice to Barth's term *Trägheit*, which is the German term in physics for inertia: it means indolence, that stubborn laziness that just sits there, refusing to get up and do anything. (My wife admitted to me later, 'I thought you'd never get up from that computer and go do anything with other people!')

Among academic theologians the investigation of religious experience had begun a century earlier in the generation of thinkers struggling to come to terms with the Kantian revolution. The young F.D.E. Schleiermacher took up the challenge in the first book ever written about 'religion' understood in the modern way as something generic, distinct from Christianity (now viewed as just one of its historical forms), a transcultural and transhistorical *something* that is basic to human life and irreducible to any other cultural realm. Titled *On Religion: Speeches to its Cultured Despisers*, Schleiermacher's book is a frankly apologetic work, couched in the rhetoric of Early Romanticism, the avant-garde movement of the day, of which Schleiermacher was a charter member. Though far removed from the language of modern science, the book nevertheless shares one of its most basic traits: it appeals to *experience*. But it does so in a novel way, designed to free religion from the rationalistic straightjacket imposed by the Kantian dichotomy of theoretical and practical reason. What Schleiermacher does, methodologically speaking, is to extend the dichotomy into a trichotomy, giving religion its own experiential realm. 'Religion,' he claims, 'maintains its own sphere and its own character only by completely removing itself from the sphere and character of speculation, as well as from that of praxis.'[5] That third sphere, according to Schleiermacher's later formulation in his systematic theology, *The Christian Faith*, is 'neither a Knowing nor a Doing, but a modification of Feeling, or of immediate self-consciousness'.[6] Religion, Schleiermacher is telling us, is at home not among our ideas or our morals but rather in the realm of our affections.

> Come to think of it, I did in fact have prior experience with prisoners. Towards the end of my teaching career I led a group of students from my college to a study away program in Athens. One weekend several students (including two of my own) were arrested and charged with an act of vandalism and actually stood trial in a Greek court (they were acquitted after the true perpetrators came forward). While they were being held at the local police station, I visited them – the first prisoners I had ever visited! I later jokingly told one of them (who subsequently did honors study in Karl Barth's theology under my direction) that when I appear before the Son of Man in his glory (cf. Matt. 25:31 ff.), and he asks me if I ever visited any of 'the least of these' in prison, my student is to raise his hand vigorously and testify on my behalf. Well, the joke turns out to have been on me, though another six years were to go by before I realized it.

Schleiermacher's important recovery of religious affections led him to take a fateful turn as a systematic theologian, one that had a momentous influence on the direction of Christian theology in the following century, and remains a significant factor in theology to this day. Having recognized that Christian religious experience is rooted in our affective nature, he tried to use this insight to resolve the epistemological quandary of modern theology by treating Christian feelings as the foundation of our knowledge of God. He accordingly transformed dogmatics into *Glaubenslehre* ('faith-ology': the name commonly applied to his two-volume systematic theology, *The Christian Faith*), effectively transferring the object of theological inquiry from the Word of God to the experience of faith. 'Christian doctrines,' he writes in his classic reformulation of theological method, 'are accounts of the Christian religious affections set forth in speech.'[7] Intended to set theology on a secure foundation in a world dominated by empirical science, Schleiermacher's redirection of theology had virtually the opposite effect. As theologian after theologian in the nineteenth and twentieth centuries sought to identify the anthropological locus in human experience that could provide an incorrigible foundation for Christian truth, the net effect was to lead theology on a fruitless search for a secure foothold somewhere in the experience of human subjectivity.

Karl Barth recognized the futility and the danger of this project: it misrepresented both the situation of the human being before God and the radical disjunction between all human experience – especially *religious* experience – and the self-revelation of the living God of biblical faith. He parodied the theological quest for God through religious experience as the absurd attempt to 'speak of God simply by speaking of man in a loud voice'.[8] That quest is theologically incoherent because it seeks to know God on the basis of an alleged inherent human ability to know God; but such a knowledge could not be knowledge of the gracious God, who grants knowledge (and experience) of himself to human beings in spite of the fact that such knowledge is humanly impossible. Barth revises the classic Reformed formula, *finitum non capax infiniti* ('the finite cannot comprehend the infinite'), to read: *homo peccator non capax verbi Domini* ('the human sinner cannot comprehend the Word of God'). This principle means that the human quest for knowledge of God is seeking to do the impossible. Yet we know that knowledge of God is possible, Barth maintains, because it is actual; and this fact must be the starting point for inquiry into its possibility. In other words, the possibility of knowing God is presupposed in the Church, which hears the Word of God in faith. If we approach the knowledge of God from the human side, we can see it only as an impossibility. But if we view it from the standpoint of God's self-revelation in Jesus Christ, our knowledge of the Word of God is certain (and must therefore be possible). 'The reality of the Word of God,' Barth writes, ' ... is grounded only in itself' and not on any human ability or possibility. Human knowledge of that Word, therefore, 'can consist only in its acknowledgment'.[9] Trying to secure theology by showing how it is humanly possible is both futile and faithless, missing the heart of the gospel message. 'With man this is impossible, but with God all things are possible,' said Jesus to his disciples (Matt. 19:26). Oswald Chambers draws the conclusion for Christian experience today: 'God can do nothing for me until I get to the limit of the possible.'[10] The task of theology is to describe God's possibilities in the face of their apparent human impossibility.

Six years after the Athens experience, I found myself retired from teaching and struggling to climb out of the spiritual pit into which I had fallen. I happened one day to mention to a friend in my church who had worked with ex-offenders that I had long had this 'thing' in my head about prisons. He suggested that I email a friend of his, an ex-offender who now runs an aftercare program for former inmates in my town. Still I procrastinated another four months before following up on his advice. Then one day I was seated at my desk reading that section of Barth's dogmatics that had long intrigued me but I had never read, §65 on 'The Sloth and Misery of Man'. I had already read Barth's discussion of the first aspect of sinful sloth, which he describes in that trenchant German term *Dummheit*. Now he was describing a second aspect, which he calls *Unmenschlichkeit*, inhumanity. The sinner in his laziness is not only stupid but inhuman, isolating himself in self-protective loneliness, refusing to come out of his shell and be a human being together with others.

Suddenly, the text before me became a mirror. Without stopping to reflect, I set aside the heavy volume of dogmatics, reached for my keyboard, and sent an email message to the man who works with ex-offenders. From there, things took off with a rapidity that made my head spin. He suggested that instead of talking about prisons, I come to a session of his program for former inmates, which I did that same week. At the conclusion of the meeting, I met him for the first time and he introduced me to another man, who was not only the pastor of the church where we were meeting but also the chaplain at the local men's medium-security prison. (He also lives just two blocks from me, but we were unaware of one another's existence.) Since the prison was currently on lockdown, the chaplain told me that the next day would be a good time for him to show me around and describe the programs he oversees. I filled out a volunteer application and underwent a brief background check. It was the only way I could get into the prison to visit and observe the various activities to see where I might fit in. As far as I was concerned, all was still tentative, but the hook had been set (cf. Matt. 4:19).

Experience, therefore, cannot be the *source* of our knowledge of God, despite all the attempts by modern theologians to treat it as though it were the ground of faith. George Lindbeck has argued that this kind of theology assumes what he calls an 'experiential–expressivist' model of religion, which arose in opposition to the traditional 'cognitive' model that interpreted religion as a set of 'informative propositions or truth claims about objective realities'. Because the cognitive model appeared to clash with modern science, many modern theologians found the experiential–expressivist alternative attractive. This model of religion 'interprets doctrines as noninformative and nondiscursive symbols of inner feelings, attitudes, or existential orientations',[11] which means that religious faith will never come into conflict with modern science. But it also means that theology gets things backwards, seeking its object in the inner depths of human experience rather than in the Word that God utters beyond the limits of human possibility. Lindbeck proposes to put an end to this modern tradition of seeking God through 'religious experience' by reversing the terms. 'A religion,' he writes, 'is above all an external word, a *verbum externum*, that molds and shapes the self and its world, rather than an expression or thematization of a preexisting self or of preconceptual experience.'[12] The problem with experiential–expressivism is that it 'reverses the relation of the inner and the outer'. His alternative, which he calls a 'cultural–linguistic' model of religion, seeks to undo this reversal of inner and outer. On this view, religion is 'a kind of cultural and/or linguistic framework or medium that shapes the entirety of life and thought', and instead of deriving external features of a religion from inner experience, it is the inner experiences which are viewed as derivative. Such a view sees religious experience not as the source but rather the fruit of the encounter with God and returns theology to its proper task as the interpreter of the Word of God.

My first experience inside the walls was the Sunday evening worship service, held in the large visitors' room and attended by more than fifty men. As the inmates filed in through the door from the prison in their uniforms (the inmates call them 'browns', but to me they looked like hospital workers in khaki scrubs), each one shook hands with the chaplain and greeted him. I had been bracing for this moment, assuming that I would encounter at least some latent hostility: what kind of do-gooder from the outside was I, anyway, and what was I doing as a spectator in their cramped little world? But nothing of the sort occurred, either then or since; instead they treated me just as they had the chaplain, shaking my hand with a slight nod of the head and a 'God bless you'. When they filed out after the service, many of them shook my hand again and thanked me warmly for coming, even though I had not said a word. How could I resist coming back to a place where people thank God for my mere presence among them?

I started attending a small-group mentoring program, in which one to three inmates with less than a year remaining before release meet with an experienced mentor from Prison Fellowship. In such an intimate setting it was impossible for me to remain a mere observer, and soon I was joining in the Bible study, conversation, and prayer. If there was one experience that finally 'hooked' me, it was the first time I heard an inmate pray for me, thanking God for sending 'Brother G.' to be with them and mentor them. After just a few sessions, thanks to a couple of snow storms that kept the designated mentor from getting out of his driveway, I found myself 'flying solo'. My nervousness quickly evaporated, and soon I was looking forward to mentoring on my own.

The critique of experiential–expressivism has played an important role in recent discussion by diagnosing a deep-seated flaw in modern theology, one reaching back to the age of Kant and Schleiermacher. Under the cultural pressure of modern scientific empiricism, too many Christian thinkers have yielded to the temptation to refashion theology as a kind of empirical enterprise in which religious experience (however defined) is treated as data from which we might derive knowledge of God. Lindbeck's proposal to replace this flawed method with a cultural–linguistic model of religion has had a salutary effect in recent theology, but it remains too abstract and undeveloped to offer a way forward. It has provided a necessary negative critique of the misuse of experience in Christian theology but offers little positive guidance to the question of how the affective heart of Christian experience can find adequate theological expression. Lindbeck acknowledges in passing that 'the relation of religion and experience ... is not unilateral but dialectical',[13] but he is unable to make good on this insight in his cultural–linguistic proposal.

As I drove from my home to the prison for the very first time, my route took me past my college (it was the same route I had taken every day of my working life), and I heard a voice from somewhere inside my head say, 'There's the prison where you were incarcerated for thirty-eight years.' Further up the highway, as I made the turn onto the prison grounds, I marveled that I had driven by so many times without ever noticing the prison there, just a few feet from the road. The warm September sun glistened off the chain-link fencing and the multiple coils of razor wire along its top and another at its base. Driving along the fence on my way to the parking lot at the rear, I realized with a start that it appeared beautiful to my gaze, and I thought how callous and unsuited to this ministry I must be. (It was a glorious late-summer morning – like the weather on 9/11.)

Another time along the same road I had a vision: the roof of the prison building inside the fence had been rolled back, and the inmates were being 'raptured' right up into the clouds. I know now that the beauty I beheld was not the result of my callousness but an anticipation of God's glorious transfiguration of the earth (not to mention his transformation of my own life).

Experience as a pneumatological issue

By now it should be obvious that an adequate theological account of Christian experience cannot be undertaken as an exercise in epistemology. Religious experience is not the solution to the epistemological quandary of modern Christianity. Rather, the proper locus of the theology of experience is pneumatology, for it is impossible to speak adequately about Christian experience without talking about the Holy Spirit, and it is not possible to speak theologically about the Holy Spirit without including the real life experience of Christian believers. But how are we to approach this topic in a culture whose imagination has been captivated by modern science? Perhaps the answer can be found not by submitting to the modern dogma that all truth is empirical, but rather by calling it into question. We can make a start by returning to Schleiermacher's new theological departure two centuries ago. Ever since Barth and his early associates in the dialectical theology movement burst on the scene after World War I, the theology of Schleiermacher has been repeatedly subjected to attack for inaugurating what we now call experiential–expressivism. But this well-deserved criticism should not blind us to what was right in Schleiermacher's attempt to deliver theology from Enlightenment rationalism, especially in its Kantian form. His diagnosis was on the mark, even if his attempted cure was misdirected. For he rightly recognized that the chief weakness of Enlightenment Christianity was its denial of the affective experience at the heart of Christian faith.

I am in the prison dining hall observing my first Bible study inside the walls. The leader is a seasoned volunteer from the local inner-city black Baptist church. He told me later that he is not, like so many prison volunteers, a former inmate himself but grew up in a family where nearly every other member, starting with his father, had spent time in jail. Now employed as a social worker for the state, he spends most of his free time working with prisoners as a Christian volunteer. I am standing awkwardly to one side of the room, leaning against the stainless steel rails where the inmates collect their meals when the room is serving its usual purpose. Having learned my religion in mainline churches, it had not occurred to me to bring my Bible to the Bible study. An inmate sitting in the first row – he had been the one leading the singing and praise in two languages before the program formally began – caught my eye, and making a generous come-hither gesture with one arm while pointing to the large Bible on his lap with the other, beckoned me to join him ... and when I did so my observer status dissolved. The leader was reading from the fifth chapter of John's Gospel about the paralytic lying beside the pool of Bethesda. 'One man was there,' he read, 'who had been an invalid for thirty-eight years' (v. 5). He was the one who wanted to be healed when the Spirit moved the waters but had no one to carry him there. (Thirty-eight years? I had never focused on that particular detail. Why thirty-eight? Exactly the number of years that I had spent teaching college just down the road.) Ignoring the man's excuses, Jesus says to him, '"Get up, take up your bed, and walk." And at once the man was healed, and he took up his bed and walked.'

Two weeks later I attended another Bible study in the same room, and this time the leader was an ex-prisoner – in this very facility, he told the inmates. Having no idea what text had been used in the earlier Bible study (I verified this fact with him later), he proceeded to read John 5:2–9. Sometimes the Holy Spirit has to repeat himself before I get the message.

We can find guidance and direction in our quest for a theological account of Christian affective experience by leaving European theology aside for the moment and turning to some dramatic events in colonial America, and their interpretation by 'America's theologian', Jonathan Edwards.[14]

The drama, known to history as the Great Awakening, began with an outbreak of religious fervor in 1733 in Edwards's own church in Northampton, Massachusetts; under the influence of the dynamic popular preaching of the itinerant English revivalist George Whitefield, it subsequently swept like wildfire through the American colonies from Boston to Georgia, leaving a lasting imprint on American Christianity. This outbreak of religious 'enthusiasm' also provoked severe criticism, led by Charles Chauncy of Boston, who denounced the irrationality and unseemly emotionalism of revivalist religion. Jenson comments that Chauncy's 'supposition of the irrational character of affections, the religious especially, has continued to determine American religion and theology'.[15] Edwards, seeking to come to terms theologically with the outpouring of religious feeling all around him, became the chief advocate of revivalism while nevertheless struggling to define the line between the healthy expression of genuine Christian affections and the hypocritical 'enthusiasm' exhibited by so many who were moved by the awakening.

About a year before God sent me to prison, I was lying in bed in a local convalescent facility, recovering from knee replacement surgery. My room had a large window overlooking the front lawn, where a carved wooden sign bore the name of the place: Beechwood Manor. It was an ageing facility, and my metal-frame hospital bed was too short. Sometime during my second night I awoke in considerable pain, despite medication, made worse by the fact that I could not stretch out my leg in the short bed. I lay awake for hours, staring blankly at the dark window, beyond which I could imagine the grounds and the sign. Every image and phrase that flashed through my mind seemed laden with metaphorical meaning: biblical passages, bits of gospel songs and hymns, fragments of memory from various times in my life, faces of friends and enemies old and new – all of it felt laden with meaning, and all of it was related in some transcendent and deeply-felt way that I could not have articulated. At some point during that long night, with my leg still throbbing, I thought about the sign out on the lawn and idly wondered (as I sometimes do, having spent several years of my life in Germany) what 'Beechwood' would be in German. It leapt to mind in a flash: *Buchenwald*. For a long time thereafter I drifted in and out of consciousness, feeling a kind of solidarity with all the countless sufferers past and present. I didn't know what to make of it at the time, but the vividness of that experience left it seared into my memory.

* * * * *

Hold on my child, joy comes in the morning,
Weeping only lasts for the night;
Hold on my child, joy comes in the morning,
The darkest hour means dawn is just in sight.[16]

Early in Edwards's *Treatise Concerning Religious Affections*, the book in which he struggles to achieve a theological evaluation of the dramatic manifestations of revival that he witnessed in the Great Awakening, he announces the thesis that he will expound and defend in the book: 'True religion, in great part, consists in holy affections.'[17] It is important to note that Edwards is quite aware that affections can be false as well as true: 'A man's having much affection don't prove that he has any true religion: but if he has no affection, it proves that he has no true religion.'[18] We might paraphrase his view by saying that religious affections are the *sine qua non* of genuine faith.

Writing half a century before Schleiermacher, Edwards treats the Christian religious affections not as the source of theology but as the human response to the beauty of God and his works. Jenson comments on Edwards's 'native unity of speculation and adoration' and describes his religion as 'adoration of God's beauty'.[19] The issue that Edwards is pursuing is often characterized in popular terms as a tension between 'head' and 'heart', or, expressed philosophically, between the intellect and the will; and Edwards does make use of both these terminologies. But what is most striking and theologically insightful about his treatment of religious affection is his refusal to treat the polarity as a simple dichotomy.

In his 1733 sermon 'A Divine and Supernatural Light', he appears at first to adopt the familiar duality, which had been around in the West since Augustine and had eventually calcified into the crude faculty psychology taught by some of Edwards's contemporaries. This dualistic thinking separated the mind into distinct cognitive and volitional faculties, which had then to be combined or integrated in some way in order to make sense of human experience. As Edwards pursues his interpretation of religious affection, it soon becomes obvious that there cannot be distinct cognitive and volitional 'faculties' but rather, in Jenson's paraphrase, a 'temporally extended consciousness, which is cognitive in that reality variously appears in it and is volitive in that it is drawn to or repelled by these appearances'.[20] The notion in Edwards that allows the difference of intellect and will to be transcended is what he calls 'a *sense* of the *beauty*, amiableness or sweetness of a thing; so that the *heart* is sensible of pleasure and delight in the presence of the idea of it'.[21] Unlike both the Deists and the Rational Supernaturalists of the Enlightenment, Edwards begins not with the *idea* of God, however conceived, but with the *apprehension*, which is necessarily also the adoration, of God in his beauty and majesty. Such an experience (for an experience it must surely be) has as its object something both known and valued (i.e. both 'theoretical' and 'practical'), something that combines intellect, will, and affections in a single act of consciousness.

> One morning at Beechwood, my favorite nurse's aide, a shy but friendly Haitian woman named Lourdes, bustled into my room humming as she raised the blinds and prepared the room for the arrival of breakfast. 'What are you singing?' I asked. 'A Catholic song,' she replied in her Creole accent (I loved the way she said 'Cath-o-lic'). After my recovery, we met weekly for a time at a local coffee shop, where I helped her with English as she applied for her RN in the United States and told me about life in Haiti after the earthquake and about being a Haitian immigrant in New England. The place had wireless Internet, and we worked on her applications on my laptop. Her password was ILOVEYOUJESUS. For me it was a first glimpse of what it might be like to serve Jesus among the least of these.

This understanding of 'true religion' or genuine Christian faith allows Edwards to make a distinction that gives him leverage in the task of distinguishing between the good and bad fruits of revivalism. He argues that 'there are two ways of thinking and understanding, especially of spiritual or mental things'. In the first type 'we don't directly view the things themselves by the actual presence of their ideas' but apprehend them by their signs, which constitute a 'mental reading', a kind of shorthand that takes the place of the actual ideas. This kind of thinking is 'a *mere cogitation* without any proper apprehension of the things thought of'.[22] It is unproblematic and unavoidable in most ordinary thinking, for only God is able to understand everything 'by the actual and immediate presence of an idea of the things understood'.[23] In the second type, the one 'more properly called *apprehension*', 'the mind has a direct *ideal view* or *contemplation* of the thing thought of'. Such true apprehension may be applied to matters purely of the understanding ('figuratively called the head', Edwards comments). But he is far more interested in its other application, to the will ('figuratively called the heart'), which includes this expansive list: 'things [that] are pleasing or displeasing, including all agreeableness and disagreeableness, all beauty and deformity, all pleasure and pain, and all those sensations, exercises, and passions of the mind that arise from either of these'. Out of this rather scholastic-sounding typology, he derives the distinction that will enable him to both justify and defend the genuine outpouring of Christian affections in the Great Awakening and also to distinguish between its authentic and inauthentic fruits – i.e. between true religious affections and hypocritical 'enthusiasm'. The first way of understanding mental and spiritual things Edwards calls 'mere *speculation* or the understanding of the head', and he contrasts it with the second way, 'the *sense of the heart*'.[24]

One day in my mentor group, which at that point comprised two men who had been with me for several months, the conversation came around to volunteers and what motivated them to come into the prison. I commented that I wasn't sure what had brought me to prison – though I was sure it was the place God wanted me to be – but had noticed how many of the other volunteers had been incarcerated themselves and now wanted to help others in the same situation. Since I had never been in prison, I wondered aloud if I lacked the proper credentials. One of the prisoners turned to me and said, 'No, you weren't ever an inmate, but you're in the right place, because you have the heart for it.'

As a teenage Methodist I had often heard the story of John Wesley's heart-warming experience at the meeting in Aldersgate Street. And I knew at once that here in prison is where I have felt my own heart 'strangely warmed'.

* * * * *

Poems are hard to read
Pictures are hard to see
Music is hard to hear
And people are hard to love

But whether from brute need
Or divine energy
At last mind eye and ear
And the great sloth heart will move.[25]

This way of making the distinction is no mere repeat of the traditional separation of intellect and will, for in Edwards's version knowledge and truth are found on *both* sides of the border. Yet the two are not simply juxtaposed alternatives: when it comes to the really important things in life, no 'mere speculation' will do. If we would truly *know* these realities, we must apprehend them with the 'sense of the heart'. To do otherwise is to rest satisfied with a 'nominal' Christianity and miss true living faith altogether. We might even say that for Edwards the heart has an epistemological advantage over the head. Any approach to Christian truth that leaves the affections out of the story is sure to miss the mark. And here is where the rubber meets the road in the question of 'religion and science' in the modern world. The empiricism required by the modern natural sciences must eschew the 'sense of the heart' in order to do its work. Responsible scientists must necessarily exclude the affections from the work of science. As scientists they are not wrong to do so. This fact does not mean, however, that science and religion must be continually at war; but it does mean that scientific empiricism cannot serve as our model for every kind of thinking, including theological. The religious pathos of modernity is rooted in the fact that early modern science learned that by bracketing questions of purpose or ends (i.e. by excluding Aristotelian 'final causes' from scientific thinking) it could achieve intellectual insight into, and technical mastery over, the things of this world. But then it (we) forgot that the exclusion of purposiveness was not a scientific discovery that things have no purpose but rather a choice, a deliberate decision to exclude purpose from our account of reality. Giddy with the intellectual and techno-logical fruits of empirical science, modernity has greedily wanted to apply this way of thinking to everything in sight, including the things of God and the human soul. This analogical overreaching by moderns, who have forgotten that empiricism exacts a spiritual price in return for its technological gifts, has wreaked havoc in our common culture and our individual souls.

> After a few months as a prison volunteer, I mentioned to the chaplain that I wished I had a group of Christians with whom to pray. He told me about a few guys, ex-offenders and recovering addicts and some men who work with both, who meet weekday mornings at 6:30 to pray. I decided just to try it out, though for a retiree it was an awfully early hour; but it soon became an addiction.

Another habit we have learned from modern science that gets us into trouble in theology is the disinterested posture that the empirical observer must take up in relation to the object of observation. In his sermon 'A Divine and Supernatural Light', Edwards distinguishes the two kinds of thinking ('merely speculative or notional' and 'the sense of the heart') by using some everyday analogies. He takes two examples from ordinary experience: (1) 'the difference between having a rational judgment that honey is sweet, and having a sense of its sweetness'; and (2) 'between believing that a person is beautiful, and having a sense of his beauty'. Then comes the clincher: 'The former may be obtained by hearsay, but the latter only by seeing the countenance.' The same difference pertains theologically between one who 'rationally believe[s] that God is glorious' and one who 'has a sense of the glorious-ness of God in his heart'.[26] Job, after enduring incredible suffering and at last encountering the living God, says this: 'I had heard of you by the hearing of the ear, but now my eye sees you' (Job 42:5). This distinction is what makes those reports one reads about from time to time – reports of polling data purporting to show that most Americans believe in God (better: believe that there is 'a' God) – so utterly meaningless. No quantity of merely 'notional' or nominal belief can ever amount to even a trace of heartfelt living faith, because it lacks the *sine qua non* of genuine Christianity, the conversion of the heart.

> Right after submitting my retirement letter (one year in advance), I traveled to Spain for a few months, where I noticed a large advertisement emblazoned on the sides of busses in Madrid. I don't recall what was being advertised (prob-ably some kind of investment or annuity), but the operative verb was *jubilarse*. Checking my pocket Spanish–English dictionary, I discovered that it wasn't about some kind of jubilation but rather about retirement: that's how you say 'to retire' in Spanish. I think it was a foreshadowing of my own retirement: if retiring means 'jubilating oneself' that's certainly how it's turned out for me! But at the time I had no idea.

* * * * *

I had eagerly anticipated retirement as a deliverance from thirty-eight years of correcting undergraduate prose, sitting through endless faculty committee meetings, and swimming against the cultural stream as my college, along with the rest of American higher education, succumbed to the pressures of competitive consumerism. But actual retirement was another story, unanticipated and bewildering. The inner demons I had been too busy to attend to for all those years crept out of their hiding places in my soul and began to torment me. Frightened and bewildered by what I saw myself becoming, I found my way to a wise counselor, who told me in one of our first meetings that he was not a Christian believer. I actually found that a relief because I didn't have to worry that he might cut me some slack for 'religious' reasons. No one was more amazed than I when that therapy became my road to a kind of vibrant Christian life that I had never dreamed was possible. Much later, I told my therapist the story of Balaam in Numbers 22 and my personal interpretation: if God can speak through the mouth of a donkey, why not through a Jungian therapist?

The disappearance from theology of the 'sense of the heart', the temptation to approach God 'disinterestedly', the desire to do theology from a neutral perspective – all these modern tendencies are symptoms of the neglect of the Holy Spirit. A century has gone by since the meteoric rise of Pentecostalism, which has changed the face of world Christianity so dramatically. It is tempting to view the dramatic, exuberant, and often undisciplined eruption of Pentecostal and charismatic spirituality into Christianity as a kind of 'revenge of the Spirit'. The dearth of vital experience in the religious lives of so many Christians in modern times stems from the long neglect of the Holy Spirit in modern Church life and theology. The rise of the Pentecostal–charismatic movement is both a symptom of the problem and a judgment on the churches. The continuing decline of the dispirited mainline churches is simply the other side of the coin. To respond to the new outpouring of the Spirit, as many in the mainline churches have tried to do, by condemning its emotionalism, its indifference to the niceties of theology and doctrine, and its lack of ecclesial discipline – to respond in this way is to repeat in the twenty-first century the error of Charles Chauncy and his supporters in the eighteenth. It is equally unwise for the older churches to try to ignore the Pentecostal challenge – first, because it will prove to be impossible in the end, and second, because one ignores the signs of divine judgment at one's own peril.

Living in the spirit: The pneumatology of experience

Christian theology has never been quite sure what to say about the Holy Spirit. When the fathers of the Church, responding to the Arian controversy in the fourth century, tried to articulate the rule of faith in a credal formulation that would define the essential teachings of the Church, they came up short – literally. The original creed of the Council of Nicaea in AD 325 (not to be confused with the enlarged version issued by the Council of Constantinople in 381, which became known generally as 'The Nicene Creed'), after affirming belief in God the Father in a few brief phrases, and belief in the God the Son in much greater detail, had only this to say in its third article: ' ... and in the Holy Spirit'. Period. And when they finally got around to saying something more specific about the Holy Spirit, they sowed the seeds of the first great schism in the Church, the split between the Orthodoxy of the Greek-speaking East and the Latin-speaking church of the West. To this day, there is still no agreement as to whether the Spirit 'proceeds from the Father' alone or 'from the Father *and the Son*' (the Latin *filioque* that remains a stumbling block to reconciliation between Eastern and Western Christians). But the arguments over the fine points of doctrine are only symptoms of a deeper spiritual unease.

> At one of the lowest points on my long spiritual trek to health, my wife, after hearing me weep inconsolably for some minutes, said to me, 'How I wish I could fill the hole in your soul!' The metaphor stuck with me, and some time later and further along that road (under the influence, perhaps, of the gospel music that had become my joy and comfort along the way) I had a vision: I saw the blood of Jesus flowing into that hole in my soul.
>
> * * * * *
>
> What can make me whole again?
> Nothing but the blood of Jesus ...[27]

The problem of the Spirit broke out anew in the Reformation of the sixteenth century, not in the main arena of conflict between the magisterial Reformers and the Roman Church, but within the Protestant ranks. In response to the Spirit-filled radicalism of Thomas Müntzer, who claimed to receive revelation directly from the Holy Spirit apart from Scripture, Luther replied that he would not listen to Müntzer even if 'he had swallowed the Holy Ghost, feathers and all'.[28] Luther's reaction against the radicals only became more adamant after (as he saw things) Anabaptist heresy ignited social violence. Initially sympathetic with the demands of the peasants, he turned against them once their political protest grew into the Peasants' War in 1524–25. The long-term consequences of Luther's vigorous rejection of the Radical Reformation were profound and lasting, bequeathing to later Protestantism a deep aversion to any hint of what he called *Schwärmerei*. (The usual English equivalent, with an equally pejorative connotation, is *enthusiasm*, though this term has faded over time, due at least partly to confusion with the more recent positive usage of the term.) The root of *Schwärmerei*, according to Luther and later Protestants, was the belief in any unmediated experience of the Holy Spirit. To protect against that ever-present danger, they insisted that the only valid vessels of inspiration are the written Word of God in the Bible and the sacraments authorized by it.

> For the four months we lived in Sevilla, taking Spanish classes and learning to love Andalucía, I worshiped with a tiny congregation of *anglicanos* that I found on the Internet. I had to walk for half an hour to an apartment

building in a part of the city off the tourist beat, where they rented a small, leaky basement room. Two congregants who were American expatriates served as interpreters when I couldn't follow things (I was OK with the liturgy, and song lyrics were projected on the wall, but sermons usually escaped my linguistic grasp). I was vaguely aware of the tradition of giving testimonies in church, but this was the first time I had experienced it directly. The most enthusiastic 'testifier' was a woman who had left the American Midwest in the 1960s after a traumatic childhood in the Reorganized Church of Jesus Christ of Latter-Day Saints, married a Spaniard, become an Evangelical Anglican, and had lived in Sevilla ever since. I couldn't keep up with her rapid-fire Spanish testimonies, but I was able to catch their fervent spirit.

Early in the twentieth century the theological problem of the Holy Spirit once again took center stage when the rapid growth of the Pentecostal movement led to a new confrontation between the settled doctrine of the older churches and dramatic new manifestations of the Spirit. When the Azusa Street revival in Los Angeles in 1906 exploded into a dynamic worldwide renewal movement (today we would say that it 'went viral'), the resulting controversy had a familiar ring to those who knew their Reformation history. This trajectory is nicely captured in the subtitle of a recent book by Simeon Zahl: *The Holy Spirit between Wittenberg and Azusa Street*.[29] Zahl shows how 'the primary theological distinctive of charismatic and Pentecostal Christianity – the centrality of a certain conception of personal experience of the Spirit' – allows us to explore the questions raised by the 'apparent impasse between classical Protestant critiques of "enthusiasts" (*Schwärmer*)' and Pentecostal Christianity.[30] At the heart of this impasse is the theological status of experience: how is the Holy Spirit present in the world today, and in what way do individual Christians experience that presence? For the first time since the beginnings of the Pentecostal movement a century ago, there are encouraging signs of real theological dialog. By its very nature, early Pentecostalism was uninterested in formal theology, tending to be anti-intellectual and dismissive of the Church's doctrinal and theological tradition. But now some of the younger Pentecostal theologians are showing interest in seriously engaging with that tradition. My own awareness of this new departure was first aroused by the arresting title of James K.A. Smith's book *Thinking in Tongues*.[31]

Testimonies are a familiar part of Christian life inside the walls. Many of the inmates come from churches where testimony is a regular part of worship, and once a month the Sunday evening service is led by a volunteer who simply invites anyone who wishes to testify to come forward – and there is never any shortage of takers. When I attended one of these services, the first man up was one of my favorite inmates, a regular at Wednesday Bible studies and Alpha courses; and for the past three weeks he had been part of the small group I was mentoring. A black man in his fifties (older than most of the prisoners I work with), he towers over me (a rare and sometimes unsettling experience for a six-footer like me), and is usually overflowing with affability and eager to express his gratitude for the changes God is making in his life to anyone who will listen. In his testimony that night the words flowed forth, eloquent in a way that only those with little formal education can seem to produce, rich in metaphor and biblical allusion yet utterly natural and unselfconscious, emotional and heartfelt without a trace of embarrassment. (If you hear envy in that description, I won't deny it.) He told us that he had recently turned fifty-five, and thirty of those years had been spent behind bars. A couple of weeks earlier, at a service that culminated with the worship leaders and volunteers praying individually with inmates who came forward to request it, I had seen – and heard – him weeping and praying in anguished sobs that told me vividly what I had already guessed from my conversations with him, that his overflowing joy had roots in a life of sorrow and disappointment that had nearly consumed him. I also felt echoes of his grief in myself as I recalled episodes of uncontrollable weeping not all that long ago, as my old life collapsed around me, occasioned by the catalyst of retirement, and I felt the birth-pangs of the new life I now enjoy. And I recalled my 'Buchenwald night' and caught a glimmer of what it was all about.

* * * * *

For I consider that the sufferings of this present time are not worth comparing with the glory that is to be revealed to us. For the creation waits with eager longing for the revealing of the sons of God. For the creation was subjected to futility, not willingly, but because of him who subjected it, in hope that the creation itself will be set free from its bondage to corruption and obtain the freedom of the glory of the children of God. For we know that the whole creation has been groaning together in the pains of childbirth until now. And not only the creation, but we ourselves, who have the firstfruits of the Spirit, groan inwardly as we wait eagerly for adoption as sons, the redemption of our bodies.

(Romans 8:18–23)

At the heart of the dialog between 'Wittenberg and Azusa Street' is 'the problem of the reliability of unmediated spiritual experience of any kind' and the related issue of 'Christian self-deception', often raised by critics of Pentecostalism.[32] On the one hand, the Church has a legitimate interest in restraining outbursts of direct 'spiritual' experience that are sometimes idiosyncratic, undisciplined, and indifferent or even hostile to Christian teachings based on Scripture and articulated through long centuries of Christian experience (called 'tradition'). But on the other hand, if the Church seeks to inhibit such excesses by choking off every emotional and 'enthusiastic' (in the modern sense of the term!) expression of inspiration by Christian believers, it risks cutting itself off from the springs of its own spiritual nourishment and renewal, resulting in the kind of spiritless institutional torpor that one so often finds in the once-mainline churches today. This problem has been with the Church since its beginnings and will no doubt continue till Jesus returns in glory. The ancient Church had its Montanists to deal with; the Reformation had to cope with spiritual zealots and Anabaptists of various stripes; the Great Awakening in colonial

America had to distinguish between genuine revival and bogus 'enthusiasm'; and Christians over the past century have struggled to distinguish the new outpouring of gifts of the Spirit among self-described Pentecostals as well as charismatic Christians within the historic churches from self-deceptive, and sometimes self-serving, emotional indulgences.

> The Spirit of the Lord GOD is upon me,
>   because the LORD has anointed me
> to bring good news to the poor;
>   he has sent me to bind up the brokenhearted,
> to proclaim liberty to the captives,
>   and the opening of the prison to those who are bound ...
>
> (Isaiah 61:1)

Simeon Zahl has put his finger on the crucial issue raised in all these controversies; he calls it 'the self-deception problem'.[33] How can the Church protect itself against illegitimate or even fraudulent claims of direct spiritual inspiration without closing itself off to the life-giving source of the Holy Spirit who is the Lord himself? Zahl shows how Luther's anthropological pessimism (in other words, his strong biblical doctrine of original sin) made him acutely aware of 'the proclivity ... in human beings toward egoistic self-deception'. To guard against such deception, Luther chose 'to reject all claims to unmediated experience outright'. Zahl's own solution to the self-deception problem is different and more open to direct experience of the Spirit. He proposes a principle of 'negative' experience (he always puts 'negative' in scare quotes), which he unfolds in a series of three propositions:

1 Experience of the Spirit is not *necessarily* limited to the instrumentality of the Word ... ;
2 'Negative' experience can be a sign of the presence or activity of the Holy Spirit in the life of an individual or community ... ;
3 This ['negative'] sign may be a *more reliable* indicator of such presence or activity of the Spirit [than the more 'positive' experiences reported by Pentecostals and charismatics].[34]

By 'negative' experience, he means that we need 'to look for the Spirit in day-to-day human experience, rather than exclusively in Word and sacrament, but to expect it most reliably in obstacles, difficulties, and the thwarting of ego, rather than foremost in experience of intimacy with God or convictions of clear divine guidance'. Zahl insists that this principle is not an innovation but rather articulates an insight that has long guided Christians but has been overlooked by the Pentecostal–charismatic movement. He is not saying that 'negative' experience should be viewed as the *only* sign of the Spirit's presence; rather it is the *most reliable* sign. The 'positive' is not excluded, it is just deemphasized.[35]

Zahl has identified an important key to solving the 'self-deception problem' by indicating how the Holy Spirit might truly speak to Christians today without raising the specter of 'enthusiasm'. That key is what he calls 'negative' experience. But the way in which he tries to relate 'negative' and 'positive' experience, and especially the way in which he relates both to Scripture, introduces a serious theological confusion, one that could open the way to just the kind of 'spiritual' excesses that the Reformers sought to head off. In conclusion I want to propose an alternative interpretation of 'negative' experience that will avoid those excesses and provide a clearer account of the experience of the Christian seeking to live today in the power of the Spirit.

At the root of the confusion is Zahl's attempt to play off the negative and positive aspects of Christian experience against one another as though they were alternatives that might be set in competition. He suggests that we see the Spirit *most reliably* in experience that confounds our expectations and thwarts our egos *rather than* primarily in positive experiences of divine inspiration and guidance. But the two are not in fact in competition; nor are they separable, as though we could classify particular experiences as one or the other and then 'prioritize' them. In classical Christian theological terms, the relation of positive and negative spiritual experience is the relation of God's *grace* and *judgment* in our lives. And these two are never alternatives, never in competition with one another, and it is not possible to prioritize them. They are two sides of the same coin, two faces of the one God who comes to us in gracious judgment and judging grace, moving us to respond in penitence and thanksgiving.

The other problem with Zahl's proposed solution is the role it sees for Holy Scripture. Concerning his three propositions, we need first of all to heartily affirm no. 2, while denying no. 1. (No. 3 can be set aside because of the confusion about comparing negative and positive experience already indicated.) To open the possibility of spiritual experience beyond the Bible is both to remove an essential safeguard and to misunderstand the role of the Bible in the Christian life. To suggest, as Zahl does, that 'the Bible is not the sole and absolute mediator of the Spirit'[36] is to abandon the *sola scriptura* of the Reformers and to miss its point at the same time. Saying that the Bible is the only mediator of the Holy Spirit is not to say that the Spirit speaks only *in* the Bible, as though it contained the collected works of the Holy Spirit. That way lies the deadliest kind of biblical literalism. The Bible, rather, is the criterion of spiritual experience, its touchstone, its litmus test. Not every utterance of the Spirit is to be found *in* the Bible, but every true utterance of the Spirit must be *in conformity with* the Bible. That's what the Bible is 'for': discerning the spirits, distinguishing truth from falsehood, showing us the difference between God's promises and Satan's lies. Scripture is, in Calvin's felicitous metaphor, the 'spectacles' we need to put on in order to correct the astigmatism of our sinful nature so we can see the world as it really is, the 'theater of God's glory'.

In his last university course before he retired from teaching, Karl Barth elected to teach the introductory course in theology. *Evangelical Theology: An Introduction* is the fruit of that endeavor, a kind of 'last lecture' by a revered theological teacher in which he sums up the task of the theologian. It is most fitting that a chapter on 'Experience in theology' be contained in a book on the practice of Christian theology, for, as Barth reminds us, before all else, theology is a *praxis*, something we *do* as theologians. 'It is clear,' Barth writes, 'that evangelical theology itself can only be pneumatic, spiritual theology.'[37] As such, theology always takes place *in* the Spirit, and can therefore never begin somewhere 'outside' the Spirit. This peculiar location of the discipline is what drives so many secular scholars (some of them theologians) to despair. Theology always seems to be begging the question, chasing its own tail, running in a vicious circle. As Barth reminds us, however, the circle is necessary, and it's not vicious but 'virtuous'. 'Theology can only *do* its work,' Barth writes. 'It cannot, however, seek to secure its operation.'[38] How, after all, could a practice undertaken in the Spirit ever manage to secure its operation – or want to? For 'the wind [*pneuma, spiritus*] blows where it wishes, and you hear its sound, but you do not know where it comes from or where it goes,' Jesus said to Nicodemus. 'So it is with everyone who is born of the Spirit' (John 3:8). And Nicodemus was a 'teacher of Israel' (v. 10), a Pharisee, a theologian. The whole discussion between them arose because Jesus had told him he must be born again, 'born of water and the Spirit' (v. 5). That's what has to happen if one is to become a theologian. And, late in life, that's what finally happened to me.

> O God, from my youth you have taught me,
>   and I still proclaim your wondrous deeds.
> So even to old age and gray hairs,
>   O God, do not forsake me,
> until I proclaim your might to another generation,
>   your power to all those to come.
>
>   (Psalm 71:17–18)

Notes

1 This essay is dedicated to the memory of Charles W. Colson (1931–2012), my mentor whom I never met, whose work made possible the ministry in which I now share. 'Remember those who are in prison, as though in prison with them … ' (Heb. 13:3).

2 I. Kant, *The Critique of Pure Reason*, trans. P. Guyer and A. Wood, Cambridge: Cambridge University Press, 1998, B xxx.

3 C. Wesley, 'O for a Thousand Tongues to Sing', *Hymns and Sacred Poems*, 1740.

4 C. Wesley, 'And Can It Be', *Psalms and Hymns*, 1738.

5 F.D.E. Schleiermacher, *On Religion: Speeches to Its Cultured Despisers*, trans. R. Crouter, New York: Cambridge University Press, 1988, p. 102.

6 F.D.E. Schleiermacher, *The Christian Faith*, trans. H.R. Mackintosh and J.S. Stewart, New York: Harper & Row, 1963, 1: 5.

7 Schleiermacher, *The Christian Faith* §15, 1:76.

8 K. Barth, *The Word of God and the Word of Man*, trans. D. Horton, New York: Harper & Row, 1928, p. 196.

9 K. Barth, *Church Dogmatics I/1*, Edinburgh: T&T Clark, 1975, p. 187.

10 O. Chambers, *My Utmost for His Highest*, Uhrichsville, OH: Barbour Publishing, 1935, reading for May 24.

11 G.A. Lindbeck, *The Nature of Doctrine: Religion and Theology in a Postliberal Age*, Philadelphia, PA: The Westminster Press, 1984, p. 16.
12 Lindbeck, *The Nature of Doctrine*, pp. 33–34.
13 Lindbeck, *The Nature of Doctrine*, p. 33.
14 This description of Edwards is taken from the title of the compelling study of his theology by Robert W. Jenson, *America's Theologian: A Recommendation of Jonathan Edwards*, New York: Oxford University Press, 1988.
15 Jenson, *America's Theologian*, p. 77.
16 W.J. Gaither and G. Gaither, 'Joy Comes in the Morning', 1974.
17 *The Works of Jonathan Edwards*, vol. 2: *Religious Affections*, ed. J.E. Smith, New Haven, CT: Yale University Press, 1959, p. 95. Hereafter cited as *WJE*, followed by volume and page numbers.
18 *WJE* 2, p. 121.
19 Jenson, *America's Theologian*, pp. 22, 23.
20 Jenson, *America's Theologian*, p. 65. My account of Edwards in this paragraph is dependent on Jenson's much fuller exposition in Ch. 6 of his book.
21 *WJE* 17, p. 413. Emphasis is from Jenson's citation of this passage in *America's Theologian*, p. 66.
22 *WJE* 18, p. 458.
23 *WJE* 18, p. 457.
24 *WJE* 18, p. 459. The words appearing here in italics are written in all capitals in Edwards's manuscript.
25 William Meredith, 'A Major Work', *The Open Sea and Other Poems*, New York, N.Y.: Alfred A. Knopf, 1958, p. 56.
26 *WJE* 17, pp. 413–14.
27 R. Lowry, 'Nothing But the Blood', in *Gospel Music*, by M. Doane and R. Lowry, New York, NY: Biglow & Main, 1876. Available online at http://hymntime.com/tch/htm/n/b/t/nbtblood.htm.
28 'Thomas Müntzer', in *Encyclopædia Britannica Online*: www.britannica.com/EBchecked/topic/397713/Thomas-Muntzer, accessed June 5, 2012.
29 S. Zahl, *Pneumatology and Theology of the Cross in the Preaching of Christoph Friedrich Blumhardt: The Holy Spirit between Wittenberg and Azusa Street*, New York: T&T Clark, 2010.
30 Zahl, *Pneumatology and Theology of the Cross*, pp. 1–2.
31 J.K.A. Smith, *Thinking in Tongues: Pentecostal Contributions to Christian Philosophy*, Grand Rapids, MI: Wm. B. Eerdmans Publishing Company, 2010. Smith starts with an Introduction having another arresting title: 'What Hath Athens to Do with Azusa Street?' and contains extensive further references to other Pentecostal thinkers eager for academic dialog with the broader Christian tradition.
32 Zahl, *Pneumatology and Theology of the Cross*, p. 6.
33 Zahl, *Pneumatology and Theology of the Cross*, p. 184.
34 Zahl, *Pneumatology and Theology of the Cross*, pp. 185–86 (Zahl's emphasis).
35 Zahl, *Pneumatology and Theology of the Cross*, p. 186.
36 Zahl, *Pneumatology and Theology of the Cross*, p. 193.
37 K. Barth, *Evangelical Theology: An Introduction*, trans. G. Foley, Garden City, NY: Doubleday, 1963, p. 49.
38 Barth, *Evangelical Theology*, p. 44.

22
FEMINIST THEOLOGIES

Jenny Daggers

Introduction: Locating feminist theologies

The core commitment of feminist theologies is to 'the struggle for justice'. Feminist theologies are therefore always political practices which attend to women's experiences of oppression and liberation, and seek to do gender justice in the world, the Church and theology. While the first concern is with gender justice, feminist theologies act in solidarity with other forms of this struggle for justice across such divisions as 'race', class, sexuality or (dis)ability. These practical struggles rest on an analysis of power relations in theology, Church, and society; their aim is to resist abuses of power that result in injustice, and to construct just human relations. Writings by academic feminist theologians are connected with women's movements that include women who are active both within their churches and in broader justice struggles outside church contexts.

As the Chinese American theologian Kwok Pui-lan makes clear, feminist theology has always been 'intercultural theology'.[1] In addition to this chapter, feminist theologies will also appear in the following three chapters on black theologies, liberation theologies, and postcolonial theologies, as feminist theologies emerge in diverse global contexts. From the late 1960s, feminist theologies arose simultaneously as Christian responses to the women's liberation movement in the North American and (Western) European world, and through the involvement of Latin American, African and Asian women alongside men in organizations such as the World Council of Churches (WCC) and the Ecumenical Association of Third World Theologians (EATWOT). North American feminist theologians were the first to hold academic tenured positions, and thus the first to develop feminist theologies in a systematic form. Since the collapse of the Communist 'Second World', from the 1990s, feminist theologies have also grown within East European countries, as churches re-establish themselves as a recognized presence within society after decades of repression.

The chapter title of 'feminist *theologies*', in the plural, reflects this diversity of theologies arising in different contexts. Feminist *theology*, in the singular, can also be seen as both a global network and a distinct stream of theological thought, which links women activists and theologians from diverse local situations. On the one hand, a common intercultural feminist theology emerges through the exchanges made possible by this global network; on the other, tensions and different priorities emerge, particularly between the concerns of white Western feminist theologies of European heritage and feminist theologies emerging in the postcolonial world. Postcolonial analysis reveals the power differential between white feminist theologians of 'colonizer' heritage and feminist theologians of colour, whose forebears were among the 'colonized'. The continuing privileges of the Western 'First World' of the global north, over against the 'Third World' of the global south, underpin this power differential. This discussion leads towards the ground covered in the later chapter on postcolonial theologies, so the point will not be pressed further here, but it is important to keep in mind this alternative colonizer or colonized heritage of all the feminist theologies you will encounter in this chapter. It is also important to recognize that feminist theology is an argumentative community in its own right: while feminist theologies reflect their particular contexts there is also diversity and difference among feminist theologians who share the same context.

Western Christian feminist theologies arose from a devastating critique of Christianity, which named it as a 'patriarchal' religion that is incapable of correction. Mary Daly's *Beyond God the Father* is a seminal text in this respect, while the British feminist theologian Daphne Hampson, in *Theology and Feminism*, made similar criticisms.[2] The literal meaning of 'patriarchy' is control by the fathers. Daly claims that Christianity is patriarchal through and through; you cannot imagine Christianity without this patriarchal control. For example, when the feminist biblical scholar, Phyllis Trible, recommended 'depatriarchalizing the bible' (that is removing patriarchal elements from the text), Daly responded that it would be interesting to reflect on the length of the remaining text: there might be enough to make an interesting pamphlet![3]

Some Western feminist theologians followed Daly in leaving Christianity behind to take up a postChristian position. The 1979 collection of essays, *Womanspirit Rising*, shows the presence of an interreligious conversation between Christian feminist theologians and those with postChristian 'Womanspirit' (or Goddess), and Jewish commitments.[4] Whereas Jewish and Christian feminist theologies have continued to develop alongside (see, for example, Janet Martin Soskice and Diana Lipton (eds) *Feminism and Theology*),[5] a new postChristian Womanspirit tradition has reconstructed feminist religion outside the Christian tradition. However, the concern of this chapter is specifically with the major tendency within feminist theology: Christian feminist theologies that stay with Christian community and theology, while challenging longstanding patriarchal control.

One final introductory point is to note that feminist theologies attend to 'the body' and human 'embodiment'. They advocate embodied thinking, and are critical of theologies that fail to take human bodies into account. This concern is present in feminist theologies from the global south, in their concern for the conditions of poverty and sexual violence that bear on the bodily existence of poor women, and in the different concerns with women's bodies in Western consumer culture. There is an overlap between some feminist theologies and 'queer' theologies that reflect on lesbian, gay, bisexual, transsexual, and transgender experience, and so attend to the intertwining of sexuality and gender issues.

Gender injustice in the world

The primary concern with injustice in the world, the Church, and theology includes attention to how injustices within the Christian Church and theology influence political relations within the wider world, by shoring up unjust practices and regimes, and to how just practice in church and theology might change this negative influence. Feminist theology is therefore concerned with what Mike Higton has called 'a habitable settlement', not only for Christians within the Church, but also for oppressed peoples of the wider world. Feminist theology thus shares with liberation theology a concern for the poor, and an insistence on the 'option for the poor' (see chapter 24). Feminist theology genders the critique made by liberation theology: women are the poorest of the poor, suffering patriarchal domination and sexual abuse in addition to the social, economic, and political injustices they share with men of the same context. Feminist theologies thus give attention to ongoing political analyses of ever changing global patterns which create ever changing forms of exclusion and injustice.[6]

In 1979, the Indonesian feminist theologian Marianne Katoppo wrote as follows about the exploitation of Asian women through prostitution:

> Prostitution is one of the burning issues in Asia today; there is a very real link between tourism and prostitution. It is also linked to the presence of foreign military bases and transnational companies. ...
>
> The Church does not exhibit an attitude of love and acceptance to the prostitutes. More often it is one of judgment and self-righteousness. ...
>
> An SCM report has estimated that 60% of the women in some areas of Indonesia are prostitutes. Generally, they are driven by economic necessity. Living in conditions of extreme poverty, they are ruthlessly exploited. This is a prime example of the way women tend to bear the burden of double exploitation because of their sex in an underdeveloped exploited country.
>
> In the Philippines, says the *Far Eastern Economic Review*, sex provides a major incentive to the traveller. ... a first-class (*sic*) hotel now offers a room package which includes a female companion. ...
>
> It should be noted that the women included in the package deals normally get only 15–20% of the fee paid by the clients. Perhaps there are no sufficient indicators to measure the moral degradation that prostitution brings with it. But it is clear that a country that considers tourism as a pillar of its economic development does so at the expense of human dignity, and especially at the cost of the exploitation of its women.[7]

One significant factor is the rise in global migration bringing people from Latin America, Africa, and Asia into the cities, towns and villages of the Western world. New forms of injustice are created as increasing numbers of illegal migrants perform menial tasks without statutory protection of minimum standards in pay and working conditions. New forms of indentured labour and trafficking of women for forced prostitution reinstitute practices that once flourished in Western countries, but had become illegal through progressive social policies.

Immigration has also created 'diasporic' communities of peoples who have roots in countries in the global south, but who belong – with or without legal status – in countries of the Western world. Latina feminist theologians in the US, whose families originate in Mexico or other Latin American countries, and Latin American feminist theologians have recently developed an ongoing intercultural exchange. Introducing their first book, a collection of essays based on conference papers, Virginia Vargas Valente points to these women's experiences as providing a source for critical interpretation. The practice of feminist theology is '"an alternative ethico-political project" ... which is not hegemonic or Western, but emerges from the fringes and from the frontiers'. The practice of feminist theology 'allows us to "walk toward a new world of justice", by engendering new forms of social coexistence'.[8] Jeanette Rodríguez sums up her essay in words that give a good example of the intercultural tensions between the experiences of diasporic and Latin American Latina women. It is clear that, as a Latina woman, she shows solidarity with Latino men, as well as women:

> As theologians, we promote choices for life that bring forward communities that have been marginalized, voiceless, and not allowed to the table. I do not pretend to speak as an expert in political matters, but as a theologian, I believe that our actions can be guided by the Spirit, who wants us to live in light more than darkness. ...
>
> [A]ll of us yearn for peace and justice in the world. Many of us have seen, with our own eyes, the cost of human greed and social conflict. These experiences have led us to work for the basic right of every person to a life of dignity. Building bridges [between diasporic and Latin American Latina women] has been made difficult by the cultural baggage we carry and the manner in which the dominant culture has structured our roles.
>
> This bridge work is necessary because countless communities of our brothers and sisters across the globe are being assaulted. Our role is to remember our own journeys as well as build bridges of solidarity to those communities whose members are tortured, marginalized, and whose sons and daughters are at grave risk. Our collective wisdom will build bridges to those communities in which mutilated cadavers appear in cemeteries, where those who struggle for justice and peace are assassinated. ...
>
> Intercultural dialogue and activity create communities of reciprocal care and shared responsibilities. A hallmark of Latino communities then becomes a rich pattern of life in the world we now inhabit, where every person matters and each person's welfare and dignity is respected and supported.[9]

Outside the Western world, new forms of injustice accompany the appropriation of land occupied by indigenous peoples for the exploitation of natural resources by advanced capitalist enterprises. Ecofeminist theology, which joins the wider ecological movement in working for a sustainable use of planetary resources, is partly informed by the sustainable good practice of displaced indigenous ways of life; in addition it seeks justice for communities in danger of being displaced, and it pays particular attention to the plight of indigenous women. Ecofeminist theology names the link between exploitation of women and exploitation of the earth, then sets out to address both problems. While Rosemary Ruether has written extensively on ecofeminism,[10] the following extract concerns practical ecological action taken by the African Independent Churches in Zimbabwe, during the 1990s, in which women play a major role:

> The traditional deep affinity for the earth in Africa, based on an essentially religious understanding of the universe, is vividly illustrated by the African Independent Churches' (AICs) programme of tree planting in Zimbabwe. ... [The AICs] are proclaiming a widening message of salvation which encompasses all of creation and they are dancing out a new rhythm in their services of worship which, in the footwork, spells hope for the ravaged earth. They have not worked out a new ethic on paper but they are 'clothing the earth' (*kufukidza nyika*) with new trees to cover its human-induced nakedness. In so doing they have introduced a new ministry of compassion; they live an earthkeeper's ethic. In declaring the so-called 'war of the trees' an ecumenical platform was created in order to unite the churches in a green army and to launch environmental reform in terms of creation's liberation. In the new struggle, ecclesiastical structures are changing, new perceptions of ecological responsibility are emerging and innovative liturgical procedures to integrate the environmental ethic with the heart beat of church praxis are being introduced. ...
>
> The AICs express a predominantly peasant ecumenism which rests on a common commitment to the healing of the earth. Popularly, they have been seen as healing, liberative institutions, with the history of prophetic healers and their support of the struggle for liberation (*chimurenga*). Now the focus has shifted to their role in the healing of suffering creation. Prophets are turning their healing colonies into 'environmental hospitals' in which the patient is the denuded earth, the 'dispensary' is the nursery where the correct medicine is being prepared, and the community is the healing agent.[11]

Feminist theology, like liberation theology, directs Christian attention to these injustices. With liberation theology, it insists that Christian virtue must be concerned with addressing these structural injustices, as well as with individual ethics. It is imperative that Christian theologians and communities see the struggle for justice as their responsibility. Like liberation theology, feminist theology takes injustice in the world as a starting point for theology: injustice sets an agenda that theology must address.

Gender injustice in Christianity and Christian theology

This section of the chapter turns to the Christian Church and theology. I will first clarify feminist critique in more detail, before investigating strategies for reconstructing the practices of Church and theology in order to promote gender justice: feminist theology seeks to construct a *habitable* settlement for women within the

Church, and it demands that gender justice is also done when an *intellectual* settle-ment is sought within theology. One important difference between feminist theology and liberation theology is that gender injustice is interwoven into the received tra-ditions of the Christian Church and theology. Feminist theology is therefore dealing at the same time with gender injustice outside and inside Christian traditions. It is important here to anticipate discussion of postcolonial theology in chapter 25, by making the point that white feminist theologians of colonizer heritage are likely to stand in a different relation to received tradition than feminist theologians whose formation is within churches created by the modern missionary movement, in the context of European colonialism. While both groups share similar issues concerning male domination of Christian churches and contemporary theology, Western fem-inist theologians may have a deeper investment in challenging gender injustice as it is enshrined in the long history of the Western Christian church and its theology. In contrast, Kwok states that Third World women have little time for academic 'mental gymnastics', given the plight of the Asian poor.[12] There is thus a tension to be found in feminist theology over how much attention to give to the received tra-dition, when an intellectual settlement is sought. Some Western feminist theologians are in complete agreement with the priorities emerging in the postcolonial world, so that their constructive work breaks new ground, making only a minimum engage-ment with previous tradition; others recover neglected resources from the Christian tradition, and forge new ways of approaching problematic texts and traditions. Examples given below will clarify this tension.

Within the context of Western debates, Christian feminist theologians agree with postChristian critics who claim that Christianity is both patriarchal and androcentric (that is, male-centred). Yet Christian feminist theologians must somehow negotiate a problem that postChristians solve by leaving Christianity: given that Christianity and Christian theology are so imbued with patriarchal mechanisms of exclusion and control, what strategies can feminist theologians adopt to negotiate a Christian Church and tradition that are not yet transformed in response to feminist critique? How do Christian women in church and theologians in academy or seminary conduct them-selves so that they are not subject to the patriarchal authority enshrined in text, church practice and theological tradition?

Christian feminist theologies use resources belonging to the Christian tradition itself to critique and reconstruct Christianity, as well as borrowing tools for critical thinking and reconstruction from wider cultural contexts. Four key areas of feminist critique in feminist theological practices of critique and reconstruction stand out: the maleness of Jesus and of the Trinitarian God; the patriarchal biblical text; the exclusion of women in Church and from theology; the impact of metaphysical dualisms that identify male with mind and spirit and female with body and the earth, and then privilege male over female. A range of reconstructive strategies shape alternative feminist theological practices to the patriarchal and androcentric forms made visible by feminist critique.

This list sets the agenda for feminist Christian theology. If the practice of Christian theology is to be habitable by women as well as men, these issues need to be addressed. One point to note is that it is over thirty years since powerful feminist theological critique was first articulated in its twentieth-century form. During that period there have been considerable changes in the practices of the Church and theology. However, it is important to keep in view that these changes are partial and incomplete. There is no simple one-directional dynamic at work, ensuring that feminist criticism will one day be no longer necessary, as the Church and theology will have been irrevocably changed to eradicate all traces of patriarchal control and androcentrism. Rather, a feminist hermeneutic of suspicion is a continuing necessity to monitor the ongoing practices of the Church and theology. The four areas of critique and reconstruction are now considered in some detail:

The maleness of Jesus and of the Trinitarian God

Mary Daly's critique was couched in terms that ensured it would be noticed. Daly took an idea from Elizabeth Cady Stanton, editor of a nineteenth century text, *The Woman's Bible*, that the myth of the Fall is a 'myth of feminine evil', which provides the foundation of Christianity.[13] She writes 'women as a caste are "Eve" and are punished by a cohesive set of laws, customs and social arrangements that enforce an all-pervasive double standard'.[14] For Daly, the notion that salvation comes only through the male while women are identified with Eve and evil is 'christolatrous'; she speaks of the original sin of sexism, whereby women are caste as 'primordial scapegoats'.[15] Clearly this critique mounts a powerful challenge to traditional Christologies, which have ignored the maleness of Christ and its implications for women and men. Daly's critique goes further in claiming that 'if God is male, then male is God': the elevation of maleness in Trinitarian theology uplifts all men and reduces the status of all women. Her criticism drew attention to the assumed maleness of Father and Son and its implications for the patriarchal ordering of human relations.

Feminist Christologies seek strategies for addressing problems arising from the maleness of Jesus, whereas some theologians explore the Trinitarian implications of these strategies, in addition.

In her seminal text of feminist theology, *Sexism and God-Talk*, Rosemary Ruether addresses the question 'Can a Male Saviour Save Women?' by arguing that Christ as liberator saves women, as well as the poor, from oppression: his maleness is but one aspect of his particularity. As she writes elsewhere:

> Turning to the historical Jesus, as the particular and paradigmatic expression of God's Logos–Sophia for the Christian Church, what is necessary is not a further evacuation of his particularity. Rather, we need a fuller ability to accept his particularity, without confusing one aspect of that particularity, his maleness, with the essence of Christ as God's Word incarnate. What we find in most Christology is an effort to dissolve most aspects of Jesus' particularity … in order to make him the symbol of universal humanity; yet an insistence that the historical particularity of his maleness is essential to his ongoing representation. How then should we understand the relationship of Jesus as a historical individual in all his particularity, not only as a male, but as a first-century messianic Galilean Jew, and yet also make these particularities no longer limits on his representation as the embodiment of God's universal new Word?

We should do that ... by emphasizing his message as expressed in his ministry. This message was the revolutionary word of good news to the poor. Good news to the poor means that favour with God and hope of redemption is not based on social status in the hierarchies of unjust society, but is a free grace available to all who respond to it by repenting of their hardness of heart and being open to each other as brothers and sisters. In this perspective we see the emphasis on Jesus' maleness as essential to his ongoing representation ... is contradictory to the essence of his message as good news to the marginalized *qua* women.[16]

While this first strategy downplays the significance of the maleness of Christ, a second approach explores female representations of Christ in the Christa figure, or reads Mary as a liberative figure for women. As Julie Clague comments, 'The artistic world had to wait for the twentieth century before it could give birth to the (literally absurd) visual suggestion that Jesus Christ can be represented as female'.[17] The figure is controversial both outside and within feminist theology. Similar responses followed the display of Christa figures in two different Anglican cathedrals: Edwina Sandys's *Christa* in the Cathedral of St John the Divine in New York, in 1984, and Margaret Argyle's *Bosnian Christa* in an ecumenical liturgy during the World Council of Churches Decade for Churches in Solidarity with Women (1988–98), at the Cathedral in Manchester, UK, in 1993.

A New York critic considered the *Christa* to be 'historically and theologically reprehensible' in its total change to the Christ symbol, whereas charges of blasphemy followed the Manchester service. On the other hand one supporter argued that Sandys's sculpture drew attention to the fact that

> the incarnation of the second person of the Trinity involved the taking on of humanity, of all 'flesh,' male and female. By the same token, the passion, the suffering of Christ, is shared symbolically by all members of the body of Christ, the church.[18]

Feminist opinion is equally divided, with opponents arguing that the *Christa*, with its pornographic resonance, legitimizes the violent abuse of women. On the other hand, women who have suffered abuse have testified that, for them, the *Christa* is a healing resurrection figure. While it stimulates theological imagination, the *Christa* thus remains an ambiguous figure.

Some feminist theologies have reconstructed Mariology to support the liberation of women, so foregrounding a powerful liberative feminine figure alongside the liberating male Christ. The following passage produced by Asian women gathered at a Singapore conference in 1987 is one example:

> The task of feminist Mariology is twofold:
> (1) We must name, and liberate ourselves from, the destructive effects of 2,000 years of male interpretation of Mary.
> (2) We must return to the Scriptures as women within our own cultural contexts, to rediscover the Mary who is liberated and liberator. ...

With the singer of the Magnificat as his mother, it should not surprise us that Jesus' first words in Luke's account of his public ministry are also a mandate for radical change. Predictably, however, the Church has forgotten that Mary is the first to announce this change. ... She is the woman who survives and returns from exile. ... She is present in support of Jesus' ministry, which she inspires and initiates, from its beginning to its end. Jesus' words in Luke 11.27–28, 'Rather, happy are they that hear the word of God and obey it', therefore mean that Jesus is rejecting the claims of his mother and brothers, but that he is acknowledging that it was from his mother, in his family, that he himself learned to hear and obey the word of God. ...

Each of us, within our own culture, has found different strengths in the process of reclaiming and redefining Mary. We can look at Mary the mother and see her womb as a place of the action of the Holy Spirit – a place of struggle and suffering which brings new life. The struggle of mothers in the Asia/Pacific context, who struggle with and for their children, to give birth to a new and just reality. Mary is the mother of suffering, of those who suffer.[19]

A third strategy returns to the core commitment of feminist theology by emphasizing women's communal struggle for justice, rather than individual liberative figures, as embodying the saving action of Christ. From Daly's advocacy of 'a corporate redemptive action' in *Beyond God the Father*, to Carter Heywood's emphasis on co-creative power in relation, Rita Nakashima Brock's notion of a Christa/community, to Sharon Welch's 'communities of resistance and solidarity', the communal struggle for justice is understood as itself redemptive.[20] This focus is found also in womanist theologies, such as Dolores Williams's *Sisters in the Wilderness*, and in writings from postcolonial contexts, such as Musimbi Kanyoro's 'Engendered Communal Theology'.[21] Widely held feminist values of mutual relations over against hierarchy are embedded in notions of women's redemptive communities. Feminist theology is a practice of women's communities, which provide the context for individual feminist theologies and from which they are written.

Where the first three reconstructive strategies address Christology, the remaining two place revised Christology within a Trinitarian context. Implicit assumptions that the biblical language of God as Father, Son and Spirit means that God *is* male and *is not* female, in the same sense that (the majority of) human beings are *either* male *or* female, are made visible and brought into question. The North American theologian, Sallie McFague, advocates the use of new metaphors of God, to open up understandings beyond an unexamined maleness of God that has become attached to traditional formulations. In a move that connects with ecofeminist concerns, McFague follows the feminist philosopher, Grace Jantzen, in using the metaphor of the world as the body of God, to which God is present as mother, lover, and friend: mothering is associated with the pursuit of justice; loving with the work of healing; and friendship with inclusive table-fellowship. The emphasis is on the reflection of these divine qualities in human practices:

The intention of these remarks on the ethic of God the mother-creator as justice is ... to sketch the change of attitude, the conversion of consciousness, that could come about were we to begin to live inside the model and allow it to become a lens through which we looked out on the world. We would no longer see a world we named and ruled or, like the artist God, made: mothers or fathers to the world do not rule or fashion it. Our positive role in creation ... as preservers. ... is a very high calling, our peculiar calling as human beings, the calling implied in the model of God as mother. ...

There are several characteristics of healing that make it an obvious image for the work of God as lover as well as the work of the followers of this God. First, ... the model of healing undercuts the body/spirit split in traditional views of redemption. Classical treatments of redemption, in spite of affirming the resurrection of the body, tend to separate the whole person into two parts – primarily spirit, incidentally body – and of course the body of the world ... receives no attention. The healing model, however, is based in the physical. ...

Second, the healing model [is appropriate] for imaging salvation in an ecological, evolutionary context. ... A third feature of the healing model which recommends it as a way to understand salvation is its dual emphasis on resistance and identification: resistance to disease, disorder, and chaos ... and identification with the sufferers in their pain. ...

Our model of the church as a community of friends united by a common vision of fulfilment for all can also be seen as the product of an inclusive sensibility. Beginning with the image of a shared meal open to outsiders, it expands to include the entire cosmos in its circle of care. ... Thus when we speak of the kind of care for the world that our model suggests, we extend the model ... and suggest that to befriend the world is to be its companion – its advocate and its partner. ... What we are suggesting, therefore, is that the notion of companion of the world, modeled on God as the sustaining friend of the world, comprises being with the world in two ways: as an advocate fighting for just treatment for the world's many forms of life, and as a partner identifying with all the others.[22]

A different approach is taken by a number of feminist theologians who develop the biblical figure of wisdom, Sophia, that is characterized as female, and has been linked in traditional scholarship with the Trinitarian persons of Christ and the Spirit. A reference to Logos–Sophia appears in the excerpt from Ruether given above. Feminist development of Sophia includes a significant contribution by Elisabeth Schüssler Fiorenza in her *Jesus: Miriam's Child, Sophia's Prophet*, while the Korean North American theologian, Grace Ji-Sun Kim in her *Grace of Sophia* demonstrates that the figure is not restricted to North American writings.[23] Liturgical use of Sophia is at the centre of a North American backlash against feminist theology that centred on a 1993 conference, 'Reimagining the Divine', organized under the auspices of the World Council of Churches: the following controversy demonstrates continuing resistance to 'reimagining' the Trinitarian God in the feminine, over against the assumed maleness of the classical tradition.

The following extract from Elizabeth Johnson's *She Who Is* shows a development of Sophia that reconstructs Trinitarian theology to allow the three persons to be thought of in feminine terms:

It is not essential for the truth of God's triune mystery to speak always in the metaphors of father, son and spirit, although virtually exclusive use of these names over the centuries in liturgy, catechesis, and theology has caused this to be forgotten. At this point in the living tradition I believe that we need a strong dose of explicitly female imagery to break the unconscious sway that male trinitarian imagery holds over the imaginations of even the most sophisticated thinkers. ...

God is God as Spirit-Sophia, the mobile, pure, people-loving Spirit who pervades every wretched corner. ... Sophia-God dwells in the world at its center and at its edges, an active vitality crying out in labour, birthing the new creation. ...

God is God again as Jesus Christ, Sophia's child and prophet, and yes, Sophia herself personally pitching her tent in the flesh of humanity to teach the paths of justice. ... Sophia-God is irreversibly connected with the joy and anguish of human history, in the flesh; in the power of Spirit-Sophia, Jesus now takes on a new communal identity as the risen Christ, the body of all those women and men who share in the transformation of the world through compassionate, delighting, and suffering love. ...

God is God again as unimaginable abyss of livingness, Holy Wisdom unknown and unknowable. She is the matrix of all that exists, mother and fashioner of all things, who herself dwells in light inaccessible. ... Holy Wisdom is a hidden God, [an] absolute holy mystery ... of love, bent on the world's healing and liberation through all of history's reversals and defeats.[24]

The Argentinian feminist and sexual theologian, Marcella Althaus-Reid takes a step further, in criticizing the heterosexual assumption that remains implicit in classical theology, and remains unchallenged in some feminist theologies. While Johnson's strategy provides a necessary counterbalance to an assumed maleness of God, it can be seen to reinscribe gender as a simple binary category of male over against female, in an assumed heterosexual relation. For Althaus-Reid, reimagining God in feminine terms does not go far enough; she brings 'queer' theology to bear, so that God can be imagined in terms that go beyond the heterosexual norm:

Theology has conceived God in history as a relationship (a community, for instance) expressed in the Trinitarian metaphor. That relationship has been politicised, culturalised and made a centre of gender reflections in Feminist Theologies.

However, more reflection is needed to sexualise the Trinity, in order to understand our kenotic existence not only as a sexual one, but as a dissident one. The task of Queer Theology is precisely to deepen this reflection on the sexual relationship manifested in the Trinity and to consider how God in the Trinity may come out in a relationship outside heterosexualism. The queering of the Trinity is simply the following: How might the Trinity lead us into the kenosis of sexual practices, within justice but outside the law? ... [W]e may ask, for instance ... How to complete the Queer kenosis of the divine, which is so close to the heart of the Other theologian, that is, the ultimate coming out or the complete, unabridged confession of God? ...

What is at stake [in kenosis] is not just God devolving itself in Christ but in the Trinity, and in the Trinity understood as an orgy, that is, as a festival of the encounter of the intemperate in two key elements. The first is the theological presentation of God as an immoderate, polyamorous God, whose self is composed in relation to multiple embraces and sexual indefinitions beyond oneness, and beyond dual models of loving relationships. The second is a commitment of an omnisexual kenosis to destabilise sexual constructions of heterosexual readings of heterosexuality itself, bisexuality, gay and lesbian sexual identities and transvestite identities.[25]

The patriarchal biblical text

Feminist biblical scholars have highlighted the patriarchal and androcentric nature of the biblical text and its detrimental effect on women readers in the context of the Christian Church and theology. Two figures stand out within a broad scholarly field. The Old Testament scholar, Phyllis Trible, laid bare the 'texts of terror' in the Hebrew Bible that recount the subjugation, use, and murderous abuse of women.[26] For Trible, the Bible is in need of 'depatriarchalization'. In contrast, the New Testament scholar, Elisabeth Schüssler Fiorenza, holds that the Bible is patriarchal through and through; it is so dangerous to women that it should carry a health warning.

Trible's strategy is to recover neglected biblical traditions that challenge patriarchy, and to reinterpret passages in new ways. This approach suggests that it is possible to remove a patriarchal layer – to 'depatriarchalize' – to reveal beneath it a usable biblical text. Trible recovers neglected feminine imagery for God, and reinterprets texts that have been key to the subjugation of women, such as the creation account in Genesis 2–3, where she discovers God and woman as helper, and woman as man's equal: 'Speaking with clarity and authority, the first woman is theologian, ethicist, hermeneut and rabbi'.[27] She also tells the stories of abused women *in memoriam*, so that patriarchal damage is acknowledged.

In contrast, for Fiorenza, women need a 'feminist hermeneutics of suspicion' to ensure damaging texts that insist on male headship and women's subjugation are identified and resisted. Her feminist hermeneutics of suspicion is a strategy that is used beyond the interpretation of biblical texts, as a method of engaging with the wider received tradition and its theological texts. The story of women in the early Church can be read in the light of wider available evidence of a 'discipleship of equals', which can be used to make good the 'gaps' in the patriarchal text. She argues that the task of academic biblical studies is to evaluate biblical texts and their function in contemporary sociopolitical and religious communities. This is a dialogical, practical and emancipatory model, which is shared with liberation theology, but distinctive in feminist hermeneutics of suspicion being brought to the text.

Fiorenza connects her feminist biblical criticism with the broader range of theologies that critique injustice through her concept of kyriarchy, which operates along the axes of race, class, heterosexual culture and religion. In her recent book,

Democratizing Biblical Studies, Fiorenza engages with emancipatory strands in contemporary biblical studies, to refine and rename categories she has used in previous
work, to better align her approach with other forms of biblical scholarship that
contend kyriarchal power, including postcolonial biblical studies, while maintaining
a distinctive feminist voice. In previous works, *Bread Not Stone*, then *Rhetoric and Ethic*,
Fiorenza names four paradigms as: (1) the doctrinal–fundamentalist, (2) the scientific–
historical, (3) the hermeneutic–(post)modern, and (4) the rhetorical–emancipatory. In
Democratizing, these paradigms are once again redescribed and renamed as: (1) the
religious–the*logical-scriptural paradigm, (2) the critical–scientific–modern paradigm,
(3) the cultural–hermeneutic–postmodern paradigm, and (4) the emancipatory–radical –
democratic paradigm. ('The*logical' draws attention to the assumed maleness of the
term theology, which Womanspirit feminist the*alogians have countered by coining
the term *thealogy*.) The following passage spells out the commitments embodied
in the practice of biblical studies in accordance with her fourth paradigm:

> Studying the genealogy of biblical studies from the perspective of emanci-
> patory movements and the public square helps one to realize that scriptural
> meaning-making has been practised, for the most part, not only by elite
> Western-educated clergymen, but also for the benefit of Western cultural
> and capitalist interests. A Western doctrinal or scientific approach declares
> its own culturally particular readings as universal divine revelation or scientific
> data that may not be questioned. ...
>
> The form of biblical interpretation most closely associated with colonial-
> ism is manifested not only in other worldly evangelicalism and literalist
> fundamentalism, which are oriented to the salvation of the soul, but also in
> scientific malestream biblical scholarship.
>
> Whenever we read/hear/interpret Scripture or any other text, we read/
> hear/interpret it by engaging one or more of these paradigms of interpretation.
> But whereas the three hegemonic malestream paradigms of interpretation
> do not enable a critical process of reading that indicts the dehumanizing
> power of scriptural texts, the critical–emancipatory–political paradigm seeks
> to do so by making explicit the critical hermeneutical lenses and goals with
> which it approaches the Scriptures. While the other three paradigms
> obfuscate the fact that they also have sociopolitical and cultural-religious
> interests and goals, the rhetorical–emancipatory paradigm openly confesses
> that it engages in biblical interpretation for the sake of conscientization and
> well-being.
>
> This fourth paradigm stresses experience, social location, relations of
> power, and interested perspectives of interpreters, as well as the rhetori-
> cality of text and interpretation and the institutional locations that deter-
> mine all four paradigms of biblical studies. It seeks to research and lift into
> consciousness the legitimizing, dissimulating, and reifying or normalizing
> functions of ideology at work in biblical interpretation. It does not stand
> accountable to either the academy or the Church, but seeks to analyze the
> power structures of both in relation to the wider public and political-societal
> structures.[28]

Exclusion of women in church and from theology

Feminist theology is critical of the exclusion of women: from positions of ecclesial authority in its different denominational forms, including the Catholic and Orthodox priesthood; by exclusive liturgical language for humanity as well as for the divine; and from authorized theology. Feminist theology is part of a wider development of gender theory;[29] different strands in feminist theology are congruent with different strands in wider feminist theory, which emphasize respectively gender equality or gender difference. The impact of feminist critique is evident in a reactive 'new Catholic feminism', articulated by Pope John Paul II, which argues for traditional notions of complementary gender differences over against feminist demands for equality. Feminist theologies of gender difference, in contrast, draw on postmodern feminist philosophies, informed by writings of the French feminists, Luce Irigaray and Julia Kristeva, and by Judith Butler's work.[30] Where 'new Catholic feminism' attempts to draw Catholic women back to closed notions of an essential and unchanging created difference, which posits priesthood as essentially male, feminist theologies of gender difference see gender as an open category in transformation. Critique of women's exclusion points up the formative influence of exclusive practices on the self-understandings of men and women in the churches; in contrast, inclusive practices set in motion new understandings of Christian manhood and womanhood.

Ruether defined a principle for the reconstruction of Christian Church and theology – promotion of the full humanity of women. As well as providing a critical lens for identifying problematic practices, her principle also clarified the aim of feminist reconstruction: hierarchical and exclusive practices need to give way to gender equality and inclusion.

Activist campaigns for the ordination of women, such as the Movement for the Ordination of Women (MOW) that was active in the Church of England between 1978 and 1992, worked for inclusion of women in the priesthood, whereas other feminist theologians pressed for radical reform of the churches to move beyond hierarchical clerical–lay divisions. The tension between working closely with received traditions of Church and theology, and reconstructing anew is evident in Fiorenza's notion of the *ekklesia* of feminist women and women-oriented men, and in the Women–Church movement in North America; in the UK feminist liturgical experiment is reflected in publications such as *Women Included*, and *Celebrating Women*. The founding principle of the *ekklesia* of women is the discipleship of equals; Women–Church and women's liturgies use inclusive language for humanity and the divine, so promoting the full humanity of women as well as of men. Women–Church is one site of the already-mentioned women's redemptive communities. Rita Nakashima Brock speaks of the Christa/community as a place where the erotic power within connectedness heals the broken heart of patriarchy; feminist liturgies are testament to this healing.

Metaphysical dualisms

From the inception of North American feminist theologies, feminist critique of Greek metaphysical dualisms that predate Christianity, but which have been deeply influential on Western and Eastern (Orthodox) traditions, has been articulated. An example is seen above in the excerpt from Sallie McFague's *Models of God*, whereas the negative impact for both woman and the earth of binary dualisms that make both related inferior terms to the superior terms of man and mind/spirit, is already evident in the discussion of ecofeminism earlier in the chapter.

The demand for radical gender equality that characterizes the work of both Ruether and Fiorenza is premised on the demise of binary dualisms. Feminist theologies of difference seek ways of perceiving gender differences that escape the imposed binary relation; they seek instead to forge new feminine subjectivities that can hold their own over against well-established male cultures in Church, theology, and the world. Many of the strategies considered above seek to construct alternatives to binary dualisms by bringing into being new individual and corporate feminine identities that exceed patriarchal constraints and confound patriarchal expectations.

A focus on the body and the bodily practice of the incarnation is a significant counter to the effects of binary dualisms. In the following passage, Lisa Isherwood explores the potential of an incarnational theology that begins with embodiment and transgression of the heteropatriarchal norm:

> As a theologian trained and immersed in the Christian tradition I take very seriously the idea of incarnation. By incarnation I do not mean the once and for all Son of God who saved the world through his death but rather the glorious abandonment of the divine into flesh and the passionate dance of the human/divine that ensues. And the purpose of this is *life* – life in abundance, liberating and embracing radical embodied equality. As a feminist I also take very seriously the understanding that how one's body manifests in the world affects how one is perceived, treated and the access one has to institutions as well as power over one's own life. ...
>
> By now we are all familiar with the arguments for the pervasive nature of heteropatriarchy and the way in which it begins with acts of intimacy, be they childrearing or love-making. We are bred into it and our bodies encouraged to enact it more and more, to find it attractive and attracting. We are encouraged to become willing victims of a dominance/submission discourse that does not allow for full flourishing. We know from our liberation colleagues that the oppressor is no more in touch with a free and flourishing life than the oppressed ...
>
> There is no doubt that women have become freer to understand and pursue their own desires. As we are constantly reminded, women are moving from being purely objects of desire to subjects of our own desire and this is extremely healthy. Through this knowledge we are able to make choices that are really ours and in so doing affirm more of our humanness. As an incarnational theologian I have to applaud this move and affirm that incarnational theology requires more humanness and less abstraction of the self. ...
>
> [F]eminist theology has for many years now been removing the otherness of the divine and locating it within and between people. Theologians like Heyward have located the divine within the erotic, the raw energy and power that lies within and between us, the force that draws us out, attracting us to each other and the world in a dance of justice-seeking.[31]

Conclusion

There is no clear boundary separating feminist theologies from black, liberation, and postcolonial theologies. The above excerpt from Fiorenza's *Democratization* illustrates very well the process of rearticulating feminist theologies to engage with changes in both the global kyriarchical landscape and in available academic analytical tools for critical analysis and reconstruction. Feminist theologies of the global north are in dialogue with feminist theory and philosophy, and subject to postcolonial critique arising in the global south; at the same time, feminist theology is best understood, from its inception, as a global network of feminist theologies. The closing excerpt from Isherwood, with its comment on feminist theology removing the otherness of the divine, highlights the ongoing tension within feminist theology: on one hand, a tendency to reconstruct Church and theology anew, given critique of the (hetero)patriarchal (and colonial) nature of the received tradition;[32] on the other, a tendency represented, for example, by Soskice, Tina Beattie, Sarah Coakley, and perhaps Kathryn Tanner,[33] which insists on an even-handed desire to do justice to the received tradition,[34] while insisting that, in the light of feminist critique, the tradition of Church and theology, from this time forward, does gender justice.

Notes

1 Kwok P.-L. 'Feminist Theology as Intercultural Discourse', in S. Parsons (ed.) *The Cambridge Companion to Feminist Theology*, Oxford: Blackwell, 2002, pp. 23–39.

2 M. Daly, *Beyond God the Father*, Boston: Beacon, 1973; D. Hampson, *Theology and Feminism*, Oxford: Basil Blackwell, 1990.

3 Daly, *Beyond*, p. 205.

4 C. Christ and J. Plaskow (eds) *Womanspirit Rising: A Feminist Reader in Religion*, New York: Harper & Row, 1979.

5 J. M. Soskice and D. Lipton (eds) *Feminism and Theology*, Oxford: Oxford University Press, 2003.

6 See: Kwok P.-L. (ed.) *Hope Abundant: Third World and Indigenous Women's Theology*, Maryknoll, NY: Orbis, 2010; M.M. Fulkerson and S. Briggs (eds) *The Oxford Handbook of Feminist Theology*, Oxford: OUP, 2012.

7 M. Katoppo, *Compassionate and Free: An Asian Women's Theology*, Geneva: WCC, 1979, extract reprinted in U. King (ed.) *Feminist Theology from the Third World: A Reader*, London: SPCK, 1994, pp. 114–18.

8 V.V. Valente, 'Foreword', in M.P. Aquino and M.J. Rosado-Nunes (eds) *Feminist Intercultural Theology: Latina Explorations for a Just World*, Maryknoll, NY: Orbis Books, 2007, pp. vii–xi: p. x. Valente cites Rosada-Nunes.

9 J. Rodríguez, '*Tripuenteando*: Journey toward Identity, the Academy, and Solidarity', in Aquino and Rosado-Nunes (eds) *Feminist Intercultural Theology*, pp. 70–88: p. 85.

10 For example in: R.R. Ruether, *Gaia and God: an Ecofeminist Theology of Earth Healing*, London: SCM Press, 1992.

11 D. Ackerman and T. Joyner, 'Earth-Healing in South Africa', in R.R. Ruether (ed.) *Woman Healing Earth: Third World Women on Ecology, Feminism and Religion*, Maryknoll, NY: Orbis Books, 1996, pp. 121–34: pp. 126–27.

12 Kwok P.-L., *Introducing Asian Feminist Theology*, Sheffield: Sheffield Academic Press, 2000, p. 32.

13 Daly, *Beyond*, p. 47.

14 Daly, *Beyond*, p. 62.

15 Daly, *Beyond*, pp. 47, 77.
16 R.R. Ruether, 'The Liberation of Christology from Patriarchy', in A. Loades (ed.) *Feminist Theology: A Reader*, London: SPCK, 1990, pp. 138–48: p. 147.
17 J. Clague, 'The Christa: Symbolizing My Humanity and My Pain', in *Feminist Theology* 14.1, 2005, pp. 83–108: p. 83.
18 Clague, 'The Christa', p. 95.
19 Asian Women Doing Theology, Singapore Conference, 1987, 'Summary Statement on Feminist Mariology', in King (ed.) *Feminist Theology from the Third World*, pp. 271–75: pp. 271–73.
20 Daly, *Beyond*, p. 55; C. Heywood, *The Redemption of God: A Theology of Mutual Relation*, Washington, DC: University Press of America, 1982, and *Our Passion for Justice*, New York: Pilgrim, 1994; R.N. Brock, *Journeys by Heart: A Christology of Erotic Power*, New York: Crossroad, 1988; S. Welch, *Communities of Resistance and Solidarity: A Feminist Theology of Liberation*, Maryknoll, NY: Orbis Books, 1985.
21 D.S. Williams, *Sisters in the Wilderness: The Challenge of Womanist God-Talk*, Maryknoll, NY: Orbis Books, 1993; M. Kanyoro, 'Engendered Communal Theology: African Women's Contribution to Theology in the Twenty-First Century', in *Feminist Theology* 9.27, 2001, pp. 36–56.
22 S. McFague, *Models of God: Theology for an Ecological, Nuclear Age*, London: SCM Press, 1987; excerpt reprinted in Loades (ed.) *Feminist Theology*, pp. 255–74: pp. 260–63, 272–73.
23 E.S. Fiorenza, *Jesus: Miriam's Child, Sophia's Prophet: Critical Issues in Feminist Christology*, London: SCM Press, 1995; G.J.-S. Kim, *The Grace of Sophia: A Korean North American Women's Christology*, Cleveland, OH: Pilgrim Press, 2002.
24 E. Johnson, *She Who Is: The Mystery of God in Feminist Theological Discourse*, 2nd edition, New York: Crossroad, 2002, pp. 213–14.
25 M. Althaus-Reid, *Queer God*, London: Routledge, 2003, pp. 46, 57.
26 P. Trible, *Texts of Terror: Literary Feminist Readings of Biblical Narratives*, Philadelphia, PA: Fortress Press, 1984.
27 P. Trible, 'Feminist Hermeneutics and Biblical Studies', in Loades (ed.) *Feminist Theology*, pp. 23–29: p. 27.
28 E.S. Fiorenza, *Democratizing Biblical Studies: Towards an Emancipatory Educational Space*, Louisville, KY: Westminster John Knox Press, 2009, pp. 81–82.
29 As made clear at other points in this chapter, feminist theology is also part of the wider development of *theology*. Both aspects of the identity of feminist theology need to be kept in mind.
30 G. Howie and J. Jobling (eds) *Women and the Divine*, New York: Palgrave Macmillan, 2009; E.T. Armour and S.M. St. Ville (eds) *Bodily Citations: Religion and Judith Butler*, New York: Columbia UP, 2006.
31 M. Althaus-Reid and L. Isherwood (eds) *The Sexual Theologian: Essays on Sex, God and Politics*, London: Continuum, 2004, pp. 49–50, 53–55.
32 See: M. Althaus-Reid and L. Isherwood, *Controversies in Feminist Theology*, London: SCM, 2007; C. Keller and L.C. Schneider, *Polydoxy: Theology of Multiplicity and Relation*, London: Routledge, 2011; L.C. Schneider, *Beyond Monotheism: a Theology of Multiplicity*, Abingdon: Routledge, 2008.
33 T. Beattie, *New Catholic Feminism: Theology and Theory*, London: Routledge, 2006; S. Coakley, *Powers and Submissions: Spirituality, Philosophy and Gender*, Oxford: Blackwell, 2002 and *God, Sexuality and the Self: an Essay 'On the Trinity'*, Cambridge: CUP, 2013; J. Soskice, *The Kindness of God: Metaphor, Gender and Religious Language*, Oxford: OUP, 2007; K. Tanner, 'Social Theory Concerning the "New Social Movements" and the Practice of Feminist Theology', in R.S. Chopp and S. Davaney (eds) *Horizons in Feminist Theology: Identity, Tradition and Norms*, Minneapolis: Fortress, 1997, pp.179–97.
34 The term is Rachel Muers's, in her 'Doing Traditions Justice', in J. Daggers (ed.) *Gendering Christian Ethics*, Newcastle: Cambridge Scholars Press, 2012, pp. 7–22.

23
PRACTICING BLACK THEOLOGIES, OR, CHALLENGING THE RACIAL MATRIX

Willie James Jennings

> Only the most exceptional people become aware of the matrix. Those that learn it exists must possess a rare degree of intuition, sensitivity, and a questioning nature. However very rarely some gain this wisdom from wholly different means …
>
> (Opening lines of *The Animatrix: World Record*)[1]

As this new century dawned, the North American film industry welcomed the arrival of the *Matrix* film trilogy. This groundbreaking work of the Wachowski brothers ushered in a new level of integration of technology into the craft of filmmaking, at the same time as drawing on a number of movie genres, ancient epics, and philosophical themes. What perhaps most captured the imagination of *Matrix* fans was the premise of the film – that there existed two worlds: a real world where life was rigidly controlled and an illusionary world that seemed to be free but was in fact easily manipulated. In fact, this premise was so intriguing that a group of well-known animators created nine short Japanese styled animation films (*animé*) to fill in aspects of the *Matrix* story. *The Animatrix* (2003) also presented provocative storylines that built on the central idea of a world in which people are for the most part unaware that they are asleep and under the control of a massively powerful machine.

One of the more powerful of these short films was *World Record*. This is the story of an athlete of African descent who prepares to run the race of his life – in fact, a race that will become his last race. Dan, as he is named, is a hundred-meter man, which means he is a sprinter involved in the highest profile event in track and field. As the race begins, several narrative interruptions inform us that Dan had already run a world record time that was nullified because he was accused of using performance-enhancing drugs. Now, with an excellent time in a qualifying heat, Dan is out to prove himself and break the world record again. The story thus far seems not unusual, presenting occurrences easily connected to stories of present-day athletes, but the point that will shape the story will be its unfolding unreality, a falsehood hidden to this black runner.

As the race ensues we see Dan straining every muscle in his body to push himself as hard as he can. Then his worst fears are realized; Dan's muscles begin to shatter. Yet his wounds are only the beginning of what will be his eventual revelation.

As his muscles collapse, he senses he can still run and push himself even faster. Little does he realize that he is beginning to awaken to the truth that he is in an unreal world, and that those who control the matrix are alarmed at his emerging awareness. The black athletes – Dan's co-runners – turn into white agents of the matrix itself, charged to keep all continuously unaware that they live in a world of illusions. However, the agents themselves are not real people. They are programs created to carry out the policing actions of the machine itself through body simulations.

This story provides a social analogy for thinking about race, theology, and the perceptions of reality that flow out of each, and it situates us nicely inside the fundamental dynamic explored by black theologies of liberation.

Black theologies of liberation seek to come to grips with the racial condition of modernity. Much of Christian theology in the last several centuries has refused to enter into a clear reckoning of this condition, which we could characterize as an unreal world concealing a real world. In relation to Christian faith, the unreal world is not simply the world of race, but more precisely the world of Christian theology conditioned by the racial imagination.

The making of an unreal racial world

There was a moment in history when Christian theologians entered into a unique situation so unanticipated that its effects completely overwhelmed them. This situation was the so-called age of discovery and colonialism when vast stretches of the world came under the domination of early Europeans.[2] Only something bordering on science fiction could capture what this time meant for the thinking of Christian intellectuals, who were faced with two breathtaking occurrences. On the one side, a whole host of new realities confronted them – new peoples, languages, landscapes, animals, flora and fauna, and ways of living. They were now entering fully into the geographic density of the world and they were facing far more complex questions about its actual nature. The geographic frame that had been gained from Scripture and tradition, reason and experience, no longer captured the world unfolding in front of their eyes. On the other side, theologians did not enter the new worlds alone or even first. They came as missionaries alongside and behind two other crucial types of individuals – merchants and soldiers – who were for the most part Christian as well. Together they arrived into the new lands with force, with the unbelievable power to alter the worlds of the indigenes.

This new situation was in effect a crisis for Christian theology, even if Christian thinkers did not recognize this as such. This was a crisis not about the truth of Christian faith, but about its geographic reach. This was a crisis not about the power of Christian faith, but about Christian faith resting comfortably in unprecedented power. In the face of this twofold yet hidden crisis, Christian theologians made innovations and adjustments to the doctrinal substratum of both the content of faith (the faith that is believed) and the practice of believing (the faith that believes). It was precisely the conceptual struggle of grasping the creation in the newness of discovery and then relating it to salvific history that characterized the Old (theological) World encountering the New World. A powerful and urgent new question was thrust on Christian intellectuals, a question that continues to echo to our time. How should theologians relate their understanding of the world as creation to a far more complex world unleashed on them with the discovery of the new worlds?

The first adjustment theologians made was to subtly separate geographical knowledge from theological knowledge and insert themselves and their Eurocentric gaze as the new point of epistemological stability for real knowledge of the world. In effect Old World theology and philosophy could no longer lay claim on a sure grasp of the creation. Theologians realized that much of the geographic information and speculation pronounced on the basis of philosophy, as well as on the Church Fathers and Scripture, was not accurate and was in many cases simply wrong. Their experience standing and living in the space of the New World contradicted that Old World theological vision. As a result, with the casting off of traditional understandings of the geographical world, theologians filled up the gap with their own contemporary views. By gently drawing the geographic authority of the tradition to themselves they positioned themselves as the stabilizing point of theological authority. This innovation was simple but profound. They would speak for the tradition in these new conquered spaces, re-establishing on the surer ground of their real world experience the geographic truth of the world, coordinating that new truth with the tradition.

It is with this new conceptual adjustment that theologians opened up a new discursive performance of Christian theology by enfolding it inside the surety of specific human existence – in this case, the surety of white European existence. This would open toward not only the hubris of Eurocentrism, but it would also at the same time establish a way of speaking and thinking that centralized and normalized the judgments of Europeans as the witnesses of the true, the good, and the beautiful. This was a far more comprehensive effect than simply saying that the victors of a war get to write the history of the conflict in ways that advantage them. This normalization and centralization of early Europeans in the new worlds, which has often been designated as the emergence of the centered European subject and/or the rise of white hegemony, took root inside Christian theology and the Christian theological imagination. The effect here was of an abiding merger. As Euro-theologians spoke in colonialized spaces of the world, of God and salvation, grace and faith, and of all that is seen and unseen – that is, as they spoke globally, universally – they also spoke of what should be, what should be built up, torn down, altered, or eradicated. This is what I mean by speaking universally. It is the belief that one represents the full reality of humanity coupled with the usurpation of the right to present reality for the many. However, speaking universally or globally was not the problem. Many people(s) have such discursive practices. The problem is that a marriage took place that should never have been, the Christian universal with the early European universal.

Christian theology by its very nature plays in the universal because it speaks of a God who is the creator of all. Theology gestures toward all flesh, claiming deep connection to all social worlds, places, and peoples. The European universal, by contrast, emerged out of a specific moment when European peoples began to form a world system of signification. Multiple European peoples positioned themselves across vast stretches of space, and spoke similarly about a wide range of matters and, equally important, enacted an aesthetic regime that would birth a constellation of evaluative strategies that could and would permeate every aspect of indigenous life. The energy that drove this marriage forward was on the one hand the sheer military, technological, and economic power of the emerging European nation-states, and on the other hand, the trajectory of supersessionism that allowed Christians to imagine themselves as the people of God, the new Israel, and no longer gentiles. I have written at length about the ramifications of the loss of the historical consciousness of gentile existence for Christian theology, but, in brief, the effect of that loss was to solidify the naturalness of this merger of Christian thought with European thought.

The point here is not that Euro-Christians thought as *Euro*-Christians. How else could they think? The point here is that thinking was diseased from its very beginnings in the new worlds, and this first adjustment of thought that positioned the Euro-Christian at the center of the conceptual world opened up two additional adjustments. The second adjustment followed immediately from the first. Once Scripture and tradition were mediated through the sure position of the European knower then theologians could begin to address the deep problem of history. When did God create these new lands? Why did God create these new lands and peoples? Where do they fit in the biblical drama? Such questions quickly exposed the implications of New World encounter and forced theologians to reconceptualize the issue in the language of providence.

Doctrines of providence, from the colonial moment forward, would be articulated with an incredible new elasticity. Christians and their theologians discerned the guiding hand of God in the way they arrived and remained in the New World, while discerning no such divine involvement in the lives of native peoples. The idea of providence did two important jobs in these multiple contexts, whether Portuguese, Spanish, Dutch, French, English, or German. On the one hand, it shielded the imaginations of Christians from the vulnerability of theological narratives that struggle to cover peoples, places, animals, and ways of life unanticipated by those narratives, while on the other hand it activated a new sense of agency that ran roughshod over new spaces and peoples. It was by divine sanction, the right order of the world given by God, that new peoples would be governed. The early Europeans placed Christian theology in its rightful place of imagining history theologically, but they did so wrongly.

The history that theologians imagined at this moment carried two co-actors, God and white men working to bring the good out of the weak and undeveloped. Providence in this regard generated not simply a sense of comfort in the face of the strange, the new, and the inexplicable, but it also promoted an optic, a way of seeing what ought to be in the world commensurate with the will of God. Thus the third adjustment growing out of this hermeneutic of providence is well-known as a part of historic missionary endeavors. As Christianity encountered indigenous worship practices and behaviors that opposed the European understanding of the one true God, the Christian God, a process of eradication began. The hermeneutic of providence modulated into a hermeneutic of idolatry – not only could God's hand be seen, but demonic work could also be discerned. As the decades and centuries unfolded this optic matured forming an ethnographic, anthropological vision of cultures arranged hierarchically.[3]

This would mean that the primary posture of a Eurocentric Christian theological imagination was to look out on the unknown and evaluate its otherness as disorder, distortion, and demonic rather than as realities that signify the creaturely, the shared, the created. It also meant that Christian theology would come to be encased in what I have termed a pedagogical imperialism; that is, a way of being in the world that first imagines the Christian as teacher and the world as learner.

Racial existence grew out of this theological ground. It was born of the remaking of native worlds as early Europeans positioned themselves between indigenous lands and native peoples, marking themselves as the only ones who may speak the truth of both lands and people. Early Europeans turned their piecemeal observations of people into deep truths of their ontological status. They were white and natives were black or somewhere in-between. They channeled their lust for space into the renaming of places, driving out indigenous ways of seeing and knowing themselves through landscapes and animals, pushing away memories of specific areas that formed the identities of peoples, and driving death nails in the rituals of place that had mid-wived generations of native peoples into the truth of their existence. The unreal racial world grew in reach and power until it seemed – and continues to seem – the always natural way of the world for millions of people touched by the legacies of colonial remaking. For so many people, the earth, the ground, has always been just dirt, just undeveloped segmented patches of land, ready to be formed and transformed into whatever we wish. It does not speak or gesture or suggest a movement of life that we should follow as part of its created reality. For so many people animals are not nor have they ever been our kin. They travel paths of their own choosing separate and unconcerned with us. And never do they speak to us of who we are. And people in this abhorrent vision are encased in racial truth with whiteness as both a form of preferred racial being and the centralized signifier of normal humanity.

The challenge to the unreal racial world

A miracle happened in this unreal world: native peoples designated black, red, yellow, and not quite white, became Christian. Despite the rise of white supremacy and the efforts to kill native worlds, many indigenes did become Christian. Of course, some have argued that their becoming Christian was an act of subjugation, a sign of death. The power of this argument cannot be denied, yet there emerged very early people of African descent among other native peoples who argued in subtle and sometimes pronounced ways on theological grounds against the Christianity of colonial societies, of slaveholding societies, of societies that sanctioned the rape of native women and slave women. Out of this miracle came the impulse of what we would later call black theologies of liberation. The actual history of black theologies of liberation has been told in many texts and need not be repeated here.[4] What is crucial however is to understand the challenges that black theologies of liberation inherited and the problems they struggled with as they faced those challenges.

Let us return to the *The Animatrix: World Record* for a moment to help us sense the depth of challenge black theologies of liberation were forced to face. As we noted earlier, as Dan the sprinter forced his body to perform at its highest level despite his pain, his eyes began to open to the real world. In a moment of true sight, Dan saw himself not on a track running in an honest competition, but bound, completely tethered to a machine, the extent of which he could not comprehend. The moment of sight found him pressing his body free of the machine's chains only to be spotted by the machine.

How does one name a process and articulate an operation so vast, so expansive, that even to attempt to conceptualize it brings you to the edge of perceived madness. Many African Christian intellectuals found themselves trying to do theology always on the edge of madness. Some never saw or felt the racial matrix, and some in sensing the unreal world nevertheless ignored it. But some Christian intellectuals, because of the depth of what Wendell Berry called the hidden wound or what Walter Mignolo called the colonial wound found it necessary to push themselves beyond it to survive, and in that desperate effort to live, they began to see what others could not or would not see.[5]

What did black theologies of liberation begin to see in the misty dim light cast by the racial machine? They saw at least four painful realities.[6] First, they saw God constantly and consistently projected as a white man. This was not only a matter of image and likeness, but deeds and demeanors. The colonial world both Catholic and Protestant refused to release God from its actions. It intimated divine sanction for all that it did. Even its failures – political, economic, environmental, and genocidal – were described as seeking the divinely ordered good for the native and the nation alike. The use of God-language to justify statecraft was not the new thing spied out here, but its insidious racial mixture that demanded white men be imagined and positioned at the center of every serious theological project and Christian undertaking if it were to be seen as authentically Christian. The entire Christian world was made to revolve both conceptually and materially around white male bodies as the policing center of theology.

Black theologians also saw a second reality of the unreal world. They saw a theology of history written as a theology of whiteness. Providence is a very powerful doctrine because it is more than a doctrine. It is a way of life. The life it suggests draws our attention to God working in the world, but it was precisely this work that was discerned through a distorted lens. God was rendered as always historically bound to his co-laborer the European in bringing about the new in the world, and the Christian world was plagued with a life-draining atrophied vision of history that turned nonwhite Christians into episodic actors in the grand drama of our march toward the parousia led by white Christian intellectuals. Moreover, black theologies of liberation felt the effect of this plague as they tirelessly tried to offer alternative narrations of the work of God in the world that did not yield the conclusion that God willed white supremacy.

Third, black theologies of liberation struggled even more against the power of pedagogical imperialism in which the Christian universal is married to the universal born of the colonial operation. Again, *The Animatrix: World Record* helps us imagine this struggle. Once the machine realized that Dan saw it, it bound Dan more tightly to itself, forcing his body more closely to its overwhelming power.

The revealing of the machine world did not mean escape from it. It actually meant that the black body (of Dan) was exposed and with that exposure the machine unleashed its awesome power to further bind an already bound body, pressing Dan back into the dream world, forging a path of forgetfulness on top of the illusion of that life-determining race. The pedagogical imperialism that encased Christian theology and was nurtured by it gave birth to colonial frames of education and their inescapable scholastic ecologies. Native peoples were faced with the great trauma of life in 'the prison house of language' (to quote a phrase from Fredric Jameson).[7] This was life pressed in the cauldron of European languages and made to twist and turn through their enunciative regimes, while at the same time having native tongues cut out and destroyed in the prohibition to speak the words and wisdom of the ancestors in public or private.

Language mastery in the colonial moment was certainly in the prison house of language. If one was going to argue against the given – the given systems of exchange, the given social truths, the given knowledge of God and humanity – one would first have to submit to the European given. The point was never the value, utility, or possibility of life within European languages, but the absolute inescapability of their dominant positions. Christian theology gladly built its home inside the citadel of those languages and merged with the systems of education grown on imperialist soil. Those systems of education followed the economic currents that circled around white bodies so that the material realities of education (books, buildings, systems of evaluation, methods of instruction, and rituals of scholastic demeanor, for example) complemented the centrality of European thought and the supremacy of its human vision. Christian theology never imagined a life beyond this racial magisterium. Its pedagogical imperialism was performed in church and in the academy where the Christian universal made love to the colonial universal. Black theologies of liberation have tried again and again to identify, isolate, and challenge this coupling that positions white bodies next to universal language poised to tutor all of humanity about its essential matters, such as reason, tradition, faith, doctrine, science, art, and so forth.

Nonwhite voices are locked in the position of contributors within this discursive regime. Forever situated in the space of 'particularity', nonwhite intellectuals become points of evidence that confirm the observations pronounced from the position of the white universal.

This coupling also meant the growth of canonization processes both subtle and grotesque that encircled and elevated the aesthetic sensibilities of the colonizing settlers. Black theologies of liberation have tried to register the longitudinal effects of this canonization of the true, the good, and the beautiful bound to white bodies and the formation of the idea and image of genius tied to its practices of evaluation. This has been a painfully difficult charting, not only because of its long history, but also because of its fantastic range moving from the sites of music and worship, to the work of biblical interpretation, to the shape of curriculums, to the practices of ministry, and all the way to the forms of Christian spirituality. The struggle against pedagogical imperialism has been most difficult precisely because it has been a struggle to dismantle the colonial master's house from inside that house while using his tools. How does a nonwhite Christian intellectual challenge a diabolic coupling that is at the heart of her own formation as a Christian and an intellectual?

All theologies of liberation cognizant of this racial entrapment have felt the power of this question and seen the need to find a way forward. Black theologies of liberation have also recognized the residual effect of this pedagogical imperialism in the contours of intellectual exchange within Western Christianity.

The fourth painful sighting was to see the bodies of people of color discounted as bearers of divine presence, carriers of holy knowledge, and sites of godly instruction. The world presented to native peoples by Christians coming to their worlds was one in which God was only reluctantly present, revealed as if God were a large finger pointing to the places and peoples that must be cleaned up, organized rightly, and pulled from their demonized behavior. Even as this grotesque picture faded, gently rubbed out by later missionaries embarrassed by that early mission theology, the template was fixed. It was a template mapped extensively onto the collective psyche of Christians in modernity through which people of color are rarely seen, rarely positioned, rarely received as teachers of the faith and even more inconceivably as those who might lead the Church to new places (conceptually, materially, spatially) where visions of a healthy ecclesial future might be more clearly seen.

These four painful realities – a white male God image, a theology of history bound to whiteness, a pedagogical imperialism, and the dismissal of people of color as authentic Christian teachers – constitute in part the theological habitus of the modern racial condition. Habitus, in this regard (drawing on the thought of Pierre Bourdieu), means a set of dispositions established through practices that guide the ways people understand themselves and their actions (their agency) and shape the ways people imagine life ought to be or is normally the case (structure).[8] The theological habitus is only one aspect of the modern racial condition, which in its comprehensive reach functions like a doctrine of creation guiding people in how they might envisage life. Black theologies of liberation have tried to challenge the theological habitus of the modern racial condition through a discursive practice aimed at overcoming these realities. However, few Christian theologians appreciate the massive task faced by liberationist thought as it seeks to overcome the very dynamic that it is embroiled within, thereby making itself a target of the same captivating forces it seeks to weaken and ultimately break open.

Liberationist practices of hope

Black theologies of liberation, especially Womanist liberationists, call on Christians to explore their images of God, and to ask themselves if the triune identity has been transformed into an incipient *übermensch*, a white superman who is in fact imagined as the revelation of God in flesh. This has been both a matter of the images and the language we use in theological discourse. Womanist liberationists especially have captured in multiple ways the idol production operative in much theological discourse that constantly gestures not toward the God–human, but the (white) man who is god.[9] Yet the problem of the nexus of racial image and masculine language exposes the wider network of signification at play in the unreal racial world. That wider network communicates visions of redemption that require white male bodies leading the way. The vision of a powerful white man victorious over all his enemies fills the cinematic universe and floods the collective imaginations of so many Western Christians that it constantly threatens to corrode our understanding of Jesus of Nazareth, his cross and his resurrection. Love of Jesus is always in danger of becoming simply love of his resurrected power, which mirrors the power imagined to reside in images of strong decisive white men.

The desire for white masculine form and the seductive power of its performance remain an aspect of the racial condition and white supremacy that Christian theology has yet to begin to take seriously as a problem for Christian reflection. In *The Animatrix: World Record*, the white agents who sought to control the black body were not real; they too were fabrications of the machine. Yet the machine fantasized its power in the unreal world through the fantasy of powerful white male bodies. This is a precise analogy for the fantasy work that images of white male bodies do to capture and project Western desires for supremacy, power, and self-sufficiency. Indeed all peoples, men and women, are invited to enter into such images. Black theologies of liberation have placed their finger on this pulse and continue to invite other Christian intellectuals to listen to this erratic heartbeat.

Second, black liberationists struggle against narratives of whiteness that bind a theological vision of history in a conceptual tourniquet. This struggle has been waged on multiple fields. In biblical studies, efforts have been made to read racial existence into the biblical drama by locating an African space as the context of divine action.[10] In the history of theology, many scholars of color have tried to localize early Europe as only one site among many where Christian theology was formed. This localization would, they hope, suggest an expansive framework within which to understand Christian thought, orthodoxy, and normative Christian intellectual practice. In addition, black liberationists have turned their attention to the history of black Christians and more generally African and African diaspora religious thought as the most fruitful context for narrating specific, local histories of social and political significance and theological import. These strategies in effect present a practice of historiography tied to black liberationist thought that challenges the master narratives of whiteness through the consideration and examination of specific stories of black struggle for religious and theological self-expression of beliefs.[11]

This second practice also necessitated for many liberationists the need for people of color to form their theologies from their own cultural resources.[12] This strategy was in some measure a direct response to the overwhelming problem of pedagogical imperialism. If all theology is a reflection of particular cultures, as many modern intellectuals imagine, then what follows from this premise is the commitment to articulate religious vision from the socio-cultural vision of a people. For Africans and their descendants this need was perceived as acute given the concentrated efforts of the colonialists to destroy, demonize, and transform native religious practices and perceptions. This challenge to pedagogical imperialism was in effect a work of institutionalization that paralleled the work of institution building that has been part of the legacy of black struggle from the beginning of the emergence of white colonial power. Liberationists have noted this institutionalizing operation in the creation of books, secret worship services, hidden religious rituals, churches, schools, colleges, universities, clubs, and societies both secular and religious, all aimed at not only securing the social logics of collective self-expression, but establishing intellectual vision freed from white supremacy.[13]

It is only in relation to these first three practices of challenging (a) white male image production, (b) white theologies of history, and (c) pedagogical imperialism, that we can see the full power of a fourth discursive practice of seizing the importance of experience and context for establishing didactic authority. Black liberationists caught sight of two normalizing processes endemic to the white Christian universal, even though they were often hidden or denied by the intellection of Anglo Christian theologians. First, the normalization of *Euro-Christian experience* as a crucial cultural substratum of their doctrinal reflections and theological speculations, which they exposed in everything from their examples used in teaching, their scholarly demeanor, their jokes, stories, articulated fantasies, and especially their aesthetic sensibilities. Of course, the person who teaches is fundamentally a part of the content that is taught and this should be accepted as inherent in the realities of being a teacher.[14] Yet this normalization process meant ignorance of and/or the refusal to acknowledge the depth of integration of the person into the content, as well as the ways the white aesthetic regime permeated theological work. Second, liberationists saw the full force of the erasure of *their* bodies from authorial possibilities in theology, both in terms of decisive contributions to the articulation of Christian belief and practice as well as the imagined position of consequential teachers of the Church. In this regard, liberationists saw the effects of Western educational ecologies that circulated around white bodies.

The appeal to experience and context exists in the midst of a constellation of colonial operations as an angular attempt to slice through thick processes of conceptual and social normalization. The problem is that such appeals have often been characterized by both liberationists and their antagonists as appeals that stand over against or alongside of tradition, reason, and practices of biblical interpretation, as well as orthodoxy, denominational polities, and some social mores.[15] Whether experience and context should be positioned conceptually in these ways seems to me to be beside the point. The crucial issue at play here is the importance of exposing processes of theological formation that deny the fundamental work of identity creation that flows through Christian theology and that has been caught up inside the racial matrix. Let us return to the *The Animatrix: World Record* once more to underscore this struggle of identity creation in Christian theology.

Dan, the awakened runner, after he was tightly chained back into the machine, 'woke up' back in the matrix in a hospital being pushed in a wheel chair by a babbling nurse. This nurse seems half-drugged herself as she speaks to Dan as if *she* is in a catatonic state. Ironically, she wears a cross signifying the Christian origins of her profession (and a Christian echo in the story) as she pushes him along a corridor. It seems to suggest that Christianity and social control move seamlessly together. Standing behind them is a white agent of the matrix, far enough away that he cannot be heard speaking to the machine. He assures the machine that Dan's re-assertion is so absolute that he will never awake again. He will see himself as having won the race in world record time but at the cost of losing his ability to walk or run.

Indeed the entire storyline and the operation of the matrix pivots on this struggle to control the perception of the real. As the story moves tightly toward Dan's wounded black body, we are invited to imagine what might happen now that the matrix has won and re-established its power. This seems to me to be the most fruitful conceptual position from which to analyze the practices of black theologies of liberation – what might be theorized from the site of wounded black bodies and what might be the next theological steps. Finally, this short film anticipates what has in effect been the answer given to this question by liberationists. The final word we hear Dan speak in a whisper through clenched teeth is simply 'free'. He repeats this single word and then the inexplicable happens – this tortured black body in the chair stands up.

Dan knows the truth. He is free and he must act on what he knows. Interestingly, we are not shown his face as he stands, only his body doing what it was not supposed to do. Here we encounter a specific vision of freedom that is first and foremost the freedom to live beyond the unreal world, to deny its prison, and to resist the given. As Dan stands up we hear the final words of the white agent speaking for the machine. He tells Dan, this broken body struggling to stand, to 'sit down'. The absurdity of the command can only be understood in light of the prior words of the agent, 'he will never walk or run again'. This dynamic draws yet another precise analogy with the struggle of Christian intellectuals of color and their allies who consider themselves theological liberationists. The emancipatory visions that are rising out of the practices of black theologies of liberation are works in progress that seek to address the myriad of issues, constraints, and problems that continue to come against people of color. Those visions also seek to offer new possibilities of life with God beyond the racial matrix. The real question that these practices press on us is will more Christians and their theologians actually begin to see what they see?

Notes

1 *The Animatrix: World Record*, Tokyo: Madhouse Studios, 2003.
2 W.J. Jennings, *The Christian Imagination: Theology and the Origins of Race*, New Haven, CT: Yale University Press, 2010.
3 A. Pagden, *The Fall of Natural Man: The American Indian and the Origins of Comparative Ethnology*, Cambridge: Cambridge University Press, 1982; B. McGrane, *Beyond Anthropology: Society and the Other*, New York: Columbia University Press, 1989.
4 J. Cone and G.S. Wilmore (eds) *Black Theology: A Documentary History, 1966–1979*, Maryknoll, NY: Orbis Books, 1979; C.J. Sanders, *Living the Intersection: Womanism and Afrocentrism in Theology*, Minneapolis: Fortress Press, 1995; T. Witvliet, *The Way of the Black Messiah: The Hermeneutical Challenge of Black Theology*, Oak Park, IL: Meyer Stone Books, 1987; E. Antonio, 'Black Theology', in C. Rowland (ed.) *The Cambridge Companion to Liberation Theology*, Cambridge: Cambridge University Press, 1999; H.H. Singleton III, *Black Theology and Ideology: Deideological Dimensions in the Theology of James H. Cone*, Collegeville, MN: Liturgical Press, 2002.
5 W. Berry, *The Hidden Wound*, Berkeley, CA: Counterpoint, 2010; W.D. Mignolo, *The Idea of Latin America*, Malden, MA: Blackwell, 2005.
6 This list in no way intends to be exhaustive of the important contributions black theologies of liberation are making to Christian theological work and wider scholarly endeavors

in the study of religion. My list is only suggestive of a framework within which to analyze liberationist practice.

7 F. Jameson, *The Prison-House of Language: A Critical Account of Structuralism and Russian Formalism*, Princeton, NJ: Princeton University Press, 1974. The title and thesis of Jameson's instructive text help us situate the function of language use within its specific socio-political deployments, which is also a crucial aspect of the history of theology that is yet to be told.

8 P. Bourdieu, *Outline of a Theory of Practice*, Cambridge: Cambridge University Press, 1988, and *In Other Words: Essays Towards a Reflexive Sociology*, Stanford, CA: Stanford University Press, 1990.

9 L. Phillips (ed.) *The Womanist Reader: The First Quarter Century of Womanist Thought*, New York: Routledge, 2006; D.S. Williams, *Sisters in the Wilderness: The Challenge of Womanist God-Talk*, Maryknoll, NY: Orbis Books, 1993; S.Y. Mitchem, *Introducing Womanist Theology*, Maryknoll, NY: Orbis Books, 2003; E.M. Townes (ed.) *A Troubling in My Soul: Womanist Perspectives on Evil and Suffering*, Maryknoll, NY: Orbis Books, 1993.

10 D.T. Adamo, *Africa and the Africans in the Old Testament*, Benin City, Edo State, Nigeria: Justice Jeco Press & Publishers, 2005; C.H. Felder, *Troubling Biblical Waters: Race, Class, and Family*, Maryknoll, NY: Orbis Books, 1989; E.M. Yamauchi, *Africa and the Bible*, Grand Rapids, MI: Baker Academic, 2004.

11 K.R. Connor, *Imagining Grace: Liberating Theologies in the Slave Narrative Tradition*, Urbana and Chicago, IL: University of Illinois Press, 2000; C.J. Evans, *The Burden of Black Religion*, Oxford: Oxford University Press, 2008; T.E. Fulop and A.J. Raboteau (eds) *African American Religion: Interpretive Essays in History and Culture*, New York: Routledge, 1997.

12 D.N. Hopkins, *Shoes that Fit our Feet: Sources for a Constructive Black Theology*, Maryknoll, NY: Orbis Books, 1993; C.A. Kirk-Duggan, *Exorcizing Evil: A Womanist Perspective on the Spirituals*, Maryknoll, NY: Orbis Books, 1997.

13 A.G. Miller, *Elevating the Race: Theophilus G. Steward, Black Theology, and the Making of an African American Civil Society, 1865–1924*, Knoxville, TN: University of Tennessee Press, 2003; P.R. Griffin, *Black Theology as the Foundation of Three Methodist Colleges: The Educational Views and Labors of Daniel Payne, Joseph Price, Isaac Lane*, Washington, DC: University of America Press, 1984; W.E. Montgomery, *Under Their Own Vine and Fig Tree: The African-American Church in the South, 1865–1900*, Baton Rouge, LA: Louisiana State University Press, 1993.

14 J.H. Cone, *My Soul Looks Back*, Maryknoll, NY: Orbis Books, 1986; and *Risks of Faith: The Emergence of a Black Theology of Liberation, 1968–1998*, Boston, MA: Beacon Press, 1999; K. G. Cannon, *Katie's Canon: Womanism and the Soul of the Black Community*, New York: Continuum, 1995.

15 C. Rowland (ed.) *The Cambridge Companion to Liberation Theology*; I. Petrella, *Beyond Liberation Theology: A Polemic*, London: SCM Press, 2008.

24
LIBERATION THEOLOGY
A how-to guide

Thia Cooper

[The meeting] began with everybody hearing the personal story of two elderly Blacks. A story of much suffering and discrimination. After this, all together in unison they tried to remember the history of the Blacks in Brazil. In an overview there appeared on the board the long slavery with its sequence of oppression. After this, they asked for a global overview of the history of the people of the Bible. In this way, in the end, on a big parallel board, there were two stories, distant in time, but near each other in content; two stories of oppression and struggle for liberation ... They began to look at their situation in a different way.[1]

Liberation theology,[2] defined most simply, is reflection and action that focuses on freeing humanity from oppression. This action and reflection is based on faith, Scripture, tradition, reason and experience. As this book has emphasized throughout, theology is a practice and practice itself is theological. Further, this book is organized around the Wesleyan Quadrilateral of Scripture, tradition, reason and experience. At first glance, these two pieces fit liberation theology well.

However, liberation theology is distinctive in at least two ways. First, liberation theology prioritizes the powerless,[3] the marginalized. Liberation theology argues that Christianity should free humanity and it criticizes traditional theologies, which have often been used to oppress human beings. The powerless, who have been ignored by traditional theologies, are at the center of liberation theology. Liberation theology asks how and why we are oppressed or are oppressing others. It aims to free theology itself from its oppressive uses.

Second, liberation theology prioritizes action. Reflection without action is not theology. Each person is expected to put faith into action. As Clodovis and Leonardo Boff wrote 'Liberation theology is not a *theological movement*, but *theology in movement*.'[4] Liberation theology contrasts orthodoxy (which produces dogma, right rules) with orthopraxis (which produces praxis, right action). Praxis is practice that has been reflected upon. Reflection and action produce a spiral known as the hermeneutical circle, the method central to liberation theology.

These two distinctions lead to four further emphases in liberation theology, absent from some traditional theologies. First, the fact that theology is praxis also means that every person can be a theologian. Gustavo Gutierrez stated, 'There is present in all believers – and more so in every Christian community – a rough out-line of a theology.'[5] Theologies are developed as people act and reflect in community. No issue or action is decided by one individual, or hierarchically; the issues are worked out collectively. The role of the 'formal' theologian, minister, or scholar is to draw together the threads of this reflection, to write 'academically', to introduce new audiences to these themes.

Second, liberation theology emphasizes the need for a 'hermeneutic of suspicion'.[6] A hermeneutic of suspicion initially accepts nothing as fact: what we understand our situation to be, what academics or our faith traditions state, and so on. Each piece will be set beside the others and they will all be examined together.

Third, liberationists argue that theology is not neutral; it always takes a stand. If a theology claims neutrality, then it supports the status quo. For example, if theologians claimed to be neutral with regard to slavery, this stance would allow slavery to continue, implicitly supporting it.

Finally, liberation theology focuses on God's kingdom, a new heaven and new earth.[7] There will be a new earth, not just a heavenly afterlife. This new earth is to be worked toward now. Liberationists argued that the emphasis on the 'here and now' was missing from much traditional Christian theology. A focus on the new heaven rather than the new earth allowed this life to remain oppressive.

Liberation theologies emerged first in Brazil among poor Catholic communities in the 1960s. These communities came to be known as 'base ecclesial communities', groups of fifteen to twenty people who met to discuss life and the Bible.[8] The excerpt beginning this chapter is one example. Priests and nuns encouraged their expansion; in Brazil alone they grew to several hundred thousand in number. As these communities reflected and acted, the hermeneutical circle and a new theology, called liberation theology, emerged. This theology focused on analyzing and improving the economic and political situations facing the poor communities.

Liberation theologies expanded to address issues of gender, race, ethnicity, ecology, sexuality, and others where people find themselves oppressed, marginalized, powerless to act. The wealthy were prioritized over the poor, but so too white was prioritized, male prioritized, heterosexuality prioritized. And liberation theologies have moved beyond Catholicism into other Christianities and have emerged in other religions including Judaism and Islam. Some of the Latin American communities were and continue to be multi-religious themselves. In Salvador, Brazil, for example, some people practice Christianity and Candomblé or other indigenous or African-derived religions together.

Since theology is practice, we[9] will be liberation theologians later in this chapter and work our way through the method of the hermeneutical circle central to liberation theology. We begin with a brief history of liberation theology's emergence. Then we work through the four steps of the hermeneutical circle, with examples. By the end of this chapter, you should have a sense of how this tradition is situated in history and culture and how you could begin the process of liberation in community.

A brief history

Several pivotal events in Latin America's history set the scene for liberation theology's emergence. From European colonization in 1492 through independence in the

1800s, Church and state were combined on the continent. The Catholic Church directly influenced politics. With independence, most countries separated Church from state and the Catholic Church lost influence. In the early to mid-1900s, the Church began a project called Catholic Action, to educate its parishioners as to how they should vote, in part to regain some influence over the state.

This move had unintended effects. First, the Church was hoping to influence wealthy and university-educated parishioners. However, in most countries this group was less than 5 percent of the population. Instead, Catholic Action influenced the practice of the 95 percent who were impoverished. Second, the churches began to promote a method which they called 'See, Judge, Act'. They wanted people to become aware of the issues important to the Church (see), judge the issues based on the Church's advice, and then act: vote. Catholic Action ended up influencing an entirely new movement of Latin America's poor, who had never before been encouraged to 'see, judge, act'. They saw their own situations, judged injustice, and acted to improve their situations.

This shift from a focus on the actions of the wealthy to the actions of the poor themselves mirrors a debate occurring globally in the 1960s between development and liberation. Development theorists and practitioners aimed to raise the living standards of the poor to those of the wealthy through economic growth. In contrast, those in favor of liberation argued that the poor could improve their own situations. What poor communities needed was for the powerful to lessen their control. Liberation practices tended toward socialist economics where development practices tended to be capitalist.[10]

Let's take Brazil as an example. In the early 1960s, some Brazilians shifted from support of development policies to liberationist policies. For example, Paulo Freire, a Brazilian philosopher of education, who grew up extremely poor in the northeast of Brazil, developed a holistic philosophy of education based on his experience.[11] His work inspired the Basic Education Movement, which encouraged adult literacy. Archbishop Helder Camara, and other members of the Catholic Church in northeast Brazil, began to call for more liberationist practices including land reform to redress the extremely unequal distribution of land.[12] These policies aimed to enable the poor to determine their own problems and solve them. In this context, the first base communities gathered together to struggle against economic poverty.

The landscape quickly shifted from a focus on economics to one on politics. In 1964, there was a military coup, overthrowing Brazil's democratically elected government. The military feared that the calls for adult education and land reform, which President Joao Goulart supported, were heading toward socialism. And with the recent Cuban revolution (1959), the military would take no chances.[13] For the next twenty years, opposition to the military government was not allowed. People who spoke out against the government 'disappeared',[14] were arrested, and tortured. The military also took over universities and other organizations. Freire was exiled and the Basic Education Movement was disbanded and outlawed. Camara's life was threatened and in 1969 his assistant Father Antonio Neto, a twenty-eight-year old, was tortured, tied to the back of a car, dragged through the streets, hung and shot in the head three times.

Facing these experiences, the communities developed a hermeneutic of suspicion. Rather than accepting the issues as presented by a church, the communities worked through them themselves. As they wrestled with the social sciences, the Bible and Catholic tradition, they came up with interpretations that differed from the official Church.[15] The theology of liberation emerged from these communities in Brazil first and spread across Latin America. In 1968, the Latin American bishops held a meeting in Colombia to respond to Vatican II and stated publicly their support for Vatican II and the emerging theology of liberation. Liberation practices appeared to agree with the general changes in Roman Catholicism through Vatican II.[16] Two years later, Gutierrez's *A Theology of Liberation*, the first formal work on liberation theology, was published in Spanish. Theologians like Gutierrez, Camara, Ernesto Cardenal[17] and many others began to write about this emerging theology and so it entered the public realm, the academic realm and became part of the purview of academic theologians.

Liberation theology increased in stature throughout the 1970s and 1980s and spread throughout the world.[18] In a few Latin American countries, liberationists gained political power: Cardenal, for example, was Nicaraguan Minister of Culture from 1979 to 1987 during the Sandinista administration. Three other liberationist priests served in this government as well. However, their successes were short lived. The USA actively sought to counter any government that leaned toward socialist policies.

In the 1980s, the Roman Catholic hierarchy began to condemn liberation theology. The Vatican issued an *Instruction on Certain Aspects of the 'Theology of Liberation'* and Cardinal Ratzinger (Pope from 2005 to 2013) strongly opposed liberation theology, investigating several of its theologians. Leonardo Boff, for example, was silenced by the Vatican. There were two main objections to the emerging theologies. First, liberation theology took Marxism seriously and the Pope disapproved of Marxist policies, fearing a turn to atheism. Second, the theologies emerged from communities rather than from the Pope. The Vatican re-articulated the importance of hierarchy stemming from Peter down through the history of the papacy. This condemnation led to the disappearance of liberation theology from the media and other aspects of the international scene. At the local level, many churches stopped supporting the base communities. Yet, communities continued their work and theologies continued to emerge. But liberation theologies simply were not acknowledged by people with power. The global North tended to assume that liberation theology was dead and gone. This assumption was also strengthened as many governments began to return to democratic rule. In the late 1980s and early 1990s the fall of the Berlin Wall and the apparent demise of communism led to further assumptions that 'there is no alternative'.[19] In reality, liberation theology continues to call for alternatives to any policies that oppress or marginalize others.

In the past ten years, there has been a resurgence of liberation theologies in academic circles. For example, in 2007, a new Consultation on Liberation Theologies was formed at the American Academy of Religion's Annual Conference.[20] Over four hundred people attended its first session. Liberation theologies once again have representatives in the academic realm from around the world who participate in liberationist communities. And liberation theologies continue to emerge from communities working through the hermeneutical circle.

The hermeneutical circle

The hermeneutical circle is similar to the method of 'See, Judge, Act', put forward by Catholic Action. However, the judging is split into two parts: one based on faith and another based on reason. Communities see, communities analyze from their faith (sacred text, tradition, and theologies) and their reason (academic knowledge), and then they act. In this method liberation theology's two foci, acting and prioritizing the marginalized, are evident.

The first step in the hermeneutical circle is to assess our situation in community, to see. What is our reality? How are we poor, powerless, oppressed? How might we be impoverishing, oppressing or dominating others? This step requires a process of becoming self-aware, conscientization.[21] Through conscientization, the community becomes aware of its situation and how that situation sits in its larger history and culture.

The second step is to analyze our situation in community with academic tools, to judge. Our situation may be helped with academic tools and our situation may help us to critique academic tools.

The third step is to analyze our situation with theological tools, to judge. Our understanding of our situation may be enhanced by our theology, faith traditions, and sacred texts. And our situation may help us to critique our faith traditions, sacred texts, and theologies.

The fourth step is to act, to put the reflection into practice. And the spiral continues. In this way, liberation theology emerges, grows, and is refined.

Four qualifications need to be stated here. First, if a community assumes that it has found the correct practice and no longer needs to reflect, then it has lost the hermeneutic of suspicion critical to liberation theology. Second, this spiral is messy. Sometimes action has to be taken without full reflection. Sometimes in assessing the situation, steps are already intertwined. I separate them out here to emphasize the importance of each piece. Third, the reflection is not always overtly theological. Base communities are no longer explicitly ecclesial. And fourth, even the academic theologian comes from a community and should represent, in part, the views of the community, not solely his/her own. Where the theologian departs from the community, this should be made clear.

Let's see how this circle works in community.

Step 1: Conscientization: Recognizing our situation (see, experience)

Conscientization is:

> The process in which men [sic], not as recipients, but as knowing subjects, achieve a deepening awareness both of the sociocultural reality that shapes their lives and of their capacity to transform that reality.[22]

So first we assess our situation in community. We use our eyes and ears to see what is around us, and to listen to our neighbors in community. We go through a process of conscientization whereby we take charge of our own reality, become active participants in our own lives. We need to decide who our neighbors in community are, what our situation is, and how that situation sits in history and the wider global community.

There are four pieces that help us determine who our neighbors in community are. First, we need to decide the parameters of the community. Who will be part of this community and why? Who are we excluding and why? Is our community diverse in opinions, in age, race, ethnicity? If not, why not? And how can we ensure we do not oppress those who are outside the community? Second, once the parameters of the community have been chosen, we need to ensure every voice of the community is heard at each stage of the circle. Third, and related to this is that each member of the community should actively participate. The working of the community should be made comfortable for each person to participate in his/her own way. And fourth, no one should dominate or be seen as the leader. There may be a facilitator or someone who coordinates aspects of the community but it can rotate. Hierarchy can have a negative impact on the prior aspects.

Keeping in mind who our community is, we then assess what our situation is. This may be obvious at some times and completely hidden at others. Further, it will change over time, which is why this circle becomes a spiral. First, we ask what our reality is. What situation are we living in? What problems are we having? We need to be willing to share our own perceptions and listen to the perceptions of others in the community. Together we come to an assessment of our situation in community. Then we ask how others outside the community perceive our situation. Who are we comparing ourselves to? Who are others comparing us to? And finally, we assess what is unique about this situation. Why is it that we have come together now?

Once our community has assessed its situation, we need to situate it in the wider history and global community. What has happened in our community in the past? How have things changed? How does this relate to other communities and situations around the world? We cannot know this fully but it serves as a check to ensure that we are not prioritizing ourselves over other people and communities who may be more marginalized, to ensure that we examine our own oppressiveness.

To take one example, the Center for Studies and Social Action (CEAS, Centro de Estudos e Ação Social) supports base communities in and around Salvador, Brazil.[23] It is a Jesuit-based organization established in 1967 in the aftermath of the military coup. It has consistently tried to create a space for reflection and action and has embraced the method and theology that emerged from base communities. CEAS describes itself as using a method of *andade* (walking with) the groups. Its own goal is to work with the most marginalized people in and around Salvador. CEAS argues that the poor communities quickly learn and many times already know their rights. What they want is help building their capacity to demand that those rights be fulfilled.

Twice a year CEAS reviews its links with communities. As part of this process it thinks through the following questions: Who are we excluding? Who is still marginalized? These reviews have led it to work with homeless people with HIV/AIDS, prostitutes, street youth, and others. It is consistently trying to figure out how to include the most excluded in its community. This is the important first step of determining who our neighbors in community are.

Next, a community needs to see what their situation is. CEAS worked with a poor coastal community in Salvador known as Gamboa de Baixo. In the past, they eked out a living on the steep cliff on the coast through fishing. Now they faced at least two forms of poverty: economic and political. Their traditional livelihood of fishing had disappeared. And they could not get the municipality to respond to any of their demands for help. So they faced a physical lack: a lack of money, food, electricity, etc. Their perception of this lack was not solely economic. They saw the problem as political. Where other communities were provided with sewers, water and electricity, theirs was not. Outsiders' perception of the community differed. The municipality saw this community as a barrier to tourism. They wanted that part of the coast for cruise ships to dock. They planned to build a huge pier to reach the top of the cliff. And in fact, they had already built a major road jutting out over the edge of the cliff. The people living in the community could now only access their dwellings by a steep walkway under the road itself. The municipality was trying to drive them out. Knowing others' perceptions, the residents can work to change them.

Then there are the particulars of this time and space. The sea has fewer fish and more pollution. The residents cannot get jobs in the tourist trade because their health is bad, their teeth are bad, they are dark skinned, and they have no education. No one comes into the community because it is cut off by the main road. No public services are available because the town wants the residents to leave.

The situation will of course change in that community over time. Issues emerge and disappear and take precedence over others. For example, the city of Salvador received a World Bank loan to develop the Gamboa area. It intended to use this loan to make the area attractive to tourism. Lawyers advising the Gamboa Residents' Association, however, found a clause that said the government had to provide shelter for the residents. Hence, the government found itself forced to build the shells of concrete buildings in which the residents now live. Now they struggle to gain access to water, electricity and sewer services to make their houses habitable.[24]

In assessing the situation it is also important to look at the wider history and culture. The Gamboa situation is not unique to Gamboa alone. They have linked to other communities in and around Salvador to see how other neighborhoods have responded when the government tries to push the residents out to increase the tourist trade. They have learned how to demand public services, etc. CEAS plays an important role here offering them advice, linking up the various groups, and finding lawyers and other important connections. At this point, the lines between the first and second step begin to blur.

Step 2: Analysis of academics and situation (judge, reason)

Obviously, the prime object of theology is God. Nevertheless, before asking what oppression means in God's eyes, theologians have to ask more basic questions about the nature of actual oppression and its causes. The fact is that understanding God is not a substitute for or alternative to knowledge of the real world.[25]

Once we have used our eyes and ears, we then need to use academics. Having assessed our situation, we can determine what our community knows that can help us. We can also ask what more we need to know. And then finally, we need to get access to and learn that knowledge. This and the previous piece may not appear to be theology to many in the global North; however, it is all part of the theological process.

So what knowledge do we already have as a community? There is no required minimum education although 'analysis of academics' appears to suggest this. In fact, in the base communities, they often studied as a group, sharing their accumulated knowledge and figuring out where to learn more. Some of this analysis begins to occur in our previous step of conscientization but it is separated out into a second step to emphasize its importance in the process. It is often the case that we already have academic knowledge that we can apply to our situation. Each person's experiences are valued in this piece of the conversation. If my experience disagrees with an academic text, the text does not override my experience. It may be that our knowledge of a situation can apply to and change academic assumptions.

Next, we address the gaps in our knowledge. The first subjects to be addressed here, historically, were the social sciences, in particular, economics and politics. This made sense because the first issues to be addressed were economic and political poverty. They also analyzed the field of development studies. Today too, we still analyze issues and situations with: Economics, Politics, Development Studies/Globalization, Sociology, Anthropology, Gender and Sexuality Studies, and so forth. Any academic subject can be helpful here. I simply highlight those most commonly used.

It is important to have a hermeneutic of suspicion when approaching the literature. To take economic poverty for example, it has been argued that poverty is caused by laziness, wickedness or ignorance. Poverty has also been viewed as a lack of resources or knowledge of how to use resources. Here, development can be pursued: teach them how to be like us. Another view argues that poverty is the result of oppression; the powerful need to give up oppressing others. We will see these three aspects in other forms of poverty.[26] From a liberationist perspective, the discussion starts from the margins, with those who have been dismissed for whatever reason.

Turning to history, this step, analysis of academics, is the one that received the most condemnation. As I mentioned above, the Vatican condemned liberation theology in part because of its use of Marxism. Many liberationists were and continue to be influenced by Marxist economics, politics, sociology and so forth. These liberationists distinguished between Marx's analysis of class struggle and the atheist worldview that emerged. The Boff brothers in response to the accusation that liberationists were too influenced by Marxism said,

> Marx (like any other Marxist) can be a companion on the way, ... but he can never be *the* guide, because 'You have only one teacher, the Christ' (Matthew 23:10). This being so, Marxist materialism and atheism do not even constitute a temptation for liberation theologians.[27]

What is important in any use of academics is the hermeneutic of suspicion. No one economic or political or sexual or ecological analysis can be assumed to be correct: capitalist or communist, democratic or dictatorial, patriarchal or matriarchal and so forth. Experience should help us to critique these academic tools.

I'll give you two brief examples of this step in action. First, on Itaparica Island, a forty-five minute boat ride from the city of Salvador, CEAS worked with a group of pre-school teachers. The government only funds primary school on this island (ages eight to twelve), although children have a constitutional right to pre-school and secondary school. The city government states that children can attend pre-school on the mainland. In response to this situation, several churches and other organizations have set up private pre-schools on the island. Yet problems remain. CEAS works with the community's teachers to address two further issues: 1. improving the teachers' pedagogy; 2. increasing the capacity of the teachers to demand provision of pre-schools by the state.

The teachers meet every two weeks, dividing their meetings into two parts: pedagogy and capacity-building. The teachers keep diaries of their work in the classrooms and at each meeting one teacher shares a portion of their diary with the group. In one meeting, a teacher shared a story of one of her youngest students. The four-year-old girl did not interact with other students. In trying to figure out what the problem was, the teacher learned that the girl's father mistreated her. The teacher wanted advice on how to deal with the situation. The teachers then brainstormed strategies to help build the child's self-esteem.

At another meeting, a lawyer for the city visited the community and blamed bureaucracy for the lack of response from the government. The teachers accused the city of not addressing the 'root of the problem of social injustice'.[28] The lawyer left and the women began to discuss the public budget. They wanted to adjust resource allocation to include pre-schools and force the government to implement their plan. They were beginning to participate actively in the democratic process, arguing that education is a right not a privilege. They were deepening their study of the democratic process in general, amassing a variety of ways to approach the government.

An example of a larger scale movement that has developed is the Landless Movement in Brazil (MST, Movimento dos Trabalhadores Rurais Sem Terra).[29] Emerging from the calls for land reform, it became a national organization in 1984. A clause in the new Brazilian Constitution enabled takeover of land that was considered productive but was unused by its owner. The landless movement brought together communities to reclaim this land. As the MST developed, their academic resources developed too. They now have sectors focused on communication, culture, education, gender, health, human rights, international relations, production, and youth.

Alongside these analyses, and intertwined with them, are faith-based responses.

Step 3: Analysis of faith and situation (judge, sacred text, tradition, theologies)

We've assessed our situation and analyzed it with academics. Now we will analyze our situation with sacred texts, tradition, and theologies. Helpful questions and analyses emerge from many areas of theology: queer, feminist, womanist, black, economic, political, ecological, etc.[30] As with the previous step, we have some personal experience with text, tradition, and theologies and some new knowledge to attain. Further, one does not need to be literate to 'read' the sacred text;[31] there is no minimum required education.

Sacred texts

In a small basic ecclesial community made up of very poor farmers, the group read the text which prohibits the eating of pork. The people present at the meeting asked,

'What message does God have to give us today through this text?' They discussed the matter and decided, 'Through this text God wants to tell us that we, today, should eat pork!' The argument went as follows: God's main concern is with the health and life of God's people. Pork, when it's not treated properly, can cause disease and lead to death. Therefore in biblical times God forbade the people to eat pork. But today we know how to treat this type of meat. It's no longer a danger to our health. Besides that, it's the only meat we have to eat. If we don't eat this meat we'll be endangering the lives and health of our children. So today we ought to eat pork. That's being faithful to God![32]

Before we start to read the sacred text, we need to unpack our assumptions and attitudes. Reading the Hebrew and Christian Scriptures, for example, documents produced by and addressed to people a long time ago and in very different economic, political, ecological and other contexts can feel like being in a twilight zone. The 'hermeneutic of suspicion' is very helpful here. We must be aware that the Bible does not clearly reflect on the themes we would most like to see there. And yet, we try to read the Bible to analyze our situation. We also need to understand that while for many Christian communities the Bible is authoritative, for many others its harm has been such that this authority is now in question.

Second, we need to remember that we read texts from our social location. While a middle-class white male student in the USA may read the text from one perspective, a mixed race Brazilian farmer may read it from a very different perspective. Mesters points out that the base communities tended to read the Bible with 'freedom, familiarity, and fidelity'.[33] Having a 'free' approach to reading it, means they are not bound up in a prior tradition of reading. In fact, here they came up with the opposite interpretation to what the text literally said. Third, it feels familiar to the communities. Mesters describes this familiarity as 'people who feel at home in the Bible'.[34] It does not seem to be a strange text. Finally they want to be faithful to the text. However, this faithfulness is: 'not primarily to the meaning the text has in itself (the historical and literal meaning), but to the meaning they discover in the text for their own lives'.[35] They read the text in order to be able to act to change their situation.

There are two lenses in particular that liberationists use. First, do no harm. Miguel De La Torre states,

> Jesus Christ, in the gospel of John said it best, 'I came that they may have life, and have it abundantly (10:10).' … Only those interpretations that empower all elements of humanity, offering abundant life in the here-now, as opposed to just the here-after, are biblically sound.[36]

And you can see this in the biblical quote used to introduce the section. Their analysis of the text was that where pork caused death in the past, it now brings life. Hence they should eat it. As we read the biblical texts, we constantly need to be on our guard for our own biases in readings that would cause harm.

Second, prioritize those who have been most oppressed and marginalized. De La Torre notes that 'We can begin by realizing that some biblical verses have been misinterpreted, consciously or unconsciously, to protect the power and privilege of the dominant culture.'[37] We tend not to focus on the poorest in our global society; to offer humanity only to those with status. Instead our 'reading' of reality and faith should focus on the victims, the marginalized, in all realms: economic, political, gender, sexual, environmental, and so forth. We continually need to assess whether our reading of the Scriptures prioritizes those in our community who are most ignored.

Faith traditions

> In responding to Matthew 12:1–8, Quique said: 'People are more important than laws, Jesus is teaching. But for the Christians of today as for the Pharisees of those times, it's just the opposite. Before birth-control pills became popular throughout the world the United States experimented with them on thousands of poor women in Puerto Rico. As a result of those experiments a great number of monstrous children were born. The church protested, not because of the monstrous children nor because they were experimenting on poor people. It was because the birth control was through pills and not through some other method, for example, rhythm. For them what was sacred was a law or rather a legality, not people.'[38]

Those same lenses are used when examining faith traditions. Asking 'What do the traditions say?' or 'What does my denomination think?' are important questions. However, they are only one aspect of the conversation. We need to ask the following questions too. Where did the doctrine come from? Who does it benefit? Who does it harm? Does it prioritize the marginalized? The religious traditions themselves are not assumed to be authoritative, rather they are representative of how others have interpreted text, tradition, reason and experience in the past. Further, they need to be examined to see if they are based on practice.

In practicing liberation, all is subject to suspicion. There is no automatic adherence. This critical suspicion of tradition is not just within the Roman Catholic Church, it is for any church tradition. While Protestant communities are freer to question aspects of the tradition, many Protestant churches still have creeds and dogma to which members are expected to adhere. Tradition can help to illuminate our situation and our situation can help to critique tradition.

Formal liberation theologians refer to the creeds and councils of the faith more so than the communities do. In part, academic theologians try to show how the liberation emerging from the communities can be understood already to be part of the Church tradition. For example, many liberation theologians have referred to the Second Vatican Council.[39] It is important to note that the theologians are not showing how liberationists submit to the Church but rather how the Church illuminates the theologies emerging from community. This is in distinct contrast to the hierarchy of the Roman Catholic Church, among others, and has led to criticisms of liberation theology, as I noted above.

The base communities tended to distrust the Church's teachings, as the excerpt beginning this section shows. This is particularly true of the Latin American context where people have seen the churches side with the rich against the poor throughout history. And it is also true of other communities who have been marginalized or excluded by churches. The more that religious traditions focus on dogma rather than praxis, the more communities tend to distrust tradition.

Theologies[40]

If we find an individual who is a poor, black, lesbian, AIDS-infected, disabled, ugly, an old prostitute, and still we see this individual as a human being in her fundamental dignity, we will be undergoing a spiritual experience of grace ... and faith.[41]

When the base communities were first reflecting, other theologies did not make much of an appearance. Rather, as these communities became literate and had access to the sacred text for the first time, that tended to be the focus. However, as time has passed and liberation communities have expanded around the globe, you can find communities who are reflecting on theologies. In addition, communities reflect on the theologies that they themselves have constructed through their praxis. As a community works through theologies there are important questions to ask. Who is writing? On whose authority do they speak? And what are their biases? Who are they prioritizing?

As we have seen throughout this chapter, there are common hallmarks of theologies that emphasize liberation. First, liberationists tend to produce theologies that focus on the margins. In the base communities, people often use the actions of Jesus as a guide. Here, they tend to refer to the gospels where Jesus was often associated with those on the margins. We too should teach each human being as human, as Sung noted above. In denying humanity to anyone we deny humanity to Jesus.[42] Jesus is the other, the homeless woman suffering from HIV, the mass murderer jailed for life, a child slave working in the cocoa fields of West Africa. It is not 'what would Jesus do?' but 'what would we do to Jesus'? If I thought of the elderly prostitute as Jesus, would I be indignant that she is denied enough food and water and shelter to survive?

So as you read theology, think about whether it is considering those most marginalized, and if so, on what authority? Is the theologian him/herself a part of the marginalized community? If not, what contact does he/she have with that community? As we assess our situations we need to ask: where are we enabling humans to be fully human? Where are we denying others their humanity?

Liberationists also tend to focus on theologies and theologians who prioritize community. Liberation theologians argue that we come to know God through knowing others. Gutierrez stated, 'In his perceptive homily at the closing of the Council (Vatican II), Paul VI commented on Matthew's text saying that "a knowledge of man is a prerequisite for a knowledge of God"; and he summarized the objective of the Council as "a pressing and friendly invitation to mankind of today to rediscover in fraternal love ... God."'[43] My personal understanding of God is based only on my own experiences; in communion with others I gain broader knowledge and experiences. Such knowledge and experiences enrich and deepen my own. Blending this with the focus on the margins, the poor, the oppressed, the marginalized then becomes the starting point for theology, for knowing God. Not only does the quote from Sung show this, you can also see that he is being inclusive with his language, using 'we'. As hard as it is to come to decisions in community, these decisions, if taken collectively and without domination by some, will tend toward distributing power equally.

So when reading ask: Is this person writing theologically from his/her own perspective? Are they incorporating the perspective of others in their community as well? How does my community's experience support or critique this theology?

And based on the emphasis on the marginalized in community, liberation theologians tend to focus on justice. Justice is crucial because it is only through just community that people could know and love God. Further, in God's kingdom (the new heaven and new earth), justice will rule. Sin is any form of injustice and salvation will be this new earth with justice. The struggle for justice is the struggle for God's kingdom, literally in this world. This hermeneutical circle itself brings us closer to the kingdom. The Boffs state that 'the kingdom ... is not a kingdom "of this world" (John 18:36), but it nevertheless begins to come about in this world.'[44] There are three critical aspects here. First, Christians should work toward the kingdom now, critically assessing this world in the light of God's kingdom. Where injustice lies, justice should be sought. Second, the kingdom is both here and not here. None of our decisions will be perfect but they can help us move closer to the full kingdom. Third, God will fully bring about the new heaven and new earth; so God is on the side of those marginalized.

In our current situations we often find injustice, which liberationists describe as sin. Sin breaks the relationship between human beings and God. Injustice must be eradicated to build right relationships between human beings and with God. Salvation then is liberation from sin. It brings about communion with God and unity with each other, including an 'ugly', 'old' prostitute. This praxis is of love, of justice; it is a sharing of power.

So when reading theology ask: Is this theology oppressing others? Is it searching for just treatment of all? And we should ask these questions of our community itself.

It is also important to note that theological concepts are not limited to the Christian tradition. Although this chapter has focused on Christianity, many of the communities are multifaith. They integrate a variety of texts, traditions, and theologies.

Our theological assessment needs to be blended with the sacred text, the tradition, the academic judgment and the assessment of our situation in order to act. Remember that none of these theological foci can be taken as fact. Any theme may turn out to need adjustment in the future. None of this is permanent. We will act and rethink and re-act.

Step 4: Taking right action: Praxis (act)

In one sense, this step is straightforward: take action. However, often this step is avoided or undoes much of the previous reflection. First, it can be tempting to keep on reflecting in order to be sure the action will be the correct one. However, this spiral only works when you act. Second, in taking action, be sure it is the action agreed to in community. It can also be tempting to run off in our own individual direction rather than the community's decision. Third, our action will not be perfect. We need to be aware of this and be prepared to reflect on our actions again. And fourth, start this reflection even as you are acting. Ask, who are our actions benefitting? Who are we excluding? How does this affect our situation? How does it affect our academics, our faith communities, etc? Our actions can be the beginnings of right praxis. As equality of power grows our situations may be improved in a way that leads us closer to justice.

Let's look at three examples of action. On a local level, let's return to the Gamboa community, introduced above. Recognizing that there was a disparity between their own perception of their living situation and the perception of others, they decided to host a photographic walkabout. Reporters and photographers from the newspapers, magazines and even radio stations were invited to the community for a day to see what life was like for the residents. As they worked to produce their promotional material, they added captions like: 'From here I am not leaving; from here no one can take me away.' And 'Watch out people, here comes Via Nautica.' These captions encapsulated their determination to remain a community in the face of the tourist plan (Via Nautica) to build a pier above the community for cruise ships and other boats to dock and disembark. As they planned their agenda, they talked about how this walkabout could change their relations with the media. For example, the previous week, about forty masked people wearing police uniforms had come into the community assaulting several residents. Three residents ended up in hospital. Despite the residents giving the license plate number of one of the cars to the newspapers, nothing was reported. This day, however, would give them another chance to tell their story.

A second and larger scale example is that of the MST, which emerged from liberationist reflection. As I mentioned above, the movement works to build communities to reclaim land. It begins with the resettling of families into tent communities near the property. The families can then farm the land. After having farmed the land for one year, they can apply for legal ownership. The process takes several years to go through the court system and the families cannot live on the land until they own it. It is also extremely dangerous as the landowners often hire people to forcibly remove the landless from the land. While some of the communities are predominantly Catholic, others are multifaith and liberation theology is integrated to varying extents.

My final example is international, that of the Jubilee Debt Campaign.[45] This campaign argues for the cancellation of the debts of the world's poorest countries. In 1997, the Jubilee 2000 Coalition was formed, working for cancellation by the year 2000. Since then, faith-based organizations in the UK and around the world have continued to work on this issue. As with the MST, not everyone involved is a liberationist and not every liberationist supports this campaign. However, it shows three pieces of an effective struggle for liberation. First, people of different faiths come together around this issue. Jews, Christians, and Muslims are involved with this organization. Second, based on the theological principles I articulated above, it works with the most marginalized countries and aims to enable them to improve their own situations. Third, it has integrated economics, politics, and faith to act.

Conclusion

Liberation theology is reflection and action that focuses on freeing humanity from oppression. This theology emerges from community through the process of the hermeneutical circle and prioritizes those who have been most marginalized. A community can move through the steps in any order and often simultaneously. It can have local, national and even international impacts.

So how do you read liberation theologies? Ask whether or not pieces of this hermeneutical circle have been followed in community. If some or many are missing, ask who is the theologian speaking for? Although we are working in community, we cannot always see our own biases. So be on the lookout for them and point them out to us when you find them.

And how do you do liberation theology? Act and reflect and include. First, practice. Second, critique your experiences, your academics, and your faith. Third, continue making your communities more diverse and inclusive.

Notes

1 C. Mesters, 'The Liberating Reading of the Bible', in SEDOS, June–July 1996, pp. 164–70: p. 165. Carlos Mesters is a Dutch priest who has lived and worked in Brazil since 1949.

2 I define liberation both as 'freedom from' and 'freedom to'. While liberation is freedom from powerlessness and oppression, it also must be freedom to act. I define theology in the traditional Anselmian sense of 'faith seeking understanding'. It encompasses the study and action of every person of faith. The action is critical to liberation theology.

3 Powerlessness may be economic, political, sexual, racial, ecological and so forth.

4 L. Boff and C. Boff, *Introducing Liberation Theology 1: Liberation and Theology*, trans. P. Burns, Tunbridge Wells: Burns & Oates, 1987, p.83. Leonardo Boff is a Brazilian priest and theologian. Clodovis, his younger brother, is also a priest and university professor.

5 G. Gutierrez, A *Theology of Liberation: History, Politics and Salvation*, trans. C. Inda and J. Eagleson, London: SCM Press, 1974, p. 3. Gutierrez, a Peruvian priest, is considered to be the 'father' of liberation theology. He was the first to publish a book on the subject in English, based on his work with communities in Peru.

6 This phrase was initially developed in the work of Paul Ricoeur.

7 See Isa. 65:17, 66:22, 2 Pet. 3:13, Rev. 21:1. This concept is described further in the 'faith' step of the hermeneutical circle section.

8 'Base' denotes that they are from the grassroots, the poorest segment of the community. 'Ecclesial' means they were part of the church structure. Today 75 percent of Brazilians consider themselves Catholic. The numbers were even greater in the 1960s. And 'community' emphasizes that they were groups of people reflecting and acting together. Groups and communities and organizations now exist in many different sizes from less than ten people to more than two hundred. It is the method practiced rather than the size that is important.

9 I use 'we' to be inclusive. For the purposes of this chapter, you are welcome to include yourself as a theologian to test it out, whether you consider yourself to be a person of faith or not. In many liberation communities, faith and practice are so blended that practice is assumed to be theological even if the person is unclear about their faith, agnostic, or atheist. You will also note that I use the personal I, at times, rather than the third person. It is because I want you to be clear that this is my own perspective. This is important to liberationists because often theology was taken as if it represented everyone or applied to everyone, when it was often from the perspective of white European men and did not represent or apply to many of the world's faithful.

10 See my book *Controversies in Political Theology: Development or Liberation?*, London: SCM Press, 2007, for the history of this conversation and that of the associated theologies.

11 Freire wrote a ground-breaking book, *Pedagogy of the Oppressed*, trans. M.B. Ramos, New York: Herder & Herder, 1970, which continues to influence educational practices today.

12 Statistics are notoriously varied. However, most sources, including several in Brazil itself, say that 1 percent of the population owns between 45 and 50 percent of the land. And the poorest 40 percent of the population owns less than 1 percent of the land. To take two examples from INCRA (Instituto Nacional de Colonizacao e Reforma Agraria), Brazil's National Office of Colonization and Agrarian Reform: 79 large landowners own 4.5 percent of Brazil's rural area. Twenty of them own 2.2 percent or 18.88 million hectares in Brazil's rural area. For those readers who read Portuguese, see www.incra.gov.br.

13 The USA supported military dictatorships across Latin America as they feared the calls for liberation were socialist and they did not want any country aligning with the Soviet Union. The military dictatorships enacted policies of economic development that the USA promoted around the world.

14 The 'disappeared' are people who were taken from their houses by police or the military and never seen again.

15 See the section on the hermeneutical circle for details.

16 For details of the changes to Roman Catholicism in Vatican II, see M. Lamb and M. Levering (eds) *Vatican II: Renewal Within Tradition*, Oxford: Oxford University Press, 2008.

17 Cardenal is a Nicaraguan priest, who was part of the Sandinista government in the 1980s.

18 See, for example, K. Koyama, *No Handle on the Cross*, Maryknoll, NY: Orbis Books, 1977; A. Pieris, *An Asian Theology of Liberation*, Maryknoll, NY: Orbis Books, 1988; A. Boesak, *Farewell to Innocence: A Social-Ethical Study on Black Theology and Black Power*, Maryknoll, NY: Orbis Books, 1976, and the Commission of Theological Concerns of the Christian Conference of Asia (ed.) *Minjung Theology: People as the Subjects of History*, London: Zed Books, 1981.

19 This famous phrase is attributed to former British Prime Minister Margaret Thatcher. It refers to the assumption that democratic capitalism is the only possible system.

20 To see the state of liberation theologies today, consult my book publishing the first five years of the consultation's presentations: T. Cooper (ed.) *The Reemergence of Liberation Theologies: Models for the Twenty-First Century*, New York: Palgrave MacMillan, 2012.

21 This word is directly transposed from the Portuguese *conscientizacao*. It is more than just becoming self-aware. It is also situating oneself in the larger cultural, historical, economic, political and other contexts. See Freire's definition at the beginning of Step 1.

22 P. Freire, *The Politics of Education: Culture, Power and Liberation*, trans. D. Macedo, London: Macmillan, 1985, p. 93, n. 2.

23 For those who read Portuguese, consult their website: www.ceas.com.br.

24 See the excellent article by Professor Keisha-Khan Perry addressing the spatial injustices in and around this community, including the building of a high-rise apartment building for the white elite that destroyed some homes in the Gamboa community. (K.-K. Perry, from the 'Margins of the Margins', in *Brazil: Black Women Confront the Racial Logic of Spatial Exclusion*, Inaugural Working Paper Series 1.5, Hartford, CT: Center for Urban and Global Studies, Trinity College, 2009; available online at www.trincoll.edu/UrbanGlobal/CUGS/Faculty/Rethinking/Documents/Margin%20of%20the%20Margins%20in%20Brazil.pdf; Accessed January 15, 2012.) The article discusses the conflicts emerging between the elite wanting the coastal waters for their yachts and the Gamboa community's fishermen and women. It also contains photos that show how the neighborhood is physically changing. And finally, it contains several negative descriptions of the community by outsiders.

25 Boff and Boff, *Introducing Liberation Theology*, pp. 24–25.

26 So for example, with regard to gender, one may find literature that argues women are simply less intelligent than men and dismisses them. One may find books and articles that state that women need to learn to be like men: teach them. Or one may read that women have been oppressed by men and that men need to give up oppressing and holding power over women. The same has been applied to race, sexuality, politics, etc.

27 Boff and Boff, *Introducing Liberation Theology*, p. 28.

28 CEAS, *Equipe Urbana: Linha Programatica II/ Organizacao e Educacao Popular no Meio Urbano: Relatorio Semestral de Atividades, ano: julho de 2001*, Salvador, Brazil: CEAS, 2001, p. 3.

29 See www.mstbrazil.org for details of the history of this organization, its objectives, its links to liberation theology and the progressive Catholic Church and its academic emphases.
30 The other chapters in this section have excellent links to the practice of theology in general and mirror many of the practices of liberation theology.
31 Many of the people in the original base communities were not literate. However, after Vatican II, masses were no longer celebrated in Latin. Instead, they were in Spanish, Portuguese and other local languages. For the first time, people heard the biblical texts. In some communities, they reflected on what they had previously heard. In others, one person could read the text and others could then comment.
32 C. Mesters, *Defenseless Flower: A New Reading of the Bible*, trans. F. McDonagh, Maryknoll, NY: Orbis Books, 1989, p. 4.
33 Mesters, *Defenseless Flower*, p. 5.
34 Mesters, *Defenseless Flower*, p. 6.
35 Mesters, *Defenseless Flower*, p. 9.
36 M. De La Torre, 'Scripture', in M. De La Torre (ed.) *Handbook of U.S. Theologies of Liberation*, St. Louis, MO: Chalice Press, 2004, pp. 85–100, p. 87. Miguel De La Torre is professor of Social Ethics and Latino/a Studies at Iliff School of Theology in Denver, Colorado. He has written extensively on aspects of Latino/a theology.
37 De La Torre, 'Scripture', p. 86.
38 E. Cardenal, *The Gospel in Solentiname*, vol. 2, Maryknoll, NY: Orbis Books, 1978, pp. 18–19.
39 See for example the quote from Gutierrez in the following section. He refers to the Pope's sermon, which ended the Second Vatican Council.
40 Burns and Oates published a series of books in a Liberation and Theology Series that is excellent. The Boff brothers' *Introducing Liberation Theology* is the first book in that series. To see the development of liberation theology throughout the 1980s, please consult any of those works.
41 J.M. Sung, 'The Human Being as Subject', in I. Petrella (ed.) *Latin American Liberation Theology: The Next Generation*, Maryknoll, NY: Orbis Books, 2005, pp. 1–19: p. 5. Jung Mo Sung is a Korean-Brazilian theologian who is Dean of the School of Humanities and Law at Methodist University in São Paulo, Brazil.
42 Matt. 25:35–40: 'For I was hungry and you gave me food, I was thirsty and you gave me something to drink … ' and 'Then the righteous will answer him, "Lord, when was it that we saw you hungry?" … And the king will answer them, "Truly I tell you, just as you did it to one of the least of these who are members of my family, you did it to me."'
43 Gutierrez, *A Theology of Liberation*, pp. 200–201.
44 Boff and Boff, *Introducing Liberation Theology*, p. 52.
45 In the USA, see www.jubileeusa.org; in the UK, see www.jubileedebtcampaign.org.uk.

25
POSTCOLONIAL THEOLOGIES

Susan Abraham

The long history of modern European colonization is widely known. What is not so widely known and acknowledged is that the colonial aftermath led to the process called decolonization, a condition that has been engaged by theologians widely in the past twenty years.[1] Decolonization is an uneven process that has brought ambivalent gains to the newly 'independent' nation-states of the world. Among the academic responses to decolonization has been the development of a form of critical thinking in the academy called 'postcolonial theory', which not only investigates the colonial archive (the literary records reflecting on the experience of colonialism) but also tracks the effects of post-colonialism[2] on newly independent nation-states. Post-colonial theory is a sustained reflection on the modern colonial encounter between Europe and the rest of the world.

The aim of postcolonial *theory* is to decolonize Western modes of knowing. That is, it operates as an ongoing major critical discourse within the Western academic division of the humanities in colleges and universities. One might think that decolonization happened automatically and as a matter of course when various parts of the world emerged from under modern European colonial rule. However, decolonization does not mean the simple uncoupling of colonizer and colonized. In contemporary postcolonial theory, decolonization is a complex and intellectually strenuous activity spurred by varieties of political, cultural, and critical interventions in a number of disciplines. These efforts have encountered various difficulties and resistances, but they have also made important inroads and effected significant changes in how we in the Western world see things.

One of the ongoing challenges of postcolonial theory is to communicate these insights to a wider audience than the academy alone. An inherent feature of this critical discourse, which has given rise to much specialized writing in the academy, is that any attempt to define it remains difficult and elusive. It has no single, organized methodology nor even an originating moment since academic postcolonial theory ranges far beyond the historical legacy of the modern European colonial encounter. For example, as world histories of colonialism show, European colonial projects are not unique or singular. One can argue that the Rome of Christian antiquity was a colonial power[3] as was the colonization of Ireland by England or the colonization of Korea by Japan.[4] However, what goes by the name 'postcolonial theory' refers to the European colonization of various parts of the world in the past five hundred years and the continuing form it takes in neo-colonial globalization.

As a number of postcolonial theorists have indicated, postcolonial theory is also complicated by its twin methodological convictions – that of Marxism[5] on the one hand, and poststructuralism[6] and postmodernism[7] on the other. Thus, a distinction can be made between the Marxist-based political convictions of postcolonial theory which analyze class issues, and the postmodern and poststructuralist theoretical allegiances that advance a compelling critique of Western forms of knowing, thinking, and doing. The emphasis on Marxism, poststructuralism, and postmodernism also reflects the academic disinterest in religious or theological ideas. In a manner of speaking, therefore, one can say that academic postcolonial theory is largely a 'secular'[8] enterprise.

In a similar vein, for postcolonial Christian *theology*, the question of how to decolonize theological knowledge leads to critical and constructive engagement across a number of methodological and political commitments. For example, some postcolonial theologians engage in a historical critique of postcolonial contexts by way of race, class, gender and sexuality analyses. Others are more concerned with the manner in which certain theological ideas such as freedom, liberation, or religious identity and belonging are constructed in, and gain their intelligibility in relation to, a particular cultural framework that often goes unnoticed. Another approach has been to constructively rethink the grammar of theology. For example, reflecting on the manner in which many Christians presume the cohesiveness of theological terms such as God, Christ, Human Being and Church, postcolonial theologians wonder if the symbols operate in culturally distinct frameworks. Could a Christian theologian who is doing theology in an Arabic-speaking context, for example, use the symbol 'Allah' for God?[9] Or, when Christians consistently use male pronouns when referring to the transcendent divine, are they naïvely borrowing from culturally specific patterns of gender superiority? Or, when Christian churches around the world are styled in the line of Gothic cathedrals in Europe, which are themselves abstract reflections of European natural beauty, are they simplistically reinscribing European cultural norms of architectural beauty?

In postcolonial theology, these three approaches – the materialist, the conceptual or symbolic, and the grammatical – are certainly not exclusive of each other. Thus, postcolonial theology, in its critical attention paid to traditional symbols, argues that there is a connection to be established between how we think about God, Christ, the Human Being, and the Church and how imperial systems of domination are created and sustained. Theology cannot be seen apart from the cultural, political, and economic systems it presumes or in which it is unavoidably embedded. Consequently, any postcolonial constructive proposal that is advanced is cognizant of and attentive to the complex contemporary context. Finally, most postcolonial theologians will point to the limits of Western ways of knowing when it comes to articulating theological ideas such as freedom, liberation, and religious identity and will advance instead cultural proposals which are largely ignored or unknown in traditional Western theology.

The trajectory of 'experience' in postcolonial theology

Each of these related theoretical emphases in their practical delineation examines the modern category of 'experience'. This has been a traditional source for theology. However, instead of merely focusing on experience of God (as if that were direct and immediate), postcolonial theology critically examines 'experience' as mediated through the multiplicity of methods presented by Marxist, poststructuralist or postmodern emphases. One manner in which 'experience' comes into focus for postcolonial theology is through examining how culture operates in theology. In the contemporary complex context, 'culture' is necessarily post-colonial since there is no culture on earth that can exempt itself from the experience of colonialism.

In an earlier phase of decolonizing theology, the category 'culture' simply meant the sense in which cultural location modified theology. Proposals for African American, Latin American, Asian and African theology highlighted ways in which cultural particularity challenged the presumption of Western forms of theology to speak from a universalizing position – that is, a God's eye vantage point. The idea that culture has a role to play in theological thinking is not itself a new idea and it certainly was not the invention of postcolonial theory. Doing theology using cultural analysis and cultural criticism has been part of varied forms of theology such as political theology,[10] correlation theologies,[11] ethnographic theologies,[12] feminist,[13] womanist,[14] *mujerista*,[15] and *minjung*[16] theologies. In the past decade, a number of theological studies have reflected on the significance of culture as important for theology and pressed the argument that theology itself as a genre ought to be seen as a mode of cultural production. In other words, Western theology that persisted without reflecting on its own cultural matrix was shown to be rather provincial in its language, unreflective of its philosophical and political orientations and sanguine in its understanding of power.

The emphasis on culture is reflected in a concentration on personal and social identity and how it shapes experience. For instance, in a statement on the significance of culture for theology, Sheila Greeve Davaney argues that the turn to culture[17] in theology acknowledges that human beings are historical creatures that inhabit particular social worlds.[18] As she asserts,

> Over against notions of rationality and experience as ahistorical, commonly structured and temporally invariant, there have emerged assumptions of the located, particular, pluralistic and thoroughly historical nature of human existence, experience and knowledge.[19]

To take culture into account is therefore already to think of 'rationality' and 'experience' as radically and inescapably historical. In such a view, theologies of culture were also emphasizing what postcolonial theologies emphasize – namely that experience and rationality must be understood in particular historical frames. Such a view of how culture plays a role in religious beliefs, practices, identities, values, institutions and even texts, led to innovative methodological proposals in theology. Analyses following the postmodern analysis of culture borrow the language of post-colonial theory, including its presentation of cultural location as a complex site from which to speak of experience. It is important to understand, however, that the category 'culture' is a complex and highly differentiated category in many of these proposals.

The complexity of the category 'culture' has not always been apparent. This has limited the critical impact of some third-world theologies. R. S. Sugirtharajah in his book, *Postcolonial Reconfigurations*, argues that the anti-colonial and national rehabilitation movements of the nineteenth century gave rise to the development of strategies of interpretation in constructive theology:[20]

> A number of critical theories, both foreign and local were tried and discarded. It was in this dialectical tension between the colonized and the colonizer, recuperating and rejecting one's own culture, and both imported and indigenous methods, that Third World hermeneutics was fashioned.[21]

These 'third-world hermeneutics'[22] emphasize experience utilizing a certain fixed notion of identity. As he points out, third-world theologies arising in postcolonial contexts are basically 'experiential discourses' which reflect people's experience of living in impoverished conditions. He also points out that the perception that third-world theologies only dealt with 'experience' ultimately compromised their importance in the eyes of Western academic theology, which perceived in them a lack of rational argumentation. That is, third-world theologies were understood to problematically present experience as opposed to reason. How, then, can postcolonial theologies make clear the *analytical* framework in which 'experience' complicates the traditional formulations of theological categories such as God, Christ, Human Being and Church? Sugirtharajah provides us with an important warning: do not draw simplistic correlations between human experience and theological ideas.

Unfortunately, many third-world theologies and experience-based theologies have fallen into this trap, simplistically correlating experience and theological language, leading to what has been widely decried as 'identity politics' in theology. Identity politics, arising from the uncritical use of cultural identity categories such as 'Asian' or 'Black,' do not necessarily decolonize theological knowledge. Instead, by aggressively presenting themselves as 'marginal' to academic theological discourse, these forms of identity-based theologies function to reinscribe highly problematic relations between the so-called 'center' and 'margin'. Furthermore, they rarely acknowledge the immense pluralism that words such as 'Asian' as a blanket name (among other such names) hide. Finally, the uncritical presentation of identity as something homogenous and static fails to acknowledge the power involved in the very act of naming. Thus, in the UK only people from the Indian subcontinent – including Pakistan and Bangladesh – are 'Asian'. In the US, on the other hand, this designation marks people from a vast swath of eastern parts of Asia while people from the Indian subcontinent are not usually considered as belonging to 'Asia'. Of course, the name 'Indian' in the US context carries with it a particular history of cultural naming and misrecognition. Each uncritical use of the name 'Asia' also veils the fact that cultural naming in our time still memorializes the colonial encounter. Cultural expressions such as 'Middle East', 'Latin America', or 'Africa' used as homogenous wholes are all reflective of European views of cultural others with whom they were and continue to be in a colonial (i.e. superior/subservient) relation.

So how do postcolonial theologians take account of these pitfalls in their attempt to decolonize theology? Here, I present two points of exploration. The first issue is that of identity and experience which has been complicated in different ways by secular postcolonial theory and by postcolonial theology. It should be noted, however, that these two stances – that of theology and that of theory – are not mutually exclusive insofar as the theoretical framework of secular postcolonial theory consistently informs and challenges theological production. Theology has always demonstrated the ability to constructively bridge disciplinary boundaries as any cursory survey of titles on theology and postcolonial theory will demonstrate. The opposite is less true. Theology and the study of religion have not significantly influenced the academic and secular stance of postcolonial theory. Some thinkers such as Gayatri Chakravorty Spivak, however, have begun to integrate religion into their analyses.[23] The next section therefore presents postcolonial theologian R. S. Sugirtharajah, postcolonial theorist Homi Bhabha, and practical theologian Marion Grau in order to track the development of postcolonial theology with postcolonial theory.

The second issue concerns postcolonial writing and reading as ethical practices that attempt to decolonize knowledge. Thinkers such as Edward Said and Homi Bhabha have from the outset criticized the 'orientalist'[24] frame of Western academic knowledge. Rather than taking the Western orientalist frame as a given, Bhabha, for example, writes about postcolonial theory and writing as a way to identify new and surprising forms of agency. In *The Location of Culture*, Bhabha writes:

> I have chosen to demonstrate the importance of the space of writing, and the problematic of address, at the very heart of the liberal tradition because it is here that the myth of the 'transparency' of the human agent and the reasonableness of political action is most forcefully asserted. Despite the more radical political alternatives of the right and the left, the popular, common-sense view of the place of the individual in relation to the social is still substantially thought and lived in ethical terms molded by liberal beliefs. What the attention to rhetoric and writing reveals is the discursive ambivalence that makes 'the political' possible.[25]

Reading and writing for postcolonial theorists is a highly political activity. For example, writing is a revolutionary activity for 'what was some people's modernity was someone else's colonialism'[26] and agency cannot be simplistically sought for colonized subjects under the aegis of Western modernity. It is for this reason that a dependency on cultural identity constructed through postcolonial cultural categories is highly problematic. Consequently, postcolonial theology does not result in easy strategies for decolonizing theology, implicated as it is in the colonial and civilizing mission; for this very reason, however, grappling with such strategies is important. Reflections on theological writing in the post-colonial context have led thinkers such as David Tracy to assert that religious or theological language is *sui generis* in nature. Religious and theological writing therefore are of a unique kind since the primary referent in such writing is God. However, postcolonial theological writing goes further than Tracy's analysis. Postcolonial theological writing is able both to make room for the kind of transcendent referent that Tracy is interested in preserving as the domain of religious language, while also showing how the immanent human other and her agency ought to be preserved with equal attention.

Decolonizing experience and identity

In ordinary parlance, 'identity' refers to a unified and cohesive name for oneself, one's community, or one's nation. For many of us, the identities of gender and race are self-explanatory and coherent. The problem with this assumption, however, stems from the recognition that all identity categories have been shown to circulate in a historically-specific cultural context marked by power differentials which value and reward different identities differently. For postcolonial theology, the quadruple issues of race, class, gender and sexuality form a constellation of oppressive strategies that shore up and perpetuate colonial forms of Christianity. Moreover, the political development of decolonization did not automatically provide direct and immediate solutions that could remedy the deep colonial patterns embedded in Christian forms of thought and practice. In his suggestions for theology in a postcolonial framework, R.S. Sugirtharajah argues that it is best to understand the development of decolonization in historical view and to mark the accompanying moments of ambivalences attending the attempts to decolonize Christianity.

In India, the experience of narrating the colonial encounter began with the anticolonial and national rehabilitation experiences of resistance in the nineteenth century.[27] These experiences created the following ambivalence: while the anti-colonialists raided the cultural and philosophical heritage of their past, they also discovered to their horror 'that the indigenous heritage they so eagerly turned to contained several contaminated aspects, customs and practices such as untouchability, caste distinctions, polygamy, female circumcision, and widow-burning'.[28] The ambivalence, however, enabled the development of what can be legitimately called 'Third-World hermeneutics', an approach to interpretation which borrowed methodological insights from the Europeans while inflecting it with aspects of indigenous culture and everyday experience. The consequent theology thus came to emphasize local experience and identity-based hermeneutics. Like other third-world theologies, postcolonial theology from India begins with the experiences of actual people. Thus, the idea that theology ought to be universalizable is called into question. As Sugirtharajah's epigraph to Part II articulates,[29] theology remains the same whether done at 120°F or at 70°F. What does *not* change is the object of theology and the theological imagination – God. What does change is the *theologian*. Thus, identity-based hermeneutics have given rise to a number of ways of doing theology, including feminist, Dalit,[30] indigenous. These and other strategic theological discourses are in large part attempts to think through personal experience and the position of inferiority accorded to the experience of being female, marginalized, or otherwise erased from traditional theology. In the same vein, postcolonial theology has emerged as a particular form of theological thought, as a reflection on experience as it is constructed through the flows of global geopolitical power:

> The term [postcolonial] generates at least three meanings; first, in a historical sense, it encapsulates the social, political and cultural conditions of the current

world order, bringing to the fore the cultural, political and economic facts of colonialism, and aiding the recognition of the ambiguities of decolonization and the ongoing neo-colonization. Secondly, as a critical discursive practice, postcolonial criticism has initiated arresting analyses of texts and societies. It provides openings for oppositional readings, uncovers suppressed voices and, more pertinently, has as its foremost concern victims and their plight. It has not only interrogated colonial domination but has also offered viable critical alternatives. Thirdly, the term implies the political and ideological stance of the interpreter who is engaged in anti-colonial and anti-globalizing theory and praxis. Applied to biblical studies, it seeks to uncover colonial designs in both biblical texts and their interpretations, and endeavors to read the text from such postcolonial concerns as identity, hybridity and diaspora.[31]

In other words, postcolonial theory influences postcolonial theology in terms of present configurations of neocolonialism and globalization. Secondly, as the quote emphasizes, identity, hybridity,[32] and diaspora[33] experiences are the standpoints from which neocolonialism and globalization are critiqued. At this point, it is pertinent to examine these interlocking categories of identity, hybridity, and diaspora in postcolonial theory to make clearer their impact on postcolonial theology.

The postcolonial theorist with whom the ideas of identity, hybridity, and diaspora have been most associated is Homi Bhabha. In terms of Bhabha's work, one could enter almost anywhere and perceive his concern with articulating the complicated and complex nature of identity, particularly in view of the fact that one of the primary material consequences of post-colonial history was the creation of 'independent' and secular nation-states. For Bhabha, and a host of others, speaking of culture in terms of national identity is *the* problem to be overturned in a postcolonial academy. Braiding together poststructuralism, psychoanalysis,[34] cultural studies and Marxism, Bhabha argues that the postcolonial subject is best understood in a framework of temporality rather than spatiality. That is, identity is to be thought of as a signifier[35] that circulates in a particular *time* period instead of being reified in terms of the clear cut 'space' of the nation. Identity instead belongs to the *time* of the nation. Thus, cultural identity marked by geopolitical constructs such as nation is a very modern, post-colonial development. As a result, experience constructed in the time of the nation is significantly different in kind from the identity of culture advanced in earlier forms of identity-based theories.

In an essay titled 'DissemiNation,' Bhabha argues that the postcolonial condition is best understood in a temporal milieu, which brings the concept of nation as culture to the foreground. Temporality, rather than spatiality (in this case the geographical territory with political borders defining distinct nation-states from one another), brings into focus the dominant means of locating culture. But culture is not a transparent identity marker. Culture instead is a way of life into which one is initiated and disciplined. That is, one learns how to behave in one's culture through a myriad of strategies imposed by culture's homogenizing impetus. In this manner culture is the bedrock of experience:

> The discourse of national*ism* is not my main concern. In some ways, it is the historical certainty and settled nature of that term against which I am

attempting to write of the Western nation as an obscure and ubiquitous form of living the *locality* of culture. This locality is more *around* temporality than *about* historicity: a form of living that is more complex than 'community'; more symbolic than 'society'; more connotative than 'country'; less patriotic than *patrie*; more rhetorical than the reason of the State; more mythological than ideology; less homogenous than hegemony; less centered than the citizen; more collective than 'the subject'; more psychic than civility; more hybrid in the articulation of cultural differences and identifications than can be represented in any hierarchical or binary structuring of social antagonism.[36]

Identity therefore must be constructed in terms of the life and experiences of people in the nation, but not in the manner that makes the nation appear as a universal, timeless, and invariant reality. 'Culture' is to be observed in the dynamic negotiations between local and global forces (both national and international) that are always challenging static forms of identity. Culture is the space of negotiation; that is, it refuses to capitulate to the kind of historicism[37] that tends to be assumed when we speak about nation or national identity. For example, Bhabha points to the problem of naming any of our cultural identities with names such as 'Indian' 'American' or 'Palestinian'. Any of these names, indeed any national name at all, is a highly contested one. Each name runs several risks. A name either suppresses the radical heterogeneity of peoples within the imagined borders of a nation (for example, when one speaks of 'India', one speaks of a radical plurality of 1.2 billion people), usurps for itself the radical heterogeneity of a whole continent (as in the case of 'America'), or, in other cases, animates a form of recognition that can then be refused by international bodies seeking to preserve current political allegiances (Palestine would be a case in point). Thus, 'nation' is created in a complex matrix of political negotiations, cultural self-articulation, and historical self-definition.

Since these are all particularly modern marks of authenticity, 'nation' really ought to be understood more in a temporal frame rather than in a spatial one. For nation is a narrated reality rather than an ontological reality. That is, the nation is an idea that comes into being in the wake of Western modernity and then exists in the complex of ongoing negotiations with other nations. Such an idea is best understood in the distinction Bhabha makes between the 'pedagogical' and 'performative' strategies of national identify formation. Bhabha argues that national identity is a negotiation between the pedagogical narrative of nation – in history and geography (modern notions of time and space) – and the performative, in which national identity is performed in spectacular events celebrating its 'independence' or in ceremonies celebrating its national uniqueness. For Bhabha, in the pedagogical narrative of nation, the idea of 'The People' is as an *a priori* historical presence. That is, in the pedagogical framework, the nation assumes the homogeneity of 'The People' in its linear narration of history. The performative, on the other hand, occurs in the 'enunciatory present'[38] that is, in the actual moment of articulation. The performative therefore 'introduces the temporality of the "in-between"'[39] and calls attention to the lack of ability in national discourses to truly accommodate the heterogeneity of its people.

The goal of using the category 'culture' is not merely to bring forth the 'free play of polarities and pluralities'[40] in the space of the nation. Rather, it is to bring forth a 'jarring of meanings and values' in the process of cultural interpretation. This is a subtle but exceedingly important point that Bhabha introduces into the study of culture and one of critical importance for theology. When culture becomes a part of theological thinking, what surfaces is not some exotic identity category that gives the impression that experience is a single, cohesive, and unified whole. Rather, the enterprise of thinking theologically undergoes a transformation as perplexing interventions performed by all culturally significant others that changes the 'scenario of articulation'.[41] It is what creates the jarring of meaning and values. An example of such a changed scenario of articulation is to be seen in the recent work of constructive theologian Marion Grau, whose reflections on missionary activity in the colonial context of South Africa have much relevance for postcolonial constructive theology.

Marion Grau's book, *Rethinking Mission in the Postcolony: Salvation, Society and Subversion*,[42] presents a historical and theological analysis through the framework of cultural negotiation as presented in Bhabha's theories of identity, hybridity, and diaspora. Mission is a theological area that is of great interest to postcolonial theologians, particularly in the wake of secularized and Western critiques of the missionary activity of Christianity that frequently accompanied the military conquests and colonization of the non-Western world. Much historical work has been done to overturn such a view of mission without denying the reality of the colonial violence in which Christian missions sometimes participated. However, in a theological exploration of the issues surrounding mission, Grau argues that mission practices demonstrate the same kind of ambivalence about identity that Bhabha charts, and furthermore, that missions' scenario of articulation is far more complex than merely the exercise of brute power by the colonizer over the colonized. She writes:

> Encounters in mission involve one type of hermeneutical action in imperial zones of interaction. We hear of interpreting bodies: bodies interpreting and bodies interpreted. Of messages getting scrambled, reinterpreted, as different communal bodies manifest: not just the colonially approved churches, but independent churches and 'syncretistic' movements like Ratana in Aotearoa/New Zealand or the Shembe Church in Kwa-Zulu Natal.[43]

That is, the category 'culture' is a vast field of networked relations in which everyone, not just the missionary and his hapless convert, is operating. A postcolonial theology of mission must take cognizance of mission history and point out, first of all, that flat description of national identity such as 'fifteenth-century Portugal' or 'the British Navy' are fundamentally metaphors. These metaphors ought to signal something about the porous and shifting nature of intercultural encounters. For example, more than half of the British Navy was not British and Napoleon's 'French' army included Poles and Germans.[44] When this is taken into account, we begin to see that certain theological ideas such as conversion necessarily meant conversion to a religio-cultural identity, already mixed or hybrid, and conversion did not just happen to the convert. Both religious and cultural systems exhibit a two-way 'commerce,' as Grau argues and as she ably traces in the historical archive of the Anglican Colenso Mission in South Africa.

In a fascinating exploration of the Zulu, the Colensos, and the hermeneutics of salvation, Grau presents the contours of a 'polydox'[45] theology of mission. She tracks the manner in which identity in the colonial encounter remains just one signifier amidst a series of colonial interventions. Here, conversion to Christianity cannot be seen apart from the socio-political and economic context in which Christian identity operates. Conversion to Christianity is therefore not simply a private experience of a soul 'getting saved' but is grounded in economic and cultural experiences. Missionary institutions attracted 'physically or socially orphaned persons, the disenfranchised, women, and persons of lower class or status'[46] by offering what Grau calls 'an opening in the density of established relationality'.[47] Missionaries of course were never the sole agents in the colonial encounter. Colonized people, by engaging in resistance and negotiation, and by using missionary institutions to advance themselves and improve their station in domestic contexts, effectively challenged patriarchal, social, cultural and theological norms. The complex and complicated motivations of converts to Christianity are finely illustrated in Tsitsi Dangarembga's novel *Nervous Conditions*, in which the protagonist Tambu's reasons for conversion include her hunger for education, the urgent need to transcend the patriarchal and chauvinist world of village and family, and her preference for the cultural, economic, and social privileges of the colonial cultural world.[48] Furthermore, the growth of indigenous Christian churches developed forms of Christianity that allowed them greater agency to function as institutions independent of colonial churches in Europe. In these cases, resistance required both adaptation and appropriation. Missionaries themselves 'converted' and 'went native' in efforts to make syncretistic[49] negotiations in culture and theology.

In Bishop John William Colenso's case, Grau contends that he eschewed the evangelical theology and hellfire preaching of his contemporaries and reformulated Christian ideas of salvation in universalist terms. Thus, he reiterates Irenaeus' soteriological theology of recapitulation, in which Christ recasts the idea of the 'First Adam' by repudiating and transforming the sin and separation from God. This constructive theological argument allows Colenso to 'assume the presence of a natural theology in every culture and person as an expression of the sacred'.[50] This effectively enabled him to struggle against egregious forms of racist imperialist strategies in the colony, believing that 'theology needs to be open to questions, preached in humility, while claiming neither divine nor missionary omnipotence or omniscience'. In other words, converts from both camps – the colonizer and the colonized – have struggled in complex ways for personal or social liberation. Mission and subversion have happened on multiple levels and conversion has been demanded of all, not just the recipients of missionary preaching.

The manner in which Scripture arrives in the missionary context also demonstrates complex negotiations between the message, the messenger and the medium of the message. In the section 'Translating God: What is the Message?' Grau points out that translating the Bible into African tongues functioned to relativize the grip the missionaries had on the Bible. Such a phenomenon is also charted by Bhabha in his chapter 'Signs taken for Wonders: Questions of ambivalence and authority under a tree outside Delhi, May 1817.'[51] There, Bhabha demonstrates, albeit from a non-theological and secular standpoint, the surprising forms of agency operative in the colonial encounter as a consequence of the Bible having been translated into vernacular languages. Similarly, Grau asserts that one cannot evade the 'politics of translation' in which the translators 'inscribe the incarnate faith of those who communicate the faith as much as they transmit faith in an incarnate God. Such an incarnate faith becomes reincarnated when its flesh moves and relocates.'[52] Colenso, for example, translated words from the Greek to suit his theological position: the term *pistis* as a case in point. It was translated as *temba* – meaning confidence, hope, and trust. This choice runs contrary to contemporary translations that use *kolwa* instead of *temba*, suggesting faith as assent to a creed, rather than, as Colenso preferred, faith as a sense of trust in God.[53] In other words, from the missionary and colonial context, Colenso has been able to argue that an experience of trust in God better defines the stance of the Christian believer than the Western emphasis on assent to beliefs and creeds. The subtle theological issue here unsettles certain unquestioned, taken-for-granted notions of Christian identity. A Christian becomes one who stands in a particular relationship to the divine, as opposed to one who stands in a particular relationship to a human community. While this may seem like an overly sharp distinction, since no Christian is in a lone relationship with the divine, what Colenso accentuates in mission theology is the practice of a disposition of trust towards the divine as enacted in the community.

If we take a look back at this section on how identity is construed in postcolonial theology, it is important to underscore the way in which the contemporary critique of identity, arising in postcolonial theory, challenges the assumption that because cultural and national identities are singular and cohesive they are able to provide clear and transparent accounts of experience in the colonial context. Bhabha's work demonstrates that identity operates as a term in global cultural contexts that emphasize temporality more than spatiality. Such a presentation of identity decolonizes it because it enables us to note the ways in which identity is a continually negotiated and constructed *argument*, one that is recurrently created and recreated in multiple forms of negotiation. The 'experience' to be tracked here is not some singular, monolithic and cohesive experience arising from geopolitical identity established by the nation-state; it is instead the experience of negotiation on multiple fronts and in conversation with various interlocutors which consequently functions to recreate identity. Along these lines, Grau's postcolonial presentation of mission theology alerts us to the idea that the marginalization and demonization of mission theology in contemporary theological or religious contexts needs to be nuanced and qualified through a study of how religious and theological identity was in fact negotiated in the colonial space. Thus, resisting what one might presume to be an 'orthodox'[54] theology of mission operative in missionary contexts, Christian missionaries often demonstrated far more empathy and imagination on how shared identity was created through processes of conversion. Mission theology in such instances was also subversive and not straightforwardly imperialistic; it transformed not just the objects of mission, but also the subjects of mission and the theology of mission.

In decolonizing contemporary Christian theologies of mission Grau demonstrates a two-fold task. On the one hand, decolonizing Christianity does not mean that Christian theologians simply capitulate to the demands of secular studies of religion, which often simplistically argue that mission theology went hand in hand with imperial Christianity. In fact, the capacity to rethink colonial encounters and to trace how agency was enacted in surprising and novel ways complicates the position not only of theologians, but also of secular thinkers of postcolonial *theory* such as Homi Bhabha. On the other hand, Grau's book is a provocative and thoughtful suggestion to think about mission theology anew. Mission, after all, is a concrete and formative practice of Christian traditions that is as new and as different as every instance of its expression. Its colonial heritage, however, has given progressive theologians pause and has made it difficult for many to think of mission theology in language other than the imperial language of exclusivist Christianity. This is all the more problematic because conversion, understood as the transformation of identity, is a flashpoint for religious violence around the globe today. However, Grau's historical survey – followed by her constructive theological arguments – shows that decolonizing Christian mission theology must take into consideration both the *disruption* of local cultures and life logics that occurred in the colonial encounter along with the *recognition* of how local populations used this alternate logic to redemptive effect. Following these implications, constructive theologies of mission can begin to think of 'mutual mission'[55] in which Christian belonging, and therefore identity, cannot be uniformly 'orthodox'. In other words, in the colonial context, mission theology is necessarily polydox in which the message, the medium, and the recipients of the message are all actively constructing new paradigms of meaning and relationship. In a milieu of shared experiences, conversion is a mutual experience of transformation and trust of human relations. This idea is in no way meant to assert that the colonial encounter was unmarked by the dehumanizing violence of imperial Christianity. On the contrary, and in the face of that reality, Grau underscores that a theology of mission must situate relationality at the heart of the identity negotiations since it constitutes the basis of mutual conversion and transformation – relationality between the divine and the human as well as that between human beings.

The practice of postcolonial theological writing and reflection

Without a doubt, the missionary and colonial context of European modernity was marked by the circulation of texts and discourses that established unilateral lines of authority and forced legitimacy. Perhaps one of postcolonial theory's strongest contributions to the decolonization of knowledge in the academy can be located in its critique of texts and discourse. This strand of postcolonial theory comes by way of poststructuralism, which is a radicalization of structuralism presented by the Swiss linguist Ferdinand de Saussure. Poststructuralism may be defined as a 'transdisciplinary critical examination of how we represent the world through language and ways of thinking'.[56] Thus, it takes into account the central problem at the heart of knowledge production and intellectual practice. In the study of religion, poststructuralist theory has variously been employed in fields such as biblical studies, the study of Buddhism, Islam, mysticism, and theology among others. There is no unified method operating in these studies. Nevertheless, scholars of religion employing poststructuralist theories commonly point to the problems of epistemology, semiotics[57] and ideology.[58] It is in the context of the academy and the university that theologians can begin to reflect on the nature and task of theological writing and the role of theological discourse in postcolonial contexts.

The ideological frame in which colonial and imperial power effectively operate can be seen in the control employed over language. Bill Ashcroft, Gareth Griffiths, and Helen Tiffin,[59] in their early analysis of the theory and practice of postcolonial literatures, argue that one of the main features of imperial oppression is control over education and language. Those in power use language – aided by its institutional structures and arguments about 'truth', 'order', and 'reality' – to create, sustain, and to guarantee control over other mechanisms of disciplining life. How is authority established in and through language? In the colonial context, it is clear that language is used in a way that consolidates imperial power. Nevertheless, the idea that language is the site of ideological persuasion is not an unfamiliar idea to theology. The debate over texts – the reading as well as the writing – has been extensively studied by theologians committed to writing theologically in the context of pluralism.[60] For example, in his essay 'Writing',[61] David Tracy points out that written texts play a certain role in religious contexts. However, his analysis represents in some ways a form of post-colonial response from within the Western academic and institutional enclave. In the essay, Tracy is primarily concerned to present a hermeneutics of writing where

> the greatest puzzle and complexity lie not in traditional Christian theological debates on 'scripture alone' vs. 'scripture and tradition', but rather in the Christian self-understanding of the hermeneutical relationship of the presence-oriented category 'Word' to Scripture as *written* text, and thereby, to writing.[62]

In other words, the Christian understanding of Scripture has to do with an event, an event of divine self-manifestation in the Word which is Jesus Christ. Tracy is attempting here to overturn the secular 'linguistic turn' in religious studies – a strategy or line of analysis which examines religious and theological language for the ways they create and sustain imperial power. In this essay, however, he is clearly challenging proponents of the secularized analysis of language by asserting that scriptural language as normative language can only be analyzed in terms of its referents. That is, because religious language has God as its primary referent, it is of a *sui generis* (unique) nature, which means that it can only be understood in theological terms, and is not reducible to ethics or political power (although it does concern itself with both). Tracy's argument, in other words, presents a form of constructive theological thinking that counters secular accounts of language as nothing more than sites of power negotiation. Postcolonial theology goes a step further as we shall see.

In an argument such as Tracy's, the Christian idea of 'event' underscores the gratuitous and gracious nature of divine revelation in the 'Word-as-Word-event' and is a happening of language itself not under the control of the subject. The act of writing therefore reveals a capacity for excess beyond human control which has been left largely untheorized. While it is true that Tracy is making room here for divine action and agency, postcolonial theorists and theologians will demur that room ought to be made also for the differently construed human other. Tracy, for his part, spends no time analyzing the authorized reader and writer of Scripture, such as Grau demonstrated in her analysis of missionary dynamics. For Tracy, revelation as an event of divine self-manifestation is not about supernatural truths, but rather an encounter in which God reveals person-like characteristics such as intelligence and love. Of course, divine excess and human anthropocentricism are thwarted by reference to the Schleiermacherian understanding of the 'living' God as opposed to the understanding of God as simplistically personal. That is, 'God' always exceeds human grasp and knowledge in the manner that God continually relates to human beings. God is not just 'Father' to me in my individual reality. Yet, I can call God 'Father'[63] because analogical and personalist[64] language for the divine is appropriate and embedded in the tradition. Language – or, more specifically, language in Scripture – is thus both the site of an encounter and an event of revelation itself. Tracy's theological stance, it must be noted, is a riposte to secular structuralist and poststructuralist analyses of language.

In Tracy's view, language is not simply related to secular concerns about meaning and intelligibility. It is part of the Christian tradition, arising, as Tracy argues, in keeping with Barth's emphasis on the ability of the Bible as Word of God to produce the miracle of faith in Jesus Christ. In Barth's nuanced understanding of the role of the medium of scriptural language, the Word of God is both *Logos* and *Kerygma*. As *Logos*, Word is both disclosure and manifestation of Jesus Christ. As *Kerygma*, Word is proclamation, distance and disruption of all our attempts to speak, write, and think of faith in Jesus Christ. Such a dialectic or tension can be observed widely in Christian thought and practice: for Catholic and Protestant theology alike, revelation as Word means that Jesus Christ is both self-presencing *Logos* and self-distancing *Kerygma*. Barth therefore preserves the theological force of language vis-à-vis God's self-disclosure which is at the same time God's self-concealment. Tracy (with Barth) is primarily concerned to preserve God's freedom and agency from capture in human anthropocentric language. Nevertheless, the intuition that the medium of communication (human language) is a complex area of theological investigation and reflection has resonances with postcolonial strategies that present language as a series of complex and contested negotiations.

In Tracy's theological argument, the Christ experienced as present to the community in proclaimed Word and sacrament is the same Christ who was present to the original apostolic communities who 'wrote' the texts of Scripture. This emphasis on writing therefore has an important hermeneutical or interpretive emphasis.[65] Only in light of such a principle is the dialectic of self-presencing *Logos* and self-distancing *Kerygma* made clear. For Tracy, this dialectic (back-and-forth movement) functions in the genre of the written testimony – which in this instance, is that of the gospels where its unique compositional mode unites disclosive Word and Word as proclamation. In such a view, writing is neither a derivative of speaking and nor is it merely a technical form of speaking. Writing, particularly in the genre that is the gospels, demonstrates that self-presence is never full, simple or whole since it operates in a dialectic of disclosure and distance.

Thus, the *materiality* of writing has an important function to play in Christian self-understanding. First, the emphasis on the materiality of writing has the capacity to reveal the impossible – the repressions, power conflicts, and silences that are inscribed in a text. Here Tracy acknowledges that writing has been used not simply to present pure ideas, but also to enforce otherness, i.e. to distinguish and then marginalize a certain group or set of peoples, with the implicit valuation that 'they' are somehow not as important as 'us'. Writing itself has been used in colonial contexts to dominate cultures with non-literate or non-alphabetic traditions of writing. For scholars of religion in particular, there has been much concern that the study of religion has overly emphasized writing to the exclusion of other forms of expression and communication and the wider materiality of culture. Tracy writes:

> the capacities to conceptualize and to be reflective are deeply influenced by the particular matter given primacy by a culture. In Western cultures, that reflexivity is grounded principally in the materiality of writing. But in non-text-centered cultures, reflexivity may be rendered more authentically by such materials as performance, manual labor, pictures and above all the body. Hence representation of the principal *ideas* or *concepts* of a religious culture is more accurately described as a *presentation* or *rendering present* of the ideas in and through a particular form of materiality.[66]

What is clear in such a view of theological writing is that *writing is but one modality* in which the principal ideas of a religious tradition may be understood. Tracy presents a theological argument in which theological language is a practice of and by the Christian practitioner. Would such a view of language be inimical to secular postcolonial analyses of language, which may not agree with the *sui generis* claims of theology that theological language is a site of divine revelation?

Here I turn to one of the more subtle thinkers in postcolonial theory, Trinh T. Minh-ha, who has influenced a generation of thinkers in postcolonial religious and theological thought. Postcolonial theology, in this vein, is not a straightforward concern for the Christian Church. Postcolonial theology instead is a constructive enterprise aiming to think theologically using the many critical tools of postcolonial theory. An exploration of Trinh's work provides us with a starting point to think of how postcolonial thinkers may use postcolonial theory to think theologically. Trinh herself is not a theologian. She is a writer, filmmaker, and composer, but her reflections on writing in order to decolonize it have influenced many who want to think of the material reality of religion and not just a belief system.

Trinh's most often quoted work in postcolonial studies of religion and theology is *Woman, Native, Other: Writing Postcoloniality and Feminism.*[67] Here, writing is put forward as a project to examine postcolonial processes of displacement (that is, experiences of migration and crossing of national borders), cultural hybridization (in the era of globalization, no culture is 'pure'), decentered realities (the globe is now poly-centered), fragmented and multiple selves (again, depending on migration patterns, one inhabits at least two contexts simultaneously), marginal voices and languages that intervene and rupture (at the heart of postcolonial strategies to limit the reach of homogenizing narratives of nation or globe). These are themes, as we have seen, that operate across postcolonial writing and thinking. Consider some lines of poetry penned by Trinh, which serve as the epigraph to her chapter 'Commitment from the Mirror-Writing Box':

> i was made to believe
> we who write also dance

yet no dancer writes
(the way we write)
no writer ever dances
(the way they dance)
...
whoever pretends to deed
walks skip run while writing
must be flying free[68]

Here she explains in her poetic political writing that the act of writing is a 'triple bind' for postcolonial gendered subjects: 'we are (therefore) triply jeopardized – as a writer, as a woman and as a woman of color.'[69] In such a view, writing must be akin to a mirror, a mirror that is able to show reflections, albeit the reflections of other mirrors.[70] Moreover, writing as a mirror demonstrates that no one can own the image thus produced. When a woman writes, she must assiduously avoid repeating the 'priest–God' scheme, in which language as mastery and knowledge functions as 'truth'. Writing charged with intentionality in this way is construed as revealing hidden knowledge, a form of disclosure in which the reader is invited to believe. Writing cannot be the mere description of the 'sovereignty' of the author.[71] Post-colonial writing has to avoid such 'euphoric narcissistic accounts of yourself and your own kind'.[72] Writing is not a projection of the sovereign and isolated self, but the shared manner in which we read other texts. In making such a subtle point, Trinh argues that the 'me' of writing must disappear to make room for the 'I' of reading and writing. Writing and reading is not about 'me'. Yet, one may not read or write without the 'I', that is the postcolonial gendered subject reflecting on herself. She writes:

> For writing, like a game that defies its own rules, is an ongoing practice that may be said to be concerned, not with inserting a 'me' into language, but with creating an opening where the 'me' disappears while 'I' endlessly come and go, as the nature of language requires. To confer an Author on a text is to close the writing ... When you are silent, it speaks; when you speak, it is silent. Writing is born when the writer is no longer.[73]

Thus, it is not postcolonial heroic identity that must feature in postcolonial writing. It is rather a manner of deconstructing language and its power frameworks so that the elusive 'I' of gendered postcolonial subjectivity may find room to speak and to be heard. Such a form of subjectivity, however, is more about surrender to one's work than total mastery of it – our work writes itself through our bodies. Similar to Tracy's argument, that meaning can only be produced in encounter, meaning here is produced by the unsaying body that nonetheless presents a more-than-linguistic meaning in and by the means of the writing. Only such an embodied use of language, always anterior to the writer,[74] makes of writing a form of nurturing or *nour-ricriture*.[75] Thus is writing able to connote 'material, a linguistic flesh'.[76] Only in this way can postcolonial thinkers write the body, so to speak. Body writing does not mean that one raises problematic ways of seeing race or gendered roles as signifying the difference that postcoloniality underscores. Instead, the attempt to decolonize the written body means that the body surrenders to the work of nourishing the world through its incarnating words. It is the right use of body instead of raising its contingent marks of race, gender or sexuality as 'nourishing' for postcolonial subjects.

Trinh's evocative and deeply challenging call was a significantly early intervention in the academic study of US politics, but it has not so far made the impact that postcolonial theorists such as Homi Bhabha and Gayatri Chakravorty Spivak have made in the study of religion and theology. Nevertheless, her imprint can be discerned in many anthologies. One such practical example of postcolonial reading and writing is the essay by Sharon Ringe entitled 'Places at the Table: Feminist and Postcolonial Biblical Interpretation'.[77] Ringe's argument is clearly indebted to a point that Trinh and Spivak make, which is that feminists in the dominant culture of the US are in a position to be *both* colonizer and colonized. Thus, the dimensions of the postcolonial project are not limited to theorizing the oppressed. Participation in this elite discourse (because it requires a high degree of education and immersion in particular academic frameworks) also renders one an oppressor. And the oppression is and has been accomplished by inadequately theorizing a category which seemed 'natural' for feminists – 'woman'. Ringe points out that when US feminists theorize about gender, they fail to think beyond the 'caricature of Everywoman'.[78] Instead of identifying gender as an interpretive category that changes the shape of the entire analysis of literature, history or philosophy (as Trinh would argue), gender in this instance functions to erase fundamental differences of race, culture, class, marital status, sexual orientation and a myriad of other factors. This point concretizes Trinh's idea that the body (both in its individual and social manifestations) is what should write. The body is not simply a category, which even when used with theoretical sophistication can obfuscate even as it attempts to unravel. It is thus that the writer nourishes her world; she is not the hero of her work, but heroically places herself in an incarnational posture to reveal the suffering of the world.

In her reading of Luke 14:1, 7–14, Ringe examines the values, assumptions, and social standpoints encoded in banquet etiquette. She argues that reading Scripture is akin to a spiritual practice. Like Trinh, who moves in and out of poetry, narrative and prose as argument, Ringe moves in and out of analytical modes of engagement – the reading of the text on the one hand and the reader's perspective as reader on the other. Thus, in the reading of the text she is able to point out how social class dominates the Gospel stories in a number of ways. Gender is an implicit issue as well, since women are not mentioned at all as participants of the banquet in Luke 14. Feminist readings of the passage argue that in the cultural context in which such a banquet might take place, women would have been present – a wife perhaps, female servants and female children. However, such an assumption is premised on the experience of the modern reader, particularly North American or Western. In many parts of the world, though, women and children eat in seclusion. Western feminists simply 'read themselves into the text'.[79] A postcolonial reading further asks us to examine the conditions under which Luke's Pharisee host is throwing a banquet and interrogates our own relative power to host, invite, or not invite participants to banquets we may throw. Thus, it is not the straightforward reading of humility and charity that is of use to postcolonial feminists. Reading Scripture becomes a way to read body into the text, not to identify self in the text, but for transformation, to examine relative privilege. Such a method of reading is the opposite of the 'heroic' reading or writing of the sovereign self that writes oneself into the text. Postcolonial reading of Scripture is a spiritual practice of 'unselving', one might say.

Each of these thinkers of the practice of reading and writing – David Tracy, Trinh T. Minh-ha and Sharon Ringe – makes very particular arguments that touch upon the concerns and the spirit of 'postcolonial theology'. As was asserted earlier, there is no such thing as postcolonial theology if what is understood by this term is merely an identity category. Postcolonial writing is not heroic writing about unique private experiences or even a unique individual consciousness. It is reading and writing in order to make room for the humbling surprise of revelation. Admittedly, in secular forms of postcolonial writing, the 'revelation' is that of the incarnated one of the forgotten and erased postcolonial subject and her body – *she* is the incarnated one. In postcolonial theology's disavowal of heroism and unique privilege, however, it seeks to heal the damage of Western modernity and the timely appearance of the marginalized subject as a character in heroic writing. For Trinh, such writing capitulates to the demands of Western modernity and the Enlightenment's bourgeois hero. In its stead is the 'nourishing' writing that attempts to create by displacing the established conventions of the sovereign author and reader, re-learning the conventions of postcolonial writer and reader. Again, following on Trinh's work, Sharon Ringe argues that feminist writing and interpretation of Scripture should not present an imperial model of 'reverse' power. That is, feminists cannot present themselves as sovereign and autonomous masters of the texts they seek to interpret. A postcolonial feminist stance is instead a position in which feminists examine their relative positions of privilege and power in relation to the text. In other words, reading and interpreting marks a process of self-transformation. Such a stance is remarkably resonant with Tracy's argument that Scripture and theological language belong in a different genre of writing than other forms of writing. However, his deconstructive nerve seeks to make the argument that normative texts such as Scripture are sites of divine revelation. That is, Scripture, when encountered as *Logos* and *Kerygma* conveys forms of knowledge that escape human control of every kind. Postcolonial *theology* attempts to formulate the practice of Christian thought in ways that overturn the expectations of what Bhabha would call the 'timely' bourgeois subject. It is instead, an exercise in undoing privilege to make the space for surprising divine and human revelations.

Conclusion

This chapter has proceeded in two major steps. First, the section on negotiated identities and pluralized experience argued that postcolonial theology cannot use national or cultural identities as if they provide clear and unambiguous categories for understanding experience. For example, though I am from India, when I do theology I cannot present what I do simplistically as 'Indian' theology. For one thing, a question that arises immediately is what one means by 'Indian', especially if one presumes to speak for over a billion people! On the other hand, I cannot *but* present an 'Indian' perspective, given that I do not want my theological thinking to replicate the colonizing and universalizing moves of traditional forms of theology. It is a fraught enterprise. Postcolonial theology does not begin from cultural identity. Instead, it attempts to present decolonizing theology to speak to the kind of experience of Christianity that formerly colonized people have. The identity 'Indian' provided by the national frame alerts us to modernity and the time of nationhood. There is no Indian 'essence' that can be an eternal resource for experience. Rather, as postcolonial theorists and theologians argue, what is 'Indian' (or 'Latin American' or 'African' or 'American') is a shifting signifier depending on the international stage on which the name is being used. Since the *meaning* of 'Indian' shifts, a decolonizing theology cannot depend on the name 'Indian' to speak of experience. Instead, one examines the experience of cultural, social, and political negotiations that crop up in the colonial encounter.

For postcolonial Christianity, a theology of mission must be able to reflect such a complex reality. As is well known, Christian mission theology has been vilified greatly for having been part of the imperializing agenda of modern Europe. However, Christian missions often stood apart from the mercantile and military interests of European powers. A theology of mutual mission, in which the asymmetrical relationship between Christian missionary and the recipients of missionary work is transformed, is the critical and constructive work of decolonizing theology. Of course, there is no attempt to cover up the actual context of colonial violence in which such attempts came to bear fruit. Hence, postcolonial theology must remain critical of the violence of colonial and neo-colonial power even as it seeks to subvert the binary frame of oppressor and victim. The reason for doing this is to avoid the kind of victim-oriented identity politics of a few decades ago. Postcolonial theology is keenly aware that the colonial encounter did not just create the conditions for the victimization of native populations. Many stories of survival need to be unearthed in the colonial archive and retold in order to provide for the complex agency required to counter contemporary forms of neo-colonialism. Speaking of agency thus depends on nuancing the kind of 'experience' that colonized peoples had in the aftermath of the colonial encounter. It is for this reason that Grau represents the kind of constructive theological argument that unearths the theological agency of both missionary and the ones who were recipients of missionary activities. For Grau, what is critical in the colonial context is more the relationship that circulated as part of the power dynamic between the two groups and less the one-sided telling of a story of the power of one group over another.

In the second section, the practice of postcolonial writing and reflection both argues for the special status of religious and theological language and for the ways in which language, particularly the written form, can colonize. Even a theologian such as David Tracy – who writes from the North American theological center attempting to counter the secular analyses of language – is cognizant of oppressive power exerting itself through the mode of script. His point is that theological language is of a unique variety that speaks to a capacity for divine revelation in the manner that it is written, spoken, and transmitted. Conversely, Trinh T. Minh-ha is in agreement that writing does indeed have the capacity to reveal. However, in her case the revelation is more mundane. Revelation here is of the human being, whose incarnational posture attempts to heal the suffering of the world. Postcolonial writing therefore is also of a unique kind. However, it is not unique because it attempts a particular identity position. It is unique because it eschews the kind of bourgeois heroism that was enshrined in identity politics. While Tracy and Trinh may not be in agreement over what constitutes the *sui generis* nature of post-colonial or postcolonial writing, Sharon Ringe in her constructive theological argument challenges Western feminists to do more in the face of reading Scripture than reading themselves into it. Ringe's decolonizing move thus preserves the unique nature of religious language and writing while simultaneously providing a reading that is truly 'nourishing' for complex forms of decolonizing theology. Unselving, as a spiritual goal for feminists, may sit uneasily with Western ideals of agency. Even postcolonial feminists may wonder what it might mean for women who were and are consistently 'unselved' by imperial power to think of reading and writing as a program of unselving. For Ringe, the issue here is the special nature of sacred Scripture. It is not the 'heroic' body that is nourishing in postcolonial contexts; it is the incarnate body that humanizes both colonial power and powerlessness. That is, the postcolonial human body adopts the disposition of an incarnational response to the suffering following the colonial aftermath. Postcolonial theological writing and reading therefore are primarily *spiritual* activities. Such an articulation of the goal of postcolonial writing and reading will fly in the face of those secular forms of agency invested in a binary account of identity. Yet, it is the only way in which we may decolonize to prepare for the revelation of the incarnating divine and the incarnating human in the dehumanizing contexts of colonial and neo-colonial violence. If postcolonial theological writing and reading are spiritual activities, then what is 'postcolonial' is not bound to any geography. After all, contemporary geography is a consequence of colonial history. However, it is bound to be theological in content and transformative in intent. Nevertheless, a warning is in order. R. S. Sugirtharajah articulates the fraught nature of postcolonial theology:

> Postcolonialism may be a trendy substitute for what is known as Third World Theologies, and a convenient label for lumping together all Asian, African, Latin American, Caribbean and Pacific theologies... Postcolonialism could become 'another fashion in the international methodological market', or another 'new tool shaped in the West's critical foundry'... [Are] our writings replicating orientalist tendencies? I too am haunted by the question whether I am a postcolonial orientalist perpetuating the European representations of the orient within the space provided by the academy.[80]

It is little wonder, then, that what ought to bear the name of postcolonial theology is fundamentally a spiritual exercise of unselving rather than the demarcation of problematic cultural or national identity.

Notes

1 Relevant works include: S. Abraham, *Identity, Ethics, and Nonviolence in Postcolonial Theory: A Rahnerian Theological Assessment*, New York: Palgrave, 2007; D.T. Adamo, 'Decolonizing

the Psalter in Africa', in *Black Theology: An International Journal* 5.1, 2007, pp. 20–38; M.I. Aguilar, *Theology, Liberation and Genocide: Reclaiming Liberation Theology*, London: SCM Press, 2009; M. Althaus-Reid, *Indecent Theology: Theological Perversion in Sex, Gender, and Politics*, New York: Routledge, 2001; E.P. Antonio, *Inculturation and Postcolonial Discourse in African Theology*, New York: Peter Lang Publishing, 2006; S.A. Bong, 'An Asian Postcolonial and Feminist Methodology: Ethics as a Recognition of Limits', in *Gender, Religion and Diversity*, U. King and T. Beattie (eds), New York: Continuum, 2005, pp. 238–49; M.G. Brett, *Decolonizing God: The Bible in the Tides of Empire*, Sheffield: Phoenix Press, 2008; S. Burns and M.N. Jagessar, *Christian Worship: Postcolonial Perspectives*, Sheffield: Equinox, 2011; J. Daggers, *Postcolonial Theology of Religions: Particularity and Pluralism in World Christianity*, New York: Routledge, 2012; M. Dube, 'Searching for the Lost Needle: Double Colonization and Postcolonial African Feminisms', in *Studies in World Christianity* 5.2, 1999, pp. 213–28; M. Grau, *Rethinking Mission in the Postcolony: Salvation, Society and Subversion*, London: T&T Clark, 2011; D. Joy, *Mark and Its Subalterns: A Hermeneutical Paradigm for a Postcolonial Context*, Sheffield: Equinox, 2008; C. Keller, M. Nausner, and M. Rivera, *Postcolonial Theologies: Divinity and Empire*, Saint Louis, MO: Chalice, 2004; J.K. Kim, *Women and Nation: An Intercontextual Reading of the Gospel of John From a Postcolonial Feminist Perspective*, Boston: Brill, 2004; P.-L. Kwok, *Postcolonial Imagination and Feminist Theology*, London: SCM, 2005; B. Lee, 'When the Text is the Problem: A Postcolonial Approach to Biblical Pedagogy', *Religious Education* 102.1, 2007, pp. 44–61; S.D. Moore and F.F. Segovia, *Postcolonial Biblical Criticism: Interdisciplinary Intersections*, London: T&T Clark, 2005; F.F. Segovia and R.S. Sugirtharajah, *Postcolonial Commentary on the New Testament Writings*, London: T&T Clark, 2009; T.-S.B. Liew and R.S. Sugirtharajah (eds) *Postcolonial Interventions: Essays in Honor of R.S. Sugirtharajah*, Sheffield: Phoenix, 2009; and V. Westhelle, *After Heresy: Colonial Practices and Post-Colonial Theologies*, Eugene, OR: Cascade, 2010.

2 The hyphen between 'post' and 'colonial' has generated much conversation. For some theorists, the hyphen indicates that the 'post-colonial' refers to the aftermath of the colonial encounter, while 'postcolonial' without the hyphen refers to a locus of theorizing. See Ella Shohat: 'Notes on the Post-Colonial', in F. Afzal-Khan and K. Seshadri-Crooks (eds) *The Pre-Occupation of Postcolonial Studies*, Durham: Duke University Press, 2000, pp. 126–39.

3 See W. Carter, *Matthew and Empire: Initial Explorations*, Harrisburg, PA: Trinity, 2001; R.A. Horsley, *Paul and Empire: Religion and Power in Roman Imperial Society*, Harrisburg, PA: Trinity, 1997; S. Moore, *Empire and Apocalypse: Postcolonialism and the New Testament*, Sheffield: Sheffield Phoenix, 2006; S. Samuel, *A Postcolonial Reading of Mark's Story of Jesus*, London: T&T Clark, 2007.

4 On Ireland, see B. Mac Cuarta (ed.) *Reshaping Ireland, 1550–1700: Colonization and Its Consequences*, Dublin: Four Courts, 2004; C.E. Manathunga, 'Ireland', in *Colonialism: An International Social, Cultural, and Political Encyclopedia*, ed. M.E. Page, Santa Barbara, CA: ABC-CLIO, 2003, pp. 280–81. On Korea, see A. Dudden, *Japan's Colonization of Korea: Discourse and Power*, Honolulu, HI: University of Hawaii Press, 2005; R.H. Myers and M.R. Peattie (eds) *The Japanese Colonial Empire, 1895–1945*, Princeton, NJ: Princeton University Press, 1984.

5 Marxism is a worldview initiated by the work of German philosopher Karl Marx (1818–83). His work is characterized by its critique of capitalism tied to his central argument that social class divisions constitute the fundamental structure of materialist history and social power dynamics. Since its inception Marxism has spurred numerous critical appropriations and developments, from the Frankfurt School to Neo-Marxism. While a number of 'communist states' appealed to Marxism during the twentieth century, many intellectuals contest the conflation of Marxist thought and these communist movements. See R.C. Tucker (ed.) *The Marx–Engels Reader*, New York: W. W. Norton, 1972; J. Mepham and D.-H. Ruben (eds) *Issues in Marxist Philosophy*, Brighton: Prometheus, 1979.

6 Poststructuralism is an intellectual movement associated with the larger movement of postmodernism. Introduced by French intellectuals in the 1960s and 1970s, poststructuralism contests the argument for a universal structure of culture that was central to structuralism – another prominent intellectual movement of the day. Whereas structuralists believe

that social observation and critical reflection enables scholars to identify foundational characteristics of human culture such as 'human nature', poststructuralists use methods like deconstruction to expose the historical contingency and particularity of claims about human life. See 'Post-structuralism', in *The Oxford Companion to Philosophy*, ed. T. Honderich, Oxford, New York: Oxford University Press, 1995, p. 708; C. Belsey, *Poststructuralism: A Very Short Introduction*, Oxford: Oxford University Press, 2002.

7 While postmodernism is sometimes used to refer to a historical era in the West following World War I, postcolonial theory is a product of the vast intellectual movement known as postmodernism which transcends historical era and exists alongside other 'pre-modern' and 'modern' intellectual commitments. Postmodernism is distinguished by its suspicion of universal truth claims, which it deems relative interpretations of reality influenced by the radical difference that characterizes each individual. See G. Kaufmann, 'Christian Thought at the End of the Twentieth Century', in J. Livingston and F.S. Fiorenza (eds) *Modern Christian Thought*, Minneapolis, MN: Fortress, 2006, pp. 494–95; 'Post-modernism', in *The Oxford Companion to Philosophy*, p. 708.

8 See C. Calhoun, M. Juergensmeyer, and J. Van Antwerpen (eds) *Rethinking Secularism*, New York: Oxford University Press, 2011, p. 8: the word 'secular' 'referred to the affairs of a worldly existence and was used in the Middle Ages specifically to distinguish members of the clergy, who were attached to religious orders, from those who served worldly, local parishes (and who were therefore, secular) ... In the two centuries in which the Enlightenment's secular/religious distinction has been prevalent in European and American thought, it has come to be accepted as a commonplace dichotomy. It is still not clear, however, exactly what the distinction demarcates. One way of thinking about it is in strictly legal and political terms, that public institutions should be unfettered by influences that privilege particular moral creeds and associations ... In another view, secularism implies a framework of nonreligious ideas that is explicitly contrasted with religion. To be a secularist, in this sense, is to adopt a stance toward life that clearly separates religious from non-religious ways of being.'

9 See T. Tennent, *Theology in the Context of World Christianity: How the Global Church Is Influencing the Way We Think about and Discuss Theology*, Grand Rapids, MI: Zondervan, 2007.

10 A term coined by German Catholic theologian Johann Baptist Metz, 'political theology' refers to a movement among European and American theologians who emphasized theology's obligation to address power and oppression in society and the Church following the horror of the Holocaust. Political theology is also used more broadly to describe any theology aimed at transforming society and/or the Church for the sake of the most vulnerable. See G. Gutiérrez, 'Political Theology and Latin American Liberation Theologies', in Livingston and Fiorenza (eds) *Modern Christian Thought*, pp. 273–308; J.B. Metz, *Faith in History and Society*, trans. J. Matthew Ashley, New York: Crossroad, 2007; J. Moltmann, *Theology of Hope*, Minneapolis, MN: Fortress Press, 1993.

11 Correlation theologies 'correlate' the Christian message and the human situation. Popularized by twentieth century theologian Paul Tillich, and further developed by contemporary Catholic theologian David Tracy. See R.P. McBrien, *Catholicism*, San Francisco, CA: Harper, 1994, pp. 22–25; P. Tillich, *Systematic Theology*, vol. 1, Chicago, IL: University of Chicago Press, 1973; D. Tracy, *Blessed Rage for Order: The New Pluralism in Theology*, Chicago, IL: University of Chicago Press, 1996.

12 Following postmodern theology's turn to the particularities of socio-historical context, ethnographic theology relies on the ethnographic methods common to the social sciences for contextual theological reflection. See A.M. Vigen and C. Scharen (eds) *Ethnography as Christian Theology and Ethics*, New York: Continuum, 2011.

13 Feminist theology addresses gender inequality that constitutes society, church, and theological truth claims, and calls for the eradication of sexism based on the Christian tradition. See S. Abraham, *Frontiers in Catholic Feminist Theology: Shoulder to Shoulder*, Minneapolis, MN: Fortress Press, 2009; S. Briggs and M.M. Fulkerson (eds) *The Oxford Handbook of Feminist Theology*, Oxford: Oxford University Press, 2012; S. Coakley, 'Feminist Theology', in Livingston and Fiorenza (eds) *Modern Christian Thought*, pp. 417–42.

14 Womanist theology engages the Christian tradition to address the realities of African American women. See K.G. Cannon, E. Townes, and A.D. Sims (eds) *Womanist Theological Ethics: A Reader*, Louisville, KY: Westminster John Knox, 2011; S.Y. Mitchem, *Introducing Womanist Theology*, Maryknoll, NY: Orbis, 2002.

15 *Mujerista* theology addresses the experiences and oppressions of Latina women, especially those experiencing poverty. See A.M. Isasi-Díaz, *Mujerista Theology*, Maryknoll, NY: Orbis, 1996 and *La Lucha Continues: Mujerista Theology*, Maryknoll, NY: Orbis, 2004.

16 *Minjung* theology addresses the social and political realities of South Korean Christians, especially their struggles for social justice. See W.A. Joh, *Heart of the Cross: A Postcolonial Christology*, Louisville, KY: Westminster John Knox, 2006; V. Küster, *A Protestant Theology of Passion: Korean Minjung Theology Revisited*, Leiden, Netherlands: Brill, 2010.

17 A modern and anthropological sense of culture has functioned in theology since the 1920s. As Kathryn Tanner argues in *Theories of Culture: A New Agenda for Theology*, Minneapolis, MN: Fortress Press, 1997, p. 38, a more plausible account of culture is the postmodern view of culture with an emphasis on 'interactive process and negotiation, indeterminancy, fragmentation, conflict and porosity'.

18 S.G. Davaney, 'Theology and the Turn to Cultural Analysis', in D. Brown, S.G. Davaney, and K. Tanner (eds) *Converging on Culture: Theologians in Dialogue with Cultural Analysis and Criticism*, New York: Oxford University Press, 2001, pp. 3–16.

19 Davaney, 'Theology and the Turn to Cultural Analysis', p. 5.

20 In their book *Constructive Theology: A Contemporary Approach to Classical Themes*, Minneapolis, MN: Fortress Press, 2005, co-editors Serene Jones and Paul Lakeland distinguish constructive theology from other theological forms by explaining, 'We are not interested in merely describing what theology has been; we are trying to understand and construct it in the present, to imagine what life-giving faith can be in today's world' (p. 2). As such, constructive theology engages the classical doctrinal categories of theology (God, Christ, Salvation, etc.) with and for the social, political, and intellectual landscape of the present.

21 R.S. Sugirtharajah, *Postcolonial Reconfigurations: An Alternative Way of Reading the Bible and Doing Theology*, London: SCM, 2003, p. 2.

22 Hermeneutics refers to a lens of interpretation. In this case, those who appeal to a 'Third World Hermeneutics' argue that those who share an experience of the 'Third World' also possess a distinctive interpretive lens through which they encounter knowledge and the world.

23 See G. Spivak, 'Moving Devi – 1997: The Non-Resident and the Expatriate', in *Other Asias*, Oxford: Blackwell, 2008; S. Abraham, 'The Pterodactyl in the Margins: Detranscendentalizing Postcolonial Theology', in S. Moore and M. Rivera (eds) *Planetary Loves: Spivak, Postcoloniality, and Theology*, New York: Fordham University Press, 2011.

24 In the eighteenth and nineteenth centuries in Western Europe, 'orientalism' referred to the study of the languages and literatures of the 'Orient' – that is, the whole of Asia from Turkey to India to Japan. During the late twentieth century, however, scholars such as Edward Said began to employ the term critically to describe how European orientalists 'invented' a false and homogenizing depiction of the diverse peoples across the vast Asian continent. See E. Said, *Orientalism*, London: Pantheon, 1978; A.L. Macfie, *Orientalism: A Reader*, New York: New York University Press, 2000.

25 H. Bhabha, *The Location of Culture*, London: Routledge, 1994, p. 24.

26 From an interview with Homi Bhabha in G.A. Olson and L. Worsham (eds) *Race, Rhetoric, and the Postcolonial*, Albany, NY: State University of New York, 1999, p. 17.

27 Sugirtharajah, *Postcolonial Reconfigurations*, p. 1.

28 Ibid.

29 See the epigraph from Klaus Klostermaier in Sugirtharajah, 'Postcolonialism and Indian Christian Theology', *Postcolonial Reconfigurations*, p. 117: 'Theology at 120°F in the shade seems, after all, different from theology at 70°F. Theology accompanied by tough chapattis and smoky tea seems different from theology with roast chicken and a glass of good wine. Now who is really different, *théos* or the theologian?'

30 Dalit theology engages the Christian theological tradition to address the realities of those occupying the Dalit caste in India; See A.P. Nirmal and V. Devasahayam, *A Reader in Dalit*

Theology, Madras: Gurukul Lutheran Theological College & Research Institute, 1990; P. Rajkumar, *Dalit Theology and Dalit Liberation*, Aldershot: Ashgate, 2010.

31 Sugirtharajah, *Postcolonial Reconfigurations*, p. 4.

32 Hybridity is a central term in postcolonial theory. The process of hybridity occurs when individuals or groups interact with the normative cultural categories of their context (e.g. race, gender, religion) in a way that illuminates the inability of these norms to represent human life fully. In turn, hybridity negotiates these normative categories to generate a new space of representation. See Bhabha, *Location of Culture*; R.J.C. Young, *Postcolonialism: A Very Short Introduction*, Oxford: Oxford University Press, 2003.

33 Diaspora is an evolving term, but it essentially denotes a movement or migration of people away from their native land. Diasporas sometimes occur against the will of those in migration, while other times they are the result of willful migration. See R. Baubock and T. Faist (eds) *Diaspora and Transnationalism: Concepts, Theories and Methods*, Amsterdam: Amsterdam University Press, 2010.

34 Psychoanalysis is a theory of psychology and psychotherapy founded by Sigmund Freud. See A. Elliott, *Psychoanalytic Theory: An Introduction*, Durham, NC: Duke University Press, 2002.

35 A signifier is a sign that denotes a meaning within a given context.

36 Bhabha, 'DissemiNation', in *Location of Culture*, pp. 139–70: p. 140, emphases in the original.

37 Historicism is a theory of history that assigns a fundamental significance or meaning to an historical period or event based on the interpreters' interpretive commitments. See S.G. Davaney, *Historicism: The Once and Future Challenge for Theology*, Minneapolis, MN: Fortress Press, 2006.

38 Bhabha, 'The Commitment to Theory', in *Location of Culture*, pp. 18–28, explains the 'enunciatory present' thus: 'The concept of cultural difference focuses on the problem of the ambivalence of the cultural authority: the attempt to dominate in the *name* of a cultural supremacy which is itself produced only in the moment of differentiation. And it is the very authority of culture as a knowledge of referential truth which is at issue in the concept and moment of *enunciation*. The enunciative process introduces a split in the performative pre-sent of cultural identification; a split between the traditional culturalist demand for a model, a tradition, a community, a stable system of reference, and the necessary negation of the certitude in the articulation of new cultural demands, meanings, strategies in the political present, as a practice of domination or resistance. The struggle is often between the histori-cist teleological or mythical time and narrative of traditionalism – of the right or the left – and the shifting, strategically displaced time of the articulation of a historical politics of negotiation which I suggested above' (pp. 34–35, emphases in the original).

39 Bhabha, *Location of Culture*, p. 148.

40 Bhabha, *Location of Culture*, p. 162.

41 Ibid.

42 M. Grau, *Rethinking Mission in the Postcolony: Salvation, Society and Subversion*, New York: T&T Clark, 2011.

43 Grau, *Rethinking Mission*, p. 7.

44 Grau, *Rethinking Mission*, p. 10.

45 Literally meaning 'multiple-beliefs', Polydoxy is a theological idea championed by L.C. Schneider and C. Keller that concerns the multiple and sometimes competing belief claims from which theologies emerge. See Keller and Schneider (eds) *Polydoxy: Theology of Multiplicity and Relation*, London; New York: Routledge, 2011; L.C. Schneider, *Beyond Monotheism: A Theology of Multiplicity*, New York: Taylor & Francis, 2007.

46 Grau, *Rethinking Mission*, p. 162.

47 Grau, *Rethinking Mission*, p. 163.

48 Grau, *Rethinking Mission*, p. 167.

49 Syncretism is the combination of differing beliefs to establish a unity among otherwise distinct and even conflicting views or traditions. See A.M. Leopold and J.S. Jensen (eds) *Syncretism in Religion: A Reader*, New York: Routledge, 2004.

50 Grau, *Rethinking Mission*, p. 174.

51 Bhabha, *Location of Culture*, pp. 102–22.

52 Grau, *Rethinking Mission*, p. 181.
53 Ibid.
54 In Grau's book, 'orthodox' is contrasted with 'polydox'. What Grau has so well demonstrated in her work is that in the colonial context, 'polydox' is a better term to describe the kind of negotiations and hybrid moments for theology. Orthodoxy presumes that there is 'right' belief as opposed to 'polydoxy' which asserts that multiple beliefs, sometimes competing, are operating in contexts of asymmetrical power.
55 Grau, *Rethinking Mission*, p. 280.
56 J. Carrette, 'Post-structuralism and the study of religion', in J.R. Hinnells (eds.) *The Routledge Companion to the Study of Religion*, London: Routledge, 2010, pp. 274–83.
57 Semiotics concerns the processes of language and communication through the study of signs, symbols, metaphor, and analogy. See D. Chandler, *Semiotics: The Basics*, New York: Routledge, 2007.
58 Ideology is an all-encompassing system of ideals structured according to particular biases in power. See M. Freeden, *Ideology: A Very Short Introduction*, Oxford: Oxford University Press, 2003.
59 B. Ashcroft, G. Griffiths and H. Tiffin, *The Empire Writes Back: Theory and Practice in Postcolonial Literatures*, London and New York: Routledge, 1989, p. 7. The epigraph to the book ascribes the phrase 'The Empire writes back' to Salman Rushdie.
60 Pluralism describes a context wherein a diversity of religions is recognized and tolerated. While pluralism is commonly celebrated in the post-Enlightenment West, it in fact maintains a fundamental uniformity by representing difference through a pre-determined category of 'religion' that does not necessarily encompass the unique particularities of the cultural and theological landscape. Plurality, by contrast, does not assume a fundamental unifying category in its expression of difference within a given context.
61 D. Tracy, 'Writing', in M.C. Taylor (ed.) *Critical Terms for Religious Studies*, Chicago: University of Chicago Press, 1998, pp. 383–93.
62 Tracy, 'Writing', p. 385.
63 See J.M. Soskice, *The Kindness of God: Metaphor, Gender, and Religious Language*, Oxford: Oxford University Press, 2008, and *Metaphor and Religious Language*, Oxford: Oxford University Press, 1987.
64 'Personalist' language in theology means that we can use words that reflect our experience in the world as human beings. Thus, to call God 'Father' is to use personalist language that is also analogical, meaning that God is like a Father in our experiences of human fathers, but also that God infinitely exceeds representation as a human being with a gendered nature.
65 Tracy, 'Writing', p. 389.
66 Tracy, 'Writing', p. 392, emphasis in the original.
67 Trinh T.M.-H., *Woman, Native, Other: Writing Postcoloniality and Feminism*, Bloomington and Indianapolis, IN: Indiana University Press, 1989.
68 Trinh, *Woman, Native, Other*, p. 5.
69 Trinh, *Woman, Native, Other*, p. 28.
70 Trinh, *Woman, Native, Other*, p. 22.
71 Trinh, *Woman, Native, Other*, p. 29.
72 Trinh, *Woman, Native, Other*, p. 28.
73 Trinh, *Woman, Native, Other*, p. 35.
74 Trinh, *Woman, Native, Other*, p. 36.
75 Trinh, *Woman, Native, Other*, p. 38. '*Nourricriture*' is Trinh's word to describe 'organic writing' or 'nurturing writing'.
76 Ibid.
77 S.H. Ringe, 'Places at the Table: Feminist and Postcolonial Biblical Interpretation,' in R.S. Sugirtharajah (ed.) *The Postcolonial Bible*, Sheffield, UK: Sheffield Academic Press, 1998, pp. 136–51.
78 Ringe, 'Places at the Table,' p. 138.
79 Ringe, 'Places at the Table,' p. 147.
80 R.S. Sugirtharajah, *Postcolonial Reconfigurations*, p. 32.

26
ENGAGEMENT WITH THE ARTS

Richard Viladesau

The engagement of Christianity with the arts has been a reality nearly since the beginnings of the Christian community. However, through most of the Church's history that engagement was practical rather than theoretical. Christian theology shows itself implicitly in the artistic practice of Christian communities. Over the centuries artistic genres, styles, and forms that were derived from Christian doctrines and ideas developed. For example, in ritual drama, there are the Eucharistic liturgy and Holy Week services; in rhetoric, there are the homily and sermon; in painting and sculpture, there are specifically Christian genres like the crucifix, the 'Madonna and child', and there are Christian styles like the Byzantine icon; in music, we have 'Gregorian' and Byzantine chant, sacred oratorios, and the Lutheran oratorio-Passion; in architecture, we see the basilica church and the cathedral; in literature, we find sacred poetry and legends of the saints; and there are many mixed forms, like the illustrated book of hours or sacred dramas, from which Western theatre eventually evolved.

However, theological reflection on the arts was mostly *ad hoc* (literally 'to this' or 'for this' – that is, directed toward particular issues that were pressing at the moment). Furthermore, such reflection was directed almost exclusively to questions regarding *sacred* art: art that was explicitly religious and was intended to be used in a religious context. Medieval theology indirectly reflected on the arts in its development of a theology of *beauty*, but there was little or no theological engagement with the arts as such, that is *as art*. This could only come about once the arts had separated themselves from the church context. That separation was part of the process of secularization that began in the early modern period, during the Renaissance and the European Enlightenment. Since that period, Western culture's secularization has entailed the separation of religion not only from the sciences and political life, but also from the arts. The latter increasingly looked to worldly life for their subject matter, and to the secular marketplace (rather than ecclesiastical or aristocratic patronage) for their economic sustenance.[1] The independence of the arts from religion also raised the theoretical question: is art an end in itself – and, if so, can it be subjected to a purpose outside itself – including morality, or religion, or even beauty?[2]

The philosophical discipline of aesthetics (the study of sensation, of beauty, and of the arts) arose in the eighteenth century; but it was not until the mid-twentieth century that Christian theology began considering the arts in a significant way. The direct engagement of theology with the arts can be considered under four aspects: 1) the arts in the service of religion, as sacred communication and sacred decoration; 2) the arts as a repository of the theological tradition; 3) the arts as a dialogue partner for theological reflection; 4) the arts as an independent mode of thinking that can be seen as a different kind of theology, standing on its own. In the following sections, we shall look first at theology's engagement with sacred art, art explicitly in the service of religion, and then at examples of the three forms of theological engagement with the arts in general, as art.

Art as sacred communication and as sacred decoration

Of all the arts, it was rhetoric that received the most explicit attention in the early centuries of the church, because of its practical relevance. The Greek and Roman orators had developed theories and styles of public speaking that were largely taken over into Christian preaching and theological debate. There were also theological discussions concerning the legitimacy or the suitability of various kinds of music in church. But the most significant theological reflection on the arts regarded the use of pictures, and this was because the use of the graphic arts aroused considerable controversy.

Sacred images were forbidden in the rabbinic Judaism that early Christianity came out of. On the other hand, the 'worship' of idols was a prominent feature of the popular level of pagan religion. It was therefore logical that opposition to images was present to some extent in the church from very early on. This opposition reached its apex in the iconoclast (literally, 'image-breaking') movement of the eighth and ninth centuries. This movement was initiated by the Byzantine emperors with the support of a majority of the bishops. The issues at stake in the iconoclast controversy were complex, and included political and social factors; but on both sides the dispute was carried out largely on theological grounds. The theological question centered not on the possibility of representing the invisible Godhead *in itself* (which everyone admitted was impossible), but on representations of Christ as the divine-human. An important corollary issue involved the reverence or 'adoration' that was given to images of Christ, his mother, and the apostles and saints.

Let us look first at the pronouncement of the iconoclast church council held in Constantinople in the year 754, denouncing the use of images in church:

> Satan misguided people, so that they worshipped the creature instead of the Creator. The Mosaic law and the prophets cooperated to undo this ruin; but in order to save humankind thoroughly, God sent his own Son, who turned us away from error and the worshipping of idols, and taught us the worshipping of God in spirit and in truth. As messengers of his saving doctrine, he left us his Apostles and disciples, and these adorned the Church, his Bride, with his glorious doctrines. This ornament of the Church

the holy Fathers and the six Ecumenical Councils have preserved inviolate. But the before-mentioned demi-urgos of wickedness [Satan] could not endure the sight of this adornment, and gradually brought back idolatry under the appearance of Christianity. As then Christ armed his Apostles against the ancient idolatry with the power of the Holy Spirit, and sent them out into all the world, so has he awakened against the new idolatry his servants our faithful Emperors, and endowed them with the same wisdom of the Holy Spirit. Impelled by the Holy Spirit they could no longer be witnesses of the Church being laid waste by the deception of demons, and summoned the sanctified assembly of the God-beloved bishops, that they might institute at a synod a scriptural examination into the deceitful colouring of pictures which draws down the spirit of man from the lofty adoration of God to the low and material adoration of the creature, and that they, under divine guidance, might express their view on the subject.[3]

The bishops of the council explicitly state what their theological method will be: they will examine the Scriptures and will be faithful to the teachings of the six previous Ecumenical Councils. Their method therefore is essentially dogmatic, based on authority. They claim that the bishops and emperors have this authority because Christ has endowed them with the Holy Spirit. They begin with a reference to the first commandment of the Law of Moses (the Ten Commandments), which explicitly forbids the worship of images (and, according to some interpretations, even the making of images of any kind):

I am the LORD your God, who brought you out of Egypt, out of the land of slavery. You shall have no other gods before me. You shall not make for yourself an image in the form of anything in heaven above or on the earth beneath or in the waters below. You shall not bow down to them or worship them ...

(Exodus 20:2–4).

The prophets also inveighed against idolatry. And Christ said that his followers should worship 'in Spirit and in truth'. But Satan, the bishops say, reintroduced idolatry under a Christian guise by deceiving people into thinking they could worship God by adoring images. The bishops continue:

After we had carefully examined their decrees under the guidance of the Holy Spirit, we found that the unlawful art of painting living creatures blasphemed the fundamental doctrine of our salvation – namely, the Incarnation of Christ, and contradicted the six holy synods. These condemned Nestorius because he divided the one Son and Word of God into two sons, and on the other side, Arius, Dioscorus, Eutyches, and Severus, because they maintained a mingling of the two natures of the one Christ.

Wherefore we thought it right, to show forth with all accuracy, in our present definition the error of such as make and venerate these, for it is the unanimous doctrine of all the holy Fathers and of the six Ecumenical Synods, that no one may imagine any kind of separation or mingling in opposition to the unsearchable, unspeakable, and incomprehensible union of the two natures in the one hypostasis or person.

As we have seen, the iconoclasts appealed first to the explicit prohibition of images in the first commandment. But then they move to a dogmatic argument. They insist that any portrayal of the divinity is impossible; but to represent Christ simply in his humanity – as is inevitable in any picture – implies the denial of the real unity of his person as being both human and divine, as was defined in the earlier councils. In other words, any picture will necessarily eliminate Christ's divinity.

> What avails, then, the folly of the painter, who from sinful love of gain depicts that which should not be depicted – that is, with his polluted hands he tries to fashion that which should only be believed in the heart and confessed with the mouth? He makes an image and calls it Christ. The name Christ signifies God and man. Consequently it is an image of God and man, and consequently he has in his foolish mind, in his representation of the created flesh, depicted the Godhead which cannot be represented, and thus mingled what should not be mingled. Thus he is guilty of a double blasphemy – the one in making an image of the Godhead, and the other by mingling the Godhead and manhood. ... When, however, they are blamed for undertaking to depict the divine nature of Christ, which should not be depicted, they take refuge in the excuse: We represent only the flesh of Christ which we have seen and handled. But that is a Nestorian error. For it should be considered that that flesh was also the flesh of God the Word, without any separation, perfectly assumed by the divine nature and made wholly divine. How could it now be separated and represented apart? ... For where the soul of Christ is, there is also his Godhead; and where the body of Christ is, there too is his Godhead. If then in his passion the divinity remained inseparable from these, how do the fools venture to separate the flesh from the Godhead, and represent it by itself as the image of a mere man? ... Whoever, then, makes an image of Christ, either depicts the Godhead which cannot be depicted, and mingles it with the manhood (like the Monophysites), or he represents the body of Christ as not made divine and separate and as a person apart, like the Nestorians.

Those who make images, then, fall into one of the heresies that were condemned by the early councils. If they claim that by representing the human Christ they are also representing the divinity, they fall into the heresy of the Monophysites, who claim that Christ has only one nature, and thus neglect the difference of the human and divine natures. Furthermore, they would be claiming that the divinity can be pictured, which is impossible. On the other hand, if they claim that they are picturing only the humanity of Christ, then they fall into the opposite heresy, associated with Nestorius, that separates the two natures.[4]

Christ can indeed be represented materially, they say, but only by symbol: namely, by the sacrament of the Eucharist:

> The only admissible figure of the humanity of Christ, however, is bread and wine in the holy Supper. This and no other form, this and no other type,

has he chosen to represent his incarnation. Bread he ordered to be brought, but not a representation of the human form, so that idolatry might not arise.

Hence the council concludes:

> Supported by the Holy Scriptures and the Fathers, we declare unanimously, in the name of the Holy Trinity, that there shall be rejected and removed and cursed out of the Christian Church every likeness which is made out of any material and colour whatever by the evil art of painters.

On the other side, the iconodule ('image-honoring') position was based on a notion taken from Plato, that the image participates in the reality of the one it portrays, and is thus a way of bringing about that person's presence (to the mind or spirit). So the veneration of the image was considered a legitimate way of honoring not the image itself, but the person represented in it. The iconodules dealt with the Old Testament prohibition of images by saying that it applied to the Godhead in itself. But now God had become human, and in Jesus God has given us a visible image of the divinity. Although the divinity of Christ cannot be pictured in itself, his humanity can be portrayed; pictures remind us of the mystery of the Incarnation, in which the invisible God becomes flesh. Therefore, according to the iconodules, to reject the possibility of portraying Christ implied a denial of the Incarnation. In using and honoring images, there is no idolatry, because the image itself is not worshipped. Rather, the worship or honor goes to the one that the image represents.

The theology of the iconodules finally triumphed, and was proclaimed in the decree of the Second Council of Nicaea (787):

> We, therefore ... define with all certitude and accuracy that just as the figure of the precious and life-giving Cross, so also the venerable and holy images, as well in painting and mosaic as of other fit materials, should be set forth in the holy churches of God, and on the sacred vessels and on the vestments and on hangings and in pictures both in houses and by the wayside, to wit, the figure of our Lord God and Saviour Jesus Christ, of our spotless Lady, the Mother of God, of the honourable Angels, of all Saints and of all pious people. For by so much more frequently as they are seen in artistic representation, by so much more readily are people lifted up to the *memory of their prototypes*, and to a longing after them; and to these [images] should be given due salutation and honourable reverence, not indeed that true worship of faith which pertains alone to the divine nature; but to these, as to the figure of the precious and life-giving Cross and to the Book of the Gospels and to the other holy objects, incense and lights may be offered according to ancient pious custom. For *the honour which is paid to the image passes on to that which the image represents, and he who reveres the image reveres in it the subject represented.* For thus the teaching of our holy Fathers, that is the tradition of the Catholic Church, which from one end of the earth to the other has received the Gospel, is strengthened.

We see in these documents that the essential method of both sides in the theological dispute was an appeal to authority, namely to the teaching of the Councils on the unity of humanity and divinity in the single person of Christ. Each tried to show that its position on images was logically implied by that doctrine. Neither side gave any serious consideration to the nature of visual art as such; but both presumed that the purpose of visual art is a representation of reality.

Western theology generally accepted the decrees of the Council on images,[5] but the Western justification of images (both in the medieval church and in the later response to Reformation iconoclasm) was based more on their teaching value than on any sense of 'presence' of a person or of a divine power in the image. Western theologians constantly repeated the saying of Pope Gregory the Great (reigned 590–604) that 'the illiterate can see in pictures what they are unable to read in books'. In the sixteenth century, certain Reformation movements (especially in Calvinism) once again challenged the legitimacy of sacred images, and Roman Catholic and Lutheran theologians once more affirmed it.

Sacred art was also seen as having a cultic function as adornment or '*decoratio*' – i.e. as a means of making the church *decus* (fitting, suitable, beautiful) for the worship of God. This embellishment or beautification was seen as a proclamation and extension of the universal reflection of God's beauty in creation. It was therefore also a means of the 'ascent' of the mind from the material to God. Western theology therefore accorded to images a primarily functional role, rather than the quasi-sacramental status that they attained in the East.

The arts as a repository of the theological tradition: art as a theologial 'text'[6]

The nineteenth century critic John Ruskin wrote:

> Great nations write their autobiographies in three manuscripts; – the book of their deeds, the book of their words, and the book of their art. Not one of these books can be understood unless we read the two others; but of the three the only quite trustworthy one is the last.[7]

What Ruskin says of great nations is also true of the great religions. They constitute and communicate themselves not only through their scriptures and theological writings, through their institutions, movements, and ethical practices, but also through their rites, poetry, architecture, music, painting, and sculpture. And although the third 'book,' consisting of religious art, cannot be understood without the previous two, it gives us perhaps the most vivid and accurate sense of the religion as lived, thought, imagined, and felt by its adherents. For this reason the books of religious deeds and of religious words are also incomplete without the accompaniment of the book of religious art.

Of course, an important aspect of the 'art' of Christianity is that which is directly contained in its literature, including its Scriptures. Our concern here, however, will be sacred images and pictures as mediators of the Christian tradition. These have long been the subject of exploration by historians of art and culture. In the last few decades, they have assumed increasing importance in religious studies as well.

This importance is comparatively new: even more recent than the application of methods of literary theory to the Scriptures. Reasons for the previous neglect of art in Western theology are not difficult to think of. In the past a certain 'logocentrism' – preoccupation with the verbal, and especially the written word – has in general dominated the study of Christianity. This has been the case for two major reasons: 1) Christianity's insistence on the normativity of the 'word' contained in the Scriptures, and 2) the literary emphasis that is generally characteristic of Western intellectual culture and scholarship (which in turn derives, at least in part, from the Judeo-Christian tradition of Scriptural study). In the contemporary period, however, a major shift has occurred, largely due to the emergence of the study of religion as a cultural phenomenon. Here the influence of anthropology, especially in the study of non-literate religious traditions, has led to the study of material culture as an auxiliary means of examining scriptural religions, in particular Christianity.[8]

This marks a change in the method and style of theological inquiry. As Frank Burch Brown writes:

> religious truth that is expressed beautifully, figuratively, and artistically has long had the reputation of being (at the very most) a vivid but less precise expression of what can be said more properly in systematic, conceptual discourse ... Similarly, for the Church's ongoing interpretation of the truth *as* truth, the inquirer has looked not to its poetry and art or even to its liturgy (though these are acknowledged to have their own unique value) but rather to doctrinal statements and theological texts.[9]

But even study that concentrates specifically on 'intellectual history' must take account of the cultural contexts in which thinking inevitably takes place. One of the most revealing aspects of such contexts is the history of religious art. (Naturally, visual 'texts' do not stand alone, but are illuminated by Christian literature.) In their origins religion and art formed a unity, and even when they became conceptually differentiated in Western culture, the two remained closely united: so much so, that until the modern era the greater part of Western 'fine' art was explicitly tied to religious themes and patronage.

One very influential figure in the movement to recognize the arts as an important repository of the theological tradition was Professor Margaret Miles of Harvard Divinity School. Her ground-breaking book *Image as Insight: Visual understanding in Western Christianity and Secular Culture*[10] provides an illuminating example of the method of engagement of historical theology with the arts, in this case the visual arts. She both discusses method, and in her discussion itself gives an example of what she is talking about.

Miles begins by noting the constant association of religion with sight. We frequently use words like 'sight' and 'insight' as a metaphor for knowledge: knowing something is *like* 'seeing' it. But Miles insists that the relationship in religion is closer. To describe religion as 'a way of seeing' is not just a figure of speech; in religion we literally have a different way of processing what comes to us through our physical eyes. The religious person senses a 'numinosity' or divine quality in the visible aspect of the world:

> Religion has ... repeatedly been described as a way of seeing. 'Seeing,' in academic parlance, has been used so frequently as a *metaphor* for understanding that its primary *literal* sense has been neglected. Religion is a way of seeing not merely in the figurative sense. Religious 'seeing' implies perceiving a quality of the sensible world, a numinosity, a 'certain slant of light,' in which other human beings, the natural world, and objects appear in their full beauty, transformed.[11]

Naturally, this kind of spiritual seeing that awakens spiritual awareness does not happen all the time. It is religious art that records it, reminds us of it, and attempts to awaken it in us. 'Religion needs art to orient individuals and communities, not only conceptually but also affectively, to the reality that creates and nourishes'.[12] Religion is not only a complex of *concepts* about God and the world; 'it is also an altered *perception* of the meaning and value of the sensible world, a different way of seeing'.[13] Hence the history of religious art is important not only as a record of 'illustrations' of ideas, but also as a record of ways of seeing the world. The art of a period reveals not only explicit ideas that are expressed verbally in a period's theology and are *also* illustrated by pictures, but also the values, presuppositions, and biases of the period that are *not* expressed verbally, but that are shown in the way of portraying things or events. The examination of art may reveal things about the artists' and theologians' 'point of view' that they themselves were unaware of.

It follows that art is an important source of information about what people actually thought and believed; what their 'faith' actually was: how they 'saw' the world because of faith. In order to use this source, Miles says,

> We must reconstruct on the evidence of the images themselves the spectrum of messages that were likely to be received by the people who lived with them in vitally interested contemplation on a daily basis.[14]

Note that Miles speaks of a 'spectrum' of messages. We cannot assume that everyone saw the same thing in a picture, or interpreted it in the same way. Moreover, Miles continues, we must take into account three major differences between our experience of seeing art and that of past ages in the Christian tradition.

First, most pre-modern people had a very different understanding of what happens in the act of seeing itself.

> In the theory of vision described by Augustine, the most influential author of the medieval and reformation periods, a fire within the body – the same fire that animates and warms the body – is collected with unique intensity behind the eyes; for an object to be seen by a viewer, this fire must be projected in the form of a ray that is focused on the object, thereby establishing a two-way street along which the attention and energy of the viewer passes to touch its object. A representation of the object, in turn, returns to the eye and is bonded to the soul and retained in the memory.

This strong visual experience was formulated negatively as the fear of contamination by a dangerous or 'unsightly' visual object or positively as the belief in the miraculous power of an icon, when assiduously gazed on, to heal one's disease …

This heightened, even exaggerated, respect for the power, for good or evil, of visual experience is very far from modern understandings of what occurs in vision. Modern theories of vision concentrate on the mechanics of vision without attention to the psychological, moral, or spiritual effects of visual experience … Modern people prefer to think of themselves as disengaged voyeurs. This is a form of self-deception that makes it difficult for us to sympathize with what we think of as the 'superstition' of medieval people who were very conscious of themselves as powerfully and intimately affected by visual images.[15]

Second, Christians in the past experienced religious images in specific contexts: namely, liturgy (public worship) and devotion. The individual did not interpret sacred art according to his or her individual background, but as a member of a community with pre-established meanings in mind. The architecture of the space in which images were viewed, as well as the liturgical actions celebrated there, contributed to the image's meaning. All were elements of cross-referential symbols within the apprehension of a well-ordered cosmos.

In other words, the contemporary viewer is likely to miss the meaning of religious art because it has been taken out of its living *context*, which included a whole view of the world and an active participation in that sacred world. Contemporary people are used to looking at art from a purely *aesthetic* point of view, valuing it for its beauty or its decorative quality or the pleasure it brings, or the cleverness of its execution, etc. But all of this is quite foreign to the original context and meaning of most sacred art of the past.

Third, the modern person sees many more artistic images than the ordinary person of the past could possibly have done. We see so many images that we have to limit our attention to them to protect ourselves from sensory overload. Common people in the past may have seen only a few artworks in their entire lives.

Pre-sixteenth century women or men, depending on the social class to which they belonged, may have seen only the relatively few images in their local church throughout their lives. The visual, as well as the verbal, overload of modern people requires that all the senses, and especially vision, act much more as 'data reduction agencies' than as windows. It is likely that our capacity for vision is … congenitally fatigued by the sheer volume of images with which most modern people cope.[16]

These three factors present a serious challenge to the use of art from the past as a theological source of information. Most modern people, including historians, 'are usually not prepared – either educationally or psychologically – to give to historical visual evidence the same interest and attention that they give to verbal texts'.[17] Yet that is exactly what is needed, because verbal theological texts give a very inadequate representation of history:

[I]t is inadequate, to say the least, to attempt to understand a historic community entirely from the study of the writings of a few of its most uncharacteristic members.

Recognition that the full task of historical understanding involves the interpretation of both verbal and visual texts will have important results for the reconstruction of a usable history for many people who have not found their own situations and interests reflected in historical verbal texts. These texts, almost exclusively the product of culturally privileged, highly educated, male, and most frequently monastic authors, constitute the great bulk of the literary products of Christianity before the modern period. From these writings, we can learn a great deal about how their authors thought, something about how they felt, and sometimes a bit about how they lived. But we cannot expect to learn from them how the large majority of the people in their culture thought, felt, and lived.[18]

Miles notes that the use of images as texts of historical theology will be especially relevant to women. Here Miles's method intersects with that of feminist theologians. One of the goals of feminist theology is precisely to reinterpret the historical place of women in the Church, which has often been overlooked because of the predominance of male voices and interests in written texts. But in looking at Christian art, we find that

from the earliest christian images there is a continuous depiction of women and the developments of subjects and themes based on the experience of women. For a woman whose daily life centered around the worship of a christian community, these images may have been powerfully affirming in a way that twentieth-century women find difficult to imagine, flooded as we are with exploitive commercial images of women.[19]

Miles cites the representations of events in the lives of the Virgin Mary, Saint Anne, and other female saints as sources for the reflection and interpretation of the experiences of women. In a later chapter of her book, she gives an illustration of her method of including the visual arts along with written texts by an examination of the portrayals of women in fourteenth century Tuscan painting. She notes that these images illuminate the written texts from the period, and are illuminated by them. Both kinds of 'texts', written and visual, are needed 'if the worlds of historical people are to be understood'. The relation of the two kinds of text to each other is complex:

The relation of texts to images may ... be seen as one of (1) complementarity or even redundancy, in which image and text offer similar and mutually reinforcing messages; (2) tension, in which text and image offer differing evidence that can be used to understand the community from which they come; or (3) contradiction, in which fundamental dissonance between texts and images signals either that texts and images represent different and unreconcilable groups within the community or that texts and images should be understood as mutually compensatory in the community they represent. At this point, we can describe the messages available from both texts and images and who within the community was likely to have received them.[20]

Miles's reflections on the place of images in the doing of history represent an important element in theological method, and in particular the method of historical theology: in the passages we have read, she shows us how the theologian must first of all identify the relevant data; then attend to those data, making explicit their limitations; then analyze them, comparing them to data from other sources; and finally relate them to current perspectives and experience. This method of engagement of theology with the arts from a historical point of view is basic, and to a greater or lesser extent underlies every other kind of engagement.

The arts as a dialogue partner for theological reflection

The German-American theologian Paul Tillich is famed for his insistence that theology must be practiced in dialogue with the contemporary world. In this dialogue, the arts play a particularly important part.

> Theology moves back and forth between two poles, the eternal truth of its foundation and the temporal situation in which the eternal truth must be received.[21]

There is a kind of theology that is 'kerygmatic' – that is, a theology that simply preaches the Christian message, on its own terms. But to be relevant to contemporary people, theology must also be 'apologetic', in the original Greek sense of the term 'apologia'. This has nothing to do with expressing sorrow or making excuses, but rather means giving an explanation of the meaning of and the reasons for one's faith.

> Apologetic theology is 'answering theology.' It answers the questions implied in the 'situation' in the power of the eternal message and with the means provided by the situation whose questions it answers.[22]

Tillich explains what he means by 'the situation' that theology must address:

> The 'situation' to which theology must speak relevantly is not the situation of the individual as individual and not the situation of the group as group ... The 'situation' theology must consider is the creative interpretation of exis-tence, an interpretation which is carried on in every period of history under all kinds of psychological and sociological conditions. The 'situation' cer-tainly is not independent of these factors. However, theology deals with the cultural expression they have found in practice as well as in theory and not with these conditioning factors as such ... The 'situation' to which theology must respond is the totality of [humanity's] creative self-interpretation in a special period.[23]

Tillich calls the practice of theology that relates the message of Christianity with the contemporary situation the 'method of correlation'. The method of correlation is

> a way of uniting message and situation. It tries to correlate the questions implied in the situation with the answers implied in the message. It does not derive the answers from the questions ... nor does it elaborate answers without relating them to the questions as a self-defying kerygmatic theology does. It correlates questions and answers, situation and message, human existence and divine manifestation.[24]

Where do we find humanity's 'creative self-interpretation' – the 'situation' that theology must address? Where do we find the 'question' to which God's 'answer' is addressed? For Tillich, we find this 'situation' expressed especially in philosophy, literature, and the arts.[25]

His conviction of the importance of the arts as a cultural expression of the human condition led Tillich to be a pioneer in theological engagement with the arts, especially painting and architecture. We find a good example of his method at work in the essay 'Religion and Art in the Light of Contemporary Development', written a year before his death in 1965.

Tillich's concern in this essay (and in most of his writings on art) is not primarily sacred art, but rather the religious dimension in secular or 'nonreligious' art. It is here that we find one important expression of the cultural situation, the contemporary 'question' that theology must give a Christian answer to. We will note, however, that here theological correlation is not seen merely in terms of question (the situation) and answer (Christian revelation). Rather, the arts here are seen as also contributing to the 'answer' to the meaning of life. But that answer – the creative interpretation of life in a particular period – is itself still a kind of 'question' – a 'situation' – that confronts Christian theology and calls out for a response. The correlation with theology is in showing how the cultural contribution or anticipation corresponds to the explicit answer that is given in religion and specifically in the Christian vision of the new life.

Tillich attempts first to specify just what the religious dimension in art consists of:

> What is the nature of the religious dimension in culture generally, and the arts particularly? What makes a cultural function religious, even if it does not deal with religion? The answer is: Everything in human culture has a religious dimension if it points to the holy, that is, to that which is the ground and aim of everything that is. Or, in another terminology, every cultural creation has a religious dimension insofar as it contributes to the answer of the question of the meaning of our existence and existence universally. The religious dimension in a work of art is that element in it which participates in the answer to the question of the meaning of existence.[26]

Tillich notes that he is here using the word 'religious' in a very wide sense:

> In calling this religious, we deviate from the ordinary concept of religion as the activities of a human group in which the direct relation to a divine being

is expressed in ritual and doctrinal symbols. If religion were only this, one could not speak of a religious dimension in culture. But the basic nature of religion is the answer one receives in oneself, or through others, to the question of the meaning of life. Being grasped by the power of this question, its answer and its ultimate source, being penetrated by it in one's whole existence, being infinitely concerned about it – that is religion. Religion in this sense can appear in all expressions of [humanity's] cultural creativity, both in the created works and in the creating person. It appears in the arts of shaping [humanity's] social existence though law and politics, through educational ideas and economic aims, and it appears in the acts of receiving the universe in knowledge and aesthetic vision.[27]

Tillich asserts that it is the particular 'style' that reveals the element of 'ultimate concern', the 'religious' dimension, in human creative works. It is the artistic 'style' that points to a self-interpretation and to the artist's 'ultimate concern'. Therefore it is the stylistic elements in art that engage the theologian as a point of correlation with religion and with the Christian message.[28]

Theology of the arts, therefore, means, trying to find what a particular artistic style reveals about the religious dimensions in the creations under the domain of this style. How is the question of the meaning of life answered in a particular work of art under the predominance of a particular style?[29]

Tillich discerns three conflicting 'styles' or 'stylistic elements' that are found in every work of art:

These elements are the naturalistic, the idealistic, and the expressionistic ... Naturalism in this context refers to the artistic impulse to present the object as ordinarily known or scientifically sharpened or drastically exaggerated. ... Idealism in this context refers to the contrary artistic impulse, that of going beyond ordinarily encountered reality in the direction of what things essentially are and therefore ought to be. It is the anticipation of a fulfilment that cannot be found in an actual encounter and that is, theologically speaking, eschatological. Most of what we call classical art is strongly determined by this impulse, although not exclusively, for no style is completely ruled by any one of the three stylistic elements.

The third stylistic element is the expressionistic. Expressionism in this context refers to the artistic impulse (which is predominant in most periods and in most phases of history) to break through the ordinarily encountered reality instead of copying it or anticipating its essential fulfillment. Expressionism uses pieces of the ordinarily encountered reality in order to show a meaning which is mediated by the given object but transcends it. This is the reason why much of the great religious art is determined by this stylistic element, although it appears also in styles that have not or have not yet produced important religious works.[30]

Naturalist and idealist styles (including Impressionism) tend to present forms of 'self-sufficient finitude',[31] either in the object itself or in the subjective vision of the artist. They can indirectly evoke the ultimate: in naturalism, by presenting the finite world as being in need of salvation;[32] in idealism by evoking a final perfection that is never found in this world.[33] But it is the 'expressive' element that is able to directly represent the ultimate; the other elements can only do so indirectly. This is because

> The expressive element in a style implies a radical transformation of the ordinarily encountered reality by using elements of it in a way which does not exist in the ordinarily encountered reality. Expression disrupts the naturally given appearance of things ... that which is expressed is not the subjectivity of the artist in the sense of the subjective element which is predominant in Impressionism and Romanticism. That which is expressed is the 'dimension of depth,' in the encountered reality, the ground and abyss in which everything is rooted.[34]

Note that Tillich's 'stylistic elements' do not correspond to artistic styles as they are usually defined by art critics or art historians. (Tillich has been criticized by art historians on exactly this point.) For example Tillich considers a portrait by John Singer Sargent and an impressionist landscape by Monet both to be 'naturalistic', while he considers 'idealist' style to be represented by both Byzantine art and by the early Renaissance painter Perugino.[35] He considers the 'expressionist' to be the most widespread stylistic element. It is found in such diverse forms as Asiatic art, Gothic painting, and contemporary abstract art. The discernment of the stylistic elements in art is itself an art[36] – or rather, a theological interpretation of art. Hence Tillich's analysis of stylistic elements does not allow us to place every work of art within one or another category. It gives rather a philosophical interpretation of the idea of 'style', used in an analogous sense. The analysis of 'style' is meant to point to the different ways in which art can express the human questions and answers about the meaning of life, or the ultimate reality.

Note also Tillich's value judgments about kinds of art. These also are based on theologial criteria. Tillich considers art to be valuable and deep insofar as it in some way expresses the concern for ultimate meaning. The 'ambiguities' that Tillich talks about are the possibilities in each style to miss that concern, and therefore miss what for Tillich is the most important function of art.

In the passages quoted, we have seen Tillich's 'method of correlation' in operation: in works of art he is able to discern the 'question' posed by the situation *in light of the 'answer'* that is given in Christian revelation; and, on the other hand, the correlation to the situation allows that answer to become relevant to the contemporary person. In the analysis of 'stylistic elements' he gives a theologial interpretation of the different means by which the dimension of ultimacy in a particular 'situation' can be made present.

The arts as an independent mode of thinking

Both Miles's and Tillich's practice already imply a third way in which theology can be engaged with the arts: by recognizing in them an independent way of encountering reality that cannot be reduced to conceptual thinking. The arts may therefore be seen as a different way in which a revelation of God may come to humanity: a non-conceptual form of practicing theology.

It is in this sense that the highly influential Swiss theologian Karl Barth wrote in a famous passage that the composer Mozart has a place in theology:

> Why can one hold that Mozart has a place in theology (especially in the doctrine of creation, and then again in eschatology) – even though he was no Father of the Church, nor even, apparently, a particularly assiduous Christian (and who was a Catholic, besides!), and who, when he was not actually working, seems to our way of thinking to have lived somewhat superficially? One can say that Mozart belongs in theology because precisely in this matter, namely the goodness of creation in its totality, he knew something that neither the real Fathers of the Church, nor our Reformers, neither the Orthodox nor the Liberals, neither the adherents of natural theology nor those powerfully armed with the Word of God, and certainly not the Existentialists, knew as he knew it – or at least they did not know as he did how to express it and show its worth; something moreover that the other great musicians before and after him likewise did not know the way he did. In this matter he was pure of heart, head and shoulders above both optimists and pessimists. 1756 – 1791! It was just during this time that the theologians and other honest folk were having a hard time defending the good Lord, who was placed in the dock because of the Lisbon earthquake. But in the face of the problem of Theodicy, Mozart had the peace of God, which surpasses all reason – whether praising or blaming, speculative or critical. The problem caused him no struggle – it simply lay behind him. Why concern himself with it? He had heard – and he allows those who have ears, even to this day, to hear – what we shall only *see* at the end of time: the total coherence of the divine dispensation. As though from this end, he heard the harmony of creation: a harmony to which the darkness also belongs, but in which the darkness is not blackness; where there is deficiency, but without being a defect; sadness, without becoming despair; gloom that nevertheless does not degenerate to tragedy; infinite sadness that nevertheless is not forced to make itself absolute. And for this very reason, this harmony contains cheerfulness, but within limits; its light shines so brightly, because it shines forth from the shadows; it has a sweetness that is also sharp, and therefore is not cloying; it has a life that does not fear death, but knows it very well. *Et lux perpetua lucet (sic!) eis*[37] – even the dead of Lisbon. Mozart saw this light as little as any of us; but he *heard* the entire world of creation that is encompassed by this light. And it was fundamentally right that he did not hear a middle, neutral tone, but heard the *positive* tone *stronger* than the negative. He heard the latter only in and with the former. But in this inequality he nevertheless heard both together (one example, among many: the Symphony in G-minor of 1788!) He never heard abstractly only the one side. He heard *concretely*, and therefore his compositions were and are *total* music. And insofar as he heard the created world entirely without resentment or bias,

what he brought forth was not his, but creation's own music: its dual, but nevertheless harmonious praise of God. He really never had to or wished to express himself in his works: neither his vitality nor his sorrow nor his piety, nor any program at all. He was wonderfully free from the constriction of needing or wanting to say something himself in his music. Rather, he simply offered himself to be to some extent the opportunity through which a bit of wood, metal, or cat gut could let themselves be heard and played as the voices of creation: the *instruments* – from the piano and violin, through the horn and clarinet, down to the venerable bassoon, and somewhere in their midst, without any special pretension, and precisely for that reason distinguished, the *human* voice – sometimes leading, sometimes accompanying, sometimes in harmony, each giving its particular contribution. He made music from each of them, using human emotions as well in the service of that music, and not vice-versa! He was himself only an ear for that music, and its mediator for other ears ...

... [W]e find in the music of Mozart – and I wonder whether one can find it so strongly in any of those who came before or after him – a shining and (I might say) a convincing proof that it is a *slander* on creation to ascribe to it a share in chaos because it includes in itself a 'Yes' and a 'No,' because it has a side turned toward God but also a side turned toward nothingness. Mozart allows us to hear that even in this second side, and therefore in its totality, creation praises its Master, and thus is perfect. On this threshold of our problem – and this is no small thing – through Mozart order is created for those who have ears to hear: and better than any scientific deduction could have done it.[38]

In his praise of Mozart, Barth makes a remarkable admission, coming from a theologian: theologians do not know everything about theology's object. The artist may know more, although art expresses the truth in a different way. In this passage, Barth sees Mozart as particularly relevant to the problem of 'theodicy': that is, the explanation of how evil in the world can be reconciled with a good God. He claims that Mozart's music – for those who can hear it properly – allows us to realize that for the Christian the evil in the world cannot be the last word, but must be placed in the perspective of God's good creation and God's gracious triumph over evil. In this sense, Mozart's music (and all beautiful art) fulfills the function that Tillich ascribes to the 'idealistic' style: an 'eschatological' anticipation of a final beauty and goodness.

Conclusion

Besides the four we have considered, there are also other ways in which theology may engage with the arts in a more indirect manner: for example in a theology of beauty. Also important is a consideration of the ethical relationship between asceticism and pleasure, a theme pursued by the novelist Leo Tolstoy in his religious writings. In line with our last section, the twentieth-century philosopher and novelist Irish Murdoch has argued powerfully for seeing the arts as moral educators. They serve this function not merely by communicating a moral content, but precisely in their aesthetic nature, whatever their content. They concentrate our attention on something estimable in and for itself, apart from the ego, and thus they lead us toward transcendence and even toward love of something 'other' than ourselves.

Notes

1 See Hans Belting, *Likeness and Presence: A History of the Image before the Era of Art*, trans. Edmund Jephcott, Chicago and London: University of Chicago Press, 1994. Belting refers to the 'era of art' as the period when the arts became independent of religious purposes, following the breakdown of the medieval synthesis and the hegemony of Christianity in Western society.

2 Already Aquinas had distinguished between the 'formal object' or goal of art and that of ethics or religion; but the notion that art forms a norm unto itself began to attain currency with the Renaissance ideal of the artist as a creative genius, and achieved theoretical justification in Kantian aesthetics.

3 The quotations from the Second Council of Nicaea and from the iconoclast council are all taken from Philippe Labbé, S.J. and Gabriel Cossart, S.J. (eds) *Sacrosancta Concilia Ad Regiam Editionem Exacta*, Venice: Sebastian Coleti, 1729, Tome VII, col. 389. Emphasis added.

4 It is debated whether Nestorius and his followers actually held the position attributed to them.

5 But see Helmut Feld, *Der Ikonoklamus des Westens*, Leiden: E. J. Brill, 1990, pp. 11–32, for exceptions and qualifications to this statement.

6 Parts of this section are adapted from the chapter 'Art as a Theological Text' in my book *Theology and the Arts*, New York: Paulist Press, 2000, pp. 123–64.

7 John Ruskin, 'Preface' to *St. Mark's Rest*, in *Ruskin Today*, Harmondsworth: Penguin Books, 1964, p. 196.

8 See John E. Cort, 'Art, Religion, and Material Culture: Some Reflections on Method', in *Journal of the American Academy of Religion* 64.3 (1996), pp. 613–32.

9 Frank Burch Brown, *Religious Aesthetics. A Theological Study of Making and Meaning*, Princeton, NJ: Princeton University Press, 1989, pp. 40, 165.

10 Margaret R. Miles, *Image as Insight: Visual Understanding in Western Christianity and Secular Culture*, Boston: Beacon Press, 1985.

11 Ibid., p. 2. Emphasis added.

12 Ibid., p. 4.

13 Ibid. Emphasis added.

14 Ibid., p. 7.

15 Ibid., pp. 7–8.

16 Ibid., p. 9.

17 Ibid.

18 Ibid., pp. 9–10.

19 Ibid., p. 11.

20 Ibid., p. 12.

21 Paul Tillich, *Systematic Theology*, vol. 1, Chicago: University of Chicago Press, 1951, p. 3.

22 Ibid., p. 6.

23 Ibid., p. 4.

24 Ibid., p. 8.

25 Ibid., p. 49.

26 Tillich, 'Religion and Art in the Light of Contemporary Development', in Paul Tillich, *On Art and Architecture*, John Dillenberger and Jane Dillenberger (eds) New York: Crossroad, 1987, pp. 166–67.

27 Ibid., p. 167.

28 Tillich, 'Protestantism and Artistic Style', in *On Art and Architecture*, p. 123.
29 Tillich, 'Religion and Art', p. 167.
30 Tillich, *Systematic Theology*, vol. 3, Chicago: University of Chicago Press, 1963, pp. 71–72.
31 Tillich, 'Art', in *The Religious Situation*, trans. H. Richard Nieburh, New York: Henry Holt and Company, 1932, pp. 55–70, quoted in *On Art and Architecture*, p. 68.
32 See Tillich, 'Art and Ultimate Reality', in *On Art and Architecture*, pp. 139–57, at p. 147.
33 Ibid., p. 149.
34 Tillich, 'Protestantism and Artistic Style', p. 123.
35 Tillich, 'Religious Dimensions of Contemporary Art', in *On Art and Architecture*, pp. 171–87, at pp. 175–78.
36 Tillich, 'Contemporary Visual Arts and the Revelatory Character of Style', in *On Art and Architecture*, pp. 126–38, at p. 130.
37 Barth's text substitutes the indicative *lucet* for the subjunctive *luceat* in the second phrase of the Introit of the requiem mass: *Requiem aeternam dona eis Domine, et lux perpetua luceat eis* ('Eternal rest grant unto them, O Lord, and may perpetual light shine upon them') – so that the last phrase is no longer a prayer, but a statement of fact: 'eternal light shines upon them'.
38 Karl Barth, *Kirchliche Dogmatik* III, 3: *Die Lehre von der Schöpfung*, Zollikon-Zürich: Evangelischer Verlag: 1950, pp. 337–40 [my translation].

27
THEOLOGY AND
POPULAR CULTURE

Michael W. DeLashmutt

That a volume such as this necessitates a chapter written about theology and popular culture indicates just how explosive the growth in this interdisciplinary nexus has been over the course of the last two decades. Though theology (or religion) and culture have been paired together as topics for exploration and scrutiny since well before Matthew Arnold's *Culture and Anarchy* (1869),[1] H. Richard Niebuhr's *Christ and Culture* (1950)[2] or Paul Tillich's *Theology of Culture* (1959),[3] approaches to theology and culture from the nineteenth century to the latter half of the twentieth have gravitated towards two biases which are not particularly helpful for our present discussion. In general terms, such approaches have either centered on the relationship between theology and *high* culture (arguing that certain sorts of culture are particularly effective at achieving certain sorts of theological ends) or have implicitly adopted what Kathryn Tanner describes as both a modernist and an anthropological approach to studying culture.[4] In regards to this latter point, this has meant a tendency to study culture from the 'outside' and (especially in the case of theological studies) a neglect of the cultural embedding of the scholar. For those interested in a serious engagement with popular culture, either of these tendencies will prove problematic.

As an alternative to the assumptions which underpinned previous approaches to the study of culture, the emergence of Cultural Studies as a legitimate academic discipline in the 1960s changed both the way in which culture was theoretically understood and deepened the methodological resources for studying culture. Beginning with the work of Richard Hoggart, E.P. Thompson, Raymond Williams and later Stuart Hall (all of whom were associated with the Centre for Contemporary Cultural Studies at the University of Birmingham), Cultural Studies offered a renewed theoretical framework for understanding cultures. Cultural Studies differed from more established approaches to studying culture that were gleaned from either cultural anthropology or Marxist readings of culture (such as those associated with the Frankfurt School). These scholars, and those who would come after them, gave special consideration to how the various practices, beliefs, institutions, and political and economic structures of a culture, as influenced by issues of class, ideology, gender, ethnicity, nationality and sexuality, shaped the construction and distribution of meaning within a culture.

Parallel to the growth of Cultural Studies in the English-speaking world, the study of everyday culture has also occupied an important position in twentieth-century Continental thought. In particular, one could note Roland Barthes' *Mythologies* (1957)[5] which applied semiotic theories to cultural texts as varied as advertisements for washing powder and popular fashion magazines; Michel de Certeau's *The Practices of Everyday Life* (1984)[6] which discusses the strategies or tactics which one employs in the process of meaning making in a highly consumerist culture; or the various academic and popular works of Slavoj Žižek, who uses Lacanian psychoanalysis to read the deep meanings present within the texts and practices at the margins of popular culture. These parallel trends in the academic study of everyday life have provided dialogue partners, theoretical frameworks, and an impetus for much of the ongoing work in the theological and religious studies approaches to engaging with popular culture.[7]

One element of what distinguishes work being done today in the field of theology and *popular* culture from earlier attempts at studying theology and culture (as such), is the extent to which contemporary authors are squarely situating the subject matter of theology within their own experience of the complex inter-relationship between the meaning-bearing texts and the meaning-making practices which make up everyday life.[8] Out of this experience, scholars are giving evidence to at least one of three assumptions about the relationship between theology and/or religion and popular culture. First, there is the belief that some degree of knowledge about God (or religion) can be gained through a considered reflection on everyday life. Second, and related to the first, is the belief that God can choose to reveal Godself through any of a variety of cultural texts, objects or practices. Third, there is a belief that studying popular culture is best done from the inside, thus making the study of theology and popular culture partially an exercise in what practical theologians refer to as theological reflection.[9]

Like many people who work in this field, my interest in theology and popular culture began first as a way of putting together – into some kind of coherent whole – two seemingly divergent parts of my life; my involvement as a participant in – or consumer of – popular culture and my growing interest in a critical and creative reflection on my Christian faith, which took the form of an interest in Christian theology. The process of making sense out of theology and popular culture was not, for me, a straightforward matter. The church tradition that I was a part of during my early twenties was by all accounts remarkably conservative. As inheritors of the American Holiness–Pentecostal tradition, we didn't drink or smoke, we shied away from cinema (unless it was rated PG or below) and we exclusively listened to Christian Contemporary Music. There was a bawdy (or bawdy for us) joke that was frequently told about people who went to my conservative Christian university. It was said that on our college campus we didn't allow premarital sex because sex could lead to dancing! If a cultural form or practice was secular, we avoided it like a spiritual plague.

In the mid-1990s I was a pastor at a small non-denominational charismatic church near Seattle. It was the evening of the fourth of July and my wife and I were at a

BBQ at the house of a parishioner. The parishioner's small bungalow had an exceptional view of our town's harbor where later in the evening the annual fireworks display would begin. The mood was light and cheery and in addition to the sounds of the bonfire crackling in the background and children running around playing, a nearby radio was tuned to a local pop-music station on which Joan Osbourne's 'One of Us' was softly, but recognizably, playing. In light of our avoidance of all things secular, it was unusual to hear a mainstream song playing on a mainstream radio station at a social gathering of our church friends (though of course the fact that I could recognize this pop song shows that my strict devotion to this form of cultural conservatism was already fraying at the edges).

As I listened to the lyrics of this unremarkable pop song, something in me switched on. I was amazed to hear such a theologically important question about the nature of God's relationship to humanity discussed with such honesty and such directness in the context of (of all places!) secular music. I found Osbourne's lyrics to be a compelling indictment of the Contemporary Christian Culture which I was so uncritically consuming at the time. In Osbourne, I found someone who came from outside of 'the Church' yet who was asking the kind of deep questions about the nature of God's relationship to the world in her trite pop music which I would have expected (though frequently didn't find) in the trite songs broadcasted on the local Christian radio station. It shocked me that 'out there' in 'the world' one could find matters relating to God being discussed in deeper, messier, and perhaps more authentic ways than what I could frequently find in the Christian cultural ghetto within which my church and I were situated. Encountering discourse about God outside of the Church started me on a journey to look for God 'out there in the world'. I wanted to know if there were other forms of culture that raised similarly deep questions about faith and to see if in culture itself there might be a way in which the knowledge of God could be found. It turns out that by looking for God in literature, cinema, music, art, and all manner of 'secular culture' I have learned far more about love, beauty, value, community, and indeed God, than I would have ever done by turning my back on the world.

In this chapter, I will outline some of the ways in which theologians and scholars of religion are today attempting to make sense out of, with and through popular culture. I'll begin by offering four examples of how we define popular culture, and then move into a discussion of four basic trends that are prevalent among the work that's being done in the study of theology and/or religion and popular culture. Finally, I'll conclude by describing my own threefold approach to understanding theology and popular culture, as grounded in my experience of teaching the subject to students in the USA and the UK. Though this is hardly an exhaustive survey of the contemporary state of this emerging theological sub-discipline, as you read this you'll gain a sense of where you can move forward in your own work in this field.

A popularity contest

One of the initial questions that students ask me when encountering this subject for the first time is, 'How do we know what makes up *popular* culture?' We may, for example, have an intuitive sense that the music of U2 is popular culture and that a performance of Bach's 'Goldberg Variations' is somehow a different kind of culture, but such tacit knowledge alone does not explain why it is that we make such a distinction. Our assumptions are further complicated in light of how the reception of cultural goods changes over time. What happens to our arbitrary differentiation between popular and other kinds of culture when the music of U2 becomes increasingly the music of a certain generation and no longer the music of the majority? Moreover, what if Bach's 'Goldberg Variations' becomes 'popular' when it is featured in the soundtrack of a Hollywood film or becomes the object of celebrity endorsements?[10] When we talk about 'popular' culture we must be precise about how it is that we are using this adjective (popular) to modify its noun (culture). Let me suggest four potential meanings: Quantitative, Accessible, Populous, and Oppositional.

Quantitative: First, we could say that something is popular if it has wide appeal. Popular culture could be identified by looking to the Billboard Top Twenty charts for music, a newspaper's listing of the top-selling fiction books in a given week, or a list of the top-grossing films of a particular year. Though popularity is easy to determine by using such metrics, the problem with the quantitative approach is that it ignores those elements of popular culture that may not be blockbusters, yet nonetheless share a popular cultural aesthetic. For example, I am a fan of the Scottish band Belle and Sebastian, whose intentionally playful sound has lent to them the genre label of 'twee-pop'. Though they play in a popular style, their fan base is relatively small and their music has infrequently been on the top of the charts. So although the band is certainly a part of popular culture in terms of style, genre, and aesthetic, if we applied a strictly quantitative approach to defining popular culture, we'd have to rule them out.

Accessible: If the quantitative approach fails to convince us, we could choose to call something popular if it enjoyed wide availability. In this sense, popular culture is that which the majority of the population has access to. Though I am nearly persuaded by this definition, again it places perhaps too much emphasis on only those forms of popular culture that the majority of people can (or would want to) consume. As with the quantitative approach, defining popular culture by availability marginalizes those aspects of popular culture that may be slightly less commercially successful. Moreover, defining the scope of 'wide availability' in a multi-national context is not at all straightforward. Is something part of popular culture only when it is available for global consumption? If this is the case, we could consider the music of Michael Jackson as part of popular culture (in addition to online retailers, there is hardly a brick-and-mortar record shop in the world that wouldn't be able to sell at least some of his music), but what about the status of something that is faddishly popular in one location and not the other? In Britain, I have been struck by the popularity of news quiz shows like *Mock the Week* or *8 Out of 10 Cats*, but such genres have no meaningful correlate in American popular culture. In America, Country and Western music is extremely popular and one can find a wide selection of Country and Western radio stations all over the country. Yet in the UK, Country and Western is rarely broadcasted on popular radio. Are quiz shows and Country music not part of popular culture because their popularity is limited to particular national contexts? Clearly, we need to consider the local, as well as the global, if we use availability as a means of defining popular culture.

Populous: Third, we could define popular as that which originates from the people (as in the sense of something being populous). This view is distinct from those above, in that the way we arrive at our definition is informed by the creation of a cultural good rather than exclusively the consumption of that good. Along these lines, something is popular culture when we can say that it emerges from the work of the people (akin to what is frequently described as 'folk culture'). However, though we could look at podcasts, flashmobs, 'independent music' and film as potential examples of populous popular culture, most of the cultural goods which we consume are actually produced through vastly complex processes. Whether we think of television programs, film, music, or consumer goods, rarely are popular cultural objects created by identifiable individuals or groups. If popular cultural goods and practices must be restricted to only those objects that can be traced back to a particular author, we'll find ourselves engaging with a very sparsely populated popular cultural world.

Oppositional: If we have found the meaning of 'popular' in popular culture evasive, perhaps we could attempt to define popular culture by identifying what it is not. This oppositional approach tends to differentiate between authentic and inauthentic cultural forms as they relate to their origins or use among certain social classes (e.g. high, folk, and low culture). In the UK, for example, we could talk about the difference between the popular press (*The Sun* and the *Mirror*) and the 'quality press' (*The Times* and *The Guardian*) or more generally we could talk about the difference between popular cinema (*Transformers*) and art house cinema (*Dogville*). Though, intuitively, this may appear like a natural way of delimiting 'popular' (or perhaps disposable) and quality (or perhaps enduring) culture, there are a number of problems with this last view. Most importantly, differentiating between authentic and inauthentic cultural forms relies on a number of unspoken and unidentified class and value statements that one may unwittingly utilize when distinguishing between cultural forms. Indeed, rather than strictly analyzing culture, in so doing we may actually be imposing our cultural prejudices upon those individuals who consume particular cultural goods.

If a firm definition of the 'popular' in popular culture escapes our grasp, perhaps we can identify some common themes from the four definitions advanced above. I would argue that despite their many differences, the quantitative, accessible, populous, and oppositional approaches all share a common theme that will prove useful in our ongoing discussion of popular culture in this chapter. I would suggest that 'popular' is used in the four examples above to denote a space within our common life where there exists both the interchange between the consumption, production and application of artifacts and the emergence of a context for shared corporate practices. Seen in this way, the study of popular culture (including artifacts and practices) is ultimately a way of uncovering and identifying our varied participation in the process of meaning making. Though we must take seriously the 'stuff' that populates the cultural world, our goal when studying popular culture is not simply to develop a deeper appreciation of cultural forms, but to seek a clearer understanding of the meanings that emerge through our engagement with popular culture.

Though the study of popular culture can be cool, hip or fun, it also represents very important work. Popular culture is the place in which the big issues of our day can be expressed, developed or satirized. We see in popular culture both representations of our greatest hopes for ourselves and our society, as well as images which depict our deepest fears and anxieties. To be sure, some popular cultural texts and practices provide more fruitful resources for such reflections than others. But even things as apparently trite as an episode of *Desperate Housewives* or the pop music of Lily Allen can provide us with important insights into pressing cultural concerns. For theologians who are interested in understanding the way in which the Gospel is interpreted or enacted in our present day, we cannot afford to ignore the important role played by popular culture in shaping our contemporary imaginative frame of reference.

Theology and/or religion and popular culture

Because of the central role it plays in our collective life, particularly in the West, theologians and scholars of religion have recently begun to give considerable attention to the significance of popular culture. Four examples are worth noting here: First, during the last decade the international professional organization for religion scholars, the American Academy of Religion, has run several panels on 'Religion and Popular Culture' along with whole program units dedicated to studying the interplay between religion and new media, religion and film, and religion and music. Second, several research networks and organizations have been formed which encourage dialogue between theologians, scholars of religion, and cultural scholars (UK Research Network for Theology, Religion and Popular Culture, The International Conferences on Media, Religion and Culture). Third, a handful of online and offline journals (*The Journal of Religion and Popular Culture, The Journal of Religion and Film, Cultural Encounters*) have been produced which serve to provide a forum for developing scholarship in the field. Finally, in both the academy and for the general reader, there has also been a proliferation of books written on a myriad of cultural topics from a theological or religious studies perspective, including several excellent general introductory texts and essay collections,[11] as well as a number of books specializing on film, media, fiction, sport, video games, and consumerism.[12] Even the most recent Routledge textbook, *Religions in the Modern World*, includes a chapter on religion and popular culture, alongside chapters on the major world religions and key trends in the study of religion (e.g. globalization, secularization, and religious violence).[13]

Tricks of the trade

There are many ways in which one could propose to examine the relationship between theology and or religion and popular culture. Here, I wish to begin by walking through the approach noted by Bruce Forbes and Jeff Mahan in their edited volume, *Religion and Popular Culture in America*, and conclude by reflecting on my own threefold approach, which has been informed primarily by my experience teaching theology and popular culture in the context of formal theological education.

Forbes and Mahan identified what they saw as four prominent trends which are reflected in the current work that deals with religion and popular culture: 1) religion *in* popular culture; 2) popular culture *in* religion; 3) popular culture *as* religion; 4) religion and popular culture in dialogue. According to the first approach, religion *in* popular culture examines the role played by religious themes within cultural texts and practices. One could think of the religious themes in popular music (like Lady GaGa's 'Judas' or Madonna's 'Like a Virgin'), films (the important function of the priest in Clint Eastwood's *Gran Torino* or the religious symbolism of the Matrix Trilogy) and fiction (the role played by faith in Yann Martel's *Life of Pi* or in Dan Brown's *Da Vinci Code*). Using this approach, religiously minded cultural scholars (or culturally minded religion scholars) can identify how religious themes are interpreted within contemporary culture and can identify the continued role played by religion in shaping our cultural imagination.

In their second approach, the study of popular culture *in* religion, Forbes and Mahan note how religious groups make use of cultural forms in order to effectively adapt their religious beliefs and practices to their surrounding cultural context. An example of this could be the hugely popular *Left Behind* series of Christian fiction, or the multi-million dollar Christian Contemporary Music industry. In both of these cases, the normative influence of what is largely an Evangelical Christian faith has led to the creation of cultural goods that utilize the *forms* of popular culture as a way of expressing and underlying religious content.

In describing popular culture *as* religion (the third approach), Forbes and Mahan touch upon the body of work which describes how popular culture can serve a function in contemporary society which was once largely the purview of traditional religions. Popular culture, according to many scholars, takes on such a religious function when it is used as a means of creating communities, serves as a hermeneutic lens through which one could interpret the world, provides a set of meaningful practices, or perhaps gives participants a sense of something larger than themselves. A frequently cited example of popular culture *as* religion is sport fandom (cinema going, popular music fandom, and even aspects of contemporary celebrity culture have also been described in this manner). Though considerable scholarly work has been directed at such an approach, the extent to which the parallel between religion and popular culture marks popular culture *as* a religion rather than *like* a religion is hotly contested.[14]

Finally, Forbes and Mahan suggest 'religion and popular culture in dialogue' as something of a catch-all category for those examples of religion and popular culture which don't neatly fit into the other three categories. One could find here examples of the dynamic interchange between popular culture and religion, where religion is neither necessarily the subject of cultural creations (the first approach) nor the content of cultural objects and practices (the second and third approach), but rather a site for creative religious meaning making within the context of popular cultural production and consumption. According to Gordon Lynch's fourfold typology, this is the place where 'popular cultural texts and practices' are used as a 'medium for theological reflection'.[15]

Teaching theology and popular culture

As noted above, religious scholars and theologians work very closely with one another in this field and it is difficult, at times, to distinguish what is 'theological' as opposed to 'religious' about such analyses of popular culture. In what remains of this chapter, I want to offer a somewhat autobiographical reflection on a few lessons that I have learned as both a theologian and a theological practitioner (that is, the kind of person who tries to work out the practices of theology in the life of faith and ministry) whilst doing work with theology and popular culture. As I seek to articulate what is a distinctively theological approach to popular culture, I have found it useful to learn from the attitudes which have emerged from my interactions with students, during the few years that I have been teaching theology and popular culture in secular and religious universities, with theological courses, colleges, and seminaries in traditional and adult-education contexts, in the UK and the USA. As I will describe below, I see three approaches in the theological study of popular culture (which I'll refer to as the moral, missional, and theological reflection approaches), that correspond to three types of students who I will call the Marketer, the Curate, and the Disaffected Churchgoer.

The Marketer

For some time, I have been teaching an introductory course on theology and popular culture which has served as an elective or optional module at a number of different institutions. Because students are seldom required to take the course, I make a habit of asking students why it is that they've signed up to study theology and pop culture in the first place. Amongst the expected answers on one such occasion ('I like the idea of watching films in class'; 'I don't know much about popular culture and I think I should learn something'; 'It worked out well with my schedule'), I received an answer from a student that has stuck with me for the past five years: 'I signed up to Theology and Popular Culture because I think it will help me to be a more effective marketer in my ministry'. In chasing up this answer I found that this student had cannily created a bespoke ministry preparation program at his American Christian university by combining courses from the university's new business school program with more conventional ministry courses (leadership, theology, pastoral counseling, and my elective in theology and popular culture), to help prepare himself to more effectively apply the lessons of the Church Growth Movement with a modicum of cultural sensitivity.

The Marketer wanted to use the theological study of culture as a tool which would enable him to effectively communicate a theological message in as attractive and intelligible a way as was possible. In so using culture as a missional tool, the Marketer's theological and moral sensibilities controlled the terms of the relationship. If a cultural form offended or challenged those sensibilities it needed to be sanitized or avoided. For example, in his class work he was very excited to think about how social networking sites like Facebook or MySpace could be used as a way of extending his church's ministry, or in learning about how principles drawn from advertising and marketing could produce more effective forms of church publicity.

However, when he and his classmates were asked to engage with music that had explicit lyrics, or fiction and film that may have had some sexual content, the Marketer would refuse to engage with these materials beyond what his moral sensibilities would allow.

The Curate

Before reflecting in more detail about the Marketer's moral approach to theology and popular culture, let's contrast the Marketer who came from a US university with an adult learner from an undergraduate ministry training course in the UK, who we will call the Curate. Most of my teaching experience in the UK has been within the context of adult education, primarily with students who are either preparing for some form of public Christian ministry or who are returning to higher education to gain a new focus for their Christian ministry. The students in my modules have had ages ranging from their mid-thirties to their mid-eighties. It is hard enough to speak about popular culture with any degree of credibility to a group of eighteen- to twenty-four-year-olds, who may at least hold a tenuous agreement about what popular culture for them is made up of; but, when popular culture can mean anything from Tony Bennett to Terry Wogan, Bonanza to Bono, scrambling for definitions can be challenging.

When I would ask these students why it was that they were studying theology and popular culture, without fail they would talk about their desire to understand what exactly popular culture *was*; many had a sense that it was important, but most couldn't quite articulate why this was the case. When pressed further, students would describe how they wanted to be able to talk about their faith in a way which made sense in the context of contemporary culture (not unlike, I suppose the marketing approach noted above), or they would say that they wanted to be able to use film clips or music or television as a way of initiating conversations about religious topics, or they would say that they felt that in order for their Christian faith to be relevant to those around them, they needed to understand their own missional context.

Though, on the surface, this missional approach to popular culture may seem to unite the Marketer and the Curate, across their different church traditions, their different nationalities, and their different demographics, there is a profound difference to their general orientation to culture. Whereas the Marketer is content to fix his gaze on the surface appearance of culture, the Curate is prepared to enter into a conversation with culture on issues of some depth. The difference between the UK mid-life Curate and the young US Marketer is best expressed through one of my favourite teaching anecdotes.

Since it was released in cinemas, I've been using the 2006 Alejandro González Iñárritu film *Babel* in a variety of teaching contexts as a way of getting students to think theologically about film. I have been surprised by the different ways in which my UK and US students have responded to the film. Whilst some of the students in the Marketer's cohort found the film to be very compelling viewing, the vast majority were unable to recognize any redemptive quality in the film because of its infrequent profanity and scenes of a mild sexual nature. In fact, so upset were several of the students that they made a formal complaint to the Dean about my showing the film on a module in the university's school of ministry. In contrast, when showing the film to my UK Curates, nearly all of the students have been profoundly moved by the film and offered some very robust theological reflections stemming from the film (on topics like the weak depiction of women; questions of international justice; the theme of interconnectedness, etc.).

Although both Marketers and Curates were coming to popular culture in order to achieve a missional objective, they can be distinguished from each other by the degree to which they operated a generous reading of culture or allowed the cultural form to speak on its own terms. This is not to say that in either case it is possible or preferable to bracket out religious presuppositions. If Ricoeur's hermeneutics teaches us anything, it's that our reading of texts is always mediated through the complex detours of which religious faith is an example. Unlike the Marketer, the Curate was able to maintain a dialogue where faith informed culture and culture informed faith. In the case of *Babel*, the Marketer's concern for sexual purity, informed by his interpretation of Jesus' teaching about lust and adultery made it impossible for him to watch the film in a way which opened him up to any redemptive or transformative encounter with the film's narrative. The Curate was able to watch the film and think about the theological message conveyed by the film (in terms of social justice, the nature of familial love, care of neighbour), but was also able to offer a theological critique of the film stemming from her strong reaction against the depiction of gun violence. Indeed, in every screening of the film in the UK, students have consistently focused on the ethical problems of gun violence as depicted by the film – a topic never once identified by my American students.

The Disaffected Churchgoer

I want to conclude by describing a third type of student with whom I've worked on issues in theology and popular culture. Whilst in my experience of teaching in the context of accredited (that is, degree-leading) education my students have largely been thinking about theology and popular culture with particular ministerial concerns in mind, when working in non-accredited lifelong learning environments, I have found students use popular culture largely as a way of expressing their inner spiritual journey. This was especially the case with those who felt that their spiritual or intellectual needs were no longer being addressed by their home congregations. In one such course on Popular Culture and Spirituality, a group of these disaffected churchgoers described how traditional Christian theology, the Creeds, prayer, and the liturgy had gradually, over time, stopped making sense to them and (in many cases) to their adult children. In response to this, I asked students to bring with them a video clip, a song, a passage from a novel, or another cultural object that they had found spiritually nourishing. These students, many of them clergy, found in popular cultural forms – whether the *Twilight* series of novels, films like *Gran Torino* or *About a Boy*, or pop/folk music like that produced by Mumford and Sons – a language that spoke to their deep spiritual needs. They shared a profound sense of disaffection from traditional Christian symbols and felt isolated from their received understanding of Faith, Religion, or God, but were able to find a common language to express their spiritual sensibilities by appealing to popular culture as a source of theological reflection or as a site in which God was able to authentically disclose Godself to them.

The Marketer, the Curate, and the Disaffected Churchgoer demonstrated three different motives for engaging with popular culture, which could otherwise be described as a Moral, a Missional, and a Theological Reflection approach. For the moral approach to popular culture, how we engage with culture is determined largely by our moral and theological frameworks. Culture is regarded as distinct from, or even subordinate to, the moral universe of Christian theology. Though culture may be appropriated for missional purposes, popular culture must be scrutinized in order to prevent the moral contamination of the individual Christian by cultural goods. In the missional approach, though Christian theology still largely controls the terms of the relationship between theology and culture, the guiding concern is less private morality than it is public mission. If culture can aid in the effective promotion of the Christian Gospel, the missional approach would encourage the Church to be emboldened to use culture in whatever way is most effective. In the approach that I am referring to as the 'theological reflection',[16] popular culture and theology are given even footing and are allowed to interpret one another, as dialogue partners. In this way, we allow culture to first speak to us, in its own language, before we seek to scrutinize culture for its missional worth or moral risk. Through such a relationship to culture, we are leaving open the possibility that God may choose to reveal God-self (or not!) through the texts and practices of our cultural world. Through the theological reflection approach, by remaining open to God's self-disclosure in popular culture, we may discover something about God that perhaps we may not have already known.[17]

Conclusion

Given the increased pace at which books are being written (and new courses are being taught), it appears to me that this particular theological sub-discipline is addressing a deep concern held by many of our readers and students (and perhaps also our colleagues). Like them, I feel the intense disparity between the imaginative frame of reference that is populated by our popular cultural world, and the imaginative frame of reference populated by Scripture and tradition. By studying popular culture, as theologians and theological practitioners, we are provided with an opportunity to engage in what a previous generation of scholars described as the task of 'inculturation'. Inculturation is

> the incarnation of Christian life and of the Christian message in a particular cultural context, in such a way that this experience not only finds expression through elements proper to the culture in question, but becomes a principle that animates, directs, and unifies the culture, transforming and remaking it so as to bring about 'a new creation'.[18]

Rather than a therapeutic attempt to make theological sense of our particular hobbies, passions or interests, and more than simply an opportunity to exhibit our cultural acumen for the benefit of our peers or readers, I would hope that the theological study of popular culture would enable us to discover the ongoing self-disclosure of the Incarnate Christ in our changing world.

Notes

1 M. Arnold, *Culture and Anarchy*, ed. D. Wilson, Cambridge: Cambridge University Press, 1960.
2 H.R. Niebuhr, *Christ and Culture*, New York: Harper Brothers, 1950.
3 P. Tillich, *Theology of Culture*, New York: Oxford University Press, 1959.
4 K. Tanner, *Theories of Culture: A New Agenda for Theology*, Minneapolis, MN: Augsburg Fortress Press, 1997.
5 R. Barthes, *Mythologies*, New York: Harper, 2001.
6 M. de Certeau, *The Practices of Everyday Life*, Berkeley, CA: University of California Press, 1988.
7 For a fuller exploration of both the history of cultural studies and popular cultural studies, see J. Storey, *An Introduction to Cultural Theory and Popular Culture*, Harlow, England: Longman, 1997.
8 A good example of this in the theological study of popular culture can be noted in the work of Tom Beaudoin (especially *Witness to Dispossession: The Vocation of a Postmodern Theologian*, Maryknoll, NY: Orbis Books, 2008), which effectively uses autobiographical theological reflection as a means of engaging with popular culture, amongst other issues.
9 See E. Graham, H. Walton, and F. Ward, *Theological Reflection: Methods*, London: SCM, 2005.
10 This was the case with Simone Dinnerstein's rendition of the Bach piece after it was featured in the 2008 film *The Day the Earth Stood Still* and subsequently received an endorsement from Oprah. The resulting popularity launched Dinnerstein's rendition of 'Goldberg Variations' into the top of the Billboard classical charts for several weeks.
11 On the Theology and Popular Culture side of things, see W.D. Romanowski, *Eyes Wide Open: Looking for God in Popular Culture*, Grand Rapids, MI: Brazos, 2001; C. Detweiler and B. Taylor, *A Matrix of Meanings: Finding God in Pop Culture*, Grand Rapids, MI: Baker, 2004; G. Lynch, *Understanding Theology and Popular Culture*, London: Blackwell, 2006; K. Cobb, *The Blackwell Guide to Theology and Popular Culture*, Oxford: Blackwell Publishing, 2005; E. Mazur and K. McCarthy, *God in the Details: American Religion in Everyday Life*, London: Routledge, 2000; B. Forbes and J. Mahan, *Religion and Popular Culture in America*, Berkeley, CA: University of California Press, 2000.
12 C. Marsh, *Theology Goes to the Movies: An Introduction to Critical Christian Thinking*, London: Routledge, 2007; J. Lyden, *Film as Religion*, New York: New York University Press, 2003; C. Deacy, *Theology and Film: Challenging the Sacred/Secular Divide*, Oxford: Wiley-Blackwell, 2008; H. Campbell, *When Religion Meets New Media*, London: Routledge, 2010; S.J. Hoffman, *Good Game: Christianity and the Culture of Sports*, Waco, TX: Baylor University Press, 2010; V. Miller, *Consuming Religion*, New York: Continuum, 2006; C. Detweiler, *Halos and Avatars: Playing Video Games with God*, Louisville, KY: Westminster John Knox, 2010.
13 L. Woodhead, H. Kawanami, and C. Partridge (eds) *Religions in the Modern World: Traditions and Transformations*, 2nd edn, London: Routledge, 2009, pp. 489–522.
14 To varying degrees, this approach has been taken by Lyden's *Film as Religion*; R. Till, *Pop Cult: Religion and Popular Music*, London: Continuum, 2010; P. Ward, *Gods Behaving Badly: Media, Religion, and Celebrity Culture*, London: SCM Press, 2011, and by many of the authors in Mazur and McCarthy's *God in the Details*.
15 Lynch, *Understanding Theology and Popular Culture*, p. 21.

16 I am indebted here to Gordon Lynch's four-fold typology: '1) the study of religion in relation to the environment, resources, and practices of everyday life; 2) the study of the ways in which popular culture may serve religious function in contemporary society; 3) a missiological response to popular culture; 4) the use of popular cultural texts and practices as a medium for theological reflection' (Lynch, *Understanding Theology and Popular Culture*, p. 21).

17 As David Bosch has noted, 'The early Christians did not simply express in Greek thought what they already knew [about Jesus Christ]; rather they discovered through Greek religious and philosophical insights, what had been revealed to them. The doctrines of the Trinity and of the divinity of Christ ... for example, would not be what they are today if the church had not reassessed itself and its doctrines in the light of the new historical, cultural situations during the third through the sixth centuries.' (D. Bosch, *Transforming Mission: Paradigm Shifts in Theology of Mission*, Maryknoll, NY: Orbis Books, 2001, p. 190).

18 P. Schineller, *A Handbook on Inculturation*, New York: Paulist Press, 1990, p. 6.

INDEX